THE UNKNOWN CIVIL WAR
IN SOVIET RUSSIA

THE UNKNOWN CIVIL WAR IN SOVIET RUSSIA

A Study of the Green Movement in the Tambov Region 1920-1921

Oliver H. Radkey

HOOVER INSTITUTION PRESS
Stanford University, Stanford, California 94305

Hoover Institution Publication 155

International Standard Book Number 0-8179-6551-3
Library of Congress Card Number 75-41905
Printed in the United States of America

To the elder friends of my student years Dr. Alexander F. Iziumov and his wife, Alexandra Stepanovna, born Shcherbatova, and to their friend and mine, Professor Michael Karpovich.

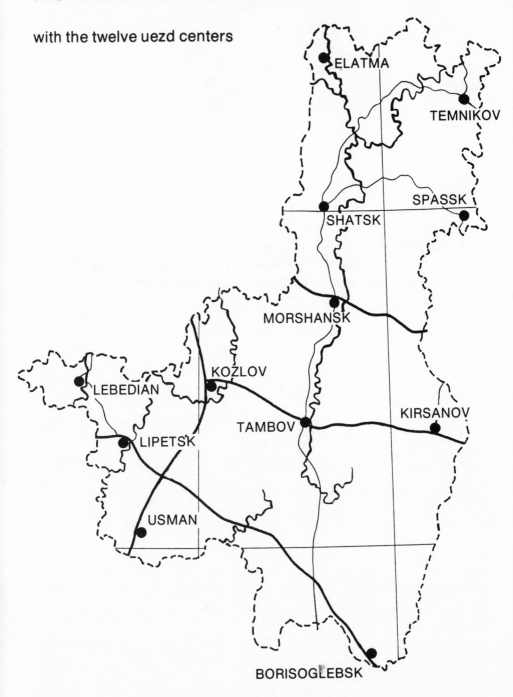

HISTORIC PROVINCE OF TAMBOV

with the twelve uezd centers

ELATMA

TEMNIKOV

SPASSK

SHATSK

MORSHANSK

KOZLOV

LEBEDIAN

KIRSANOV

TAMBOV

LIPETSK

USMAN

BORISOGLEBSK

Contents

TAMBOV REGION

As of Today
With Main Area of
Insurrection

(The region is the cut-down core
of the
historic province.)

Foreword

The Green movement is one of the aspects of the Russian Revolution which constitute its challenge and fascination. The significance of the movement will be adjudged differently according to whether the historian is conventional in outlook or independent in spirit, but its interest to the scholar is equalled only by the difficulty of disclosing its essence, of rescuing it from the oblivion to which it has been consigned by force of circumstance and by conscious design of the Soviet government. To the mystery of the unknown and the obstacles placed in the way of any approach to its sepulchre has been added its appeal as a third force arising out of the convulsive writhing of the peasantry—and not of the peasantry alone—against being further victimized by Reds and Whites in their contention for the privilege of abusing the population. That this genuine third force operated for all too short a time and ended in failure cannot militate against its claims for recognition by those who refuse to idolize the State and who do not limit historical validity to the winning side.

The fascination of the unknown has as its obverse side the difficulty of moving the subject into the realm of the known. Although the author never inclined to optimism, any lingering illusion he might have harbored disappeared within the Hoover Library. Here, in a collection noted for its excellent coverage of the early years of the Russian Revolution, he found only two titles listed under the heading of the Tambov or Antonov insurrection. Of these two titles one had been lost and has never since been found. The single most informative source—one of provincial origin, by no means free of error, and described by its compilers as only the raw material for a history of the uprising—could not be located outside the Soviet Union.

A grant from the American Philosophical Society sent the author to the USSR in the summer of 1965 to inspect this source and several

others of lesser importance. The inveterate suspicion first encountered at the frontier and not abating until departure should have
negated the notion that Soviet authorities would permit an independent investigation of the subject, even on the basis of materials
exclusively of Soviet origin and after the lapse of forty years.
Nevertheless, it proved feasible to study and to take notes on these
materials. But after a trip to Leningrad and a return to Moscow en
route to the Rumanian frontier, the author's car was broken into
under obvious circumstances while parked in front of the main
entrance of one of the principal Moscow hotels.

It might seem stupid to steal notes on Soviet publications, yet it
was by no means a stupid action. These sources of the early 1920s
contain information on sensitive matters which would never appear
in later Soviet publications. The author retained some of the information in his memory, not committing it to paper until he was out
of the country and out of the satellite orbit. Something saved from
the disaster thus appears in this study despite the inability to give
page references; when the author is not sure of the facts he says so.

It was a matter of bitter regret that the locale of the uprising could
not be visited. It is always well to see what one is writing about—in
this case, the Vorona (crow) valley and some of the villages that
figured in the story. The road lay through neighboring Orel and
Kursk provinces, yet the scene of operations in the Tambov region
some four hundred kilometers to the east might as well have been on
another planet. Restrictions were so great that in White Russia it
seemed inadvisable to deviate two kilometers from the established
route to inspect the site of the battle fought in 1708 at Lesnaia.
Nevertheless, it can be said that an extensive trip by automobile
through Soviet Russia is well worth the time, money, discomfort,
and even the apprehension it occasions.

The resources for study of the Russian Revolution in the United
States are so great that they did not fail even this difficult test. It had
been hoped that recourse to newspapers could be avoided because
of the poor paper and miserable print of that time, but the Moscow
misfortune threw the author back on *Pravda* and *Izvestiia,* restoring
some of what had been lost and yielding additional information that
can be found nowhere else. The Trotsky Archive in the Houghton
Library of Harvard University affords the backstage illumination so

often lacking in treatments of Soviet policy. Scattered materials in the aggregate have helped to reconstruct an episode which has been intentionally blotted from the pages of history.

It cannot be said that the present study offers an exhaustive— much less a definitive—account of the Antonov uprising in Tambov province. Intended as a study in depth of one phase of the Green movement, in all too many instances the depths could not be plumbed. The author has not succeeded in giving conclusive answers or, at times, any answer at all to questions no serious endeavor can hope to evade. Freedom of investigation in the Soviet Union doubtless could clear up some of these matters. Others, most likely not. Too much time has gone by, the work of effacement has been too thorough, the obsession with secrecy and suppression of unpalatable facts too great. Published accounts based on archival material suggest that the archives themselves are in disarray— cluttered with reports filled with inaccuracies and hyperbole, yet never subsequently revised. Nowhere is there a reconstruction of military events or even of the skeleton of these events—something the author had hoped to present in partial redemption of his failure in other respects.

So it is that only modest claims can be made for the present study. The author has done the best he could with what has been available. It was possible to assemble a considerable amount of information on a subject about which almost nothing has been known, to answer some questions and to suggest tentative answers to others. The causes of the insurrection are clear enough; its spontaneity is reasonably well established as is the essential character of the Green movement; a rough outline of the course of developments has been sketched; the reasons for the failure of the uprising are apparent; and we are rather well informed of what lay behind decisions on the Soviet side.

But areas of darkness remain. What prompted decisions on the part of the Greens, in fact, is not an area of darkness but one which is pitch black and will ever remain so. The Green leaders were ex-terminated and their records destroyed. Files of the Soviet secret police doubtless contain a certain amount of valid testimony from squealers and turncoats; other captives divulged nothing and those entrusted with the innermost secrets of the movement fell in action.

Critics are wont to say that a definitive study must await the future. They will say so in this instance, and they will be wrong.

This study concerns a major episode in the struggle of a genuine revolutionary force against Communist tyranny. The last chapter attempts to fit the Tambov insurrection into its general setting. The conclusions are tentative, however, and subject to revision as further investigation of this widespread phenomenon confirms, refutes, or modifies these views.

Whatever the deficiencies of this work—and the author is only too painfully aware of them—the conviction remains that his interpretation of the Green movement is both original and correct. He is also convinced that this account and analysis of the Tambov phase of the Green movement affords rather searching insight into the character of the Communist regime—not as it became under Stalin, if his rule was indeed an aberration, but as it already was under Lenin—especially in relation to that large and unfortunate peasant class which found itself in the grip of devotees of the cult of heavy industry, to which inanimate object of worship all human values were to be offered in sacrifice.

The study of the Antonov or Tambov phase of the Green movement has been unfailingly interesting and inordinately difficult. Words of appreciation are due those who helped to smooth the way. The staff of the Hoover Library could not have done more to create pleasant working conditions, both technically and subjectively. To his friends Mrs. Arline Paul, Mary Gillmor, Dorothy Godsall, Hilja Kukk, and Marina Timkoff-Utechin the author wishes to say that the favors and consideration shown him will always be a fond remembrance.

Another friend, Anna Bourgina, has helped to fill out the inevitably thin bibliography by producing from the Nicolaevsky Collection of the Hoover Institution several important documents. Professor Anatole Mazour and Mr. Gregory Lounz of New York have helped with bibliographical suggestions. Professor Peter Scheibert of the University of Marburg called the author's attention to an obscure but valuable source that provided welcome confirmation from the Communist side of the inadmissibility of correlating the strength of the Green movement in its citadel with the proportion of kulaks in the population. Mrs. Helen Pashin called attention to the Virta novel as something more than fiction, and Mrs. Xenia J. Eudin has generously shared the knowledge gained from a parallel study. Professor Terence Emmons volunteered his assistance in trying to overcome certain difficulties that arose in connection with the work. And Professor Thomas Riha assumed the task of establishing, as a by-product of his own research, whether the chief Russian newspaper in exile would yield any substantial amount of information about Tambov. The negative result—and dry runs are an essential part of research—detracts in no way from his service, which can be remembered though not requited as a result of his tragic destiny.

Years before the investigation was undertaken, Professor Merle Fainsod of Harvard University informed the author of what awaited him in the Trotsky Archive and, when the time arrived, arranged for him access to this collection in the Houghton Library. A special debt is owing Professor Witold Sworakowski, who in a dark hour urged the author to persevere in his work and not allow it to be ruined by malevolent forces. In general, the author wishes to thank all these friends and others for their help and unfailing goodwill.

Financial assistance has come from a number of sources. First from the Hoover Institution itself through Dr. W. Glenn Campbell. Then from the American Philosophical Society in the form of a travel grant to see what could be done in Russia. The Graduate Research Institute of the University of Texas granted research leave in 1969, and the next year added an equal sum to an award from the American Council of Learned Societies. To all those who helped in procuring financial assistance the author acknowledges his indebtedness, and especially to W. Gordon Whaley, Dean of the Graduate School of the University of Texas, and to John Silber, Dean of the College of Arts and Sciences until its disruption and now President of Boston University.

No series of acknowledgments would be complete without words of appreciation to the author's wife, Jakoba B. Radkey, for the many ways in which she has furthered this work and for typing the manuscript, willingly and without complaint, over a lengthy period beset with other duties.

The choice of an editor by the Hoover Institution was singularly fortunate. The author is grateful to Sallie Jaggar Hayes not only for the professional competence she has brought to her task but also for the understanding and sympathy she has so graciously displayed.

Last, not least, the author is indebted to his friend, Glenn Campbell, Director of the Hoover Institution, for the ultimate favor of making possible the appearance of this study in its entirety, free of the gutting operation that so often is imposed by publishers, particularly in the case of an independent investigation addressed to unsealing one of history's byroads instead of moving down its beaten track.

— 1 —

Introduction: Subject and Setting

The Subject

The civil war in Russia which followed the October Revolution and lasted from 1918 through 1920 has commanded much attention, both at home and in the West. Few people have realized, however, that it was followed by a second civil war of comparable duration and destructiveness but of quite different character. If the first, well-publicized civil war found two mail-fisted minorities contending for mastery of the Russian people, the second, muted civil war was a convulsive movement of the people itself—and particularly the peasantry—to shake off the tyranny imposed by the victorious Red minority. Why has Red against White engaged the attention of a world somehow color-blind to the conflict between Red and Green?[1]

A number of considerations come to mind in casting about for an answer. First and foremost, the Soviet regime was and is embarrassed to disclose the dimensions of a movement that forced the "workers' and peasants' "government to send the Workers' and Peasants' Red Army into savage combat with large numbers of peasants. What happened to the state and its emblem when the Sickle ceased to be an adornment and cut at the roots of the regime? A veil of silence was drawn over the whole affair for more than forty years. Only in the 1960s have studies of any consequence appeared on the Green movement—from the official point of view. Even today an independent investigation in Russia itself is quite impossible, as this author has discovered to his sorrow.

The Soviet regime also sought to conceal its embarrassment by misrepresenting the character of the Green movement. It decreed

1

the suppression of the name "green" and, with its skill in separating words from their meaning, applied the term "bandit" in its stead. To strengthen the indictment and afford variety, the term "criminal" is also used. The slander began early and was by no means a Stalinist innovation. In the section of the Green movement here to be studied, the satrap on location, V. A. Antonov-Ovseenko, made no distinction between Greens and Whites, nor did Maxim Gorki, despite the intervals of independence that characterized his relationship with the Communist regime.

Secondly, the second civil war has for various reasons been neglected by Western scholarship. What embarrasses Soviet Russia is not pleasing to those Western intellectuals who share the prejudice of Gorki against peasants as people who live in darkness, are not identified with progress, do not take readily to socialism, and yearn for private property. Working class movements are preferred to peasant, and intellectual movements to either. Western intellectuals are not so independent of official policy and popular currents in their countries as they like to think, and the fact that the Western Allies had nothing to do with the second civil war in Russia, whereas they had been very active in the first, no doubt has contributed to intellectual oversight and to positive neglect.

Finally, a formidable barrier to investigation was posed by the nature of the subject. Peasant movements tend to be locked within the country of their origin and to have a minimum spill-over into the outside world. When the movement unfolds in the interior of a vast country like Russia, there is no spill-over at all. Peasants are rooted in the soil; it is hard for them to run away; their horizon is limited; they do not know where to go or how to make a living. On occasions when compassion broke through his veneer of cynicism, Frederick the Great referred to peasants as "the beasts of burden of human society." For the most part, they exist and suffer, and are mute like the beasts in the field.

Peasants do not write, nor do their leaders, who have been exterminated by the Soviet regime. The Communist technique of pulling the backbone of a social group and leaving a mass of human jelly, added to Lenin's conviction that the Green movement—or the petty bourgeois *ochlos*, as he thought of it—constituted a mortal danger to his regime, led the authorities to leave no stone unturned in their efforts to run to earth the Green leaders. The rank and file might or might not be let off—many of them were also killed and others transplanted—but the leadership had to die. Nearly all trace of the movement was wiped out; even the name was taken away.

And so little is left by which to study this second civil war. Scattered scraps of information, for the most part of extreme rarity, have to be assembled to give a picture which in no sense can be termed conclusive. The platitude that a definitive study must await the future will not be repeated here, for the long life of what may be the most oppressive regime in history, combined with the normal attrition of time, makes it extremely unlikely that such a history can ever be written. Yet something can be done to rescue the subject from the oblivion to which it has been consigned naturally by force of circumstances, and unnaturally by design of the Soviet regime.

When the investigator rolled back the curtain far enough to envisage the scope of this second civil war, he was confronted with a breathtaking spectacle. In the late winter and spring of 1921, small fires nearly everywhere in Russia threatened to merge with half a dozen major conflagrations into one vast funeral pyre for the Communist hierarchy. Only two of the conflagrations, at Kronstadt and in the Ukraine, have received attention and they are imperfectly known. With no desire to detract from Nestor Makhno or his truly popular cause, it must be said that the insurrection under his leadership was not typical of the Green movement in all respects because it was Ukrainian rather than Great Russian, and because he operated for the most part on the edge of the country whence he was able to flee across the border and live to tell his tale. The Kronstadt rebellion occurred on the doorstep of the West, flaring up like a comet and going out as fast. It was peasant only by derivation and was exposed to proletarian influence.

More knowledge is needed of the great dark area of the interior before valid conclusions can be drawn about the second civil war and before its history as a whole can be written. Kronstadt was more than a streaking comet, despite its brief life, and Makhno belongs to Russian history as well as to the folk tradition of his native Ukraine. Yet somehow neither brings us to the heart of the movement which nearly ended the Soviet regime in the fourth year of its existence, at the very time when it was celebrating the successful outcome of the first civil war and its emergence from under the sword of the past.

Another phase of the Green movement has been chosen as the subject of this study, a phase more central in location, purely Russian in ethnic complexion, no less formidable in numbers nor less tenacious in resistance to communism, better organized if less free-ranging, and even more tragic in its outcome. The insurrection in Tambov province associated with the name of Alexander S. Antonov, which began in August of 1920 and went out in streams of blood in the spring and summer of 1921, drove the Soviet regime into a frenzy of repression because of a strategic position which—under only slightly more favorable circumstances—would have made it the key link in the chain of insurrections dooming the existing order to extinction.

It cannot be claimed for the Tambov uprising that it produced the dramatic effect of the Kronstadt rebellion or that it matched the upheaval in western Siberia as the primary factor in bringing about the New Economic Policy (NEP). But it exercised a strong and continuing influence on the evolution of Soviet policy toward an accommodation with the peasants which would release them from the hell into which they had been plunged, and nothing afforded the masters of the Kremlin more relief than when the Tambov stone was finally removed from their throats. Despite the all but insuperable difficulty of getting at them, the events in this province and the conditions that provoked them afford a case study in depth of the Green movement as typical as any and more interesting than most.

The setting of the Antonov movement will first be examined in its geographical and socio-political aspects. An analysis of the movement will follow, and then the dark story of the uprising itself insofar as it can be reconstructed. Finally, the possibility of a more fortuitous outcome will be weighed.

The Geographical Setting

The administrative structure of the Russian Empire, like so much else, proceeded from the hands of the Enlightened Empress. The Soviet government in its early years was too preoccupied with other matters to meddle with her work, so Tambov province was essentially as she had left it, with its twelve subdivisions or *uezds*[2] and its strategic south-central location athwart the lines of communication between Moscow and the lower Volga. According to the German railroad manual, the provincial capital of the same name lies at kilometer 465 from Moscow on the trunk line through Kashira, Ranenburg, and Kozlov, and becomes the point of bifurcation of two lines to the lower Volga, one to Saratov via Kirsanov and Rtishchevo and the other to Kamyshin via Uvarovo and Balashov. North of the provincial capital the main line from Moscow to Samara (Kuibyshev) also passes through Tambov province, and to the south another major line takes off from the Moscow–Rostov railway at Griazi and runs diagonally across Tambov province via Borisoglebsk on the way to Tsaritsyn (Stalingrad, Volgograd). Thus the most direct routes between Moscow and all important points on the Volga from Syzran and Samara on its middle course to Astrakhan[3] at its mouth pass through Tambov province.

Along with the sister provinces of Penza, Voronezh, Kursk, and Orel, Tambov made up the Central Black Earth zone of European Russia—in a sense, the heartland of Russia—and had become densely populated as the Russian people moved out of the northern forest onto the fertile soil after the Tatar sway over the steppe had been broken. The province had long since ceased to be colonized, however, and had itself become a base of colonization for newer regions. From being the third most populous province in Russia in 1851 it slipped to ninth position by the census of 1897.[4]

The configuration of Tambov province resembled an irregular square at the base with a sizable northward projection from the eastern half of the square. This extension to the north, rectangular and resembling a smokestack in shape, contained four *uezds*, Shatsk and Elat'ma on the western side and Spassk and Temnikov on the eastern, with Morshansk *uezd* at the foot connecting them with the squarish base. The interior of the base, the main part of the province, was occupied by the two most populous *uezds*, Tambov to the east and Kozlov to the west. Beyond Kozlov three *uezds* extended along the western border of the square: Lebedian' *uezd* in the northwestern corner, Usman *uezd* in the southwestern, with Lipetsk *uezd* in between. To the east of Tambov *uezd* and bordering on Saratov province (Balashov and Serdobsk *uezds*) was Kirsanov *uezd*. The southeastern corner of the squarish base consisted of Borisoglebsk *uezd*, twelfth and last of the subdivisions comprising Tambov province. The chief town in every instance had the same name as the *uezd* itself, and Tambov—the only town with pretensions to being a city—was central both to its *uezd* and to the province as a whole.

The seven *uezds* constituting the base of the province differed from those in the northern annex—or smokestack—in three major respects: fertility, woodlands, and ethnic composition. These seven were on the black earth, they were populous and relatively prosperous, but had seen their woodlands recede before the ravages of the axe and the plow. Nature had been less generous in the north where much of the soil was sandy, but a good deal of the original cover was preserved there precisely because she had rewarded more stingily the rapacity of man. In her work of conservation, however, nature had not taxed her generosity. The trees on the inferior soil of the northern *uezds* were of the softwood, coniferous variety, mainly pine with some fir in the northeast, whereas the slaughtered trees on the black earth had offered many fine specimens of the hardwood, broad-leaved variety, particularly of oak. Thirty-four percent of the northern area was still forested at the beginning of this century as against only eight percent of the black earth zone.[5]

More than conifers had survived in the northern *uezds*. The Finnish aborigines were still there, reinforced by the Tatar descendants of the Golden Horde. Spassk *uezd* was not even Russian in the sense that it had a Mordvin majority of 53 percent and a small Tatar element of 2 percent; Temnikov *uezd* was nearly a third non-Russian, and Shatsk and Elat'ma had lesser but still appreciable minorities of Mordvins and Tatars. On the other hand, the black earth portion of Tambov province to the south—including Morshansk, which was partly *chernozem* and partly not—was all but exclusively Great Russian in population. The three southeastern *uezds* of Tambov, Kirsanov, and Borisoglebsk are most pertinent to our story. They were quite fertile, largely denuded of forests, and almost purely Russian.

If the main part of Tambov province afforded little in the way of forest cover, no part of it provided the other traditional refuge from tyranny—a mountainous terrain. The plainlike character of the province was barely disturbed by the scattered low ridges acting as watersheds for the streams. There were no mountains nor even any respectable hills. A forsaken spot to the northwest of Tambov town known as the Lysye Gory (bare hills) owed its neglect to its barrenness and not to its elevation.

With three exceptions, the watercourses were too small to have cut deeply into the level country through which they flowed. The Voronezh river in the west does not figure in our story; it is otherwise, however, with the Tsna in the center and the Vorona (crow) river in the east. The Tsna arises from the union of small streams in the southern portion of Tambov *uezd* and flows northward past the capital on its way to the Moksha and the Oka; on its right or eastern bank across from the city a large forest stretched for some distance upstream and downstream and attained some breadth toward the east—the only extensive forest in the entire main part of the province. It consisted of pines with an admixture of deciduous trees, mainly birch and—in the lower places—alder and willow, only rarely oak or aspen. An inferior forest standing on inferior soil—which had preserved it—this forest had the saving grace of being virtually unbroken, of being connected with northern forests extending all the way to the Volga in Nizhni Novgorod province, and of being criss-crossed with large and densely wooded ravines or hollows (*ovragi*).[6] Here in the most central and populous *uezd* there was a place of refuge, at first for robbers and murderers—the human driftwood of revolution—and then for those who had lost out on the plain, for the strong and desperate men to come.

Some settlements of significance bordered the forest: Pakhotnyi Ugol (plowable place) to the northeast and Nizhne Spasskoe and Rasskazovo to the southeast (the station of Rasskazovo on the Tambov–Saratov line lay within the forest), but most of the villages that will claim our attention were in open country in the southeastern part of Tambov *uezd*. Verkhne-Spasskoe, Khitrovo, Koptevo, Verkhotsene, and Sampur were all situated on one or another of the headwaters of the Tsna in the direction of Kirsanov *uezd*. Sampur station was on the Tambov–Balashov–Kamyshin railroad line as was also the village of Rzhaksa at the point where Tambov,

Borisoglebsk, and Kirsanov *uezds* came together. In the thickly settled country west of the city of Tambov and almost into Kozlov *uezd*, the peasants of the village of Belomestnaia Dvoinia sought to diversify their agriculture by specializing in raspberry culture—betokening a spirit of enterprise probably not unconnected with what would happen to them under the Soviet system. The size of some of these villages at the beginning of the century might be noted: Rasskazovo had 7,500 inhabitants, Verkhne–Spasskoe 6,500, and Pakhotnyi Ugol 5,300, so the comment to be made below about villages in the Vorona valley applies also to these sister villages in Tambov *uezd*.[7]

The Vorona river is a story all to itself. Its headwaters rose in what was then Penza province but its main course lay through Kirsanov and Borisoglebsk *uezds*, its considerable volume of water[8] drifting southward toward the confluence with the Khoper. The Khoper in turn is tributary to the Don, of which the Vorona, albeit indirectly, is one of the important feeders.

Descriptions of the Vorona valley vary somewhat in detail, and the xenophobia of the Soviet regime renders it impossible for the foreign tourist—much less the investigator—to view it at first hand, but the valley is said to be of singular beauty, at least in its original state: deep and wide and covered with trees of the superior broad-leaved, hardwood varieties. Even into the twentieth century, however, stretches of the *urema* or *urman* (*orman* is the Turkish word for "forest") have been preserved, recalling the Tatar past. These lie in a thin band along either side of the valley between Kirsanov and Borisoglebsk. In the vicinity of the latter town there is a magnificent stand of oak and ash with maple, elm, and linden, the celebrated Tellermanovskii or Tilleormanovskii forest (Turkish *tilki* for "fox" and *orman* for "forest"?) which so captivated the fancy of Peter the Great—not, of course, for its own sake—but because he saw the great oaks of excellent quality transformed into ships and moving relentlessly forward against the Turks. Even the Soviet regime suddenly awoke in 1948 to realize the value of these woods in helping to break the east wind that blows from the deserts of Turkestan, and placed them high on the list of natural features to be conserved.[9]

Elsewhere the woods were less impressive, but in general the Vorona valley was still forested in the earlier part of the century as were the valleys of the tributary streams and the network of *ovragi* into which much of the terrain had been carved. The cover of these hollows might be cut-over growth or simply brush, but it sheltered wild life and would soon do the same for men. These hollows were going the way of those in the neighboring province of Voronezh, where aged villagers preserved the memory of running water in the troughs of the depressions. The same fate—though in lesser measure—overhangs the fertile provinces of the Central Black Earth Region as those further east on the Volga: Russia is drying up. The desert of Central Asia is reaching into Europe, unhindered by the monarchy in its quest for prestige and for war, and actively assisted by the Soviet regime in the desperate struggle for food to which its dogmatism condemns it, including the virgin lands program on the edge of the desert. In the case of the Vorona river, attempts to revive navigation finally were abandoned after 1865 because of growing shallowness. The river also undercut its banks and threw large oaks into the channel, further obstructing movement.

But for the time being there was enough water—on the surface, at least—especially during the spring floods, when the low-lying left or eastern bank of the river became a flood plain. Preserved as a permanent feature after the water had receded was a maze of lakes and swamps extending over a considerable distance. These lakes—Ramza Lake, Ilmen Lake, Snake Lake, and others—were not large but were very densely wooded, not only along their shores but on the islets or mounds of dry land with which they and the nearby swamps were interspersed. And in the shallow stretches there were reeds in profusion—reeds as tall as a man. In one wild and secluded spot was a stand of virgin forest entirely surrounded by deep water and known as the Zolotaia Kletka—the Golden Cage.

The opposite bank of the Vorona tends to be higher and less subject to inundation. Here to the west of the river the fertile soil created a zone of denser settlement and a number of large villages had grown up, either in the valley itself near the river, or on the uplands in the distance: Inokovka, Parevka, Inzhavino, Uvarovo in the valley; Kalugino and Karavaino on tributaries further west. All of these villages were in Kirsanov *uezd* except Uvarovo, which was across the line in Borisoglebsk. These were not the only villages, of course, but they were to be the more eventful ones. Nor does this imply a dearth of villages on the other side of the river; there were some, but relative infertility and flooding combined to spread them out and make them less prominent. Three, however, deserve to be remembered: Ramza on the lake of that name, Balyklei further south, and especially Nizhni Shibriai in the Uvarovo area. These villages in the Vorona valley and on the plain were very large by Western standards, in conformity with the rule that on the black earth the people lived bunched together in big settlements. Inokovka had 7,096 inhabitants and Parevka 5,408 in the 1890s; Uvarovo at the turn of the century had 10,000.[10] They would be called "country towns" in the United States—large country towns—yet in Russia they were true villages despite their size, overwhelmingly peasant in cast and outlook with only the rudiments of a middle class.

The Antonov insurrection would not be confined to Tambov but would spill over into Voronezh province, and military operations would extend into portions of Saratov and Penza provinces as well. The connection would be closest in the case of Voronezh as the result of a local uprising under Kolesnikov, destined to become virtually a wing of Antonov's movement. Voronezh was the neighbor of Tambov to the south; it was another component of the Central Black Earth Region, even more fertile and even less forested. The terrain exhibited the same features as those noted for Tambov. The over-all extent of the forested area—less than 9 percent of the total or only 7 percent in the case of the Soviet region which, however, coincides only in part with the former province— was very little more than in the case of the most denuded *uezds* of Tambov province. There were several substantial patches of pine forest in the north on the sandy terraces of the Voronezh, Usman, and Bitiug valleys.

Toward the southeast, on the watershed between the lower Bitiug and the Osered' rivers in Pavlovsk *uezd*, a truly fine stand of trees had survived the depredations of man. This Shipov forest is noteworthy in several respects: there is an extraordinarily high proportion of oaks—89 percent—which are distinguished by their height and the excellent quality of their wood. Beyond them the steppe holds sway and there is no further cover of consequence clear to the Caucasus range. Small wonder, then, that this splendid stand of oak should have impressed everyone from Peter the Great in 1709 to the Soviet authorities of the present time. The forest extends along the Osered' for some forty kilometers and attains a breadth of eight to ten kilometers. It occupies an area of 32,300 hectares and is divided by deep hollows into three sections.[11]

The Shipov forest resembles in quality and composition the Tellermanovski or Tilleormanovski forest in the Vorona valley of Tambov province. The latter forest, in fact, continues into Voronezh province along the Khoper river after the confluence with the Vorona, relieving the otherwise steppe-like character of Novokhopersk *uezd*—the most eastern subdivision of Voronezh province and immediately to the south of Borisoglebsk *uezd* in Tambov. The two forests together comprise the last major stand of the oak tree on the fringe of the southeastern prairies. Unfortunately, a wide stretch of open country intervenes to prevent them from forming a continuous protective belt—against the encroachment of the desert from Asia and in favor of men persecuted from Moscow.[12]

Less closely connected than Voronezh with events in Tambov, the eastern provinces of Saratov and Penza nevertheless were affected. In Saratov province, Balashov and Serdobsk *uezds* shared the same characteristics as the adjacent *uezds* of Tambov province—Borisoglebsk and Kirsanov—in respect to the prevalence of black earth, the open character of the country, and the homogeneity of the population. But Chembar *uezd* of Penza deviated from the pattern in ethnic composition. One-fourth of its inhabitants were of non-Russian stock: Finno–Ugrian (Mordvins 12 percent), Altaian (Tatars 7 percent), or intermediate (Meshcheriaks 6 percent).[13] It thus had an affinity with Spassk *uezd* in the northern tier of Tambov province although physical features linked it to Kirsanov *uezd*, its neighbor to the west.

The geographical setting of the Antonov movement suggests that a better place could have been found—one with mountains and more woods. Unfortunately, mountains are relegated to the rim of European Russia and the unsystematic Russian people have systematically ravaged their forests.[14] Little logic can be found in ordinary political events, and still less in the case of insurrections that grow out of a complex of political, social, economic, and psychological conditions among which the conscious choice of terrain is a decidedly secondary factor.

The Social and Political Setting

If the geographical setting offered little in the way of advantages for a peasant uprising, the social structure of the Tambov–Voronezh region was far more favorable. Two small cities, a number of district towns or *uezd* centers, a few professional people, and the rudiments of a village middle class did little to relieve the overwhelmingly peasant cast of the population. The rural component was 91.8 percent of the whole in Tambov[15] and 88 percent in Voronezh province.[16] V.A. Antonov-Ovseenko, Chairman of the Plenipotentiary Commission of the All Russian Central Executive Committee of Soviets for Fighting Banditry in Tambov Province (this institution had a real Communist title), asserts that his satrapy was the most peasant of all Russian provinces.[17] It is true that the upheaval since 1917 had even increased the already enormous proportion of the rural population; the figure cited for 1920, the year of the insurrection, is 92.7 percent.[18] Whether or not Antonov-Ovseenko's assertion is correct—Kursk province, for example, had also been 92.7 percent rural in 1895,[19] and several other provinces would qualify as strong rivals—Tambov was unquestionably one of the most rural sections of the country.[20]

But it is not enough to say that this region was peasant like few others. What kind of peasants lived there; what gradations existed within the class in this fat farming country? And—especially—how numerous were those blood-sucking vampires of the village, the kulaks or "wealthy" peasants? We are not able to say how many there were, if only because no one has ever offered a precise definition of the term. For the Communists a kulak is the black beast, the source of most—if not all—evil after the elimination of capitalists and landowners, an object at once of intense hatred and intense fear, as familiarity with Lenin's works will attest. Criteria for determining the proportion of kulaks shift from the number of horses owned, the number and type of machines employed, the amount of labor "exploited"—that is, hired—to the amount of land held or rented and back again. Always the concept has been kept fluid for a very good reason: in the last analysis it is extended to all peasants who oppose the regime. The author has his own definition, the validity of which he is prepared to defend: a kulak in Russia is a less miserable peasant.

It has not been possible, however, for the Communists to avoid concrete estimates of the number of kulaks; in the present instance M. N. Tukhachevski fixed it at the time of the uprising at 20 percent.[21] His words carry weight, since he suppressed the uprising. And yet in all probability he was merely repeating the conventional Communist estimate for this part of the country, as the same figure is used for the same purpose in respect to Voronezh province.[22] An explanation of how such a figure is determined is not offered, strengthening our contention that the Communists, for all their fixation on kulaks, do not have any "scientific" formula for measuring this stratum of the population and apply the term to any peasant who is—or may be presumed to be—against their regime.

A less hazy claim is that 14 percent of the holdings in Tambov province belonged to kulaks in 1917, and 9 percent to better-to-do peasants.[23] The first figure is obviously based on the 13.8 percent of households with mechanical sowers, harvesters, or other complex machinery according to the general economic census of 1917, a proportion much greater than in Riazan, Tula, Kursk, and Orel—provinces to the north and west—and hence supporting evidence for the view that Tambov stood out as a kulak stronghold. The second figure is also taken from Communist party sources with no indication as to how it was derived. The 23 percent total for the upper strata of the peasantry can be closely approximated on the basis of other criteria. Twenty-three and four-tenths percent of the households had owned three or more horses apiece at the turn of the century;[24] and 20 percent of them each had six or more *desiatinas* of land under plow in 1917, while 8 percent had over ten *desiatinas*.[25]

Aside from the question of the degree of wealth reflected in the ownership of three horses or fifteen acres of land, none of these means of weighting the kulak element apply to 1920, nor do they measure the levelling in the size of holdings during the period of wartime communism or the general impoverishment of the peasantry during those dreadful years. A source speaks of 6 percent of households with three or more horses in 1917,[26] but whether the cumulative effect of the war, the introduction of machinery, and the steady increase in horseless households—a process which began in the previous century—would have been so hard on the horses as to cause the figure in question to tumble from 23.4 percent to 6 percent in twenty years seems more than dubious.

Data in the possession of the *uezd* committee of the Communist party purported to show that one-tenth of the households in Kirsanov *uezd* were still kulak in January 1921 after wartime communism had run its course.[27] According to Antonov-Ovseenko, the number of households in the same *uezd* with six *desiatinas* or more of cultivated land had fallen between 1917 and 1919 from 30.4 percent of the total to 16.3 percent, and households with over sixteen *desiatinas* had completely disappeared. In the province as a whole, holdings with six *desiatinas* or more had shrunk from 18 percent to 6.3 percent.[28] This information strengthens the impression that kulaks were indeed numerous in Kirsanov and Tambov *uezds*, as generally throughout the southern areas at the base of the province.

We may conclude from this scattered and not very satisfactory evidence that on the eve of the revolution one of every five peasants in Tambov province was less miserable than the other four, and so could be called a kulak. Even such a degree of affluence had been lessened during the upheaval with the levelling of the peasants themselves and the excesses of wartime communism; kulaks nevertheless managed to survive—or to revive—particularly in those areas that became the hearth of the insurrection. It can also be concluded that former kulaks who had seen their holdings levelled or had been set upon by agents of the Communist regime preserved the memory of a better day along with a hatred of the order which had dragged them down into the squalor of the average peasant. Communist propaganda is most likely correct in depicting them as a significant factor, though not at all accurate in blowing them up into monsters of evil and attributing to them sole responsibility for agrarian insurrections. It is absurd to speak of Kirsanov, Tambov, and Borisoglebsk *uezds* as "mainly kulak"[29] when—even under a strained interpretation of the term—that element was less than a third of the village population, and by more realistic standards would have been still smaller.

Nevertheless, by the mere fact of standing out from the herd the kulaks evidenced qualities that caused their social weight to exceed their numbers and made them—for certain purposes—the mouthpiece of the aspirations of the village as a whole. They were more enterprising and self-willed, they could more easily achieve organization, they were more conscious of their grievances and more prone to seek redress, they were probably more intelligent, and certainly they were more capable than the mass out of which they had so painfully emerged. It is likely that they would have formed the backbone of resistance to the surgery performed on the Russian people in the name of social experimentation even if they themselves had not been selected for excision.

The proletariat in Tambov province did not have to be sought with a microscope; it could be found in the war industry and railroad shops in the city of Tambov and in the cloth factories and beet sugar refineries distributed over the countryside. Yet it was a tiny element compared to the peasantry, and its scanty numbers had been thinned further by the adverse conditions created in part by the ascendancy of its own self-appointed vanguard, the Communist party. Industrial workers numbered 14,000 at the opening of the century,[30] 25,327 by 1918, but only 17,426 in 1921.[31] Although these figures are restricted to workers in plants and factories—that is, to industry in the strict sense—and do not include those engaged in crafts, they still do not include proletarians as the Communists would like them to be, for the cloth factories, distilleries, and sugar refineries were in bucolic surroundings and for many workers their wages merely supplemented the family income from agriculture as a result of the retention of holdings. The half-proletarian, half-peasant type flourished here as well as further north. Communist sources, both of that period and later, complain that the Tambov workers could not serve as the proper basis for a strong Communist organization since they not only could not pull the village after them but in all too many instances themselves succumbed to village influence.[32] The commissar of repression limits basic support to the two thousand-odd workers of the recently-equipped munitions plant—the Powder Works—and to the several hundred workers of the artillery repair shop in Tambov,[33] yet Communist control even here left something to be desired.

We may treat with reserve the Communist strictures on the Tambov working class, since it will be one of our theses that by 1921 the proletariat manifested sympathy for the peasant cause, whether it were a case of the worker who had remained half a peasant or of the simon-pure proletarian who had severed ties with the village. In general, the disjunction of the two classes is not so sharp as the Communists like to make it, and certainly by 1921 the harsh conditions under which the Russian workers lived were alleviated very little by the claim of the governing party to be their vanguard.

Notes

1. The color of the woods and the countryside, and so of the peasant cause.

2. This Russian word will be retained, as the possible translations—"district" or "county"—do not satisfy the author.

3. The Moscow rail connection with Astrakhan extended southward from Saratov through the arid steppe east of the Volga.

4. N. Romanov, "Tambovskaia guberniia," *Entsiklopedicheskii slovar'* (Brockhaus-Efron), vol. 32 (St. Petersburg, 1901), p. 560.

5. Ibid., pp. 559–60.

6. N. Romanov, "Tambov: Tambovskii uezd," ibid., p. 568.

7. Ibid., pp. 568–69.

8. References to the respectable flow of the Vorona can be taken in the relative sense only, for the new issue of the Soviet encyclopedia reveals the average discharge over the year as that of a modest stream—41.5 cubic meters per second at Borisoglebsk. See *Bol'shaia sovetskaia entsiklopediia*, 3rd ed., vol. 5 (1971), p. 361, col. 1070.

9. "Borisoglebskii lesnoi massiv," ibid., 2nd ed., vol. 5 (1950), p. 580.

10. Figures from *Entsiklopedicheskii slovar'* (Brockhaus-Efron) under the entries for the respective places.

11. See the short but informative article, "Shipov les," in the *Bol'shaia sovetskaia entsiklopediia*, 2nd ed., vol. 48 (1957), pp. 51–52. Ash make up 5 percent of the total, aspen 4 percent, and linden, elm, and maple 2 percent. All trees are broad-leaved and most are hardwood. It is thought that the name of this forest came from the English word "ship," and that that is what Peter meant the trees to become.

12. The information on Voronezh is drawn mainly from the encyclopedia articles on the subject in the *Entsiklopedicheskii slovar'* (Brockhaus-Efron), vol. 7 (1895), pp. 205–9, and in the *Bol'shaia sovetskaia entsiklopediia*, 2nd ed., vol. 9 (1951), pp. 108–14 (see picture of Shipov Forest on p. 111), and from articles on the various *uezds*. It is regrettable that the base of reference for the geographical setting must be twenty to thirty years before or thirty to forty years after the events in question; thus the forested area at the time of the insurrection (1921) had lessened somewhat in comparison to the turn of the century and possibly also when compared to the present, if recent plantings are included in the figures.

13. See the description of Chembar *uezd* in *Entsiklopedicheskii slovar'* (Brockhaus-Efron), vol. 38 (1903), p. 495.

14. The forested area in Penza province had shrunk over a period of sixty years from 1,349,868 *desiatinas* in the 1830s to 572,436 in 1896. See the article on Penza

province in ibid., vol. 23 (1898), p. 135. The steppelike character of Novokhopersk *uezd* in Voronezh province effaced the memory of the time when it had been a continuous forest through which no one could pass.

15. Apparently by the last Imperial census of 1897, although not explicitly so stated. See the article on Tambov province in *Entsiklopedicheskii slovar'* (Brockhaus-Efron), vol. 32 (1901), p. 560.

16. V. Shilov, "Voronezhskie ocherki: 1. nasha guberniia" [Sketches of Voronezh: our province], *Pravda*, no. 160, 20 July 1922, p. 5. Figure given is for 1916.

17. V. A. Antonov-Ovseenko, "O banditskom dvizhenii v Tambovskoi gubernii" [About the bandit movement in Tambov province], typescript, Document T–686 of Trotsky Archive, p. 1.

18. I. P. Donkov, "Organizatsiia razgroma antonovshchiny" [Organizing to crush the Antonov movement], *Voprosy Istorii KPSS*, no. 6 (June 1966), pp. 60–61. In certain *uezds* the figure neared 98 percent; these *uezds* are not specified.

19. See the article on that province by N. Kudriavtsev in *Entsiklopedicheskii slovar'* (Brockhaus-Efron), vol. 17 (1895), p. 121.

20. It may be interesting to note that the sister provinces of Tambov, Voronezh, and Kursk had almost exactly the same number of people and the same ratio of town to country population. The Empress Catherine liked symmetry and uniformity, and her laying-off of administrative divisions in the Central Black Earth Region conformed brilliantly to her predilections.

21. M. N. Tukhachevski, *Voennym kommunistam* (Tambov, 1921), p. 4, cited in Donkov, "Organizatsiia razgroma antonovshchiny," *Voprosy Istorii KPSS*, no. 6 (June 1966), p. 62.

22. I. Ia. Trifonov, *Klassy i klassovaia bor'ba v SSSR v nachale nepa (1921–1923gg.)* [Classes and the class struggle at the beginning of the NEP (1921–1923)], part 1, *Bor'ba s vooruzhennoi kulatskoi kontrrevoliutsiei* [The struggle with the armed kulak counterrevolution] (Leningrad, 1964), p. 78.

23. Ibid.

24. See article on Tambov province in *Entsiklopedicheskii slovar'* (Brockhaus-Efron), vol. 32, p. 562. The year of reference is presumably 1897.

25. Antonov-Ovseenko, "O banditskom dvizhenii v Tambovskoi gubernii," p. 1.

26. Trifonov, *Klassy i klassovaia bor'ba v SSSR*, part 1, p. 78.

27. From the Central Party Archives, cited in ibid. A study of the map would repay even Russian authors. This one does not know that Inzhavino was in Kirsanov *uezd;* he wants to place it in Tambov *uezd*, although he says "province." Of course it was; all of Kirsanov *uezd* was in Tambov province.

28. Antonov-Ovseenko, "O banditskom dvizhenii v Tambovskoi gubernii," pp. 2-3. Lenin made marks in the margin of this manuscript opposite the figures showing the decline of large holdings, no doubt with mixed emotions: pleasure at the misfortune of the kulaks, sorrow over the increase in smaller individual holders.

29. A. Girshfel'd [Hirschfeld], "Tambovskii krovopodtek" [The Tambov bloodletting], *Izvestiia*, no. 247, 3 November 1921, p. 1.

30. *Entsiklopedicheskii slovar'* (Brockhaus-Efron), vol. 32, p. 563.

31. Donkov, "Organizatsiia razgroma antonovshchiny," *Voprosy Istorii KPSS*, no. 6 (June 1966), p. 61.

32. Ibid.; see also V. I. Lenin, "Novye vremena, starye oshibki v novom vide" [New times and old mistakes in new form], in *Polnoe sobranie sochinenii* [Full collection of his works], 5th ed. (Moscow, 1958–1965), vol. 44, p. 103, and "Predislovie" [Foreword], ibid., vol. 42, p. viii.

33. Antonov-Ovseenko, "O banditskom dvizhenii v Tambovskoi gubernii," p. 1.

— 2 —

Causes of the Insurrection

Why did the province of Tambov become the center of a formidable insurrection, one of the key episodes in the second civil war and the best-organized of all the peasant attempts to free themselves from the iron grasp of the Soviet regime? The causes were in part social and economic and in part political and personal; some were common to the whole country, others were of a regional character. One primary cause was peculiar to Tambov province.

The peasants there shared the privations of peasants everywhere as a result of the Great War, the civil war, revolution, and communist rule. Already in the fall of 1919 these privations had been recounted to President Kalinin as he passed through Morshansk *uezd*: the village had been without nails for a whole year; there were no implements and no kerosene; salt was so scarce that one pound brought in barter eight pounds of grain. Matches and ironware of all kinds could have been added to the list. Kalinin upbraided the complaining peasants and admonished them that they were not badly off.[1] That depends on the point of view. In the light of what was to come, it may be conceded that he was correct.

Lenin spoke with authority when he said that revolutions require sacrifices. His certainly did. He seemed to feel that the worth of a revolution depended on the amount of sacrifice it entailed, for he berated the Czech communist Šmeral for wanting a revolution that would not be too hard on the people.[2] A difficult task, according to Lenin, was the distribution of privations in a revolution. The correct solution was to proceed along severely practical lines: "We help peasants because it is indispensable to the retention of power. . . . It is this motive of expediency that for us has been decisive, and not any consideration of just distribution." Some months earlier he had felt constrained to admit that the peasants, who had been better off than the workers until the winter of 1920–1921, were now indeed worse off.[3] In reality both were utterly miserable. Now, however, he apologized to the Communist International for helping peasants while workers starved and "the peasant exploits us."

These words and those above were spoken in the summer of 1921[4] at a time when a large segment of the Russian peasantry had been gripped by a famine of Asian proportions, fully comparable to the great famines of Chinese and Indian history. They are the words of a man who was primordially anti-peasant, and they reveal—as do few of his utterances—his inner essence. There was reason to revolt against this man.

Wartime conscription had weighed upon the Russian people for six full years by the time the Tambov insurrection began. The war weariness which had contributed so powerfully to the triumph of Bolshevism in 1917 had been still further intensified by three years of civil war, and the disinclination of the population to fight for either Reds or Whites showed in a flood of desertions from the contending armies—especially from the numerically superior Red Army. The woods were full of these desperate characters. In fact, one derivation of the term "Green" is that it was applied in irony by the population to the soldiers hiding out in the forests.[5] Soviet authorities would bestir themselves periodically and send out punitive detachments to round up deserters, some of whom would be shot as an example to others. Small wonder that deserters furnished many recruits for the Green bands, although Soviet sources differ as to the magnitude of the contribution, most of them blowing it up while others refuse to treat it as a factor of primary significance.[6] Not only conscription itself but the way it was administered constituted a grievance: corruption permeated the system and in one area there was a regular tariff for relief from the draft, payment being made either in inflated roubles or—presumably at a more favorable rate—in moonshine. One village of 170 dwellings had eighty deserters, some of whom had been bought out and others of whom had simply absconded.[7]

The end of the war with the Whites and the demobilization of much of the Red Army did not allay this discontent but merely changed its form. The disgruntlement of the conscripted was succeeded by that of the demobilized, who returned to their villages after vexing delay to find conditions bad and their families in need.[8] It was hard for them to settle down to peaceful pursuits, due both to the psychology bred by living at the expense of the country and to the difficulty of absorbing such numbers into a ruined economy. Only at the cost of unprecedented exertion, according to Lenin, had it been possible to disband an army in wintertime with any degree of dispatch in the face of transportation problems then existing in Russia.[9] He stated flatly that "demobilization bred banditry," and it is evident that he had a very real fear of turning loose so many peasants with military experience and regarded the situation as dangerous in the extreme.[10] Actually, demobilization was only a single contributing factor to the Green movement.

The same can be said of religion. While the clergy does not seem to have exercised any more influence in Tambov province than elsewhere, religious sentiment was not negligible and merged with the powers of darkness in such manifestations as the vogue of Anna the Prophetess and the sale of water from a sacred spring in Morshansk *uezd*, reputed to induce visions of Christ, of his mother, or of the saints. Especially did the primitive Mordvins succumb to the lure of the spring—the one form of peasant exploitation which aroused Soviet indignation.[11] It was not only the antireligious policies in themselves that offended sensibilities, but the crude manner in which they were carried out. Women and older persons may have constituted the core of the aggrieved,[12] but now and again there are indications that the peasants as a whole resented the atheism of the Soviet regime.[13]

A major irritant of the rural population was the institution by the Communists of state and collective farms between 1918 and 1921 in the first flush of collectivizing zeal. All accounts without exception, Soviet and non-Soviet, agree that these enterprises were intensely unpopular. It was not merely that they held back land—in a sense preserving certain former estates which the peasants would have liked to divide—but that the makeup of their personnel affronted the toilers' conscience and evoked ridicule, indignation, and ire. One element the farms preserved was the *dvorovye*, the household or courtyard menials under serfdom, who had lost out all around: the emperor had given this element nothing at the time of emancipation and the peasants had given it nothing in 1917 and 1918, shutting it out from the proceeds of expropriation. But the Soviet regime admitted it to the collectivized farms since ordinary peasants did not seek admission and this element had no other place to go.

State and collective farms also sheltered remnants of the former possessing classes—the managerial personnel of the estates and sometimes the estate owners themselves. Wounded veterans lived on the farms, and idlers were attracted to them as a natural place of refuge. The motley population of collective enterprises seemed to be animated by a collective desire to do as little work as possible, and of the relatively large number of them in Tambov province—which had a higher degree of collectivization, in part because of artificial stimuli—not one was doing well.[14]

The men in the Soviet hierarchy found excuses for them—nothing could shake their dedication to dogma. Kalinin told the comrades that they should not be astonished at the failure since these enterprises had so little in the way of technical equipment or comforts,[15] and Lenin attributed their unsatisfactory performance to lack of experience in collective operation. "The experiment with these farms that have been collectivized merely affords an example of how not to operate; the peasants in the vicinity make fun of them or wax indignant."[16] There was no use in giving more latitude to the state farms at the present time, Lenin said. "They are very bad."[17] This blunt confession was offset by his faith in the future. Dogma obstructed his vision, and he did not foresee that fifty years later they would still be bad.

The waste on state farms and the trifling character of their work force further irritated the peasantry. There was duplication of labor, crops were poorly attended, and livestock badly cared for; theft was rampant. The peasant economy may have slipped but it was far above the level of the state farms, whereas under the Tsar a superior form of agriculture had been practised on private estates. The peasants not only resented the state farms but held them in contempt. And the peasants had to make good what the loafers did not do, for they were dragooned into labor service, certain villages being assigned to certain farms in a manner not unlike the practice of Peter the Great in binding villages to factories or to plants. The peasants, seeing in this practice a return to the old system, said that only the landowners were lacking, and there were even some of those around—as we have seen—although not in their former capacity. Far from serving as examples of better farming, the collectivized enterprises became a cancerous growth on the rural economy, preparing the ground for armed revolt against the regime that sponsored them. What happened in the course of that revolt would attest more clearly than any sources the depth of peasant revulsion against them.[18]

The revolution had had the effect of equalizing landholdings throughout the country, reducing the number of kulaks and poor peasants at either end of the scale and swelling the number of middle peasants, who were henceforth enthroned in the village—until Joseph Stalin saw fit to undo this most fundamental of all the results of the revolution with his program of forced collectivization, with his "revolution from above" which was in the strictest sense of the word a counter-revolution. It was the contention of the commissar of repression in 1921 that the knife of equalization had been especially sharp in Tambov province. The kulaks most adversely affected by this levelling process formed the backbone of the Green movement, in his opinion, seeing in it the opportunity not only of striking at the hated Soviet order, but also of regaining their lost position in the village. He cited some figures for Kirsanov *uezd*—home ground of the Antonov bands—according to which households with more than eight *desiatinas* (twenty acres) each had decreased by some eight times while those with over sixteen *desiatinas* had completely disappeared. Without specific reference to Kirsanov, he said that kulaks suffering from this process had at times even been reduced to the pauper category.

It is an interesting contention, yet one that is hard to evaluate.[19] Certainly there were better-to-do peasants adversely affected by the revolution, but whether they formed a definite substratum of the kulak class is questionable in view of the fact that any kulak would be set against the Soviet regime and that any peasant, irrespective of economic standing, would be resentful of one or another of its policies.

When everything has been said about plural causation in the case of the Antonov insurrection and all allowances have been made for other factors, there remains one overwhelming cause: the food levy of the early years of Soviet Russia—the years of militant communism. Lenin conceded that it was the main cause of general disaffection,[20] and no source has contradicted him, with one minor exception. In the fever of the civil war and the fight for survival— with a feeling of desperation and without regard for its own theory of a lengthy period of transition—the party plunged straight into communism by taking the produce of the peasantry for distribution to the factories, which would then supply the peasants with whatever they needed. But the factories in reality could supply the peasants with little or nothing, and in effect the surplus food was confiscated—and sometimes more than the surplus. The peasants, with the shortsightedness common to all classes, had approved expropriation of the landowners' property without compensation; and now they had their own produce—and, a decade later, their holdings—expropriated without compensation. They had been paid—it is true—in paper money, but inflation rendered it valueless.

Lenin acknowledged the true state of affairs, though only after the Green movement had forced abandonment of the levy. He asserted that the regime had been able to survive only by taking the produce of the peasant without recompense, "since paper money, of course, was no recompense,"[21] and depicted the levy in terms of a loan with payment deferred until industrial recovery.[22] Fifty years later the debt is still unsettled and is compounded annually by the procurements which have become a permanent part of the system, contrary to Lenin's intent.[23] Apparently the present Soviet contention is that the peasants received payment at the time in the form of expropriated land and the protection afforded by the Red Army against restoration of the old order.[24]

A grievous burden everywhere in Russia—"unbearable" though "temporary," in the words of L. D. Kamenev,[25] who made a career of being a moderate in an extremist party—the food levy was exceptionally severe on Tambov province because of its reputation as a food-producing area and because of special circumstances. But the performance no longer justified the reputation. It is true that in normal times Tambov was a surplus food area, but the surplus had become modest relative to the North Caucasus, western Siberia, and the Ukraine—and the times were not normal. The proximity of the front in the first civil war had depleted its food resources, serious losses of equipment had been sustained, and in general the level of agriculture had declined. Yet Tambov continued to figure as highly productive in the calculation of the Food Commissariat, and much was exacted of it.[26]

Special circumstances, however, aggravated a burden that would have been heavy in any event. The areas of maximum surplus grain production had been held fitfully during the first civil war; even at its conclusion they were not as firmly in hand as provinces like Tambov, where Soviet control had been all but unbroken. Moreover, the true breadbaskets were remote and transportation problems in relation to them were difficult. Tambov, on the other hand, was closer to the food-deficient center of the country and bound to it by convenient means of shipment.

And so it was milked dry, both on its own account and to compensate for failure to extract more from the outlying regions. It paid dearly in the food years 1918–1919 and 1919–1920, and even worse was to come in 1920–1921 when the potential of western Siberia, the North Caucasus, and the Ukraine had been included in the schedules of the Food Commissariat at a time when the Soviet apparatus was not strong enough to fulfill such expectations.[27] It was so bad that the commissar of repression himself told Lenin that if the levy on Tambov province had been fully realized, a person would have been left with one *pood* of grain and one and six-tenths *poods* of potatoes, whereas the average consumption in the years 1909–1913 had been seventeen and nine-tenths *poods*. Even at that, he added, the levy had been nearly half fulfilled.[28]

The incidence of the food levy thus fell most heavily on areas of no great surplus, simply because they were more accessible. The agencies of the Food Commissariat—praised by Lenin for its relative effectiveness and the steady rise in its level of achievement[29]—could get at Tambov more readily and remove the grain more easily. The significance of the province in this respect was marked in the year of the first food levy, 1918–1919. It then figured as second only to Samara province in both levy and actual procurement,[30] and ranked first in food requisitioning personnel (numbered appropriately in bayonets: 4,816 out of a total of 25,408 actively engaged as of 1 November 1918)[31] and third in the number of committees of the poor (3,011, or about a tenth of the whole).[32] Tambov was therefore a main arena for the application of Lenin's second social war in the village. Its preeminence appears to have been steadily maintained, and in 1920 it was the main source of potatoes for Petersburg, although eclipsed by Tomsk province in respect to grain.[33] Finally, it will be remembered that the importance of Tambov province transcended its own resources: through it passed major lines of communication between the center and the fertile southeast.

There is a single source that denies the significance of the food levy as a mainspring of the Green movement in Tambov province and brands the notion of its crushing incidence as a myth needing to be exploded. According to this source, the full weight of the levy fell on the northern, infertile, and relatively submissive *uezds* where the degree of fulfillment ranged from 74 percent to 146 percent (the latter a revealing figure in itself) as against only 20 percent to 30 percent in the future "bandit" *uezds*—those most disaffected in the center and southeast: Tambov, Kirsanov, and Borisoglebsk. As these were the fertile areas, however, one would need further information before evaluating the claim, for partial compliance in a rich district might outweigh full compliance in one from which little could be expected.

Since no other figures are reproduced, and as the bulk of evidence—Soviet as well as anti-Soviet—is in the other direction, the contention[34] must be disallowed. In asserting that the Socialist Revolutionaries (SRs) had blown up the impact of the food levy, this "attentive witness" of their actions in Tambov province probably was personally engaged in distortion by attempting to portray the Antonov uprising as the product of SR manipulation rather than as a genuine peasant movement born of grievous conditions. The Soviet leadership took much the same line until the upheaval of early 1921 forced it to confront reality.

As in the case of conscription, though with still broader repercussions, the food levy embittered the population as much by the way it was carried out as by its intrinsic harshness. Its administration was attended by all manner of abuses. When the dam of popular patience had burst earlier in 1921 and had forced its abolition, the Soviet leadership conceded these abuses and sought to play them down. Lenin admitted that the state apparatus was permeated with bureaucratism—a whole lot of bureaucratism—but he was optimistic that these so roundly cursed abuses could be overcome.[35]

He could feel optimistic because of his faith in terrorism, which he would apply to the bureaucracy in order to root out saboteurs who

had wormed their way in and were abusing the peasants: they were
to be tried and shot on the spot. This proposed action must have
been the high-water mark of Lenin's concern for the peasants. He
fell upon the Martovs and Chernovs for their abhorrence of such
methods. He maintained that terrorism had to be either the White
Guard or bourgeois terrorism on the order of the English in Ireland,
or the Red terror of his own regime.[36]

Lenin conceded more than bureaucratic evils. The food policy of
Soviet Russia from 1917 to 1921 without doubt was crude, imperfect, and fraught with abuse, and serious mistakes had been made in
its execution.[37] Twice he acknowledged that at times not only the
peasant's surplus produce but a part of what was necessary for his
subsistence had been claimed by the levy.[38] Kalinin, the nominal
head of state, confirmed the words of his party chief—the real
head—and went even further. Upholding the necessity of compulsion in matters of taxation, he nevertheless confessed that at times
officials resorted to measures "harsh in the highest degree"[39] and
that, while reproaches about plundering the peasants contained
more noise than truth, there were occasions "here and there" when
everything, up to the last grain, had been taken from them.[40] As a
consequence, the decline of the rural economy had been
hastened—an understatement no British leader has ever matched.

The All-Russian Central Executive Committee, in a circular to
local soviets, affords insight into specific abuses committed by
agencies entrusted with putting the food levy into effect: arbitrary
arrests, incarceration in unheated quarters, physical violence,
unnecessary brandishing of arms, and so on. The committee pointed
out that it was a grave offense to collect more than the levy called for
or to divert the proceeds to private needs or to the distillation of
spirits, especially when such offenses were committed by food levy
personnel in public view.[41] Heavy penalties for these abuses were
enacted on 3 March 1921 in the midst of a fearful crisis, leading one
to question why they had not been enacted previously in view of the
fact that the food levy had been in operation since the latter half of
1918. Outright criminality on the part of some local officials was
mentioned in the government newspaper.[42]

Lenin put his finger on perhaps the gravest of all abuses when he
made it clear that by collecting two or even three times over from the
peasant, the government had actually been guided—not by its own

standards in fixing the food levy—but by the principle of taking all that the traffic would bear. As a result the peasant who strove the hardest suffered the most. Any possibility of stable economic relationship had thus been destroyed.[43] The repeated upward revision of the exactions was also a consequence of what Lenin termed the inability of the Communists to figure correctly even five weeks in advance.[44]

So far the recitation of abuses concerns the country as a whole. What about Tambov itself? We have the testimony of the military commander who suppressed the uprising and the commissar who oversaw the repression. Taking the latter first, Antonov-Ovseenko starts by denying that pressure on the Tambov peasantry had been any more severe than in the case of other "grain" provinces. A careful investigation had turned up only two or three instances of grave illegalities; the excesses imputed to the food detachments were exaggerated, and in general these organs had kept within the limits of what he significantly termed "severe decrees and circulars."

Indirectly, the commissar seems to be saying that it was the government and not its agencies which was to blame, especially when he states the food levy of 1920–1921 was wholly beyond the ability of the peasants to meet.[45] Directly, he says a good deal more about what was wrong in Tambov province at the end of his memorandum, when he details for Lenin the measures necessary to insure against a repetition of the uprising. In general the soviets were to be brought closer to the people, who were to be drawn into their work and given assurance that local needs and conditions were being taken into account. There would be merciless prosecution of all forms of economic mismanagement; the population must be shown that what was taken from it was being conserved and used to best advantage. There were to be no promises incapable of being redeemed. The relations of the state to the village were to be precisely defined, and the village must know precisely what was demanded of it and when. Never were demands to be made exceeding limits already established, and never were obligations to be imposed impossible of fulfillment. Decrees must not be issued belatedly but must precede the actions taken under them. There must be no relapse into methods now abandoned, such as inflicting a collective penalty on a village because of the default of a part of its citizens or levying a supplementary tax after the regular imposts had been collected. This prescription in the negative sense of things which were not to be done, of course, reveals those things that had been done by the Soviet administration in Tambov province.[46]

The testimony of the military commander is terse and matter-of-fact. The Soviet regime used its best general against the Greens in Tambov, and the memorandum Tukhachevski wrote for Lenin is a model of succinctness, of clarity, and also of honesty. He did not dissemble the reasons for the insurrection. They were those common to all of Russia, he told Lenin: disaffection over the food levy, and the "incompetent" and "exceptionally harsh" way in which it was carried out in the localities by the food administration. Tukhachevski apparently felt no need to go into the other causes in view of the extent to which they were overshadowed by the food levy.[47]

Testimony of equal importance is that of the Chekist M. Pokaliukhin or Pokoliukhin, an agent of the Extraordinary Commission who was intimately involved in combatting the Green movement and who was there at the end.[48] Pokaliukhin relieves the studied anonymity of Communist accounts by giving the name of the official in charge of executing the food levy program in Tambov province. His name was Golvin, and although Pokaliukhin mentions him in only one sentence, what he says is revealing enough: Golvin "did not spare harsh measures" in dealing with the peasantry.[49]

Testimony from the Soviet side naturally is not given to elaboration in such matters, yet is indicative of what went on in the unhappy province. Details may be filled in from non-Soviet sources, at least to some extent. The committees of the poor, recruited from the hooligan castoffs of society with a generous injection of criminal elements and practising every kind of abuse—including the settling of personal accounts on the side—dealt an irreparable blow to the moral authority of the regime. Later they were abolished, but the memory of them remained.

Representatives of the central government irritated the rural population by their tactlessness and cruelty, their round ignorance of agricultural matters, and their "bad Russian speech" (the latter presumably a reference to their Jewish or Lettish background).[50] The hard-driven local officials, if they were honest, writhed under the orders from Moscow, and one commissar—a member of the party—receiving an impossible order to take five more *poods* per person after two such levies had already been made, found a solution in suicide.

Shootings perhaps were not common but neither were they unknown. A specific example was Dukhovka in Tambov *uezd*, where two of the villagers were killed, one wounded, and one shot as an example to the others.[51] Several sources mention the taking of hostages; and the peasants of Novaia Derevnia (somewhere in Tambov province), recounting their woes to a sailors' detachment sympathetic enough to listen, added flogging to the list—the time-honored expedient of dealing with peasants in eastern Europe which always crops up under regimes of the most diverse character. Elected members of village and *volost'* soviets who responded to the will of their constituents rather than to that of the central government were cast into prison and their beheaded soviets had chairmen from the towns imposed in their stead.[52]

Plundering for private gain accompanied the food levy and rendered it still heavier. A peasant observer of conditions in Talitski *volost'* of Usman *uezd* saw how members of requisitioning detachments sent cattle, grain, and fowl to their own homes. But it was not merely a question of diverting from public to private use what was lost to the peasant in either case. If the food detachment people saw something not subject to requisition that excited their cupidity, they took that, too. Our peasant source (and that is the rarest of sources) witnessed the appropriation of wearing apparel by despoilers so lacking in a sense of shame that they took warm clothing off the owner and put it on themselves in the home of the victim, before his very eyes.[53] In Usman *uezd* generally the Communist youth was in the saddle. Most responsible positions were held by eighteen- to twenty-four-year-olds whose approach to Communism was simple and materialistic: everything was for themselves and they rode on the best horses as by natural right.[54]

In noting the aspects of Soviet policy that provoked armed resistance, it should be borne in mind that not only articles of consumption were levied. The peasant might have his horse and wagon or cart requisitioned or be forced to use them himself for conveyance duty, either to carry officials in need of transportation—and Soviet officials even in this early stage were already quite numerous—or to transport military personnel who preferred to move through the villages instead of going by rail.[55] Or the peasant might have to haul wood in a land where oil has only recently superseded coal as the chief source of fuel, but where at that time wood was more important than either for industry, railroads, and heating the cities. The conveyance weighed heavily upon the peasant under ordinary circumstances, and its weight was intolerable when he did not have enough fodder to maintain the strength of his horse. Lenin recognized the significance of the peasant and his horse for the nonagricultural sector of the economy and the burden that rested upon them[56]; and Antonov-Ovseenko recognized the load as being very heavy in Tambov province, especially in the northern *uezds* where the poverty of the soil had preserved the forest from the ravages of the plow.[57]

Had they known any history, the peasants of Tambov province would doubtless have agreed with the summation of their plight by Socialist Revolutionaries in exile when they wrote that "as in the days of Batu a tribute had been laid upon the village population" and another numberless horde with its extraordinary commissions and its whole machinery of merciless exploitation had come down upon them.[58] Lenin had been actually weaker than Batu, if not less merciless, and the peasants would have to wait for Joseph Stalin before experiencing a yoke equal to or surpassing that of the Mongol conqueror. Lenin said that it had been "unimaginably difficult" to put through the food levy,[59] less because of the inadequacy of his administration—one may well imagine—than because of the rapaciousness of the decree. He also said that it had been "burdensome beyond measure."[60] and capped his confessions by telling the Tenth Party Congress that "we will not conceal the fact that the peasantry has profound reason to be dissatisfied."[61]

But he made no such statements reflecting on a measure he had unswervingly sponsored until the events of early 1921 forced his hand. For these events to happen, it was necessary that the rural population be shaken out of its Oriental passivity and be made to realize as intolerable what had long since become so in fact. Two developments effected the transformation.

The first of these was the cessation of the civil war in the fall of 1920. It will be our thesis that this was the first civil war, before whose ending the second could not begin. The Whites under

Wrangel had been overrun in the Crimean citadel by mid-November, relieving the Russian peasantry of the fear of a restoration. This fear had been a very real one, according to a peasant in Usman *uezd*—the inevitable consequence, we may add, of expropriation without compensation. By playing upon this fear and meeting criticism with cries of "Denikin!" the Soviet authorities had been able to stifle dissent and hold the peasants in line.[62] As long as the civil war raged and the Denikins and Kolchaks were visible on the horizon, the peasants gave little trouble. To quote the nominal head of the Soviet state: "They gave grain, they gave cattle for the army, they fulfilled onerous duties. They put up with it all."[63] But when the danger was no longer palpable they would no longer bear the burden, and the way was open for the enemies of the Soviet to reach them.[64]

The second development stirring the village to desperate resistance was the appearance of the most terrible of all the enemies of the Russian people—the desert of Central Asia. The foolishness of governments has never been better illustrated than by the failure of those in Russia to contain or even seriously to contest this powerful, elemental force of nature. By 1914 the Tsarist government ceased to try and turned away to save Serbia and seize the Straits. In that year began the downward slide of agriculture. The desert marched from one triumph to another and carpeted whole stretches of arable land with a thick layer of sand.

Political and economic conditions added to what Kalinin has so aptly termed "a solid preparation for disaster," even if he was reticent about the contribution of his own regime. The year 1919 was the reprieve before execution of the death sentence. The harvest proved to be exceptionally good, the best in many years. But things were deranged by the civil war, according to our Soviet source, and by the food levy, according to the Socialist Revolutionary, which states that the Soviet government left little margin for the peasant and his livestock—only about half of what was normally used by a peasant in the northern black earth zone and only a third of what a German peasant would have used.

And so with little to go on the peasant entered the fateful year of 1920, when the desert would show what it could do. There had been nothing like the drought of that year for a period stretching back to

1840, with the exception of 1869 and 1885.[65] The result was a harvest classified as bad—that is, not giving back even the amount of seed used to produce it—in eleven provinces, and outright disastrous—famine-provoking—in five. The eleven included the most productive in European Russia in respect to grain export. Both Tambov and Voronezh as well as Saratov were among them although not figuring as yet on the list of starvation areas—at least not as a whole. One source states, however, that the southern and southeastern parts of Tambov province were already hungering[66]; these would be the ones nearest the Volga, the most fertile ones, and the "bandit" *uezds*. By the end of August 1920 Lenin complained in a telegram to provincial executive committees of the Volga region about the difficulty of moving shipments of petroleum up the river because of its unprecedented shallowness.[67] He always concerned himself primarily with industry, but the drought was severe enough to affect everything.

There followed a winter of little snow before the catastrophe of 1921. By May and June it was clear that the desert had not relented and that the drought was as bad as ever. The winter grain crop was ruined and the summer crop damaged.[68] The average temperature at Saratov on the Volga equaled that of Cairo on the Nile; in the annals of the city there was no precedent for such heat.[69]

The crop failure of 1921 was unique in its extent and devastation. Only the north central and lake regions of European Russia were exempt from the influence of the desert; here the crops were good—or as good as they could be on the generally infertile soil. Elsewhere more or less successful harvesting occurred only on the rim of the desert's vastly-expanded zone of activity, as on the right-bank Ukraine or in some parts of Siberia other than the Omsk region. Surprisingly, the yield in the Kuban valley did not greatly diminish and this fertile area continued to supply the cities of Russia, in part via Tambov province. The 1922 harvest was average, but until it came in most of southeastern Russia remained a disaster zone, with 22,558,500 people starving by official estimate out of a total population in the stricken areas of 31,922,000 as of 1 July 1922.[70]

The famine did not flail Tambov province as it did the provinces on the Volga, yet there was ample misery. The commissar of repression himself is authority for the statement that by January 1921 half the peasantry was starving. It would be unique for a commissar to exaggerate the plight of peasants under Soviet rule, even in a secret memorandum, so we may interpret his statement to mean simply that about half the people in Tambov province did not have enough to eat—although he speaks of them as chewing on bark and dying from hunger in the worst-stricken areas such as Usman *uezd* and parts of Lipetsk and Kozlov *uezds*.[71] As he does not mention the "bandit" *uezds* of Tambov, Kirsanov, and Boriso-glebsk in this connection, his account varies somewhat from the much later Soviet source cited above,[72] which places the worst conditions in 1920 in these southeastern districts, closer to the Volga and so to the desert.

But it is idle to be concerned with degrees of tragedy—it was bad everywhere. Desperately the peasants sought to make their flour go further by finding substitutes for grain. Potatoes and acorns served the purpose, but potatoes also were scarce and acorns were available only in limited areas. Even this modest boon of nature was in large measure denied the peasants, for the Soviet government levied even on acorns. So recourse was had to unacceptable ingredients—to weeds and chaff. As the peasants failed to keep out the wormwood while gathering pigweed, the bread turned black and bitter. It was estimated that less than a third of the population ate good bread, and then only for a part of the year.

The situation in regard to livestock had long been deteriorating and now became catastrophic. Two-cow families gave way to one-cow families, and many had no cows at all. Horses lost their value, since in many instances they either could not be fed or were given straw and became too weak to work. They were not killed—to kill a horse was a crime to a peasant—they were simply driven away and left to fend for themselves. Behind the yards and out in the fields were many of their carcasses. The number of work horses in 1922 was only 59 percent of that of the previous year,[73] which in itself had represented a serious shrinkage from the past. The peasant was deprived of the materials for heating his domicile by the scarcity of manure and the use of straw for fodder. It was a vicious circle. But the peasant's lot was less monotonous, since he could now freeze as well as starve.[74]

Thus far stress has been placed upon the weight of the burdens borne by the rural population, and upon the abuses connected with the food levy, but not upon the sheer waste accompanying its administration. The Soviet regime has never had a deft hand in agriculture and this characteristic was pronounced from the start. Its head prided himself upon the relative effectiveness of the food-collecting apparatus in contrast to other branches of the Soviet administration.[75] But Antonov-Ovseenko in his secret memorandum told Lenin that however effective the food organs had been in separating the peasant from his produce, they were guilty of gross negligence in conserving the fruits of their enterprise. He felt constrained to admit that a large number of livestock had perished for want of attention, that much grain had been allowed to spoil or to be consumed by fires—here more was involved than official slackness, as shall be seen—and that quantities of assembled potatoes had been left to freeze.[76] The effect of such visible waste in a province where half the population was hungering may easily be imagined.

To the economic and social conditions underlying the Tambov tragedy must be added the political conditions productive of armed revolt. Briefly stated, these were two, one the logical consequence of the other: the strength of the Socialist Revolutionaries and the weakness of the Communist party.

It was customary to regard Tambov as an SR patrimony. There some of the most prominent members of the party had been born, among them Stephen Sletov, one of its founders, his sister Anastasia Sletova, the wife of V. M. Chernov, and Maria Spiridonova, executrix of the people's vengeance against Councillor Luzhenovski in 1906 and leader of the Left SRs a decade later. There V. M. Chernov himself, the chief intellectual force of neo-Populism, had won his spurs in the 1890s by conducting agitation among the peasants of Borisoglebsk *uezd*[77] when it became possible to move again after the death of Alexander III and the retirement from the scene of the two Durnovos—I. N. Durnovo, minister of the interior, and P. N. Durnovo, head of the police department—exceptionally able men who between them had created the trough of the revolutionary movement under Alexander III.

Tambov had been surpassed in turbulence during the revolution of 1905 by the neighboring province of Saratov, together with which it had lapsed into sullen passivity after the triumph of the old order. But in the open year of 1917 the SRs finally came into their own, and politically Tambov presented the view of a grey mass of centrist SRs. Their predominance, however, did not restrain the peasants from staging disorders in September on a scale so broad as to constitute the most graphic evidence of the impatience of the countryside at the record of the Provisional Government.[78] The November election for the Constituent Assembly gave the SRs an overwhelming victory, although not quite as lopsided as in Kursk and Voronezh.[79] Lenin's skill prevented the SRs from mobilizing the peasantry during the earliest and weakest period of Communist rule; their organization was damaged under that rule, and the Left SRs, who were locally little in evidence during 1917, gained ground thereafter and drew off some strength—though how much it is impossible to say since no element of opposition can be measured under the Soviet system.

The food levy and the other harsh features of that system restored to the Socialist Revolutionaries their ability to mobilize the peasantry for political action. There is some evidence of a rather fragmentary character that they had really never stopped trying, but now—in 1920—their efforts bore fruit in a network of clandestine units known as the Union of Toiling Peasantry—*Soiuz Trudovogo Krest'ianstva* (STK)—which will be called the Peasants' Union.

This was a strong organization—by Russian standards of peasant action, a very strong one. It was the civilian arm of the Green movement. An examination of its structure and functions will be deferred until the chapter on organization; here we shall note merely the problem involved in its relationship to the military branch of the Green movement. Did the Peasant's Union serve as the seedbed from which the bayonets sprouted, or did the union itself grow up in the shadow of the military force that Alexander S. Antonov had carefully been putting together? Restated in personal terms, did the SR intellectuals who had always formed the party organization produce the Green movement or was it the outgrowth of peasant desperation skillfully channeled by a man of action, himself a Socialist Revolutionary but not an intellectual, not a party functionary, and never a man to be trammelled by party instructions or regulations?

The factors accounting for the strength of Social Revolutionism in Tambov province explain in large measure the weakness of Communism. The results of the voting in 1917 would lead to the conclusion that the Communists did rather better here than in other overwhelmingly rural constituencies, since they were outvoted less than four to one by the SRs and counted nearly a quarter of a million supporters. But the figures are deceptive, for they reflect a yearning for peace rather than for Communism. Once peace had been attained and Lenin had inaugurated the food levy in conjunction with his second social war in the village (the "rich" peasants versus the poor with the average or middle peasants being held to neutrality)—that is, once Bolshevism had dropped the mask and revealed itself as Communism—the circumference of support contracted drastically and came to embrace little more than the party membership, which in this inhospitable territory was impressive neither in numbers nor in quality.

At the time of the formation of the provincial party organization in May 1918 there were only fifteen hundred members. A year later there were some eleven to twelve thousand; obviously too rapid an intake, for the shake-up of July 1919 eliminated about five thousand from the rolls and left less than seven thousand members, or one Communist for every five to seven hundred inhabitants.[80] The ratio of a minority to the mass it rules need not be high, but it has to be higher than this if it is to rule firmly. The next figure we have is for New Year's Day, 1920, and is an exact one: 11,113 people were in the party at that time, of whom 7,297 had entered on the occasion of the last "party week" toward the end of 1919 when all workers and peasants so desiring had been taken in without the formality of recommendation.[81] Half a year later, in July 1920, membership stood at 14,200.

Thereafter a second period of "re-registration"—shake-up or purge—ensued and continued for the rest of the year. There were 13,490 Communists, including candidates for admission, in Tambov province in August 1920; they were grouped in 685 organizations, 285 of them in the towns with 8,498 members, and 400 in the country with 4,992 members. This was the month when the peasants rose in revolt. By January 1921 the membership of the Communist party had fallen to 9,100.[82] The party was like a sponge, soaking up water and then having it squeezed out—quite a bit of water in both instances. The personnel expanded and contracted so drastically that the organization was deprived of a firm footing and was unable to meet the challenge of the Antonov insurrection.

Not only the thinness and instability but the quality of its membership weakened the Communist party. The proximity of the province to the firing line of the first civil war caused a heavy draft on its personnel for military assignment: fifteen hundred Communists went off to fight Denikin alone. There may have been a correlation between participation in the civil war and dedication to the cause; probably the true believers went more readily and incurred graver losses. In any event, the repeated mobilizations diluted the membership[83] and opened the way to elements less desirable from the partisan standpoint.

Soviet sources inevitably deal with the problem in terms of proletarian versus nonproletarian content. The breakdown for 1921 is said to have shown that only about 30 percent of the party was drawn from the working class and the remainder from the peasantry and the "old intelligentsia,"[84] which in this province had been overwhelmingly Populist. As a matter of fact, by 1921 the proletarian component is not so significant, whether high or low, for the proletariat had become only less disaffected than the peasantry. Of more significance is the probability that the crude half-intellectuals who always have constituted the backbone of Communism had receded before an influx of former Populist or nondescript intellectuals, who for one reason or another had decided to take advantage of the wider opportunity for enrollment in the party. It is reported that some village cells consisted almost entirely of former SRs and Mensheviks, and that among them not a few sought admission in order to sabotage from within.[85] Allowing for the Communist compulsion to drag Mensheviks into any situation as villains, however improbable the setting—and Mensheviks were as scarce as hen's teeth in the rural areas of Tambov province—the rest of the statement is probably true.

The Communists had but a tenuous hold on the soviets—their chosen organs—not just on the village and *volost'* levels where they could have been expected to have difficulty, but also on the *uezd* or district level where things presumably would have been better in hand. The peasants in their majority are described as not taking part in the electoral assemblies, and the opposition parties had been excluded from the soviets. Nevertheless, only a small number of Communists were elected, and in three *uezds*—Usman, Lipetsk, and Temnikov, none of them primarily "bandit" *uezds*—anti-Communist majorities were reported in the soviet congresses, presumably in 1920 although dates are not given. In the Lipetsk congress the Communists had only nine—and sympathizers eight—of the two hundred delegates.

The rule was that Communist success was inversely proportional to the distance from Tambov—the further away from the city, the fewer Communists in the soviets.[86] Only through pressure and strong-arm tactics could they maintain their position; of spontaneous support there was very little in this sullen and hostile sea. The peasant observer makes the interesting comment that in the soviets as a whole control rested in the hands of undesirable characters who also hated Communism, but who had so compromised themselves by nefarious actions as to be committed to upholding the regime out of an instinct for self-preservation.[87]

Another aspect of Communist weakness in Tambov province reflects more credit on that party. Mistreatment of the peasantry provoked decided opposition in the ranks which found expression in the emergence of a right wing dedicated to a conciliatory policy and to softening the impact on the localities of harsh decrees from the center. Needless to say, this wing collided with the adherents of the general line and acute tension arose which came into the open at a peasants' congress in Usman *uezd*. Here the toe-the-line people, in the name of party discipline, undertook to deprive dissenters of the privilege of participation; the dissenters refused to submit to exclusion, the left resorted to the power of the state, and the right had its leaders arrested—including a physician named Ispolatov.[88]

Here in the provinces—already in 1920, at a time when Bukharin himself belonged to the inner core of leadership, directed *Pravda* along orthodox lines and probably had no thought of any such future course of action—the wing of the party was forming that would later come to prominence and experience a tragic fate under his leadership along with that of Rykov and Tomski. There were other issues at stake, but then—as later—the peasant question dictated the line of cleavage between those who would uphold the urban and industrial bias of their party and those who would adjust to the agrarian society over which it had come to rule.

The Communist party in Tambov was a composite of discordant elements. Along with the social dregs and cast-offs, along with the distinctly criminal element—if we are to believe the hostile sources[89]—there were honest people divided between those who nursed Marxian fanaticism and those who were determined to improve relations with the peasantry. With all its diverse elements, the composite was not large. Soviet writers acknowledge the party's weakness but seek to explain it along different lines: they stress the large nonproletarian element and find a further source of weakness in the fact that so many members had not undergone Bolshevik tempering and that their political preparation was weak.[90] In whatever terms the weakness is explained, there is no doubt that the Communist party in Tambov was at low estate when struck by the Antonov insurrection.

The causes examined so far account for the Green movement, but only in lesser part for its virulence in Tambov. Seemingly, the outbreak could have occurred in any of the provinces with similar characteristics and similar experiences. The incidence of the food levy was heavy everywhere, the other exactions no less burdensome, war weariness was felt at every hand, the agrarian component of the population was scarcely less pronounced, and Social Revolutionism had its strongholds—and Communism its weak spots—throughout the Central Black Earth and Volga regions. Kursk and Voronezh provinces resembled Tambov most closely, Samara had a high proportion of kulaks—as Soviet sources never tire of pointing out—and Saratov, with its distinguished record of agrarian revolt, differed only in the sense that Tsaritsyn raised somewhat the proletarian component.

Any one of these provinces could have been the scene of a formidable insurrection, all of them witnessed manifestations of the Green movement, and yet only in Tambov did it materialize in a form that may be said to have endangered the Soviet regime. The conclusion is inescapable that Tambov owed its preeminence in the Green movement to the presence of Alexander S. Antonov.

Notes

1. M. I. Kalinin, *Za eti gody: stat'i, besedy, rechi* [In these years: articles, conversations, speeches] (Leningrad, 1926–1929), vol. 3, pp. 65–72.

2. One is reminded of the confrontation forty-seven years later between Brezhnev, the disciple of Lenin, and Dubček, advocate of a brand of Communism that served the population rather than the cult of heavy industry.

3. Speech to the metal workers' conference in Moscow, 4 February 1921, in Lenin, *Polnoe sobranie sochinenii*, 5th ed., vol. 42, pp. 307–8.

4. Report to the Third Congress of the Comintern, 5 July 1921, in ibid., vol. 44, pp. 45–47.

5. Nadezhda P. Zybko, *Tambovskaia partiinaia organizatsiia v gody grazhdanskoi voiny i inostrannoi interventsii (1918–1920gg.)* [The Tambov party organization in the years of the civil war and foreign intervention (1918–1920)] (Tambov, 1961), p. 27.

6. See the article by A. Kazakov in *Krasnaia Armiia*, no. 9, 1921, cited in Trifonov, *Klassy i klassovaia bor'ba*, part 1, p. 9; see also Zybko, *Tambovskaia partiinaia organizatsiia*, pp. 27–28, where it is claimed with very dubious validity that desertion from the Red Army virtually ceased after the summer of 1919.

7. "Kommunisty na rabote (Pis'mo krest'ianina iz Tambovskoi gub.)" [Communists at work (a peasant's letter from Tambov province)], *Revoliutsionnaia Rossiia*, no. 5 (April 1921), pp. 25–26. Although the name of the peasant who wrote the letter was withheld and the village shared the name of Borisovka with many others, it may be surmised from the context that the setting was in Usman *uezd* and the time was the fall of 1920.

8. "Brozhenie v krasnoi armii" [Ferment in the Red Army], *Volia Rossii*, no. 137 (24 February 1921), p. 4.

9. Speech to Moscow party workers, 9 April 1921, in Lenin, *Polnoe sobranie sochinenii*, 5th ed., vol. 43, p. 153.

10. Report to the Tenth Party Congress on the activity of the Central Committee, 8 March 1921, in ibid., pp. 10, 16–17; see also comment in speech to transport workers on 27 March in ibid., p. 138.

11. N. Pilatskaia, "Dela chudesnye" [Wondrous doings], *Pravda*, no. 167 (28 July 1922), p. 6.

12. "Usmirenie krest'ian v Tambovskoi gubernii" [Peasant pacification in Tambov province], *Na chuzhoi storone* [In foreign parts], no. 3 (1923), p. 129.

13. See chapter eleven.

14. Antonov-Ovseenko, "O banditskom dvizhenii v Tambovskoi gubernii," pp. 1–2. The reader is reminded that this appraisal comes from the commissar of repression himself and was written for the edification of Lenin.

15. Kalinin, *Za eti gody*, vol. 2, p. 118.

16. Report on the replacement of the food levy by the tax in kind, 15 March 1921, in Lenin, *Polnoe sobranie sochinenii*, 5th ed., vol. 43, p. 60. This passage was suppressed in the 3rd edition under Joseph Stalin (see vol. 32, p. 194), and not without reason.

17. Statement at the Tenth Party Conference, 28 May 1921, in ibid., 5th ed., vol. 43, pp. 337, 458 n. 110.

18. -skii, "Po Rossii: Zhizn' sovetskoi derevni (Pis'mo iz Tambovskoi gubernii)" [Around Russia: life in the Soviet village (letter from Tambov province)], *Revoliutsionnaia Rossiia*, no. 3 (February 1921), pp. 21–22; "Kommunisty na rabote," ibid., no. 5 (April 1921), p. 28; Antonov-Ovseenko, "O banditskom dvizhenii v Tambovskoi gubernii," pp. 1–2. The first two sources, which are Socialist Revolutionary (SR), give the distinct impression of forced labor but Antonov-Ovseenko says peasant labor on the state farms was on a share-cropping basis. Thus the obligation would not be in the category of a *corvée* although probably elements of compulsion, indirect if not direct, were present. Antonov-Ovseenko states that there were 150 state farms in operation in 1920 in Tambov province, which was ahead of other provinces in respect to the degree of collectivization; he admitted, however, that this distinction had not come as a result of natural growth. In every case the state farm drew on peasant labor from outside. The higher degree of collectivization no doubt helps to explain the virulence of anti-Soviet sentiment in Tambov in contrast to certain provinces which resembled it in other particulars.

19. Antonov-Ovseenko, "O banditskom dvizhenii v Tambovskoi gubernii," pp. 2–3, 31; see also Kalinin's speech to the Central Executive Committee, "V dni Kronshtadta: Ot voiny k mirnomu khoziaistvennomu stroitel'stvu" [At the time of Kronstadt: from war to peaceful economic upbuilding], in Kalinin, *Za eti gody*, vol. 2, p. 106.

20. Statement on the New Economic Policy and the tasks of political agitators, 17 October 1921, in Lenin, *Polnoe sobranie sochinenii*, 5th ed., vol. 44, pp. 156–59.

21. Speech to the party workers of the Moscow area about the tax in kind, 9 April 1921, in ibid., vol. 43, p. 151; see also concluding remarks on report about replacement of food levy at the Tenth Party Congress, 15 March 1921, in ibid., p. 79; and Lenin's speech to transport workers' congress on 27 March 1921 in ibid., p. 141.

22. See report on Central Executive Committee and Sovnarkom, 22 December 1920, in ibid., vol. 42, p. 148; report on activity of the Central Committee, 8 March 1921, in ibid., vol. 43, p. 14.

23. "O prodovol'stvennom naloge" [About the tax in kind], in ibid., pp. 220–22.

24. Donkov. "Organizatsiia razgroma antonovshchiny," *Voprosy Istorii KPSS*, no. 6 (June 1966), p. 60. Such a justification was given already by Lenin but the sacrifice exacted of the rural population was, even so, viewed as a loan to be later repaid with the restoration of large-scale industry; see Lenin's theses of a report to the Third Congress of the Comintern written on 13 June 1921, in Lenin, *Polnoe sobranie sochinenii*, 5th ed., vol. 44, p. 7. The idea of borrowing from the peasantry has long since been discarded by his successors; too much was borrowed, and the idea of the function of industry as supplying in abundance the needs of the peasants is something about which it is better not to speak.

25. *Izvestiia*, no. 291, 25 December 1921, p. 2; the occasion was the 9th All-Russian Congress of Soviets.

26. Antonov-Ovseenko, "O banditskom dvizhenii v Tambovskoi gubernii," pp. 3–4.

27. Lenin, report on the political activity of the Central Committee to the 10th Party Congress, 8 March 1921, in *Polnoe sobranie sochinenii*, 5th ed., vol. 43, pp. 11, 13–14; Donkov, "Organizatsiia razgroma antonovshchiny," *Voprosy Istorii KPSS*, no. 6 (June 1966), pp. 60–61; P. A. Borisov, *Chernym letom* [Black summer] (Moscow, 1965), pp. 6–7.

28. Antonov-Ovseenko, "O banditskom dvizhenii v Tambovskoi gubernii," p. 4. A letter from a Tambov peasant published in an SR source tells of a family with five mouths to feed that gave up 37.5 *poods* to the food levy out of 85–87 *poods* produced. As 20 *poods* were needed for sowing winter grain, only about 30 were left for the family of five to eat, and it is specifically stated that this included potatoes. The family could have more only by going into the seed reserve. See "Kommunisty na rabote," *Revoliutsionnaia Rossiia*, no. 5 (April 1921), p. 27. It is evident that the official but secret Soviet source and the SR peasant are close to one another in their figures. Generally it is held that the acreage sown contracted because of peasant dissatisfaction with government policy. It was more grim than that. The area shrank because of the struggle to stay alive and the consumption of seed grain.

29. Lenin, *Polnoe sobranie sochinenii*, 5th ed., vol. 43, p. 72; see also speech to the 3rd All-Russian Food Conference, 16 June 1921, in ibid., p. 355.

30. *Iz istorii grazhdanskoi voiny v SSSR: Sbornik dokumentov i materialov v trekh tomakh 1918–1922* [From the history of the civil war in the USSR: a collection of documents and materials in three volumes, 1918–1922] (Moscow, 1960–61), vol. 1, no. 295, pp. 305–6.

31. Ibid., no. 286, pp. 296–97.

32. Ibid., no. 314, p. 326.

33. "Kto snabzhaet Petrograd" [Who supplies Petrograd?], *Volia Rossii*, no. 141, 1 March 1921, p. 4, quoting the *Krasnaia Gazeta* of 5 February 1921. Already by November 1918 the cutting off of the breadbaskets from the center had imposed upon "the remaining grain-producing provinces and Tambov in particular" the task of provisioning Petersburg and Moscow. See comment of Borisoglebsk food committee in *Iz istorii grazhdanskoi voiny v SSSR*, vol. 1, no. 317, pp. 329–30.

34. It was advanced by one B. V. in the *Tambovskaia Pravda*, as reproduced by S. Ch., "Tambovskaia pamiatka ob eserakh" [Tambov record book on the SRs], *Izvestiia*, no. 121 (1560), 2 June 1922, p. 1. The atmosphere of the time, the beating of the drums against the SRs on the eve of their trial, also renders the argument suspect.

35. Speech at the plenary session of the Moscow soviet, 28 February 1921, in Lenin, *Polnoe sobranie sochinenii*, 5th ed., vol. 42, p. 363.

36. "O prodovol'stvennom naloge," in ibid., vol. 43, pp. 234–35.

37. Theses of report on tactics of his party to the Comintern congress, 13 June 1921, in ibid., vol. 44, p. 9.

38. Report to the party workers of the Moscow area in ibid., vol. 43, p. 150; "O prodovol'stvennom naloge," in ibid., p. 219.

39. Remarks before the city soviet of Chita, 27 July 1923, in answer to the peasant Pokrovski, in Kalinin, *Za eti gody*, vol. 3, p. 301.

40. "Ot voiny k mirnomu khoziaistvennomu stroitel'stvu," in ibid., vol. 2, p. 114.

41. "Oprichniki v derevne" [Agents (of Ivan the Terrible) in the village], *Volia Rossii*, no. 154, 16 March 1921, pp. 3–4; Trifonov, *Klassy i klassovaia bor'ba v SSSR*, part 1, p. 216.

42. D. Petrovski, "Bor'ba s banditizmom i krasnye kursanty" [The struggle against banditry and Red Army trainees], *Izvestiia*, no. 133 (1276), 23 June 1921, p. 1.

43. Report on the tax in kind to the 10th Party Conference, 26 May 1921, in Lenin, *Polnoe sobranie sochinenii*, 5th ed., vol. 43, pp. 312–13.

44. See concluding remarks the next day in ibid., pp. 330–31.

45. Antonov-Ovseenko, "O banditskom dvizhenii v Tambovskoi gubernii," p. 4.

46. Ibid., pp. 33–36.

47. M. N. Tukhachevski, "Zapiska," typescript dated 16 July 1921, T–685 of Trotsky Archive, p. 1.

48. The long and informative account by Pokaliukhin I consider to be the best source on the Tambov insurrection; unfortunately, the notes taken from it were lost in the Moscow disaster mentioned in the foreword of the present study.

49. "Po sledam Antonova" [On Antonov's trail], in *Put' Bor'by* [The path of struggle] (Tambov, 1922–1923), vol. 2, *Antonovshchina*, pp. 65–91 (specific page unknown).

50. "Usmirenie krest'ian v Tambovskoi gubernii," *Na chuzhoi storone*, vol. 3, pp. 128–29. Even the Central Party Archives attest the necessity of "reorganizing" some committees of the poor because of the infiltration of "undesirable elements"; see, for example, *Iz istorii grazhdanskoi voiny v SSSR*, vol. 1, no. 286, p. 297.

51. "Po Rossii: Zhizn' sovetskoi derevni," *Revoliutsionnaia Rossiia*, no. 3, February 1921, p. 23.

52. Ibid.; M. Fomichev (Michael Lidin), "Antonovshchina: Iz vospominanii antonovtsa" [The Antonov affair: recollections of a follower of Antonov] (Santiago de Chile, 1955), typescript from the Russian Archive of Columbia University, p. 34.

53. "Kommunisty na rabote," *Revoliutsionnaia Rossiia*, no. 5, April 1921, p. 25.

54. Ibid., p. 28.

55. "Po Rossii: Zhizn' sovetskoi derevni," *Revoliutsionnaia Rossiia*, no. 3, February 1921, p. 24.

56. "O prodovol'stvennom naloge," in Lenin, *Polnoe sobranie sochinenii*, 5th ed., vol. 43, p. 218; speech on same subject in ibid., p. 246; report of Central Executive Committee and of the Sovnarkom to the 9th Congress of Soviets, 23 December 1921, in ibid., vol. 44, pp. 316–318.

57. Antonov-Ovseenko, "O banditskom dvizhenii v Tambovskoi gubernii," p. 5.

58. "Vynuzhdennyia ustupki" [Forced concessions], *Volia Rossii*, no. 162, 25 March 1921, p. 1.

59. Speech to a gathering of the party forces of Moscow city, 24 February 1921, in Lenin, *Polnoe sobranie sochinenii*, 5th ed., vol. 42, p. 349.

60. Speech on the tax in kind recorded on a phonograph, in ibid., vol. 43, p. 246.

61. Speech at the close of the congress, 16 March 1921, in ibid., p. 120.

62. "Kommunisty na rabote," *Revoliutsionnaia Rossiia*, no. 5, April 1921, p. 26.

63. Kalinin, "Ot voiny k mirnomu khoziaistvennomu stroitel'stvu," in *Za eti gody*, vol. 2, p. 115.

64. See also the leading editorial by Iuri Steklov, "Derevnia i novaia ekonomicheskaia politika," *Izvestiia*, no. 203 (1346), 18 September 1921, p. 1; Donkov, "Organizatsiia razgroma antonovshchiny," *Voprosy Istorii KPSS*, no. 6 (June 1966), p. 60.

65. See M. B. Gurevich, *Golod i sel'skoe khoziaistvo Ukrainy: Ocherk* [Essay on the famine and rural economy of the Ukraine] (Kharkov, 1923).

66. Donkov, "Organizatsiia razgroma antonovshchiny," *Voprosy Istorii KPSS*, no. 6 (June 1966), p. 61.

67. Lenin, *Polnoe sobranie sochinenii*, 5th ed., vol. 51, appendices, no. 28, p. 351.

68. A. V. Eiduck, *Die russische Hungersnot 1921–1922 und ihre Bekämpfung im Lichte der Tatsachen* [The Russian famine 1921–1922 and its control according to the facts] (Berlin, 1922), p. 3. Eiduck was the Soviet envoy to foreign relief agencies.

69. Kalinin, "Po golodnym mestam" [In the famine areas], *Izvestiia*, no. 199 (1342), 8 September 1921, p. 2.

70. Kalinin, "Itogi golodnoi kampanii" [Results of the efforts to control famine], in *Za eti gody*, vol. 1, pp. 203, 214. Much information on the famine is given by Kalinin in two sections of this volume: "Neurozhai i golod 1921 goda" [The crop failure and famine of 1921], pp. .179–86, and "Itogi golodnoi kampanii," pp. 187–221. Another source of importance for 1919 and.1920, based on a survey in the *Ekonomicheskaia Zhizn'* for 2 September 1920, is found under the heading "Sovetskaia Rossiia" in the SR émigré paper, *Volia Rossii*, no. 196, 6 May 1921, pp. 3–4.

71. Antonov-Ovseenko, "O banditskom dvizhenii v Tambovskoi gubernii," p. 4.

72. See note 66 above.

73. Eiduck, *Die russische Hungersnot 1921–22 und ihre Bekämpfung*, pp. 8–9.

74. "Kommunisty na rabote," *Revoliutsionnaia Rossiia*, no. 5, April 1921, pp. 27–28. Most of the above information is drawn from this peasant source.

75. Lenin, *Polnoe sobranie sochinenii*, 5th ed., vol. 43, pp. 72, 355.

76. Antonov-Ovseenko, "O banditskom dvizhenii v Tambovskoi gubernii," p. 4.

77. The story is told by V. M. Chernov in his *Zapiski sotsialista revoliutsionera* [Memories of a Socialist Revolutionary] (Berlin, St. Petersburg and Moscow, 1922), vol. 1, pp. 249–335; see Oliver H. Radkey, *The Agrarian Foes of Bolshevism: Promise and Default of the Russian Socialist Revolutionaries, February to October 1917* (New York and London, 1958), pp. 56–57.

78. See Radkey, *The Agrarian Foes of Bolshevism*, pp. 437–39.

79. See table of election returns in Oliver H. Radkey, *The Election to the Russian Constituent Assembly of 1917* (Cambridge, Mass., 1950), p. 78.

80. Plus some two thousand sympathizers. Evidently persons connected to a certain extent with the organization are meant, for surely there would have been more than a couple of thousand sympathizers as the term is generally used—that is, in the loose sense.

81. "Po Rossii: Zhizn' sovetskoi derevni," *Revoliutsionnaia Rossiia*, no. 3, February 1921, p. 24.

82. Donkov, "Organizatsiia razgroma antonovshchiny," *Voprosy Istorii KPSS*, no. 6 (June 1966), p. 61; Trifonov, *Klassy i klassovaia bor'ba v SSSR*, part 1, p. 36. The figures given in these sources are drawn from the party archives.

83. On this subject see Trifonov, *Klassy i klassovaia bor'ba v SSSR*, part 1, pp. 36–37; Zybko, *Tambovskaia partiinaia organizatsiia v gody grazhdanskoi voiny*, p. 37; "Antonovshchina," in *Sovetskaia istoricheskaia entsiklopediia* (Moscow, 1961–), vol. 1, p. 636.

84. Trifonov, *Klassy i klassovaia bor'ba v SSSR*, part 1, p. 37.

85. Donkov, "Organizatsiia razgroma antonovshchiny," *Voprosy Istorii KPSS*, no. 6 (June 1966), p. 61.

86. "Po Rossii: Zhizn' sovetskoi derevni," *Revoliutsionnaia Rossiia*, no. 3, February 1921, p. 24.

87. "Kommunisty na rabote," ibid., no. 5, April 1921, p. 26.

88. Ibid., p. 28.

89. Ibid., p. 25; "Po Rossii: Zhizn' sovetskoi derevni," ibid., no. 3, February 1921, p. 24.

90. Donkov, "Organizatsiia razgroma antonovshchiny," *Voprosy Istorii KPSS*, no. 6 (June 1966), p. 61.

— 3 —

The Leadership of the Insurrection

It is difficult to exaggerate the significance of leadership—or the lack of it—in human affairs. While Carlyle and Joseph Stalin may have succeeded in doing so, their cult of personality has as its counterpart on the other extreme the unwillingness to recognize that the fortunes of an historical development are always conditioned and often determined by the quality of the men who stand at its head. Regrettably, in the present study it is not possible to do justice to the factor of leadership, and for two reasons: the character of the movement itself, and the character of the regime that suppressed it.

The Green leaders were men who acted and wrote not. They were a wholly different breed from the SR intellectuals to whom the Soviet regime has sought to subordinate them. They resembled the Tatar warriors of yore who fought and died with little or no thought of leaving a record of their deeds for posterity. Moreover, the interior location in which the action unfolded prevented the world from taking note of them and prevented them from breaking through to attract external attention. What little is known comes mainly from hostile sources, and Soviet historiography has been wont to play down the individual in favor of impersonal factors—always excepting the Stalinist period, when it received a draught of horse-like proportions in the opposite sense. More important than any prescription for writing history, however, has been the conscious effort to destroy every trace of the Green cause by running down and exterminating every one of its leaders and by mentioning them only to defame. The Soviet regime, it must be repeated, has betrayed a special sensitivity on this subject. And so there is little to go on, even in the case of Antonov, not to speak of his lieutenants.

One approaches the personality of Antonov through a swamp of ignorance and uncertainty by stepping from one small island of fact to another. To find his first name required effort, and even more was needed to learn the patronymic. The year of his birth is unknown and the time, place, and circumstances of his death could be established only after long and patient research. Whole periods of his life are blacked out and the short years of his struggle against Communism are full of problems that cannot be solved, either because information is inaccessible or because it does not exist. He was not prominent enough in the open year of 1917 to receive national publicity and local sources of information are closed to investigation; most likely they would not yield much in any event. After 1917 the veil descends; he was either in hiding or locked in mortal and unequal combat with an enemy determined to erase him from history. It is not possible, therefore, to do him justice, but enough is known to mark him as a leader sprung from the people, and one of the first magnitude.

Alexander Stepanovich Antonov was born into a petty burgher family in the town of Kirsanov, probably not earlier than 1885 and not later than 1890. He thus conforms to the well-established tradition—erected into a law by Lenin and Stalin—that peasant movements are not led by men of peasant origin, a tradition that holds with few exceptions from Žižka and Florian Geyer to Antonov and Nestor Makhno.[1] But as the son of an artisan in a small provincial town, Antonov could no more escape the impact of the agrarian problem than did the SR intellectuals from whom he otherwise differed so greatly.

Information about his early years is scanty and contradictory. His father is said to have been from north Russia but the son passed his life in Tambov province and largely in Kirsanov *uezd*, except for sorties into Saratov province and for the years of his Siberian confinement. Either because of hooligan acts or because of an early manifestation of independence, he was expelled from school and later accused of being illiterate.[2] But we have clear evidence from a primary and hostile source that Antonov was decidedly literate and even well-read.[3] He was either a person of unusual talent, in learning as in other respects, or he had been reinstated and allowed to finish his studies.[4]

Still as a youngster—one source even says as a boy—he was drawn into the revolution of 1905. The next year he became a member of the Socialist Revolutionary party and soon defined the position he would occupy ever after in relation to it when he described himself as an "independent SR." The type of activity which appealed to him was economic terrorism, and he became a "typical expropriator" of the 1905 era. Supposedly such deeds of violence were committed to finance partisan enterprises, yet the line between idealistic purpose and personal gain was always in question. From the start, the Communists eagerly attributed bandit proclivities to Antonov, and indicted him as a drunkard as well; they achieved both purposes by having him engage in the plunder of liquor shops. They also have him killing police. As the few sources of a neutral or friendly cast do not expressly contradict such charges, and as Antonov does seem to have been hard-drinking as well as hard-driving, the question is left open. The Imperial authorities were not too concerned with the line between expropriation and robbery, and when Antonov was implicated in the robbery of a Saratov capitalist—he operated in two provinces at this stage of his career—they convicted him as a criminal and gave him a stiff sentence of penal servitude. This happened either in 1907 or—more probably—in 1909, and one source specifies a twelve-year penalty. He was sent to Siberia as a convict, not as an exile, and there he remained until liberated by the March revolution of 1917.[5]

Still young, with his spirit unbroken, Antonov returned to his native heath in a state of grace, since he had the right political affiliation, had incurred sacrifice in the cause of the revolution, and enjoyed the reputation of being a brave man. He did not at first go back to Kirsanov but went to the provincial center, where he entered that branch of the administration with which he had once been at war. Now, however, the police served the revolution. It had been renamed the militia, it needed to be staffed with trustworthy men, and Antonov was a likely candidate. So he became head of the militia in one of the districts of Tambov *uezd* and remained in this position, as best we can determine, until October of 1917.

Antonov resumed his ties with the Socialist Revolutionaries. Before long, however, his independence asserted itself and he grew dissatisfied with party attitudes of the Kerenski era, particularly with the flabbiness displayed toward hostile groups; he desired a much stronger line against both the reaction and the Bolsheviks. Thus he unerringly placed his finger on the cardinal weakness—not only of the SRs but of socialists everywhere—as people who are essentially pacifist and unable to stand up to their enemies as fighters willing to incur the blood sacrifice.

There was only one place for him to go; he moved over to the left wing of his party. The Left SRs—soon to become an independent party (PLSR)—had not been growing as rapidly in the Central Black Earth Region as in some areas, yet were distinctly on the upgrade. Apparently Antonov owed his promotion to this shift of allegiance, for he became chief of militia for all of Kirsanov *uezd*, his home district, either in or right after October as a result of Left SR sponsorship during the period of collaboration with Bolshevism.[6] If this most plausible account of his good fortune is followed, he received the appointment from the Soviet government. A Soviet account in two versions at first has Antonov advancing because of his harshness toward Bolsheviks,[7] while the later version drops this particular piece of embroidery and merely notes the fact of the appointment, presumably because admitting the truth would refute the infallibility of the Soviet regime.[8]

In his new office Antonov displayed his usual independence. He is represented as backing away from the Left SRs because of their stand in favor of dissolving the Constituent Assembly, an entirely plausible reaction since provincial revolutionists—even those of extremist tendencies—were running behind their central committees in Petersburg in continuing to regard the assembly as something of a shibboleth. But Antonov was careful to preserve the Left SR *yarlyk* or stamp as a means of staying in office, since the hard-pressed Soviet government could thus regard him as somewhat of an ally. There may have been other and more honorable considerations as well, for Antonov continued to be as independent of his former party as of his new one. He succeeded in being on good terms with both sets of SRs, whose mutual hostility would soon be submerged in mutual adversity. There was no rupture with the Left SRs, and several years later the nominal head of the Soviet state would refer to Antonov as "Left SR."[9]

Antonov succeeded also in pulling the wool over the eyes of the Communists for some months, during which he laid the groundwork for an armed insurrection against their regime. From the first he had no illusions about Communism and the incompatibility of its rule with peasant interests. He was remarkably consistent in this respect, and proceeded in systematic fashion. Cultivating ties with the peasantry from the vantage-ground of his official position, he sought out secluded villages where reliable confederates could be found; he collected arms in devious ways[10] under the nose of a regime intent upon disarming the populace, and secreted these arms for safe-keeping in the villages of his choice. His work was facilitated by the necessity of making the rounds of the *uezd*, and by good relations with SRs of both stripes. As lieutenants he selected former officers of the Imperial army—not because of reactionary proclivities, of course, but because of their fighting skill—placing them in key positions as chiefs of militia for the districts comprising the *uezd*. The names of two of them, Loshchilin and Zaev, have been preserved.[11]

Antonov could not hope to get away indefinitely with this risky business of plotting the overthrow of an order while serving it in an important capacity. It is not certain when his tenure as chief of police in Kirsanov *uezd* ended. Possibly it was soon after the withdrawal of the Left SRs from the Soviet government in March 1918, for one source has him trying to get through to the Samara front after it erupted in May of that year. When he did not succeed, he returned to Kirsanov and engaged in peaceful propaganda.[12] If such were his real course of action, he could scarcely have still been holding his position. It seems more likely that he continued in office until the Left SR uprising in Moscow in the summer of 1918. Removal of Left SRs from responsible positions in Tambov province was ordered on July 9.[13] It is even possible that Antonov, dissembling his true feelings, managed to hang on till August.[14]

The only certainty is that August 1918 marked the definitive break between him and the Soviet regime. The Che-ka or Extraordinary Commission had been gaining in effectiveness and now it came on his trail. Loshchilin and Zaev were seized and shot, but Antonov was tipped off and got away. His hiding place is variously described as the wooded swamps of Kirsanov *uezd*, the Ramza swamps, the Inzhavino forest, the fat kulak villages of Inzhavino, Koptevo, Tugolukovo, or the plain villages of Ramza, Parevka, Kalugino, Karavaino, and Treskino. Since the choice is open, the author will state his own: Antonov found refuge in the forest lakes and swamps of the Crow or Vorona river in the southeastern corner of Tambov province, where he always went when in deep trouble and where the final act of his life would be played out in June 1922. The Inzhavino Communist congress anathematized him and pronounced upon him sentence of death.

Antonov lived for almost four years with a price on his head. He was sometimes up and more often down, but as long as he had life within him he was never to be counted out. Almost immediately he showed his mettle. He was hunted like a wild beast but—a predator himself—he could hunt on his own. Gathering about him a band of like-minded men—described by the same source first as considerable and then only as small, and estimated in Soviet sources to have been about one hundred fifty strong—he entered upon a campaign of terrorism against Soviet personnel and institutions, employing stealth and hit-and-run tactics. His first victims were the Communists responsible for his death sentence at the Inzhavino congress. Other targets were found such as a *volost'* soviet, and by the end of 1918 Antonov had become—one would not say a danger—but a source of trouble for the Soviet regime and thus the hero of the day to that large element of the population which felt aggrieved at its actions.[15]

His activities broadened in 1919, but more slowly than one would have expected. Two factors seem to account for the lag. First, Antonov was lying low until he could see how the civil war developed. The Communist stereotype is that he was whetting the knife, waiting to plunge it into the back of the Soviet republic at the moment when it was most heavily engaged with the Russian and the foreign reaction.[16] Nothing is further from the truth. Antonov himself, the Left SRs in general, and most of the regular SRs were adamant against jumping from the Soviet frying pan into the fire of a monarchist restoration. If anything, they over-stressed the danger from the right to the detriment of their own cause. The second factor accounting for the slow accretion of strength was that the peasants had to suffer repeatedly at the hands of the food levy despoilers before their bruised feelings reached the pitch of rebellion.

Neither the effort nor the response sufficed in 1919 to produce an insurrection or even to put Antonov at the head of a large force. In

1922 Antonov's brother-in-law testified at the SR trial in Moscow that all during 1919, when they were constantly together, Antonov engaged in no public work, undertook no agitation among the peasants, and restricted himself to small-scale guerrilla actions.[17] The testimony of Bogoliubski[18] is all the more valuable in that he could not be shaken on the witness stand and did not give the prosecution the evidence it wanted to incriminate the accused. For once we have solid information about an elusive subject.

Notwithstanding his reluctance to undertake decisive action as long as the issue of civil war remained in doubt, Antonov waged a systematic though restricted campaign against the Communists in 1919 on two fronts. He carried out a series of expropriations and he decimated government personnel, particularly in the case of obnoxious officials.[19] It was the latter activity that endeared him to the populace and laid a solid foundation for the moral authority he would later enjoy. Viewed in one light, he had simply resumed the terrorism which the SRs had practised against Tsarist officials in the early years of the century, but in the present instance both the initiative and the execution proceeded from a single will. His was an individual, not a corporate enterprise. The Soviet authorities responded with Che-kas "on mission"; they "rode out" against him and a number of armed clashes ensued without decisive results. Hatred was being built up, and the countryside prepared for the insurrection.

By the end of 1919 and the beginning of 1920 Antonov was ready to enlarge his sphere of activity. For the first time he took in hand the organization of the peasantry, at first on his own and then in conjunction with the SRs, precisely at the time when Denikin's recoil on the Moscow front and the ensuing rout of the White armies left little doubt that the Reds had won the civil war. With the Whites all but swept from the field, the Greens could now move. Antonov also—and even more significantly—sought to tone up and to augment the armed force at his disposal. We are told that at the close of 1919 he stood at the head of several thousand "dark, befuddled" peasants.[20] He made it his business to end their befuddlement so far as the use of arms was concerned, and to convert the ill-assorted band into a hardened instrument of warfare. He succeeded beyond measure and by the fall of 1920, when he assumed leadership of the peasant bid for freedom, he had a miniature army at his command.[21]

However meager and inadequate our knowledge of Antonov's career until the insurrection, it nevertheless affords some insight into the man and his character. Here was no drawingroom revolutionary. Rather was he a man of action who did not shrink from fire but passed through it and came out hardened for further exploits. His spirit had not been broken by the Siberian servitude when the revolution was only a hope, nor by the termination of his professional career when the revolution was submerged in the tide of success. He would try again. Unlike a number of Left SRs and a host of others, he sought no accommodation with Bolshevism to save his position—opportunism was foreign to his nature. Unswervingly anti-Communist throughout his career, despite—or rather, because of—his own extreme revolutionism, he understood Communism as so many with greater cultural advantages have failed to do; for all of its fulsome phrases about the "broad masses," he realized that it held nothing good in store for either peasants or workers.

He was endowed by nature with the priceless gift of clear vision which a higher education had neither implanted nor obscured, and he possessed talent of a high order to pierce sham and delusion and to go to the heart of things, as is seen not only in relation to Communism but also in relation to its opponents. In the case of the political movement with which he himself was nominally associated, Antonov understood—as it never would—that a cause is hopeless unless it can defend itself with arms in hand. At the May congress in 1920 he told the peasant and political opposition that what it must have above all else was armed strength to combat both Communism and monarchist restoration; that without it the people—the workers as well as the peasants—were doomed to be trodden upon by one or the other of the iron-fisted minorities contending for mastery over them. Antonov intended to address himself to the creation of this armed strength.[22]

It will be observed that Antonov spoke of the need to defend both the workers and the peasants. The point is that he was a broader man than the movement he headed, which was inevitably tainted with antiproletarian bias since the simple people—seeing how all acts of the Soviet government were executed in the name of the workers—extended their resentment to the ostensibly favored class as well as to the regime that arrogated to itself the right to speak in its name.

But Antonov was not a peasant and could take a wider view. He favored collaboration between the two toiling classes. He seems to have realized that without support in the cities a peasant movement could not succeed, even in Russia. And he could appreciate the senselessness of a feud between two elements in the population, both of whom were victimized by the same regime. According to a peasant from a "remote village" who was one of his followers, Antonov steadily countered expressions of hostility to the proletariat by observing that not all workers were Communists by any means.[23] This statesmanlike attitude not only strengthened his own movement but could be used to drive a wedge between the self-proclaimed vanguard of the proletariat and the proletariat itself, a vulnerable link in the hook-up of Communist forces, and particularly so in the circumstances of 1920–1921.

If Antonov were capable of true statesmanship in certain respects, he was severely earthbound in others. He could not operate beyond his native heath. Rarely has a revolutionary leader been so hobbled to home base. In this respect he differed completely from his Ukrainian counterpart, Nestor Makhno, whose Green bands could cut loose from Guliai Pole and range far and wide, moving not only from *uezd* to *uezd*, but through entire provinces and even beyond the confines of Little Russia. Part of the explanation lies in the fact that Antonov had a more elaborately organized force, the territorial complexion of which made it difficult to move away from the sustaining area. Another factor may have been that Makhno could count more on spontaneous popular support, since the Little Russian peasantry had a dual motivation for fighting Moscow, animated as it was by nationalism as well as by a sense of economic grievance.

But in the last analysis it was not simply that Antonov found it difficult to operate in unfamiliar terrain; he could not bring himself to make the effort. He seems to have drawn spiritual strength from his presence in Kirsanov *uezd* and adjoining areas of Tambov and Borisoglebsk *uezds*, above all in the deep woods of the Vorona valley where, in the words of his younger brother, "each nook, bush, dale and grove were known to us."[24] If ejected in battle, he would double back and make for his accustomed haunts. Thorough knowledge of the terrain undoubtedly told in favor of the Greens as long as some kind of equilibrium prevailed; but once the balance of force was drastically altered to the benefit of the enemy, the commitment to a fixed area devoid of extensive cover became a fateful disadvantage.

Those fighting against Antonov on the Soviet side sometimes asked themselves whether it had ever "occurred to him that there were people beyond Kirsanov *uezd*?"[25] Such comment is exaggerated in the case of a man who had engaged as a youth in expropriations in Saratov province and had been condemned to years of penal servitude in some remote part of Siberia, and yet there is more than a little truth in it. Antonov must have believed, without ever having heard it, in the American adage that "every dog is stronger on his own home ground."

Other salient features of the leader of the Tambov anti-Communist uprising may be briefly pointed out. Having known little mercy in life, he gave none in return. The Communists denounced him for cruelty—nothing is said about their own—and the accusation seems to have been justified; in fact, the excesses later to be noted which Antonov either perpetrated or permitted to be perpetrated may have detracted seriously from whatever prospects of success his movement might have had. The editor of *Izvestiia* called him a "bloodthirsty criminal" and a *bashibuzuk* ("head-smasher" will do as a translation of this Turkish term). Referring apparently to manifestos which have not survived, Steklov wrote that Antonov summoned his "bandits" to wipe Communists from the face of the earth, along with the term "comrade" and their whole hateful jargon, then to burn their bodies on the spot and to sow their ashes to the wind. Antonov, according to this source, respected neither age nor sex.[26] It must be said that not only the enemy but his own men feared him, for he was a stern and perhaps even harsh disciplinarian.

But his command could never have withstood the blows that came its way had it been held together by fear alone. Antonov may have intimidated his following, but he also inspired admiration and respect. His personality, outlook, and judgment dominated the whole movement. Even the Communists of the early twenties who fought against him—not those of a later period—grudgingly concede his virtues. He was a foe never to be underestimated who made the most of modest means. He was resourceful in planning his campaigns and intrepid in their execution. He was adept at devising stratagems and laying traps. Above all, he was an organizer of the first magnitude, converting bands of deserters and rustics into a regular army—the most formidable of all the Green forces—and mounting a system of communications and espionage that was the envy and—for long—the despair of his enemies. M.N. Tukhachevski acknowledged his organizing talent without reservation.[27]

No one questioned his personal bravery, aside from the party hacks and pseudo-historians of the later Soviet period. Although the means were at hand,[28] Antonov never entertained the thought of fleeing the country. Emigration had no appeal for him, nor did any other flight from reality. At the end of the road he chose neither surrender nor suicide; in the face of hopeless odds, sick and deserted, he shot it out and went down fighting. Like the Elector Albert Achilles, he could think of no better place to die than in the midst of his enemies.[29]

What little we know about Antonov seems rich in comparison to our knowledge concerning his lieutenants. Their very names are in question. The only source that gives any extensive information about them—one that is closed to independent investigation—does not, after all, give very much.[30]

Antonov had a younger brother, Dmitri, who was his faithful servitor and constant companion-in-arms. According to a hostile source, Dmitri yielded his brother "dog-like" devotion.[31] In any event, the younger Antonov was not a mere shadow but had a significant role of his own in the Tambov affair as the author of the manifestos of the Green army. The editor of *Izvestiia* is twice in error when he attributes these manifestos to the elder Antonov and describes them as "illiterate."[32] They were literate enough to disturb the Communist hierarchy and were composed by Dmitri under the name of "Young Lion"—Molodoi Lev—which he seems to have chosen out of a child-like sense of his own importance.

As may be imagined, the manifestos were thoroughly destroyed. One survives, however, in the Soviet publication mentioned above[33] and is by no means a discreditable piece of work. It is written in a semipoetic vein with distinct and regular cadence—very simple, and very pleasing. The young man undoubtedly had literary talent which, under other circumstances, might have flowered. It was not that of Lermontov, but it was not bad. He wrote in the language of the people, moreover, and what he said was more likely to register on their murky consciousness than the proclamations of party intellectuals. The correspondent who looked over the last thing that he would ever write—the account of their exploits which Dmitri was preparing for his brother when they were cut down—pays him a certain respect and notes the correct placing of the commas as well as the absence of grammatical mistakes.[34] So much for Yuri Steklov's charge of illiteracy, parroted ever since in Soviet publications. As one endeavors to break through the cloud of oblivion and obfuscation that envelops his memory, one cannot but feel a measure of sympathy for this young man who had elected to share his brother's fate and who shared it to the full.

An associate high in the favor of Antonov, and a peasant leader of some eminence, was a man named Peter M. Tokmakov. He is one of the most interesting of the Green leaders, yet almost nothing is known of him and even his first name and initial are taken from the novel. He came from the peasantry and was a Left SR. In fact, from shreds of evidence available, he may have been the most important member of his party in Tambov province, for he had been chairman of the committee of the Peasants' Union (STK) for the whole province and had left that position (in favor of Pluzhnikov?) only to become Antonov's right-hand man and the commander of one of the two armies into which the Green forces were divided. The other was led by Antonov in person. Except in the field the two men were always together, an indication of Tokmakov's high standing in view of Antonov's habit of keeping a certain distance between himself and the other commanders, and of dealing with them on a basis of formality rather than of intimacy.

A hard-line revolutionary and extremist in his own right, Tokmakov was a Communist-hater of the first water and acquired a reputation for cruelty in a struggle where cruelty was the order of the day. A feud among extremists is like a feud among relatives in degree of hatred engendered, and the Communists were as justified in seeing in him an implacable foe as was he in seeing in them the enslavers of his class. The Left SRs were true representatives of the agrarian revolution and true champions of the interests of the average peasant, whatever the Communists might say about their affinity for kulaks. Tokmakov was a typical Left SR also in being a homegrown revolutionary, sprung from the peasantry and rooted in the Tambov countryside, devoid of intellectual pretension and with a penchant for action that distinguished him from the SR intellectuals, who do not even mention him among Antonov's lieutenants although they mention others of lesser significance.[35]

A romanticized version of the Tambov insurrection makes Tokmakov out to be a Tatar,[36] but whether that really was his ethnic group or was merely fictional fancy on the basis of his Tatar name—"tokmak" in Turkish means "mallet"—is not known. Many Russians bear Tatar names, though the connection with the name-giving forebears would be less remote for commoners than for noble families.

Left SRs coexisted in the Green movement with regular SRs, and ordinary peasants with more affluent ones. The common affliction of the food levy and other features of Communist rule caused them to sink their differences, at least under the given circumstances. The presence of the kulak Ivan E. Ishin among the collaborators of Antonov has been blown up by the Communists as evidence of the kulak character of the Green movement. But who should know better than the Communists that the assistance the kulaks gave Antonov no more made him a kulak agent than that the assistance the Germans gave Lenin made the latter a German agent? Ishin was an important figure among the Greens, yet not so important as Tokmakov.

A member of the PSR since 1905, Ishin had suffered in the cause of the revolution. Upon his return from exile in 1909, he settled down and opened a grocery store in the village of Kurdiuki. His business activities were rather extensive, for in addition to his store he rented up to eighty *desiatinas*—some two hundred acres—of land and several large gardens, using hired labor on a considerable scale.[37] This most grievous of sins according to SR dogma did not lead to excommunication, and with the success of the revolution he rose steadily from head of a *volost zemstvo* to be member of the provincial committee and treasurer of the PSR, handling the party funds of tens of thousands of roubles. In his private affairs, Ishin repeated the pattern of the previous revolution: he bought some forty *desiatinas* of land in the wake of the February revolution, built a solid house, and opened a store.[38] Manifestly, he was settling down to enjoy the new conditions; the only trouble was that the revolution would not settle down and that it fell into the hands of the Communists.

Ishin very likely was one of those kulaks who suffered from the October revolution and who found in the Green movement the promise of rectifying his wrongs. He became a sort of business manager for Antonov and seems to have passed as his theorist and master of propaganda, since he did not want for words and the peasants would listen to him. Ishin is said to have saluted Bacchus both day and night.[39] Whatever his drinking habits and transgressions as a kulak, Ishin displayed one admirable trait of character: at a time when the SR intellectuals were crawling out of their skins to get away from the taint of Antonov, and just before Antonov himself had been run to earth, Ishin in testimony for the SR trial of 1922 did not disown the past but spoke of Antonov as his "old party comrade."[40]

The Communists discovered several other representatives of the kulak class in their search for the cloven hoof of Antonov's movement. M. Yurin came from Ramza in the heart of Antonov country and held a position of leadership in the provincial SR organization. A more colorful figure was Marusia Kosova, daughter of a kulak speculator, and leader in her own right of a band which included all five members of her family.[41] This female "bandit" was for a time a thorn in the flesh of the Tambov soviet.

A brave and steadfast confederate of Antonov was a character called "Grach," a nickname borrowed from a member of the crow family in eastern Europe. Just how he earned this term is uncertain, perhaps by having a gloomy and taciturn nature. Soviet sources differ as to his real name, giving it either as Finakov[42] or Simakov[43]; the latter comes from the primary Tambov publication, so it will be accorded preference. The issue usually is dodged in favor of the sobriquet. "Grach" was a trader of some kind—in what is not specified—and a personal friend of Antonov. He was given command of one of the large operational groups, and was a stern taskmaster and a dangerous foe. He never wavered in his loyalty to the Green cause but went through to the end, recanting nothing and betraying no secrets. The Extraordinary Commission got nothing out of him.[44]

Less shadowy than other Green leaders is Ivan S. Matiukhin who was the victim of a plot in which the Soviet cavalry commander, G. I. Kotovski, figures as hero. We even know how Matiukhin looked, something that cannot be said of any of his confederates including Antonov himself. He is described as a "dark-haired peasant of massive build with pronounced facial features and a fierce and furtive gaze."[45] The Communists considered him a dangerous and "not stupid" enemy, and an exceptionally cruel one whose forte was said to be head-twisting—[46] a not illogical accusation in view of his physical strength. Matiukhin commanded a regiment in the Green army and had under him as a squadron leader his brother Michael, described as his right hand.

Ivan S. Matiukhin and the Zheltov spoken of in the Fomichev manuscript[47] may well have been the same man, as the way in which they met their end[48]—by falling into a trap baited with treachery—is identical, and two such ruses could scarcely have been made to work. Very possibly the Greens used assumed names as had the SRs before 1917, and the Bolsheviks as well. None of these cover-up terms are known, unfortunately, and there is no way of determining whether I. S. Matiukhin ever used the alias of Zheltov. Though the fate of the two is similar, the background is quite different, for Zheltov is said to have been a Molokan from the village of Rasskazovo who forsook his sectarian pacifism only under the spur of Communist violence. Matiukhin, however, is described by the defector Ektov as having been a horse thief before the revolution and a member of a Soviet food detachment afterwards, in which capacity he wronged some peasants and was arrested, only to be released by Antonov as head of the *uezd* militia.

Exception may be taken to this account on the ground that the interval between the formation of food detachments and Antonov's flight from his post—if there was such an interval at all—was too short for the wrongdoing, the arrest, and the release to have taken place. It is all barely possible but not likely; and the contradiction must be resolved in favor of the first version of his background and the conjecture that Matiukhin and Zheltov were one and the same person.

If Matiukhin actually was set free by Antonov, he repaid him in bad coin, for he is said to have thought of himself as Antonov's rival and to have aspired to sit on his throne. The two men once quarreled bitterly over the distribution of trophies which Matiukhin had taken and did not wish to share with other regiments. Matiukhin sought to use Antonov's errors against him, and cultivated persons whose feelings he had bruised.[49] Doubtless there were jealousies and frictions in the Green as in other movements, but their gravity cannot be assessed due to the silence of other sources on the subject.

The names so far mentioned do not exhaust the list of Green leaders who attained a certain level of distinction, but information about the others is too scant for treatment. We know they existed and very little more. An officer named Boguslavski succeeded Tokmakov in his command and was in turn succeeded by Kuznetsov, an officer of experience and highly respected in the partisan movement.[50] The Communist press assigned importance to the elimination of one Boltnev, political commissar of a Tambov "bandit" regiment.[51] Vas'ka Karas' must have been a colorful commander; everywhere he is mentioned and nowhere is anything said about him.[52] Averianov also draws a blank, although he headed an important segment of Antonov's army. About characters with obvious pseudonyms such as Bat'ko, Maksimka, Monakh, only the standard Soviet charge of barbarous conduct can be cited.[53]

Interesting though very brief information about participants in the Green movement may be found in the Fomichev manuscript; the only trouble is that in every instance except Antonov himself the name mentioned does not occur elsewhere, leading to the conclusion that the author of the manuscript knew only the assumed and not the real names of the persons about whom he writes— Zheltov (Matiukhin?), Yaryzhka, Mishin, Shornikov, and Ivan Nikiforovich Petukhov. There is much confusion in the manuscript, and the fact that Fomichev was cut off from the Green movement before the decisive events of 1921 severely limits his knowledge, as does also the belated character of his memoirs; they were written some thirty years after the events in question and in such improbable places as the Philippines and Santiago de Chile, with no materials at hand.

There is no reason to doubt, however, that the anarchist Yaryzhka participated in the Green movement as head of a detachment. His early death in the fall of 1920 may account for the absence of his name in reports more concerned with leaders of the later and decisive phase of the insurrection, or it may be that he had another name. Yaryzhka had struck an officer of the Imperial army in 1916, was imprisoned, and came out an anarchist. Member of a commune in 1918, he found the straitjacket of Communism even less to his liking than what had gone before. Under the black flag of anarchism he began operations in the summer of 1918 and, adhering to Antonov's movement, fought until killed in action in the fall of 1920 under the same colors.[54] The Green cause had no flag of its own and the black banner of anarchism was no less appropriate to its character than the red banner of the regular and left-wing Socialist Revolutionaries.

Not enough is known about the men who headed the Tambov uprising to pass judgment upon them, with the possible exception of Antonov himself. All that can be said is that their movement foundered for reasons other than faulty leadership, although tactical and more particularly strategical errors were not lacking.

Notes

1. The only exceptions known to the author are Bolotnikov, Gonta, and Zalizniak, and the latter two qualify but imperfectly.

2. See, for example, Yuri Steklov, "Ot Chernova do Antonova" [From Chernov to Antonov], *Izvestiia*, no. 71, 2 April 1921, p. 1. Steklov was an able and not hopelessly prejudiced editor but he simply did not know much about this subject.

3. S. E., "Na mestakh: Konets esero-bandita Antonova" [On the local scene: end of the SR bandit Antonov], *Izvestiia*, no. 145 (1584), 2 July 1922, p. 4. S. E. was Tambov correspondent for his paper. He examined the effects found on the body. We are grateful to him for an oasis of honesty in a desert of defamation and ignorance.

4. Fomichev (Lidin), "Antonovshchina: Iz vospominanii antonovtsa" (Philippines, 1950–1951), p. 18, where it is definitely stated that he finished high school. But see Borisov, *Chernym letom*, p. 36, an extremely prejudiced source, which makes Antonov a dropout or rather a castout.

5. Anonymous (Iuri Podbelski; see bibliography), *Kak tambovskie krest'iane boriatsia za svobodu* [How Tambov peasants fight for freedom] (n.p., 1921), p. 5; Fomichev (Lidin), "Antonovshchina: Iz vospominanii antonovtsa" (Philippines, 1950–1951), p. 18; Trifonov, *Klassy i klassovaia bor'ba*, part 1, pp. 54–55; Borisov, *Chernym letom*. pp. 35–36; "Antonovshchina," *Sovetskaia istoricheskaia entsiklopediia*, vol. 1, p. 635.

6. Fomichev (Lidin), "Antonovshchina: Iz vospominanii antonovtsa" (Santiago de Chile. 1955), pp. 3–4; and especially ibid. (Philippines, 1950–1951), p. 18; Trifonov, *Klassy i klassovaia bor'ba,* part 1, p. 55. The last source is less explicit but does not contradict the first two.

7. Borisov, "Konets antonovshchiny" [The end of the Antonov affair], in *Nezabyvaemoe: vospominaniia uchastnikov grazhdanskoi voiny v SSSR* [What is not being forgotten: recollections of civil war participants in the Soviet Union] (Moscow, 1961), p. 286.

8. Borisov, *Chernym letom*, p. 37.

9. Kalinin, *Za eti gody*, vol. 2, p. 107; see also idem, *Izbrannye proizvedeniia* [Selected works] (Moscow, 1960), vol. 1, *1917–1925 gg.*, p. 268; Trifonov, *Klassy i klassovaia bor'ba*, part 1, p. 104.

10. See below, chapter six.

11. Vladimir Dokunin, "Tambovskii schet sotsial-banditam" [The Tambov bill of reckoning for the social bandits], *Pravda*, no. 123, 4 June 1922, p. 3.

12. Anonymous (Podbelski), *Kak tambovskie krest'iane boriatsia za svobodu*, p. 6.

13. *Bor'ba rabochikh i krest'ian pod rukovodstvom bol'shevistskoi partii za ustanovlenie i uprochenie sovetskoi vlasti v tambovskoi gubernii (1917–1918 gody): Sbornik dokumentov* [The workers' and peasants' struggle under the guidance of the Bolshevik party to establish and consolidate the Soviet regime in Tambov province (1917–1918); a documentary collection] (Tambov, 1957), nos. 127, 130, pp. 171, 173. This source could have yielded something had it been prepared properly, but a studied effort is made to keep the opposition faceless. There is a survey of developments in Kirsanov *uezd* (ibid., no. 167, pp. 223–26) without mention of Antonov and with only the general statement that "as far as petty counter-revolutionary activities originating with individuals are concerned, there were plenty of them, and all materials bearing on them are concentrated in the local Extraordinary Commission." It would take another revolution to jar these materials loose for the benefit of scholars.

14. The author's surmise, also implied in Hirschfeld, "Tambovskii krovopodtek," *Izvestiia*, no. 247 (1390), 3 November 1921, p. 1.

15. Dokunin, "Tambovskii schet sotsial-banditam," *Pravda*, no. 123, 4 June 1922, p. 3; Leonidov, "Eshche ob eserakh v Tambovskoi gub." [Something more on the SRs in Tambov province], *Izvestiia*, no. 155 (1594), 14 July 1922, p. 3; anonymous (Podbelski), *Kak tambovskie krest'iane boriatsia za svobodu*, p. 6; Trifonov, *Klassy i klassovaia bor'ba*, part 1, p. 55; Fomichev (Lidin), "Antonovshchina: Iz vospominanii antonovtsa" (Philippines, 1950–1951), p. 18; Hirschfeld, "Tambovskii krovopodtek," *Izvestiia*, no. 247 (1390), 3 November 1921, p. 1; Borisov, *Chernym letom*, p. 37.

16. Borisov, *Chernym letom*, p. 37.

17. From the proceedings of the trial in *Pravda*, no. 153 (1592), 12 July 1922, p. 4.

18. Bogoliubski was Antonov's *shurin*—the brother of his wife. This is the only evidence we have that Antonov was a married man. His wife is never mentioned. She may well have been taken as a hostage.

19. See below, chapters six, seven.

20. Dokunin, "Tambovskii schet sotsial-banditam," *Pravda*, no. 123, 4 June 1922, p. 3.

21. Bogoliubski testimony at the SR trial in *Pravda*, no. 153 (1592), 12 July 1922, p. 4; Iuri Steklov, "Vol'nitsa i podvizhniki" [Freebooters and fighters], *Izvestiia*, no. 96 (1239), 6 May 1921, p. 1; anonymous (Podbelski), *Kak tambovskie krest'iane boriatsia za svobodu*, p. 6; Antonov-Ovseenko, "O banditskom dvizhenii v Tambovskoi gubernii," p. 5; Trifonov, *Klassy i klassovaia bor'ba*, part 1, p. 55.

22. See Fomichev (Lidin), "Antonovshchina: Iz vospominanii antonovtsa" (Santiago de Chile, 1955), p. 31, for statement to this effect.

23. Ibid., p. 28; see also ibid., p. 4.

24. S. E., "Na mestakh: Konets esero-bandita Antonova," *Izvestiia*, no. 145 (1584), 2 July 1922, p. 4.

25. *Put' Bor'by*, vol. 2, *Antonovshchina*, passim.

26. Steklov, "Ot Chernova do Antonova," *Izvestiia*, no. 71, 2 April 1921, p. 1.

27. Tukhachevski, "Zapiska," p. 1.

28. Fomichev (Lidin), "Antonovshchina: Iz vospominanii antonovtsa" (Santiago de Chile, 1955), p. 39.

29. There is no reliable description of Antonov. In fact, there is nothing at all on his appearance save the words of a novelist who is at pains always to depict him in an unfavorable light. According to this account, Antonov was slender and of medium stature, with lips that were pale and thick (this novelist invariably comments on lips) and sunken eyes which imparted an owlish cast to his features. He had prominent cheekbones and hollows at the temples. He wore his whiskers in a distinctive manner, refusing to droop them in the Cossack way as did all others on his staff and even the civilian leader of the uprising, G. N. Pluzhnikov, head of the Peasants' Union. And that is about all. See Nikolai E. Virta, *Odinochestvo* [The lone one: a romance] (Moscow, 1962), pp. 8, 77. The novelist is ordinarily well-informed about the events he describes, was himself an eyewitness to some of them as a boy, and may have seen Antonov on one or more occasions. Or he may describe him from hearsay or from imagination. As for photographs of Antonov, the author knows only of those in the files of the political police (see below, chapter twelve).

30. *Put' Bor'by*, the second volume of which has the special title of *Antonovshchina*.

31. Ibid., page unknown. Probably from the memoirs of the Chekist Pokaliukhin, pp. 65–91.

32. Steklov, "Ot Chernova do Antonova," *Izvestiia*, no. 71, 2 April 1921, p. 1.

33. *Put' Bor'by*, vol. 2, *Antonovshchina*, about pp. 33–34.

34. S. E., "Na mestakh: Konets esero-bandita Antonova," *Izvestiia*, no. 145 (1584), 2 July 1922, p. 4.

35. See anonymous (Podbelski), *Kak tambovskie krest'iane boriatsia za svobodu*, pp. 15–16. The above information is taken from what is remembered about the short passage on Tokmakov in *Put' Bor'by*, and also from Ektov's comment as reproduced in Borisov, *Chernym letom*, p. 32.

36. A Strygin, *Rasplata: Roman* (Voronezh, 1965), pp. 119–20. Here the first name of Tokmakov is also given as Peter, and that it may be, but what is fact and what is fiction in this novel is not for this author to say.

37. Trifonov, *Klassy i klassovaia bor'ba*, part 1, p. 79, drawing on the information in *Put' Bor'by*, vol. 2, *Antonovshchina*, p. 28.

38. Borisov, *Chernym letom*, p. 32, based on Ektov's account. It is possible that instead of a repetition of pattern, two sources are relating the same set of facts to two different periods. Neither Trifonov nor Borisov are reliable from the standpoint of research, but the latter is a primary source and the former had access to archives, and so both must be used *faute de mieux*.

39. Borisov, *Chernym letom*, pp. 32–33. This commissar was a prohibitionist and a Communist prig in general, but in this instance seems to be telling the truth.

40. "Za chto ikh sudiat": P. L., "Kratkaia istoriia partii eserov" [For what they are tried: short history of the SR party], *Pravda*, no. 125, 8 June 1922, p. 3.

41. Trifonov, *Klassy i klassovaia bor'ba*, part 1, p. 79.

42. "Na mestakh: bor'ba s banditizmom" [On the local scene: the fight on banditry], *Izvestiia*, no. 217 (1360), 29 September 1921, p. 1; ibid., no. 224 (1367), 7 October 1921, p. 3.

43. Trifonov, *Klassy i klassovaia bor'ba*, part 1, p. 79.

44. From the author's recollection of what was said about "Grach" in *Put' Bor'by*, vol. 2, *Antonovshchina*. This source was also used by Trifonov, but

anything in the early Soviet sources in any way reflecting credit on the Greens is suppressed in the later ones—a measure of the deterioration of historiography in the Soviet Union.

45. Borisov, *Chernym letom*, pp. 50–51.

46. Trifonov, *Klassy i klassovaia bor'ba*, part 1, p. 123.

47. Fomichev (Lidin), "Antonovshchina: Iz vospominanii antonovtsa" (Philippines, 1950–1951), pp. 26, 29–32; ibid. (Santiago de Chile, 1955), p. 25.

48. See below, chapter ten.

49. Ektov's characterization of Matiukhin is recorded by Borisov, *Chernym letom*, p. 33; see also ibid., pp. 40–41.

50. Ibid., p. 32. See below, chapter ten.

51. "Na mestakh: bor'ba s banditizmom," *Izvestiia*, no. 217 (1360), 29 September 1921, p. 1; ibid., no. 224 (1367), 7 October 1921, p. 3.

52. Except that he was from the village of Padov and gathered around him a bunch of desperate men. See anonymous (Podbelski), *Kak tambovskie krest'iane boriatsia za svobodu*, p. 15.

53. S. E., "Antonovshchina," *Izvestiia*, no. 122 (1561), 3 June 1922, p. 3. It will be observed that S. E. was on the spot within a year of the failure of the insurrection and less than a year after mopping-up operations, that he had a favored position as Tambov correspondent of the government newspaper, and yet knew very little. The real trouble with this whole subject is the locked-up character of the Soviet regime, which divulged very little even to its own representatives. The information is in the files of the Extraordinary Commission and its successors, where it was secreted and continues to be so fifty years later.

54. Fomichev (Lidin), "Antonovshchina: Iz vospominanii antonovtsa" (Philippines, 1950-1951), pp. 23, 28–29.

— 4 —

The Character of the Green Movement

In considering the nature of the Green movement, ideology is the aspect most easily disposed of. The simple truth is that it had no ideology, and only a negative program. The Green partisans knew what they were against—they had a better understanding of Communism than had its intellectual opponents—but only the haziest of notions as to how to order Russia in the hour of victory. They had a sure intuition, however, which in the end might have availed more than a detailed program of reconstruction.

What passes as the program of the Tambov insurrection—and so as the reflection of its ideology—was the statement of purpose drawn up in the name of the Tambov Committee of the Peasants' Union (STK) and adopted by a provincial peasants' congress in May 1920,[1] some three months before the beginning of the insurrection. This program or code (*ustav*) of the Peasants' Union demanded the overthrow of the Communist regime for having led the country to misery, ruin, and shame.[2] It may also have called for the destruction of the Communist party,[3] since the peasant delegates at the congress meant to tear Bolshevism up by the roots and to hang all Bolsheviks who persisted in going against the people,[4] whether this purpose was explicitly stated in the program or not. All citizens, irrespective of class, were to enjoy political equality except for members of the Romanov family. The destinies of the country would be entrusted to a Constituent Assembly, elected on the same basis as in 1917 but subject to the right of constituents to recall their representatives; until it could meet, power would rest in the hands of associations and parties fighting Communism. It was not even clearly stated that the assembly would be a new one rather than the one-day assembly of 18

January 1918 recalled from the grave, but it seems reasonable to infer from the context that a new one was intended.

Among the more significant features of the program was the acceptance of full-scale socialization of the land as enacted into law by the former Constituent Assembly. Industry would be partially denationalized, but large-scale enterprises such as coal mining and metallurgical plants would remain in the hands of the state. At the same time there would be workers' control and government supervision of industry; nothing had been learned from the experience of 1917, when such muddy and misconceived formulas as this had contributed to economic breakdown. Domestic or craft industry could operate freely. Political and economic relations with foreign countries would at once be reestablished, and foreign as well as Russian capital would be admitted for purposes of restoring the economy. Finally, broad state credits would be afforded the personality (sic).[5]

Along with the usual pledge of civil liberties, the noneconomic sections of the program contained a reaffirmation of the right of self-determination for the nationalities and population of the former Russian Empire, and a commitment to the eradication of illiteracy and to free teaching in the schools (freedom from Communist dogma, or freedom to impart religious dogma?). The final point in the program—sixteenth on the list—might under other circumstances have become the most significant of all. It stated that the guerrilla bands and volunteer formations now waging war on Communism would not be dissolved until the Constituent Assembly convened and decided the question of an army.

Aside from the fact that some of these provisions were fuzzy enough to merit inclusion in the platform of an American political party, the entire program is a very clear reflection of SR influence on the Tambov Peasants' Union. A Soviet source states, in fact, that the provincial committee of the party proposed it to the union.[6] Whether or not technically true—the Communists have always exerted themselves, then and now, to pin responsibility for the Antonov uprising on the SRs—the statement is essentially true. The practised eye sees everywhere the SR imprint. There is the point about the Soviet regime having led the country into shame; the shame, of course, being the Treaty of Brest-Litovsk, although the treaty is not mentioned—and could not be mentioned with any grace—since the great majority of the peasantry had acquiesced in this "shame." Nothing in the whole range of Bolshevism had so outraged the right-wing Populist intelligentsia as a treaty that flew in the face of their anti-German and pro-French as well as their nationalist sensibilities.

The points about the immediate reknitting of ties with foreign countries and the admission of foreign capital onto the Russian economic scene are assuredly to be correlated with the views of the SR intellectuals rather than with any compelling urge on the part of the Tambov peasants to rescind the annulment of foreign indebtedness, which inevitably would have been a pre-condition for further investment of French and British capital.

After the February revolution, the SRs—in this case the right SRs—had deadlocked the commission on the election of the Constituent Assembly with their demand for the exclusion of members of the Imperial family from electoral rights. Are we now to believe that the House of Romanov was to be excluded on demand of the Tambov peasants? Not to suggest, of course, that the peasants harbored monarchist sympathies, but merely to point out that their limited horizon was sufficiently obscured by more tangible grievances to nullify any concern with the defunct dynasty.

Typical of the Populist intelligentsia, likewise, was the distaste for peasant militia and plebeian leadership implicit in the provision for dissolution of partisan bands once the Constituent Assembly had reconstituted the Russian army. The intellectuals' conception of that army had been clearly revealed at the time of the Samara front in 1918 as a regular army with an officers' corps of the conventional type, not drawn from the depths of the population as in the case of the Green movement.

The most palpable evidence of SR influence, of course, is the inclusion in the program of the point about socialization of the land. Land would be treated as a gift of nature like air, not subject to private ownership but open on a basis of equality to all who wished to work it with their own labor.[7] Just how this grand concept would be applied in practice had never been worked out, and it remained a characteristic construction—or myth—of the Populist mentality. But myths everywhere enjoy popularity, and this particular one had

been embraced by countless peasant gatherings in 1917. The
question here is how well did socialization of the land accord with
the peasant outlook in 1920, after three years of sobering
experience? If we are to follow one Soviet source, it accorded not at
all with their outlook, which had developed further until it had come
to uphold the principle of private property. The program of the
Peasants' Union and so of the insurrection, according to this source,
came out for the inviolability of private ownership of the means of
production, with land being given over to those who worked it
themselves.[8]

There is a great temptation to accept this statement, which would
make it easy to substantiate our thesis as to the true relationship
between the Green movement and the SR party. Unfortunately, the
statement is not true; the Tambov peasants had not progressed to
the point of throwing overboard the shibboleth of socialization in
favor of holding the land as private property, although they were
moving in that direction. Socialization of the land certainly figures in
the program, and is not to be glided over as the Soviet author has
done. It was clearly incompatible with the principle of private
property at the beginning of an evolutionary process which would
nevertheless have ended by swallowing up the features of
socialization. This point about acceptance of private ownership of
the means of production in the program of 1920 has simply been
injected from the outside and is not to be found in other and more
authentic versions of the program.[9]

There is no record of any dissent in peasant ranks over adoption of
socialization in 1917, but three years later "heated debates"
preceded reaffirmation of belief in this cardinal tenet of Socialist
Revolutionism. The decisive argument in favor of socialization
seems to have been that if the purchase and sale of land were
permitted, a new class of landowners would arise from the town
population and the peasantry itself, and a renewed need for
expropriation would confront the levellers in the village communities or *mirs*. If loafers and drunkards wished to sell out and go
to the towns, the attitude was to let them go, but their land could be
disposed of only to the *mir*.[10] V. M. Chernov would have found here
interesting confirmation of his thesis—advanced at the time of

Stolypin's assault on the *mir* for the purpose of reassuring panic-stricken members of his party—that the real strength of the socialization program lay not in any collectivist proclivities that it was supposed to preserve or inculcate, but in its equalizing features which harmonized so perfectly with the egalitarian spirit of the peasantry in both Great and Little Russia.[11]

The success of the SRs in grafting their program of land socialization onto the Tambov Peasants' Union did not extend to the prohibition of hired labor, which is not included in the union's list of principles and about which no consensus seems to have been reached in popular discussions.[12] The failure to accept, if not to reject, this Populist phobia against hired labor may be an indication that the SRs had slipped since 1917, when they had had everything their way in the Tambov countryside.

Nevertheless, they had preserved more influence here than elsewhere, and one of the primary differences between Antonov's insurrection in Tambov and Makhno's in the Ukraine is that the former was to some extent still held in leading strings by the Populist intellectuals, whereas Makhno had scraped off the socialist encrustations on his movement and had met squarely the peasant desire to be rid of rulers and to own land in full right. This combination of anarchism with the right of private ownership appealed to more than the Ukrainian peasantry; it was winning ground in Great Russia as well.

The editor of *Izvestiia* had secured three sheets handed out by "bandits" on 21 March 1921 in a village of Saratov province. He proceeded to analyze their content and found not a word about socialization of the land. Instead he found praise of the West as the source of progress and condemnation of Communism as a throwback to Asia. The "bandit" program sang of free labor in place of the commune and of private property in land and even in industry. There was, to be sure, an expression of hostility to large-scale capitalism, betraying a residue of SR sentiment. The editor contrasts the two variants in the Green movement, the Antonov admixture of SR and Black Hundred elements with the Saratov combination of SR and bourgeois ideology. He says no word about any commitment to private property or any backing away from socialization in the case of the Tambov variant; the whole burden of his analysis is that the Saratov variant under the leadership of Popov and Shkuratov had moved further in the direction of private property.[13]

Thus the present-day Soviet imputation of a like stage of development to the Greens in Tambov, noted above, may be dismissed out of hand. In general, the editor of *Izvestiia* in the early 1920s stands on a higher cultural plane than a Soviet "historian" of the 1960s.

Too much should not be made of the faithfulness of Tambov to the heart of the SR program. Viewed in broad perspective, socialization of the land was a way station on the road from the primitive collectivism of the *mir*, with its submergence of the individual, to the peasant proprietorship of the West, with its emancipation of the peasant who wanted to work. If the Greens in Saratov province had progressed further along this road, and those in the Ukraine further still, there is no reason to think that those in Tambov would have lagged far behind.

Moreover, it is well to remember that the STK or Peasants' Union was itself only the civilian adjunct of Antonov's movement, the core of which consisted of the leader and his fighters. What the STK did is of significance for the movement, yet is not of its inner essence. Antonov had teamed up with an organization in the SR mould and went along with its ideology as a kind of reflex action. That the program of the STK was no model of clarity helped to iron out any differences that might have arisen. A socialist coloration came easily to Antonov, who had been an SR and even a Left SR, and to Tokmakov, who was still a Left SR, while in no way cramping their actions. If Antonov as a youngster had been a free spirit in the 1905 era of expropriations, it stands to reason he was not going to wear a party halter as a mature leader. He was simply not concerned with ideology; he was a man of action who, in the last analysis, was his own ideology.

At first he had no program of any kind,[14] not only during the period of incubation but even after the insurrection had started. It ran for four full months without his making a statement of purpose or issuing a single proclamation, so far as is known.[15] No meetings were held to propagandize the population. Few revolutions have been so silent. Most drown in words even more than in blood. But in this instance there were no words, only war to the hilt. "Naked guerrilla warfare, without slogans, without ideas, without program—such is the Tambov uprising in its second phase."[16] The first phase had witnessed spontaneous action without leadership; now there was leadership without words. Gradually the insurrection worked into its third phase, that of leadership and some words. The STK program was taken up as the basis for speechmaking in villages that had passed under Green control; meetings were held and there was talk of the Constituent Assembly, of land socialization, and of the rights of the citizen.

The essential character of the insurrection, however, is to be seen in the earlier and ideologically barren phases; the words came as an afterthought, they were tacked on—as it were—without changing the character of the movement which had already set, hard and fast. The SR intellectuals recognized the true state of affairs, and even after the insurrection entered the vocal stage they still were not satisfied. They could not conceive of life without ideology and they wrung their hands at the spectacle before them. For them the weakness of the insurrection lay in the vagueness of its purpose, and they beheld the tragedy of the Tambov peasantry in the absence of ideological leadership.[17]

Actually, the Green movement was better off for not being contained in a rigid ideological framework—assuming, that is, that any movement is ever so contained. Its strength lay in the spontaneous support of the people, who were as little concerned about ideology as was Antonov himself. The peasants knew quite well what they did not want—well enough for them to sustain his movement—and no amount of ideological window-dressing on the part of the intelligentsia could clarify their minds as to exactly what they wanted in the way of a new order. The peasants had to find their own way.

One could say they wanted the February revolution without the war and without a regime suffering from a chronic paralysis of the will; or they wanted the October revolution without the food levy, the communes, and the state farms. They may have thought they wanted socialization of the land, but this shibboleth of the Populist intellectuals would have yielded almost as quickly to peasant proprietorship as Lenin's brand of collectivism did under the New Economic Policy. The peasants would have discovered that they wished to own as well as to hold the land, and the Populist intellectuals would have capitulated to them or lost their following.

Socialization of the land, therefore, cannot serve as a means of establishing the essential difference between the Socialist Revolutionaries and the Green movement which flew their red banner for want of a symbol of its own. Both would have given up on socialization, the SRs because they must either yield to the peasant tide or break, and the Greens as a matter of course—not because they had to go with the tide but because they were the tide.

The true distinction between Socialist Revolutionism and peasant insurrectionism, shorn of ideological encrustations foisted upon it, would have appeared in connection with another matter, something that was clear and tangible and could not be conjured away. We have seen that the SRs, in gaining acceptance of their program by the Peasants' Union, had magnanimously consented to put off dissolution of the guerrilla and volunteer formations responsible for victory over Bolshevism until the Constituent Assembly had met and decided on the question of an army. It was a typical formulation of the Populist intellectuals, and betrays clearly their aversion to anarchistic elements that had taken the field without asking their guidance and were conducting the struggle independently with only some ideological borrowings from them. The intellectuals would inevitably have striven to get rid of these elements as soon as possible in favor of a regularly constituted army which would have secured the Russian state from enemies either real or imagined.

In view of their state-mindedness and their phobias and predilections, they assuredly would have found enemies or created them where they did not exist. They would have been hostile to the Turkish Republic and to Finland and the Baltic States, and they would have discerned a menace in Japan, perhaps even in the Weimar Republic. How they would have viewed Poland is impossible to say, since Pilsudski's imperialism would have embarrassed acutely their pan-Slavist sentiments. The SR intellectuals further to the left—those of the Chernov school who did not share the chauvinism and did not suffer from the Germanophobia, Turkophobia, and Finnophobia of their right-wing colleagues— would have struggled against these tendencies with uncertain results, probably not too successfully in the light of the 1917 experience. All of the SR intellectuals, however, both those on the right because of their state-mindedness and those on the left because of their pacifism, would have instinctively feared the partisan bands with their penchant for violence and their willingness to shed blood. Only the Left SRs would have felt an affinity for them, for the Left SRs also were a product of the elemental passions of the population.

As for the Green bands and their leaders, nothing is surer than that they would have refused to dissolve. In the hour of victory, feeling their power, they would have sought to preserve it and would have pointed to the danger of letting things slip back into the old groove as the result of the reconstitution of an officers' corps drawn from the upper levels of Russian society. Such a conventional European army would have been the result if previous educational qualifications were to govern the selection of officers. The Green leaders would have insisted that only officers from the depths of the people and of proven dedication to its cause could be entrusted with the creation of the new Russian army, the foundation of which would be laid by incorporation into the military structure of the forces under their command. Both personal ambition and political calculation would have impelled them to take this stand. Some of them were too lacking in discipline, too prone to anarchism, to make their will effective. But not Antonov. He had the strength of character and the organizing ability to do what he had felt to be necessary already in May 1920 when he told the first congress of the STK that the peasants and the workers, too, must have the armed force needed to deal with danger from the right.[18]

Sooner or later the quarrel over the army would have been connected with the divergence between the collectivism of the Populist intellectuals and the growing property-consciousness of the peasantry, who would have wished to break the bonds of socialization and to convert their holdings into full and heritable property. The former Green leaders would have gone along with their peasant following easily and as a matter of course, since they had no ideological rigidity but only intuitive desires, and the Populist intellectuals would have sustained a double defeat. They might have bent on the matter of socialization, never on that of the army; but if they would not bend they could be broken, and the best guess is that Antonov would have gotten the army he wanted with the support of the Left SRs and the peasantry.

Thus if Communism had foundered, the distinction between Social Revolutionism or Populism and the Green movement would have been clarified by further developments on the military and agrarian fronts, and the Greens would have stood forth as men of action attuned to the peasant consciousness for whom intuition and feeling took the place of ideology.

The foregoing argument, of course, rests on the assumption that Antonov was as hostile to the Whites as to the Communists. His whole past supports such an assumption. From the first to the last he pursued a course of unswerving loyalty to the revolution. Penal servitude in Siberia, after all, did not endear the Russian monarchy to the victim. And green is the color of those who chose to be neither red nor white. Nevertheless, a consistent attempt has been made in Soviet historiography to represent Antonov, if not actually as an agent of the Whites, at least as a counter-revolutionary who sought to link his movement with theirs and always, it seems, in a subordinate position.

First an attempt was made to provide a theoretical setting for Antonov and the Green movement elsewhere. Instead of recognizing it as an independent phenomenon leading to a second civil war, it was treated as a later and degenerating phase of the same civil war in which the Greens were portrayed as tools of the vanquished Whites and the latter, in turn, as those of the Paris bourse.[19] The process of counter-revolution began with the attempts to restore the Constituent Assembly and then the throne, and ended in the "swamp of banditry."[20] The editor of one of the two main Soviet organs stated flatly that there was no essential difference between the Tambov "toiling peasantry" and the Constantinople monarchists. Wrangel and the remnants of his army were at that time interned in the vicinity of the Straits. "In the person of Antonov and others like

him, Chernov stretches out his hand in friendly fashion to
Wrangel.'' Having thus abandoned all restraints, the editor went on
to say that ''the bandits represent the right SRs, directed and guided
by the White Guards.'' The latter were undoubtedly among them
(he could name none), and directed their actions as at Kronstadt.
And why? Because otherwise it could not be; such was the law of
counter-revolution.[21] If the Green movement flourished and spread
it would inevitably end by erecting the Romanov banner.[22]

Here is not the place to deal with people who discover laws
governing human behavior. It will be enough to observe that the
''law'' of counter-revolution here set forth is based on the wild
peasant thrashings of the seventeenth and eighteenth centuries with
their search for the ''good Tsar'' and espousal of the ''old faith.''
Such a ''law'' throws out the whole social evolution of Russia since
emancipation, without which the formulators of the ''law'' would
themselves never have come to power or even existed.

The Communists do not deal with the peasant in theory any more
successfully than in practice. Steklov's falsification of the Green
movement holds to this day with some variations. Instead of the last
stage of a single civil war, the Green movement has recently been
viewed as a new aspect of the class struggle in the period of
transition.[23] Or it has been viewed as one of a number of attempts on
the part of the Russian and international bourgeoisie to set the
peasants against the workers and their vanguard for the purpose of
putting an end to the dictatorship of the proletariat.[24]

Whatever the variation, the purpose is always the same: to deny
any independence, any character of its own to the Green movement.
This purpose accords with Lenin's teaching that economic forces
would never permit the peasantry to achieve cohesion but would
always subject it to the domination—he said guidance—of a class
solidified under capitalists or Communists.[25] Yet this same Lenin at
the height of the March crisis of 1921, when he was badly shaken and
less sure of Marxian infallibility, said that the relationship between
the peasantry and the proletariat posed a danger ''surpassing by
many times that of all the Denikins, Kolchaks and Yudeniches taken
together,''[26] and that the defeat inflicted on the Soviet regime in the
spring of 1921 by this headless class had been ''far more grievous
and dangerous'' than any experienced in the civil war.[27]

Perhaps it was less an obsession with the White Guard reaction than fear of truly independent action on the part of the traditionally submerged peasant class, now at last threatening to come into its own, that lay behind Soviet misrepresentations[28] of the Green movement. In any event, the Communist intellectuals shot as wide of the mark with their historical parallel between the Tambov and Vendée insurrections as the Populist intellectuals did with theirs between the October revolution and the Paris Commune.[29] Both sets of intellectuals had absorbed a smattering of history but had learned as little from it as the Soviet and Provisional governments they represented: Russia was not France, and 1920 was not 1793.

Examination of specific Soviet charges reveals vagueness, confusion, and the entire emptiness of the contention that the Green bands "were an instrument of the outcast exploiting classes and international imperialism."[30] Exponents of such a view have to scrape desperately to establish even a tenuous connection, much less a subordination of the Green to the White movement.

The attempt has centered around the events of the summer of 1919 when the White cavalry leader, Mamontov, raided deep into Soviet territory and occupied for a brief time portions of Tambov province. According to the story, Antonov established contact either with Mamontov or with his superior, Denikin, or both. A political commissar in the Red Army says that Antonov not only entered into relations with Denikin but got aid from him.[31] But since this commissar arrived on the scene much later—in the spring of 1921—and since his is one of the most prejudiced accounts, it need not be taken seriously.

Other information along the same line, however, is more specific. Somewhere[32] it has been stated that Antonov chose as his emissaries to Denikin the brothers Santalov, who certainly held positions of responsibility under him though presumably less prominent ones than the men mentioned in our foregoing sketch of leadership. Most specific is a statement in the Soviet press later on to the effect that at the time of Mamontov's ride in August 1919 Antonov had sent to Denikin's headquarters two representatives, Yakimov and one of the Santalov brothers, ostensibly in the name of the Greens but actually on behalf of the SRs. Furthermore, the fact had been established that Denikin, on his part, had despatched an airplane with counter-revolutionary proclamations to fly over "bandit" territory, and that this literature had been dropped in the vicinity of the village of Chernavka in Kirsanov *uezd*.[33]

A search of maps fails to yield a village of this name, but it may be assumed—since Kirsanov was Antonov's home district—that his band was the object of the propaganda; and it is plausible, though by no means certain, that the Whites were responding in this fashion to the Yakimov and Santalov mission. As to what went on between the mission and Denikin—if it actually was sent and reached its destination—there is no information whatever.

Still another version of the eventful summer of 1919 has Antonov sounding out the peasants as to what course to adopt when Mamontov knifed into Tambov province. The peasants preserved neutrality in the face of the crisis; they favored no deal with the invader. Antonov's confederates were of the same mind. It was decided, on the other hand, at least not to engage the invaders, and instructions to that effect went out to all those in the incipient Green movement.

After Mamontov had seized Tambov, a confrontation took place in the village of Mordovo at which Antonov was represented by one of his officers, the rural school teacher Luzin, an ensign in the World War. After belittling the guerrilla effort and contrasting its primitive set-up with Denikin's regular army and duly constituted government, Mamontov offered to intercede with Denikin to incorporate the bands into the Volunteer Army as special behind-the-lines units. But Luzin thought no arrangement was possible because his side stood for liberty and Mamontov's for the old order. Mamontov disclaimed belief in a restoration, upholding merely the need for a strong national authority, while Cossacks who were present expressed definite aversion to the monarchy. And there the matter rested. The interview yielded one tangible if modest result: in exchange for some fresh peasant horses, the White general left the Antonov forces several hundred rifles with cartridges and two Colt machine guns. It will be observed that the peasants, as usual, footed the bill.[34]

It is all an interesting story. The question here is whether it was anything more than a story. The episode is related in direct discourse, strictly in accordance with Russian custom and strictly in disregard of historical accuracy, since the author was not there and did not have the minutes of the meeting—in all probability there were none. Furthermore, the episode is not included in the second manuscript of his memoirs.[35] Omission the second time around is not necessarily an indication of error the first time, for both manuscripts—though highly interesting and undoubtedly containing valid material—are poorly organized and afford evidence that the narrator was carried away with his own words.

What does he say in the second manuscript about Antonov and the Whites? There are some general observations stressing the republican character of Antonov's movement—about which there is never any doubt—and the republican sentiment of the peasantry. Throughout 1919 and into 1920, when the civil war was at its climax, Antonov undertook no embarrassing action against the Bolsheviks such as cutting railway communications behind the front lines, but contented himself with combatting punitive detachments sent out against the peasants. He was restrained not only by his own attitude but also by the strong peasant feeling against the Whites, which left no doubt in his mind that Denikin would share the fate of Kolchak.

After these general observations, which are wholly in agreement with sources other than hopelessly prejudiced ones from the Soviet side, the author proceeds to relate another and very different episode from that mentioned above. Hearing from peasant sympathizers of a mysterious band hiding in the woods of Lebedian *uezd*, Antonov sent one of his associates to investigate. His emissary, Mishin, came on a small band of men from a vanished world: the marshal of the nobility of that *uezd*, the chief Tsarist official—*zemskii nachal'nik*—several officers from the Imperial army, and some deserters, all under Lieutenant Petrovo-Solovovo. of noble origin. Mishin summoned the band in the name of the peasantry either to get out or to join Antonov—the woods were reserved for the Greens. After some hesitation the forlorn group opted for the second alternative and was distributed among Antonov's units, a certain Captain Egorov being assigned to Zheltov's command.

This unfree union ended in tragedy. It was consummated sometime in 1919 before the failure of Denikin's offensive against Moscow—a more definite date cannot be given. But in April 1920

Captain Egorov, having fallen into the hands of the Reds, betrayed Zheltov and caused him and his whole command to be cut to pieces in an ambuscade. On that very night Antonov settled the question of White elements in his Green forces by having every officer from the old army killed save only the few who had been with him from the beginning.[36]

Again we have an interesting story. The only trouble is that in relation to the ambush the author of the manuscript seems to be in error. If, as we suspect, Zheltov is Matiukhin and Captain Egorov is Staff Captain Ektov, then the ambuscade took place—not in April 1920—but more than a year later, at a time when Antonov's army had been so thoroughly beaten and dispersed that he could scarcely have undertaken a purge of the scope described.[37] Furthermore, and with reference not only to the two Fomichev manuscripts under discussion but also to other sources, the whole question of Antonov's relations with the Whites in 1919 is bedeviled by the fact that at that time he seems to have had no more than a hundred to a hundred and fifty men in his "forces" and to have been lying low, mounting no major enterprises until the smoke of the first civil war had cleared away. Why then should he have engaged the attention of Denikin, Mamontov, or any other White commander? And if the initiative came from Antonov, the most likely explanation is that he was simply fishing for arms. One can only conclude that this question of relations with the White movement is as treacherous for the historian as it was for Antonov himself.

As for the later period of the actual insurrection, the effort to convict Antonov of being in the toils of the Whites hinges on the role of D. F. Fedorov, a Constitutional Democrat (Kadet) of provincial significance, formerly a large landowner and a lawyer by profession. There is little doubt that Fedorov was associated with Antonov in an important capacity. He seems to have been a member of the Supreme Operational Staff and specifically to have been in charge of counterintelligence in the city of Tambov, masking his activity as a branch manager of a Petersburg firm for the purveyance of horses or of some other commodity. When he went to Moscow in May or June 1921 along with several others to muster support for the movement, he posed as the "SR Gorski." A source otherwise free of exaggeration has Fedorov carrying on his espionage with the aid of

dyed-in-the-wool monarchists and adherents of the old regime—the
former procurator of the Vilno district court Chekhovski, the Baltic
baron Colonel Taube, the ex-Tsarist General Esipov, Colonel
Minski, and others—a rather imposing array of shadows from the
past.[38]

Thus the contention that the "bandits" and the SRs were
associated with Kadets and monarchists in their fight against the
Soviet republic may well be true. But the legend fostered at the time
and never since abandoned—that Green was a false coloration and
that these White elements dominated the movement—is not for a
moment seriously to be entertained.

According to the legend, Fedorov actually headed the whole
affair and financed it as the intermediary for counter-revolutionary
circles in Moscow and Petersburg, which in turn had international
connections. More specifically, the threads ran from Fedorov to
N. M. Kishkin, member-in-residence of the central committee of
the Constitutional Democratic party, then mainly in exile; the
committee in turn transmitted the will of international capital.[39] In
other words—and reversing the order—the chain of command
emanated from Parisian financial circles to the central organ of the
Constitutional Democratic party; from this organ to Kishkin in
Moscow; from him to Fedorov in Tambov, and thence to Antonov
in the field.

Much evil may have come from Paris, but not the Antonov
insurrection. The earlier Soviet sources themselves do not sustain
the legend. When Fedorov and his comrades[40] went to Moscow in
the late spring or early summer of 1921 they did not receive through
Kishkin instructions from the Constitutional Democratic central
committee abroad—as the legend has it—but were merely trying to
get in touch with him as representative of the committee; before they
succeeded they were arrested and their purpose disclosed. The
Extraordinary Commission (Che-ka) itself, in a public statement,
made it clear that the attempt to link Kishkin to Antonov had
failed,[41] whatever might be the justification of its effort to get at the
Kadet leader from another angle.[42] The Che-ka at that time did
occasionally come out into the light of day and under Dzerzhinski
had not learned to lie inordinately.

The reaction of the insurrectionists to the studied defamation of their movement may be judged from one communication intercepted by the Soviet authorities. Cut off as they were from the outside world, the Greens became prey to wild rumors. Their organizer in the Pavlov area, a man named Vasin, advised the provincial committee of the Peasants' Union (STK) in June 1921 that word had come to him that Wrangel had taken Kiev, that Poland had resumed war on the Soviets, and even that Ataman Semenov with the aid of Japan had burst into the Urals, taken Ufa, and was advancing victoriously on Samara. Vasin did not know what to believe and begged for information. Far from being elated, he said that "such rumors can only harm our work. We need light as to what groups are acting and whether their actions may be viewed as useful."[43] The Soviet press assured the SRs that the actions were useful to them and to all others working for the same master, the world bourgeoisie.[44]

But the point to be noted here is that rumors of reactionary successes did not help the Greens and were not welcomed by them. Aside from this one scrap of evidence culled from the Soviet press, their voice is mute on this as on other matters; but Vasin's attitude may be taken as typical, for the two causes were alien, one to the other, and the Soviet insistence on splashing White on the Green cause should not be allowed to delude the truth-seeking student of history.

The Green movement was never strong on paper work and its meager output has been thoroughly destroyed. There is in existence, however, a single copy of a proclamation over Antonov's name, addressed to Red Army men, which seems to bear out everything the Soviet has said about his movement. The very first charge brought against the "red autocrats" who were nesting in "Moscow of the white walls" is that they have "defiled our shrines, our ikons with the sacred relics." The message not only admonished Red Army men to desert to Antonov but summons the Russian heroes of the past—Ilya Muromets, Dobrynia Nikitich, Minin, and Pozharski—to awaken and heed the call of the fatherland to further exploits. Antonov, in fact, compares himself to Minin and to Pozharski, and Tambov to Nizhni Novgorod.

There is a curious passage about how the Red Army men were to
get to Tambov: they were to move in any way possible, even by
whole echelons on railroads and steamers, yet were advised to avoid
highways and to give preference to country roads. Curious also is
the reference to the Ukraine. The soldiers were told that the
commissars would try to hold them in the Ukraine. They must bear
in mind that "the Ukrainians are preparing a general insurrection
and you will not be able to cope with them, for they are a cunning and
capable people."[45]

The whole document is curious, in fact, and merits closer
examination. There is no date. The place is given as Tambov where
Antonov had not been since 1917. If unwary soldiers had gotten
there they would have found a strong Red garrison. There were four
other names on the proclamation besides Antonov's: Turin,
Voskresenski, Ivanov, Kutepov—none of them known to this
investigator, either as real names or as pseudonyms. Turin figured as
"Chairman of the United Civilian Committee of the Supreme
Command of the National Militia." None of these three organizations existed. In the proclamation Antonov boasts of having an army
of one hundred twenty thousand at his command—a figure too high
by ninety-nine thousand. And, finally, is it not unusual that
Antonov, the former Siberian convict who had himself been a Left
SR and whose favorite and closest friend was the Left SR leader in
Tambov province, should have been so concerned about shrines,
images, and sacred relics?

The proclamation is faked from beginning to end. The very first
statement about the religious objects betrays its monarchist origin.
So also does the pompous, almost bombastic tone, so different from
the genuine manifesto noted below.[46] The reference to the
Ukrainian people as being cunning or tricky—khitryi—tinged with
unfriendliness, may betoken the chauvinism of former ruling
elements which had served them so badly. Similarly the denunciation of the commissars for "having converted into an impassable
wasteland our strong and rich state" smacks both of state adulation
and hyperbole, since Russia had hardly been a strong and certainly
not a wealthy state.

This proclamation did not emanate from the people; everything
about it rings false. But its fakery does not deprive it of historical

value, for it affords graphic evidence of an effort on the part of dispossessed elements to graft themselves onto a truly popular movement which later they assuredly would have attempted to repress. Along with Kishkin's federalist plan, the Che-ka had unearthed in the possession of P. T. Salamatov another plan impregnated with rigid centralism and slated for implementation in case coordination at the center succeeded in fusing local uprisings and sweeping out the Soviets.[47] Reactionary forces undoubtedly sought to capitalize on the Green movement, but their machinations no more made Green into White than the machinations of Imperial Germany made Bolsheviks into German imperialists. The combined efforts at distortion of Reds and Whites cannot efface the fact that in Russia there was—for a time—a genuine Third Force.

Inevitably the Soviet attempts to portray the Greens as tools of reaction were accompanied by accusations of anti-Semitism and of a resort to religious obscurantism. Bearing in mind that anti-Semitism of the less virulent type was endemic in Russian society, these charges should be examined. At the outset it may be noted that mention of anti-Semitism in connection with the Green movement, while frequently encountered in Soviet sources, is made *en passant* and without specification.

Not all references to the matter, to be sure, are as vague as the one that Antonov incited his men against "those of other faith" who were seeking the ruin of Russia.[48] The "SR bandits" are said to have egged peasants on to cut up and to exterminate the "kike-Communists,"[49] which is definite enough but still not specific as to time or place. An officer of the Red Army who fought against Antonov confided to the press that the SRs—by which he meant the Greens—mingled their slogans for the Constituent Assembly with other slogans such as *"Bei zhidov, spasai Rossiiu!"* (Beat [or kill] the Jews and save Russia!),[50] thus imputing to them the old war cry of the Black Hundreds. As these statements were made when the drums were beating on the eve of the SR trial of 1922—and were themselves part of the drum-beating—they are less worthy of credence than the secret testimony of the commissar of repression, who makes the point that it is not the program or code of the Peasants' Union that breathes the true spirit of the Green movement, but the handwritten resolutions of village meetings and the broadsides of the Green commanders; in other words, the genuine literature of the insurrection, which he had and we do not. Here, crassly formulated, was the sentiment of the rebellion: "Down with the Jew Communists!" On the manuscript of his report in the Houghton Library it is fascinating to see how Lenin underscored these words and marked in the margin beside them; evidently they engaged his attention as much as anything in the report.[51]

And so there was anti-Semitism in the Green movement. How much, and with what justification? There could not have been much coming down from the past, because Tambov had never been a part of the Pale and because the Jewish population of the province was so microscopic as not even to be mentioned in the ordinary sources of information. The census of 1897 gave 98.6 percent of the population as Orthodox, 0.7 percent Moslem, and 0.6 percent sectarian—mainly Molokans.[52] That leaves 0.1 percent, or less than three thousand people, to be distributed among Jews, Lutherans, and Roman Catholics; at the turn of the century Tambov town had a Lutheran church, a synagogue, and a Catholic church was under construction.[53] Probably the one city and few towns of the province had received an increment of Jews as a result of the Great War,[54] but the number would have shrunk again in the wake of revolution and civil war.

Though reticent on the Jewish question, the Soviet press contains one interesting item about the situation in Tambov. At the time of the removal of church treasures, a measure which the Soviet government with its consummate skill of propaganda had tied to famine relief, Rabbi Gurevich in Tambov is represented as stubbornly refusing to part with those of the synagogue until the Orthodox Church had yielded its vessels of gold and silver. Gurevich must have been a lonely figure amid his treasures, for the revolution had decimated his fold and removed from it virtually all well-to-do Jewish families. They had all faded from the scene and gone elsewhere.[55]

Anti-Semitism in the Green movement, then, must have sprung from the circumstances of the time instead of being handed down from the past. There is, of course, no way of knowing how many

Communist officials in Tambov province or in the associated province of Voronezh were Jewish at the time of the insurrection or in the years immediately preceding. Only scraps of information can be provided, far too few to measure the resentment against ravishers of the people who were Jewish.

In connection with the initial imposition of the food levy in Voronezh in 1918, there is reference to a Comrade Golman as a plenipotentiary with jurisdiction over a food army large enough for him to order it to be broken up into detachments of a hundred men each.[56] Nothing is known about his further actions, but the nature of his work would not have endeared him to the population. After the assassination of M. D. Chichkanov in 1919,[57] A. G. Schlichter (1868–1940) became chairman of the Soviet Executive Committee of Tambov province—that is, the chief government official—and member of the collegium of the Commissariat of Trade, both in the same year of 1920. In 1919 he had been food commissar of the Ukraine.[58] His appointment probably betokened the agrarian significance of Tambov and the expectation that he would be able to extract from it yet greater quantities of food. The nearer he came to fulfilling the expectations of Moscow, of course, the greater would be his unpopularity in Tambov.

Of most immediate concern to this study, however, were the depradations of an official named Golvin who, during an unspecified period, directed the collection of produce from the peasantry under the food levy program. What he was like may be judged from the admission of another Soviet official that Golvin did not "spare the harsh measures."[59] This testimony of a member of the Extraordinary Commission (Che-ka) is an extraordinary disclosure which might possibly appear in an early Soviet source but assuredly not in a later one. The same source reveals the dispatch from the center of a "Comrade Levin" to reorganize the Che-ka in Tambov province, and says that after this shake-up its service was improved.

Levin would have done his work in devious ways, secluded from the public gaze, and his Jewishness would not have registered on the public consciousness. But the grievous actions connected with the administration of the food levy would inevitably have been associated with the names of Golman and Golvin, and would have aroused resentment against Jews as well as against Communists. It is here that the roots of whatever anti-Semitism there was in the Green movement of Tambov province may be found. There does not seem to have been a great deal, if only because there were so few Jews in the province. One source denies there was any. It says that anti-Semitism had been proscribed by Antonov, and cites the confrontation between some of his men and the reactionary young lieutenant mentioned above, Petrovo-Solovovo, who had been telling the peasants that the Jews had ruined Russia and were exterminating the Orthodox population. He had been hushed up and compelled to join the Green army, only to perish later in Antonov's purge of White elements.[60]

As further evidence of the absence of popular feeling against the Jews, mention is made of an incident in the village of Znamenka in 1918. After Bolsheviks had plundered a pharmacy and killed the Jewish proprietor who tried to defend his property, the local peasants had taken in his family and managed to send it to Saratov. Such incidents may well be true, but to maintain that anti-Semitism was wholly unknown in the Antonov movement and the Tambov peasantry generally seems to be going too far.[61] The best surmise is that Judeophobia was not lacking but that it was less pronounced than in the case of the Green movement in the Ukraine, with its large Jewish population and with a long tradition of ethnic or religious friction.

In conjunction with the charge of anti-Semitism, the Communists have sought to convict Antonov of fomenting religious feeling. Here they seem to have even less to go on than in the case of anti-Semitism. Steklov attributed to Antonov a verse in which the Green leader speaks of having dedicated his host to Faith, Fatherland, and Justice and of having blessed it with the cross.[62] If true, these three lines of bad verse would represent all that has come down to us from Antonov's pen; since it was not used for prose, it is not likely that it would have been used for verse, and our conjecture is that this doggerel belongs in the same category as the above-mentioned proclamation or manifesto.

Soviet sources are credible, however, in assigning to Antonov's army a field church that accompanied it on its campaigns, or at least served it in its marshy place of refuge; this tiny structure was made of reeds and mounted on poles.[63] There appears to have been some contact between the Greens and members of the clergy, both white and black or secular and regular. At least one priest fled the approach of a Red force and sought refuge with Antonov, "to provide his men with pastoral care and the blessing of the Lord." This priest, however, by admission of his pursuers, was scarcely an obscurantist; in his well-stocked library many authors were represented, including Tolstoy and Gorki.[64]

One of the greatest handicaps of the insurrection must have been the dearth of medical services. It is all a blank in the record, but many a wound which in an army with a state behind it would not have been lethal must have ended in death for a luckless guerrilla. At least to some extent, however, a modicum of care was provided by monks in the role of medical attendants. Thus members of the Vyshinski Monastery served Antonov's forces and cared for the wounded in some lonely forest nook. The conditions under which they worked may be imagined from the fact that even in the large Russian cities pharmaceutical supplies were scarce in these terrible years. One monk nevertheless rescued Yaryzhka and gained the affection of the hard-bitten anarchist leader.[65] Even the Left SRs, as will be noted,[66] concealed their insignia and valuables in a village church; whatever discoveries may be made in a church, this particular one could not have been foreseen.

As to Antonov's peasant following, as distinct from his military command, it is likewise not possible to say very much on the score of religion. In general there was some religious resentment on the part of the peasantry against the actions of the Soviet regime, but not as much as could have been expected. The Bolsheviks in 1919 had exposed the remains of a Tambov saint, Pitirim. The peasants viewed these proceedings with imperturbability; the Tsar, they said, had exposed Pitirim's remains upon mobilization in 1914 to aid in overcoming the Germans but without discernible effect, so what kind of a saint was he?

Even the closing down of churches in the villages occasioned little open resistance, but the inhabitants are said to have made every effort to save the priests—sometimes secluding them in the forests and taking care of their families by means of an assessment on each household. Persecution of the clergy and repression of the peasantry became entwined, and priests died with peasants in the course of the punitive operations. Though manifesting little will to resistance so long as the civil war was on, the peasants stored up resentment over the closing of churches and the hounding of the clergy. Their anger was directed particularly against the workers, who were often used by the Communists to commit antireligious acts as well as to confiscate the peasant's grain. The workers, said the peasants, "believed neither in God nor the devil and tried to drag others down their road to hell." In the course of the insurrection such sentiments occasionally merged with others of an economic character to produce bestial treatment of captured workers.[67]

It seems that Antonov neither fanned religious fanaticism nor strenuously combatted it; he gave free rein to his men and to the peasants to do as they pleased. If his men wanted a field church, he offered no objection; if the peasants tortured helpless workers, it was only another incident in a merciless struggle. In the absence of any knowledge as to whether he himself entered the field church, we may conclude that he remained essentially indifferent to religion[68] and that the grievous events of the revolution had not thrown him back into its arms but had at most converted his earlier aversion into a tolerance born of persecution from a common source. Since he maintained his opposition to the White movement, there is no reason to suspect him of forsaking in the field of faith his former dedication to the revolution. Moreover, his men were by no means always considerate of the feelings of the religious-minded. On Easter Sunday, 1921, in Nikolskoe village near Sampur in Tambov *uezd*, his men relieved worshippers of their footwear and articles of clothing as they were coming out of the church, and in Dvorianshchina village they appropriated the Easter comestibles of the believers.[69]

Neither in respect to collaboration with the Whites, in anti-Semitism, or in the cultivation of religious fanaticism does the Soviet indictment of Antonov hold water. The thinness of the charges against him at times approaches the ludicrous; there is a fanfare of accusation, the drums are beaten, and nothing comes forth. The attempt to link the SRs—if not the Green movement—to the pogrom of Jews and workers in Kozlov at the time of the Mamontov raid is an exercise in futility.[70] The Communists produced at the time of the

SR trial the worker I. N. Chemriaev, member of the PSR from 1904 to 1919 and at one time member of the praesidium of the Tambov soviet, but the sole contribution he made to the arraignment was to call Antonov a "hooligan bandit."[71]

Not everything was this vacuous. At times there was a modicum of truth in the charges. The Greens were not paragons of revolutionary virtue. Neither, we might add, are the Communists. The whole matter may be reduced to a formula: for the Communists, anything that promotes their cause qualifies as revolutionary or at least as "progressive," anything that obstructs it is branded as counter-revolutionary. From this point of view the Green movement, naturally, was counter-revolutionary. But history admits pluralism in revolution as in other matters; it is not necessary for a movement to enthrone Communism in order to qualify as revolutionary. From the objective point of view, the revolutionary credentials of the Greens were as good as those of the Communists, and in some respects better.

A consideration of the ideology and program of the Tambov insurrection may conclude with an analysis of the one true reflection in writing of its spirit and purpose. In the primary Soviet source on the subject there is preserved the text of a manifesto of which the authenticity cannot be doubted.[72] The rhythmic, semipoetic style reveals the handiwork of Dmitri Antonov or the "Young Lion," to give him the literary name that he had devised for himself and preferred to use on the manifestos of his composition (it is doubtful there were any others). The language is rather pleasing in its rhythmic simplicity; it is written with feeling and is straight from the people. Here is something untouched by the verbiage and the theoretical constructions of the Populist intellectuals. The manifesto appeals to the soldiers of the Red Army to desert their masters and come over to the side of the people so that oppression will end and the "fat life" prevail.

The Communists pounced upon these guileless words as indisputable evidence of a bourgeois, counter-revolutionary mentality. Their indignation is understandable, as life would never be fat under them. The SR leaders would have spoken of prosperity, had they been writing the manifesto, but the phrase of Dmitri Antonov

had its place in an appeal to Russian peasants for whom the vision of
the fat life to come might have been an interval of light between their
dark past and darker future.

The whole burden of the manifesto with its message of subversion
bears witness to political instinct, for only through a break in the Red
Army could the Greens hope to win. There is a single line of
anti-Semitism, something about overthrowing the rule of the Jewish
Communists. Was it inserted by the editors? Probably not, for again
a son of the people is addressing other sons of the people and Dmitri
Antonov knew that in the lower ranks of the Red Army there was
latent anti-Semitism. But the issue is not belabored as it would have
been in a White proclamation. A single line in a manifesto is about
the correct proportion for anti-Semitism in the Green movement, at
least in the province of Tambov.

The same political instinct as in other matters is seen in the
absence of any invocation of the deity; God is left to his chosen
neutrality. Once more we are reminded that this is a Green, not a
White, manifesto. The "Young Lion" either calculated that the
residue of religious sentiment in the Red Army was too small to
justify such an approach or he himself did not care to make it, or else
his indifference was such that the thought did not occur to him.

In general, the manifesto convincingly refutes the Soviet effort to
slander the Tambov insurrection as counter-revolutionary. Nothing
in it can be construed as incompatible with the Russian Revolution
in the true and broader sense. In all other cases the overlay of SR
formulations and of Soviet distortion has to be stripped away to get
at the essence of the Green movement; nearly always it must be
appraised by its deeds instead of by the words put into its mouth by
Populist intellectuals for want of words of its own, but in this rare
instance the otherwise so inarticulate movement speaks for itself.

Notes

1. *Pravda*, no. 153, 12 July 1922, p. 4; testimony of Bogoliubski printed under the proceedings of the SR trial. See also Trifonov, *Klassy i klassovaia bor'ba*, part 1, p. 96.

2. Text of the program in anonymous (Podbelski), *Kak tambovskie krest'iane boriatsia za svobodu*, pp. 13–14.

3. Not listed among the sixteen points in ibid., but given among the eight to be found in Trifonov, *Klassy i klassovaia bor'ba*, part 1, pp. 96–97. Here the weight of evidence is on the side of the Soviet source.

4. Fomichev (Lidin), "Antonovshchina: Iz vospominanii antonovtsa" (Santiago de Chile, 1955), p. 20.

5. Leonidov, "Esche ob eserakh v Tambovskoi gub.," *Izvestiia*, no. 155, 14 July 1922, p. 3. This point was smoothed over by Podbelski in anonymous, *Kak tambovskie krest'iane boriatsia za svobodu*, when he records only the "opening of broad state credits" without saying to whom they would be extended. But later, after being arrested and having to exculpate himself before the Soviet authorities, Podbelski sought to put distance between SR intellectuals and the peasant rebellion by disparaging as illiterate this very point in the program. See his typescript in the Nikolaevsky Collection in the Hoover Institution entitled "Predsedateliu moskovskogo soveta r. i k. deputatov" (n.d., but known to be most likely July 1921), p. 2.

6. Trifonov, *Klassy i klassovaia bor'ba*, part 1, p. 96.

7. Socialization of the land is discussed in Radkey, *The Agrarian Foes of Bolshevism*, pp. 25 ff. and passim.

8. Trifonov, *Klassy i klassovaia bor'ba*, part 1, pp. 96–97. The author relies on other Soviet sources of the time, and by no means the best ones. Another example of the present state of Soviet historiography.

9. It is repeated in a non-Soviet source, apparently because the author followed the partial and inaccurate list of provisions presented by Trifonov. See Iuri S. Srechinski, "Zapechatannaia stranitsa" [The sealed page], *Novoe Russkoe Slovo*, 25 April 1969.

10. Fomichev (Lidin), "Antonovshchina: Iz vospominanii antonovtsa" (Santiago de Chile, 1955), p. 20.

11. See Radkey, *The Agrarian Foes of Bolshevism*, pp. 84–85.

12. See Fomichev (Lidin), "Antonovshchina: Iz vospominanii antonovtsa" (Santiago de Chile, 1955), p. 20, for inconclusiveness of discussion on these matters; see absence of reference to ban on hired labor in summary of program presented in Leonidov, "Eshche ob eserakh v Tambovskoi gub.," *Izvestiia*, no. 155, 14 July 1922, p. 3; also anonymous (Podbelski), *Kak tambovskie krest'iane boriatsia za svobodu*.

13. Steklov, "Banditizm, kak avangard burzhuaznoi restavratsii"♭[Banditry as the vanguard of bourgeois restoration], *Izvestiia*, no. 88 (1231), 23 April 1921, p. 1. Although moving within the circle of Marxian dogma, Steklov was a man of relatively wide vision with regard for the truth. The author has not caught him lying about the Green movement or otherwise, although he is quite capable of shifting an emphasis. Even his use of the term "bandit" instead of "green" was a case of straining the truth rather than of subverting it.

14. "Krest'ianskoe dvizhenie" [The peasant movement], *Volia Rossii*, no. 172, 8 April 1921, p. 1.

15. Anonymous (Podbelski), *Kak tambovskie krest'iane boriatsia za svobodu*, p. 11.

16. Ibid., p. 12.

17. Ibid., pp. 13, 16; see also editorial, "Povstanchestvo" [Insurgency], *Volia Rossii*, no. 199, 10 May 1921, p. 1; and especially pronouncement of the central committee of the PSR of 26 April 1921 under the heading "Partiia s.-r. o zadachakh momenta" [The SR party on current problems], ibid., no. 218, 2 June 1921, pp. 3–4.

18. Fomichev (Lidin), "Antonovshchina: Iz vospominanii antonovtsa" (Santiago de Chile, 1955), p. 31.

19. Petrovski, "Bor'ba s banditizmom i krasnye kursanty," *Izvestiia*, no. 133 (1276), 23 June 1921, p. 1; "O kulakakh, banditakh i pozharakh" [On kulaks, bandits and conflagrations], *Volia Rossii*, no. 207, 20 May 1921, p. 1.

20. Steklov, "Bandity, esery i kadety" [Bandits, SRs and Kadets], *Izvestiia*, no. 97 (1240), 7 May 1921, p. 1.

21. Steklov, "Ot Chernova do Antonova," ibid., no. 71, 2 April 1921, p. 1.

22. Steklov, "Nashi vandeitsy i shuany" [Our Vendéens and Chouans], ibid., no. 112 (1255), 25 May 1921, p. 1.

23. "Antonovshchina," in *Sovetskaia istoricheskaia entsiklopediia*, vol. 1, p. 635.

24. Donkov, "Organizatsiia razgroma antonovshchiny," *Voprosy Istorii KPSS*, no. 6 (June 1966), p. 71.

25. Speech at the All-Russian Congress of Transport Workers, 27 March 1921, in Lenin, *Polnoe sobranie sochinenii*, 5th ed., vol. 43, pp. 136–41; "O prodovol'stvennom naloge," in ibid., pp. 239–40; report on the tactics of the Russian Communist Party to the Third Congress of the Comintern, 5 July 1921, in ibid., vol. 44, p. 42.

26. "Otchet o politicheskoi deiatel'nosti TsK RKP (b)," 8 March 1921, in ibid., vol. 43, p. 18.

27. "Novaia ekonomicheskaia politika i zadachi politprosvetov," 17 October 1921, in ibid., vol. 44, pp. 158–59.

28. See further Ia. A., "K 4-letnei godovshchine VChK" [On the fourth anniversary of the All-Russian Extraordinary Commission], *Izvestiia*, no. 279 (1422), 11 December 1921, p. 1; Steklov, "Derevnia i novaia ekonomicheskaia

politika" [The village and the new economic policy], ibid., no. 203 (1346), 18 September 1921, p. 1; Trifonov, *Klassy i klassovaia bor'ba*, part 1, pp. 298–301.

29. See Radkey, *The Sickle under the Hammer: The Russian Socialist Revolutionaries in the Early Months of Soviet Rule* (New York, 1963), pp. 328–29.

30. Trifonov, *Klassy i klassovaia bor'ba*, part 1, p. 301.

31. Borisov, "Konets antonovshchiny," in *Nezabyvaemoe*, p. 286.

32. Probably in *Put' Bor'by;* the author remembers mention of the Santalov brothers in this source, but is not sure whether it was in this connection.

33. Dokunin, "Tambovskii schet sotsial-banditam," *Pravda*, no. 123, 4 June 1922, p. 3. Whether the assertions made here are accepted or not, they contain one unmistakable touch of propaganda. If Antonov did send men to Denikin, he acted on his own and not on behalf of the SRs. Dokunin's article was part of the warm-up for the SR trial of 1922 and sought to incriminate further these unfortunate people. The responsibility of the SRs for Antonov's insurrection will be dealt with in the following chapter.

34. Fomichev (Lidin), "Antonovshchina: Iz vospominanii antonovtsa" (Philippines, 1950–1951), pp. 14–15.

35. Ibid. (Santiago de Chile, 1955).

36. Ibid. (Santiago de Chile, 1955), pp. 25, 34–36.

37. See chapter ten.

38. S. Ch., "Tambovskaia pamiatka ob eserakh," *Izvestiia*, no. 121 (1560), 2 June 1922, p. 1 This article is based—at least in part—on an account in the provincial press by a certain B. V. in the *Tambovskaia Pravda*.

39. *Put' Bor'by*, volume and page cannot be given; "Zagovoro-boiazn'" [The phobia about conspiracies], *Volia Rossii*, no. 305, 14 September 1921, p. 1; Dokunin, "Tambovskii schet sotsial-banditam," *Pravda*, no. 123, 4 June 1922, p. 3; Trifonov, *Klassy i klassovaia bor'ba*, part 1, p. 43.

40. Including N. Ia. Gerasev, an SR who bore the assumed name of "Donskoi." Probably this was also the mission that brought into the clutches of the Che-ka staff Captain Ektov (Egorov?), whose apprehension and subsequent defection wrought such damage to the uprising and specifically to Matiukhin's (Zheltov's?) command.

41. "Soobshchenie Vserossiiskoi Chrezvychainoi Komissii ob arestakh vo Vserossiiskom Komitete pomoshchi golodaiushchim" [Announcement of the All-Russian Extraordinary Commission about the arrests in the All-Russian Committee of Aid to the Starving], *Izvestiia*, no. 199 (1342), 8 September 1921, p. 3; this report was republished without change in *Iz istorii Vserossiiskoi Chrezvychainoi Komissii 1917–1921 gg.; sbornik dokumentov*, no. 340, pp. 464–66; it was reproduced at the time with only slight error in "Fabrikatsiia zagovorov: Chrezvychaika o Vserossiiskom Komitete" [The fabrication of plots: Che-ka's report about the All-Russian Committee], *Volia Rossii*, no. 307, 16 September 1921, p. 3.

42. A scheme for the reconstruction of Russia along federal lines, written in his handwriting, was found with his secretary, Kafieva. Kishkin was no reactionary. His conduct had been commended in the Soviet press only a month before his arrest; see "Zagovoro-boiazn'," *Volia Rossii*, no. 305, 14 September 1921, p. 1. A. F. Kerenski once told this author that Kishkin had stayed clear of the Kornilov conspiracy in 1917.

43. S. E., "Antonovshchina," *Izvestiia*, no. 122 (1561), 3 June 1922, p. 3.

44. "Na mestakh: Bor'ba s banditizmom," ibid., no. 177 (1320), 12 August 1921, p. 3; see also "Krest'ianskoe dvizhenie v Tambovskoi gubernii," *Volia Rossii*, no. 290, 27 August 1921, p. 5.

45. The surviving copy of the proclamation is in the B. I. Nicolaevsky Collection of the Hoover Institution, Stanford, California. It was shown to me by courtesy of Anna M. Bourgina.

46. See p. 93.

47. "Soobshchenie Vserossiiskoi Chrezvychainoi Komissii ob arestakh vo Vserossiiskom Komitete pomoshchi golodaiushchim," *Izvestiia*, no. 199 (1342), 8 September 1921, p. 3.

48. Steklov, "Ot Chernova do Antonova," *Izvestiia*, no. 71 (1214), 2 April 1921, p. 1.

49. Dokunin, "Tambovskii schet sotsial-banditam," *Pravda*, no. 123, 4 June 1922, p. 3.

50. "Banditskie prestupleniia partii eserov: Antonovshchina: Iz besedy s genshtabistom t. Davydovym" [The bandit crimes of the SR party: the Antonov affair: from conversations with General Staff member Comrade Davydov], *Pravda*, no. 116, 27 May 1922, p. 3.

51. Antonov-Ovseenko, "O banditskom dvizhenii v Tambovskoi gubernii," p. 6.

52. *Entsiklopedicheskii slovar'* (Brockhaus-Efron), vol. 32, p. 560.

53. Ibid., p. 566.

54. The Imperial government had adopted the policy of uprooting a part of the Jewish population in the zone near the front, which coincided with the Pale, and of settling it in cities of the interior; some have seen in this forced migration of a wretched population and its congregation in garrison cities of the rear a cause for the revolution, or at least of its spread.

55. See under heading "Bor'ba s golodom" [The fight against famine] Zaezzhii, "Tambovskie vesti: iz'iatie tserkovnykh tsennostei" [Tambov news: the removal of church treasures], *Izvestiia*, no. 96 (1535), 3 May 1922, p. 3.

56. *Iz istorii grazhdanskoi voiny v SSSR*, vol. 1, no. 289, p. 299.

57. On 14 October at Lake Ilmen in Kirsanov *uezd*. See Zybko, *Tambovskaia partiinaia organizatsiia*, p. 37; Virta, *Odinochestvo*, p. 53. The novelist has him killed by one of Antonov's lieutenants. No specific information elsewhere.

58. Lenin, *Polnoe sobranie sochinenii*, 5th ed., appendix of names, vol. 51, p. 530.

59. *Put' Bor'by*, vol. 2, *Antonovshchina*, page unknown. From the memoirs of Pokaliukhin.

60. The confrontation is related somewhat differently in the two versions of the source (see note 61). The later version does not play up the anti-Semitism angle and names a different officer as Antonov's emissary.

61. Fomichev (Lidin), "Antonovshchina: Iz vospominanii antonovtsa" (Philippines, 1950–1951), pp. 25–26, 32; see also ibid. (Santiago de Chile, 1955), p. 25.

62. Steklov, "Ot Chernova do Antonova," *Izvestiia*, no. 71 (1214), 2 April 1921, p. 1.

63. Borisov, *Chernym letom*, p. 71. Reference was made to the church in another source—an article in a military journal, probably *Voina i Revoliutsiia*—which this author read in Moscow and the notes on which perished with the others.

64. Borisov, *Chernym letom*, p. 68.

65. Fomichev (Lidin), "Antonovshchina: Iz vospominanii antonovtsa" (Santiago de Chile, 1955), p. 21.

66. See below, chapter five, six, ten.

67. Fomichev (Lidin), "Antonovshchina: Iz vospominanii antonovtsa" (Santiago de Chile, 1955), pp. 20–21. On bestialities, see below, chapter eleven.

68. According to the novel, Antonov issued no decrees as to religion, neither as to its teaching in school nor as to anything else. Virta, *Odinochestvo*, p. 179.

69. *Put' Bor'by*, vol. 2, *Antonovshchina*, p. 135, as cited in Trifonov, *Klassy i klassovaia bor'ba*, part 1, p. 118.

70. See A. Luk'ianov, "Mamontovskii pogrom i rol' v nem eserov" [The Mamontov pogrom and the part of the SRs therein], *Izvestiia*, no. 129 (1568), 13 June 1922, p. 2.

71. S. E., "Pokazaniia byvshikh eserov (Ot nashego tambovskogo korrespondenta)" [Deposition of former SRs (from our Tambov correspondent)], ibid., no. 128 (1567), 11 June 1922, p. 2.

72. *Put' Bor'by*, vol. 2, *Antonovshchina*, about pp. 33 or 34.

— 5 —

Who Were the Greens?

What kind of people were drawn into the army of insurrection or supported it from the sidelines? Peasants, of course, but what kind of peasants? And did other elements of the population find representation? The Soviet stereotype has the movement made up of "criminals, deserters, and kulak sons."[1] Splinters of the White Guard frequently appear as another component, but in a position subordinate to the three core elements. Here the Soviet sources inadvertently make a distinction between the Greens and the Whites whom otherwise they seek to confound.

Some divergence is apparent, however, in weighting or in ordering the core elements: a contemporary source has a reservoir of deserters swelling the mainstream of kulaks and criminals,[2] whereas a present-day writer fashions the skeleton of the Green movement generally out of marauders, murderers, criminals, and deserters who move about as roving bands of desperados and spark kulak uprisings.[3] Whether admitted to the ground floor of developments or coming in on the second story, the kulaks cannot escape their fate as the inevitable scapegoats of communism. The Voronezh soviet executive committee defined "banditry" in the region as an elemental protest on the part of the more prosperous peasants growing out of the conscious discrimination against them and attaining form and direction with the adherence of officer-adventurers.[4] Here is the simplest formulation: kulak base and upper-class direction. Generally a somewhat broader make-up is admitted, however, with each of the components receiving at least perfunctory attention.

The criminal element always figures without specification, so that one is left with the impression that it is thrown in for the sake of opprobrium. The line between criminal and free-booter or expropriator is tenuous at best and is drawn now to one side and now to the other, depending on the point of view. In the Tsarist setting Antonov himself and Yaryzhka, the anarchist, were criminals and had been duly imprisoned, but would they be classified as such in a revolutionary society? Here is one reason for the vagueness of Communist charges on the grounds of criminality. Doubtless there were people of a criminal bent among the Greens just as there were such among the members of the food detachments of the Soviet government. In both instances, however, such tendencies were cramped by the rigid discipline which was maintained. The Communists are on firmer ground when they speak of the Green movement harboring declassed elements set adrift by the war;[5] the war's backwash carried many individuals into the stream of revolt, while the war itself influenced or scarred the psychology of those who would fight on both sides of the second civil war.

The White Guard element is also played up for purposes of denigration, although in its case some concrete, individual examples can be cited in the Communist indictment: officers from the old army such as Ektov, Boguslavski, and Kuznetsov, here and there a Constitutional Democrat on the order of Fedorov, the local manufacturing family of the Cheremyshkins in Rasskazovo—in their case it seems to have been merely a matter of seeking contact with Antonov—and that is about all.[6] It follows from what has already been said about the character of the movement that the Communists would be unable to establish the presence of any considerable White element; in fact, they tacitly abandoned the attempt in dealing with the specific make-up of the movement, contenting themselves with vague references to the adherence of remnants of the former privileged classes in addition to the very limited number of individuals they are able to name.

Among these remnants the Borisoglebsk *uezd* committee of the Communist Party in June 1921 singled out priests and teachers as being for the most part undoubtedly "pro-bandit" and right SR in their sympathies;[7] priests and teachers, it may be supposed, had been as "privileged" as kulaks were "rich." Village traders and petty officials of the old order are added to the list of those who once had had some sort of position and who saw in the Green movement the last chance to restore the good old times.[8] Nevertheless it is apparent that the Communists viewed deserters and kulaks as the backbone of the Green movement.

Desertion from all armies—Tsarist, Red, and White—on the part of the population victimized by war-making minorities—imperialist, Communist, and reactionary—became a mass phenomenon in Russia and not least in Tambov province, where a contemporary Soviet military source estimates the number of deserters in the fall of 1920 at the incredible figure of 250,000.[9] Whatever the figure, it was swelled in Tambov and everywhere else by the absence of any social compulsion for inclusion in the armed forces comparable to that in American society, in which the outcry against "slackerdom" attained unbelievable intensity in the First World War, only to abate in the second. As not the tenth part of such a host found its way into Antonov's army, even assuming it to have been composed exclusively of deserters, it is apparent that only a special kind of deserter joined the Greens.

A recent Soviet investigator, more sober than others, comes close to the truth when he describes the deserter element as "wrathful" or "malevolent," thus excluding the mass who were sick of any kind of armed activity.[10] How large a proportion of Antonov's army was made up of these wrathful deserters cannot be said, but that they were numerous enough to exert a marked influence on its character and its actions can be seen in an incident that occurred in the first weeks of the insurrection. A Green band in good military order and knowing just what it wanted descended on a cantonal (*volost'*) soviet in Borisoglebsk *uezd*, shot the secretary of the executive committee, broke open the money box, and scattered papers all over the office. Accounts differ as to whether the box contained any money, but the real objective was destruction of records. All materials bearing on military service and on taxes or levies were destroyed.[11] Here can be clearly discerned the two main components of the Green movement: the deserters went after the military service records and the peasants got rid of those upon which the levies and contributions were based.

In the fall of 1917 small groups of deserters began to form in the wooded areas of Tambov province, both in the forests themselves and in the hollows (*ovragi*) which were so prominent a feature of the topography and which, because of the absence of fertile topsoil, were not farmed and were densely wooded, due to the greater amount of moisture. These groups of army men who had voted for peace by absconding did not consist merely of local peasants from the front or from reserve units; some were from hospitals and shuddered at the thought of returning to the carnage, yet were afraid to appear at home. All were hiding out from the Provisional Government. They were quiet and peaceful and bartered with the peasants, who were tolerant of them and asked no questions.

With the coming of 1918 and mobilization for service in the Red Army, a change ensued. A new wave of desertions brought many recruits to bands already in existence; they began to feel their strength—all deserters were armed—and to be less timid in their actions. Soldiers entered the villages freely to seize a sheep or a calf or to ravish a peasant girl. They even regularized their depredations by levying a kind of tribute on the village, usually in the form of produce or of livestock. The peasants met to discuss the situation and were of a divided mind: they noted the harm done by the deserters but they conceded their usefulness in combatting the food levy detachments, which were a greater source of woe. As the peasants felt the need of protection from the greater evil and as the deserters realized how hard it would be for them if the peasants were rendered hostile, one side bridled its resentment and the other its despoliation, resulting in a *modus vivendi*.[12]

The accommodation came all the more easily when the peasants themselves began to join the deserters, at first those especially aggrieved by treatment at the hands of Soviet authorities and then in increased numbers as tension mounted. A development of equal importance was the linking together of various groups and the growing tendency to coalesce under the leadership of A. S. Antonov.[13] Awareness on the part of the Soviet government, both of the problem of desertion and of its broader social and political implications, led to strenuous measures to halt the drift. According to information in the regional party archives, armed detachments were set on foot expressly for the purpose of catching deserters; with a strength of 1,800 men, these detachments were reported to have "brought thousands of deserters to justice," of whom around a hundred of the worst offenders were sentenced to be shot.[14]

Russian statistics must always be approached with caution; these particular figures are cited without recommendation. If there were a quarter of a million deserters in Tambov province and 1,800 men could round up thousands of them, then they must have been demoralized to the point that Antonov—to have constituted a fighting force out of any number of them—would have had to be more than a genius. He would need to be a superman. And one hundred death sentences awarded by the Soviet government seems much below its capacity in such matters. All sources, Soviet and anti-Soviet, treat deserters with disdain, but how else could a helpless population react when it was being tortured by war-making minorities whose zeal for fighting was limited only by their disinclination for personal participation? And if deserters were so undependable,[15] how did Antonov fashion out of them a first-rate fighting force? Their big role in the Green movement is seen in the likelihood that its name was derived from them: the peasants referred to them as "green" soldiers because of their forest habitat.[16]

If deserters were the nucleus of the Green movement, the kulak stratum of the peasantry is generally regarded as its chief sustaining element by the time of the insurrection. The shift in composition is not explained, aside from references to kulak resentment over the discrimination inherent in the food levy program. The kulak core of the insurrection is everywhere affirmed and nowhere proven. Nevertheless, it is reasonable to assume that kulaks are at least a key element, although it is impossible to cite even a bad estimate of the social composition of Antonov's force, much less of the outer ring of sympathizers.

An anti-Soviet eyewitness volunteers the information that it was the "solid" peasants who furnished the inspiration and leadership and the youth with military training who served as executors of their will.[17] He makes one very interesting observation, albeit on the basis of scant evidence. He talked in a village with a young man who seemed to speak for the Greens and yet was well educated. From this circumstance he infers that there must have been a connection between the *khutoriane* and the Green movement, since children of this social group sometimes received a higher education.[18]

Reference is to the Stolypin land reform, which envisioned as the highest form of peasant economy the detached farmstead (*khutor*) on the American model. Such a peasant (*khutorianin*, plural *khutoriane*) who had cut loose from the village community and had secured a consolidated holding on which he lived, separately from other peasants, can be dignified with the name of farmer. Despite the flimsy evidence, the eyewitness would seem to have made a valid observation. Such farmers had the most to lose from a continuation of the Soviet regime. Having only recently emerged from the communal cocoon, they were now threatened with being forced back into it or—and this was even worse—into a state or a collective farm. By the mere fact of cutting loose and going on their own they had displayed a sturdiness and independence of spirit that would make them resist communism to the bitter end.

The conjecture regarding the farmers may be linked to the thesis of the commissar of repression about kulaks who had suffered from the levelling process being a mainstay of the insurrection (see chapter two). Certainly the owners of the detached farmsteads would have been prime targets for the egalitarian-minded villagers, even more than the better-to-do peasants who for some reason had not yet separated themselves from the village. The only possible objection to this line of reasoning is that peasants who had seen their holdings levelled had no commitment from Antonov to restore to them what had been taken away; in fact, the strong Left SR influence on the Green movement argues that they would not have obtained satisfaction, and the socialization shibboleth of the other SRs points in the same direction even though they might show more indulgence to kulaks in practice. At the very least, however, Antonov would have left the more prosperous peasants free within the limits prescribed by the average peasantry, whereas under the Soviet regime only the worst could be expected. In these two instances, then—the anti-Soviet observer Okninski, and the Soviet commissar of repression Antonov-Ovseenko—we encounter some plausible considerations in respect to the kulak factor.

Otherwise there is only a flow of stereotyped—and sterile—denunciations of kulaks available in Soviet sources. They do name some individual kulaks like Ishin who occupied an important post in

Antonov's shadow, but they convey little real information. They seem consciously to strive to create the impression that only wealthy peasants supported the insurrection. But if one reads further in them or goes to better sources, he discovers that the participation of ordinary peasants is conceded.

Conceded with all kinds of qualifications to soften the blow of having to inform the Soviet public that "some part of the toiling peasantry" (thus excluding the kulaks, who never toiled but only exploited) had risen in arms against the "workers' and peasants' government." They had done so "temporarily and by accident, against their basic class interests"[19] because of "their darkness and ignorance or their economic dependence on kulaks."[20] Such peasants had to be "backward"[21] or "misled and confused."[22] Already by the end of 1919 Antonov had gathered around him several thousand "dark, bamboozled" peasants.[23] Unable to maintain the fiction that only kulaks backed the Greens, Communists have tended to limit defections from the toilers' camp to the middle stratum of the peasantry in the hope of upholding the further fiction that the poor were impervious to the Green appeal. In the effort they still further compromised the argument for the kulak character of the insurrection: a political commissar in the armed forces by acknowledging that the Greens were drawn largely from this middle stratum,[24] and the historian of the Che-ka by recognizing that a "considerable part of the middle peasantry" had adhered to the insurrection.[25]

A witness from the other side avers that poor peasants and landless peasants fought for the Greens and that the Bolshevik stake on pauperdom in Tambov province had not been justified.[26] No doubt he is correct. Why should a poor peasant have been less dark or backward, less misled and confused, less bewildered, befuddled, and bamboozled than a middle peasant? If anything, these terms would have been more applicable to the poor peasant.

Only in the case of the former *dvorovye* (menials, household or courtyard servants) was there an element in the village upon whom the Communists could count. These people had not been allotted land at the time of emancipation, they had to engage in crafts or else become agricultural laborers on estates; they had been left out a second time in the "black repartition" of 1918 when the mass of the peasantry refused them a share on the ground that they were not really cultivators and would only sell or rent their land.[27] Subservient to the Soviet regime by force of economic circumstance, they went into the committees of the poor or the food army detachments or staffed the officially-favored collective agrarian enterprises—communes or state farms.[28] The Soviet regime commanded the support of a part of the poorer peasantry, but by no means all.

To refute the Soviet stereotype of the Tambov insurrection as a kulak affair, it is not necessary to search for furtive admissions in Soviet writings, to have recourse to the scanty literature on the other side, or to rely on reasoning from fragmentary facts. In at least two instances representatives of the Soviet regime with greater authority—and hence with less need of painting out the truth—have put matters in their proper perspective.

Soon after the crest of the Green wave had receded, M. I. Kalinin publicly acknowledged that "peasant disaffection over the [food] levy had manifested itself not only in the kulak upper crust but also in the middle and even the poorest segments of the rural population."[29] Kalinin, it is true, was talking about the Green movement in general rather than the Antonov uprising in particular.

But recently, in an official publication with specific reference to the Tambov affair, it has been candidly admitted that—along with the kulaks, deserters, and criminals—in the ranks of the rebels were to be found "honest toiling peasants, both middle and poor." Some were there because of lack of a toiling consciousness under kulak and SR pressure, some out of blind protest against their hard life or the unjust acts of a food levy organ, some as a result of compulsory mobilization and because of kinship or neighborly ties with confirmed bandits, since the tradition of collective responsibility or, better, of standing together was still strong in the village.[30] It is a remarkable admission to find in a present-day Soviet source, and one wishes that others might be as honest. And so we have confirmation of our thesis from an incontestable source that the Tambov insurrection caught up not only kulaks, but was broadly representative of the peasantry as a whole.

The crowning embarrassment for the Communists comes, however, with the revelation that the insurrection enjoyed support among the workers as well as among the poorer peasants, despite

Communist dogma and despite the dull, bovine resentment of the peasants themselves against worker identification with the Soviet system. The Communist leaders, at least on occasion, recognized that the proletariat could not be insulated from the mood of the peasantry,[31] so great was the degree of interpenetration between the two classes—particularly in Russia, where the rural antecedents of the workers were still green in their memory and were continually refreshed by still-existing ties with the village.

As Lenin told the Third Congress of the Communist International, "the ferment in the peasantry was very strong; among the workers, also, discontent was rife."[32] He railed repeatedly at the "petty bourgeois, anarchistic elemental mass [that is, the peasantry] which surrounds us like air and reaches deeply into the ranks of the proletariat."[33] In the midst of the February–March crisis of 1921 he denounced this mass as the main danger to proletarian dictatorship, as able to gather more strength than any other force in a country like Russia, and to contaminate even a section of the nonparty workers.[34] He must have had a bad night or the situation must have taken a turn for the worse, for he discarded this limitation on the very next day in acknowledging that the contagion had spread to the mass of the workers and even "inside our party."[35] He was referring to the "workers' opposition," which refused to subordinate itself to the vanguard to the degree he desired. Several months later in a desperate telegram that was not made public until 1959 he spoke of the "catastrophic situation" as inducing in working-class circles a "most undesirable strain" which, in turn, was "fraught with serious political consequences."[36]

Other Communist sources lack Lenin's authority and so tread more cautiously in respect to the degree of proletarian defection. Preobrazhenski could not deny the pull of the peasantry on the proletariat in 1921 as in 1918, but sought to limit it to a part or parts of the proletariat.[37] More specific are the editors of Lenin's collected works, who define the segment of workers suborned by the "petty bourgeois elemental mass" as those with special ties to the village.[38] A man assigned to historical writing, whom one would not call a historian, still further narrows the range by saying that "individual" workers might be found in the peasant bands.[39]

Leaving the national scene and coming to the local arena of struggle, the small working class in Tambov province was also caught up in the wave of disaffection. Harsh measures had not been spared the workers: they were forced to acquiesce in a lengthened working day, they had imposed upon them "Saturdays" and "Sundays"—as days for the donation of free labor were called—they had been hard-driven and deprived of rest at a time when more was needed because of the shortage of food, and they too had suffered from the trampling on the most elementary personal rights which has always accompanied Communist rule.[40]

Lenin's commissar of repression did not conceal from him the extent of worker unrest, but preferred to attribute it to difficulties in respect to food rations. The commissar admitted that the Communist party had lost ground, even in the class it was supposed to represent. As the spirit of opposition mounted among the workers, the influence of the party weakened. A stubborn strike movement had not yielded to measures taken with the support of his own Plenipotentiary Commission, the trade union council, and other agencies under the Communist system for stifling popular resentment. The leather workers in Lipetsk, the cloth workers in Tambov and other types of workers in that city are mentioned, but above all it was the railwaymen who gave trouble. The regime could least tolerate strikes among them, and those in the railroad centers of Griazi, Rtishchevo, and in the marshalling yards of Tambov were broken by arrests and other measures.[41] Among the latter was incarceration in unheated cars on sidings during the wintertime.[42] The effectiveness of this antistrike measure cannot be denied.

Even had the railroad workers not had such fuel to fire their resentment, they probably would have been opposition-minded. At the time of the October revolution the Left SRs had controlled the All-Russian railwaymen's union (the chief organ of which was the Vikzhel), and in the absence of information about this branch of labor in Tambov province several years later it is reasonable to assume that their influence still was strong. As for the SRs, their activity among workers had usually been less successful than among peasants, but delegates from Tambov at their All-Russian conference in September 1920 reported success in fomenting a strike of railroad shopmen.[43] Actually, Left SRs probably had as much to do with it, and general conditions were more responsible than either. Antonov was known to have more than a few sympathizers among railwaymen.[44] One of them named Firsov, who belonged to the SR party organization, acted as a go-between, travelling to Antonov's hideout in wintertime with a consignment of cartridges and receiving money in return.[45] Discontent was rife among workers in general, but it seems to have centered in those on the lines of communication, touching a raw nerve of the Soviet government and adding to its difficulties in provisioning the urban centers of the north.

An attempt to determine the social composition of the Green movement in Tambov would not be complete without reference to the non-Russian ethnic groups which constituted a not inconsiderable segment of the population in the northern *uezds* and a much larger segment in certain adjoining provinces. For some reason the sources—with a single exception—have nothing to say on the matter, although it definitely bears on the fate of the uprising. The Mordvin settlements and the much smaller Tatar element in the north were closed to the Green movement. So were the rather extensive native areas, Mordvin, Cheremis (Mari), Tatar, and Bashkir beyond the confines of Tambov province. Russification under the tsars had stirred no spectacular acts of resistance as in outlying portions of the empire among more advanced peoples, but it left a smoldering resentment which the Bolsheviks knew how to turn to account. Already they were developing the techniques of playing upon the divisions of a society which would serve them so well.

And so they conferred autonomy upon these native peoples, who gratefully received it and regarded it as emancipation from the ills they had suffered, and who looked on the Bolsheviks as their benefactors. A revolt against the Soviet regime would not enlist their sympathies and, under the influence of Communist propaganda, might even convert latent into active hostility. Punitive detachments of Tatars and Bashkirs are said to have dealt cruelly with Tambov peasants in revolt, seeing in them Russian nationalists who would enserf again the native peoples.[46] The information, however, is vague. Two Tatar regiments, the 202nd and the 204th, distinguished themselves in fighting against the Greens in neighboring Saratov province.[47] Sensitivity to charges of having to use non-Russian units to hold down the Russian people may account for Soviet reticence on this topic.[48] In any event, Antonov found few recruits among the non-Russian population, but rather a wall of hostility; other Green leaders appear to have fared no better, always excepting Makhno in the Ukraine. The curse incurred by the Tsarist authorities had been transmitted to the hapless Russian peasants.

Summing up what is known of the social composition of the Tambov insurrectionary movement, it was overwhelmingly a peasant movement in the broadest sense—that is, it was drawn from all strata with the strong probability that the average middle peasant predominated over the kulak. The deserters, of course, were themselves nearly all peasant. But the Greens also found backing in both the middle and the working classes, the modest contribution in each instance being due more to the slender representation of the class in Tambov province than to any weakness in the spirit of opposition. Finally, the Green bands and their sympathizers were all but exclusively Russian, a characteristic in no wise mitigated by the presence in an elevated position of a man with a Tatar name, Tokmakov, who was also the Left SR leader in Tambov province. The Asian name, and perhaps origin, of this interesting man about whom so little is known and who now is lost to history, no more detracts from the purely Russian character of the movement than does the Asian name of the province itself.

The general impression is that the political complexion of the Tambov insurrection was as overwhelmingly Socialist Revolutionary as its social composition was peasant. Like so much else in connection with this subject, it is a false assumption. It has been shown already that under an SR overlay the Green movement preserved its own character, essentially nonpartisan and truly popular, with a penchant for anarchism contained only by Antonov's genius for organization. Now we shall learn that the SRs were of a divided mind regarding the insurrection and that large numbers of Antonov's followers were SRs only in name or not even that.

The standard Soviet view is that the insurrection was an SR affair from beginning to end. It was put forth at the time and is still maintained.[49] In its crass form, Antonov's command is only an instrument of nefarious party policy, an ordinary band of deserters hiding in the forest until the SRs take it over and make something out of it, using it as a core around which to assemble a large-scale "bandit" enterprise. A direct line runs to the Central Committee, whose agents arrive on the local scene and "insist in its name on the necessity of mercilessly exterminating" Communists wherever they may be found.[50] At times the onus lightens a little on the Central Committee, only to fall more heavily on the provincial organization: "all actions of Antonov were strictly controlled by the provincial SR center."[51] Antonov descends to the level of an agent or puppet; the weight of his crimes rests more easily upon him, though that is not the intent. State prosecutor Krylenko refers to him as a "political illiterate," bereft of organizational talent on any broader scale.[52]

At other times, however, more of a balance is held between the party and the "bandit" leader, who is elevated to the status of an equal partner in crime. The situation is portrayed in terms of a *mariage de convenance* between a leader in need of a political organization with ideas and trained workers and a party in need of a man of action who was popular and stood at the head of a spontaneous movement.[53] When the Voronezh committee of the Communist Party said that the SRs tried to give "banditry" an ideological foundation and organizational stability[54] it was getting close to the truth, as is seen in the continuous effort of the SRs to make the movement run in their channel—as one of their leaders expressed it[55]—or to convert an elemental into a creative force, as the party organ put it.[56]

This more plausible Soviet version of the relationship between the SRs and the Greens tends to shift the emphasis to the ultimate responsibility of the SRs and away from actual direction of the uprising; it may coexist with the crass version in one and the same source. Krylenko achieves the feat of merging both in one proposition by noting compliance of the local SRs with the injunction of the Central Committee to form committees of the Peasants' Union, and then by vaulting over all that lay in between to assert that the result was insurrection. He thus establishes SR responsibility, wrenching truth in the process, while skirting the question of who guided the insurrection.[57] It is an exercise in casuistry worthy of theologians and Communists but not of honest men.

Even the more plausible Soviet version, circumspect in loading all culpability on the SR Central Committee, is nevertheless unwilling to abandon the effort to convict it of actual direction as well as of ultimate responsibility for the enterprise. Repeatedly the link between the national and local party members is upheld; unfortunately for the credibility of this thesis, there is no unanimity in naming the intermediaries involved. According to the allegation more publicized than others because it came from the Extraordinary Commission, Iuri Podbelski, the anonymous author of the pamphlet we have been using,[58] served as emissary for the Central Committee.[59] Testimony presented at the SR trial the next year named other people as responsible for maintaining ties with the center through trips to Moscow; curiously, one newspaper gave Egorev and Dankovski as the intermediaries[60] and the other named a different pair, Bondarenko and Grigoreva,[61] although both drew their information from one and the same source, from Bogoliubski, the brother-in-law of Antonov.

The conflicting information on this crucial point, which does not help the Soviet case, is avoided in respect to the link-up between the Tambov provincial organization and Antonov, since both sources agree that this function was performed by one Bereznikov who visited Antonov either in his own right as a member of the SR provincial committee or at its behest. Bereznikov seems to have negotiated with Antonov over the coordination of activities and to have received money from him for the party coffers in full knowledge, according to the Communists, that it was derived from the proceeds of his "expropriations," the chief activity of Antonov at the time Bereznikov began to visit him early in 1920. Antonov did not give all of the seized funds to the SRs, it should be noted; he appears not as a party agent but as an independent collaborator willing to share with the PSR, in what proportion we are not told. And it should further be noted that the party came to him; it was not he who figured as the suppliant.[62]

The whole question of the relationship of the Central Committee to the Tambov SRs and of the latter to Antonov presents many difficulties that cannot be satisfactorily resolved, but it may be that the testimony of Antonov's brother-in-law comes rather close to the truth. It is definite and rather detailed, even if not free of contradictions as reported in the press. Certainly it is greatly to be preferred to the one indirectly available account in the provincial press, which gives a rather lurid and altogether improbable account of the machinations of the Central Committee while carefully refraining from naming a single one of its agents who travelled back and forth to Tambov.[63]

Since at the SR trial in 1922 the Soviet government could not establish as firm a tie between the party and the Tambov uprising as it desired, in view of its unwillingness as yet to abandon all semblance of justice, it shifted ground somewhat and sought to make the SRs look even worse by charging them with throwing overboard what they had instigated and abetted. The prosecution bore down heavily on this theme in an effort to make the SRs appear to be base and cowardly, and as treacherous in relation to their peasant following as in relation to the Soviet regime. Citing such statements in the clandestine Tambov *Zemlia i Volia* as "How long are the Communists going to get away with their mockery of the *muzhik*?", Krylenko asked how else were the dark people to interpret these words than as a call to arms? Through their activities the SRs had engaged in the "most shameless provocation" of politically backward elements, had seen their slogans adopted by the aroused population, and then had left them in the lurch, surrendering them to the first adventurer who came along.[64]

The SR side of the controversy also is marred by distortion. The desire to put distance between themselves and an uprising that failed was only natural when it is remembered that so many of them were at the mercy of the Communists, but the lengths to which the Socialist Revolutionaries would go are a matter of surprise and even of reprehension. The most serious attempt to absolve their party of responsibility for the uprising was made at the trial in 1922 by D. F. Rakov, a member of the Central Committee and a factional colleague of V. M. Chernov, in what *Izvestiia* describes as an "extremely long and boring" disclaimer of any connection.

According to Rakov, neither the central nor the provincial organization of the PSR had anything to do with the affair, the provincial organization because it did not exist at the time of the uprising as a result of disruption in the wake of Che-ka arrests. If Bereznikov (the name appears here as Berezniakov) had gone to Antonov beforehand it was not to establish ties or to get money either for a bicycle for himself or for broader party purposes, but to admonish Antonov "to desist from his bandit activities or else to cease calling himself an SR." Rakov went on to affirm that Antonov had never belonged to the party (!) and that he only pretended to be an SR. He generously conceded—both to Antonov and to the Bolsheviks—that Antonov and his peasant followers may have adopted the style of "independent SRs," the implication being that such a term would not have been too wide of the mark. As for bonafide members of the party, only certain individuals like George and Nicholas Muraviev had adhered to the movement, on their own initiative and at their own risk.

Rakov even denied SR enterprise in respect to the Union of Toiling Peasants (STK), maintaining that this organization was the handiwork of Antonov, not of the party; a few days later he backed water somewhat in admitting that some local unions had been founded under party auspices while insisting that any organization on a broader scale, above the *volost'* level, stemmed from Antonov. Finally, Rakov contended, the testimony of Antonov's brother-in-law, Bogoliubski, had not really established SR participation in Antonov's course of action.[65]

Another member of the Central Committee, E. M. Timofeev, found satisfaction in the circumstance that Bogoliubski, the sole witness produced by the state for that period, had not been able to link the provincial SR committee with Antonov until the Bereznikov visit in May 1920, although Antonov had begun his activities in August of 1918.[66] Actually Bereznikov had gone to Antonov at the beginning of 1920,[67] but, even so, the interval of nearly a year and a half does indicate that Antonov had assembled the nucleus of his movement independently of the PSR as a corporate entity.

The most extreme action on the part of the SRs to dissociate themselves from Antonov came after the back of the insurrection had been broken on 2 July 1921, when the Central Organizational Bureau of the PSR drew up a statement entitled, "An Answer to Slanderers." Soviet authorities described the statement as an official communication of the SR Central Committee to the Soviet government. The text was not reproduced, only some excerpts. The SRs acknowledged the false path of violence, killings, and pogroms often taken by peasant uprisings. "The Bolsheviks know that the party regards the Antonov movement as half-bandit and that members of the party are not to be found in its ranks." Only when an uprising had the approved character of a struggle against the Communist dictatorship for the purpose of securing the rights of the toilers, and only when it rigidly excluded elements alien to the revolution, would it meet with support from the party. In the light of evidence in its possession, the Soviet government pronounced the message a lie through and through. It had value, however, as an illustration of SR technique in first instigating an uprising and then in disowning it when it was found to be "unhealthy"—that is, inconvenient.[68]

It is not, however, the veracity of the Central Committee that is at stake here so much as is its honor. As shall be seen in a moment, the declaration was not a lie so far as the upper levels of party life are concerned, but the propriety of drawing it up and sending it to the Soviet government is quite another matter. A peasants' revolt had been beaten into the earth by the whole apparatus of oppression, only a flicker of life remained, and then came the SR party and cast its pebble also. To be sure, the revolt jeopardized the status of the party—such as it had become—and endangered the lives of those members of the Central Committee within reach of the Extraordinary Commission, but a modicum of pride would seem to be essential to a revolutionary organization which, in this instance, was not going to escape its fate in any event. When the SR leaders characterized Antonov's movement as "half-bandit," they moved halfway toward the position of the regime they ostensibly were combatting. The moral capitulation conveyed in this message is hard to believe. The only record of it is in an official Soviet publication, but the verisimilitude is convincing enough.

How may the truth be established amid this welter of accusation and self-exculpation? To what extend was the Tambov insurrection an SR undertaking and to what extent a "bandit"—that is, independent—enterprise? In a subject cursed by a dearth of material there is suddenly too much. Yet surprisingly enough it is possible to cut through the conflicting assertions and to emerge with the true picture, even if a few doubts still cast their shadows.

The leadership of the Socialist Revolutionary party accepted the inevitability of armed struggle against the Communist regime. At the same time, and for honorable reasons, it wished to avoid any action that would entail useless sacrifice. An insurrection, to enlist its support, must be general and free of any taint of collaboration with counter-revolutionary elements. Neither cruelty, rapine, plunder, nor anti-Semitism might sully the honor of those upholding the people's cause. Outbursts from below that resulted only in destructiveness and in dispersion of effort must be avoided. Peasant rebellions were all too likely to be of that type. "The peasantry first of all reaches for the rifle to chase away commissars and food detachments, without thought of what will happen the next day." Only a well thought-out, concerted program of action stood any chance of success. And so the Central Committee condemned spontaneous resort to violence and guerrilla warfare.[69] Since insurrections are as imperfect as other forms of human endeavor, the conditions imposed by the SR leaders in effect ruled out support of any insurrection that was likely to develop.

Though the day of deliverance might never dawn in the face of such a prescription, the SR leadership wished to prepare for its arrival. And so on 13 May 1920 V. M. Chernov sent out a circular letter to local organizations recommending 1) a campaign of remonstrance based on village and *volost'* meetings which would challenge the Soviet regime to submit its rule to a vote of confidence, 2) the formation of nonpartisan peasants' unions (STK) to gather in all active forces of opposition, 3) the creation of a parallel network of party cells to acquire ideological dominion over the unions and to vest in the PSR the leadership of the entire mass peasant movement.[70] This initiative of the Central Committee met with an energetic response, particularly in Tambov province where local party forces either established unions or fused with those already set on foot by Antonov (a relationship difficult to determine; see chapter six). The purpose of these illegal peasant unions, according to one of the more sober Soviet sources, was to serve as the base of a broad insurrection.[71] The Central Committee itself intended the movement it was sponsoring to be effective, yet peaceful and quiet; if it became otherwise, the "Bolshevik ravishers" would be to blame.[72]

With the campaign to blanket the countryside with a network of peasant unions—an enterprise that actually succeeded, at least in the southeastern *uezds* of Tambov province, in creating a corporate force out of the traditionally dispersed and downtrodden rural population—the SR leadership had taken a long step toward armed revolt. But to pass from preparation to combat was—for these leaders—a matter of extraordinary difficulty. They could bring conditions right to the point of insurrection, yet they never took the final step. Even the provincial SRs, more inflamed than those in the center, likewise held back from the fateful decision. For all of their militancy the Tambov SRs, at their congress or conference held in July 1920 on the former estate of the Sheshlavtsevs in Kareika village of Alexandrovsk *volost'*, rejected the use of arms as premature in view of the need for further organization and for completing the task of gathering forces. Antonov was notified of the decision. In fact, the whole question of his relationship to the party came up at the convention. At least one delegate—Shishkin of Kirsanov *uezd*, Antonov's home district—objected to the admission of his representatives on the ground that organizations of the Savinkov type had no place in the councils of the party[73]—the most graphic evidence yet of friction between Antonov and the Socialist Revolutionaries.

It was apparently at this convention or immediately afterwards that the SR provincial committee summoned Antonov either to conform to party tactics or to cease using the SR label. Above all, he must discontinue his haphazard and sterile terrorist acts and turn to "peaceful organizational and cultural work." For that purpose he was invited to leave his native heath and to go to the northern *uezds* where he had no roots and no reputation, where the peasants were poor and dispirited, and where the Finnish aborigines would be cold to a call to arms. Small wonder that Antonov did not act on this summons to self-banishment.

His detractor, the SR intellectual Iuri Podbelski, asserts that he yielded to the demands, then failed to honor his commitment. The author of this book very much doubts that he yielded, even in words; Podbelski himself says that Antonov had no firm tie with the PSR and was little inclined to be bound by party discipline. In any event, nothing came of the attempt to divorce Antonov from his habitat. He did not go north but stayed on the scene, where his guerrilla tactics soon would be greatly extended by a spontaneous insurrection which neither he nor the PSR had started although both had contributed to its coming, Antonov by the example of his punitive raids and the PSR by encouraging the formation of peasant unions.[74]

The Soviet editor thought that by proposing to send Antonov on mission to the north of Tambov province after his depredations had become well-known the SRs had incurred moral and political responsibility for his actions.[75] Such casuistry betokens a determination to incriminate the SRs no matter what they did; the whole purpose of their move had been to end guerrilla warfare. Whatever may be thought of the SR action, it was not the program of an organization bent on making war.

Once the insurrection had begun the Tambov SRs swung over to its support, although not without vacillation even then. Some kind of staff was set up for the purpose of procuring arms for the insurgents. Unfortunately, it is quite impossible to say when the staff was constituted, who took the initiative, and who served on it. Sources contradict one another and the same source contradicts itself. All that can be said is that the staff was set up either just before or—more probably—just after the insurrection began and that it was a joint enterprise of the SRs and the Left SRs. Only one name is definitely connected with the staff, that of Nicholas Karpukhin, and nowhere is there any further mention of his name.[76]

Inability to clear up the uncertainty surrounding this staff is an irritation but not a matter of great importance, since it would never really function. Fate overtook it in the form of the Extraordinary Commission. Arrests by the Soviet organ shattered not only the staff but the entire organization of the PSR on the provincial level. The arrests occurred in August 1920, at the very beginning of the insurrection according to our most reliable source,[77] in September according to the next most reliable one,[78] in the wintertime according to one less reliable,[79] and in early 1921 according to the least reliable.[80] The divergence is all too typical of our subject. We shall give the preference to the date specified by Antonov-Ovseenko, working as he would later be in Tambov with the Che-ka at his elbow, and we shall follow him also in relation to the scope of the arrests when he states that a considerable part of the provincial committee was taken into custody.

The SRs, on the other hand, desirous of establishing their innocence at the trial in 1922, exaggerate the blow that fell upon

them—Podbelski by saying that the whole SR organization in
Tambov was arrested to a man, and Rakov by observing that the
party was *hors de combat* at the time of the uprising.[81] The blow was
severe enough, in any event; only gradually did the SR organization
recover, and then to assume an Antonovist cast if one is to judge by
the assertion that his lieutenants, Tokmakov and Ishin, became
members of the provincial committee, the latter in November of
1920.[82] The disarray in SR ranks left the field to Antonov. He would
have led the insurrection in any case.

The dualism in the Socialist Revolutionary party came to a head at
its All-Russian conference in Moscow in September 1920; on the
one hand, the warlike spirit of the delegates from the localities
clamoring for action; on the other hand, the caution and vacillation
of the central organization hanging back as always and desperately
trying to sit on the lid. Distinguished for their militance were the
delegations from Tambov and the Kuban. The latter demanded a
general insurrection without further delay and an end to squeamishness in working with enemies of Bolshevism; any hostile force could
be utilized, and no longer should attention be paid to keeping one's
own vestments clean. The Tambov delegation, pointing to the major
work accomplished in respect to peasant unions since turning away
from legal action in May, called on the party to support the
insurrection that had already started and to guide it in the right
direction. The local SRs, in short, had come down on the side of
Antonov.

But the SRs at the center were not to be diverted from their
endless swaying. By the narrowest of margins in a very thin vote
they put through a decision that acknowledged the inevitability of a
resumption of armed struggle with Bolshevism at some time in the
future, yet posed as the party's present task the continuance of
organizational work in view of the dispersion of the masses. This
was no decision-making, but a side-stepping operation, for when
would the rural masses not be dispersed? To the Soviet government,
however, the guilt of the PSR in fomenting counter-revolutionary
outbreaks had been established.[83]

The Central Committee, or those who acted in its name (the PSR
was illegal, yet enjoyed a degree of fitful and capricious toleration so
that everything functioned abnormally, if at all), repeatedly tried to

dampen the ardor of insurrection. Though the evidence is exasperatingly vague, it seems likely that the Volga bureau of the PSR, headed by N. I. Rakitnikov, sent a mission into Tambov province toward the end of 1920 to investigate the situation and to get in touch with the leaders of the rebellion. It counselled abandonment of the effort in order to forestall further useless sacrifices and the destruction of villages. Advice of this tenor would certainly have been in line with Rakitnikov's character and with the mood of the Central Committee, influenced as it was by V. M. Chernov, long the associate of Rakitnikov but a man who combined the same vacillating disposition with much greater intelligence. But the delegates from the localities involved in the uprising refused to heed the advice, preferring to believe that the SR leaders opposed Antonov only for the sake of appearances.[84]

SR leaders persevered in their refusal to sanction the Tambov uprising or any like development elsewhere. They caused to be distributed—it is said in large numbers—among the peasants of the central provinces a manifesto of the Socialist Union of Toiling Peasantry (STK). The emphasis in this title should fall on the word "Socialist," for its presence indicates that the organization was an agency of the leadership, distinct from the local peasant unions which in Tambov and Voronezh provinces formed the civilian backbone of the insurrections. The manifesto called on the peasants to restrain their just wrath and not to be led into fruitless endeavors. It singled out for express condemnation the Kronstadt uprising in the north, the Makhno movement in the south, and the Tambov insurrection in the center as examples of isolated attempts to subvert the regime that were easily overcome and that only frittered away the strength of the village. The peasants must forswear such actions and must conserve their strength for the general decisive struggle.

This fainthearted proclamation contained some worthwhile admonitions, however; it warned its rural constituency against the idea that the worker was the peasant's enemy, against being used by reactionaries, and against showing hostility to other peoples in a multinational country. Finally, it coupled a defense of socialism with the strange injunction to "remember and remember well that without land you are a slave as a peasant." The target here appears to be Communism. It was good advice, but did it go with any kind of socialism?[85]

The SR Central Committee in a resolution on tactics adopted 26 February 1921 had cautioned against uncoordinated, spontaneous outbreaks. We are indebted to the Extraordinary Commission for this information, along with the assertion that the resolution secretly meant to signal to the faithful that if an uprising were succeeding it should be shown the true way and should undertake to set up local, anti-Bolshevik organs of government.[86] In its statement of 26 April 1921, later printed in the party newspaper abroad and noted in our discussion above,[87] the Central Committee repeated its injunction against sporadic outbursts in its ceaseless quest for the perfect insurrection, one which would occur everywhere at the same time and be free of any taint of corruption by alien influences or even by human frailty.

While the Central Committee continued to ride the high horse of revolutionary principle, the local SRs, confronted with the realities of life, were going their own way. How far the superstructure and the base of Social Revolutionism had diverged may be seen from the action of the Voronezh Southeastern Regional Committee at its secret session of 28 April 1921, almost precisely at the time the Central Committee was reiterating its aversion to sporadic outbursts. With jurisdiction presumably—though not certainly—over the whole southeastern region of which Tambov was a part, the committee dealt first with the affairs of the Voronezh organization and then with the relationship to Antonov's movement. It voiced satisfaction over the work of Antonov's army and undertook to coordinate the action of guerrilla forces throughout southeastern Russia and to coordinate specifically Antonov's operations with the plan of the Military Council of the Central Committee through itself as intermediary. It proposed to strengthen Antonov's staff with both political and military personnel from the Voronezh organization. Finally, it proposed to step up efforts at subversion of Red Army units. The deliberations were held and the decisions made in the presence of members of the Central Committee.[88]

A second press report at the same time, based on the confession of a captured SR, differs from the first in having Antonov himself present at the committee session. He gave an accounting of his operations and needs and received the approval of the Regional Committee, except for criticism on the score of inadequate work in the military units and in the population at large. This second report stresses the attempt to be made at subversion of the Red Army through infiltrating agents into its ranks.[89]

The stated intent of the Regional Committee to establish the closest possible tie between Antonov, the Central Committee, and the other measures of active support for the insurrectionary movement would, of course, invalidate the thesis here presented of a divergence between the central and the local SR organizations and would sustain the Communist contention that the Central Committee was up to its ears in insurrection, its hypocritical pronouncements notwithstanding. But let us look more closely at the two press reports. The first does not name the members of the Central Committee who are said to have been present; the second does not even mention their presence. The Soviet government was determined to pin responsibility for this and for other insurrections on the Central Committee, twelve of whose members were at this time (summer of 1922) going on trial for conspiracy to overthrow the regime. It is our surmise that the account of the deliberations of the Voronezh committee is true except that the references to the Central Committee were inserted to strengthen the case for the prosecution. The Che-ka had already engaged in such action the year before when it had settled on Iuri Podbelski as the purveyor of the instructions of the Central Committee to the Tambov insurgents.

The whole endeavor of the Soviet authorities may be stated simply: to depict the PSR as a monolith of treason to the Soviet state by attributing to the core of leadership the mood and the methods of local SRs in the centers of armed revolt. At times this was done deliberately in the face of knowledge to the contrary; at times it seems to have proceeded from sincere belief in the duplicity of Chernov and his associates. Podbelski had no trouble disproving the charge of the Extraordinary Commission that the Central Committee had directed through him the uprisings in Tambov and Voronezh provinces. He scarcely could have been its plenipotentiary when he had not resided in Tambov since May of 1920 but had been working in Soviet institutions in Moscow for the whole period of fighting except for two brief trips, one of which carried him to Tambov for two days and to Voronezh for four. Cut off from the affairs of the Tambov SRs, he had merely collected information from those closer to the scene and had subsequently written with sympathy for the peasantry and with none for Antonov.

We have noted how Populist intellectuals like Podbelski cherished a positive antipathy for men like Antonov and—even more—Makhno. Podbelski was no martyr to truth, but since everything he said in his remonstrance was subject to verification by the Che-ka, and since he challenged it to make the verification, we may conclude that he did not lie on this occasion.[90] No doubt the police had seized on Podbelski in a desperate search for some tangible link between the SR leadership and the events in Tambov. The materials in his possession—the manuscript of the pamphlet we have used and the raw material for another that now would never see the light of day—were evidence, not of insurrectionary zeal or complicity, but merely of the writing mania he shared with other intellectuals. The accusations of the secret police[91] are further discredited by the attempt to connect Chernov with the White Guard and even with Savinkov, whereas in reality Chernov and Savinkov had been inveterate enemies since at least 1914 and probably since the 1905 era.

Even after many years, and in a relatively sober account,[92] we find the assertion that the Central Committee sanctioned Antonov's revolt in circulars to local party groups. Discerning in it the beginning of a general insurrection, the Soviet reader is told, the Central Committee mobilized party activitists in support of Antonov's initiative. The citation in justification of these flagrantly untrue statements refers to page forty-five of the summary indictment of the SR leaders at the trial in 1922; we turn to this page of the indictment and we find nothing of the sort.[93]

In the case of Iuri Steklov, editor of *Izvestiia* at the time of the events in question and representative of the older Marxian school unaltered as yet by the crudeness of the Soviet experience, it is a rather different story. Steklov is aware of the difference between the upper and lower levels of the Socialist Revolutionary party; he admits that in the "bandit" literature at his disposal SR teachings have been simplified and vulgarized in the effort to attune them to "kulak bourgeois instincts," and he finds the result "cruder and franker" than Chernov had been. What Steklov had come upon, though he did not realize it, was the difference between Green and Red, the first effort to break out of the collectivist crust that enveloped the primitive consciousness of the peasant before it began to respond to property instincts. Steklov could not free himself from the Soviet stereotype that the "bandits" were right SRs who in turn were but the tools of reactionary or White Guard interests.[94] A short time later he had to admit that Left SRs also had a hand in Antonov's revolt.[95] The editor is not so much trying to dissemble the truth as he is floundering.

Let us rescue him, posthumously, from his predicament. To a Communist, opposition to the Soviet regime is automatically counter-revolutionary, and the greater the degree of opposition the further to the right are those who oppose. The formula will not fit in this instance—or in many others. What Steklov should have done was to adopt a different line of division and to speak of activists rather than of rightists. Had he done so he could easily have accommodated the Left SRs, who were at once more radical and more activist than the other SRs.

There is one stumbling-block to acceptance of our thesis that the SR leadership did not favor and did not support the Antonov insurrection. Ishin testified that when he became a member of the (reconstituted) provincial committee in November 1920 "we had information from Moscow, from the Central Committee, that Chernov approved the uprising in Tambov province."[96] As Ishin did not betray Antonov but continued to refer to him as "my old party comrade," it is not necessary to assume that he was currying favor with his Soviet captors by telling them what they wanted to hear. Nor is it necessary to convict Chernov of wearing two faces.

In the opinion of this author, who knew Chernov personally and has long had experience with his thinking and methods, the contradiction between Ishin's testimony and our thesis can be resolved without difficulty. Of course, Chernov sympathized with the revolt and wanted it to succeed. At the same time he did not believe it could, he dreaded the sacrifice the peasants would incur, and he mortally feared playing into the hands of the reaction. Swaying endlessly between his wish and his fear, he was quite capable of leaving with those who spoke to him on behalf of Antonov the impression that he favored his cause, while shrinking from any formal action that would commit the party to support of the insurrection. Chernov was like a ruler who agreed with whatever minister last had his ear. But left to himself, he would not sanction bloodshed after the Tsar had been deposed. Revolutionaries ought not to kill one another—such was his practice if not his theory. And so he refused to sanction the Tambov insurrection while sympathizing with it. Like the more moderate socialists everywhere, he was basically pacifistic.

Reasoning and conjecture are not essential, however, to sustain the view that the SR high command should be relieved of responsibility for the Tambov insurrection. Definitive confirmation comes from a Soviet source of unimpeachable authority. Antonov-Ovseenko in his secret memorandum to Lenin states that after the blow dealt the provincial organization by the Che-ka in August 1920, the movement went from the control of the Central Committee to the direction of local SRs in the absence of any Central Committee tie. He adds that no such tie had been reestablished up to the time of his writing the memorandum in July 1921.[97]

Assuming that he included Antonov among the local SRs, he had summed up admirably the situation. Naturally he knew the facts, as commissar of repression with the Che-ka at his beck and call. And he was free to tell the truth in a secret memorandum to Lenin, who passed it to Trotski. All this at a time when the Che-ka was informing the country of the guilt of the Central Committee in "directing the uprising of kulaks, bandits and deserters in Tambov and Voronezh provinces" through one Iuri Podbelski as plenipotentiary.[98] The credulity extended to Soviet claims in other countries arises in part from the blackout of backstage illumination. This time the illumination is there, thanks to the Trotsky Archive.

The SRs fell apart over the Antonov movement. In the absence of approval by the Central Committee, and even in the face of its express condemnation, many of the SRs in Tambov and Voronezh provinces—no doubt a majority—joined in the uprising. It was natural that such a cleavage should develop. A Soviet source of that era, following in the steps of Iuri Steklov but much better informed, argues that the local SRs moved to the right of party leadership.[99] Again, it is not a question of being to the left or to the right but of activism versus passivity.

The food levy and the other exactions of the Soviet state, the "implacable hostility to the village"[100] which no amount of drivel about a workers' and peasants' regime could paper over, had created for the peasantry an intolerable state of affairs and for the local party intellectuals a situation they could not ignore even had they wanted to. The Central Committee knew in its mind that the peasants were suffering grievously, but the peasants knew it on their hides. It was inevitable that their reaction should be more intense. How intense, one incident will illustrate. When the SR peasant organization (apparently the union founded by the party or directly under its control; see chaper six) refused at the outset to join the insurrection, an irate and independent-minded peasant exclaimed: "I see we are going to have to act alone, but in that case, beware! We will come to Tambov and kill you, too, one after the other, while we are at it!"[101]

It is possible to argue, of course, that the intensity of the reaction did actually produce a counter-revolutionary frame of mind, but the record of the first civil war indicates otherwise and the land question, if nothing else, would have prevented the peasantry from extending its rage against Communists to the revolution as a whole. In 1917 the political complexion of Tambov province had been overwhelmingly centrist SR, insofar as it was anything, and no discernible cleavage existed when Chernov was returned to the Constituent Assembly at the head of the list for this province where he had received his baptism into the revolutionary fold. He himself was left-centrist, a shading about which the populace neither knew nor cared. If the years of Soviet misrule had now created a fissure, it was not of the conventional kind: his rural constituents, in ceasing gradually to be pink, were not turning White. They were becoming Green.

The weighty role of the Left SRs in the Tambov insurrection further refutes the view that the political center of gravity had shifted rightward. To determine their role with precision is impossible, for no sooner do we approach the Left SRs on this or on any other matter than the usual difficulty arises: so much less is known about them than about the other SRs. The reason seems to be that the Left SRs commanded much less support among the intellectuals, that so many fewer of them escaped abroad, and that they were even more poorly organized. But if they wrote and talked less, they acted more, for they were the party of the agrarian revolutionaries with fire in their eyes, and of more than a few industrial workers as well.[102] The standard Soviet accusation levelled against them of being the ideological expression of kulak interests[103] may be dismissed with a phrase from Metternich as "empty twaddle."

However scanty the knowledge of their participation in the Antonov movement, it can be said with assurance that they were a major factor, thought not so major—strangely enough—as the SR organ abroad tried to make them when it attributed the organization of the Tambov uprising to Maria Spiridonova.[104] While it is true that Spiridonova enjoyed widespread popularity in "petty bourgeois peasant circles," according to the admission of the Che-ka itself,[105] and while she headed with Kamkov the faction of her party most irreconcilable to Communist rule, she could not have fomented the uprising since she was in and out of prison and constantly under surveillance, with no opportunity to appear in her home province, much less to direct an uprising. Imperfect as our knowledge may be, it leaves not the slightest doubt that Antonov made and sustained the operation that bears his name, assisted at every turn by Tokmakov as the chief Left SR representative on the scene.

At the Left SR trial in 1922, conducted simultaneously with that of the main-line SRs, it was disclosed that the Left SR Central Committee had indeed sent an emissary to Tambov province at the time of the insurrection. It had chosen for this purpose a young man only twenty-six years old, formerly a student and an ensign in the Imperial army, since 1916 in the SR and then in the Left SR movement. Gan-Pogodnik (it is not clear which was his party and which his real name) belonged to the Kamkov-Spiridonova wing of his party and was impregnated with its unbending hostility to Communism, refusing even to rise when the Soviet judges entered the courtroom. In the period of collaboration with Bolshevism, Gan had been provincial military commander at Cherepovets in north Russia; after the break between the Left SRs and the Communists he evaded mobilization into the Red Army in order to devote himself to party work, preferring not to combat Denikin in the ranks of an army based upon principles of which he could not approve. Together with six of his party comrades, whose ages ranged from eighteen to thirty-one, he was placed on trial for "counter-revolutionary" activities and for possession of arms, always a serious offense under Communism.

Although the preliminary investigation claimed to have established the fact of his participation in Antonov's "bands," the Soviet tribunal did not succeed in drawing Gan out on his mission to Tambov. He flatly refused to say what he had been about—he would report only to his Central Committee on matters involving a party trust. Gan did say that in general that body had frowned on scattered and uncoordinated outbreaks as detrimental to the peasantry in its struggle against the Soviet regime; but specifically, with reference to Tambov, he would say only that individual Left SRs had taken part in Antonov's movement. As for the rest, he read the court a lecture on the causes of the Tambov insurrection; his remarks in this connection the Soviet press preferred to pass over in silence. Finally, by using a different approach, the court succeeded in eliciting from the young man the information that he had gone to Tambov on organizational matters rather than to take part in the fighting.

Perhaps so. But there was a noticeable difference in the attitude of the accused toward the Kronstadt and the Tambov insurrections. Whereas they proudly averred—even flaunted—their solidarity with the Kronstadt rebels, there was a disposition to say as little as possible about Tambov. Maybe they were governed by fear—after all, a death sentence was possible—and knew that the Communists would be merciless in respect to a peasant rebellion although, of course, they were not models of mercy toward peasants transformed into sailors. Or maybe there was something to hide.

The previous year, when the insurrection was in its death throes, the authorities made an interesting find in the church of Khitrovo, one of the villages in Tambov *uezd* most intimately associated with the events in question. In this most unlikely of hiding-places was discovered, along with Antonov's treasury, a banner which the Left SR Central Committee had given to the Union of Toiling Peasantry. With golden braid on red velvet had been inscribed the slogan of all SRs—"In struggle thou shalt find thy rights"[106]—and the dedication to the STK together with the name of the donor. The Soviet press could not pass up the opportunity to smear the fallen foe by referring to this touching union of "SR's, Left SR's, bandits and priests."[107]

Against this line of reasoning must be set the challenge Gan issued to the court to call Kamkov and Trutovski to the witness stand, since these members of the Central Committee would be able to clear up the nature of the mission to Tambov which he was not free to do. The implication here is that the mission was innocuous. It might have been; someone else could have borne the banner to the STK. The lightness of the sentence imposed upon Gan—three years in prison—suggests that the Soviet authorities were not convinced of the truth of their own charge that Gan had participated in Antonov's guerrilla warfare. Otherwise the sentence would have been different.[108]

When everything has been considered, however, the best surmise is that the Left SR Central Committee lent its support to the Tambov insurrection, as its SR counterpart certainly did not. About the lower reaches of both political organizations there is no doubt. The Left SRs in Tambov province must have been solidly aligned behind Antonov, contributing an even higher proportion of their strength than did the SRs, among whom there was a certain amount of dissension since the town intellectuals were too unwarlike, too mindful of their own security, and too supercilious to be enthusiastic about backing a peasant enterprise headed by a man like Antonov. Support extended beyond the confines of Tambov to Voronezh and perhaps to other provinces; precisely as in the case of the SRs and with the same uncertainty as to its territorial competence, the Voronezh Regional Committee of the Left SRs was linked by Soviet investigation to Antonov's movement.[109]

Scattered support came from other political sources, in each instance individual rather than corporate. A handful of Constitutional Democrats, probably with little more influence than their numbers would suggest, despite the claims made in the Soviet press. A sprinkling of anarchists among whom Yaryzhka's is the only name—if it is his name—that has come down to us. A phenomenon so rare as to be scarcely credible: a Menshevik taking part in a peasant revolt. Dmitri Shchukin was a true white raven, a bred-in-the-bone peasant who as a soldier had gone over to Menshevism on the southwestern front in 1917. He thought of the Mensheviks as the true workers' party and of collaboration between them and the SRs as the means of realizing the union of workers and peasants. The claims of the Communists to speak for the workers he rejected as spurious. As representative of his *volost'* or canton, he had been with Antonov since the time of gathering the forces; later he commanded a detachment in Kirsanov *uezd* until captured and killed by the Communists.[110]

In conclusion, no survey of the political complexion of the Antonov movement would be valid if it concentrated on currents of opinion and ignored the nonpartisan element. Yet that is exactly what all of the sources do, leaving the investigator without anything to go on in his effort to adjust the balance. Most likely the mass of Antonov's following consisted of peasants and soldiers unaffiliated with any political organization, though no statistics are available and doubtless none will ever be. A participant declares that it is not so much a question of the rural intelligentsia and the literate peasant youth belonging to the SR party—though many did join during the era of the Provisional Government—as it is of their being influenced by its ideology. He points out correctly that the Central Committee was powerless to prevent the uprising, yet seems to think that ideology was the motivating force in bringing it on,[111] whereas it is our thesis that desperation born of the policies of the Soviet regime produced the upheaval.

The ideology never held complete sway and was becoming weaker with the passage of time. The savagery of the struggle is the best illustration of how independent the actors were of ideological constraints. What Antonov and his men did bears as little resemblance to SR ideology as does the practice of the Soviet government to the principles it so garrulously enunciates. In the last analysis, the nonpartisan mass also left its stamp on the insurrection and may be regarded as the truest representative of the Green movement, although it may be said of the leaders themselves that ideology rested lightly upon them.

Notes

1. Trifonov, *Klassy i klassovaia bor'ba,* part 1, p. 55.

2. Petrovski, "Bor'ba s banditizmom i krasnye kursanty," *Izvestiia,* no. 133 (1276), 23 June 1921, p. 1.

3. Trifonov, *Klassy i klassovaia bor'ba,* part 1, p. 90.

4. Decree of the praesidium, 9 April 1921, from the Archives of the October Revolution, cited in ibid., p. 80.

5. Ibid., p. 89.

6. Ibid., p. 87; Borisov, *Chernym letom,* p. 32; A. S. Esaulenko, *Revoliutsionnyi put' G. I. Kotovskogo* (Kishinev, 1956), p. 128.

7. From the Central Party Archives, as cited in Trifonov, *Klassy i klassovaia bor'ba,* part 1, p. 87.

8. Borisov, *Chernym letom,* p. 12.

9. Trifonov, *Klassy i klassovaia bor'ba,* part 1, p. 90, citing an article by A. Kazakov in the journal *Krasnaia Armiia,* no. 9, 1921, p. 32.

10. Donkov, "Organizatsiia razgroma antonovshchiny," *Voprosy Istorii KPSS,* no. 6 (June 1966), p. 63.

11. A. Okninski, *Dva goda sredi krest'ian: vidennoe, slyshannoe, perezhitoe v Tambovskoi gubernii s noiabria 1918 goda do noiabria 1920 goda* (Riga, 1936), pp. 296–98. The incident occurred on 10 September 1920. The author was an eyewitness. Information of this kind on this subject is exceedingly rare.

12. Fomichev (Lidin), "Antonovshchina: Iz vospominanii antonovtsa" (Santiago de Chile, 1955), pp. 8–9.

13. Ibid., pp. 10–11; Okninski, *Dva goda sredi krest'ian,* p. 311.

14. Zybko, *Tambovskaia partiinaia organizatsiia,* p. 27.

15. Srechinski, "Zapechatannaia stranitsa," *Novoe Russkoe Slovo,* 26 April 1969.

16. Zybko, *Tambovskaia partiinaia organizatsiia,* p. 27.

17. Okninski, *Dva goda sredi krest'ian,* p. 312.

18. Ibid., pp. 299–300. The observations were made in Borisoglebsk *uezd,* in the southeastern corner of the province. It was one of the three main districts involved in the uprising.

19. Trifonov, *Klassy i klassovaia bor'ba,* part 1, p. 301.

20. Ibid., p. 92.

21. "Antonovshchina," in *Sovetskaia istoricheskaia entsiklopediia,* vol. 1, p. 636.

22. Borisov, *Chernym letom,* p. 12.

23. Dokunin, "Tambovskii schet sotsial-banditam," *Pravda,* no. 123, 4 June 1922, p. 3.

24. Borisov, *Chernym letom,* p. 12.

25. Sofinov, *Ocherki istorii Vserossiiskoi Chrezvychainoi Komissii,* pp. 224.

26. Fomichev (Lidin), "Antonovshchina: Iz vospominanii antonovtsa" (Santiago de Chile, 1955), p. 43.

27. The peasants resented any deviation from uniformity. They liked neither element at the opposite ends of the social scale, neither the successful individual farmer nor the poverty-stricken landless laborer. They would take from the one and give nothing to the other. They were levellers within limits.

28. Fomichev (Lidin), "Antonovshchina: Iz vospominanii antonovtsa" (Santiago de Chile, 1955), pp. 15–16.

29. Kalinin, "V dni Kronshtadta: Ot voiny k mirnomu khoziaistvennomu stroitel'stvu: Iz rechi na sessii VTsIK i v Sverdlovskom universitete po povodu otmeny razverstki i perekhoda k nalogu" [In the days of Kronstadt: from war to peaceful economic upbuilding: from a speech at the session of the All-Russian Central Executive Committee and at Sverdlov University regarding the lifting of the levy and the shift to a tax], in *Za eti gody,* vol. 2, p. 111.

30. Donkov, "Organizatsiia razgroma antonovshchiny," *Voprosy Istorii KPSS,* no. 6 (June 1966), p. 63.

31. On this theme see Iuri Steklov, "Rabochii i krest'ianin" [The worker and the peasant], *Izvestiia,* no. 149 (1292), 10 July 1921, p. 1.

32. Report on the tactics of the Russian Communist Party, 5 July 1921, in Lenin, *Polnoe sobranie sochinenii,* 5th ed., vol. 44, p. 52. He assigned hunger and exhaustion as the reasons, ibid., pp. 52–53.

33. "Novye vremena, starye oshibki v novom vide," ibid., p. 103 (20 August 1921).

34. Report on the political activity of the Central Committee to the Tenth Party Congress, 8 March 1921, ibid., vol. 43, p. 32.

35. Concluding remarks on the report of the Central Committee, 9 March 1921, ibid., p. 47.

36. Telegram to the Siberian Bureau of the Central Committee written 13 June 1921, ibid., vol. 52, appendices, no. 42, pp. 331–32.

37. "Chto konstatiruet 'Pravda' " [What *Pravda* is bringing out], *Volia Rossii,* no. 205, 18 May 1921, p. 3. Presumably the reference is to E. A. Preobrazhenski, who wanted the Communist state to deal with the Russian peasants as Great Britain dealt with India—i.e., royally to exploit them. He got his wish, but no personal benefit from it.

38. Lenin, *Polnoe sobranie sochinenii,* 5th ed., "Predislovie," vol. 42, p. viii.

39. Trifonov, *Klassy i klassovaia bor'ba,* part 1, pp. 91 ff.

40. "Po Rossii: Zhizn' sovetskoi derevni," *Revoliutsionnaia Rossiia,* no. 3, February 1921, p. 23.

41. Antonov-Ovseenko, "O banditskom dvizhenii v Tambovskoi gubernii," pp. 29 and insert marked (29).

42. "Po Rossii: Zhizn' sovetskoi derevni," *Revoliutsionnaia Rossiia*, no. 3, February 1921, p. 23. A resort to this practice is confirmed in Soviet sources, although not with specific reference to striking railwaymen. See above, chapter two.

43. Proceedings of the SR trial in *Pravda*, no. 153, 12 July 1922, p. 4.

44. See, for example, Trifonov, *Klassy i klassovaia bor'ba*, part 1, p. 87.

45. Proceedings of the SR trial in *Pravda*, no. 153, 12 July 1922, p. 4. Antonov's brother-in-law, Bogoliubski, made the disclosure but gave no year or years. An SR witness of national prominence, Filippovski, confirmed the information and related it to 1918. From other testimony of Bogoliubski, however, 1919 is indicated. The exchange might have occurred over a two-year period.

46. Fomichev (Lidin), "Antonovshchina: Iz vospominanii antonovtsa" (Santiago de Chile, 1955), p. 38.

47. Trifonov, *Klassy i klassovaia bor'ba*, part 1, pp. 259–60.

48. The notion that the Soviets used Mongol or Mongolian troops for repressive purposes has surfaced repeatedly. It seems to have died a hard death. A. F. Kerensky affirmed their use at the time of the Hungarian national uprising of 1956; he refused to believe that Russian troops could be used for such purposes. But the Mongols are a small people and could not possibly have committed all the nefarious actions attributed to them. If the range is widened, however, to include Chinese, Turko–Tatars, and Finno–Ugrians, we move from the realm of fiction into that of fact. The Soviet regime unquestionably derived strength from their bruised feelings.

49. See "Antonovshchina" in *Sovetskaia istoricheskaia entsiklopediia*, vol. 1 (1960), p. 635, where it is asserted that the uprising was prepared and carried out under the guidance of the SR Central Committee. A. S. Antonov figures merely as the military leader.

50. S. Ch., "Tambovskaia pamiatka ob eserakh," *Izvestiia*, no. 121 (1560), 2 June 1922, p. 1.

51. From the report of the Che-ka in *Iz istorii Vserossiiskoi Chrezvychainoi Komissii 1917–1921 gg.*, document no. 333, 24 July 1921, pp. 456–57.

52. "Protsess pravykh eserov: Rech' gosudarstvennogo obvinitelia t. Krylenko" [The trial of the right SRs: speech of the State Prosecutor, Comrade Krylenko], *Izvestiia*, no. 169 (1608), 30 July 1922, p. 3.

53. Leonidov, "Eshche ob eserakh v Tambovskoi gub.," ibid., no. 155 (1594), 14 July 1922, p. 3; Borisov, *Chernym letom*, p. 37.

54. Trifonov, *Klassy i klassovaia bor'ba*, part 1, p. 57.

55. V. Zenzinov, "Krest'ianskaia stikhiia" [The blind force of the peasantry], *Volia Rossii*, no. 176, 13 April 1921, p. 2.

56. See the editorial, "Povstanchestvo," ibid., no. 199, 10 May 1921, p. 1.

57. See trial proceedings, "Rech' gosudarstvennogo obvinitelia t. Krylenko," *Izvestiia*, no. 169 (1680), 30 July 1922, p. 3. The *Pravda* version of this speech, delivered on 29 July, adds nothing although differing somewhat in detail; see no. 170, 1 August 1922, p. 3. In general there is just enough variance in the two Soviet organs to necessitate reading the wretched print of both.

58. Anonymous (Podbelski), *Kak tambovskie krest'iane boriatsia za svobodu*.

59. *Iz istorii Vserossiiskoi Chrezvychainoi Komissii 1917–1921 gg.*, document no. 333, p. 456.

60. "Sud nad eserami: Esery vozglavliali banditskoe dvizhenie Antonova" [Judgment of the SRs: the SRs headed Antonov's bandit movement], *Pravda*, no. 153, 12 July 1922, p. 4. The caption shows the way the Soviet government was determined to have it.

61. Proceedings of the trial, 29th day, morning session, *Izvestiia*, no. 153 (1592), 12 July 1922, p. 2.

62. The information about Bereznikov comes from the testimony of Bogoliubski as presented in the two sources last cited above; see also Borisov, *Chernym letom*, pp. 37–38.

63. B. V. in the *Tambovskaia Pravda* as summarized by S. Ch., "Tambovskaia pamiatka ob eserakh," *Izvestiia*, no. 121 (1560), 2 June 1922, p. 1.

64. *Obvinitel'noe zakliuchenie po delu tsentral'nogo komiteta i otdel'nykh chlenov inykh organizatsii partii sotsialistov-revoliutsionerov* [Summation of the prosecution in the trial . . . of the SR party] (Moscow, 1922), p. 43; "Rech' gosudarstvennogo obvinitelia t. Krylenko," *Izvestiia*, no. 169 (1608), 30 July 1922, p. 3. Report of same speech with variations in *Pravda*, no. 170, 1 August 1922, p. 3.

65. "Protsess pravykh eserov," 39th day, evening session, *Izvestiia*, no. 164 (1603), 25 July 1922, p. 3; 44th day, evening session, ibid., no. 172 (1611), 3 August 1922, p. 2; "Sud nad eserami," 39th day, evening session of 24 July, *Pravda*, no. 164, 25 July 1922, p. 3; 44th day, evening session of 1 August, ibid., no. 172, 3 August 1922, p. 3.

66. "Protsess pravykh eserov," *Izvestiia*, no. 153 (1592), 12 July 1922, p. 2.

67. "Sud nad eserami," *Pravda*, no. 153, 12 July 1922, p. 4.

68. *Obvinitel'noe zakliuchenie po delu tsentral'nogo komiteta p. s.-r.*, p. 43.

69. "Partiia s.-r. o zadachakh momenta" [The SR party on the tasks of the hour], *Volia Rossii*, no. 218, 2 June 1921, pp. 3–4, reproducing the announcement of the Central Committee of 26 April 1921; see also appeal of the Socialist Union of Toiling Peasantry, "Po Rossii: Sotsialisticheskii soiuz trudovogo krest'ianstva: *Zemlia i Volia:* Pamiatka trudovogo krest'ianstva" [In Russia: Socialist Union of Toiling Peasantry: *Land and Liberty:* instruction of the toiling peasantry], ibid., no. 186, 24 April 1921, p. 2.

70. Antonov-Ovseenko, "O banditskom dvizhenii v Tambovskoi gubernii," p. 5; *Obvinitel'noe zakliuchenie po delu tsentral'nogo komiteta p. s.-r.*, pp. 40–41.

71. Donkov, "Organizatsiia razgroma antonovshchiny," *Voprosy Istorii KPSS*, no. 6 (June 1966), p. 62.

72. *Obvinitel'noe zakliuchenie po delu tsentral'nogo komiteta p. s.-r.*, p. 41.

73. Antonov and Savinkov had in common only their authoritarian temperaments and their armed conflict with the Soviet regime—Savinkov with fanfare, espionage, and conspiracy, and Antonov with deeds. Otherwise they were totally different men. Savinkov is an interesting figure, the prototype of European Fascism, distinctly favorable to the upper levels of society but able to communicate with the masses, whom he detested; Antonov was a son of the people, he was "Green," and he stood for the peasant interest. Savinkov affected to be a man of action; Antonov was a man of action. One may read about Savinkov in his own

productions, for he attained a certain literary distinction. His lurid role in the PSR is described in Radkey, *The Agrarian Foes of Bolshevism* and *The Sickle under the Hammer*.

74. Anonymous (Podbelski), *Kak tambovskie krest'iane boriatsia za svobodu*, p. 7; Antonov-Ovseenko, "O banditskom dvizhenii v Tambovskoi gubernii," p. 5; "Sud nad eserami," *Pravda*, no. 153, 12 July 1922, p. 4.

75. Steklov, "Vol'nitsa i podvizhniki," *Izvestiia*, no. 96 (1239), 6 May 1921, p. 1.

76. "Sud nad eserami," *Pravda*, no. 153, 12 July 1922, p. 4; "Protsess pravykh eserov," *Izvestiia*, no. 153 (1592), 12 July 1922, p. 2; *Obvinitel'noe zakliuchenie po delu tsentral'nogo komiteta p. s.-r.*, p. 44. The last source, which might have been of material assistance, is at this point so miserably organized and written as to defeat research; the other two are merely muddy.

77. Antonov-Ovseenko, "O banditskom dvizhenii v Tambovskoi gubernii," p. 5.

78. Podbelski, "Predsedateliu moskovskogo soveta r. i. k. deputatov," p. 2.

79. S. Ch., "Tambovskaia pamiatka ob eserakh," *Izvestiia*, no. 121 (1560), 2 June 1922, p. 1.

80. Trifonov, *Klassy i klassovaia bor'ba*, part 1, p. 56.

81. "Protsess pravykh eserov," *Izvestiia*, no. 164 (1603), 25 July 1922, p. 3. The pertinent section is the evening session of the 39th day of the trial.

82. *Obvinitel'noe zakliuchenie po delu tsentral'nogo komiteta p. s.-r.*, p. 44; see also Trifonov, *Klassy i klassovaia bor'ba*, part 1, p. 56. It has not been possible to ascertain the membership of the committee at this or at any other time. The four members (there were an undisclosed number of others) named in the Che-ka report (*Iz istorii Vserossiiskoi Chrezvychainoi Komissii 1917–1921 gg.*, no. 333, p. 456), and accepted by Trifonov as members prior to the arrests, are stated by Podbelski not to have belonged, in fact, to the committee. With one exception, none of these names appears in another list of four mentioned by Bogoliubski at the trial (see his testimony at the morning session of the 29th day in *Izvestiia*, no. 153 (1592), 12 July 1922, p. 2). The discrepancies when any information is divulged, the silence otherwise, and the absence of dates make the reconstruction a hopeless task.

83. On the September conference, see "Sud nad eserami," *Pravda*, no. 153, 12 July 1922, p. 4; *Obvinitel'noe zakliuchenie po delu tsentral'nogo komiteta p. s.-r.*, pp. 41–42; Antonov-Ovseenko, "O banditskom dvizhenii v Tambovskoi gubernii," p. 5; *Iz istorii Vserossiiskoi Chrezvychainoi Komissii 1917–1921 gg.*, no. 333, pp. 455, 456; Podbelski, "Predsedateliu moskovskogo soveta r. i k. deputatov," p. 2; Trifonov, *Klassy i klassovaia bor'ba*, part 1, p. 56.

84. "Usmirenie krest'ian v Tambovskoi gubernii," *Na chuzhoi storone*, vol. 3 (1923), p. 127; Fomichev (Lidin), "Antonovshchina: Iz vospominanii antonovtsa" (Santiago de Chile, 1955), p. 3—the only sources that mention the incident. The editor of the journal was in possession of a manuscript in the form of a remonstrance drawn up by a group of SRs and addressed to the supreme organs of the Soviet state. He relates it either to the end of 1919 or to 1920, but places it before the Antonov insurrection. The subject of investigation was disorders in November, year unspecified. There were no major disorders in November of 1919, whereas there were big ones in November of 1920. Moreover, the second source states unequivocally that the mission arrived in the midst of the insurrection. We may

conclude, therefore, that the editor of the journal is wrong and that the Volga bureau acted in the wake of the bloody events of the late summer and fall of 1920.

85. Text of the manifesto, or at least excerpts from the text, in "Po Rossii: Sotsialisticheskii soiuz trudovogo krest'ianstva," *Volia Rossii,* no. 186, 24 April 1921, p. 2. Not mentioned elsewhere. I have no authority to attribute this manifesto to the influence of the SR leadership except for its general line, the tone of the manifesto, and its reception in the SR organ. One might regard it, in fact, as a product of Soviet cunning, so discouraging is it to the insurrectionary movement. But the editors of *Volia Rossii* looked on it as bona fide and so shall we.

86. *Iz istorii Vserossiiskoi Chrezvychainoi Komissii 1917–1921 gg.,* no. 333, pp. 455–56.

87. See p. 117.

88. "Banditskie prestupleniia partii eserov: Antonovshchina: Uliki na-litso" [The bandit crimes of the SR party: the Antonov affair: the evidence is at hand], *Pravda,* no. 116, 27 May 1922, p. 3.

89. "Banditskie prestupleniia partii eserov: Antonovshchina: Iz besedy s genshtabistom t. Davydovym," ibid.

90. Podbelski, "Predsedateliu moskovskogo soveta r. i k. deputatov," pp. 1–3.

91. *Iz istorii Vserossiiskoi Chrezvychainoi Komissii 1917–1921 gg.,* no. 333, pp. 456–58.

92. Donkov, "Organizatsiia razgroma antonovshchiny," *Voprosy Istorii KPSS,* no. 6 (June 1966), p. 63.

93. *Obvinitel'noe zakliuchenie po delu tsentral'nogo komiteta p. s.-r.*

94. Steklov, "Ot Chernova do Antonova," *Izvestiia,* no. 71, 2 April 1921, p. 1.

95. Steklov, "Vol'nitsa i podvizhniki," ibid., no. 96 (1239), 6 May 1921, p. 1.

96. *Obvinitel'noe zakliuchenie po delu tsentral'nogo komiteta p. s.-r.,* p. 44.

97. Antonov-Ovseenko, "O banditskom dvizhenii v Tambovskoi gubernii," pp. 5–6.

98. *Iz istorii Vserossiiskoi Chrezvychainoi komissii 1917–1921 gg.,* p. 456; first published in *Izvestiia,* no. 161 (1304), 24 July 1921.

99. A. Kazakov, *Partiia s.-r. v Tambovskom vosstanii 1920–1921 gg* [The SR party in the Tambov insurrection of 1920–1921] (Moscow, 1922). One of the relatively truthful sources. It appears to be the pamphlet which the author read in Moscow and on which he had taken notes, only to be robbed of them as recounted in the foreword. Although bowing in that direction, the source does not uphold the official line as to the responsibility of the SR Central Committee.

100. "Usmirenie krest'ian v Tambovskoi gubernii," *Na chuzhoi storone,* vol. 3 (1923), pp. 127–28.

101 *Obvinitel'noe zakliuchenie po delu tsentral'nogo komiteta p. s.-r.,* p. 44.

102. This opinion does not rest on the independent investigation of the author alone. It was the view of the Menshevik B. I. Nikolaevsky, whose knowledge of the Russian revolution may be said without exaggeration to have been immense, and of V. M. Zenzinov, member of the Central Committee of the PSR. Needless to say, the latter was not prejudiced in favor of the Left SRs but regarded them as having a strong following, albeit one largely vitiated through inferior organization, a weakness the Left SRs shared with their peasant constituency.

103. See, for example, Trifonov, *Klassy i klassovaia bor'ba*, part 1, p. 74, citing statements by Lenin and Sverdlov.

104. "Pechat' i zhizn': O levykh es-erakh zagranitsei prebyvaiushchikh" [The press and life: about Left SRs who are sojourning abroad], *Volia Rossii*, no. 165, 30 March 1921, p. 2. The title of the article is not directed against Spiridonova, who never left Russia.

105. "Za kulisami pravitel'stvennogo mekhanizma: Tsirkuliar po bol'shevistskoi zhandarmerii" [Behind the scenes in the mechanism of government: the circular to the Bolshevik gendarmery], *Revoliutsionnaia Rossiia*, no. 7, May 1921, p. 9; reprinted also in "Rukovodstvo dlia bol'shevistskikh shpikov" [Guidance for Bolshevik detectives], *Volia Rossii*, no. 175, 12 April 1921, p. 5. The SR organs had gotten hold of this circular letter (no. 5 of 1 June 1920) to all branches of the Extraordinary Commission.

106. The author has seen banners of this kind in the fall of 1934 at the funeral of E. K. Breshko-Breshkovskaia in a village near Prague. They were an artistic triumph, something not often achieved by revolutionaries.

107. "Na mestakh: Bor'ba s banditizmom," *Izvestiia*, no. 177 (1320), 12 August 1921, p. 3; reproduced in "Soobshchenie *Izvestii* o zagovorakh" [*Izvestiia* communication about plottings], *Volia Rossii*, no. 290, 27 August 1921, p. 4.

108. Information about the Left SR trial has had to be taken exclusively from the press. See "Sudebnyi otdel: sud nad levymi eserami" [Court proceedings: judgment on Left SRs], *Izvestiia*, no. 138 (1577), 24 June 1922, p. 4; ibid., no. 141 (1580), 28 June 1922, p. 2; "Delo levykh eserov" [Case of the Left SRs], ibid., no. 142 (1581), 29 June 1922, p. 5; ibid., no. 143 (1582), 30 June 1922, p. 5; "Protsess levykh eserov" [The Left SR trial], *Pravda*, no. 141, 28 June 1922, p. 6; ibid., no. 142, 29 June 1922, p. 5.

109. Dokunin, "Tambovskii schet sotsial-banditam," *Pravda*, no. 123, 4 June 1922, p. 3. Despatch from Tambov dated 25 May.

110. Fomichev (Lidin), "Antonovshchina: Iz vospominanii antonovtsa" (Santiago de Chile, 1955), p. 28.

111. Ibid., pp. 37–38, 44.

— 6 —

Organization and Tactics

An examination of the organization of the uprising divides easily into analysis of the civil structure—to all intents and purposes identical with the Union of Toiling Peasantry—and of the military set-up devised by A. S. Antonov. After both have been considered, the tactics of the Green force will be noted before proceeding to the story of the insurrection itself.

There is no doubt that its strength and stubborn character, its ability to withstand crushing losses in an unequal struggle and to intersperse these with moments of victory, owed much to the supporting network of peasant societies. The Communists might play upon the STK—*Soiuz Trudovogo Krest'ianstva* (Union of Toiling Peasantry)—and call it *Soiuz Tambovskogo Kulachestva* (Union of Tambov Kulakdom),[1] but their grudging recognition of its effectiveness belied the derision implicit in the parody. The Red Army commander who finally overcame the Green "bands" noted the skill that had gone into creation of the STK network.[2] And the Central Committee of the Communist Party in its report for the period 15 March–1 May 1921 conceded that in Tambov and again in Siberia it had run onto a "widely ramified and well-organized" union of peasants.[3] It was something unique in peasant annals.

How had it come about? Who was responsible for giving form and cohesion, albeit over a limited territory, to a class that never before had known either? A definitive answer is as elusive here as in other aspects of this fascinating and baffling subject. The sources are in even greater disarray. Not only are they fragmented and contradictory, but the omission of dates at crucial points doubles the difficulty of attempting to fit developments into their proper setting and sequence. There is some rather substantial information, however;

the rest is a matter of the author's judgment. He thinks he can give the answers, but is not sure.

We may begin with the version of Iuri Podbelski, the Populist intellectual whom the Extraordinary Commission wanted to hold responsible for directing the insurrection as delegate of the SR Central Committee—a lapse into ineptitude on the part of the secret police that is not easy to explain, since the Che-ka should have known that Podbelski was the type who would stay as far away from an insurrection as it was possible to get. But chosen he was, and he crawled out of his skin in an effort to prove his innocence which should never have been in question.

Podbelski distinguishes between two peasant unions with the same name, the one an SR enterprise and the other a creation of Antonov. The SR peasants' union (STK) he dates from the spring of 1920 when the SRs joined hands with other revolutionary groups—mainly the Left SRs—to engage in this work. Though a network of these unions soon covered Tambov *uezd*, it failed either to bind the peasants firmly together or to impose its ideological leadership, it was overtaken by insurrection—against which it had warned—and it ceased to exist immediately thereafter as a result of the arrests carried out by the Che-ka. Certain local units, deprived of guidance from above, may have joined in the insurrection. But the SR-sponsored union as such, insisted Podbelski, had nothing in common with Antonov's union, which was formed during the insurrection itself and apparently existed for the most part only on paper.[4]

To determine the worth of Podbelski's contention, it is necessary merely to note that he affirms the nonexistence of the STK after the beginning of the insurrection and the nominal existence of Antonov's union. Podbelski thus has waved aside the robust organization that constituted the civilian backbone of the rebellion, aroused the envy of Tukhachevski, earned a grudging tribute from the Central Committee of the Communist Party, and is everywhere in evidence as one studies the course of events. There are other defects in his contention, quite apart from the Soviet claim to have the documents disproving it,[5] but this *reductio ad absurdum* will do: his version of the origin and duality of the STK must be totally rejected.

Unfortunately, eliminating Podbelski's misrepresentation does not clarify the situation. There is still wide disparity in the sources as to the origin of the Peasants' Union. The lone participant in Antonov's movement who lived to write about it attributes the organization of the peasantry to Antonov himself as a result of meetings he arranged with peasant representatives soon after he went on an illegal footing in the second half of 1918. These secret meetings set up committees which had led an underground existence till the middle of 1919[6] and which were certainly the forerunners, if not the actual nuclei, of the peasant unions of 1920. A Soviet encyclopedia, on the other hand, does not trace the origin of the unions any further back than May 1920, the month in which the Central Committee of the PSR instructed the Tambov provincial committee to proceed to their formation.[7] Other sources follow the same scheme.[8] If their view is sustained, then it was the SR party and not Antonov which founded the unions.

There are two sources, however—both contained in the press reports of the SR trial of 1922—that are more plausible and more authentic than any others; they may be reconciled, one with the other, and will be followed in our account with certain adjustments of our own where these seem necessary. One is the report of the Tambov delegation to the All-Russian SR conference in September 1920 which was read at the trial by the chairman of the Soviet tribunal, and the other is the testimony of Bogoliubski, Antonov's brother-in-law and his close associate until 1920. As previously noted, the words of Bogoliubski carry weight, not only because of his relationship to Antonov but also because he did not give the Soviet government what it wanted when it placed him on the witness stand—namely, confirmation of SR responsibility for the insurrection—so that there is a presumption of honesty on his part.

Bogoliubski credits Antonov with taking the initiative in organizing the peasantry. It was at the end of 1919 that the work began, just about the time—according to Bogoliubski—of his withdrawal from active collaboration with his brother-in-law. Significantly, this was also the time of Denikin's debacle after his precipitous advance on Moscow and his even more precipitous retreat. The day of the Whites had passed, Wrangel would wage only a twilight campaign, and Antonov seems to have sensed that the day of the Greens had come. When the Tambov provincial committee of the PSR entered into relations with him early in 1920 by sending Bereznikov with a request for money, an undisclosed number of peasant "cells" had already come into being. The discovery must have excited Bereznikov, who informed the committee upon his return to Tambov after having proposed to Antonov their conversion into peasants' unions, presumably with a broadened base and running more in the SR groove. Individual SRs had joined these cells, but there were no purely SR organizations in the village. The SRs themselves, according to Bogoliubski, had done nothing to form such cells. Now they reaped the harvest when "they received them already organized from Antonov, who at the same time handed over to them the threads"—presumably the names of the organizing personnel, leaders, and intermediaries.

It may be surmised that Antonov wanted to devote himself to military matters and was glad to have a corporate body take over the work of preparing the civilian population for support of his armed forces. But he kept a hand in the process. According to his brother-in-law, the negotiations with the SRs had concerned a cooperative effort to form peasant unions and Antonov is credited with organizing the majority of unions or "brotherhoods" in Tambov *uezd*, though whether as outgrowths of cells already formed or as new creations in the era of cooperation is not clear.

The first stage in the process, the formation of cells, had been the work of Antonov. The second stage, as best we can reconstruct events, was the conversion of these cells into SR peasant unions as a result of cooperation between Antonov and the party. The third stage would be the broadening of these unions into nonpartisan ones through the joint enterprise of the SRs and the Left SRs on a basis of parity, with help from anarchists or whoever else would join in and doubtless under Antonov's watchful eye. As Antonov was he who had given and the SRs those who had received—in a double sense, both organizationally and financially—it would be interesting to know what stipulations he had made and, specifically, whether he had insisted upon giving the peasants' union a nonpartisan cast, as well he might have in view of his having been both an SR and a Left SR and of his dependence on neither.

In any case, the Central Committee of the PSR issued its call in May 1920 for the formation of nonpartisan peasant unions or STKs, and the Tambov delegation to the national party conference in September reported that after having established their own peasant organizations (time unspecified), the local SRs had proceeded to the formation of the broader, nonpartisan STKs. Work with Left SRs had been so harmonious that in the end a "complete fusion" of the two sets of SRs had occurred. A Soviet observer suggested that the nonpartisan tactics were dictated not so much by the stated aim of assembling the fragmented forces of the village as by the belief that an organizing movement under the SR banner alone had no chance of success.[9] Be that as it may, Antonov may have insisted on such a course and the need of enlisting the considerable peasant following of the Left SRs worked in the same direction. The decisions made and the tactics pursued paid off handsomely.[10]

The first peasant unions were formed in Tambov *uezd* in villages such as Khitrovo, Rasskazovo, Koptevo. Here they were especially strong and here the insurrection began[11] (according to a Soviet estimate, 40 percent of the population of Khitrovo was actively involved in the uprising).[12] The movement caught on rapidly and soon the unions covered half [13] or more[14] of the *volosts* of Tambov *uezd*. From this largest, most advanced, and prosperous subdivision of the province the unions spread to other *uezds*, an extension that was spurred by instructions for further organization and activity worked out at the SR provincial conference in July 1920 in collaboration with representatives of the nonpartisan peasantry. These instructions were duly communicated to Antonov, it should be noted.[15] When the movement attained its fullest development in January 1921, with the insurrection in full swing, there were as many as 900 village unions in five *uezds* according to secret official figures of the Soviet government.[16] Nor was the contagion limited to Tambov province, for Voronezh and Saratov also had peasant unions, at least in the *uezds* adjacent to Tambov.[17]

The STK as a whole represented a well-knit, hierarchical structure of committees or unions at five levels, the four devised by Catherine in her administrative subdivision of the empire—village, *volost'* or canton, *uezd* or county, and province—and one put in by the STK people themselves, the *raion* or district level which grouped several *volosts* within an *uezd*.[18] The principles of nonpartisanship and parity appear to have been observed everywhere and not solely on the occasion of drafting instructions for the expansion of the network noted above, when the SR party conference met with representatives of the nonpartisan peasantry and worked out a joint decision. There is mention of a district committee grouping unions in several *volosts*, which consisted of one "right" (regular) SR, one Left SR, and one SR sympathizer.[19] Apparently the last term denoted a nonpartisan in general sympathy with revolutionary Populism. The Central Archives of the Communist Party preserve the record of a staff set up to guide the insurrection which consisted of two SRs and two Left SRs;[20] mention is made at the SR trial in 1922 of a tactical bureau which achieved more than parity since it was composed of two Left SRs and only one SR.[21]

The confusion in the sources regarding these staffs and the superior organs of the STK is so great, however, that it is impossible to dispel the uncertainty surrounding them except to say that nonpartisanship was more than the façade depicted in Soviet accounts. The personnel of the SR party and of the peasants' union certainly overlapped but were by no means identical, if only because Left SRs were also there. The Left SR Tokmakov headed the provincial committee of the STK until taking the field; he was followed—though perhaps not immediately—by the SR Pluzhnikov. The STK cannot be represented simply as the handiwork of the SRs.[22]

In the last analysis this powerful organization, almost unique in peasant annals, was born of the organizing genius of A. S. Antonov and of the desperation of the rural toilers in the face of an oppression—perhaps not unique—but merely unsurpassed. The program of the peasants' union was not a stirring one. The driving force of the insurrection was negative, not positive; the peasants scarcely knew what they wanted, but they knew very well what they wanted to get rid of. A Soviet observer may have said more than he intended in favor of the STK when he wrote of its holding out the bait of an end to strife and of the establishment of a peaceful life.[23] After six years of unbroken hell such a vision was indeed "bait" for the miserable Russian peasant. Otherwise the STK had not much to promise; its strength lay in what it opposed. The main features of its program, as already noted,[24] parroted the views of the SR intellectuals instead of the inner desires of the inarticulate mass behind it.

It is necessary only to add that the Tambov delegation at the SR national conference in the fall of 1920 did sound one new note: instead of once again going through the sterile ritual of calling up the long-dead Constituent Assembly, it defined the aim of the STK as the convocation of an All-Russian Congress of Toilers.[25] So far had the STK moved the local SRs. It is true that socialization of the land was reaffirmed as having the support of the peasantry, whereas we have attempted to show that such support would not have held for the future. But the point about the future national assembly, the thought of shifting the base from universal suffrage to class representation, betokens the fissure already existing between Populist intellectuals and peasant followers which could only widen with the passage of time.

Finally, in respect to the program of the STK, it must be stressed that it contained no call to insurrection; here the STK and the SRs were as one. Both were preparing for armed resistance to Soviet oppression and both would swing behind the insurrection when it came, but the record is clear that neither provoked it—though both, of course, contributed indirectly to its coming by playing upon peasant grievances. Antonov's brother-in-law was quite explicit in denying any intent of insurrection either in STK or in party circles, where the talk was all of further organization.[26] No doubt his words were most displeasing to the Soviet government which had placed him on the witness stand in an attempt to strengthen the case against the PSR. Manifestos of the STK in possession of the Soviet authorities calling on the populace to revolt almost certainly are from the time of the insurrection; they were presented as evidence without any attempt to date them,[27] for the government evidently wished to create the impression that they antedated the outbreak.

The duties or functions of the peasant unions were manifold and important but not all-inclusive. Ishin confirms that their competence did not extend to military operations: he states that their role was sharply differentiated from that of Antonov's Supreme Operational Staff. He further states that the Tambov provincial committee of the PSR gave instructions to the provincial committee of the STK, a process without friction since the same people served on both; he says nothing about either giving instructions to the operational staff.[28] One more indication that Antonov held the upper hand in this whole business. He wanted assistance but not direction in what was foreordained to be a back-breaking task. And the STK gave him assistance. It acted as his quartermaster-general, his ministry of supply, his intelligence department, and his government in civil matters. It was, in brief, the intermediary between the Green army and the general population, doing everything in its power to sustain the guerrillas and to impede repression.

The peasants' union acted as the agency of recruitment, either by finding volunteers for Antonov or by conducting mobilizations. It provided the social pressure for keeping unwilling fighters at their task by denying deserters a place of refuge in their native villages. It collected money, food, and equipment for the Greens at the same time as it sought to block removal by government agencies of horses, grain, and other food supplies from the areas of insurrection. It saw to the quartering of Green units in villages through a special branch known as the "Komendatura." It organized efficiently and on an elaborate scale the relays of horses that lent wings to guerrilla movements. It undertook to provide medical aid for the troops and to care for the families of breadwinners at the front. It organized a system of espionage to watch over and report on movements of the enemy, and on Red Army men arriving on leave in their villages for the purpose of seeing that they did not return to their units. It devised a system of fast communications, employing couriers and signaling methods such as the stopping of windmills.

The unions maintained close contact, keeping in touch with one another not less than once a day. They even had their own armed force with the same name as a coercive branch of the Soviet system—BOXP or VOKhR, from *Vnutrenniaia Okhrana* (Internal Security). This force protected the unions or their committees, kept open communications, punished Red collaborators, struck at small Red units, and cut down stragglers. It might consist of from five to fifty members in a single village. Finally, the STKs carried on work of a general economic and administrative nature, discharging, in short, the basic functions of government. From all accounts, Soviet and non-Soviet, they did their work well.[29]

Concrete examples of what the STK was doing cannot be given. There is fleeting reference to a remote village in Tambov *uezd* near the edge of the northern forest, the village of Pakhotnyi Ugol, mistakenly given in the source as "Pakotnyi lug." Here a model functioning community had been organized, a veritable SR commune—or, better, a Green commune. Virtually the entire male population was engaged in drill and in the handling of arms.[30] The Soviet commander seems startled at having found an island in the Soviet sea from which everything Soviet had been totally banished. Similar situations existed elsewhere, though scarcely carried to such a stage of perfection. Unfortunately, our knowledge of the STK ends at this point.

The military organization of the Greens in Tambov thus rested on a broad and solid civilian foundation. It is absurd to speak of a lack of organization in the rear of Green forces without making at least this one exception, and ridiculous when the author in question—engaged in the kind of commissioned research that flourishes in Soviet Russia—has himself noted the STK network only a couple of pages before.[31] The commissar of repression termed it "an organized peasant army, resting on a powerful and intricate network" of peasant unions.[32]

Antonov's force followed with remarkable fidelity the model of the Red Army, not only in respect to having political sections[33] but in other matters as well. One Soviet observer called it the "distorted mirror" of the Red Army.[34] It even looked like what it was fighting, and on more than one occasion a state farm welcomed troops and furnished them with food and fodder only to discover with horror at the farewell that the "guests" were going to sack it.[35] Red Army headgear and the leather jackets ineluctably associated with Communists were often in evidence among the Greens and served as a means of deception and as a basis for stratagems in a type of warfare noted for its cruel and cunning character.[36] Asserting that the whole structure of the rebel force duplicated the Red Army, a Soviet author nevertheless admits of one innovation: the office of executioner in each regiment.[37] The Red Army could dispense with such an office; it had the Extraordinary Commission at its side.

The Green army was based on the principle of territorial militia. Each *volost'* involved in the movement furnished a quota of men and maintained them in the field with provisions, horses, and arms. This recruitment and upkeep devolved upon the peasant unions or, more precisely, upon the committees acting in their name. In a Soviet military journal the statement is made—referring to the movement in general and not specifically to Tambov—that each village put into the field a hundred (actually from eighty to two hundred and fifty men), and each *volost'* a regiment.[38] The author considers such quotas too high. The sources dealing with Tambov cannot be so precise for, as the commissar of repression points out, the precise rosters on paper that fell into the hands of the government do not correspond to the reality of regiments which were agglomerations of varying degrees of armament, organization, and personnel. A cavalry regiment might range from two to seven squadrons and from two hundred to two thousand sabers, of whom a considerable part would be virtually without arms. From scattered bits of information, it seems that on the average a regiment would have in the neighborhood of five hundred men.[39]

What would a Green regiment have, besides the normal complement of fighters? It would have a machine gun unit, a mounted intelligence service, and a communications service—also mounted. It would have an economic unit or section, a commission in charge of horse purveyance, and a supply train—supposedly light and mobile but often unwieldy and a drag on operations. It would have a tribunal, sometimes a special executioner, always a special section—the Green counterpart of the Red Che-ka. Here were to be found the "most desperate hooligans," the killers and torturers who hunted down Communist party members and Soviet employees.[40] The regiment would have a political section staffed by political preceptors handpicked by the STK and corresponding to the political commissars in the Red Army. Finally, it would have a well-appointed office for the transaction of business.[41]

The Green army assumed the character of horseborne guerrillas; infantry was the exception, though there might be small groups loaded on wagons.[42] The army consisted of both volunteers and conscripts, in what proportion is not known. The Soviet line, of course, is to play down the factor of free enlistment and magnify that of impressment through the contention that deception, provocation, intimidation, social pressure, and other nefarious means were used to produce "volunteers," quite apart from the widespread resort to conscription. Yet even those who push such a line are constrained to admit that some Greens fought of their own volition.[43] The stubbornness with which the field was held, the resilience in the face of great adversity, argue in favor of a high volunteer component. There are concessions in unfriendly accounts that every effort was made to impart a professional cast to the Green forces; they were constituted as a regular army and everywhere could be detected the skilled hand of military specialists. Though often operating in small detachments, Green forces were grouped in regiments, in brigades, and in two armies.

As best can be determined, there were twenty duly constituted, numbered regiments together with the Special Regiment, an elite force of "carefully selected, splendidly armed desperados" always in attendance upon Antonov. The uncertainty arises from the state of the basic source: in the Antonov-Ovseenko manuscript one digit overlaps another and both are blurred, so that the figure pertaining to the number of regiments could be either twenty or thirty.[44] It is sufficient commentary on the working habits of the Soviet state to observe that even in a document intended for perusal by Lenin a key figure cannot be deciphered. No wonder that Trotski, after inspecting a German sanitation train, sat down and wrote an article with the heading, "O, How We Lack Precision!"[45] If by fiat we make the figure twenty and add in the Special Regiment, we reach the twenty-one regiments given in another source.[46] But this calculation, in turn, is disturbed by the assertion of the commissar of the Kotovski brigade that Antonov had as the core of his army a total of eighteen cavalry regiments.[47]

If a round figure of twenty is adopted, we come to the question of special formations—and again the sources assume their normal state of disarray. There is mention of a separate brigade without further identification.[48] There is mention of separate detachments, also without elucidation.[49] The encyclopedia speaks of several "flying" detachments in addition to two armies, and also speaks of the special Kozlov brigade[50] by which it means apparently a detached force operating in Kozlov *uezd* under the command of Vas'ka Karas'. It mentions also the Kolesnikov detachment, which certainly existed as the wing of Antonov's movement in Voronezh province. About all that can be said with safety is that there were special formations in addition to the core of two armies and twenty-odd regiments. But it is mostly a matter of exasperating uncertainty. Even the irreducible

minimum of truth we have sought to present can be challenged. The
SR organ in exile talks in terms of only ten regiments of unknown
strength;[51] to be sure, it cannot be as authoritative as some of the
Soviet sources and yet what it says cannot be wholly disregarded
since it would be in line with other accounts, Soviet and non-Soviet,
that have preferred to set a low figure for the numerical strength of
Antonov's movement. There is also the question of how to fit into
the picture the Internal Security force of the STK, which stood in
relation to Antonov's soldiers as militia to army and constituted by
all odds the most numerous of the ancillary forces.

How many men did Antonov command? What has been said
already about disarray in the sources is as nothing compared to what
is now encountered. Estimates range from a few thousands up to
fifty thousand. But an investigator must do better than merely state
the range, even if variables and uncertainties interpose well-nigh
insurmountable difficulties. At what time is the count to be taken?
Are only men constantly under arms to be considered or are
occasional soldiers—those who fought some of the time and farmed
some of the time—to be included? A peasant insurrectionary force is
like a swamp, now swelling to cover the entire area, then shrinking
to the clear water in the center. What about the distinction between
troops with standard arms and rustics with pitchforks, scythes,
stakes, clubs, and flails? And the spatial and perhaps qualitative
disjunction between core regiments and the special formations?
These questions afford some idea of the difficulties involved.

Conventionally Antonov's strength has been placed at fifty
thousand. It was the figure used then and it is still being used.[52]
Originally it was probably no more than a guess by local
Communists with good reason to be impressed by Antonov's
strength; thereafter it was picked up uncritically by other writers, for
once an historical error gains currency it tends to be endlessly
repeated. But what cannot be so easily explained is that the
commissar of repression in his report to Lenin used the same figure.
After all, he should have been in a position to evaluate the estimate
of local Communists. Alloting forty thousand men to Antonov in
February 1921, the head of the Plenipotentiary Commission says
that a considerable number were deserters and that not many of

them had gained experience on the battlefields of the World War and the (first) civil war. Besides the field troops, he sets at ten thousand the strength of the militia or Internal Security forces of the STK, arriving at a total of fifty thousand.[53]

A recent Soviet investigator, obviously with more authority than others and having access to all the materials denied an independent scholar, scales the figure down to thirty thousand for the same date.[54] But then he hedges by saying that the number of those who participated in the uprising cannot be accurately determined, for sometimes calculation is based on the registers of detachments which count in the whole male population subject to call-up in the villages under insurgent control. He concludes by adhering to the lowest estimate with the assertion that "the core of the rebel army did not exceed several thousands."[55] Another Soviet historian with obviously less authority but still with every facility for getting at the truth has sprayed the landscape as with a shotgun, fixing the figure at sixteen thousand five hundred on 1 January 1921, at fifty thousand "at the beginning" of January 1921 (the strength was always fluctuating, he says, but hardly to that extent), and at twenty thousand for the period January to April 1921.[56] Still another way of dealing with the problem is to weasel out with words about Antonov disposing of "many thousands" of soldiers.[57]

The lowest estimates of Antonov's strength range from a couple of thousand to ten thousand. The latter figure merits serious consideration and has been advanced by the widow of the Red cavalry commander, G. I. Kotovski.[58] Next in descending order would be the Soviet encyclopedia which assigns to Antonov seven to eight thousand infantry and horse at the end of 1920—the same encyclopedia that allots him fifty thousand or so at the beginning of 1921.[59] A member of Antonov's army until the end of 1920 flounders like a Soviet writer before settling on a total of five thousand for his regular force.[60] His allotment of only two thousand hard core troops after Kronstadt (March 1921) is drawn from thin air and must be dismissed out of hand.[61] Our Populist intellectual who sympathizes with the peasants in their plight but dislikes Antonov as a brave man of action refers to official but nowhere published information in giving him only one thousand horse and two thousand infantry at the end of 1920; as for himself, this intellectual would prefer a still lower figure.[62] Together with Donkov's afterthought noted above, his would be the lowest estimate.

The author of the present study has long struggled to arrive at a reasonable figure, partly because of his statistical interest but mainly because the number of soldiers at Antonov's disposal is a matter of capital importance. An early decision was made to reject the conventional figure of fifty thousand if only because Antonov, with so many factors weighing against him, could not have provided arms for so many followers. As for the very low appraisals, Podbelski's is motivated by a subconscious desire to belittle the Green leader, and some Soviet sources find it hard to recognize that Antonov could have marshalled so many peasants against what was called the workers' and peasants' government. The untenability of Podbelski's appraisal appears in his juxtaposition of a few thousand troops for the Greens and a flood of one hundred thousand Soviet soldiers in Tambov province: either Antonov is made into a superman, something furthest from the wish of Populist intellectuals, or the Soviet becomes a monument of inefficiency; it may have been inefficient, but not to that extent and not in its specialty of repression. So the extremes had to be discarded, not because they were extremes but because they did not stand the test of logic. Through reasoning and prolonged consideration and plain guesswork, the author reached the conclusion that in Antonov's army there must have been some twenty thousand men.

It was therefore most gratifying, late in his investigation, to find in the Trotsky Archive the memorandum which the commander of the troops in Tambov province had written for Lenin, and to learn that M. N. Tukhachevski had placed Antonov's strength at twenty-one thousand.[63] Here at last is an unequivocal and authoritative statement. Against it must be set the estimate of Antonov-Ovseenko, more than twice as high and stemming from the other Soviet official best in a position to know the facts. But Tukhachevski has the greater verisimilitude, and in the last analysis it would seem that the commander in the field would know better the strength of the enemy than would the commissar behind the lines. Furthermore, the reading of the respective memoranda leaves no doubt as to the intellectual superiority of the general, the lucidity and the precision of his exposition differing so markedly from the diffuse and labored efforts of the commissar. The only drawback is that the military technician used so few words. The Tukhachevski memorandum is a model of laconic comment. As such, its usefulness is circumscribed for it does not go into the composition of Antonov's force.

But if loose ends are tied together and advantage is taken of scattered bits of information, a reasonable analysis can be made of its composition which will be in line with the general's disclosure. As indicated previously, there seem to have been twenty numbered regiments and Antonov's own Special Regiment. Regimental strength fluctuated over a considerable amplitude with a complement of five hundred as the median, not only for the Greens but also for the Soviet cavalry[64] upon which, of course, Antonov had modeled his own. If we figure on this basis there would be about ten thousand men in the numbered regiments, precisely the strength assigned to Antonov by Kotovski's widow. This figure may have been derived from the lists of members of the partisan bands drawn up for each village by the Extraordinary Commission in the spring of 1921; the commissar says that over ten thousand names were entered on these lists.[65] If the militia or Internal Security force of the STK—stated by Antonov-Ovseenko to have numbered ten thousand—and the Special Regiment are added, the resulting total closely approximates the figure of twenty-one thousand given by Tukhachevski. It may not be the correct breakdown of Antonov's army but it is a reasonable surmise and may help those who would object to taking Tukhachevski's testimony on faith—something that this author is quite ready to do. As for the swollen conventional estimate of fifty thousand, it could be approached only by including the rustic horde that on one or more occasions assembled for a march on Tambov.

A fighting force of twenty-odd thousand nevertheless marks a considerable achievement for a peasant insurrection in light of the historical record. While it may be doubted whether anyone really knows how many men assembled at a certain time in a given place under the leadership of Bolotnikov and Razin, Bulavin and Pugachev, the size of their "armies" is usually fixed between twenty and thirty thousand during the insurrections that covered a vast area of southeastern and middle-eastern Russia. Moreover, these "armies" were nothing but peasant hordes. If Antonov fashioned a real army of twenty thousand men in one province—or actually in parts of one province—he was not doing badly, however deficient his force may have been in instruments of mass destruction, through no fault of his. Nothing is more difficult than to impart organization to a peasant rebellion. And this may well have been the best-organized peasant rebellion in history.

Antonov's record of achievement is impressive in other particulars. The usual disarray of the sources vanishes in respect to his intelligence and communications services: regardless of point of view, they are unanimously pronounced to be excellent. Even the political commissar attached to Kotovski's brigade, a down-the-line Communist fanatic inflamed with hatred against everything that was not, concedes that the devil should be given his due, that Antonov's espionage was "well-organized."[66] His agents were to be found everywhere, in the town as in the country, and long constituted a block to effective counter-measures.[67]

Acknowledging that the network of espionage was widespread and that it functioned well, Antonov-Ovseenko advised Lenin that at one time it had extended even into the provincial Che-ka, the *uezd* committees of the Communist Party, the management of the railway department, the Soviet military apparatus, and the economic organs of state, particularly in Kirsanov *uezd*. The Greens usually knew in advance about Red troop movements and about shipments of food and military stores. They could to some extent get what they needed from arsenals and sanitation bureaus—presumably weapons, ammunition, and medical supplies.[68] Although Antonov-Ovseenko complains specifically of Kirsanov *uezd*, the degree of penetration could scarcely have been less in Tambov *uezd*, the nerve-center of the province and of the STK as well. The Soviet military organization by its own admission[69] had spies coming out of its seams. They scouted, agitated stealthily, and did damage where least expected.

For purposes of espionage and information-gathering, unlikely types were used. Women, aged beggars, and adolescents were pressed into service and ranged over distances of twenty-five miles or so.[70] The impression is that adolescents proved most serviceable, their immaturity being offset by zealousness and fanaticism. It was hard to do anything about these boys and girls; before, during, and after their missions they were equally a part of the village scene. For courier service—the "flying post" of the Greens—girls and children were often used. Signaling might be done by the ringing of church bells, by the free or arrested motion of windmills (the shutting down of windmills from one point of visibility to the next gave warning that the Reds were coming), and by similar devices.[71] The widespread character of the network of espionage, the effectiveness of its operation, the low incidence of betrayal despite the employment of immature and impressionable agents, the swiftness with which word was passed on, all argue a high degree of support for the Greens in rural and even in urban society, at least in the Tambov area.

An army without arms has been all too often the fate of peasant rebellions, and so it might have been in this case but for the able and skillful man at the head. The Tambov insurrection has A. S. Antonov to thank for not having to fight with bare hands or rustic implements in a struggle that was foreordained to be unequal enough. How the nest egg of arms was acquired is a story of the weakness and confusion of the early months of Soviet rule, the boldness and ingenuity of Antonov as chief of police (militia) of Kirsanov *uezd*, and the next-to-the-last act in the drama of Slavic "brotherhood" played out by the pan-Slavist version of Russian imperialism.

The Soviet government decided that the Czechoslovak Legion recruited from Austrian prisoners of war under Nicholas II should be disarmed. Antonov was glad to oblige, but instead of the weapons he lifted from Czechoslovak units being sent to government warehouses, they mysteriously melted away—not, however, to the black market, but to repositories in secluded villages where they would be under trustworthy supervision until the day should come for which Antonov and his confederates were planning—even in the heyday of collaboration between Lenin and the Left SRs.

It was a unique opportunity and Antonov took advantage of it. Everywhere the Communists were running circles around the Left SRs, childlike in their revolutionary faith; everywhere except in this bucolic setting. And the reason for this distinction may be summed up in one word—Antonov. As we have seen, Kirsanov lay on an important railroad between central Russia and the Volga; considerable numbers of Czechoslovaks must have passed through in early 1918 to be relieved of their arms, but nowhere are any details provided with which to enrich our story: we do not know what types of arms were taken except that machine guns were involved, or in what quantity except that it was large, nor how Antonov carried out his plan, nor do we have a single name of any principal involved save that of Antonov himself. One meager source of information merely states that arms confiscated from the Czechs were transported to certain villages in Kirsanov *uezd* where underground SR cells flourished, causing these villages later to become points of supply for the "bandits," but offers no examples—probably because none were known.[72] Only the bare fact of passing the sequestered arms to the villages is acknowledged; everything else is shrouded in darkness and may have been lost to history.[73]

Concerning the importance of what Antonov had done, there is no question; it was recognized by the general who destroyed his army. To the large hidden reserve of arms assembled by Antonov while heading the militia in Kirsanov *uezd* Tukhachevski attributed much of the credit for the "organized character" of the uprising that so justly bears his name.[74] It should be borne in mind that Czechs denuded of arms were not the only source of Antonov's accumulation for the future. Around the original nest egg other eggs were laid. Tambov society was overwhelmingly agrarian; brain-workers in their great majority were Populists or Populist sympathizers, Communists were not numerous, and it had been necessary to staff soviets and soviet agencies with politically unreliable employees, particularly during the early period of Communist rule but to a lesser degree even later. These disaffected civil servants opened so many leaks in the system that ammunition and even machine guns found their way from government stores into "bandit" hands as a result of the connivance of sympathizers in key positions.[75]

Particularly rife in 1918, such leakage continued on a reduced scale thereafter. Antonov is credited in that year with having robbed the *uprava* (provincial board) of three loads of military rifles and the Tambov artillery depot of several more loads of arms and military supplies. It is not possible to say whether all this came from what had been taken from the Czechs, overlapped with it, or was in addition to it, nor what kind of load is involved (car load? wagon load?), nor how a board of Tsarist times—if indeed it were—could be functioning under the Soviet system, especially one in charge of arms. But these are examples of the uncertainties never absent from this study.

Besides the Bohemian nest egg and the leaks in the Soviet system there were other ways in which enough arms were assembled to make an insurrection feasible. The fate that had overtaken the Imperial army benefited subversive movements by causing the countryside to bristle with arms when soldiers deserted before October or simply walked away thereafter, taking their weapons with them. Despite the general anarchy they maintained a modicum of cohesion after returning to their homes by forming unions of front fighters which merged with SR organizations in the country while retaining their separate identity in the towns.[76] As they melted back into the peasant matrix out of which they had so unwillingly emerged, the ex-front fighters—SR and nonpartisan alike—became so many links between the Imperial army of the past and the Green bands of the future.

Another cycle of desertion and demobilization set in with the first civil war and, while the Soviet government doubtless did better than in 1918 in relieving demobilized soldiers of their arms, there were still plenty of leaks in a procedure described by Lenin as entailing "unparalleled exertions."[77] In a word, and through force of circumstance, Russia now had an armed peasantry—something the Tsarist government had never intended to bring about and something the Soviet government was determined to undo, since on this front there was no difference between them: arms must be kept from the people so that oppression could go on unhindered and officials could live longer lives.

Communists complained continually about weapons in the possession of the people. One commentator wrote that the majority of village youth had cold arms and often firearms as well, and what he was driving at is readily apparent in the heading of his despatch.[78] The mortal fear of citizens having weapons is attested by a whole series of decrees, but Section VI of the *ukaz* of the Moscow Che-ka will have to suffice: "For hunting guns the Moscow Extraordinary Commission will issue no permits whatsoever."[79] Not even Communists were entrusted with weapons except when circumstances rendered it unavoidable, and military personnel had to have the type and number of the weapon they carried noted on their papers.[80] (Russians bear internal passports; before the revolution and after the revolution, it makes no difference.) As to class distinction, there was none: the proletariat was to be disarmed as well as the peasantry, and factories were ordered to turn over all weapons to the central authorities. Even collectors' items had to be registered as a means of drawing out information about anything that citizens might use against oppressors.[81] Truly, the Green tide and the knowledge of their own deeds had thrown a scare into the new masters of Russia.

As for the rest, it was a question of the Greens seizing arms by surprise or taking them from the enemy on the battlefield. The spoils of war constituted a major though fitful and indeterminate source of supply. Perhaps the main reason for inability to measure its impact has been the reluctance of Communist writers to dwell on reverses that befell Soviet forces. But one can say with assurance that the retreats were numerous and that Antonov's men amassed a large amount of war booty. The battlefield was indispensable in supplying lighter arms and equipment without which the insurrection must soon have come to an end. Whether the heavier equipment thus obtained helped the Greens very much may be doubted. Thus the seizure in March 1921 of four cannon from a cavalry regiment of the 15th rifle division[82] would at first glance appear as a windfall for an army bereft of artillery until one considers the effect on mobility of dragging these cannon around and the difficulty of replenishing the shells.

But the brave showing and the ingenuity could never offset the inherent disadvantages of a rustic rebellion cut off from the outside world, denied access to the techniques of modern warfare, and facing the organized repression of a state whose resolution and ruthlessness went far to offset its bad condition. The Greens never had enough in the way of armaments and military supplies. Their artillery was pitiable when it existed at all: primitive, homemade cannon, or antique specimens of bronze taken from the estate of some vanished nobleman. When real cannon were available, as in the case of the three left behind by Mamontov at the time of his retreat from Tambov in 1919[83] and the four captured in battle in 1921, the difficulty of utilizing them without crippling the mobility upon which the Greens depended for so much of their success counterbalanced the gain, since they almost never fought from fixed positions. Nor could they manufacture shells or provide maintenance facilities for ordnance—naturally not, since they held no towns. It goes without saying that they had no armored trains, no armored cars, or aircraft to counter those of Tukhachevski.

Thus from the standpoint of heavy armament one could not even say they were hopelessly outclassed—they had almost nothing. In the range of medium weapons they had at least something, though far less than needed. A report speaks of three Colt machine guns, one heavy Maxim, and a sufficient number of grenades as being in the possession of the Greens before the insurrection began. No figures can be given for the period of rebellion, but there seems to have been a fair number of machine guns and some ammunition, doubtless as a result of leaks or ambuscade and conquest on the battleground.

The most heartbreaking feature of their armaments, however, was the deficiency even in light weapons—the mainstay of guerrilla warfare, at least at that time. Rifles were of assorted types and at best sufficed for certain units. Peasant recruits might have only shotguns, as though they were going out to hunt instead of going into battle. Many who turned out to back up the Green warriors had only implements instead of firearms: pikes, scythes, axes, pitchforks, and clubs. And always weighing upon the spirit of the Greens was the knowledge that they had no factories or arsenals behind them, that they had only the ammunition they started out with, that could be acquired through raids or wrested from their foes. It must have been truly disheartening to have to think always of the need of conserving ammunition when faced with a choice of objectives and even in the heat of battle.[84]

Evidence of the basically unsatisfactory state of affairs in respect to arms may be found at the beginning of the insurrection in the desperate plan hatched to raid the artillery depots or warehouses (actually arsenals, since many kinds of ordnance were kept there) at Tambov and Morshansk in order to provide more arms for the insurgents, to distribute weapons over the whole province, and to raise a general insurrection. The plan was conceived—in great haste, it seems—by a military-operational staff that had sprung up apparently by decision of the provincial authority of the Peasants' Union, although that organization was in disarray at the moment. Both SRs and Left SRs were involved. It stood a serious chance of success at Tambov because the plotters had confederates inside the warehouse, especially the Left SR Poluboiarinov (half-lord), head of the convoy command, who had placed his men on guard that night. All was in readiness within the arsenal at the appointed time. A band of two hundred deserters had been called in from the villages of Spasskoe and Khitrovo—the latter the hearth of the insurrection that had just broken out (August 1920)—and lay in the forest near the warehouse waiting for members of the staff to appear.

But something went wrong. According to the *Pravda* version, the staff members were delayed purely by accident—the accident is not explained—and the deserters lost heart in the enterprise and were sent back to Spasskoe. According to the *Izvestiia* version, it was not the tardiness of the staff but faintheartedness on the part of the deserters that was to blame: only thirty of them had arms and the majority feared under such circumstances to go through with the plan. While these events were transpiring, Antonov received instructions to move against Kirsanov. The projected raid on the Morshansk armory, sponsored by the SR Fetisov, a former émigré, never got beyond the discussion stage.[85]

Plans had miscarried and the opportunity to arm the insurrection so that it could vie on more or less even terms with the Soviet units sent against it had passed, never to come again. Obviously the wrong dispositions had been made. Instead of trying to take the Tambov armory with the aid of deserters, the staff should have relied on a serious fighting force such as Antonov already had. To invite this force to move in the opposite direction against Kirsanov—never a major prize—was a strategical error for which Antonov must share the blame since he was under no compulsion to follow staff orders and could have countered by offering to take the armory.

The only mitigating circumstance is that the insurrection began spontaneously, as a surprise to everyone, and the defenders of the peasantry could not take advantage of the confusion in Communist ranks because they, too, had been caught off guard. The handicap of arms disparity could have been overcome—of course, not permanently—only by a bold stroke of this kind which had been correctly envisaged but badly executed. That handicap now imposed a burden that no amount of bravery and daring could lift in the cruel months ahead. Antonov-Ovseenko later informed Lenin that the fire of the Greens was ragged and of no great effect,[86] and Tukhachevski appraised their battle-worthiness as not comparable to that of the Red Army.[87]

From all accounts, Antonov was a stern if not a harsh disciplinarian. That he had his men well in hand is attested by the entire course of the uprising, the swift and stealthy movements, the success achieved in the face of heavy odds, the ability to absorb grievous losses without damage to morale, and by the whole record of ten months of desperate struggle—the last seven of them against a state relieved of the burden of the first civil war. Such a record could never have been compiled on the basis of compulsion alone; a large number of his men were fighting because they wanted to fight. As for the others, there was both corporal and capital punishment to keep them in line.

Soviet critics speak of the birch, but it is evident from the code of discipline preserved in the basic source[88] that it was the whip that was used. Observing that this code established floggings as the basic measure of discipline, Antonov-Ovseenko gives the range as from two stripes awarded by the corporal to twenty by the regimental commander and more by the court. The next measure, he says, was shooting. To judge from detailed orders that came into his hands, Green commanders made a stubborn effort to curtail marauding, drunkenness, and dissipation, but he believed that these orders were seldom carried out and that the results were negligible.[89]

In their zeal to blacken the Greens, the Communists are not careful of logic. Or, to put it differently, they are concerned only with Marxian logic, and not with logic per se. The orders discovered by a Soviet military authority—orders that must have been available also to Antonov-Ovseenko—give a very different impression of the state of affairs in the Green army than that of the laxness of discipline imputed to it in the latter's memorandum. We owe this countervailing evidence to the desire of the Soviet military critic to ridicule the "democratic discipline" of Antonov's "army."

And so he cites, for the year 1921, Section 6 of Order No. 12 for the Elabushinski detachment wherein it is disclosed that guerrilla fighter Glinikov had allowed the saddle to rub a sore on the back of his horse without reporting it to his superiors and that, for this slackness in the care of the animal, he would now receive fifteen lashes. Squadron commander Pivovar (beer-brewer) would undergo the same punishment for "not knowing service obligations." The order concludes with the injunction: "Not even the smallest failing must be left unpunished." Further citations follow, and of a graver nature. Court proceedings of the 12th Tokiiski and the 13th Okhotnitski regiments[90] showed that two partisans, Korovin and Moschin, had been shot for conducting "searches on their own," and that a third, Klochkov, had been given fifty lashes. These were the penalties for pillaging, "the main occupation of Antonov's army," according to the Soviet writer, who adds that even such severity could not prevent the men from robbing the peasantry.[91] That the Green requisitioning practices burdened the peasantry there is not doubt, but Antonov was obviously doing all in his power to discourage marauding and the net total, authorized and unauthorized, of what the Greens took did not compare with the systematic despoliation of the countryside during the three-year period of militant communism.

Closely connected with discipline was the matter of drink. To listen to their enemies, one would think that life among the Greens was a continuous bacchanalia. A political commissar fanatical enough to be a prohibitionist as well as a Communist compares the Greens to the Whites in point of drunkenness; they drank enormously, he says, until they passed out, drowning in moonshine the residue of a conscience as well as the "rising fear of retribution for their bloody deeds."[92] There was also method in their preoccupation with liquor: they are said to have used it as a lure for peasants. "In order to attract a greater number of peasants into their bands, they assiduously addressed themselves to distilling moonshine."[93]

However unlikely it may seem, Russia at the time had prohibition. What Nicholas II had instituted as a war measure the Communists continued in time of "peace." Not until 22 October 1921 did the Soviet regime legalize lighter wines of not more than 14 percent alcoholic content. Thereafter it improved rapidly in this one respect, and on 8 December of the same year sanctioned wine of up to 20 percent.[94] As for beer, it was subjected to various regulations and was not to exceed 4 percent in strength.[95] Thus at the time of the Tambov insurrection—August 1920 to August 1921—Russians were supposed to have neither vodka nor anything else.

Under the circumstances the Greens would certainly have lured the peasants into their ranks by going into the distilling business if the peasants had not been doing so well on their own. As it was, we may doubt whether there was any such drawing card except insofar as the Greens drove off government snoopers and enabled the peasants to enjoy their freedom of distillation. Drunkenness among the Greens themselves had limits. To judge from their exploits they were sober enough in the saddle. Off duty, and as a means of release from danger and tension, doubtless they did immerse themselves in drink. No blame attaches. Drunkenness and death have been the traditional avenues of escape for the unfortunate Russian people.

Medical service and finance are the darkest provinces of the insurrection. Almost nothing is known concerning them. The charge has been made that the Greens left their wounded to the care of the inhabitants in the locality or else abandoned them to their fate.[96] In many instances the charge was all too true; not, of course, because of the heartlessness it was meant to convey but because Antonov's men had no other choice. They had no network of medical facilities behind them and no organized corps of doctors and nurses. At most they would have a few SR or KD physicians, and there is record of one "equipped hospital" with one hundred fifty beds.[97] As for the rest, it was a question of a peasant family taking in a wounded fighter and of a peasant woman nursing him as best she could. The wounded person redeemed from the battlefield must have been entrusted to the Peasants' Union which arranged for his humble care or returned the man to his family.

It may be conjectured, however, that many were not redeemed. The Greens depended above all on mobility, and mobility meant being unencumbered by wounded. Particularly when rapid maneuvers or precipitous flight were involved, little thought could be given to those who could not keep up and they would be left behind to be taken by the enemy or to crawl off into the bushes and die like a wounded animal. Even if borne away the prospects were grim: inadequate medical supervision and a dearth of medical supplies. Only through leaks in government health agencies could the latter be obtained, and while Antonov-Ovseenko intimates that something was gotten in this way[98] it could not have been more than a trickle. Monks and the few surviving monasteries made up to some extent—but only within serious limits—for the lack of physicians, nurses, and hospitals. [99] All in all, there must have been a high mortality rate attached to wounds in action, but no statistical information of any kind is available.

Nothing can be said about the finance of the Green movement except that it existed. It was not, of course, a salaried army but one that drew contributions from the Peasants' Union in the form of donations or levies on the peasantry. Otherwise it lived off the spoils of war and kept going because of the hatred of Communism. However, it did have a war chest, perhaps even a considerable one. In the village church at Khitrovo, after the insurrection had been knocked to pieces, Soviet authorities found this treasury together with the red-and-gold banner of the Left SRs, the proceedings of the *uezd* congress of the Peasants' Union, and the resolutions of the Kronstadt insurgents. It was quite a haul. The treasury consisted of five trunks of gold or gold coins and of "other valuables."[100] And that is all we know of this trove before it went into the maw of the Soviet state, inimical to the private ownership of gold and to its use as a medium of exchange yet avid for its possession.

No estimate can be made of the value of what had been seized. Nor can it be said whether the hoard represented the whole or only a part of the war chest of the Tambov insurrection. A portion could have been hidden away in another place or buried, some of it could have been lost in transit or in flight, and Antonov—perhaps several of the other commanders—may have taken something for their own use before dispersing to their respective places of refuge. No information has been found to indicate whether the treasure belonged to the STK or to Antonov's army or whether, as seems likely, it was jointly owned. The sole surviving participant who was free to write about these matters knew that Antonov's staff disposed of "rather considerable" means in gold and infers that Antonov could have drawn on these resources to flee abroad had he been so minded.[101]

The tactics of the Tambov insurgents, like those of the Green movement elsewhere, may best be described as those of the weaker side in warfare. Rarely had guerrilla practices been raised to such a level. They rested upon certain substantial advantages which went a long way toward offsetting the handicaps of insufficient armaments and numerical inferiority, though they could never completely close the gap.

Knowledge of the terrain was one such advantage, knowledge that was not only thorough but well-nigh absolute. In the words of Antonov's younger brother, the Greens fought "where every vale and nook, every bush and grove were known to us."[102] Or to quote the Soviet political commissar, where "every draw and thicket, every swamp and ford, every road and trail" were familiar ground, where the most promising spot for defense came readily to mind, or the most favorable setting for an ambuscade.[103] The Greens were rooted in their native soil through the territorial structure of their army and clung to it tenaciously. If dislodged, they would double back to their base at the earliest opportunity.

Severe localism was an attribute of the movement; the leader himself never quite trusted those of his men who came from some other part of the country.[104] It is not meant to suggest, of course, that a unit operated only in the area from which it was drawn and on which it was based. An eyewitness, in fact, makes the point that in the course of their depredations the Greens preferred to have acts committed by peasants who lived outside the canton in question so that they would be unknown to the population[105] and—we may conjecture—less easy to trace. In conducting their operations the Greens kept to the rural areas and only rarely ventured to attack a town. Their disinclination in this respect was natural, for almost never did they succeed in taking a town.[106]

The first major advantage underlay a second, for without familiarity with the terrain it would not have been possible for Antonov to develop the mobility that enabled him to run circles around all units of the Red Army but the elite, which arrived late on the scene. Antonov's troops could deal swift and devastating blows and could cover eighty to one hundred or even one hundred fifty kilometers in a day and a night. An important factor in this was the horse relay system of the STK, but when this did not function the Greens simply exchanged—if necessary at gun point—their worn-out horses for fresh ones at the expense of the peasantry and rode on. Resaddling was relatively simple; many of the soldiers had only pillows and rope stirrups, so that at times they rode in a cloud of down feathers, strewing the way with tell-tale evidence that aided Red scouts in tracking them. Poverty of appurtenances thus complemented poverty of armaments, and the dearth of heavy weapons was converted into an asset in the one respect of added mobility. Without a wagon train the Greens attained ultimate mobility, though at the expense of cutting down their fire power and irritating the peasants through requisitions.[107]

The third advantage of Antonov's army proved even more unnerving to those who had to face it. Now it was there and now it wasn't; it could fade from the scene as though endowed with some supernatural power, some gift of invisibility that rendered it a wraith of war. What it possessed was the capability of being reabsorbed at will into the rural matrix, so that peasants working peacefully in the fields may have been warriors only a day or so before. Lightness of equipment and the lack of any particular uniform aided in the reabsorption. Again it was a question of turning to account a major disadvantage. But above all it was the sympathy of the peasant mass—what Antonov-Ovseenko terms the "organized coopera-tion" of the local population—that enabled the Greens to vanish from the scene or, as he puts it, to lessen their vulnerability, increase their mobility, and multiply their presence so that they seemed to be everywhere.[108]

The ability in large measure to elude pursuit over a period of nine months is perhaps the best proof of the broad degree of popular support for the Green cause. Between operations, we are told, Antonov's men could not be distinguished from the peasant mass. Naturally not, for so many were peasants themselves. While deserters were footloose and free to camp in some secluded place, the peasant component of the Green army had to work as well as to fight and so could be only part-time soldiers—always a weakness of peasant rebellions. But the fluidity of their occupational life long overshadowed the weakness by affording them a means of concealment.[109]

The actual conduct of operations may now be considered. A hard core in each village rallied the disaffected or adventurous element and at a given signal took to the field, joining with deserters from encampments in the hollows and contingents from other villages to fill the ranks of the regiment or detachment for that area. Movements were executed as unobtrusively as possible, using back roads and forest trails and generally keeping in small groups; only as an exception did the Greens move as a column[110] and burden themselves with a wagon train. Even when in motion, however, their true character could not easily be detected; they might draw along hitched-up plows and harrows, looking for all the world like innocent peasants going about their daily tasks. Only a slightly quickened gait could betray their real identity. It took the practised eye to discern what was going on, even when meeting them face to face. Not before time to prepare for action did the groups draw together and begin to resemble an army.[111]

The Greens preferred to avoid frontal attack in favor of unexpected blows from behind or on the flanks, and used encirclement tactics whenever feasible. They often operated after dark, not only to conceal their movements but also to heighten the element of surprise. They liked to take the enemy in his quarters, in the camp at night, or during rest intervals in the daytime. Antonov-Ovseenko says they enjoyed nothing better than to encircle "our small and somnolent units" with concentric rings of cavalry. When it involved major action the Greens hit hard and fast, engaging in hand-to-hand combat and trusting in the resourcefulness and personal initiative of their commanders. If they induced confusion and panic such tactics paid off, but if they did not they exposed the Greens to crushing losses from the superior fire and manpower of the Reds. What the Greens sought to avoid above all else was a formal pitched battle. On this point all observers agree. "Almost never did they take our attacks." In general it was a question of attrition tactics, of seeking to wear down a superior foe.

In order to forestall attack after an action had disclosed their whereabouts or in case of a reverse the Greens split into small groups, scattering over the woods or slipping back to the farms, only to rendezvous again at some previously fixed point of assembly to which the staff had directly repaired. Or numbers of them might stay together but shift their base to some other area. In any event they were not to be found where they had been. Once off the battlefield it was almost impossible to catch them, not only because of their swiftness and the sympathy of the population but also because of the admirable espionage system which kept them much better informed of the movements of the Reds than the Soviet commanders were of their own. The espionage system could also be used in reverse—to spread rumors about their location or destination so as to send the enemy off on a false scent or else royally to confuse him until he would not know what to believe.[112]

The impression should not be left, however, that in these hit-and-run operations the Greens had it all their own way. They, too, had their troubles. To ford or to bridge a deep river like the Vorona was not a simple task and to cross a railroad was especially dangerous. The river at least would have many bends but the railroad tended to be a long, straight cut through the forest or brush, opening up a distant line of vision for enemy observers. Worse still, the defenders of the peasantry risked falling under the guns of armored trains that cruised about in Tambov and neighboring provinces after the first civil war had ended in November 1920 and Wrangel had departed the scene. And so they learned to go over an embankment in extended order, in small groups, and at a rapid gait.[113]

They held up least well under air attack, according to a Soviet military commentator. Since rifle or machine gun fire upon an airplane demanded great experience, knowledge, and self-possession, an aviator risked nothing in attacking the Greens unless his motor failed, as in the case of commander Tishchenko.[114] When subjected to a hail of bullets and grenades from above they grew terrified and their detachments lost any semblance of battle-worthiness. The ground troops only had to move in and take them individually like so many stranded, flopping fish. The commentator compared the impact of an air attack to a "thunderbolt on the head." He exulted in the experience and thought the answer to "banditry" had been found.[115]

Despite the disparity in means of combat, it was the Reds who were long kept off balance and who underwent a string of humiliations until their advantages finally told in their favor.

Speaking of the Greens in general, and under the whip of Lenin's impatience, Red Army chief of staff S. S. Kamenev dwelt on the difficulty of contending with such groups in the midst of a sympathetic populace which enveloped the harassed Reds like air and exposed them to attack from the rear as well as from the flanks. Numerous adherents of the rebellion seeped into the military structure along every fissure or seam, sapping, subverting, and sabotaging. The damage wrought would surface suddenly where least it was expected.[116] Speaking of the Tambov Greens in particular, the commander of the military district that embraced Kirsanov explained to a conference of the Communist party how hard the struggle was and how wearing on his troops, with Antonov using every known method of guerrilla warfare at the head of bands which had mastered the terrain and which dissolved into thin air after each engagement. The Green tactics frayed the nerves of their Red pursuers, the overstrain and frustration induced an unfavorable mood—in other words, the Red units tended to become demoralized.[117]

There was only one way out for the Communists, and that was to make an unequal struggle more unequal still. They would finally reach this conclusion; but before recounting the story of the insurrection it is necessary to deal with such remaining aspects of tactics as deception, depredations, and decimation, with reference to the ruses of a cause that could live only by the use of skill and wits, and with reference to the specific objects of its wrath and to the victims it had chosen.

The Soviet court historian says with a mixture of honesty and self-righteousness that the numerically-inferior Greens, lacking sufficient arms and bereft of the advanced techniques of mass destruction, fell back on the arsenal of age-old peasant cunning.[118] Treachery and trickery permeated their operations, and a cruel type of warfare was made more cruel still by the stratagems and snares so prevalent everywhere. Depredations were committed under the guise of Red soldiers and redress made as Greens to win themselves sympathy. Two forces moved along parallel roads, one posing as Reds and the other as Greens, the first behaving abominably and the second in exemplary fashion—yet both were segments of Antonov's army. After a Green raid on a village under Soviet control life would be frozen and the Soviet personnel in hiding. Presently men appeared in leather jackets and Red Army caps and asked for the chairman of the local soviet. He was reproached for inactivity and ordered to convene the soviet. When its members had assembled they were asked whether all were there, and once all were accounted for they were told to stand against the wall; thus a village would be without a soviet.[119] We are assured, however, that Antonov did not misuse the Soviet uniform as much as did Makhno in abusing the population.[120]

Needless to say, Green propaganda abounded in lies like any other propaganda. Successes were trumpeted and weaknesses concealed; every effort was made to disparage the Soviet in an effort to stir doubt in the peasant mind as to its stability and to afford further stimulus for volunteers to come forward.[121] Wild claims were made about seventeen provinces being in rebel hands, about the fall of Moscow, about the invulnerability of Antonov, and so on, at the same time that news of the repression at Kronstadt was withheld from the Green army.[122] Thus the leaders were not above deceiving their own followers, as also in the case of the Cossacks-are-coming legend woven about the name of a certain Ataman Frolov who materialized only toward the end of the insurrection in the form of a Red stratagem which dosed the Greens with their own medicine.[123]

As to depredations, they were at first directed against Soviet institutions of various types and description, above all against those in any way connected with collectivized farming—a very clear reflection of the character of the Green movement. State farms or *sovkhozes*, collective farms, and communes drew the lightning like nothing else and the night sky over Tambov, Kirsanov, and Borisoglebsk *uezds* was lit up by flames arising from their installations. Hard after them came the assembly points for grain and other produce taken from the peasantry. These were mercilessly ransacked; if time allowed, the peasants were summoned to take back the "tribute" levied upon them and the Greens assisted; without time the torch might be applied—in a country on the verge of one of the great famines of history, or already in it.

Next in line of attack were the soviets themselves, their quarters, their personnel, and especially their papers and the records containing information about what had been extorted from the population—the same instinct that had prompted French peasants to plunder *chateaux* and American mobs to burn courthouses. The Greens also went after court records; they ravished the judicial apparatus and paralyzed the functioning of courts in the three main *uezds* of the insurrection and partially in Usman *uezd* during 1921. Cultural centers seem to have suffered less, aside from the reading rooms established by the Soviet regime. The official historian includes schools on the list of devastations,[124] but as other sources say little or nothing about them, the question may be left open. In any event, cultural institutions probably suffered more as propaganda centers than as dispensaries of learning. Violent dismantling of the whole Soviet set-up was the rule wherever the Greens prevailed.

As might be expected, the communication system sustained severe and repeated damage at their hands. They pulled down telegraph lines, burned railroad stations, wrecked freight trains, sent locomotives over embankments, and in general played merry hell with the steel strips linking the seats of Soviet power with the fertile southeast. Sometimes the work was carried out with non-Russian thoroughness, as when over a stretch of ten to fifteen *versts* of the Tambov–Balashov line the tracks were torn up and the rails ruined by harnessing teams of horses to bend them—presumably against trees.[125] The Communists complained that the Southeastern Railway had been severed and the hauling of grain to the center impeded[126]—probably the most intolerable of all the Green depredations in the eyes of the masters of Moscow. Somehow Antonov's men found the means of blowing up such obviously vulnerable targets as railroad bridges, though there is no way of telling how many were destroyed or how the explosives were obtained.

The ravaging extended to at least one sizable textile mill and to other unnamed enterprises. The Greens must have had a sweet tooth in view of their marked predilection for raiding beet-sugar plants. Thus on 19 November 1920 Antonov's men mounted a major attack on the Novo Pokrovsk sugar refinery and took it by storm in a deft operation.[127] Sugar-seeking did not attain the epic proportions registered in the Ukraine in conjunction with Makhno's and other operations,[128] probably because there were in Tambov so many fewer plants to seize. Last, not least, there was the prize no Russian army could forego—distilleries. Despite everything, some were still in operation and nothing could lessen the interest in their product. Several were raided inside Tambov province and the most distant undertaking of Antonov's army—the furthest it ventured from home base and its deepest penetration of enemy territory—was marked by the seizure of one distillery and two state farms in Chembar *uezd* of Penza province.[129]

The Communists have acknowledged that Antonov directed his plundering and punitive expeditions in the first instance against Soviet institutions or enterprises while refraining as a matter of policy from despoiling the peasantry. When the public sector had been so thoroughly plundered as to yield nothing more, the incidence of depredations fell increasingly on the peasantry.[130] November 1920 is cited as the time when raids on state farms and the like reached the point of diminishing returns. Just how despoliation of the peasantry squares with kulak direction of the uprising is not readily apparent, since kulaks would be the peasants most worth despoiling. But it is as useless to expect logic in the available sources as to expect accurate statistics.

The Borisoglebsk *uezd* committee of the Communist party reported to the central committee in December 1920 the sowing of panic among the population in villages under "bandit" control.[131] It seems too early to make this charge. At the end of 1920 and well into 1921 peasants were cooperating with the Greens, not because of intimidation but because they wanted to. Later, it is true—in the degenerative phase of the insurrection after the promulgation of the New Economic Policy and the appointment of Tukhachevski—the element of coercion came to the fore and the exactions of the Greens weighed heavily on the peasantry, above all in respect to the draft of horses. It was then that Antonov's men resorted to such desperate, last-throe measures as forbidding peasants to plow and to sow and flogging them on the abdomen if they did.[132]

Even then, however, the charges of arson and well-poisoning appear to be false.[133] They do not accord with objective facts. Russia was swept by forest fires at the time, no doubt some of them of incendiary origin inspired by hatred of the regime, but most of them due to the hot and hateful pulsation of the desert of Central

Asia. Iuri Steklov sounded the alarm in his newspaper—he had so many occasions for alarm in the years of his editorship—and pointed the accusing finger at "bandits" motivated by considerations of strategy, plunder, or rage.[134] But for Tambov province, at least, his accusation is disproved by his own newspaper. A table shows only a slight loss from forest fires in the province during the period from 15 April to 15 July 1921 when the most desperate fighting was taking place and the Greens would have been most prone to resort to tactics of despair: only 40 fires and 573 *desiatinas* of forest burned over as against 1,337 fires and 59,155 *desiatinas* lost in the province of Nizhni Novgorod.[135]

There were, of course, more forests to burn on the middle Volga, but not in the ratio of one hundred to one, and the figures make it clear that in Tambov the factor of arson pretty well may be disregarded. The Greens would have been crazy to burn their means of concealment, of which they had all too little in any event. Nor in the face of so dreadful a drought would they have poisoned a well at any place where they thought they might pass again. And where could they get the poison? Peasants and deserters are not manufacturing chemists, and on their raids it would not be poison that they bore away.

Under the heading of decimation we have chosen to consider the categories of the population most likely to be killed by the Greens in the course of the savage warfare. Communists and Soviet personnel naturally headed the list. More specifically, the Greens liked nothing better than to get their hands on Che-kists and members of the food-collecting agencies. Once, at Inzhavino in Kirsanov *uezd,* they captured the entire staff of the Tambov Che-ka on circuit, together with a group of executioners, and "cruelly disposed of them."[136] On another occasion, 4 May 1921, after taking the village of N., they seized thirty Soviet workers and hacked them to pieces.[137] But the recitation of horrors may be deferred to the chapters on operations.

The Greens also went after members of the Communist youth league or Komsomol, either to repay cruelties or harassments perpetrated by these youngsters or because their fanaticism and stupidity rendered them easy prey. As for the simple soldier, Soviet sources—as may be imagined—convey the impression that torture and death awaited him at the hands of the Greens. Yet the latter were doing what they could to encourage the enemy rank and file to desert or to come over to their side.[138] Here was another of the contradictions in which this study abounds.

It was resolved by Antonov-Ovseenko. The commissar of repression, surprisingly, does not repeat the Communist stereotype of atrocities committed on helpless prisoners. Instead he tells the truth—secretly to Lenin. He says that the Green command made a distinction between the rank and file Red Army men on the one hand and the officer personnel and especially Communist party members on the other. The former were usually given a pass and released with the recommendation to go home. The commanders and the Communists were killed with torture.[139] It would be interesting to know what proportion of the released rank and file heeded the injunction and succeeded in escaping the slaughter, and what proportion returned or were dragged back into the service.

The Greens could only have done as the commissar says, for they could not maintain prisoner-of-war camps. Compelled to adopt the tactics of the weaker side, engaging in hit-and-run maneuvers, they could not be burdened with the care of prisoners—even less than with care of their own wounded. These were major handicaps in a conflict marked by butchery on both sides and tempered only by the release system practised by the Greens out of necessity or out of propaganda considerations. The reader is not to infer that Red Army men were never the victims of excesses. It seems clear that they were. But such instances were apparently more often the result of the Greens leaving captives in the hands of the peasants who were capable of any barbarity. On their behalf it can only be said that a thousand years of history had taught them little else.[140]

Notes

1. S. E., "Antonovshchina," *Izvestiia*, no. 122 (1561), 3 June 1922, p. 2.
2. Tukhachevski, "Zapiska," 16 July 1921, p. 1.
3. Cited in Trifonov, *Klassy i klassovaia bor'ba*, part 1, p. 56.
4. Podbelski, "Predsedateliu moskovskogo soveta r. i k. deputatov," p. 2; anonymous (Podbelski), *Kak tambovskie krest'iane boriatsia za svobodu*, pp. 2–3, 6.
5. *Obvinitel'noe zakliuchenie po delu tsentral'nogo komiteta p. s.-r.*, p. 43. The documents consisted of proclamations of an SR *uezd* (Tambov?) committee and of manifestos of the Tambov provincial committee of the STK. They were even presented at the SR trial in 1922 and appear to be genuine. See also—and more specifically—"Protsess pravykh eserov," *Izvestiia*, no. 153 (1592), 12 July 1922, p. 2.
6. Fomichev (Lidin), "Antonovshchina: Iz vospominanii antonovtsa" (Santiago de Chile, 1955), pp. 12–13, 30.
7. "Antonovshchina," *Sovetskaia istoricheskaia entsiklopediia*, vol. 1, p. 636. For action of the Central Committee, see above, chapter five.
8. See Zybko, *Tambovskaia partiinaia organizatsiia*, p. 36.
9. Leonidov, "Eshche ob eserakh v Tambovskoi gub.," *Izvestiia*, no. 155 (1594), 14 July 1922, p. 3.
10. "Sud nad eserami: Esery vozglavliali banditskoe dvizhenie Antonova," *Pravda*, no. 153, 12 July 1922, p. 4; "Protsess pravykh eserov," *Izvestiia*, no. 153 (1592), 12 July 1922, p. 2. Here—and here alone, it seems—will be found both the Bogoliubski testimony and the gist of the report of the Tambov delegation to the September 1920 SR party conference, insofar as the Soviet press cared to reproduce it.
11. Testimony of Bogoliubski in *Pravda* as cited in note 10 above. *Pravda* prints the third village as Kopytovo, but its name should be as given in the text.
12. *Put' Bor'by* vol. 2, p. 24, as cited under the title *Antonovshchina* in Trifonov, *Klassy i klassovaia bor'ba*, part 1, p. 93.
13. "Sud nad eserami: Esery vozglavliali banditskoe dvizhenie Antonova," *Pravda*, no. 153, 12 July 1922, p. 4.
14. "Protsess pravykh eserov," *Izvestiia*, no. 153 (1592), 12 July 1922, p. 2.
15. Testimony of Bogoliubski as cited above, notes 10–14.
16. Antonov-Ovseenko, "O banditskom dvizhenii v Tambovskoi gubernii," p. 6.
17. *Iz istorii Vserossiiskoi Chrezvychainoi Komissii 1917–1921 gg.*, no. 333, p. 456.

18. In the case of the district in Tambov *uezd* centering around the aggressive village of Khitrovo, five *volosts* were included. See anonymous (Podbelski), *Kak tambovskie krest'iane boriatsia za svobodu*, p. 3.

19. From report of the Tambov delegation to the SR conference, September 1920, in "Sud nad eserami: Esery vozglavliali banditskoe dvizhenie Antonova," *Pravda*, no. 153, 12 July 1922, p. 4.

20. Donkov, "Organizatsiia razgroma antonovshchiny," *Voprosy Istorii KPSS*, no. 6 (June 1966), p. 62.

21. *Obvinitel'noe zakliuchenie po delu tsentral'nogo komiteta p. s.-r.*, p. 44.

22. Commander B. Shneerson, former head of the Fifth Military District of Tambov province, "Neskol'ko slov o tambovskom esero-banditizme" [Some words about SR banditry in Tambov], *Izvestiia*, no. 118 (1557), 30 May 1922, p. 2; S. E., "Antonovshchina," *Izvestiia*, no. 122 (1561), 3 June 1922, p. 2; Trifonov, *Klassy i klassovaia bor'ba*, part 1, p. 56. On the organizational hierarchy, see Leonidov, "Eshche ob eserakh v Tambovskoi gub.," *Izvestiia*, no. 155 (1594), 14 July 1922, p. 3; Antonov-Ovseenko, "O banditskom dvizhenii v Tambovskoi gubernii," pp. 6-7. Antonov-Ovseenko says the local committees of the union were elected by village assemblies. He does not say how the committees on the four higher levels were chosen.

23. S. E., "Antonovshchina," *Izvestiia*, no. 122 (1561), 3 June 1922, p. 2.

24. See chapter four.

25. "Sud nad eserami: Esery vozglavliali banditskoe dvizhenie Antonova," *Pravda*, no. 153, 12 July 1922, p. 4.

26. Ibid. Bogoliubski was referring specifically to the provincial peasant or STK conference and to the SR party conference in July 1920, at which representatives of the non-partisan peasantry were brought in. See above.

27. "Protsess pravykh eserov,"/*Izvestiia*, no. 153 (1592), 12 July 1922, p. 2. See also above, note 5.

28. *Obvinitel'noe zakliuchenie po delu tsentral'nogo komiteta p. s.-r.*, p. 44. Ishin's testimony is compressed into one short but valuable paragraph. He could not have been wholly correct about the two committees having the same personnel—the Left SR Tokmakov was on the STK committee, in fact, for a time was its head—unless the reference to fusion mentioned above is to be taken literally, and that would be going too far. For while the insurrection may have induced cooperation locally between the two SR parties, it certainly did not end their schism nationally.

29. On the duties or functions of the STK, see especially Antonov-Ovseenko, "O banditskom dvizhenii v Tambovskoi gubernii," p. 7; Leonidov, "Esche ob eserakh v Tambovskoi gub.," *Izvestiia*, no. 155 (1594), 14 July 1922, p. 3; Shneerson, "Neskol'ko slov o tambovskom esero-banditizme," *Izvestiia*, no. 118 (1557), 30 May 1922, p. 2; Donkov, "Organizatsiia razgroma antonovshchiny," *Voprosy Istorii KPSS*, no. 6 (June 1966), p. 63. All four sources are authoritative, albeit hostile, and the first three are primary.

30. V. Alekseev, *Oktiabr' i grazhdanskaia voina v TsChO* [October and the civil war in the Central Black Earth Region] (Voronezh, 1932), pp. 104-5.

31. See Trifonov, *Klassy i klassovaia bor'ba*, part 1, p. 111; cf. ibid., p. 109.

32. Antonov-Ovseenko, "O banditskom dvizhenii v Tambovskoi gubernii," pp. 9–10.

33. "Banditskie prestupleniia partii eserov: Antonovshchina: Iz besedy s genshtabistom t. Davydovym," *Pravda*, no. 116, 27 May 1922, p. 3; Trifonov, *Klassy i klassovaia bor'ba*, part 1, p. 110.

34. D. Petrovski, "Borba s banditizmom i krasnye kursanty," *Izvestiia*, no. 133 (1276), 23 June 1921, p. 1.

35. Anonymous (Podbelski), *Kak tambovskie krest'iane boriatsia za svobodu*, pp. 8–9.

36. Hirschfeld, "Tambovskii krovopodtek," *Izvestiia*, no. 247 (1390), 3 November 1921, p. 1.

37. Alekseev, *Oktiabr' i grazhdanskaia voina v TsChO*, p. 105.

38. "Zelenye" [The Greens], *Posledniia Novosti*, 2 September 1922, p. 3, based in turn on an article by a Soviet military observer in *Revoliutsionnyi Front*.

39. For example, Boguslavski's First Army of four regiments was estimated to be two thousand strong on the eve of its extinction. See Trifonov, *Klassy i klassovaia bor'ba*, part 1, p. 255. For a similar ratio in another connection see Strygin, *Rasplata*, p. 347.

40. Petrovski, "Bor'ba s banditizmom i krasnye kursanty," *Izvestiia*, no. 133 (1276), 23 June 1921, p. 1.

41. Antonov-Ovseenko, "O banditskom dvizhenii v Tambovskoi gubernii," p. 7; Donkov, "Organizatsiia razgroma antonovshchiny," *Voprosy Istorii KPSS*, no. 6 (June 1966), p. 63; Trifonov, *Klassy i klassovaia bor'ba*, part 1, pp. 109–10.

42. Antonov-Ovseenko, "O banditskom dvizhenii v Tambovskoi gubernii," p. 7; Trifonov, *Klassy i klassovaia bor'ba*, part 1, p. 112.

43. Leonidov, "Eshche ob eserakh v Tambovskoi gub.," *Izvestiia*, no. 155 (1594), 14 July 1922, p. 3; Donkov, "Organizatsiia razgroma antonovshchiny," *Voprosy Istorii KPSS*, no. 6 (June 1966), p. 63.

44. Antonov-Ovseenko, "O banditskom dvizhenii v Tambovskoi gubernii," p. 9.

45. "Ekh, nekhvataet nam tochnosti!" *Izvestiia*, no. 289 (1432), 23 December 1921, p. 1. Trotski saw the curse of the past in the circumstance that the country was knee-deep—or even deeper—in shiftlessness during an era of socialist revolution "which ought to transform the entire economy into one combined factory where the [mechanical] teeth engage with the accuracy of the mechanism of a timepiece." Fifty years later the teeth still do not so engage.

46. Trifonov, *Klassy i klassovaia bor'ba*, part 1, pp. 109–10.

47. Borisov, *Chernym letom*, p. 38.

48. Trifonov, *Klassy i klassovaia bor'ba*, part 1, p. 110.

49. Antonov-Ovseenko, "O banditskom dvizhenii v Tambovskoi gubernii," p. 9.

50. "Antonovshchina," *Sovetskaia istoricheskaia entsiklopediia*, vol. 1, p. 636.

51. "Krest'ianskoe dvizhenie," *Volia Rossii*, no. 172, 8 April 1921, p. 1.

52. *Put' Bor'by* (citation lost through seizure of notes, but given as p. 13 of vol. 2, *Antonovshchina*, by Trifonov; my recollection is that the figure bobs up in a number of places in this collaborative work); Borisov, *Chernym letom*, p. 38; Garri, "Grigorii Kotovskii," in *Polkovodtsy grazhdanskoi voiny* (Moscow, 1960), p. 192; "Antonovshchina," *Sovetskaia istoricheskaia entsiklopediia*, vol. 1, p. 636; M.

Kubanin, "Antonovshchina," *Bol'shaia sovetskaia entsiklopediia*, 1st ed., vol. 3 (1930) p. 99; Trifonov, *Klassy i klassovaia bor'ba*, part 1, p. 4; Shatov, "Tambovskie vosstaniia" [The Tambov insurrections], *Novoe Russkoe Slovo*, 15 February 1966; Srechinski, "Zapechatannaia stranitsa," *Novoe Russkoe Slovo*, 26 February 1969. The 2nd edition of the *Bol'shaia sovetskaia entsiklopediia* gives no figures. See "Antonovshchina," vol. 2 (1950), p. 528. The 3rd edition repeats the conventional figure of fifty thousand; Trifonov, "Antonovshchina," vol. 2 (1970), p. 96, col. 276.

53. Antonov-Ovseenko, "O banditskom dvizhenii v Tambovskoi gubernii," p. 9. The reader must beware of confusing the protagonists because of the similarity of their names.

54. Donkov, "Organizatsiia razgroma antonovshchiny," *Voprosy Istorii KPSS*, no. 6 (June 1966), p. 60. This number is based on *Put' Bor'by*, vol. 2, p. 39, which he cites as *Antonovshchina*, as well as upon the *Otchet narodnogo komissariata po voennym delam za 1921 god* (Moscow, 1922), p. 172.

55. Donkov, "Organizatsiia razgroma antonovshchiny," *Voprosy Istorii KPSS*, no. 6 (June 1966), p. 60, n. 5.

56. Trifonov, *Klassy i klassovaia bor'ba*, part 1, pp. 4, 110. The first figure comes from one knows not where; the second is taken from *Put' Bor'by*, vol. 2, p. 13 (cited as *Antonovshchina*), and the third from the same source, p. 78. As Donkov's estimate of thirty thousand comes from p. 39, we have three different figures from the same basic compendium—although presumably not from the same contributor—and there may have been others.

57. Alekseev, *Oktiabr' i grazhdanskaia voina v TsChO*, p. 106.

58. See Shatov, "Tambovskie vosstaniia," *Novoe Russkoe Slovo*, 15 February 1966.

59. "Antonovshchina," *Sovetskaia istoricheskaia entsiklopediia*, vol. 1, p. 636.

60. Fomichev (Lidin), "Antonovshchina: Iz vospominanii antonovtsa" (Santiago de Chile, 1955), pp. 17, 31.

61. Ibid., p. 39.

62. Anonymous (Podbelski), *Kak tambovskie krest'iane boriatsia za svobodu*, p. 8. He admits some increase in strength in 1921 (ibid., p. 9).

63. Tukhachevski, "Zapiska," 16 July 1921, pp. 1, 2.

64. The Kotovski cavalry brigade, for example, is said to have consisted of two regiments and a horse battery with nine hundred sabers and three cannon (from the Central State Archives of the Soviet army, as given in Trifonov, *Klassy i klassovaia bor'ba*, part 1, pp. 249, 254). But for once we can emancipate ourselves from such unsatisfactory reporting of archival material. We have the actual report of Smirnov, chief of the political section of Kotovski's brigade. As of 1–5 August 1921, at the end of the campaign, the first cavalry regiment had 360 sabers out of the 696 it was supposed to have. In the case of the second regiment, he simply states that it had 537 men, for a total of 897 soldiers in the brigade at that moment. The horse battery numbered 199. See *G. I. Kotovskii: dokumenty i materialy k istorii grazhdanskoi voiny v SSSR* [G. I. Kotovski: documents and materials on the history of the civil war in the Soviet Union], L. M. Chizhova et al., eds. (Kishinev, 1956), no. 284, pp. 366–68. For a previous report some ten days earlier see ibid., no. 280, p. 358.

65. Antonov-Ovseenko, "O banditskom dvizhenii v Tambovskoi gubernii," p. 14.

66. Borisov, *Chernym letom*, p. 33. See also *Put' Bor'by*, passim.

67. Alexeev, *Oktiabr' i grazhdanskaia voina v TsChO*, pp. 105–6.

68. Antonov-Ovseenko, "O banditskom dvizhenii v Tambovskoi gubernii," p. 9.

69. From the Central State Archives of the Soviet army (TsGASA), folio 7, as cited in Trifonov, *Klassy i klassovaia bor'ba*, part 1, p. 112.

70. Ibid.

71. Petrovski, "Bor'ba s banditizmom i krasnye kursanty," *Izvestiia*, no. 133 (1276), 23 June 1921, p. 1.

72. Dokunin, "Tambovskii schet sotsial-banditam," *Pravda*, no. 123, 4 June 1922, p. 3. Another source asserts that the "SR cells" were really Antonov's, that there were more than ten of them in two *uezds* (no date is specified), and that they were ephemeral. See anonymous (Podbelski), *Kak tambovskie krest'iane boriatsia za svobodu*, p. 6. Only the first part of the assertion is correct. Antonov certainly had more than ten or so cells in the two *uezds* of Kirsanov and Tambov, and certainly the original cells dating from 1918 were anything but ephemeral—over two years later the arms entrusted to their safekeeping were still there and ready for use.

73. *Put' Bor'by*, volume and page numbers lost; Leonidov, "Eshche ob eserakh v Tambovskoi gub.," *Izvestiia*, no. 155 (1594), 14 July 1922, p. 3; Borisov, *Chernym letom*, p. 37; Sofinov, *Ocherki istorii Vserossiiskoi Chrezvychainoi Komissii (1917–1922 gg.)* [Outline history of the All-Russian Extraordinary Commission, 1917–1922] (Moscow, 1960), p. 224; Trifonov, *Klassy i klassovaia bor'ba*, part 1, p. 55; Kubanin, "Antonovshchina," *Bol'shaia sovetskaia entsiklopediia*, 1st ed., vol. 3, p. 99. Leonidov does say that machine guns figured in the windfall Antonov amassed at the expense of the Czechs (and of the Soviet government). He errs in having the Czechs divested of their arms as they passed through Kozlov; Antonov did not operate in Kozlov in 1918, but in Kirsanov.

74. Tukhachevski, "Zapiska," p. 1.

75. "Banditskie prestupleniia partii eserov: Iz besedy s genshtabistom t. Davydovym," *Pravda*, no. 116, 27 May 1922, p. 3. These revelations came from an SR of some eminence, evidently a member of the provincial committee of the STK, who had been taken prisoner by Davydov, chief of staff of the first military district under Tukhachevski. On penetration of the soviets and even of the Communist party, see also Borisov, *Chernym letom*, p. 36; Trifonov, *Klassy i klassovaia bor'ba*, part 1, p. 54; Dokunin, "Tambovskii schet sotsial-banditam," *Pravda*, no. 123, 4 June 1922, p. 3.

76. "Protsess pravykh eserov," *Izvestiia*, no. 142 (1581), 29 June 1922, p. 2.

77. Report on the tax in kind to a meeting of party workers of the Moscow area, 9 April 1921, in Lenin, *Polnoe sobranie sochinenii*, 5th ed., vol. 43, p. 153.

78. G. Neradov, "Zhizn' provintsii (Beglye ocherki): probuzhdenie 'zelenogo zmiia' " [Life in the provinces (cursory comments): the awakening of the 'green viper'], *Izvestiia*, no. 296 (1439), 31 December 1921, p. 2.

79. "Ot Moskovskoi Chrezvychainoi Komissii," *Izvestiia*, no. 294 (1437), 29 December 1921, p. 4.

80. Ibid.; Trifonov, *Klassy i klassovaia bor'ba*, part 1, pp. 150, 185, 186, with reference to White Russia, the Ukraine, and Ukhta *uezd* in Karelia.

81. "Boiazn' vosstanii" [The fear of uprisings], *Volia Rossii*, no. 79, 15 December 1920, p. 4, quoting a special decree in the Soviet press.

82. Trifonov, *Klassy i klassovaia bor'ba*, part 1, p. 111, based on information in the Central Party Archives.

83. Leonidov, "Eshche ob eserakh v Tambovskoi gub.," *Izvestiia*, no. 155 (1594), 14 July 1922, p. 3.

84. Scattered information about the state of Green armaments may be found in Fomichev (Lidin), "Antonovshchina: Iz vospominanii antonovtsa" (Santiago de Chile, 1955), pp. 31, 43; ibid. (Philippines, 1950–1951), p. 23; Antonov-Ovseenko, "O banditskom dvizhenii v Tambovskoi gubernii," p. 7; Trifonov, *Klassy i klassovaia bor'ba*, part 1, pp. 110–12; Srechinski, "Zapechatannaia stranitsa," *Novoe Russkoe Slovo*, 26 April 1969.

85. "Sud nad eserami: Esery vozglavliali banditskoe dvizhenie Antonova," *Pravda*, no. 153, 12 July 1922, p. 4; "Protsess pravykh eserov," *Izvestiia*, no. 153 (1592), 12 July 1922, p. 2; *Obvinitel'noe zakliuchenie po delu tsentral'nogo komiteta p. s.-r.*, p. 44. The information is drawn from the testimony of A. S. Bogoliubski.

86. Antonov-Ovseenko, "O banditskom dvizhenii v Tambovskoi gubernii," p. 9.

87. Tukhachevski, "Zapiska," p. 2.

88. *Put' Bor'by*, vol. 2, *Antonovshchina*, page unknown but at the end.

89. Antonov-Ovseenko, "O banditskom dvizhenii v Tambovskoi gubernii," p. 7. See also references to the subject in Donkov, "Organizatsiia razgroma antonovshchiny," *Voprosy Istorii KPSS*, no. 6 (June 1966), p. 63; Trifonov, *Klassy i klassovaia bor'ba*, part 1, p. 110.

90. Here are two of the twenty numbered regiments, a list of which apparently does not exist except in the archives of repression.

91. Leonidov, "Eshche ob eserakh v Tambovskoi gub.," *Izvestiia*, no. 155 (1594), 14 July 1922, p. 3. Only in the rarest instances can the veil of darkness and uncertainty that overhangs the Green cause be pierced with the aid of such definite information.

92. Borisov, *Chernym letom*, p. 47.

93. Dokunin, "Tambovskii schet sotsial banditam," *Pravda*, no. 123, 4 June 1922, p. 4.

94. "Deistviia i razporiazheniia pravitel'stva" [Actions and decrees of the government], *Izvestiia*, no. 280 (1423), 13 December 1921, p. 2.

95. "Pivovarenie i prodazha piva" [Beer brewing and the sale of beer], *Izvestiia*, no. 286 (1429), 20 December 1921, p. 2.

96. Trifonov, *Klassy i klassovaia bor'ba*, part 1, p. 111.

97. Antonov-Ovseenko, "O banditskom dvizhenii v Tambovskoi gubernii," p. 28.

98. See above.

99. See above, chapter four. In the material studied in Moscow there may have been reference to a small field or ambulatory hospital for Antonov's troops as there

certainly was to a small field church. If so, such an installation could have done little to alleviate conditions, since imminent danger of betrayal, detection, and capture would have impeded its operations. It must be remembered that there was no fixed point in the possession of the Greens which the Reds could not occupy if they so desired. And an ambulatory hospital could have been only a tiny affair, sufficient at best for officers but not for their men.

100. "Na mestakh: Bor'ba s banditizmom," *Izvestiia*, no. 177 (1320), 12 August 1921, p. 3. The report is reprinted in the SR organ in Prague under the heading "Soobshchenie *Izvestii* o zagovorakh," *Volia Rossii*, no. 290, 27 August 1921, p. 4. For the Left SR banner, see above.

101. Fomichev (Lidin), "Antonovshchina: Iz vospominanii antonovtsa" (Santiago de Chile, 1955), p. 39.

102. S. E., "Na mestakh: Konets esero-bandita Antonova," *Izvestiia*, no. 145 (1584), 2 July 1922, p. 4.

103. Borisov, *Chernym letom*, p. 11.

104. Fomichev (Lidin), "Antonovshchina: Iz vospominanii antonovtsa" (Santiago de Chile, 1955), p. 21.

105. Okninski, *Dva goda sredi krest'ian*, p. 312.

106. Zybko, *Tambovskaia partiinaia organizatsiia*, p. 38; Trifonov, *Klassy i klassovaia bor'ba*, part 1, p. 109.

107. Borisov, *Chernym letom*, p. 12; Trifonov, *Klassy i klassovaia bor'ba*, part 1, pp. 111, 112.

108. Antonov-Ovseenko, "O banditskom dvizhenii v Tambovskoi gubernii," p. 9.

109. On the subject of melting away into the populace, see also anonymous (Podbelski), *Kak tambovskie krest'iane boriatsia za svobodu*, pp. 8–9; Borisov, *Chernym letom*, pp. 11–12.

110. But see Trifonov, *Klassy i klassovaia bor'ba*, part 1, p. 111, where it is stated that they usually moved as a column with a cavalry screen fore and aft and scouts further out.

111. "Zelenye," *Posledniia Novosti*, 2 September 1922, p. 3. What is said applies to the Green movement in general; no specific area of insurrection is mentioned.

112. Antonov-Ovseenko, "O banditskom dvizhenii v Tambovskoi gubernii," p. 9; Zybko, *Tambovskaia partiinaia organizatsiia*, p. 37; Sofinov, *Ocherki istorii Vserossiiskoi Chrezvychainoi Komissii*, p. 224; Okninski, *Dva goda sredi krest'ian*, p. 312; Trifonov, *Klassy i klassovaia bor'ba*, part 1, pp. 111–13; Srechinski, "Zapechatannaia stranitsa," *Novoe Russkoe Slovo*, 26 April 1969; Shatov, "Tambovskie vosstaniia," *Novoe Russkoe Slovo*, 15 February 1966; Borisov, *Chernym letom*, passim.

113. A little on this—only a suggestion—in Trifonov, *Klassy i klassovaia bor'ba*, part 1, p. 113.

114. For this grisly incident, see chapter eleven.

115. "Zelenye," *Posledniia Novosti*, 2 September 1922, p. 3. The commentator wrote in the Soviet journal, *Revoliutsionnyi Front*, whence the resumé in the Parisian organ of the Kadet party.

116. Report of 29 March 1921, contained in folio 7 of the Central State Archives of the Soviet army and summarized in Trifonov, *Klassy i klassovaia bor'ba*, part 1, p. 112.

117. Ibid., p. 113. From the Central Party Archives, folio 17.

118. Ibid., p. 112.

119. Hirschfeld, "Tambovskii krovopodtek," *Izvestiia*, no. 247 (1390), 3 November 1921, p. 1.

120. Trifonov, *Klassy i klassovaia bor'ba*, part 1, p. 108. See also ibid., p. 105.

121. Ibid., p. 105.

122. S. E., "Antonovshchina," *Izvestiia*, no. 122 (1561), 3 June 1922, p. 3.

123. Garri, "Kotovskii," *Polkovodtsy grazhdanskoi voiny*, p. 193. See below, chapter ten.

124. Trifonov, *Klassy i klassovaia bor'ba*, part 1, p. 118.

125. Borisov, *Chernym letom*, p. 39. The author, with American equipment in mind, would not have believed that rails could be bent with horse traction had he not observed the flimsy rails in use on many Russian lines as late as 1935 (and probably later).

126. "Antonovshchina," *Sovetskaia istoricheskaia entsiklopediia*, vol. 1, p. 636; Trifonov, "Antonovshchina," *Bol'shaia sovetskaia entsiklopediia*, 3rd ed., vol. 2, p. 96, col. 276.

127. See below, chapter eight.

128. See "Grabezhi i rekvizitsii na sakharnykh zavodakh pravoberezhnoi Ukrainy" [Plundering and requisitioning in respect to sugar plants of the right bank Ukraine], *Na chuzhoi storone*, vol. 3 (1923), pp. 131–36, especially ibid., pp. 132–33.

129. On Green depredations, see the *Volia Rossii*, no. 213, 27 May 1921, p. 3, quoting *Bednota* of 15 May 1921; anonymous (Podbelski), *Kak tambovskie krest'iane boriatsia za svobodu*, pp. 8, 12; Trifonov, *Klassy i klassovaia bor'ba*, part 1, pp. 105, 116–18, 121; Borisov, *Chernym letom*, p. 39; Antonov-Ovseenko, "O banditskom dvizhenii v Tambovskoi gubernii," p. 9; Dokunin, "Tambovskii schet sotsial-banditam," *Pravda*, no. 123, 4 June 1922, p. 3; Alekseev, *Oktiabr' i grazhdanskaia voina v TsChO*, p. 103; Sofinov, *Ocherki istorii Vserossiiskoi Chrezvychainoi Komissii*, p. 224; above all, *Put' Bor'by*, passim.

130. Donkov, "Organizatsiia razgroma antonovshchiny," *Voprosy Istorii KPSS*, no. 6 (June 1966), p. 63; Trifonov, *Klassy i klassovaia bor'ba*, part 1, pp. 105, 117.

131. Donkov, "Organizatsiia razgroma antonovshchiny," *Voprosy Istorii KPSS*, no. 6 (June 1966), p. 63.

132. S. E., "Antonovshchina," *Izvestiia*, no. 122 (1561), 3 June 1922, p. 3. Is S. E. guilty of exaggeration? The author is inclined to think that such incidents occurred, but only in the later phases of the insurrection. S. E. is indefinite as to the timing, though the context suggests a later date.

133. See Trifonov, *Klassy i klassovaia bor'ba*, part 1, p. 112.

134. "Pozhary ili podzhogi?" [Fires or arson?], *Izvestiia*, no. 103 (1246), 14 May 1921, p. 1.

135. "Lesnye pozhary" [Forest fires], *Izvestiia*, no. 174 (1317), 9 August 1921, p. 2.

136. Anonymous (Podbelski), *Kak tambovskie krest'iane boriatsia za svobodu*, p. 10. Most likely early in 1921.

137. *Izvestiia* of the Tambov provincial soviet executive committee, 18 May 1921, as cited in A. S. Esaulenko, *Revoliutsionnyi put' Kotovskogo* [The revolutionary road of G. I. Kotovski] (Kishinev, 1956), p. 129. The reader will notice that the name of the village is withheld.

138. Numerous manifestos calling for desertion are mentioned, among other sources in S. E., "Antonovshchina," *Izvestiia*, no. 122 (1561), 3 June 1922, pp. 2–3.

139. Antonov-Ovseenko, "O banditskom dvizhenii v Tambovskoi gubernii," p. 9.

140. On the subject of decimation, see also Donkov, "Organizatsiia razgroma antonovshchiny," *Voprosy Istorii KPSS*, no. 6 (June 1966), p. 63; Sofinov, *Ocherki istorii Vserossiiskoi Chrezvychainoi Komissii*, p. 224; Zybko, *Tambovskaia partiinaia organizatsiia*, p. 38; anonymous (Podbelski), *Kak tambovskie krest'iane boriatsia za svobodu*, p. 8. Both Soviet and anti-Soviet sources speak of the mass killing of Communists.

— 7 —

Prelude to Insurrection

We come now to the story of the insurrection. At the outset, the author had expected to compensate in some measure for analytical deficiencies by providing a clear narration of events, particularly of the military operations that contribute so much to the interest of history. The analytical deficiencies duly materialized, but the effort to reconstruct the course of the struggle led unexpectedly into a wasteland of uncertainty and distortion. The record of events is full of holes—and full of confusion between the holes.

The Soviet attempt to efface all traces of a development that gave the lie to the very name of "workers' and peasants' " regime does not alone account for the unsatisfactory state of affairs. An additional factor has been the obsession for military secrecy in Soviet publications, including the local accounts which otherwise could be of such assistance in a study of this kind—assuming that they would ever be made available. Thus the deletion in the Tambov newspaper of the name of the village where the above-mentioned atrocity occurred,[1] together with all the other deletions, would lead one to think he was reading a puzzle instead of a report. It may be suspected, however, that the overriding reason for the unsatisfactory record of military operations is Antonov himself; during nine of the ten months he held the field he made the Soviet state look so bad that its commissioned historians preferred not to fill out the record either at that time or more recently, after the lapse of two generations.

The story of the insurrection begins in the early part of 1918, in the era of collaboration between the Bolsheviks and the Left SRs when Antonov, as head of the militia in Kirsanov *uezd*, disarmed Czechoslovak units passing through on the Tambov–Saratov line and appropriated these military stores for his own use by diverting them to trusted village hideaways instead of stacking them in state repositories. Just as the time the Left SR Central Committee was concluding that collaboration was impossible with advocates of renewed enserfment and was using the Brest–Litovsk negotiations as the pretext for a rupture, the hard-bitten Left SR official in the sticks of Tambov province was concluding that the break would take the form of warfare to the hilt and was already laying the foundations of a peasant bid for power. Meanwhile the Volga Regional Committee of the regular SRs was also preparing for an uprising, in this case actually because of Brest–Litovsk, although it was hoped to use peasant grievances and the unions of front fighters which had merged in the country districts with SR organizations. The preparations extended to Tambov as well as to Penza, Saratov, and Samara provinces.[2]

Partly—or perhaps mainly—as a result of these activities, local SRs with the help of students and officers of the old army staged a coup in Tambov town on 17 June 1918 (midway between the insurrections on the Volga from May to early June and the Savinkov coup in Yaroslavl in early July) by taking advantage of a disgruntled lot of peasant recruits assembled on this first day of mobilization of the classes of 1892–1895 into the Red Army. The SRs achieved the *tour de force* of combining advocacy of the Constituent Assembly with the slogan of free elections to the soviets; but the turbulent recruits seem to have been more impressed by the emergence of Tsarist general Bogdanovich alongside the SR lieutenant Kocharovski, and in general by old-line officers donning their epaulets and buckling on their spurs. As a result they veered around to support the returning Communists and converted the coup into a fiasco.[3]

From both the Soviet and anti-Soviet sides attempts have been made to link this affair with what came later and to establish a pedigree for Antonov going back to these Populist intellectuals and White Guard officers.[4] Not a shred of evidence is adduced beyond the fact that it all occurred in the same province. And nothing else can be adduced because Antonov's movement sprang from a totally different line of development and owed nothing to this miserable affair of June 1918 which was part and parcel of the events culminating in the Samara regime of inglorious memory—with the same claim of redemption from betrayal to Germany, the same marriage of Populist snobbery to White Guard reaction, the same rootlessness in the population, and the same washout in the face of whatever resistance Moscow could muster.

Antonov's movement was Green, not pink and white; it was deeply rooted in the peasant matrix, it represented the joint enterprise of Left SRs and centrist SRs in the villages, it had nothing in common with Tsarist generals and urban intellectuals, and it held the field through ten months of bloodstained action. In no way can it be compared with the buffoonery of June 1918 which lasted for all of forty-two hours. Its forerunners were sporadic outbursts in the villages against Communist extortion. In the last analysis, the forerunner of Antonov was Antonov himself, since he had begun to assemble weapons well before the first food detachments appeared in the villages to evoke the initial wave of peasant resentment.

Where Antonov was in June 1918 we do not know, whether still in the office of chief of police of Kirsanov *uezd* or already in hiding as a fugitive from the Extraordinary Commission,[5] which in him met its match in both ruthlessness and resourcefulness. In any event, he had no hand in the foolishness in Tambov. Certainly by August 1918 he was in his place of refuge, imbued with implacable hostility toward the Soviet regime and determined to combat it—at first by petty acts of terrorism and later by more serious means.

All Soviet accounts—or nearly all—have him starting his activities in 1918 though they contribute little else to our knowledge. The most specific assigns him a band of one hundred fifty men at the outset of his "bandit" career, formed from the material at hand in the area where he had taken refuge—the villages of Inzhavino, Koptevo, Tugolukovo, and others with a solid kulak stratum. These kulaks are said to have been "quite prosperous," as no doubt they were by Soviet standards.[6] The three villages named would indicate that Antonov's initial activities were centered away from his normal habitat, out on the plain or at least on the edge of the open country. A second account providing some real information says Antonov habitually resided during this period in Ramza, Parevka, Kalugino, Karavaino, and Treskino,[7] indicating that his activities already centered in the woods and near the marshes and lakes of the Vorona valley.

Two lists have been given here and eight villages named without a single overlap—a discrepancy all too common in this study. Preference should be accorded the Vorona valley as the place affording more cover to which Antonov always repaired when hard-pressed and in which he played out the tragedy of his life and movement. That the two accounts have either hit the mark or come close to it is attested by the exceptional strength of Antonov's movement in all eight of the villages named.[8] There is some difficulty, however, from the Soviet point of view, and that is that the second list includes villages which are on poorer land and could not have had so many "prosperous" kulaks. But Soviet writers are not bothered by such contradictions or even aware of them: the kulak is always there as devil incarnate, whether the village is "rich" or poor.

All in all, and considering evidence too scattered, elusive, or indirect to be presented here, the large village of Inzhavino may be taken as the focal point of Antonov's activities in the beginning and all the way through. It was in the Vorona valley and was the natural link between the villages on the fertile plain of Tambov *uezd* and those in the forested and swampy areas along the Vorona in Kirsanov and a limited portion of Borisoglebsk *uezds*. Probably from here or from this vicinity Antonov launched his first attempt at insurrection before the end of 1918, an effort which the first-mentioned source—Leonidov—dismisses as of little consequence because the peasants did not follow him (not even the kulaks?). The second source—Dokunin—is silent as to any attempt at insurrection in 1918 on the part of this man with a "rich criminal past." Both sources agree, however, that Antonov gathered a small group of friends, deserters, kulaks, and criminals (Leonidov fixes the initial strength at one hundred fifty; Dokunin mentions no figure) to engage in occasional raids on soviets, state farms, and cooperatives, with attendant plunder and loss of life.

Elsewhere there is mention of a major revolt (October 1918) in the northern *uezds* spreading into Riazan and Penza provinces,[9] but it may be doubted that it was so major; in any case it did not involve Antonov whose strength in the beginning as in the end was concentrated in the south central and southeastern *uezds* of Tambov, Kirsanov, and Borisoglebsk, and never extended—even in diluted form—beyond Morshansk *uezd* in the north. Closer to the

Antonov territory but still not within it were the disorders that occurred at this time in Morshansk *uezd* itself, in the adjoining northernmost strip of Kirsanov *uezd*—particularly in the village of Rudovka—and in the southwestern reaches of Tambov *uezd*. The villages or *volosts* involved do not figure in the insurrection of 1920, Soviet documents establish no link with Antonov,[10] and the presumption—though not the certainty—is that these events of the fall of 1918 are spontaneous outbursts engineered by no one.[11] Our political commissar says that the "Antonov fire" first flared up in 1918—flared but not flamed—and that thereafter it smouldered until the "imperialist reaction" raked up the coals and blew upon them.[12] The last part of the statement is Communist hogwash but the first part is a fair description of the situation. By the end of 1918 Antonov was already a cockleburr but not yet a sore under the Soviet saddle.

Nineteen nineteen may be considered in general a year of smouldering, but toward the end the embers had produced a small but hot flame. The little band had grown, though by how much is a matter of choice among widely disparate estimates. The most authoritative credits Antonov with only one hundred men,[13] whereas the Soviet military source cited above (Leonidov)—which also must be taken seriously—had already given him one hundred fifty for the previous year. The other end of the sliding scale is represented by the assertion that at the end of 1919 Antonov had under his command several thousand "dark, befuddled" peasants.[14]

The novel is nothing if not eclectic: apparently the author was cognizant of these estimates—he could hardly have come on the figures himself—and has Antonov progress from ten to fifteen followers in the fall of 1918 to one hundred fifty in the winter of 1918–1919 and then to some six hundred fifty by the next winter as a result of organizing a number of deserters hiding out in places like his own. According to the novelist, Antonov had qualitative considerations in mind as well as quantitative, for he was devouring everything on which he could lay his hands concerning guerrilla warfare, particularly during the year 1812, having conceived a boundless admiration for the protagonists of that campaign—both for the great Emperor and for Kutuzov.[15] It makes a nice story. We have seen that Antonov was well read, but he must have had slim pickings in the swamps and hollows of the Inzhavino forest unless his SR friends had come to his aid. But the quantitative angle is hard enough without venturing into the qualitative; one is left with the impression that only Antonov himself could say how many men he had at this stage of his career, and he cannot be resurrected.

Whatever the number, he had put together a lethal force and was now fairly launched on the first of two main stages of his movement—the terrorist campaign directed against Soviet officials who either had made themselves loathsome or happened to be caught in his small but productive dragnet. Nineteen nineteen was the climax of the first civil war, the year of Denikin's drive against Moscow and of Mamontov's ride through Tambov. If Antonov strove for a deal with the Whites as Soviet fictional[16] and pseudo-historical accounts[17] have him doing, he did not lack in opportunity. But he was not lying low in the hope of reaching an accommodation with Denikin. Neither he nor the peasants were willing to raise an insurrection as long as the monarchists might be the beneficiaries. And he was not lying low. Instead, he was taking advantage of disturbed conditions for his own purposes.

Numerous scouting parties roved over the region as the lines of the civil war approached or actually extended into Tambov province. Some were Red, some were White, and some were neither. Under a Red guise, roving bands of Greens had taken the field to settle accounts with their enemies. They prowled at will and killed with impunity.[18] The attention of the Soviet government was riveted to the front; it had nothing to spare. In all likelihood pure anarchism prompted some of the actions while others reflected the will of Antonov. The latter type may have predominated, for Antonov is credited with the intent of decimating the food levy personnel and Communists in general.[19]

The campaign for the elimination of obnoxious or prominent Communists culminated in the killing on 14 October 1919 of M. D. Chichkanov, chairman of the Tambov soviet executive committee—in other words, the chief Soviet official in the province. The circumstances of his death are not clear. If the novel is correct in having him cut down by Antonov's staff officer while "peacefully hunting"[20] he must have been either a very brave or a very foolish man, as indeed he would have been even if—as historical sources intimate—he had gone in line of duty to investigate disorders, for he was killed in the Lake Ilmen[21] district of the Vorona valley in Kirsanov *uezd* in the heart of the Antonov country. From the Communist standpoint his action may be compared to entering a snake pit, and for once the Soviet accounts are credible when they attribute the deed to Antonov or to his entourage.[22]

The campaign of nagging terrorism exacted a not inconsiderable toll, some one hundred victims in Kirsanov *uezd* during the summer of 1919 or around two hundred for the year.[23] And it did inspire a certain terror in the ranks of the Soviet bureaucracy which found the swift, unpredictable blows "from behind the corner" all the more unnerving because the perpetrators could not be run to earth. The provincial authorities reacted as best they could by keeping Kirsanov *uezd* under martial law after lifting it elsewhere and by instituting a special mobile unit of the Che-ka with the offending *uezd* as its field of activity.[24]

By the end of the year the exploits of Antonov had begun to impinge upon the consciousness of Soviet authorities in Moscow. Announcing arrests among the SRs carried out on 28 December 1919, *Izvestiia* stated that a connection had been established between SRs and the detachment of deserters and bandits whose operations in Tambov province had damaged railway lines in the rear of the Red Army.[25] The damage actually was not only to the Red Army but as much—or even more—to the shipments of foodstuffs from the Volga to the northern centers of power. Antonov had already touched a raw nerve of the Soviet system which eventually would make him its chief target, but for the time being it was too preoccupied elsewhere to proceed against him and contented itself with ordering the provincial authorities to keep open the railroad to Saratov, to hold the towns, and to meet the grain quotas. Moscow was already conscious of a menace in Tambov but not yet of its proportions—or rather, of its potential. Thus its policy was one of containment, not eradication.[26]

The year 1920 first would witness a basic change in the situation and then the mass insurrection. The basic change came with the formation of the STK, this healthy offspring of the marriage of Antonov's initiative with SR enterprise. We have seen in the chapter on organization how the STK came into being, how—as best can be determined—Antonov himself formed the first cells of what was to be the civilian wing of the insurrection and then passed his work to the SRs and also to the Left SRs, who took to it like ducks to water. The misconception so assiduously propagated in Soviet literature that it was all the work of the SRs must be knocked out in the beginning to make way for the truth that it was a cooperative undertaking in which the roles of Antonov and of the Left SRs are of comparable—perhaps equal—importance with the role of the SRs. One hard fact in this swamp of uncertainty leaves no doubt on that score: Peter Tokmakov, Left SR and bosom friend of Antonov, headed the provincial committee of the STK until his assumption of a military command, and only then must the succession have passed to the SR G. N. Pluzhnikov. To stress this point is not at all to disparage SR influence: it was highly significant, possibly even predominant, but very far from being exclusive. The sanction extended by the SR Central Committee in May 1920 to a process already under way must not be allowed to cast it in the founder's role or to obscure the contributions of others.

The commissar of repression himself has recognized the importance of the Peasants' Union. Commenting on the multiplicity of Green bands even in 1918 and 1919, he says in effect that they could not get off the ground because they had behind them no solid anti-Soviet organization in the villages, no definite program, no single plan of action.[27] Nineteen twenty and the emergence of the STK made the difference as far as Tambov province was concerned. The STK furnished Antonov a broad and effective base of operations with the aid of which he could both build up his forces and replenish their losses in men, provisions, and horses. The STK made possible the conversion of Antonov's band in the bullrushes into an army with a country. At the same time that due acknowledgment is made of its significance, however, it must be borne in mind that the Peasants' Union was an adjunct, never the directing force of the insurrection, and that its emergence in the first half of 1920 did not make it the cause of the explosion in the second half but only a sustaining factor.

In Soviet mythology, as we have intimated, the Central Committee of the Socialist Revolutionary party ordered the formation of peasant unions and then raised the insurrection, picking up Antonov as a convenient instrument on the way. The impulse was the party's, and Antonov an object of manipulation. Let us now roll back the myth and see how the insurrection really got under way. Enough has been said about the disarray of sources for the reader to have learned that it is a law of life in this study; but in respect to the origin of the insurrection the disarray is not so bad but that he may have confidence that the account now to be presented, while possibly erroneous in this or that detail, is nevertheless essentially what happened.

August has often been an eventful month in European history. The woes of the twentieth century stem from August 1914. And on the local scene, August 1920 would mark the point of no return for the peasant movement in Tambov province. It is the month when the harvest is gathered in. In Russian as in other more western languages the month bears the name of the Roman emperor, but the Bohemian tongue still preserves the old Slavonic term—*srpen*, the month of the sickle. As the peasants reaped the fruits of their labor, the food detachments appeared for the third consecutive season to enforce the state grain monopoly and claim—that is, confiscate—the surplus and some not-so-surplus grain.

The first such experience had been in 1918 and the fall revolts had followed; the second experience produced incidents of resistance in August and September 1919,[28] and later in the fall led to the murder of Chichkanov and other Soviet dignitaries on the southeastern prairies or in the bogs and forests of the Vorona valley. The third time around would exhaust even the peasants' oriental patience. Nineteen nineteen had been a very good year, according to Kalinin, but the only margin the peasant had left was what he had been able to conceal from the food detachments. Even under ideal political conditions 1920 would have been a year of hardship for the peasants. The desert was now actively preparing the immeasurable catastrophe of 1921–1922 while the Soviet regime was holding the line on the food levy and refusing to take into account the altered circumstances. It is not possible to determine the weight of the levy in any certain locality and it would be pointless in any event, for the real principle of collection was to take all the traffic would bear. And now the traffic would bear less.

The village of Kamenka lay near the southeastern border of Tambov *uezd*. It must have been a prosperous village with a full complement of kulaks, for it was going to conform to the Communist formula that where there were kulaks there was also trouble. At any rate, it had a strong and active peasants' union. According to an SR source, it had already undergone one visitation from the food levy people when, on 12 August 1920, a requisitioning force arrived to impose a supplemental levy. The peasants had been collectively responsible under the Tsar for tax and redemption payments, and under the Soviets for the quotas of produce. The formation of the peasants' union seems to have given them a sense of collective strength. And now there would be collective resistance. They did not dissemble their feelings. An ugly situation arose, and they killed seven members of the requisitioning force. The fat was now in the fire, a "staff" was selected, and under the guidance of the local STK cell preparations were made to meet the punitive detachment that duly materialized in the form of twenty mounted militiamen from Sampur station on the Tambov–Balashov–Kamyshin line. Shots were exchanged and the punitive force was beaten off, as were two succeeding ones.[29]

At the time of the Kamenka outbreak, a large peasants' congress was being held only fifteen *versts* from the provincial capital.[30] It was locally the highest instance of the STK and it did not favor insurrection. It felt that the requisite degree of organization had not been attained in Tambov province, to say nothing of the rest of Russia. When the congress learned of the action of the Kamenka peasants it sent two delegates to contact the insurgents, to establish an intelligence service, and to bring about a measure of discipline. The actual purpose of the mission was to quiet down the peasants. The congress was not fainthearted; rather, it wanted to restrain the peasants from plunging into a conflict which *at that moment* it regarded as hopeless and which could only end in a bloodbath for them. Thanks to the SR trial of 1922, the names of the emissaries are known: George Muraviev and Boltnev (initials unknown), both of them SR stalwarts and Boltnev soon to be a political commissar in Antonov's army.

When they arrived in Kamenka they discovered, interestingly enough, that Antonov also was sending someone to find out what *volosts* had risen. And not only sending—he came in person. Muraviev met him there. Antonov's combative instincts must have been aroused, for he was never a man to shrink from action. Muraviev—and presumably also Boltnev—clearly set forth the STK position, how it counselled against an uprising and in favor of a continuation of practical organizational work. "Antonov agreed, and we parted."[31]

The effect of the STK injunction on the peasants of Kamenka is not stated. Apparently it had none. Having been stirred up, the hornets were not returning to the nest. The local cell went its own way. But very soon a decided shift occurred in the stand of the Peasants' Union. When George Muraviev and Boltnev returned to Tambov they found the provincial union backing the insurrection, setting up a staff to provide arms for the insurgents, contemplating for that purpose raids on the Tambov and Morshansk armories, and ordering Antonov to move on Kirsanov.[32]

By provincial union is meant, presumably, the committee elected at the provincial congress of peasant delegates in May which, as best we can tell, had been responsible for forming the STK from the nucleus already assembled by Antonov.[33] A committee so constituted would be a higher instance than the congress of one *uezd*—in this case, Tambov—which was in session at the time of the outbreak in Kamenka. There is no way of knowing precisely what was going on in the STK. The best guess is that it was in as great a state of confusion as were the Soviet authorities. It is not necessary to conjure up a conflict between the Tambov *uezd* congress and the provincial committee of the STK. In all likelihood they both had opposed an insurrection at the time but both had then decided to support it, once it had begun, on the grounds that the tide could not be reversed and the peasants could not be abandoned to their fate.

For what happened in Kamenka was no isolated incident. The village of Khitrovo some forty-five kilometers to the north had a strong and active peasants' union in the form of a district committee for five *volosts*. When the news came of the uproar in Kamenka this committee called a meeting of all the members of the local peasants' union to consider what stand to take. The meeting was held in a barn at night. Podbelski has the two delegates from the *uezd* congress coming to this session in the barn at Khitrovo instead of to Kamenka village; as he does not give their names we cannot say with certainty that he is confused because it is not to be excluded that two other delegates were sent to Khitrovo. He says that the local union adhered to the position of the congress and decided not to throw in with Kamenka.

But fate intervened. Before the meeting dispersed, the barn was surrounded by a Soviet mounted detachment of about thirty men. Most of those at the meeting managed to get away under cover of darkness, but three were caught and led away under convoy in the direction of Sampur. The embattled peasants thereupon decided not to give up their fellows but to mount a rescue operation. In the morning they overtook the Soviet convoy, attacked it, and had the victory—not only redeeming the captives but forcing the surviving members of the detachment to surrender. Among them were some Communists. These were shot by the peasants. And so Khitrovo village was drawn into the quickening current. It was 15 August 1920.[34]

A somewhat different, more authoritative, but less specific account of the events in Khitrovo is furnished by A. S. Bogoliubski, Antonov's brother-in-law, who had been sent to Khitrovo to establish contact with Nicholas Muraviev and, through him, to get SR literature into the hands of Antonov. Who had sent Bogoliubski to Khitrovo he does not say, but apparently he was acting for the SR organization in Tambov; in fact, a Che-ka report makes him and one of the Muravievs members of the SR provincial committee,[35] though Podbelski denies the truth of the assertion.[36]

Bogoliubski's account broadens the significance of Khitrovo from a mere stronghold of the STK into the link between the SRs in Tambov and Antonov. When he arrived in Khitrovo he did not find Nicholas Muraviev, but he found enough otherwise. He seems to have gotten there so immediately after the events that they may have still been going on. The peasants told him that a food detachment had come, they had disarmed it, and intended to stage an uprising. He himself brought the news to Tambov, to the military operational staff which had been born shortly before out of the SR–Left SR union. What the staff decided he did not know as its decisions were shrouded in secrecy. It made no difference: the staff was soon arrested, and Bogoliubski with it.[37]

The action at Khitrovo has been viewed by some as the beginning of the Tambov insurrection. Kamenka is not mentioned or is mentioned only ex post facto as having been "seized" on 19 August by a band one hundred fifty strong. The "seizure" gave Pluzhnikov, as provincial head of the STK, the opportunity to proclaim before the village assembly the SR-formulated goals of the insurrection.[38] The journal of the Communist party, in turn, dates the insurrection from 19 August and skirts the problem of where it began by naming only the general area, Inzhavino–Sampur, without mentioning specific villages.[39]

These recent Soviet studies are serious attempts to reconstruct the past; they are not propagandistic in this instance, and yet they are not satisfactory despite all the advantages at their command. While giving a different version of how the uprising started, they actually support the version presented here. The one hundred fifty horsemen did not "seize" Kamenka on 19 August; they rode into a village that had already defied the Soviet government and had killed some of its supporters. They came because Antonov had decided to help the village. And Pluzhnikov did not proclaim the beginning of the insurrection in a village that had already been up in arms for a whole week. He did not establish the headquarters of the STK and the civil center of the uprising in a "seized" village. That Kamenka was chosen as the place to make the proclamation and that it became the capital of the Peasants' Union may be ascribed in all probability to its distinction as the cradle of the insurrection as well as to a favorable geographical location.

There are other objections to recent Soviet accounts of how the uprising began. Not Pluzhnikov but Peter Tokmakov first headed the STK; only later did Pluzhnikov succeed to the position after Tokmakov had assumed command of one of the two insurgent armies—as best we can tell, toward the end of 1920 or the beginning of 1921. And Kamenka was not in Kirsanov but in Tambov *uezd*, albeit close to the line. But the main reason for rejecting the recent Soviet accounts and holding to the one presented in this study is that the contemporaneous statements of Podbelski and of George Muraviev on which it is based are supported from the Soviet side in respect to making Kamenka the point of inception.

Antonov-Ovseenko as a source of information must always command respect; he was the commissar of repression—though not on the scene in the beginning—and he told Lenin that the insurrection opened with "organized attacks" on Soviet agencies and food detachments in the villages of Kamenka and Zolotoe, the latter an addition not verifiable in other sources.[40] He told Lenin something else. He stated that at this time was formed the "First Kamenka Partisan Cavalry Regiment" which laid the foundation of the "People's Army."[41] Thus it appears that Antonov sent one hundred fifty mounted warriors to Kamenka for another purpose besides aiding the village: he was after recruits, and evidently found them. A recently-published Soviet encyclopedia also has the flame ignited in Kamenka. This historical encyclopedia, however, commits the same historical error of placing the village in the wrong *uezd*.[42]

Before turning to the spread of the "Antonov fire," it would be well to draw out the salient facts of its inception, for no aspect of the insurrection has been more a subject of distortion. The standard Soviet line has been that the SRs carefully laid the fire and, when all was in readiness, ordered Antonov to strike the match. The kulaks, of course, were privy to the conspiracy and the peasant mass had been deluded by broadsides proclaiming the deposition of the Bolsheviks in Moscow and Petersburg, so that the Tambov toilers had but to rise to win their freedom.[43] The novel reputedly so steeped in the setting has Pluzhnikov mobilizing the kulaks, Ishin assembling the stores of provisions and arms, and Antonov readying two armies, each with ten regiments and each regiment with two thousand men.[44] Antonov, in other words, on the eve of the insurrection was poised to thrust—not a "knife into the back of the revolution"—but a whole broadsword, for with forty thousand men he would have had a larger force than Wrangel. He had decided to locate his headquarters in Kamenka—why is not explained—and declared he would give the signal from there. On 15 August preparations were completed and four days later Pluzhnikov, before five thousand rustics assembled in a meadow near a school, proclaimed the insurrection.[45]

Even more sober Soviet statements are not free of this foolishness. Antonov-Ovseenko informed Lenin that the local SRs resorted to open insurrection with "organized attacks" on Soviet agencies and food detachments in Kamenka and Zolotoe.[46] Thus in one way or another Communists insist on dragging the SRs,

Antonov, and the kulaks behind them into the focal point of responsibility, sometimes forgetting even to include the Left SRs. According to them all is contrived, all is fixed, and all is prearranged.

And all is fable. No one made this insurrection. It was ignited spontaneously from the wrath of a population about to be set upon for the third year in succession by a swarm of despoilers officially sanctioned under the guise of produce collection agents. Some Soviet commentators leave the back door open to such an interpretation. The article in the first edition of the encyclopedia does not say the SRs raised the revolt; it says that it grew up on the ground of resentment against the food levy and mobilizations into the Red Army.[47] The historian of the Che-ka, who does uphold the notion of instigation, states that it was coordinated with the onset of the food levy so as to assure a broad measure of support extending beyond the kulak stratum.[48] And Antonov-Ovseenko, while not mentioning the circumstances behind the Kamenka outbreak—particularly the imposition of a supplemental levy—recognized the existence of such practices in general and counselled Lenin against permitting their recurrence.[49] As for the SRs, so burdened with sin, they were guilty not so much of conspiracy as of confusion; the local ones at first opposed an uprising and then rallied to its support when it occurred, and the leaders in Moscow and abroad refused to sanction revolt either before or after, though undoubtedly sympathetic to the peasants who spurned their advice.

Antonov was so far removed from having touched off the insurrection that he had to send one or more emissaries and then come himself to find out what cantons were involved. Far from having forty thousand men at his command as fiction would have it (how could he have hidden so many; why would he have sent a force of one hundred fifty to Kamenka with so many thousands to draw on; why bother with Kamenka at all, why not march straight on Tambov?), he is stated by a Soviet military source worthy of respect to have taken the field in August 1920 at the head of five hundred well-armed men.[50] If in the end he was able to assemble an army of twenty-one thousand in the face of manifold obstacles, it was not because of the machinations of the SRs, the ingenuity of Ishin, the resourcefulness of Pluzhnikov, or even his own qualities of leadership; it was because a movement spontaneous in origin, worthy in the truest sense of being called popular, had furnished him with so many willing recruits.

One serious obstacle interposes itself to acceptance of the version herein presented as to the outbreak of the Tambov insurrection. It is the testimony of A. S. Bogoliubski at the SR trial in 1922 when he stated on the witness stand that the provincial SR conference in July 1920 had been averse to an uprising at the time but that soon thereafter Antonov had begun the revolt. Bogoliubski, as we have noted earlier, is a witness worthy of credence. And here he is saying—straight out—that his brother-in-law initiated the uprising. But he says something more. He says that Antonov did so claiming that he could not restrain the mass insurgency from below. The first point to make is that the claim was not an excuse but the truth. The peasants in at least two villages had risen; Antonov could either aid or abstain but he could not hold back what already was under way.

Bogoliubski continues by stating that a "major peasant movement" developed in Khitrovo canton from 15 August, that he came to the scene in the midst of the tumult and was told by the peasants that they had overborne a food detachment and "intended to rise up," and that he himself had carried the news back to Tambov.[51] Thus he confirms the spontaneity of the outbreak, at least for Khitrovo (he was not at Kamenka). First he says that Antonov began the uprising and then says that the peasants did it on their own. It is the usual story of a witness floundering on the stand—after all, he was not in an easy situation.

What he means to say is that the peasants led off and Antonov came to their aid, taking over direction of a blind revolt, providing it with eyes, a brain, a form, and an organization. Only in the indirect sense may the SRs and Antonov be said to have been responsible for the Tambov insurrection, the SRs by their agitation, Antonov by his raiding, and both by the creation of the STK which imparted a sense of corporate solidarity and strengthened the will to resist.

Notes

1. See chapter six, text and note 137.

2. "Protsess pravykh eserov," *Izvestiia*, no. 142 (1581), 29 June 1922, p. 2.

3. *Iz istorii Vserossiiskoi Chrezvychainoi Komissii, 1917–1921 gg.*, pp. 140–41, excerpting a report in *Pravda*, no. 125, 22 June 1918; Litovski, "K protsessu pravykh eserov: Iz eserovskogo sinodika" [As to the case of the Right SRs: From the SR files], *Izvestiia*, no. 115 (1554), 25 May 1922, p. 2; S. Ch., "Tambovskaia pamiatka ob eserakh," ibid., no. 121 (1560), 2 June 1922, p. 1; Dokunin, "Tambovskii schet sotsial-banditam," *Pravda*, no. 123, 4 June 1922, p. 3. The Litovski cited may well be the O. S. Litovski who helped compile the *Put' Bor'by*.

4. For the anti-Soviet side, see Shatov, "Tambovskie vosstaniia," *Novoe Russkoe Slovo*, 15 February 1966; for the Soviet side, see sources cited in note 3 above.

5. See chapter three.

6. Leonidov, "Eshche ob eserakh v Tambovskoi gub.," *Izvestiia*, no. 155 (1594), 14 July 1922, p. 3.

7. Dokunin, "Tambovskii schet sotsial-banditam," *Pravda*, no. 123, 4 June 1922, p. 3.

8. The author's remembrance is that at least six of the eight are listed in *Put' Bor'by* as having furnished a very high percentage of volunteers.

9. Srechinski, "Zapechatannaia stranitsa," *Novoe Russkoe Slovo*, 25 April 1969.

10. *Bor'ba rabochikh i krest'ian pod rukovodstvom bol'shevistskoi partii za ustanovlenie i uprochenie sovetskoi vlasti v Tambovskoi gubernii (1917–1918 gody)*, pp. 223 ff. and especially documents no. 167, pp. 225–26; no. 169, p. 227; no. 172, p. 229; no. 181, p. 240; no. 186, p. 244; no. 188, p. 245.

11. In the novel by Virta, *Odinochestvo*, pp. 39–40, Antonov bears the responsibility. The factual framework agrees with the documents. But the novelist was only twelve years of age at the time and could have known of these developments only by hearsay or through later reading. As he allows Antonov a band of only ten to fifteen men in the fall of 1918 and has him nonetheless riding around and raising village after village at a very considerable distance from his native habitat, the historian may conclude that the fictional account is—fiction.

12. Borisov, *Chernym letom*, p. 38.

13. Antonov-Ovseenko, "O banditskom dvizhenii v Tambovskoi gubernii," p. 5.

14. Dokunin, "Tambovskii schet sotsial-banditam," *Pravda*, no. 123, 4 June 1922, p. 3.

15. Virta, *Odinochestvo*, pp. 40 ff.

16. Ibid., pp. 51–52.

17. See chapter four.

18. Okninski, *Dva goda sredi krest'ian*, pp. 152, 311–12.

19. -skii, "Po Rossii: Zhizn' sovetskoi derevni," *Revoliutsionnaia Rossiia*, no. 3 (February 1921), p. 23.

20. Virta, *Odinochestvo*, p. 53.

21. Evidently the Russian colonists carried with them the name of the historic lake in the north as they moved out onto the black earth when the sway of the Tatars was broken.

22. S. Ch., "Tambovskaia pamiatka ob eserakh," *Izvestiia*, no. 121 (1560), 2 June 1922, p. 1; Borisov, *Chernym letom*, p. 38; Zybko, *Tambovskaia partiinaia organizatsiia*, p. 37. The source first cited dates the Antonov movement from this slaying; actually it was already well under way.

23. Antonov-Ovseenko, "O banditskom dvizhenii v Tambovskoi gubernii," p. 5. The figure for the summer is taken from -skii, "Po Rossii: Zhizn' sovetskoi derevni," *Revoliutsionnaia Rossiia*, no. 3 (February 1921), p. 23; this source, in turn, got it from an official bulletin published in Tambov province.

24. -skii, "Po Rossii: Zhizn' sovetskoi derevni," *Revoliutsionnaia Rossiia*, no. 3 (February 1921), p. 23. The same report appeared earlier in the SR organ abroad under the title, "Zhizn' russkoi derevni," *Volia Rossii*, no. 20, 5 October 1920, p. 4, and ibid., no. 22, 7 October 1920, p. 5. The first number carried the notation that the report went to the SR Central Committee and then was sent on to the newspaper; it added that very little such information found its way abroad, a statement that is all too true as this author has reason to know.

25. "Soobshchenie gazety 'Izvestiia' ob areste pravykh eserov" [Announcement of the newspaper *Izvestiia* about the arrest of right SRs], in *Iz istorii Vserossiiskoi Chrezvychainoi Komissii*, document no. 273, p. 354.

26. This line of reasoning is suggested in Fomichev (Lidin), "Antonovshchina: Iz vospominanii antonovtsa" (Santiago de Chile, 1955), pp. 16, 19. Certain information about developments in 1918 and 1919 will be found in the following sources in addition to those cited singly above: Hirschfeld, "Tambovskii krovopodtek," *Izvestiia*, no. 247 (1390), 3 November 1921, p. 1; Donkov, "Organizatsiia razgroma antonovshchiny," *Voprosy Istorii KPSS*, no. 6 (June 1966), p. 62; Esaulenko, *Revoliutsionnyi put'* G. I. Kotovskogo, p. 128; "Antonovshchina," in *Sovetskaia istoricheskaia entsiklopediia*, vol. 1, p. 636; Kubanin, "Antonovshchina," in *Bol'shaia sovetskaia entsiklopediia*, 1st ed., vol. 3, pp. 98–99. It is obvious that the novelist Virta has followed Kubanin's short article, but where Kubanin has Antonov forming a detachment in the summer of 1919 with an initial strength of fifty the novelist has multiplied the figure tenfold, posing the question of whether this ratio of fiction to fact holds throughout the book. In this study, however, we cannot be sure even of the "fact." It is all very discouraging, since the information everywhere is so scant.

27. Antonov-Ovseenko, "O banditskom dvizhenii v Tambovskoi gubernii," p. 3.

28. Srechinski, "Zapechatannaia stranitsa," *Novoe Russkoe Slovo*, 25 April 1969.

29. Anonymous (Podbelski), *Kak tambovskie krest'iane boriatsia za svobodu*, p. 3. This account is much more specific than any other and is here accorded the preference, though Podbelski himself was in Moscow at this time and learned of the events through friends in his home province of Tambov, probably when he returned in September. See above. Though not a primary source, Podbelski was well-informed; he is least trustworthy in respect to Antonov's personal role, having the intellectual's dislike for a bloody-handed man—that is, one of courage and action.

30. It may well have been one for all of Tambov *uezd*, as Podbelski says. But the Soviet source cited in note 31 below merely calls it an STK congress without making clear whether it had the entire *uezd* for its constituency or covered a more limited area.

31. Testimonies of George and Nicholas Muraviev at the SR trial in 1922 as summarized in *Obvinitel'noe zakliuchenie po delu tsentral'nogo komiteta p. s.-r.*, p. 44. Their version is preferred to Podbelski's because they are primary sources. The Muraviev brothers spoke only of their mission, not of the events in Kamenka.

32. Testimony of George Muraviev, corroborated by A. S. Bogoliubski in ibid.

33. Such a congress is mentioned in the testimony of Bogoliubski, *Pravda*, no. 153, 12 July 1922, p. 4, but not by Podbelski in anonymous, *Kak tambovskie krest'iane boriatsia za svobodu*, p. 3, where he speaks only of the one for Tambov *uezd* in August and of one two months earlier for five *volosts* in the Khitrovo district of that *uezd*.

34. Anonymous (Podbelski), *Kak tambovskie krest'iane boriatsia za svobodu*, pp. 3–4.

35. *Iz istorii Vserossiiskoi Chrezvychainoi Komissii*, no. 333, p. 456.

36. Podbelski, "Predsedateliu moskovskogo soveta r. i. k. deputatov," p. 2.

37. "Sud nad eserami: Esery vozglavliali banditskoe dvizhenie Antonova," *Pravda*, no. 153, 12 July 1922, p. 4. His testimony is contained in this report of the SR trial.

38. Trifonov, *Klassy i klassovaia bor'ba*, part 1, p. 245, citing the *Antonovshchina* (*Put' Bor'by*, vol. 2), p. 39, ordinarily the most complete source. Similarly an anti-Soviet source, which here is obviously following Trifonov: Srechinski, "Zapechatannaia stranitsa," *Novoe Russkoe Slovo*, 25 April 1969.

39. Donkov, "Organizatsiia razgroma antonovshchiny," *Voprosy Istorii KPSS*, no. 6 (June 1966), pp. 59–60.

40. The novelist locates the village of Zolotoe in the Khitrovo area; Virta, *Odinochestvo*, p. 325. See also below, chapter ten. Zolotoe has not been found on a map.

41. Antonov-Ovseenko, "O banditskom dvizhenii v Tambovskoi gubernii," p. 6.

42. "Antonovshchina," in *Sovetskaia istoricheskaia entsiklopediia*, vol. 1, p. 636; similarly Trifonov, "Antonovshchina," in *Bol'shaia sovetskaia entsiklopediia*, 3rd ed., vol. 2, p. 96, col. 275.

43. S. Ch., "Tambovskaia pamiatka ob eserakh," *Izvestiia*, no. 121 (1560), 2 June 1922, p. 1.

44. Virta, *Odinochestvo*, pp. 88–90, 94–97.

45. Ibid., pp. 97–100.

46. Antonov-Ovseenko, "O banditskom dvizhenii v Tambovskoi gubernii," p. 6.

47. Kubanin, "Antonovshchina," in *Bol'shaia sovetskaia entsiklopediia*, 1st ed., vol. 3, p. 98.

48. Sofinov, *Ocherki istorii Vserossiiskoi Chrezvychainoi Komissii*, p. 224; see also "Antonovshchina," in *Sovetskaia istoricheskaia entsiklopediia*, vol. 1, p. 636.

49. Antonov-Ovseenko, "O banditskom dvizhenii v Tambovskoi gubernii," pp. 35, 36.

50. Leonidov, "Eshche ob eserakh v Tambovskoi gub.," *Izvestiia*, no. 155 (1594), 14 July 1922, p. 3.

51. "Sud nad eserami: Esery vozglavliali banditskoe dvizhenie Antonova," *Pravda*, no. 153, 12 July 1922, p. 4.

8

The First Months (August–December 1920)

The fire ignited at Kamenka and Khitrovo spread rapidly. Village after village made ready for war, weapons were taken out of hiding, bands were assembled. Village cells and *volost'* soviets were swept away; the STK took over the functions of government. The Soviet authorities either withdrew into the towns and guarded railroad stations, or went over to the insurgents, or were killed. The peasants cut down to the last man the *volost'* soviet executive committee at Verkhotsene.[1] The Communist regime vanished from the countryside and continued to exist only in the towns and garrison points of the areas affected by the insurrection.

These areas were not so extensive as generally represented. It is unusual to find Soviet authors exaggerating the extent of a hostile movement when they write that by September–October the five *uezds* of Tambov, Kirsanov, Borisoglebsk, Morshansk, and Kozlov had been engulfed in the flames.[2] A more sober appraisal limits the area of the insurrection to Tambov and Kirsanov *uezds* generally, to considerable portions of Borisoglebsk and Morshansk *uezds*, and to a part of Kozlov *uezd*.[3]

This author is unwilling to accept even this constriction as accurate. He has seen little evidence that operations embraced the southwestern portion of Tambov or more than fitfully involved the northern part of Kirsanov and the southern part of Borisoglebsk *uezds*; as for Morshansk and Kozlov, they appear to have been more spillover areas than home territory for the insurgents.

The insurrection centered in southeastern Tambov, southern Kirsanov, and northern Borisoglebsk *uezds*, in the triangle formed by the Lipetsk–Griazi–Borisoglebsk–Tsaritsyn railroad on the south, the Kozlov–Tambov–Kirsanov–Rtishchevo–Saratov line on the north, and the southeastern borders of Tambov province, although operations at times extended beyond the railways, and the virulent village of Pakhotnyi Ugol lay in the northern, densely-wooded reaches of Tambov *uezd*. An aspect of this circumscribed area that merits mention, however—and one which the Tambov soviet leaders, Schlichter and Raivid, did not fail to point out to Lenin when they went to Moscow early in September—was that it embraced the most fertile parts of the province.[4]

Much of Tambov province, therefore, never experienced the warfare between the Greens and the Reds—of twelve *uezds* only five were affected—while still other portions experienced it only sporadically. Not only the towns but most of the countryside continued under Soviet rule. Here was an element of weakness, present from the start and destined never to be overcome. Nevertheless, the portions under "bandit sway" comprised agriculturally the most productive regions and imposed a severe transportation handicap upon the Soviet government, lying as they did athwart several of the main routes between the fertile southeast and the food-deficient regions in the center and the northwest. Why did Lenin's regime let such a situation develop?

It could not help itself. It was breathing heavily when the peasants rose, caught between the war with Poland in the west and Wrangel's presence in the south. The second civil war opened before the first had ended, although Wrangel's threat could not be compared to Denikin's. But the international war bound the hands of the Soviet with reference to an obstreperous province. August 1920 witnessed the rollback before Warsaw and Wrangel's operations on the mainland beyond the Crimea.

In all of Tambov province there were only some three thousand troops,[5] or three thousand bayonets and six hundred sabers according to the most trustworthy estimate. A motley array of units lessened the worth of this modest force. There were some units of the regular army, but basically it consisted of Communist party and Communist youth formations and internal security detachments, known as ChON or Units of Special Assignment—i.e., against the population.[6] We may conjecture that some units were seasoned, some more earnest than effective, and some neither earnest nor effective. Inevitably the charge surfaces that many of these troops

were non-Russian, Letts and Bashkirs being specifically mentioned,[7] and no doubt some of them were, though there is no way of
knowing the proportion.

Circumstances prevented any large-scale reinforcement of the
available troops. Thus by mid-October, after the insurrection had
been going on for some two months, Soviet strength had not grown
beyond 3,915 bayonets, 532 sabers, 22 machine guns, and 5 cannon
(it is to be hoped that specific figures mean accurate ones).[8] What is
even more surprising, the strength at the end of the year had not
increased but had actually diminished, if we are to accept
Antonov-Ovseenko's figure of 3,000 bayonets for the period before
January 1921[9] when substantial reinforcements at last were
moved in.

There were other reasons for Soviet weakness. Inferior
leadership in both party and soviet organizations can be read
between the lines and sometimes in the text of Soviet accounts
regardless of the dogma of party infallibility. And despite the
anonymity behind which Communists like to work—with the
notable exception of Joseph Stalin—the names of some of these
dignitaries can be given: the secretary of the provincial party
committee (always the key official) was N. Ia. Raivid; the chairman
of the provincial soviet executive committee, A. G. Schlichter; and
the commander of the armed forces, Iu. Iu. Aplok. None
distinguished himself. None had a Russian name. If any one of them
was tied into the population it has not come down to us, whereas the
soviet chairman whom an assassin's bullet had claimed in 1919, M.
D. Chichkanov, is said by a Soviet source to have enjoyed
"exclusive popularity" among all layers of the population, as
attested by his big funeral. The SRs and the "bandits" are reported
to have felt the need to eliminate him from the Soviet leadership;[10] if
so, they had calculated correctly for the men now on the scene seem
to have been inept, inexperienced, indecisive. They did not appraise
correctly the motivating forces of the uprising and they erred in
devising means of combating it.[11]

But not all the fault resided in the leadership. The party itself was
at low estate, wracked with dissension and low in morale. We shall
presently encounter some rather startling evidence of its moral
condition, and from an unimpeachable source.[12] More to the point,

however, it was simply worn out. It had been "mobilized" so often and for so many different purposes—all of them strenuous when not desperate—that it was drained of its energy, of its moral reserve, and of much of its better personnel. Now came the summons again: five hundred members of the party were to go on barracks duty, all party organizations were to form military units ready to act at any time, special propaganda groups were constituted as was a commission to assist victims of the counterrevolution; finally, thirty Communists were injected into the Extraordinary Commission to stiffen that organization—even it was sagging, it seems.[13]

The Communists answered the call but were too jaded to muster enthusiasm. If now the accursed peasants had gotten out of control it was only one more emergency in a never-ending series. Emergency had dulled Communist sensibilities. Much of their success—before the events and later, in Russia and elsewhere—has come from their imperviousness to the need of rest, an endurance which has enabled them to wear down their enemies. On this occasion the Communists were themselves worn out.

The insurgents, on the other hand, as the aggrieved party, fought with a lift of spirit and for a time carried all before them. The momentum of success combined with the desperation bred by the food levy, the transport *corvée*, the callousness or outright cruelty of the Communist regime, and the onset of bad natural conditions, hardened their resolve and imparted élan to their movement. Antonov-Ovseenko concealed from Lenin neither the craving to be rid of the food levy nor the ability of the kulaks, armed with this promise, to pull the other layers of the village behind them.[14] At the outset, then, the Greens held the initiative and had superior morale.

And now for the operations insofar as it is possible to reconstruct them. The reader has been warned to expect little in this regard, not because of the dearth of objective analyses but for the more serious and unsettling reason that nowhere is there a simple, orderly, chronological relation of events. The most ambitious recent Soviet study, that of I. I. Trifonov, after taxing the few earlier accounts with this and other shortcomings,[15] proceeds to do no better. The all but unbroken chronicle of Soviet victories presented here and elsewhere gives only a fragmented picture of developments and does not even indicate how the victories stood in relation to one another; the grudging mention of any Green success at all conveys the impression of an immature and even childish approach in which there is no room for objective statement of facts, much less appraisal of the results. Only access to the archives or to the provincial press could unlock the imprisoned information, thought the author, until snatches from local newspapers contained in other sources convinced him that they had been so extensively and stupidly censored as greatly to lessen their usefulness, even if they were available. An attempt will be made to fit the bits of information together, but many uncertainties will remain.

After the initial outbreaks, the first major development was the march on Tambov. Little is known about it. Embattled villagers are said to have coalesced in large numbers and moved on the capital from the southeast with almost anything that would not be conducive to success. Villages along the line of march welcomed them with the ringing of bells and furnished food, volunteers, and more pitchforks, axes, and clubs. There were even rifles. Gathering headway as they went, the peasants on 1 September 1920 occupied Kuzminka station, the last before Tambov on the Balashov line. They were only fifteen *versts* or less than ten miles from Tambov when stern resistance from the Bolshevik garrison forced them to retreat.

Podbelski disclaims any knowledge of the origin of the plan or of who was leading the peasants at this time. He leans to the view that the march on Tambov was a spontaneous affair.[16] Quite likely it was. Soviet sources do not speak of this episode, whether because they find embarrassing its popular character in the absence of any indication of Antonov's responsibility, or whether because of some other reason. The novel recasts the whole business as nothing more than a military feint on the part of Tokmakov with two regiments and some deserters' units which got up to Kuz'mina Gat', twenty *versts* from Tambov, and then receded.[17] Something must have taken place but it is impossible to speak with any assurance. For our part, we will accept the Podbelski or SR version.

The sequel, however, is more significant. Podbelski has Antonov appearing on the scene as the peasants retreat from Tambov, dismissing the larger part of them as badly armed or entirely weaponless but assuming command over those with rifles and revolvers whom he forms into a small cavalry detachment and an infantry force. His leadership is accepted because no one else is available. Thus Antonov takes over the movement, ending its first or spontaneous stage in which the peasants acted on their own and inaugurating its second or directed stage in which he engages in organized guerrilla warfare with small and elusive bands. The time is the earlier part of September 1920.[18]

The account of Podbelski received from his local SR sources of information cannot be accepted in its entirety. We know beyond any doubt that Antonov did not first appear on the scene in the wake of the fiasco before Tambov. We know from the testimony of George Muraviev how, at the very outset, he had sent to Kamenka to find out what was going on and then came himself. And there is very little doubt that his was the cavalry force shielding the assemblage at Kamenka on 19 August before which Pluzhnikov had delivered his oration. Moreover, the unidentified band which appeared on 26 August between the stations of Sampur and Rzhaksa and rallied deserters in large numbers, swelling its strength in a few days from sixty to some five to eight hundred,[19] must also have been his.

Antonov, in other words, was active before, during, and after the peasant march on Tambov. And if the chastened marchers so readily accepted his leadership it was not because they could find no one better—here the snobbery of the Populist intellectual shows through quite plainly—but out of willingness to follow a leader who had attained popularity and even had become somewhat of a legendary figure because of his exploits against obnoxious agencies of the existing regime. Antonov's raids over the two-year period 1918–1920, even though conducted on a small scale, now paid off. He promised help to the peasants and they gave recruits to his rapidly expanding forces, estimated by Soviet military sources to have numbered by 8 September some six thousand men[20]—that is, to have increased tenfold in less than a month if the Leonidov estimate of his original strength is accepted.[21]

Otherwise the information Podbelski derived from his local sources fits well into the picture. The peasants had made their own march on Tambov apart from Antonov because he knew it could only end as it did. Once chastened, they would listen to him. And so he appeared among them, separated the grain from the chaff, and capitalized on their misfortune. He had had a hand in the affair from the outset, but only now the guiding hand. Henceforth the insurrection would have purposeful leadership without ceasing to be truly popular in character.

It is with reference to the emergence of Antonov as the dominant figure in the Tambov insurrection that a passage in Tukhachevski's memorandum becomes intelligible. He told Lenin that it had begun in September 1920.[22] It is true that Tukhachevski was then on the western front and would not appear on the Tambov scene until months later in the spring of 1921. Yet he ought to have known when the insurrection began, especially when reporting to Lenin. When he gives September instead of August he is correct in the sense that the insurrection became organized under Antonov several weeks after the outbreak in Kamenka. Until then it had been only a tumult. The version of events set forth by Podbelski is further corroborated by the extremely rapid increase in Antonov's strength in early September—tenfold, according to the estimate cited above—which resulted from the peasants turning to him in the wake of their discomfiture.

Not that Antonov accomplished all this by himself. The Peasants' Union or STK, working in harmony with him, shared in the direction of the uprising. A clear understanding existed as to the respective fields of competence: the STK would handle political, social, and economic matters; it would deal with the civilian population, while military operations would be severely the preserve of Antonov and his Supreme Operational Staff. This staff seems to have come into being in November 1920 and to have consisted of five members: Antonov himself, Tokmakov, Boguslavski, Gusarov, and Mitrofanovich.[23] Another source places the Constitutional Democrat Fedorov at its head and lists as chiefs of the army—and so, presumably, as members—Antonov, Pluzhnikov, and Tokmakov, adding that there were others.[24] The only reason for asserting the primacy of a Kadet civilian was to satisfy Communist dogma by depicting Antonov as a tool of international capital, and Pluzhnikov was no sort of a soldier.

Antonov headed the staff, Tokmakov certainly served on it and Boguslavski may well have done so, whereas Gusarov and

Mitrofanovich are names never elsewhere encountered. Ishin, our authority for the sharp delineation of duties between the STK and the military command, says that the provincial SR committee gave instructions to the provincial STK committee—not unnaturally, since the same men sat on both—but he says nothing about either giving instructions to Antonov's staff, thereby fortifying us even further in our conviction that Antonov ran this insurrection.[25]

From the initial events in August and early September to the end of 1920 there is evidence of a swaying struggle, perhaps less confused than appears from the scattered and disconnected details found in the sources. Aside from the indecisiveness of the struggle, few firm conclusions can be drawn. The Soviet authorities placed the three *uezds* of Tambov, Kirsanov, and Borisoglebsk under martial law on either 21 or 22 August, and charged the Orel military district with the task of repression. The declaration of martial law entailed little change in a situation that had seen Kirsanov *uezd* in a state of siege ever since Antonov had begun his hit-and-run raids and that now saw it constituted a separate military area as a token that things were somehow worse there.

But the modest number of troops available in Tambov province could not cope with Antonov. As he held the initiative and could move with great rapidity, and as the supply situation in the northern cities continued to be desperate, a good half of the 4,447 soldiers available to the Soviet command by mid-October were tied up in garrison duty in the towns, at railroad stations where Antonov could strike with telling effect, and on state farms—those special targets of peasant wrath. Only two detachments—one cavalry under Dmitrienko, and one mixed force—together with four armored railroad cars (not trains) were free to pursue the "bandits."[26] Toward the end of 1920 an armistice prevailed on the western front against Poland and Wrangel was flushed out of his Crimean bastion, but for some reason the Soviet government warmed only slowly to the idea of reinforcing the troops in Tambov.

Inadequate numbers were not the only trouble. Mediocre leadership and lowered morale in the party induced a sluggishness in the Soviet response to a challenge the seriousness of which was not at first realized. On paper the creation of a field staff and a war council, the mobilization and partial militarization of the party betokened an energetic reaction, but a drooping spirit lessened the effect of these measures. "A battalion of the VOKhR[27] and a Communist detachment . . . operated listlessly. In addition some combattants of the VOKhR went over to the side of the bandits," wryly remarks a Soviet source.[28] Betraying signs of confusion and underestimating the breadth and intensity of peasant feeling, Soviet authorities failed to draw back in time their supporters from the areas in revolt and to concentrate them in places of safety, with the result that Communists were left out at the end of the vine at the mercy of their numerous enemies. The party paid a bloody price, alike for its policies and the ineptitude of its leaders, the Greens massacring about one thousand of its members.[29]

And so Antonov won a number of victories at the start and sporadically thereafter. He swooped down on certain railroad stations and caught and disarmed various scattered Soviet detachments. His first major action is said to have been near the village of Zolotovka in Kirsanov *uezd* where he vanquished a Soviet force that included a so-called Trotski detachment. The main theater of operations, however, seems to have been in the southeastern part of Tambov *uezd* itself, south of the line from Tambov to Kirsanov and on into Saratov province, and on either side of the line from Tambov to Balashov. Particularly stubborn fighting occurred in the areas of Koptevo and Verkhotsene, as best we can tell, not in one unbroken stretch but at intervals interspaced with action elsewhere. It was near Verkhotsene (meaning village on the upper Tsna, close to its headwaters) that Antonov had the better of the 21st Rifle Regiment, and it was between Verkhotsene and Ponzar that Dmitrienko's cavalry brigade reversed the trend by routing a large Green band about a thousand strong. Presumably the action occurred in this order, although not certainly so, because the sources are very bad about giving dates and relating events to one another.

Antonov narrowly escaped disaster at the end of September when his command was compressed into the triangle between the Tambov–Kirsanov–Saratov and Tambov–Balashov–Kamyshin lines with the capital at the apex; he broke out of the ring by a bold thrust to the north, crossing the Saratov line in the Rasskazovo[30] area. Thereafter, according to Podbelski, he no longer kept his eggs in one basket but divided his forces into several more or less independent bands and continued operations into the winter with fluctuating success, seizing the Novo–Pokrovsk sugar refinery after tearing up the roadbed of the Tsaritsyn line and, well to the north, capturing a cannon from a Soviet force at Bogoslovka—both in November—but sustaining a severe defeat in December at Kriushi and Pavlodarovo in Borisoglebsk *uezd*. Soviet reports of "bandit" causualties—on this latter occasion four hundred dead and two hundred taken—are greatly to be discounted, as best we can ascertain.[31]

It is not even possible to arrange these events in proper chronological sequence, let alone to construct out of them a strategical or tactical pattern. But Podbelski's statement about the division of Antonov's force into largely autonomous bands is corroborated from the Soviet side by an appraisal of enemy strength made in December 1920. According to this survey, preserved in the Central State Archives of the Soviet Army, the army of the insurrection consisted of four large mobile groups:

1) Antonov himself disposed of 1,000 bayonets and 1,000 sabers to the south of Kirsanov, in the Inzhavino area;

2) Tokmakov had 500 sabers to the south of Rasskazovo not far from Green strongholds such as Khitrovo, Koptevo, Verkhne Spasskoe, Nizhne Spasskoe, and within striking distance of Tambov itself;

3) to the north of Tambov and between it and Morshansk, in a section of the needle-leaved forest bounded by the villages of Chernenoe, Kulevatov, and Pakhotnyi Ugol, lurked the Selianski band of 1,500 sabers;

4) the southernmost group, also of 1,500 sabers, operated under Boguslavski astride the Tsaritsyn line between Mordovo and Zherdevka.[32]

The geographical distribution is interesting: of the four bands, three were located in Tambov *uezd*, even though Selianski's might reach into Morshansk and Boguslavski's into Borisoglebsk. The name Selianski, as noted previously, is probably a pseudonym (for

Matiukhin?).[33] The total strength of fifty-five hundred would seem low for the last month of 1920 except for the fact that nothing is said about smaller bands—presumably there were some that were not splinters of the four named—or about the large affiliated band of Kolesnikov[34] in Voronezh province which would have added another thousand, perhaps even more.

The formation of the Supreme Operational Staff also lends credence to the all-too-scanty but apparently accurate information supplied by Podbelski's SR sources. The commissar of repression states that the staff was elected by secret ballot of the commanders of the "partisan regiments" on 14 November 1920, that it consisted of five members whom he does not name, and that Antonov was styled—by himself—chief of this general staff.[35] It is remarkable how hard it is for either Communists or SRs to do justice to Antonov. There is no reason to doubt that he was generally recognized as head of this staff. But what its setting up signified is another matter. Leonidov supplies the names of the five members[36] withheld by Antonov-Ovseenko. The inclusion of two otherwise obscure officers—Gusarov and Mitrofanovich—however, makes evaluation a risky matter.

Oftentimes in such instances the simplest explanation is the correct one, and it may be surmised that the creation of this body served the purpose of securing better coordination among the bands whose separate existence was decreed as much by considerations of recruiting and maintenance as by those of a strictly strategic nature. Dissatisfaction with the course of the campaign also could have dictated such a step, while Antonov-Ovseenko opens up still a third avenue of explanation with his imputation to Antonov's associates of jealousy, a claim that will be evaluated later.

Since even the military events cannot be reconstructed with any degree of satisfaction, it follows that the life of the soldiers in camp and in the field—the story of how they existed, fought, suffered, and died—cannot be related, either because the Communists have sought to submerge the individual in mass anonymity or because the Greens left no records or saw them destroyed. Undoubtedly touches of color brightened this dark struggle but almost nothing has been preserved. We know only that Antonov cultivated the revolutionary tradition among his soldiers, that his staff sent them an old marching song from the days of the *Narodnaia Volia*—the People's Will movement of the 1870s:

> Stonet i tiazhko stradaet
> Bednyi nash russkii narod,
> Ruki on k nam prostiraet
> Nas on na pomoshch' zovёt.
>
> [Our oppressed Russian people
> Groans and grievously suffers;
> It holds out its arms to us
> And calls us to come to its aid.]

It was sung at a feast in the forest when the Yaryzhka and Mishin commands came together on the border of Spassk and Shatsk *uezds*, much further to the north than most Green operations.[37]

If the course of the warfare is confused and uncertain, its character is all too clear. It was waged on both sides with utter savagery. Just as a civil war may run more to excesses than an international war, so a civil war between two revolutionary camps may be the worst of all. The Greens cut down Communists wherever they could find them, in villages they overran or as captives taken in battle. Their excellent intelligence enabled them to ferret out Communist party members among the prisoners without too much trouble. The toll of one thousand mentioned by Antonov-Ovseenko has already been noted. The more terrible excesses committed by the Greens—or more accurately, by the villagers—will be treated after the campaign of 1921.

For a time, at least, one sustains the impression that the Greens acted out of rage and the Communists out of confusion and fear, striking out blindly at the enemy without reflecting on the measures being taken. Thus the decision to burn down villages implicated in the revolt, alternating with amnesty on a generous scale. In the words of Antonov-Ovseenko, the Red terror was tried in the absence of real strength—that is, without the means of making it truly terrible. First the burning of villages, then a sudden turn to appeasement. He cites the example of eight hundred arrested peasants being released without any sifting whatever.[38]

Though he censures the local Communists for going in for terrorism that did not terrify—a failing of which no one could accuse him personally—what they did was bad enough. The village of Koptevo had adhered wholeheartedly to the insurrection and sternly resisted repression, beating off three punitive expeditions in succession. But its proximity to Tambov proved its undoing, and when finally taken it was fired from several sides and more than half-consumed in the flames. A similar fate overtook Khitrovo—with Kamenka, the cradle of the insurrection—and the villages of Verkhotsene, Verkhne Spasskoe, and others.[39] Unfortunately, the "others" are not named in the SR source nor are the dates of destruction given for those that are. Soviet accounts do not dwell on such matters except in the case of Antonov-Ovseenko's report to Lenin—secret, of course—in which he confirms the practice of burning villages without mentioning any examples.

Other practices were equally harsh. The doctrine of collective guilt decreed the shooting of peasants in batches as well as the blotting out of their abodes. The emergency war council set up by the Tambov soviet decreed confiscation of the property of participants in the uprising, but at first with little effect,[40] probably because the measure seemed at such slight variance with what the Communists had been doing all along. They did not as yet have the strength to enact the frightful scenes that attended the "liquidation" of the uprising in the second half of 1921, but they had already embraced the theory of collective guilt—so destructive of civilized values and so typical of the twentieth century—and were striding down the path of savagery.

As the year 1920 drew to a close a deadlock developed which could not be broken despite a bloody lunge, now from one side, now from the other. The Soviet historian speaks of nearly all of Tambov province as being in the grip of the Greens, then belies this unwonted exaggeration by assigning quite restricted areas to the four major groups.[41] Five months of insurrection had brought under Antonov's sway large portions of three *uezds*—Kirsanov, Tambov, and Borisoglebsk—and ill-defined but not extensive portions of two others, Morshansk and Kozlov. But even here he dominated only the countryside; not a single town did he hold. The inability to break into the towns, which eventually would be his undoing, is something of a puzzle in view of the quite modest forces available to the Soviet authorities. Inadequate firepower certainly figures in the explanation, but whether other factors are involved is a moot question.

For this would have been the time to get into the towns. The Communist party in Tambov province was breathing heavily. It was not robust to begin with, and now it had ceased to exist in the villages where its shallow roots had been destroyed in the wake of the blood-letting in which the fearfully abused and fearfully cruel peasants had engaged. A severe crisis shook the party during the winter of 1920–1921, only in part as a result of the insurrection. Discipline had fallen and disintegrative influences grew stronger, among them something Antonov-Ovseenko called "hurrah democracy," in addition to the well-known workers' opposition (at these words betokening proletarian dissatisfaction even in Tambov, Lenin made a mark in the margin, betraying his sensitivity to anything impinging on his vanguard theory). Both the provincial party conference and the provincial soviet congress had witnessed discreditable scandals.

But the most remarkable symptom of the malady wracking the party was the loss of half its membership. Here the insurrection must be assigned the major influence, for it lent the wings of fear to the element of disillusion. Those who no longer believed—or had never believed—did not vacillate further but severed ties with what they had reason to think might be a foundering organization. The provincial committee actually ceased to function in January and February of 1921, and the Communist cause in Tambov province languished with no political direction worthy of the name.[42]

The build-up of Soviet forces proceeded with surprising slowness. Troops in the province numbered scarcely more at the end of the year than at the outbreak of the insurrection.[43] Again, no really satisfactory reason can be given. M. V. Frunze had over one hundred thirty thousand troops at his disposal in the final campaign against Wrangel, outnumbering the Black (or White) Baron by four to one; yet when the campaign was over and the Crimea taken, Frunze could not run Makhno to earth and the Greens in the Ukraine continued to tie his host in knots, to the exasperation of Lenin.

Here, certainly, was one reason for the closed season on Antonov. The problems of demobilizing an army consisting of far more eaters than fighters (Trotski) and of coping with a truly catastrophic economic situation doubtless contributed to the listlessness of the effort against Antonov. But something is still missing from the explanation. After all, Antonov was astride three railroad lines among the most important in Russia for the provisioning of Petersburg, Moscow, and other food-deficient bases of power in the north, and to free these lines from the threat or actuality of interception would seem to have been a major charge on the government in the Kremlin. The only additional explanation that comes to mind is that the Greens had ignited so many fires all over Russia that the regime could not decide where to concentrate in the effort to extinguish them.

But now, with the Communists at best holding their own in Tambov province and with the deterioration of the local party organization, the truth at last seems to have seeped through in Moscow that local means would not be enough,[44] and that if Antonov was to be overcome or even contained it would be necessary to send in substantial reinforcements. It was in December 1920 that the Red Army command, now cognizant of the scope of the insurrection, undertook to strengthen the forces under P. A. Pavlov operating in Tambov province.[45]

This decision appears to have preceded a conference in Tambov at the end of December attended by leading party, army, and Soviet figures, among them V. S. Kornev, head of the VOKhR (Internal Security Forces) of the Russian republic. Acknowledging the party's weakness in the village, the inadequacy of the information furnished to the central government, and the underestimation of the uprising, the conference advised Moscow of the need for sending more troops and experienced party personnel.[46] Already in December some additional strength had arrived, though still for the most part not regular army units. From Kazan came an infantry regiment of the ChON (Units on Special Assignment), a cavalry regiment without specifications, and several small special units; Moscow sent a whole regiment of Chekists-on-mission—evidence that the special army of the secret police antedated Stalin.[47]

They would find employment. A local unit of the ChON numbering thirty men was stationed in Inzhavino and had distinguished itself by its doughty defense of this islet in the Green sea. Why such a small force garrisoned so exposed a position is not explained.[48] On 28 December 1920, in one of those lunges that made him a dread figure, Antonov fell upon this ChON unit and extinguished it to the last man.[49] It could have been the occasion also of settling accounts with a section of the Che-ka on circuit in the area, but because of the omission of the date and the numerous raids on Inzhavino we cannot be certain. In any event, either at this time or early in 1921 Antonov caught the entire staff of the Che-ka branch at Inzhavino, together with a squad of executioners, and "cruelly disposed of them."[50]

These internal security and Che-ka units arriving in December could not hope to redress the situation, though they might help further to stabilize the stalemate. They were but the vanguard of the large-scale reinforcements that appeared on the scene in January. Even these would not be enough, however, as the sequel would show.

Notes

1. Anonymous (Podbelski), *Kak tambovskie krest'iane boriatsia za |svobodu*, p. 4. Here the village is given as Verkhodenskii but it is virtually certain that the name should be Verkhotsene, one of the villages that figured most prominently in the uprising. The Populist intellectual Podbelski resembles a number of Soviet authors in that they do not know well the geography of their own country.

2. So Trifonov, *Klassy i klassovaia bor'ba*, part 1, p. 245.

3. Antonov-Ovseenko, "O banditskom dvizhenii v Tambovskoi gubernii," p. 6.

4. Donkov, "Organizatsiia razgroma antonovshchiny," *Voprosy Istorii KPSS*, no. 6 (June 1966), p. 64.

5. Trifonov, *Klassy i klassovaia bor'ba*, part 1, p. 246.

6. Donkov, "Organizatsiia razgroma antonovshchiny," *Voprosy Istorii KPSS*, no. 6 (June 1966), p. 64, n. 31.

7. Fomichev (Lidin), "Antonovshchina: I₂ vospominanii antonovtsa" (Santiago de Chile, 1955), pp. 11 ff., 32.

8. From the Central State Archives of the Soviet Army cited in Trifonov, *Klassy i klassovaia bor'ba*, part 1, p. 247.

9. Antonov-Ovseenko, "O banditskom dvizhenii v Tambovskoi gubernii," p. 10.

10. S. Ch., "Tambovskaia pamiatka ob eserakh," *Izvestiia*, no. 121 (1560), 2 June 1922, p. 1.

11. Donkov, "Organizatsiia razgroma antonovshchiny," *Voprosy Istorii KPSS*, no. 6 (June 1966), p. 64; Trifonov, *Klassy i klassovaia bor'ba*, part 1, p. 246.

12. See below.

13. Donkov, "Organizatsiia razgroma antonovshchiny," *Voprosy Istorii KPSS*, no. 6 (June 1966), pp. 63–64. This material is taken from the Central Party Archives.

14. Antonov-Ovseenko, "O banditskom dvizhenii v Tambovskoi gubernii," p. 6; Trifonov, *Klassy i klassovaia bor'ba*, part 1, pp. 245–46; "Antonovshchina," in *Sovetskaia istoricheskaia entsiklopediia*, vol. 1, p. 636.

15. Trifonov, *Klassy i klassovaia bor'ba*, part 1, pp. 12, 18–19.

16. Anonymous (Podbelski), *Kak tambovskie krest'iane boriatsia za svobodu*, pp. 4–5.

17. Virta, *Odinochestvo*, p. 101.

18. Anonymous (Podbelski), *Kak tambovskie krest'iane boriatsia za svobodu*, p. 7.

19. Cited in Trifonov, *Klassy i klassovaia bor'ba*, part 1, p. 245, from the Central State Archives of the Soviet Army.

20. Ibid., p. 246. So much for the ridiculous fictional account (above) of forty thousand men on the eve of the insurrection. Stalin must have been easily impressed when he awarded a prize to this novelist.

21. See above.

22. Tukhachevski, "Zapiska," p. 1.

23. Trifonov, *Klassy i klassovaia bor'ba*, part 1, p. 56, citing an article by B. Leonidov, "Esero-banditizm v Tambovskoi gubernii i bor'ba s nim" [SR banditry in Tambov province and the struggle with it], in *Revoliutsiia i Voina*, nos. 14–15 (1922), p. 158, a journal not available to the author of this study. For statement of Antonov-Ovseenko regarding this matter, see below.

24. Dokunin, "Tambovskii schet sotsial-banditam," *Pravda*, no. 123, 4 June 1922, p. 3.

25. *Obvinitel'noe zakliuchenie po delu tsentral'nogo komiteta p. s.-r.*, p. 44 (testimony of Ishin); Alekseev, *Oktiabr' i grazhdanskaia voina v TsChO*, p. 105.

26. Trifonov, *Klassy i klassovaia bor'ba*, part 1, pp. 246, 247; "Antonov-shchina," in *Sovetskaia istoricheskaia entsiklopediia*, vol. 1, p. 636.

27. VOKhR is a product of the Soviet passion for shortening long institutional names, since transmitted to the rest of the world; it denotes *Vnutrenniaia Okhrana* (the Internal Security Force).

28. Trifonov, *Klassy i klassovaia bor'ba*, part 1, p. 246. On measures taken, see also Donkov, "Organizatsiia razgroma antonovshchiny," *Voprosy Istorii KPSS*, no. 6 (June 1966), pp. 63–64.

29. Antonov-Ovseenko, "O banditskom dvizhenii v Tambovskoi gubernii," p. 10. Antonov-Ovseenko does not specify the period, but clearly implies that the toll was taken in the initial stage of the insurrection.

30. Given by Podbelski as 'Raskatovo but maps do not show such a place, whereas Rasskazovo was an important station on this line in the forest east of Tambov.

31. Anonymous (Podbelski), *Kak tambovskie krest'iane boriatsia za svobodu*, pp. 7–8, 12; Trifonov, *Klassy i klassovaia bor'ba*, part 1, pp. 246, 247.

32. Cited in Trifonov, *Klassy i klassovaia bor'ba*, part 1, p. 246.

33. "Selianskii" means "rustic one" or "villager." Matiukhin already has one pseudonym ("Zheltov" in the Fomichev manuscript) and may have had this one also, especially since he was a peasant and had his base in this same forested area in 1921 at the time of the debacle. But it is only a guess—a little better than other guesses, but still a guess.

34. If little enough is known about Antonov, still less is known of Kolesnikov—virtually nothing, in fact.

35. Antonov-Ovseenko, "O banditskom dvizhenii v Tambovskoi gubernii," p. 8.

36. See above.

37. Fomichev (Lidin), "Antonovshchina: Iz vospominanii antonovtsa" (Santiago de Chile, 1955), p. 25.

38. Antonov-Ovseenko, "O banditskom dvizhenii v Tambovskoi gubernii," p. 10.

39. Anonymous (Podbelski), *Kak tambovskie krest'iane boriatsia za svobodu,* p. 5.

40. Trifonov, *Klassy i klassovaia bor'ba,* part 1, p. 246.

41. Ibid. See above.

42. Antonov-Ovseenko, "O banditskom dvizhenii v Tambovskoi gubernii," p. 10. See also N. A. Okatov, *Tambovskaia partiinaia organizatsiia v period vosstanovleniia narodnogo khoziaistva (1921–1925 gg.)* (Tambov, 1961), p. 9. Here the shrinkage in membership is given as from 14,200 in June 1920 to 7,916 in August 1921. As the latter count was taken in the period of victory, it may well exceed the figure for ebb-tide in the preceding winter.

43. See above.

44. That Antonov's movement had outgrown the available means of coping with it and that the Tambov soviet and party would have to have outside help on the national scale have been generally recognized in Soviet sources. See Donkov, "Organizatsiia razgroma antonovshchiny," *Voprosy Istorii KPSS,* no. 6 (June 1966), p. 64; Borisov, *Chernym letom,* p. 39; Zybko, *Tambovskaia partiinaia organizatsiia,* p. 38; Alekseev, *Oktiabr' i grazhdanskaia voina v TsChO,* p. 104.

45. Trifonov, *Klassy i klassovaia bor'ba,* part 1, p. 247.

46. From the Central Party Archives as rendered in Donkov, "Organizatsiia razgroma antonovshchiny," *Voprosy Istorii KPSS,* no. 6 (June 1966), p. 65.

47. Sofinov, *Ocherki istorii Vserossiiskoi Chrezvychainoi Komissii,* p. 225; Trifonov, *Klassy i klassovaia bor'ba,* part 1, pp. 232, 247.

48. Perhaps there were other, regular army, troops in the garrison. If so their fate is not indicated nor their presence even noted. Earlier Soviet studies have of late been berated for not stressing the role of the party, with the result that recent studies have gone overboard in magnifying Communist heroism. The line is laid down and Trifonov and others slavishly conform.

49. *Put' Bor'by,* vol. 2 *(Antonovshchina),* pp. 44, 45, as rendered in Trifonov, *Klassy i klassovaia bor'ba,* part 1, 231.

50. Anonymous (Podbelski), *Kak tambovskie krest'iane boriatsia za svobodu,* p. 10. It is not to be excluded that the two sources are dealing with the same incident under different guises, Trifonov having the lightning strike the ChON, and Podbelski the Che-ka. It is even possible that the ChON unit was the execution squad of the Che-ka. The author of the present study is entirely dependent upon the Soviet source for the information contained in *Put' Bor'by,* as he cannot remember what was said on pages 44 and 45. Very probably the information there is more detailed and could resolve the uncertainty. In any event, the Soviet sustained one or more disasters at Inzhavino.

Communists taxed the SRs with greeting Antonov's excesses and cited as an example Podbelski's laconic comment on this incident as reproduced in the SR press. See G. Neradov, "K protsessu pravykh eserov: Sviaz' s antonovshchinoi" [Concerning the trial of the right SRs: The connection with the Antonov affair], *Izvestiia,* no. 117 (1556), 28 May 1922, p. 2.

9

In Bloody Deadlock (January–June 1921)

The early months of 1921 would see determined efforts on both sides to break out of the deadlock that had developed with the extinction of Soviet power in the rural areas of three *uezds* and with "bandits" at large in two others. Thanks to the Trotsky Archive and Lenin's collected works as well as to the secondary accounts by Trifonov and Donkov—based, however, on the Soviet archives— we are reasonably well informed as to what went on from the Soviet side but almost totally in the dark regarding affairs in the insurrectionary camp. Two of the non-Soviet sources fall away at this point,[1] the drums of propaganda are momentarily stilled—and with them, comment in the Soviet press—while everything else yields virtually nothing. Proceeding, then, from the known to the unknown, from the realm of fact to that of deduction and speculation, we shall first examine the decisions made on high in the Soviet government, then make whatever comment is possible about the efforts of the Greens to stave off the fate closing in upon them, and turn thereafter to the military events and the execution of the Soviet program.

When he wrote on 9 September 1920 to A. G. Schlichter, chairman of the Tambov soviet, asking him to provide food for two friends of his wife and inquiring about famine conditions,[2] Lenin had not heard about the uprising, or at least it had made no impression on him. He had heard and was duly impressed when he wrote to the assistant food commissar on 27 September. He called that official's attention to the province, asked whether it was true that the food levy amounted to eleven million *poods*, and wondered whether it should not be reduced.[3] His concern had increased by mid-October when he ordered E. M. Sklianski, Trotski's assistant at the war commissariat, to bring about a "swift and full liquidation" of the revolt in Tambov and to inform him of the measures taken.[4]

Even more peremptory were his admonitions four days later to Kornev, head of the VOKhR, and to Dzerzhinski as chairman of the Extraordinary Commission, in response to an appeal from Schlichter for more aid—especially in cavalry—because of a worsening situation. Lenin's "swift and full liquidation" had now become "swiftest and most exemplary liquidation," such an outcome was termed "unconditionally necessary," and he broadly intimated that Kornev and Dzerzhinski needed to display more energy.[5] Kornev reacted promptly with a report on measures taken to quell the revolt; unfortunately, the text or even the gist of the report is not given.[6]

Lenin's sense of frustration soon deepened into rage when he learned that Antonov had seized the Boldyrev factories at Rasskazovo. Branding this reverse as the "height of absurdity," he sent off a sizzling note to Dzerzhinski wherein he found the Che-ka and soviet personnel of Tambov so grievously at fault that he wanted them brought before a military tribunal, Kornev severely reprimanded, and people of superior energy despatched to the Tambov scene.[7]

He was not a merciful man, even toward his own breed. But a special degree of mercilessness was reserved for the miserable peasantry whose women in Tambov province were disarming the food levy people and arming the bandits. The food collectors must be hard when necessary, Lenin told N. A. Miliutin, plenipotentiary of the food commissariat to Orel province; struggle is struggle and a rifle is not for ornamentation. Lenin felt uneasy over the prospect that the "Antonov fire" might leap to other provinces; Orel was near at hand, and he warned Miliutin of the danger that the flame might consume his province as well.[8]

Nothing illustrates better Lenin's preoccupation with Tambov— amid all his other preoccupations—than his words to Sklianski, either at the end of 1920 or at the beginning of 1921, about the need each day of "driving forward by the mane and by the tail, of beating and whipping the commander-in-chief [9] and Frunze[10] so that they would run down and catch Antonov and Makhno."[11] And now his imperiousness was beginning to produce results in respect to the reinforcements pouring into Tambov province and the decisions being taken in highest quarters to combat a situation that was growing worse instead of better.

Let us take first the decisions on high. Early in January 1921 the Organizational Bureau of the Central Committee of the Communist party met with Dzerzhinski, S. S. Kamenev, Kornev, and men from the local scene to discuss what should be done. Henceforth the Central Committee itself and the Soviet government—we will preserve the fiction of the Soviet system although, of course, the Central Committee made the decisions—assumed direction of the task of repression to which primary importance was assigned because of the danger involved.[12] Already the Central Committee and the Sovnarkom (Council of People's Commissars) had sent out plenipotentiaries to investigate and "assist" the Tambov organs, some as early as the first month of the insurrection.

In January 1921 A. V. Lunacharski arrived on the scene; one will note that the competence of this gentleman was not restricted to cultural matters. Things really began to move on 12 January and along two lines when the Central Committee set up two commissions, the one repressive and the other concessive, the one brandishing the stick and the other tendering some candy, the one baring the "wolf's fang" and the other waving the "fox's tail,"[13] or whatever expression one wishes to use. It was the technique of Bismarck, even if the Central Committee acted out of fear as well as calculation whereas the Iron Chancellor had acted out of calculation alone.

The commission on repression grew into the Central Interdepartmental Commission for War on Banditry which began work on 27 January. Interlocking with other key organs of the Soviet system—Che-Ka, ChON, army command, and so on—it functioned directly under the Central Committee as well as under the Council of Commissars; in fact, no less than three members of the Central Committee—Dzerzhinski, F. A. Sergeev (Artem), and L. P. Serebriakov—were also members of the commission, and Dzerzhinski in addition stood at the head of the Che-ka. This Commission for War on Banditry started off, not inappropriately, under Dzerzhinski himself, but after the magnitude of the task exceeded the power of the Che-ka and caused it to be overshadowed by the army he yielded the chairmanship to Sklianski, Trotski's deputy at the war ministry. Military operations proceeded under the supervision of the commission—not only those in Tambov, to be sure, but wherever there was an infestation of "bandits" (according to the official terminology), or wherever the Green movement had gotten under way (according to ours). In April 1921 the main attention of the commission focused on Tambov, although the province was prominent in its thoughts both before and after that month.[14]

The other commission set up by the Central Committee on 12 January had as its stated purpose the consideration of measures looking toward the "swift amelioration" of the lot of the peasantry. The hand of the Central Committee was guided on this occasion not by the plight of the peasantry, but by fear that repressive action alone might not be enough to contain the Green movement. While there had been some previous indication of a disposition in high quarters to loosen the straitjacket enclosing the peasants, the conception of what should be done bore little resemblance to the far-reaching concessions soon to be made.[15] Furthermore, with respect to the specific problem of Tambov, the proposal for relaxation now in the making would stand for only a few days before being swept away in the flood of events. This second commission, consisting of Kalinin, E. A. Preobrazhenski, and the same ubiquitous F. A. Sergeev (Artem) whom patronage by Lenin and decorative value as a proletarian had raised to high rank in this party, never achieved a separate identity of its own but seems to have functioned merely as a subcommittee of the Central Committee which not surprisingly reserved for its immediate supervision questions concerning the very nature of the regime.

The Tambov provincial committee of the party decided on 25 January 1921 to draw the attention of the Central Committee to the "exceptionally grave" political situation in the province resulting from an acute shortage of food. At its session of 2 February the supreme organ of the Communist party discussed in detail this question and recommended to the Food Commissariat a speedy reduction in the amount of the food levy where peasants were suffering intensely from failure of crops. The recommendation was made in view of the political situation in the province. Yet on 12 February—ten days later—the Central Committee and the national government found it possible, in the face of the provisioning crisis that had overtaken the whole country, to grant the request of the Tambov authorities (both party and soviet) for a complete cessation of food procurements in the province. All food detachments were removed and the flow of produce reversed through distribution of seed to the peasants for the approaching sowing campaign.

Two days later Lenin received a deputation of peasants from Tambov, no doubt hand-picked by the provincial authorities and duly deferential, as one would expect. He disclosed to them the "anti-popular character of the Antonov movement," advised them of the impending change in government policy, and summoned them to proceed mercilessly against the enemies of the state, especially those within the gates in the soviet organs of power. "What Comrade Lenin Told the Peasants of Tambov" appeared in the first number of the newly founded *Tambovskii Pakhar'* (*Tambov Plowman*), then in a separate pamphlet, and was brought to the peasants even more directly by the returning deputies who made the rounds of the villages under soviet occupation and urged the rebels to lay down their arms and return to peaceful labor.[16]

In between these events, at the fateful session of 8 February 1921, the *Politbiuro* of the Central Committee had taken the decisive step toward throwing the levers of the Soviet state into reverse by adopting Lenin's preliminary draft of theses for abolition of the food levy and its replacement by a tax in kind which would alleviate the burden imposed by the state, reward the peasant for greater effort, and leave him a surplus—after payment of the tax—which he could sell on the local market for whatever it would bring. Merely to recite the concessions is to take the measure of the aberrations of the Soviet regime as it had been in its first few years and as it would be again under Joseph Stalin and his successors. The action of the *Politbiuro* on 8 February became the basis for the decision of the Tenth Party Congress in March, ending the policies of war communism and inaugurating those of the New Economic Policy.[17]

It was quite a change and in so little time. In the fall of 1920 Lenin had thought the food levy people remiss in not using their rifles more freely when seizing the peasants' grain.[18] In December he was casting around for some means of rewarding the peasant for a better performance without rewarding the kulak, whom he baldly acknowledged to be the best performer.[19] On 8 February he capitulated to the peasantry, and on 24 February in a communication to Christian G. Rakovski, satrap in the Ukraine, he went so far as to propose rewarding the peasants at any cost, even by buying abroad with gold or oil the inducements necessary to raise production.[20]

The measure of his desperation is perhaps best seen in his willingness to subordinate even heavy industry to the supreme necessity of increasing agricultural production, although he correctly noted that there was no basic conflict of interest since the existing situation strapped down heavy industry like everything else.[21] On this occasion, addressing the Tenth Party Congress on 15 March 1921, he fairly drove his party down the path of the New Economic Policy, admonishing the congress that that very evening the word must go out to the world that the relationship between the proletariat and the peasantry had been set aright by affording the necessary stimulus to the small agricultural producer.[22]

What had happened? Not a sudden worsening of natural conditions underlying the approach of famine: nature was as harsh on 2 February when the Central Committee had contemplated a reduction of the food levy in cases of acute distress, as on 12 February when it scrapped the whole apparatus of the food levy in Tambov. And not a sudden deterioration in the military situation: from the fragmentary information available, no drastic change had ensued there between December 1920 when Lenin had in mind quite niggardly concessions on the agrarian front,[23] and 24 February 1921 when he wrote in desperation to Rakovski that he wanted to provide incentive for the peasants at any cost, after having already initiated on 8 February the reforms constituting the New Economic Policy. On the contrary, the military situation in Tambov was more favorable to the Communists in February 1921 because of a massive buildup which had already given them superiority in numbers, to say nothing of their superiority in armaments. No, something unforeseen had happened elsewhere, something in relation to which the Communists lose their accustomed volubility and over which they have laid a gravestone of silence.

A formidable insurrection had broken out in western Siberia, quite similar to the Tambov insurrection but involving a much larger force and extending over a much broader area. It lacked, however, the solid base of the Tambov insurrection, for the Siberian Peasants' Union (SKS) was not as well put together as the Tambov Union of Toiling Peasantry (STK) and the Siberian peasants had no Antonov to lead them. Hence it would not be so long sustained, but while it lasted it was quite enough to convince Lenin and his party that only a drastic change in agrarian policy could save the regime.

And so neither Makhno nor Antonov nor Kronstadt produced the astonishing reversal in the party line; the Siberian insurrection was the mainspring of the New Economic Policy. Actually it was the cumulative effect of all of these insurrections, the Siberian superimposed on the others, that brought about for all too brief a time (seven to eight years) an alleviation of the harsh lot of the Russian peasant alike under Tsar and commissar. But it was the events in western Siberia that flipped over the helm of state and if Lenin still had moments of hesitation, the uprising in Armenia which broke out on 13 February and "spread like lightning,"[24] and the Kronstadt rebellion that erupted on 28 February would strengthen his resolution.

Heavy fighting raged in Siberia from 4 February onward, and within a few days the Greens were astride the Omsk–Tiumen and Omsk–Cheliabinsk railroads, severing the twin lifelines over which moved the produce of the Siberian granary to the food-deficient Moscow and Petersburg regions. With the Ukraine a prey to anarchy and famine stalking the Volga, Lenin advised the Moscow Communists that the cities were living for the most part on supplies from Siberia and the North Caucasus, and of these two breadbaskets Siberia was the more important and the loss of its contribution could not be made good from the Caucasus.[25] Not only was that region secondary to Siberia as a source of foodstuffs,[26] but shipments from the North Caucasus were continuously threatened and at times interrupted by Antonov's movements athwart the rail lines or by Makhno's further west.

Clearing the Siberian tracks was the first charge on the Soviet regime but overcoming Antonov was a related enterprise, to say nothing of the example afforded peasants everywhere by his stubborn defiance of Soviet authority. Lenin spoke of the pressure on the southeastern railroad to compensate as much as possible for the loss of Siberian grain; he noted some improvement in respect to deliveries from the Caucasus, but warned that the situation could worsen again (as it did).[27] It was Antonov who could make it worse, and herein lies the explanation of the strenuous effort now to be directed against him.

The Tambov insurrection must have been much on the minds of the Soviet leaders, even in the midst of the Siberian convulsion, and when the danger lessened from that quarter Tambov engaged their primary attention. Already the dual method of repression had been foreshadowed: cajolery and coercion were to be tried simultaneously, the cajolery accompanied by substantial concessions, the coercion unmitigated by merciful considerations. On the day he received the peasant deputation—14 February—Lenin conferred with the Tambov party secretary,[28] and now at the end of February a decisive step was taken with the constitution of the Plenipotentiary Commission of the All-Russian Soviet Central Executive Committee for the Suppression of Banditry in Tambov Province.

The Plenipotentiary Commission was plenipotentiary with a vengeance. There was no aspect of ruling the province which it did not encompass. If the Soviet effort against Antonov had hitherto suffered from dispersion of authority and from lack of coordination among the various repressive organs, that deficiency would now be remedied by fusing all authority in the commission. Under it were formed district political commissions of similar structure and similarly endowed with the plenitude of power within the respective military districts.[29]

It must always be remembered, however, that the commission and its subsidiary organs operated under the direct supervision of the central authorities in Moscow, now determined to exert unrelenting pressure for the elimination of the Green danger in Tambov. The Central Committee of the Communist Party said in its circular to the provincial committees on 23 April 1921 that Tambov "has been in recent months and is still the unifying center of organized kulak-SR banditry."[30] Actually there was no unifying center, but if there had been one it would logically have been Tambov. The chairman of the Plenipotentiary Commission reported to the Central Committee and to the Council of Labor and Defense as well as to the Soviet Central Executive Committee to which his commission was nominally responsible; in fact he reported directly to Lenin.

The chairman was A. V. Antonov-Ovseenko, a prominent Bolshevik who had helped lead the assault on the Winter Palace at the birth of the Soviet regime and who had amassed considerable experience in party and in military affairs. Among other posts he had occupied was the chairmanship of the Tambov provincial soviet executive committee in 1919–1920. And so he did not come new to the scene of his impending exertions. His long hair and spectacles would have made him at home in a hippie haven and his facial expression suggests the intellectual who has been swallowed up in a cause. His fanaticism and ruthlessness must have commended him to Lenin as just the man for the assignment.

Though he functioned under the Supreme Soviet, his appointment emanated from the Central Committee of the Communist Party. He presided over a commission which had as its other members V. A. Vasiliev, secretary of the provincial committee of the Communist party, A. S. Lavrov, chairman of the provincial soviet executive committee, P. A. Pavlov, commander of the troops in Tambov province (later replaced by M. N. Tukhachevski), and A. I. Zhabin, head of the political section of the forces commanded first by Pavlov and later by Tukhachevski. The commission thus represented a fusion of the party, soviet and military authorities at the top level, and its six district political commissions would embody the same principle at the *uezd* and local levels. It appears that Antonov-Ovseenko was de facto dictator in the province, subject, of course, to instructions from Moscow.[31]

No sooner had the Plenipotentiary Commission been constituted at the end of February 1921 than it posed for itself certain basic tasks. First it would strive to split up the peasantry, drawing off the middle and lower strata of the village population into neutrality and then into active support of the Soviet regime, while isolating the kulak stratum and then convincing it of the "economic disadvantage" of prolonging the insurrection. The wedge was to be driven as the result of a campaign combining both military and political action—in other words, both coercion and cajolery would be

involved. It is interesting to note that in thus formulating the primary
task of the campaign of repression, Antonov-Ovseenko tacitly
admitted—in private, of course, since only Lenin and a few others
would see his memorandum—that at the outset he faced a solid wall
of peasant resistance and that the Tambov insurrection was far from
being merely a kulak affair.

The second task was the military one of driving the "bandits" out
of their strongholds from which they drew sustenance and recruits,
of subjecting these to a prolonged and rigorous occupation, and of
crushing the "bandits" in the field. The third task might be termed
removing the root of infection by "taking out" the "bandit" element
according to lists of proscription compiled by the Che-ka; on these
lists would be entered the names of Antonov's warriors, of those
who served in his internal security forces, and of those who were
members of committees of the STK. Antonov-Ovseenko stopped
here but we may lengthen the list by including members of the SR or
Left SR parties, members of liberal or conservative parties
(principally Constitutional Democrats), officers of the Imperial
army, and anyone else suspected of disloyalty to the existing regime.
In short, there was to be a purge of the population. The program was
thoroughgoing, as one can see.[32]

Before the plan could be executed, it was necessary to have
dependable instruments. The commissar of repression surveyed the
scene and found it not to his liking. Not only was the insurrection in
its seventh month and holding its own, but conditions in his own
camp looked rather bad. The Communist party itself, the political
police, the ordinary police or militia, and the troops on garrison duty
or in the field were all dispirited and promised to be so many brittle
swords in his hand. The general spirit of disaffection which had
produced the insurrection seeped also into the apparatus of the
existing order and weakened the will to subdue its enemies;
economic and climatic conditions, very bad and getting worse,
worked in the same direction. And so Antonov-Ovseenko had first
to reform his own forces before facing the foe.

He began with the party. The Communists of Tambov, never very
numerous or well-organized, had seen their ranks riddled with
dissent and even their leaders affected. The secretary of the

provincial committee—the chief party official in Tambov, N. M. Nemtsov—had sided with the "workers' opposition"; B. Ia. Pinson and others had done likewise (it has not been possible to establish the party position of B. Ia. Pinson). The provincial committee as constituted in the latter half of 1920 and the early months of 1921 is said to have been incapable of work, with the result that slackness developed in ties with local organizations and party policy was faultily executed.[33] The deplorable conditions of the time, attributable at least in some measure to Communist rule, had led some party members to move toward the right long before that deviation became prominent in the party as a whole;[34] others had taken fright at the uprising and had fallen away.

The unsatisfactory state of affairs engaged the attention of Lenin himself, for on 14 February he conferred with Nemtsov in addition to receiving the peasant deputation from Tambov. Evidently he decided on this occasion or soon after to replace Nemtsov as party secretary with V. A. Vasiliev, since the appointment was made by the Central Committee[35] rather than by the Plenipotentiary Commission. The fact that Vasiliev was shifted from the Donets Basin shows the importance attached to his new assignment. He may have been an abler man and certainly was a harder one, untainted by any suggestion of dissent.

Aside from this appointment, the Plenipotentiary Commission carried through the work of party reorganization. Like everything else in the Communist party, the decisions were made on high and imposed on the rank and file. It was decreed that a provincial party conference should be called out of turn for the purpose of reelecting the provincial committee and adopting "hard combative" decisions. The "hurrah democracy" emanating from the last regular conference was to be exorcised and all such manifestations "severely repressed" within the party. We do not know what was meant by "hurrah democracy" but entertain a healthy suspicion that "genuine democracy" would have been a synonym.

The Eleventh Extraordinary Conference of the Russian Communist Party of Tambov Province was convened on 1–3 or 2–3 March 1921 and elected a new committee with exceptional powers. This committee exemplified the same fusion of authority as the commission that dictated its election: the soviet hierarchy, the

military command, and the political police were represented along
with party functionaries. M. D. Antonov sat for the Che-ka, being
identified as its provincial chairman. Of the eight committee
members listed in the party archives, half were also members of the
commission—Vasiliev, Lavrov, Zhabin, and Antonov-Ovseenko
himself—as were four of the five members of the presidium. The
semblance of local assent to what would now take place had been
created; "hurrah democracy" had given way to manipulated
democracy. The Eleventh Conference placed the whole party
organization on a war footing preparatory to decreeing the
mobilization of the membership. The new committee, endowed with
full disciplinary powers, shook up the party over a two-week period
in the latter part of March, tightening its structure and insuring a
submissive membership. A purge of the party preceded the purge of
the population.[36]

The shakeup on the local scene preliminary to launching the
campaign against the Greens could not fail to extend to the secret
police, that indispensable arm of a communist state. Heretofore it
had not accomplished very much, aside from the arrest of the SR
leadership in the fall of 1920. It had been particularly weak in respect
to intelligence operations in the rural areas, Antonov's espionage
had run circles around it, and Antonov-Ovseenko relates how—
even as late as the middle of March 1921—rumors of attack blown up
in official quarters and not countered by effective work on the part of
the Che-ka had produced cases of absurd panic in Tambov city.
Now all that would end, he told Lenin, as a result of the "energetic
action" of comrades brought in from elsewhere and of substantial
help from the new party committee. The most specific information
concerning the influx of Chekists is offered by the Tambov
compilation, which states that in the spring of 1921 a hundred of
them arrived from Moscow.[37]

And now comes the mystery. The same source goes on to say that
among the hundred agents was the special plenipotentiary to
Tambov province, comrade Antonov. Yet other contributors to the
same compilation attribute the reorganization and toning up of the
political police in Tambov province to a comrade Levin,[38] an
assertion not contradicted by Antonov-Ovseenko who even speaks
of Levin as the plenipotentiary of the Che-ka.[39] Two plenipoten-

tiaries there could not be unless one had been superseded by the other, in this case presumably Antonov by Levin, although the dearth of definite chronological information makes it impossible to establish a firm sequence here—and often elsewhere. All we can say is that pursuant to the February decision of the Central Interdepartmental Commission in Moscow to revitalize the Tambov division of the Che-ka with experienced workers,[40] an M. D. Antonov figured as chairman of the provincial Che-ka when he was elected a member of the new party committee at the Eleventh Extraordinary Conference, probably on 3 March.[41]

The author of this study thought to resolve the difficulty by assuming that M. D. Antonov served as nominal head while Levin managed affairs from behind the scenes; but this assumption will not do, for there is record of a telegram sent by Dzerzhinski on 14 April to Levin as chairman of the provincial Che-ka.[42] If M. D. Antonov had been found wanting and was replaced by Levin no confirmation can be found in the available sources, nor is there anything to suggest that Levin might have assumed the name Antonov to conceal his Jewish origin; such an expedient, not uncommon in Tsarist times, would not likely be adopted under a regime that treated manifestations of anti-Semitism as a crime even if it could not eradicate anti-Semitism. In any event, the disappearing act of the Che-ka Antonov—if he disappeared[43]—eases a situation that would have become intolerable had three Antonovs occupied the center of the stage at the same time; as it is, the commissar of repression has a hyphenated name and the name Antonov without adornment can be reserved for the Green leader.

Whoever reorganized the Tambov Che-ka made it into an effective instrument for combatting the Green movement. By early April, according to Antonov-Ovseenko, it had been put on its feet and thereafter did a great deal of work, fruitful in the highest degree. Extension and improvement of the network of village informers, partly by bribing the miserable population with gifts of scarce products, enabled it to compile lists of Antonov's soldiers, of activists in the STK, of Soviet employees sympathetic to the Green movement, and to uncover the threads of organization and supply of Antonov's forces—even to identify elements of his army with particular localities and to establish the degree of guilt of a given village in respect to participation in the uprising.

The civilian organization behind the Green army received as much attention as the army itself, since the Communists had learned to respect that organization. Suspects were listed among the railwaymen and the staffs of cooperative societies—traditional nests, respectively, of the Left SRs and the regular SRs. An especial effort was made to tighten the espionage in depots, arsenals, and warehouses in order to plug up leaks in weapons and military equipment of all kinds. Finally the Che-ka embarked upon an enterprise peculiarly Communist: kulak families in "bandit" villages were singled out according to the (economic?) census of 1917 as prospective victims of mass deportation in case Moscow should sanction this throwback to the transplantation policy of Ivan III and Vasili III at the time of the extinction of the free communities of Novgorod and Pskov.[44]

The uprising from the day of its inception was far too formidable to be dealt with by the Che-ka, which could bring its work to fruition only in the shadow of a victorious army. And the army had not been victorious save here and there; at best it had achieved a stalemate in the first half-year of operations. Hence the decision to bring in reinforcements, now feasible—at least to a limited degree—because of the end of the first civil war and the armistice with Poland. The movement of troops into Tambov province began in December 1920[45] and continued through January and February of the new year.

Figures on Soviet troop dispositions are never easy to obtain but in this instance we are favored with some rather precise information from a credible source. In January 1921 came three ChON (Special Assignment) regiments from Moscow, the 15th cavalry division from the Kiev military district, a cavalry brigade from the Caucasus, and a rifle brigade from the Western front; the Volga military district sent another rifle brigade, and forces with equipment wholly denied the Greens were moved in from here and there, including three armored detachments, three armored trains, and an aviation unit. All in all, the month of January saw the Soviet forces in Tambov province augmented by 9,659 bayonets, 1,943 sabers, 136 machine guns, and 18 cannon. The buildup in February is not specified beyond the drawing in of partially-trained elements. On 1 March 1921 the total Soviet military strength in Tambov province is set at

32,500 bayonets, 7,948 sabers, 463 machine guns, and 63 cannon—mute testimony to the strength of the insurrection, especially when it is borne in mind that even this concentration of force would not be enough.[46]

As the Plenipotentiary Commission entered upon its labors the numerical balance inclined decidedly in its favor. Already by the end of January the Soviet side had achieved numerical superiority,[47] to say nothing of the advantage enjoyed in armaments, and by 1 March it seems reasonable to conclude that the Greens were outnumbered two to one.[48] And yet all was not well in the Soviet camp.

Some of the units made up of local deserters, presumably those who had given themselves up or had been apprehended and allowed to work off their offense, were suspect as to their mood. Military intelligence was so poor that more or less accurate information came only from aerial reconnaissance. The office personnel attached to the staffs was recruited locally and reflected local sentiment; it was lacking in zeal and often in loyalty. Political work among the troops was neglected. But probably the most serious weakness concerned supply, both of military equipment and of food; one is astonished to learn that even as late as the beginning of June soldiers in some places were quite literally starving.[49] No wonder morale among the units of the Red Army was low, probably distinctly inferior to that of the Green bands although one would never find this concession in Soviet sources.

It is apparent that the Plenipotentiary Commission faced its hardest task in respect to the military, that it would have to exert more effort and wait longer for results than in toning up either the party or the Che-ka. But it went at its task with animal vigor: it weeded out unreliable elements in the military administration, removed unreliable units from the province, strove to bring order into the supply and provisioning of the troops by gradually shifting them from living off the land to government purveyance, stirred up the political sections to work harder—clearly defining their relationship to the regular command—and tightened discipline through reorganization of the military courts.

Despite this outburst of activity the commissar of repression was constrained to admit in his report to Lenin that unsatisfactory conditions persisted for some time: lack of adequate personnel held back the work of the political section through all of April and into

May, the supply of military equipment continued to be badly handled until mid-May, and the problem of feeding the troops resisted solution until June although some improvement could be registered before then. Yet in the struggle to better the situation the Plenipotentiary Commission did not change the command; the troops in Tambov province continued to be led by P. A. Pavlov and K. V. Redzko[50] as they had been since the beginning of the year. Why the commission made no change in this respect is not apparent since the conduct of operations in January and February had notably failed to break the stalemate. It remained for Moscow to shake up the command at a later date.[51]

In all of the work of the Plenipotentiary Commission, and in the attitude of the sources of power above it, one guiding principle can be discerned. Whether in respect to the party secretaryship and other positions of party leadership, or in respect to the head of the political police and his key assistants, or in respect to the political and staff work of the army—local personnel was either replaced or rigidly subordinated to party personnel brought in from elsewhere.[52] The failure to remove Pavlov at this time is no exception in view of his previous assignment as head of the Moscow administration of the military training program.[53]

The provincial party organization, the provincial Che-ka, the army units in the province, and the soviets (about which no specific information is available) had all felt the heavy hand of Moscow. It is a very good example, and an early one, of how everything is staged and managed in the Soviet system; how the hard-core party leadership imposes its will on the party membership, then on the network of soviets, and finally on the public at large. At the same time the weeding out of "local" personnel—we are indebted for the quotation marks to Antonov-Ovseenko—is an unwilling tribute to the strength of the Green movement, for the disaffection that produced it had reached even into the organs of power and blunted the instruments in the hands of the Communist oligarchy, forcing it either to refashion these instruments or to find new ones to use in their place.

While these events were transpiring in the Soviet camp, what was Antonov doing to avert the fate implicit in the mobilization against him? Doubtless the STK, headed by Pluzhnikov, labored to develop further its supply and recruitment services with results that made this the best-organized insurrection in Russia. The blows absorbed and the resilience displayed leave no doubt as to the success attained. But otherwise there is nothing to go on—it is all a blank. If the Greens left any records they repose in the archives of the Che-ka along with so much else. Soviet agencies were badly informed of developments in the enemy camp until the spring of 1921 and have not divulged what little they knew. There is only the battle record, confused and fragmentary, out of which it is not possible to construct any definite pattern.

The winter of 1920–1921 did not lead to a suspension of operations, perhaps because of the exceptional dryness that accompanied the usual cold. In January the Soviet command attempted an ambitious operation based on the maintenance of a solid front—or rather, two solid fronts—the one assembled on the Tambov–Kirsanov line and moving southward toward a junction with the other, which took off from the line Balashov–Novokhopersk and advanced northward; the jaws would close on Antonov's army and write *finis* to the Tambov insurrection. In the heart of the "bandit" country near the villages of Treskino and Kurdiuki a three-day battle ensued at the end of January; Antonov is stated to have lost some forty-five hundred men, including three thousand taken prisoner. Even if these figures were accepted the operation failed in its broader purpose, since the bulk of his forces broke out; but what would have been a loss of less than a tenth of his total strength of fifty thousand, according to the conventional Soviet estimate, would have been a loss of between one-fourth and one-fifth on our reduced—and realistic—scale and so would have been insupportable. In general, Soviet statistics on casualties are unworthy of serious consideration.

The Soviet historian has the Greens dispersed around the middle of February 1921 and their bands shifting to the region east of the Tambov–Balashov railroad—that is, to the valley of the Vorona river—after which he has nine hundred of them destroyed in the Zherdevka area well to the west of that line. A campaign against guerrillas admittedly involved confused fighting, but hardly as confused as such reporting. February ends with an engagement near the village of Boguslavskoe, where a Green force some three thousand strong is said to have sustained severe losses and to have fallen apart into three fragments.

We are not told of any Green successes, only of their reverses, and yet it is likely that the Soviet side also knew defeat. With this meager and mutilated information[54] we come to March, the month of the New Economic Policy and of Lenin's capitulation before the peasantry, and the month that saw Antonov-Ovseenko and the Plenipotentiary Commission already dominating the local scene.

As the commission entered upon its duties, it faced a situation that for months on end had undergone no basic change. The effort of the Soviet command in the wake of substantial reinforcements to destroy Antonov by mass maneuver and by the maintenance of unbroken lines of envelopment had ended in failure. On the other hand, Antonov had not succeeded in broadening the base of the uprising by igniting peasant disaffection in adjoining provinces nor by linking up with bands already operating in them, aside from a tenuous connection with the Kolesnikov band in Voronezh province. Whether he had any wider concept of strategy may be doubted. An émigré writer discerns such a concept in the raids he made into neighboring provinces in the early months of 1921.[55] The argument has logic in its favor but cannot be proved on the basis of what little information is available. Antonov did conduct occasional forays into Voronezh and Saratov provinces, and soon into Penza as well, but the question is whether they were probing operations to test peasant sentiment or were dictated by strictly military considerations such as shaking pursuit or gathering spoils. Thus after the above-mentioned action at Zherdevka, the Greens who crossed into Voronezh and Saratov were escaping rather than carrying out a planned operation.

The relationship between Antonov and Kolesnikov is a tangled one: N. A. Miliutin of the food commissariat wired Lenin on 5 February about the serious situation in Voronezh province arising from Kolesnikov's and Varavva's operations in the southern districts and from Antonov's depredations in the north;[56] and yet when Kolesnikov was defeated on 11 February it was in the central part of the province, and when he sustained a second defeat it was in the north on the border with Tambov, into which province he fled after the initial reverse.[57] Where did Kolesnikov operate, and did

Antonov or his lieutenants campaign in Voronezh or were the depredations attributed to them committed by local bands under the direction of Kolesnikov or independent of him?

Whatever the answer, neither the Soviet forces nor the Greens had been able to gain any decisive advantage and the stalemate continued. The Plenipotentiary Commission now determined to end this situation with a campaign conducted along different lines and without awaiting the results of the measures previously examined in the civilian and military spheres. A new fate awaited the "bandits": instead of being entrapped in their lair they were to be ejected from it and eventually crushed in the field. Meanwhile the bases from which they drew sustenance and filled their ranks would be subjected to a prolonged occupation until their reservoir of sympathy had been drained and the Soviet system solidly reestablished. In other words, the victims of this campaign would be not only the Green army but the population out of which it had come. To be sure, a broad political campaign would be mounted to change the mood of the village—or more particularly, the middle and lower elements of the village—while the execution squads, the concentration camps, the transplantation vans, and deprivation of a place to live or a means of support would complete the work by pulling the kulak backbone and leaving a kind of peasant jelly.

Already at the beginning of March a precise plan of occupation had been worked out, taking into account economic as well as military factors. The triangle formed by the Tambov-Kirsanov railroad, the Tambov-Borisoglebsk railroad, and the border of Saratov province comprised the heart of the "bandit" territory and would constitute the zone of occupation. The trouble with the plan was that the commissar of repression had failed to consult a map, even when reporting to the head of the party and the government: there was no railroad from Tambov to Borisoglebsk. The Tambov–Balashov line would establish the triangle but would not encompass all of the "bandit" infested area, not even the village of Kamenka, headquarters of the Union of Toiling Peasantry and—at least at times—of Antonov's Supreme Operational Staff.

Let us say that Antonov-Ovseenko had in mind an imaginary line from Tambov to Borisoglebsk; it would serve his purpose well enough. Permanent garrisons, none of less than battalion strength, would be stationed at a number of points within the zone, six in Kirsanov *uezd* and four in Tambov, to provide backbone for the counterinsurrectionary work of combing out and overawing the population, while special units—mainly cavalry—would be assigned to each military district for the purpose of running down the bands pressed out of the zone of occupation.[58]

Even as the plan of occupation was being worked out, the Plenipotentiary Commission had inaugurated an offensive which succeeded in separating Antonov from the population that supported him. The Soviet account based on archival materials is a jumble of details without supporting information, of obscure village names with few dates and no locations, so that the pattern of operations is quite effectively concealed. The commissar's observations help to clarify the general picture but fill in very few of the details, so that the task of reconstruction may be likened to reassembling a puzzle that has been dashed to the floor. Here and there, however, something fits together.

Mention has been made of the action at Boguslavskoe,[59] of how Antonov was defeated here at the end of February. If the Boguslavskoe in the Soviet account is, in fact, the village of Bogoslovskoe,[60] then things begin to fall into place. Bogoslovskoe was virtually on the border of Kirsanov *uezd*; evidently Antonov had been forced or had elected to accept battle before abandoning home ground and being driven into Saratov province, whence he now or later would move northward into the Chembar *uezd* of Penza province. We know that he invaded Penza in March 1921 but not in what part of the month. If in the first part, the invasion is part of a continuing operation after the ejection from familiar terrain; if in the latter part there may be no continuity. Clarification comes from an engagement on 11 March some fifteen to seventeen kilometers north of Durovka, where the Reds claim to have annihilated three hundred and captured seventy Greens while losing only twenty killed and wounded of their own.[61] This village, then on the Saratov side of the border and now on the Penza side, clearly lies on the line of march which Antonov would have taken from the vicinity of the previous engagement at Bogoslovskoe into the Chembar *uezd* of Penza province. We know, then, that he invaded this district in the first half of March, one of the very few occasions on which he was willing to try his fortune away from his native habitat.[62]

It is also obvious from the numbers under his command—three thousand at Bogoslovskoe and over two thousand at Durovka[63]— that Antonov had with him as he moved northward only his own Second Army, and only a part of that unless there were other forces accompanying him which for some reason were not involved in the two recorded engagements. Probably he had with him only the core of the Second Army, the one immediately under his command. The First Army, commanded by Tokmakov and later by Boguslavski,[64] was in some other zone of operations. But where? Unfortunately, the miserable information at hand does not provide an answer. The author's surmise is that this army had been based further west, closer to Tambov city, and had been ejected from the triangle and driven to the north of the Tambov–Kirsanov railroad, particularly into the large forest east of the Tsna. Mention of an action at the Green stronghold of Pakhotnyi Ugol,[65] a remote clearing deep in the forest, points in that direction. But there is no certainty. Even the date of the action is withheld; the context suggests it occurred sometime in March but one would have to know when in March to make a firmer judgment. If the surmise be correct, the two insurrectionary armies would have been rather widely separated, the First in the forest near the city of Tambov and the Second under Antonov in the Chembar district of Penza province.

The Plenipotentiary Commission at this juncture seemed less concerned with the two armies than with taking up the roots of the uprising in the zone of occupation. For the time being the population lay at its mercy, yet the occupation had run ahead of the reorganization of the Che-ka and the work of preparing the lists of proscription; that institution was not ready to institute a reign of terror and accordingly the emphasis, in contrast to the later period, rested on propaganda and on inducements to abandon the insurrection. Chief feature of the political campaign now set on foot was the holding of nonpartisan peasant conferences for the purpose of feeling out sentiment in the villages and of undercutting the rebellion by redressing grievances where feasible. Something had been done along this line in February but the movement gathered headway after the occupation of the main insurrectionary area and culminated in a provincial peasant conference from 10–16 March 1921, which fulfilled at least partially the conquerors' desire by calling for an end to the revolt but otherwise gave them little comfort.

For once a peasant assembly convened under Soviet auspices refused to act as a rubber stamp and spoke its own mind. The Antonov-Ovseenko manuscript provides the backstage illumination that would never be found in Soviet publications; as the commissar says, the mood of the village came through with great clarity at this conference. Right off, the delegates challenged the fiction of "worker-peasant power" as being in effect the power of the worker over the peasant and as contravening in any event the natural right of the peasantry to preponderant influence in the Russian state. When a compliant delegate moved to send a telegram of greetings to Lenin, closing with the slogan "Long live the worker–peasant power," other less tractable delegates made a strenuous effort either to strike the final words from the text or at least to change the order of the adjectives so that "peasant" would come before "worker." The commissar characterizes this as a "typical episode" at the conference.

The ire of the rural toilers focused above all on the food levy, on the high-handed actions of its personnel, and on the waste that resulted from its administration. "They cause the grain to rot and the cattle to perish . . . . They hold onto land but do not know how to use it." The burden of providing transport for the state "is ruining the horses; they haul to no purpose, to places where nothing is ready." Soviet officials took bribes[66] and in general "set themselves over the village"—a basic complaint reflecting the peasant view that the existing regime was not their own but rather an alien force imposed through the local soviets or else imposed upon both the soviets and the population.

Although the peasants regarded the regime as dictatorial and as inefficient or outright foolish in its economic operations, they had little understanding for political forms which meant so much to the intellectuals and particularly to the SR intellectuals. Demands for political equality and for convocation of the Constituent Assembly evoked no enthusiasm. When a part of the conference presidium moved the adoption of a resolution in favor of "free elections and equal rights for all citizens regardless of class" these demands were eliminated—by Communist stage managers, one may suppose—without exciting controversy. On the other hand, the assembled peasants decisively threw down Communist proposals to pass village sentences upon the "bandits" and to concert measures of self-defense against them. As Antonov-Ovseenko observed, the peasants feared to collaborate openly with the occupation forces because they were not sure that they would stay. There were also other reasons for this show of independence.

But the peasants were receptive to advances made toward them, to measures of conciliation that promised to ease their lot. They were pleased with the abolition of the food levy, greeted the transition to the tax in kind, and in general manifested near the end of the conference a more friendly attitude toward the Soviet regime which found expression in the summons to the insurgents to lay down their arms.

Very interesting are the comments of our commissar containing an admixture of honesty and hatefulness or Communist dogmatism with genuine analytical ability. He admits straight out that commissars had arrived on the scene "bravely disposing" of *volost'* executive committees and village soviets, even placing their members under arrest for failure to comply with what often were foolish demands. He concedes without cavil that the food levy detachments frequently acted in a manner "directly injurious to the peasant economy without compensatory advantage to the state." He acknowledged the estrangement of the rural population from the state, which it viewed as a taskmaster that issued commands and ordered people around to the detriment of their economic interest.

But he realized the advantage to his side of the peasant disinterest in the purely political demands of the SRs and the STK looking toward the replacement of the soviet system by formal democracy: he correctly observes that the peasant mind did not conceive of any definite form of the state in place of the soviets; and—though he does not say so—he knew in his heart that the peasants and the Greens would easily settle for soviets free of Communist domination. He is only partly correct in asserting that it was the special features of the Soviet regime bred by wartime conditions, not the inevitable conflict between its essence and the will of petty property holders, which irritated the peasantry; this "essence" had had more than a little to do, even in this early period, with the measures of the Soviet government and the actions of its agents in respect to what Lenin called the many-millioned, petty bourgeois ochlocracy.[67]

This nonpartisan peasants' conference in March 1921 had been sufficiently free of Communist domination to serve as an authentic expression of peasant grievances. The concessions which the Plenipotentiary Commission found it possible to make in the wake of the conference speak eloquently of what that class had endured. Permission was granted to buy grain freely within the province when need could be proved. It was to be easier to establish a mill, to get building materials from the forest, to be assigned land by a state agency; the transport service owed to the state was to be set in order and lightened at the time of fieldwork. While collective and state farms were not sacrificed to peasant resentment, they would be converted exclusively into model enterprises for demonstration purposes—no mean undertaking. Out of a special fund of scarce materials created to reward loyalty to the regime in the three most rebellious *uezds* of Kirsanov, Tambov, and Borisoglebsk, a certain amount of manufactured articles, salt, and kerosene would be supplied to villages that had fulfilled the food levy by not less than 50 percent or—in certain exceptional cases—to those that had fallen under the mark. Complaints of abuses by officials and Red Army units became subject to immediate investigation.[68]

Whatever the record of achievement in other respects, Communists can always supply.words in abundance, and a vigorous propaganda campaign was mounted to get the message of the regime across to the rebellious peasantry, particularly the shift in policy embodied in the abandonment of the food levy. To publicize the new decrees and to show that the regime was no longer turning a deaf ear to the plight of the rural toiler, 215,000 copies of thirteen titles appeared between 20 February and the end of March, whereas the number of copies published during the preceding four months (November–February) did not exceed 180,000. Among the new titles were "What Lenin Said to the Tambov Peasants," "The Lowdown on the Bandits," and a special peasant newspaper, "The Tambov Plowman." Only six numbers of this newspaper came out; thereafter it was not necessary to have a newspaper for peasants. Antonov-Ovseenko told Lenin that the publication effort was noteworthy considering the means at its disposal.[69]

The political campaign was attended by difficulties and, in the words of the commissar, achieved only an "indifferent success."

The effort to establish "revolutionary legality" and to impress it upon the public consciousness failed through want of trained personnel. Yet something had been accomplished, according to Antonov-Ovseenko: information about abuses committed by the food levy people had been compiled; some of this personnel had been transferred, some dismissed, and some hailed before the courts, especially in Kozlov *uezd*. Not enough had been done in the way of staging political show trials both of "bandits" and of Soviet officials guilty of malpractice, yet merely by taking cognizance of these in the press the "philistine" irritation to some extent had been reduced.[70] The Plenipotentiary Commission had received no help from Moscow in respect to increasing publication activity, either in connection with the supply of paper or of printing equipment, and had had to resort to "revolutionary methods" in order to obtain paper[71]—a scarce item then as it is now, fifty years later. Above all, however, the political campaign had fallen short of expectations by failing to produce a sufficient number of repentant "bandits."

The culmination of the campaign came with the proclamation of a two-week period of grace during which "bandits" could voluntarily turn themselves in along with their arms, on the understanding that the rank and file would be allowed to go home—presumably on parole, since one of the publications in five thousand copies was entitled "Instructions for the Probationer"—and those who bore more responsibility would receive reduced sentences. The "days of forgiveness" began on 25 March and were extended to 20 April in Borisoglebsk *uezd* and to 12 April in the rest of the occupied zone. During these intervals six thousand "bandits" surrendered, two-thirds of them in Borisoglebsk *uezd* because there the local bands had been crushed rather than driven away, leaving less freedom of choice.

Yet the commissar was disappointed at the response. Probably the figure he gives included many deserters unattached to Antonov's army who were taking advantage of the opportunity to return to the Red Army and to serve out their terms without punishment. And certainly he was displeased by the fact that very few of those who surrendered had brought along their weapons, despite which his commission felt bound by its promise to release them: the Soviet government since its earliest days had been intent on disarming its subjects.[72] Nevertheless he is probably correct in claiming that the proclamation of a period of grace had exerted a certain disruptive influence upon the Green bands through increasing tension between those who were determined to fight through to the end and those who were looking for a way out.[73]

Whether the tactics of cajolery would have proved more successful had the situation continued as it was is a question that must be left unanswered. For the issue was not settled; the occupation did not hold. Antonov came back.

His invasion of the Chembar district of Penza province had not been a success, aside from overrunning a distillery and two state farms.[74] No significant accretion of strength had been registered, to say nothing of the failure to ignite another province.[75] Never able to operate for long away from familiar ground and well-organized sources of supply, Antonov resolved to beat his way back into the zone of occupation despite the odds already convincingly demmonstrated by his ejection from it. But how did he execute this daring and even desperate maneuver? Did he double back to the lower Vorona valley as he would do later in the June fighting, or did he follow a different route? Only the outcome is certain; nothing else is known.

From mention of actions in the Obval–Alexandrovka district and at Pakhotnyi Ugol, it may be conjectured that Antonov moved back into Tambov province north of the Tambov–Kirsanov railroad toward a junction with his First Army in the forested region east and northeast of the capital. There is a village Obval in Chembar *uezd* near the border with Kirsanov *uezd* in Tambov province, but the maps at our disposal do not show an Alexandrovka in that vicinity. The location of Pakhotnyi Ugol would certainly support our conclusion, though in neither instance is the date of the action indicated.

In any event, a major engagement ensued on 22 March near Tambov when six thousand Greens are said to have been encircled and to have sustained enormous losses, above all to one of their best regiments—the Fourth or Parevka—the destruction of which was claimed. With three hundred dead and ninety captured out of a probable maximum strength of five hundred it certainly would have been destroyed, yet it lived to fight again at Elan on 1 June and probably elsewhere in between, so that the report of its demise may be taken as premature. The estimate of total Green strength is likely to be more accurate and argues that Antonov had been successful in consummating a junction of his two armies; though neither would have been at full strength, a force of six thousand would have exceeded by three times the number of troops Antonov had with him in invading the province of Penza.[76]

One version of these events credits Antonov with a plan to take the city of Tambov after the failure of his attempts to extend the insurrection to other provinces, hence the concentration of troops in the vicinity preparatory to storming the city. The Reds learned of the plan and forestalled it with a counterblow leading to the encirclement and the infliction of cruel losses before Antonov succeeded in breaking out of the ring.[77] This version is all the more plausible because of the general crisis at the time, which had just found expression most spectacularly in the Kronstadt uprising. May not Antonov have decided to strike while the iron was hot in the hope of scoring a signal success, possibly even of helping the Kronstadt sailors?[78]

It is an intriguing idea that must be resisted. The primary source upon which any judgment must rest is the secret report of Antonov-Ovseenko, prepared for Lenin. While it is true that the report presents few details regarding military·operations, its failure to mention the impending attack on Tambov cannot be dismissed lightly; of even greater significance is the absence of any reference to the glorious victory of 22 March. Antonov-Ovseenko mentions only the "absurd panic" in the city touched off by "rumors" of an attack "blown up" in the staff, and mentions it only to show how unsatisfactory was the state of Soviet intelligence as late as the middle of March.[79] A recent Soviet source goes so far as to assert that the "bandits" made no attacks in the open on towns and railroads while raiding villages almost daily[80]—a statement that admittedly goes too far in the opposite direction.

If Antonov-Ovseenko had divulged nothing more, we would have been left in our accustomed state of exasperated uncertainty. But he went on to tell Lenin something that no Soviet source has printed or is likely to print: Red Army units had sustained defeats in attempting to encircle Antonov; with the core of his forces he had broken through at the end of March into his home territory out of which he had been driven earlier that month. His return marked the breakdown of the whole plan of operations devised by the Plenipotentiary Commission, the collapse of the system of occupation, and the frustration of a month and a half of exertions on the part of the commissar of repression, who candidly admitted to Lenin what Soviet historians conceal from their readers.[81]

Not only do these historians hide the truth, they do not even lie in unison. Thus one of them writes that "in a fight near Kashirovka on 6 April 1921 up to 1,000 bandits were slain and their whole supply train captured."[82] Presumably describing the same action (no date is given), another historian relates:

> Without waiting for reinforcements, the military command surrounds the staff of the bandit Antonov in the village of Kashirovka. But Antonov's men break out of the ring and cross the railroad between Platonovskaia and Kirsanov. More successful was the operation in Borisoglebsk *uezd*. There Kolesnikov's band was torn apart.[83]

What for the one is a major victory becomes for the other a tacit defeat. Neither would think of locating the village of Kashirovka, nor of placing the action in its broader setting.

Though the details are not revealed or are revealed only in a confused manner and even the main line of operations is a matter of conjecture, the outcome of the campaign of March 1921 is clear enough: a victory for Antonov and a setback for the Soviet. To make this statement is not to deny that the Greens may have suffered serious losses; losses of almost any size would have been serious for them, so great were the odds against them. Yet the figures reproduced from the archives represent field estimates made at the time by Red commanders and are more the product of fevered imagination than of sober appraisal; apparently they were never revised and so must be substantially discounted.

Whatever the casualties, they were not incurred in a chimerical attempt to take a city which had undergone no assault in 1920, when the correlation of forces had been far more favorable to the Greens, and which had now been rendered impregnable by reinforcements pouring in to create a two-to-one disparity in favor of the Reds.

Everything about Antonov suggests that he was too levelheaded to attempt so suicidal an enterprise. His purpose was more modest and more feasible: to reclaim his base of operations. Instead of breaking out of an encirclement brought on by a rash attempt to seize a point that was more an armed camp than a city, he was trying to break through the cordon that separated him from his sources of supply and recruitment, where the population had rallied to his standard and where he could maneuver to maximum advantage. And he attained his objective—by admission of his chief adversary.

With the "beast" back in his lair and the occupation policy set at nought, the war raged unabated through the month of April. It was marked by the same sanguinary character and the same indecisiveness as in March, only the end situation is less clear because of a contradiction in highly authoritative Soviet sources.

The least dependable of Soviet sources, the one conceived in a "hurrah" vein, merrily surmounts all contradictions. Declaring that April witnessed "the uninterrupted pursuit of the bands in Tambov province," Trifonov cites a remarkable engagement on 8 April near Balyklei in the Vorona valley where the second brigade of the 15th Siberian cavalry division, without loss to itself, routed two "bandit" regiments at a cost to the latter of one hundred fifty dead, two machine guns, and one hundred rifles. Then he has to back water by tacitly conceding that the pursuit was somewhat less than uninterrupted: "However, the bands were still able to resist and not infrequently staged bold and sudden sallies."[84]

The chief such sally was by all odds the raid on Rasskazovo. Here on 11 April a large force under Antonov took prisoner an entire battalion of the Red Army besides seizing 11 machine guns, 643 rifles, and 150 swords, and plundering the storehouses—information that does not come from the army archives.[85] The episode embarrassed the chairman of the Plenipotentiary Commission. He confessed to Lenin that the "bandits" had inflicted a series of defeats on Red Army units, "small-scale," to be sure, and yet "scandalous"—especially the one at Rasskazovo.[86]

Later in April Antonov became even more daring. The scene shifts to Kirsanov *uezd* where an attempt was made to take the town of that name—the only one in the overwhelmingly peasant *uezd*.

Almost never did Antonov mount such an enterprise—inability to seize towns gravely weakened his movement—and on this occasion he seems not to have abandoned his customary caution by committing his main forces to the attempt.

The episode is blown up in Soviet accounts: thus the Che-ka's first armored car detachment named for the Petrograd soviet is credited with beating off and even "destroying" the attacking band.[87] Yet it appears that the jaded town Communists, who for two months had been working by day and patroling by night, defended Kirsanov with the aid of this detachment, and that the attacking band under Selianski numbered only some two hundred fifty men when it broke into the town from three sides on 25 April. In a hot fight of some fifteen to twenty minutes' duration the band was driven out of town, with a loss of eighteen dead against one Red Army man.[88] The band had been too small to begin with, and a loss of eighteen men out of two hundred fifty hardly constitutes destruction. Here is concrete evidence of the inflation of Soviet claims in respect to victories and battle casualties.

In the really heavy fighting along the railroad outside of Kirsanov the enemy placed Antonov's strength at around six thousand, so that his effort to take Kirsanov does not appear as any substantial deviation from his policy of not sending lightly-armed troops against the firepower of Soviet units concentrated in the towns. Meeting with reverses in the countryside Antonov seems to have divided his forces, one part moving northward into territory little touched by the war and the other heading southward into the hospitable Vorona valley. Both were overtaken by disaster, according to Soviet military records; the first in the vicinity of the villages of Dmitrievka and Sofino—some thirty or forty miles north of Kirsanov—and the second near one of the places named Nikolskoe in the Inzhavino area, where some eluded death in the field only to drown in the river.

Several regiments allegedly ceased to exist at this time and Marya Kosova, Antonov's female commander and reputed lover, fell into the hands of the Reds. Most likely these were serious reverses—by 11 May news had reached Kovno or Kaunas in Lithuania of bloody open fighting in which the Reds held the upper hand, thanks to their superior numbers, but had not succeeded in running down Antonov[89]—yet a death toll of two thousand for the Greens in the fighting at the end of April, as claimed in Soviet reports, seems much too high; even half that figure would be sufficiently severe.[90]

The results nevertheless convinced Antonov-Ovseenko of the definitive ascendancy of Soviet arms and led him later to assert, in his report to Lenin, that the setback sustained at the end of March—when Antonov had regained his stamping grounds—had been overcome by the victories at the end of April, the situation restored, the best Green units severely mauled, the lost cannon and machine guns reclaimed, and the Greens again expelled from their home base.[91] One is left with the impression that for some reason the commissar had misrepresented the situation. The last claim is patently false and the other claims, as best we can tell, do not correspond to reality and certainly do not correspond to the appraisal of the situation being made in the highest Soviet circles at precisely the time when these events were transpiring in Tambov province.

Notes

1. The Fomichev manuscript ceases to be of use for the period after 1920 when the author was cut off from Antonov's movement, and the Podbelski pamphlet does not go beyond February 1921.

2. Lenin, *Polnoe sobranie sochinenii*, 5th ed., vol. 51, no. 496, p. 278.

3. Ibid., no. 519, p. 290; Trifonov, *Klassy i klassovaia bor'ba*, part 1, p. 159.

4. Lenin, *Polnoe sobranie sochinenii*, 5th ed., vol. 51, no. 548, p. 303.

5. Ibid, no. 557, p. 310; see also Sofinov, *Ocherki istorii Vserossiiskoi Chrezvychainoi Komissii*, p. 225; Trifonov, *Klassy i klassovaia bor'ba*, part 1, p. 159.

6. Lenin, *Polnoe sobranie sochinenii*, 5th ed., vol. 51, p. 460, n. 353.

7. Ibid., no. 558, pp. 310–11. Printed for the first time in this, the 5th edition of Lenin's works. The editors could not provide a specific date; they place it in October, later than the 19th. Not a word about this document in Trifonov who either overlooked it or did not wish to take cognizance of it. Apparently Soviet institutions, especially the political police, are not to be too harshly criticized, even by the founder.

8. *Vospominaniia o Vladimire Il'iche Lenine* (Moscow, 1956–1957), vol. 2, p. 411; see also Trifonov, *Klassy i klassovaia bor'ba*, part 1, p. 159, where the citation is given erroneously as p. 487.

9. S. S. Kamenev, a professional soldier and a holdover from the Imperial army.

10. M. V. Frunze, commander in the Ukraine and a self-made Bolshevik general.

11. Lenin, *Polnoe sobranie sochinenii*, 5th ed., vol. 52, no. 70, p. 42.

12. *Izvestiia TsK RKP(b)*, no. 31, 20 July 1921, pp. 2–3, as cited in Donkov, "Organizatsiia razgroma antonovshchiny," *Voprosy Istorii KPSS*, no. 6 (June 1966), p. 65.

13. The Russian figure of speech, employed in this connection by Anonymous (Podbelski), *Kak tambovskie krest'iane boriatsia za svobodu*, p. 10.

14. Donkov, "Organizatsiia razgroma antonovshchiny," *Voprosy Istorii KPSS*, no. 6 (June 1966), pp. 65–66; Trifonov, *Klassy i klassovaia bor'ba*, part 1, pp. 210–13.

15. See below, especially note 23.

16. Donkov, "Organizatsiia razgroma antonovshchiny," *Voprosy Istorii KPSS*, no. 6 (June 1966), pp. 66–67.

17. Ibid., p. 66; Lenin, *Polnoe sobranie sochinenii*, 5th ed., vol. 42, pp. 333, 487, no. 130.

18. N. A. Miliutin, "Po zadaniiam Lenina" [On assignment by Lenin], in *Vospominaniia o Lenine*, vol. 2, p. 441; see above.

19. See Lenin's remarks during the discussion of the agrarian law at the Eighth Soviet Congress in *Polnoe sobranie sochinenii*, 5th ed., vol. 42, pp. 185 ff.

20. Ibid, vol. 52, no. 144, p. 80.

21. Ibid., vol. 43, pp. 81–82, 84.

22. Ibid., p. 73.

23. See Lenin's supplement to the resolution on the land question at the Eighth Congress of Soviets, 27 December 1920, in ibid., vol. 42, p. 199; for Communist balkiness even at this modest concession to the individual cultivator, see ibid., p. 474, n. 87, p. 475, n. 93. Lenin had to use pressure to get any kind of action in the desired—thought not desirable—direction.

24. See Lenin's speech to the plenary session of the Moscow Soviet, 28 February 1921, in ibid., pp. 356–57.

25. See ibid., p. 364, and more particularly Lenin's remarks to party workers in Moscow on 24 February 1921 in ibid., pp. 348–49.

26. In March, after communications were restored, daily carloadings in Siberia averaged 158 as against 120 in the Caucasus. Thereafter the situation deteriorated once more until by the first third of May 63 cars were being loaded each day in Siberia and 10.6 cars in the Caucasus. The catastrophic fall in the latter instance is noted without specific explanation (could Antonov have been the explanation?). See A. Vyshinski, "Dolzhny pobedit'! (O prodovol'stvennom krizise)" [We must win! (On the provisioning crisis)], *Izvestiia*, no. 113 (1256), 26 May 1921, p. 1.

27. Speech to Moscow party workers on 24 February; Lenin, *Polnoe sobranie sochinenii*, 5th ed., vol. 42, pp. 348–49. Lenin's remarks on this occasion reflect a state of dejection altogether exceptional for him.

28. According to one source [V. A.] Vasiliev was the secretary with whom he talked; Borisov, *Chernym letom*, p. 39. According to another it was [N. M.] Nemtsov; Trifonov, *Klassy i klassovaia bor'ba*, part 1, p. 159. It appears that Nemtsov must have been the party functionary in question, for in the shake-up at the beginning of March Vasiliev became the secretary of the new provincial committee, evidently in succession to Nemtsov. See below.

29. At first there were five military districts for the five *uezds* caught up in the uprising. Later a sixth district was formed out of the first in the center of the "bandit" infested area; but generally speaking districts and *uezds* coincided.

30. Quoted from the Central Party Archives in Trifonov, *Klassy i klassovaia bor'ba*, part 1, pp. 160–61.

31. Information on the Plenipotentiary Commission and its subsidiaries drawn from Donkov, "Organizatsiia razgroma antonovshchiny," *Voprosy Istorii KPSS*, no. 6 (June 1966), pp. 66, 67, 70; Antonov-Ovseenko, "O banditskom dvizhenii v Tambovskoi gubernii," pp. 11, 23–24, 27; Tukhachevski, "Zapiska," p. 2; Trifonov, *Klassy i klassovaia bor'ba*, part 1, pp. 218, 220. The Antonov-Ovseenko manuscript contains little on the Plenipotentiary Commission itself but much on its work.

32. Antonov-Ovseenko, "O banditskom dvizhenii v Tambovskoi gubernii," p. 11; Trifonov, *Klassy i klassovaia bor'ba*, part 1, pp. 237–38. The latter source

states that the Che-ka took under observation all Socialist Revolutionaries in
Tambov province—a considerable undertaking—and that it engaged in a
systematic *iz'iatie* (taking out) of all politically suspicious elements.

33. Donkov, "Organizatsiia razgroma antonovshchiny," *Voprosy Istorii
KPSS*, no. 6 (June 1966), p. 64.

34. See above, chapter two.

35. Trifonov, *Klassy i klassovaia bor'ba*, part 1, p. 161; see also ibid., pp.
159–60. Borisov has Lenin conferring with Vasiliev instead of Nemtsov on
February 14, but appears to be anticipating events; *Chernym letom*, p. 39.

36. Antonov-Ovseenko, "O banditskom dvizhenii v Tambovskoi gubernii,"
pp. 11, 13; Donkov, "Organizatsiia razgroma antonovshchiny," *Voprosy Istorii
KPSS*, no. 6 (June 1966), p. 67—both text and note 54. The latter source states that
officials who had compromised themselves were removed from the province,
without saying what kind of officials (party, soviet, or both), in whose eyes they
were compromised (the party leadership or the local population), or what their
names were. Antonov-Ovseenko curiously omits the name of Vasiliev, the new
party secretary, when listing three members of the newly-elected committee who
came from the outside. Vasiliev, as previously mentioned, had been brought up
from the Donets Basin and was the most prominent of the outsiders excepting only
Antonov-Ovseenko himself. Perhaps an oversight, though more likely an
indication of friction.

37. *Put' Bor'by*, vol. 2, p. 46, as cited in Trifonov, *Klassy i klassovaia bor'ba*,
part 1, p. 238, under the title *Antonovshchina*.

38. The author definitely recalls such information as being presented in this
source although, as explained in the foreword, he cannot give the exact citation.

39. Antonov-Ovseenko, "O banditskom dvizhenii v Tambovskoi gubernii,"
p. 24.

40. Donkov, "Organizatsiia razgroma antonovshchiny," *Voprosy Istorii
KPSS*, no. 6 (June 1966), p. 67.

41. Ibid., in note 54. See above.

42. *Iz istorii Vserossiiskoi Chrezvychainoi Komissii 1917–1922 gg.*, no. 325, p.
438. The Che-ka apparently had been encroaching upon a children's home and,
while Dzerzhinski had a high tolerance for harsh measures, he could muster
indignation on this occasion. The tone of the message is peremptory and the implied
rebuke rather stiff.

43. He is mentioned in the novel; see Virta, *Odinochestvo*, pp. 221–22.

44. On the reorganization and work of the Che-ka, see Antonov-Ovseenko,
"O banditskom dvizhenii v Tambovskoi gubernii," pp. 11, 12, 14; Trifonov, *Klassy
i klassovaia bor'ba*, part 1, pp. 238–39.

45. See above, chapter eight.

46. Information drawn from B. Leonidov, "Esero-banditizm v Tambovskoi
gubernii i bor'ba s nim" [SR banditry in Tambov province and the effort against it],
Revoliutsiia i voina, 1922, nos. 14–15, p. 165, as cited in Trifonov, *Klassy i
klassovaia bor'ba*, part 1, pp. 247–48.

47. From the Central State Archives of the Soviet Army, as cited in Trifonov,
Klassy i klassovaia bor'ba, part 1, p. 247. In the face of the information thus
adduced, the Soviet author clings to the traditional estimate of 50,000 men as being

under Antonov's command in January 1921. He repeats the figure as recently as 1970; see his article, "Antonovshchina," in *Bol'shaia Sovetskaia Entsiklopediia*, 3rd ed. (Moscow, 1970–), vol. 2, p. 96, col. 276. If the Soviet side had achieved numerical superiority in January and, after further build-up, disposed of 40,448 men in Tambov province on 1 March, it is absurd to maintain that the Greens numbered 50,000 in January. Probably their strength then did not differ materially from the 21,000 figure assigned by Tukhachevski when he assumed command in May. The losses sustained in between would presumably have been made good by recruitment from the peasantry under the auspices of the STK. The figure of 50,000 must be viewed as grossly inflated; see above.

48. There is marked reluctance in Soviet sources to concede the handicaps under which the Greens fought and no willingness at all to reveal the proportions of the disparity.

49. Antonov-Ovseenko, "O banditskom dvizhenii v Tambovskoi gubernii," p. 23.

50. Donkov, "Organizatsiia razgroma antonovshchiny," *Voprosy Istorii KPSS*, no. 6 (June 1966), p. 70.

51. See below, chapter ten. On conditions in the army and the efforts of the commission to improve them, see especially Antonov-Ovseenko, "O banditskom dvizhenii v Tambovskoi gubernii," pp. 10, 11–12, 13.

52. Antonov-Ovseenko makes the point clearly enough but rather casually, without dwelling upon it; ibid., pp. 13, 14. He was reporting to Lenin; no elaboration was necessary.

53. This information from Trifonov, *Klassy i klassovaia bor'ba*, part 1, p. 250.

54. Ibid., p. 248.

55. Srechinski, "Zapechatannaia stranitsa," *Novoe Russkoe Slovo*, 27 February 1969.

56. Trifonov, *Klassy i klassovaia bor'ba*, part 1, pp. 121–22.

57. Ibid., pp. 248–49.

58. Antonov-Ovseenko, "O banditskom dvizhenii v Tambovskoi gubernii," pp. 11, 12, 14.

59. See above.

60. Such a village appears on the map of Tambov province in the Brockhaus-Efron *Entsiklopedicheskii slovar'*, vol. 32, between pp. 560–61. No village of Boguslavskoe could be found on this or on any other map. One of Antonov's commanders was named Boguslavski and it is plausible that Soviet military accounts confused the personal with the geographical name. Such errors in despatches are not rare.

61. As they were outnumbered better than two to one, this would have been a considerable feat. The cavalry brigade of Dmitrienko—two regiments and a thousand men—had engaged five of Antonov's regiments with a strength of more than two thousand. Casualties were inflicted inversely to numbers in the ratio of fifteen to one. It is not necessary to accept a claim merely because it reposes in an archive.

62. The bits of information come from Antonov-Ovseenko, "O banditskom dvizhenii v Tambovskoi gubernii," p. 14; Trifonov, *Klassy i klassovaia bor'ba*, part 1, pp. 248–49. The second is based on the archives of the army, the party, and

the October Revolution; the first is part of the archives, though the original was borne away by Trotski. Fitting the bits together is up to the investigator.

63. These may be accepted as the maximum, for the Soviet military reports tend steadily to inflate his strength.

64. Boguslavski assumed command when Tokmakov succumbed to wounds sustained in battle. Accounts differ as to the date; see below, chapter ten.

65. Trifonov, *Klassy i klassovaia bor'ba*, part 1, p. 249.

66. The age-old weakness of Russian administration, which the revolution was not eradicating but at best reducing.

67. Information on the conference and its proceedings in Antonov-Ovseenko, "O banditskom dvizhenii v Tambovskoi gubernii," pp. 15–17; for observations on peasant attitude, see also ibid., p. 5. A very different impression of the conference is conveyed by Donkov, "Organizatsiia razgroma antonovshchiny," *Voprosy Istorii KPSS*, no. 6 (June 1966), p. 68. Not a word does his article contain as to the grievances voiced by the peasant delegates, nor any intimation of the independence there displayed in refusing to toe the Soviet line on every issue. Although by no means one of the worst examples of distortion, this official study—which undoubtedly disposed of a copy of Antonov-Ovseenko's report to Lenin (and Antonov-Ovseenko had been rehabilitated by 1966)—serves as a good example of how unreliable Soviet published sources can prove to be when it is possible to check them against a secret memorandum containing the truth. In fact, it is—or should be—an unsettling experience for every scholar whose work is based wholly or even partly on Soviet publications.

68. Antonov-Ovseenko, "O banditskom dvizhenii v Tambovskoi gubernii," pp. 15, 17–18.

69. Ibid., pp. 18, 19.

70. Ibid., p. 18.

71. Ibid., p. 19.

72. See, for example, the decree of the Petrograd Che-ka signed by Moses S. Uritski, 21 March 1918, in *Iz istorii Vserossiiskoi Chrezvychainoi Komissii*, no. 87, p. 102.

73. Antonov-Ovseenko, "O banditskom dvizhenii v Tambovskoi gubernii," pp. 18–20; Trifonov, *Klassy i klassovaia bor'ba*, part 1, p. 219. The latter source mentions 5 April as the deadline for the return of property taken from state farms and cooperatives.

74. Trifonov, *Klassy i klassovaia bor'ba*, part 1, p. 117; from the Archive of the October Revolution.

75. See the conclusion for a partial explanation of this failure.

76. Actions and figures from the Archives of the Soviet Army, as reported in Trifonov, *Klassy i klassovaia bor'ba*, part 1, p. 249.

77. Srechinski, "Zapechatannaia stranitsa," *Novoe Russkoe Slovo*, 27 February 1969. It is obvious that the author bases his account on Trifonov but the interpretation of events is his own, for Trifonov does not say that Antonov planned to take Tambov although he does say that the city was threatened in March and April of 1921; *Klassy i klassovaia bor'ba*, part 1, p. 231.

78. The date of 22 March would have been too late to help them since the uprising had been suppressed by 18 March. But he might well have entered upon

such a course of action while the issue was still in doubt and might have followed through despite the unfavorable outcome, since news from Petersburg would have filtered through to him slowly and would have been clouded with uncertainty.

79. Antonov-Ovseenko, "O banditskom dvizhenii v Tambovskoi gubernii," p. 14.

80. A. Rakitin, *Imenem revoliutsii (Ocherki o V. A. Antonov-Ovseenko)* [In the name of the Revolution (sketches of V. A. Antonov-Ovseenko)] (Moscow, 1965), p. 127.

81. Antonov-Ovseenko, "O banditskom dvizhenii v Tambovskoi gubernii," p. 15.

82. Trifonov, *Klassy i klassovaia bor'ba*, part 1, p. 250; based on the Archives of the Soviet Army.

83. Rakitin, *Imenem revoliutsii*, p. 132. One may understand the word "station" after the form Platonovskaia, but the correct name of the village is Platonovka.

84. Trifonov, *Klassy i klassovaia bor'ba*, part 1, p. 250.

85. Leonidov, "Esero-banditizm v Tambovskoi gubernii i bor'ba s nim," in *Revoliutsiia i voina*, 1922, compilations 14–15, p. 165, as quoted in Trifonov, *Klassy i klassovaia bor'ba*, part 1, p. 250.

86. Antonov-Ovseenko, "O banditskom dvizhenii v Tambovskoi gubernii," p. 15.

87. Sofinov, *Ocherki istorii Vserossiiskoi Chrezvychainoi Komissii*, p. 225.

88. *Put' Bor'by*, vol. 2, *Antonovshchina*, pp. 129, 130, as cited in Trifonov, *Klassy i klassovaia bor'ba*, part 1, p. 231.

89. See *Volia Rossii*, no. 201, 12 May 1921, p. 1.

90. For a sketch of operations, confused as usual, and for figures drawn from archival sources, see Trifonov, *Klassy i klassovaia bor'ba*, part 1, pp. 250–51.

91. Antonov-Ovseenko, "O banditskom dvizhenii v Tambovskoi gubernii," p. 15.

— 10 —

Decision and Death (Summer–Fall 1921)

It was on or about 26 April 1921 that E. M. Sklianski, Trotski's deputy at the war commissariat, sent a note to Lenin regarding the province which the Central Committee had just branded as the "unifying center of organized kulak–SR banditry" in Russia.[1] The situation in Tambov, Sklianski told Lenin, had not improved recently and in places had even worsened. "I would consider it desirable to send Tukhachevski to put down the Tambov insurrection. . . . The political effect of such an appointment will be considerable. Especially abroad. Your opinion?" And Lenin answered, probably on the same day: "Turn it over to Molotov for action tomorrow by the P.–Biuro. I suggest he be named without publicity in the center."[2]

On 27 April the Political Bureau of the Central Committee of the Russian Communist Party (Bolsheviks) duly complied with Sklianski's initiative, sanctioned by Lenin, and not only named M. N. Tukhachevski as commander of troops in Tambov province but charged him with liquidating the Antonov "band" in one month's time.[3] It gave some recognition to the exertions of the Plenipotentiary Commission and of its chairman in allotting so short a time span for the bloody work ahead, but not to Antonov-Ovseenko's assessment of the situation at the end of April.

Obviously the "commanding heights" of the party were not underestimating the strength of Antonov nor the danger of the movement he headed in sending out against him an array of military talent that would soon occupy the highest positions in the Red Army. If it be objected that the party acted without awaiting clarification of the results of the fighting at the end of April, Tukhachevski's own description of conditions when he arrived on the scene removes any doubt as to the falseness of Antonov-Ovseenko's claim of having gotten the situation in hand and confirms Sklianski's judgment that only the most decisive measures on the part of the Soviet state could exorcise the "bandit" menace.

Tukhachevski assumed his command on 6 May.[4] As he entered upon his duties he found Soviet power to be nonexistent in five *uezds* of the province, aside from the towns. The STK held sway over virtually the entire countryside in Tambov and Kirsanov *uezds*; in Morshansk it was supreme south of the Syzran–Viazma railroad, in Kozlov (later renamed Michurinsk) east of the Rostov railroad, and in Borisoglebsk only the southernmost part escaped its domination. The local peasantry spoke of the uprising as "their revolution" and dated events as occurring "before the revolution" or after it.[5] Tukhachevski indirectly paid tribute to the uprising by saying that operations against it had to be conceived of in terms, not of dealing with disorders, but of waging war.

True, the battle-worthiness of the Greens could not be compared to that of a regular army; here he must have been thinking primarily of the disparity in equipment, perhaps also in generalship. But the main difficulty lay in occupying territory, in holding down the population, and in drying up the sources of provisioning and recruitment—briefly, in reestablishing Soviet authority where it had ceased to exist. This was the task that would claim most of the troops at his disposal; a relatively small, technically superior, and highly mobile force would suffice to crush the Green bands. The whole tenor of the Tukhachevski memorandum, in fact, is that it was not so much military strength that accounted for the formidable character of the insurrection as the peasant support behind it.[6]

Michael Tukhachevski was becoming the muscle man of the Soviet regime. He arrived fresh from the scene of his triumph over the Kronstadt sailors, for it was he who had directed the assault on the fortress and not Voroshilov, as the novelist would have it[7]—either out of ignorance or because of his effort to crawl into Stalin's favor. Although he had not received a higher military education, holding merely the rank of second lieutenant in the Imperial army, Tukhachevski had accumulated a rich battle experience in both the civil war and the Polish war of 1920. He had commanded the Fifth Army on the eastern front against Kolchak and in December 1919 had been singled out for distinction due to his part in the campaign culminating in the fall of Omsk, capital of the White regime. After service in the North Caucasus and elsewhere, he commanded on the western front against Poland in 1920. The discomfiture before Warsaw had not discredited him and rightly so, since Lenin bore the responsibility for that rash adventure. Only later—in the years of the cult of Stalin's personality—would an insidious undermining operation be mounted against him on this score, foreshadowing his ultimate doom. Now his subjugation of the Kronstadt "anarchy" had raised him high in the favor of Lenin, who personally expressed his satisfaction with Tukhachevski's performance and commissioned him to do the same for Tambov.[8]

Yet it might be an injustice to cast Tukhachevski in the role of muscle man. A perusal of his despatches leads to a better opinion of him. They are models of conciseness and clarity, free of bombast and notably free of servile disparagement of the foe such as so often disfigures Communist writings. If it cannot be positively affirmed, neither can it be excluded that the despatches repress a tinge of sympathy for the Tambov peasantry in its miserable condition. The ability of Tukhachevski is reflected in his reports. One is led to the conclusion that here was a military technician who happened to be in the service of the Soviet regime. He could have served some other regime with equal distinction and, very likely, his ultimate reward would have been other than a death sentence.

His subordinates were a chosen lot. Second in command came Ieronim P. Uborevich. He had been an army leader in the civil war and later would stand at the head of several of the most important military regions until he, too, perished in the 1937 blood bath. Of comparable status in the Soviet military hierarchy was Ivan F. Fedko who had led a brigade in the assault on Kronstadt and now would command the armored column against Antonov; later he would rise to second position in the commissariat of defense. G. I. Kotovski, a colorful civil war figure, and Ivan V. Tulenev, commander of the southern front in the second world war, likewise were assigned to the impending operation in Tambov—Kotovski at the head of his cavalry brigade. N. E. Kakurin served as chief of staff to Tukhachevski. Finally, G. K. Zhukov was there.[9] The future marshal and conqueror of Berlin commanded a squadron of the first regiment of the 14th cavalry brigade under Dmitrienko.[10]

Part of his military experience would come from fighting against his own Russian people in what Uborevich, at least, would have the grace to term a campaign "in the highest degree unpleasant."[11]

If Tukhachevski and Fedko had conducted operations against Kronstadt, Fedko, Kotovski, and Zhukov among others had already combatted Green bands elsewhere before coming to Tambov province. These men were specialists in both civil and international warfare. The Soviet government had not stinted on talent in assembling the force to strike down the Antonov uprising.[12]

How large was this force? Certainly it did not number one hundred thousand, the figure that gained currency in anti-Soviet circles[13] just as fifty thousand has become the conventional Soviet estimate of Antonov's strength. Zhukov places Soviet strength at 37,500 bayonets and some 10,000 sabers, based on figures of Leonidov as probably furnished him by Trifonov.[14] But Tukhachevski himself would later say that in May he disposed of 35,000 bayonets, 10,000 sabers, some hundreds of machine guns and over 60 cannon, together with the subdivisional units of trainees[15]—that is, over fifty thousand troops, a numerical superiority of 2.5 to 1.0. It would appear that this is the correct figure. The degree of exaggeration can thus be determined: the conventional totals for both sides in the Tambov warfare are twice or more than twice the actual totals.[16]

The advantage conferred by greater numbers was compounded by superior knowledge of the art of warfare on the part of the Soviet commanders—not only Tukhachevski but Uborevich and Fedko as well—and, above all, by vastly superior equipment. In line with his conviction—all too justified—that guerrillas could oppose only a low degree of battle-worthiness to regulars backed by the power of the state, Tukhachevski proceeded to form a relatively small but technically advanced and highly mobile force which would hopelessly overbear Antonov's men if they were flushed out of the forests. And they would be flushed out because the mass of Red troops were to occupy and garrison the villages that were the source of supply and recruitment, leaving Antonov's regiments to wither on the vine after the roots had been destroyed.[17] Furthermore, their numerical superiority and their command of the means of communication would enable the Reds to threaten the Greens with encirclement in their forest lair.

The "first" or striking force is stated to have comprised the Kotovski cavalry brigade with 900 sabers and 3 cannon, the 14th cavalry brigade with 1,000 sabers and 2 cannon, the 21st armored detachment, and the 1st and 52nd armored detachments of the Che-ka—a total of 1,900 sabers, 5 cannon, 6 armored cars, 10 trucks, and 4 automobiles.[18] As usual the sum of the vehicles for the individual units does not equal the announced total, and the Soviet historian who cites the two cavalry brigades cites three on the preceding page,[19] making no effort to reconcile his sources. This issue is settled authoritatively by Tukhachevski, who states that he used three cavalry brigades in field operations.[20] Thus the striking force would have a strength of over three thousand. The force as a whole was commanded by Uborevich, and the armored section by Fedko.

The armor seems modest indeed. Fedko at first had only an automobile and six trucks. But he realized the potentialities from his experience in the North Caucasus. Mounting a Colt machine gun in the Packard car used by himself so that it could be turned in any direction, he caused two Maxim machine guns to be emplaced on each truck. Later the armored cars and the other vehicles were added.[21] One might wonder what such a force could achieve, bearing in mind the Russian roads and the quality of the cars and especially of the tires of that time in any country.

The cannon of Gustavus Adolphus seem ridiculous today, but they were not ridiculous in the seventeenth century. Similarly, Fedko's force was formidable when pitted against guerrilla horsemen with a few cart-borne machine guns and no cannon—or one or two cannon with almost no shells. The mobile column could outdistance even the fleetest of steeds; it could cut in ahead of the Greens, intercept their line of movement, and either rake them with concentrated fire or drive them back against the pursuing Red cavalry. The pursuit would thus be rendered effective whereas otherwise it might not have been; Uborevich is quoted as complaining that "their horses are better than ours; we can't run them down."[22]

This was an unwilling tribute to Antonov, to Ishin, his commissar of supply, and to Pluzhnikov, head of the STK. These men had made the most of whatever peasants could supply and whatever ingenuity could add from the side. But there were limits to what could be derived from their rustic sources. Besides the armored column of the enemy there were the armored trains in the background, the airplanes overhead, the infantry, and the artillery with shells in unlimited quantities. Antonov's homespun regiments could not withstand the whole apparatus of repression of a modern state now being assembled against them. Aside from the human factor it had never been an equal fight; it was now becoming hopeless.

While the military preparations were being made, the Plenipotentiary Commission and the Che-ka had completed their plans for dealing with the civilian population and with the Green fighters themselves after the army had crushed their corporate strength. A series of arrests had greatly facilitated the work. The Kadet attorney in Tambov, Fedorov-Gorski—a central figure in Antonov's espionage system—had been apprehended, perhaps sometime during the spring though it is impossible to know for certain. Then Ishin was lured to his doom through a ruse, ostensibly to confer with representatives of the SR Central Committee but actually with agents of the secret police. Both these men are believed to have divulged a great deal of information about the inner workings of Antonov's movement. The novelist claims with verisimilitude that before his execution the Che-ka pumped Ishin dry[23]—alcohol could always loosen his tongue—yet he did not renounce Antonov, according to indications from the Soviet side.[24]

Numerous arrests of less consequential people also aided the reorganized Tambov branch of the secret police in deranging the admirable intelligence system of the Greens and in uncovering the threads that ran from the civilian population to the force in the field. The Che-ka had developed the technique of playing upon the less admirable traits of human nature to extract information and even to press captives into service by dangling before them the prospect of redeeming their "guilt" in proportion to the damage they inflicted on their erstwhile comrades. As a result the territorial system of Antonov's army was pieced together, the connection of a given canton or village with a certain unit established, and the scheme of organization of the STK laid bare.

But the chief fruit of all this activity were the proscription lists on which were entered the names of individual members of the Green bands or of the STK committees, together with the names of the members of their families—the indispensable prelude to the *iz'iatie* (taking out) of the "bandit" element. By the end of April the lists were ready with more than ten thousand names of those who fought for the Green cause.[25] As the lists were assembled by villages, the proscription could be extended easily to members of a fighter's family whether or not they were individually inscribed on other lists. Antonov-Ovseenko gives no figures for families, though he definitely states that they were likewise to appear on the rolls.[26]

The dragnet of proscription would reach still further. Suspects in the public service were listed, particularly those among railroad employees and the personnel of cooperative societies—strongholds, respectively, of the left and right SRs.[27] Known members of dissident parties had been under strictest surveillance for months and would certainly be caught in the net.

Nor would the kulak escape. On the basis of the 1917 census registers were compiled of members of kulak families as well as of heads of households in "bandit" villages, and permission was sought in Moscow for the mass exile of such families from Tambov province. Moscow responded in the "positive" sense and kulak registers were prepared for twelve *volosts* of Tambov *uezd*. Presumably in other cases expulsion proceeded by rule of thumb, and peasants who appeared to be less poverty-stricken than their neighbors were as liable to be victimized by the Communists as had been lonely old women by the witch-hunters of seventeenth-century New England. An early example of the condemnation by category which would later receive a hideous extension and become the blight of the twentieth century.

Additional preparations supplemented the program of proscription. Corrals were needed to hold those destined for exile, so concentration camps made their appearance in Tambov province. Extension of the network of village informers received a great deal of attention as the indispensable basis for the uprooting of elements supporting the insurrection. The setting up of a special "material fund" of scarce products out of which informers could be rewarded, together with procedures and pressures available to the government, attracted the requisite corps of squealers. Bribing and blandishment, cajolery and intimidation finally enabled the commissar of repression and his helpmates to put intelligence on a satisfactory footing, whereas even as late as March—according to his testimony—it had left much to be desired.

Paralleling the plans for coercive measures was a strident propaganda campaign to change the attitude of the village or, more specifically, to drive a wedge between the kulaks and the mass of peasants. The widest publicity was given the NEP decrees in conjunction with a program designed to increase the flow of revolutionary literature.[28] Peasant conferences were organized, as we have seen, to create at least a semblance of popular sanction for the official course of action in the hope that such assemblies could later be induced to vote "sentences" against the "bandits."[29]

Revolutionary legality became a watchword in the endeavor to convince the population that past abuses of a bureaucratic or dogmatic nature would no longer be tolerated. Show trials, both of "bandits" and of abusive Soviet officials, were held to educate the public. The Central Committee acclaimed the results of the political campaign as having produced a shift in the mood of the village which made it possible on 27 April to undertake a program of "bandit" eradication in one month's time.[30] But the Central Committee has *pravda* (truth) inscribed only on the masthead of the central organ. The commissar of repression wrote Lenin that the political campaign had had "indifferent success."[31]

The Soviet historian blandly observes that in the war on kulak bands the political police (Che-ka and then the OGPU) made use of certain practices and methods which "inhered" in its nature.[32] No exception can be taken to this statement. In fact, it may be broadened to include the Soviet regime as a whole. The nature of the regime was such that it would go beyond the preparations mentioned above; it would resort to "exceptional" measures.

And such measures materialized with a vengeance. The fears of the Communists had been excited, their dogma outraged, by the spectacle of peasant defiance in Tambov province—more prolonged and stubborn than in other Great Russian provinces and much better organized. As long as Antonov stood, Lenin might fear that the "many-millioned, petty bourgeois ochlocracy" would get out of hand in the country as a whole. Hence the exceptional measures.

They were embodied in two decrees which were publicized in Tambov province but not elsewhere: Order No. 130, directed against "bandit" families, and Order No. 171, directed against families befriending "bandit" families. Together they marked the inauguration of the Red terror in Tambov province. We shall limit ourselves for the present to noting the contents of the first decree, since the second developed later in the heat of the impending campaign.

Order No. 130 provided for the application of "mass terror" in the case of villages noted for their commitment to the Green cause. The Soviet authorities would impose a special "sentence" on such villages bringing their crimes to the attention of the toilers, and would declare the entire male population to be under the judgment of the revolutionary military tribunal—in other words, would institute martial law to which even male children were subject.

All "bandit" families would be removed to concentration camps as hostages for members who served in Antonov's army, and the families' property would be seized. At the expiration of a two-week period, if a "bandit" had not surrendered, the property would be confiscated and the family itself banished from the province—that is, dumped at some distant point, destitute, to fend for itself in an environment noted only for the severity of its climate and the poverty of its soil (observation of this author—not from the text of the decree). In connection with imposition of the "sentence," every household in the village would be searched for arms; if any were discovered the senior breadwinner might be shot on the spot. Measures were taken to give wide publicity—in Tambov province—to the provisions of Order No. 130.

As always in the case of laws and decrees, it is necessary to know how they were applied as well as how they read. Enforcement in this instance devolved upon the political commissions set up directly under the Plenipotentiary Commission in each of the six military districts into which the area of the insurrection was divided. The makeup of these commissions has already been examined.[33] They received precise instructions as to carrying out the decree, particularly in respect to the order in which hostages would be taken. Special care was to be exercised in regard to Red Army families,[34] and they were not to take people who were ill, or women with babes in arms, or those who were pregnant and would soon give birth. Forms were provided for the inventory of property subject to confiscation. The district commissions would render a daily accounting to the Plenipotentiary Commission and to military headquarters, and would provide summaries every three days in a prescribed format. Despite these provisions for strict supervision, the execution of the decree might assume such extreme forms as the destruction of whole villages and the shooting of hostages in batches.[35]

Little latitude was left for more drastic action than had been authorized under Order No. 130, and that little would be exhausted by Order No. 171, the culmination of what Soviet publications call "severe measures" of counteracting "banditry"[36] and what the commissar of repression in his secret memorandum to Lenin called "mass terrorism."[37] The military commander in his secret report used similarly straightforward language.[38] They were at liberty to do so, since only the heads of party and government would read what they had written.

The "taking out" of the disaffected population in conjunction with the destruction of Antonov's army is said to have been delayed by the change in military command and by the need for the new commander to familiarize himself with the situation before deciding on the proper distribution of his forces. Tukhachevski arrived on the scene on 6 May and spent some three weeks in preparing for his campaign. On the civilian front also certain things remained to be done, for if the proscription lists were ready, the concentration camps were not; nor had all of the machinery for the administration of Order No. 130 been completed.

Reinforcements continued to pour into the province to strengthen party, government, and army. By the end of May twelve hundred Communists had arrived from other parts of the country to stir up local personnel and to provide more effective—or merciless— direction of the campaign of liquidation. The militia (ordinary police) of Tambov province had ceased to function in the rural areas of the five *uezds* caught up in the insurrection. Now several thousand Red Army men from the class of 1897 who had been released from service were imported into the province and given crash training so that the militia could be reintroduced into the disaffected areas.[39]

All these preparations, however, did not prevent an effort to get the "taking out" process under way even before the military campaign had broken through the protection afforded by the Green bands to the peasantry. Already in March, according to party records,[40] the removal of "bandit" families and the purging of soviet and railroad personnel had begun. But the commissar of repression dates the introduction of the hostage system from the end of April, when this borrowing from Chingis Khan and the Golden Horde was first applied to villages along railway lines,[41] and he asserts that the extraction of "bandits" began at the same time.[42] Perhaps he means as a major enterprise, since an effort as early as March—if we are to credit the other source—would have yielded modest results because of the fluid military situation. Now more would be accomplished since the lists of proscription were ready, and the party archives are said to disclose the "taking out" at the beginning of May of some two thousand persons.[43] A good start from the Soviet point of view, but the main work of decimation would have to await the campaign to break the military strength of Antonov's bands.

Toward the end of May Tukhachevski on the military front and the Plenipotentiary Commission on the civilian had completed their varied preparations and were ready for action. The interval between the fighting at the end of April and the launching of the decisive campaign at the end of May had passed in desultory fighting, principally in the form of bloody but indecisive cavalry skirmishes. The most active—or at least the most advertised—of the Soviet units involved was the elite cavalry brigade of G. I. Kotovski which had been transferred from the Kiev region and arrived in Morshansk on or about 1 May. According to one of his men,[44] Kotovski had long dreamed of true cavalry action out in the open country and away from the concentrated firepower of modern armies which had caused his brigade to be badly cut up during the civil war between the Reds and the Whites, sometimes with the loss of half his horses and men. Now in Tambov province he would get what he wanted, fighting against rustic bands who had no British Empire behind them to furnish such means of destruction.

His horsemen rode southward amid clouds of dust under a merciless sun that yellowed the vegetation before it had become green, through villages without any sign of life, to the first encounter at Bolshaia Sosnovka. The main engagement, however, came later at a place of uncertain location against a shadowy commander, perhaps on 22 May. The large Green band may have numbered five hundred or it may have numbered a thousand; it may have been commanded by Selianski or by Averianov, neither of whom have any certain existence among Antonov's lieutenants.[45] The Reds may have been led by Kotovski or by his deputy, Nicholas N. Krivoruchko, but the Soviet sources agree on at least one thing: the band was duly liquidated. The most remarkable feature of this unusual action was that the Reds cut up seven hundred "bandits" without losing a man. Kotovski's brigade was ever victorious, it is true, yet on this occasion it must fairly have outdone itself. Soon it would be integrated with the striking force of Ieronim P. Uborevich and his detached cavalry campaign be merged with the general onslaught against Antonov.[46]

We do not know what measures Antonov took to ward off impending doom. After all, there was little he could do. He could damage lines of communication but not take them over, despite strong sympathy for his cause among railway workers; he could skirmish around towns but not occupy them; his intelligence system had been gravely impaired and he was cut off from the rest of the world, aside from occasional contact with the equally isolated Kolesnikov band in Voronezh province. He could only make such dispositions of his heavily outnumbered and technically outclassed troops as would diminish, however slightly, the danger to which they were exposed. Whether his arrangements were made to least disadvantage only a military expert immersed in the subject could say.

On the eve of the decisive campaign Antonov had divided his forces, the Second Army under his immediate command concentrated in the Vorona valley in the southern portion of Kirsanov *uezd*, one of the heartlands of the Green cause and the one to which Antonov invariably repaired in times of extremity. One source assigns a strength of five thousand to this Second Army;[47] the others evade the issue. It had some cover from the relatively thin belt of forest along the Vorona and amid the swamps and small lakes of the area.

The First Army, on the other hand, with perhaps two thousand effectives,[48] had taken position well to the west in the south central portion of Tambov *uezd* around the villages of Verkhotsene and Bakharevo. One of Antonov's best regiments, the seventh, had been recruited from this area and bore the name of Verkhotsene, so that here again was one of the hearths of the insurrection, but one virtually without cover. There may have been some woods along the headwaters of the Tsna but not enough to appear on a map such as that in the old encyclopedia which shows forested areas.[49] Here was an open country of farmlands, out on the rich black earth.

A distance of some forty to sixty kilometers separated the two armies. Logistical problems may have dictated this spreading out of at best inadequate forces, but it is more likely that Antonov was seeking to give some protection to the populations that constituted the backbone of his movement.[50]

The First Army from the outset had been commanded by Peter Tokmakov. It was now led by Boguslavski. What had happened, and where was Tokmakov? The question must be posed since there is reason to regard Tokmakov as the second man of this insurrection. Unfortunately even so cardinal a question cannot be answered with assurance, for only enemy sources deal with his fate and they are contradictory and have only their customary imprecision in common. One version is that Tokmakov had been drawn into the Second Army and fell in the final campaign between 29 May and 7 June without indication of the manner, place, and day of his death.[51] It is, of course, possible that Tokmakov had ceased to command the First Army and had joined Antonov in the Second, particularly since the main strength appears now to have been shifted to the Second Army; furthermore, the basic source is emphatic in asserting that Tokmakov was very close to Antonov, who liked always to have him near at hand.[52]

Yet the likelihood is that the novelist is closer to the truth in this instance and that Tokmakov had been grievously wounded in action near Chemlyk toward the end of March or in early April, not long after the fall of Kronstadt, and had died before they could get him to headquarters at Kamenka. Antonov held the wake the whole night through at the bier of his friend. The succession occasioned a sharp conflict between Antonov and Pluzhnikov before Boguslavski was chosen.[53]

Still a third version, that of the Red Army commissar P. A. Borisov and based on the revelations of one Captain Ektov who had fallen into the clutches of the Che-ka and was trying to buy himself out by squealing on his comrades, has Tokmakov killed in action at Ozerki without specifying the location of that village or the date of the action.[54] The only Ozerki that can be located is a village in Kozlov *uezd*, much to the west of the usual theater of operations, and the only Chemlyk (or Chamlyk—Russians spell Tatar names freely) to be found is Talitski Chemlyk on the Bitiug river in Usman *uezd* near the Tambov–Voronezh border, a locale also well removed from the customary cockpit of the insurrection. It is entirely conceivable that Tokmakov with elements of the First Army might have ventured westward into Kozlov *uezd* to help one or another local band, even though Kozlov was much less caught up in the insurrection than the *uezds* further east, or that he might have concerted action with Kolesnikov to the south in Voronezh province.

Some indirect evidence exists to support, though not to prove, the latter assumption. The Archives of the Soviet Army record a defeat for Kolesnikov in his province south of the station of Liski on 11 February 1921, as a consequence of which he sought refuge in neighboring Tambov.[55] They record also an engagement at a place called Chemlyk where Kolesnikov's band lost some eight hundred killed and wounded, six machine guns, and other arms.[56] Unfortunately, the date is not given and only Kolesnikov's band is mentioned. But could Tokmakov's First Army, or elements thereof with its commander, have been trying to reintroduce Kolesnikov into his home province in this engagement at a village near the border, and could Tokmakov have here sustained the fatal wounds?

The Archives of the October Revolution preserve information regarding a raid in force by Kolesnikov the night of 17–18 March 1921 upon the village of Sadovoe in Bogorovski *uezd*, Voronezh province, cited by the secondary source as evidence of the resilience of the bands in the face of overwhelming—and doubtless exaggerated—defeats.[57] The time sequence is ostensibly the battleground south of Liski/Chemlyk village/Sadovoe village, which would throw the engagement at Chemlyk into the first part of March instead of the latter part, as in the novel. But it need not necessarily be so, considering the way Soviet history is written, any more than the geography is as stated; for there was no Bogorovski *uezd*. There was only a Bobrovsk *uezd* and in it a village of Sadovoe near the

Bitiug river. The geographical sequence from south to north would be Liski/Sadovoe/Chemlyk; if it were also the battle sequence Kolesnikov would have been moving up the Bitiug toward Tambov province and the engagement at Chemlyk would have occurred toward the end of March, as the novel says.

We do not know the place, time, or circumstance of Tokmakov's death; we know only that he died fighting bravely and that command of his First Army passed to Boguslavski. The two men had much in common. Both had served in the Imperial army in which both held officers' commissions. Both had gone through the fire of the Great War. Both were distinguished for their bravery, Boguslavski to the point of intrepidity. Both were committed body and soul to the peasant cause, in the service of which both would fall. And the new army commander, like the old and like Antonov himself, was Left SR. The Tambov uprising owed as much to that party as to the SRs, perhaps even more.

Only in two respects did the two men differ: Boguslavski is described as both handsome and popular, whereas Tokmakov was not handsome and was merely respected. Soviet observers imputed to Tokmakov a strain of exceptional cruelty, with how much justice it is impossible to say; no such aspersion is cast upon Boguslavski.[58] The two commanders probably did as much with the First Army as anyone could have done under the circumstances.

And that is about all that can be said of Antonov's forces on the eve of their supreme ordeal. Three weeks had sufficed for Tukhachevski to draft his plans, for Uborevich under him to assemble the special striking force, for Fedko under him to get the mobile column in hand, and for an officer under him named Konopko—about whom nothing is known—to be ready with the armored cars.[59] Tukhachevski had decided to concentrate against the Second Army as being now the main one and that immediately under Antonov; after it was disposed of, the lesser force under Boguslavski in its exposed position would present no great problem.

The thousands of military trainees brought in from Moscow and Orel provinces and concentrated in the special or sixth military district under P. A. Pavlov had occupied key villages such as Karavainia, Kalugino, and Treskino which had stoked the fire of the insurrection with men and provisions. They had intercepted the main lines of movement and had pressed the Green forces out of the nonforested, fertile farming areas of the Inzhavino region back into the woods along the Vorona, and they were everywhere restoring the soviets in what had been the strongholds of the Union of Toiling Peasantry.[60]

Contrary to the impression conveyed in Soviet literature, however, the cadets were otherwise only a passive factor, for Antonov-Ovseenko says that not until mid-June did they receive special fighting assignments,[61] and by then the climax of the campaign had passed. The task of flushing Antonov's Second Army out of its forest lair devolved upon regular army units although, of course, the cadets did weigh in the scales as a back-up force.

The campaign that would mark the end of the Green movement as a serious military factor opened on 27 May with an encircling movement by the Soviet troops. The next day Antonov tried to break out to the north into the Inzhavino area, encountered strong resistance from Kotovski's cavalry brigade, and fell back toward the east. Why did he not stay in the forest and defy encirclement? Probably because of the fateful drawback of his chosen terrain, pointed out in our geographical introduction: the wooded zone along the Vorona was not broad enough to render ineffective an encircling movement, particularly when the enemy disposed of superior numbers.

On 29 May Antonov, holding tenaciously to the principle that every dog is stronger on his own home ground, tried once more to redeem the situation by driving with one part of his army into Tambov *uezd* and with the other deeper into Kirsanov; again he was thrown back, and this time had to retreat precipitously into Saratov province. Once he had lost the protection of the dense belt of vegetation along the Vorona the armored column could take after him and henceforth he would be hunted like a beast in the field. The machines had been brought in by rail on flat cars[62] and so could enter fresh into the fray; doubts that they would hold up on the poor country roads and overcome the obstacles of the forest, hollows, and watercourses were resolved in their favor.[63]

Blocked off from his haunts to the west and the north and unable to stand his ground, the Green leader sought to shake the enemy by moving due east into Saratov province, where he came first into the valley of the Khoper river. The Khoper afforded less cover than its tributary, the Vorona, for its high right bank was wooded only in spots while the low left bank was steppelike in character;[64] this was, therefore, no place to tarry. It was a fine river with clean, unspoiled water flowing evenly and rather swiftly over its bed of sand; but as the chief stream between Don and Volga it interposed a serious barrier to movement both for guerrillas, who did not command the few towns with bridges, and for the armored column, which could not cross anywhere else.

Thanks to a Soviet source with both clarity and sequence we know that on 30 May Antonov crossed the Khoper at the village of Perevesenka,[65] but we do not know whether by ford or by ferry. The river had a number of shallows and such a boon may account for Antonov's choice of the crossing, although the village was straight east from the area where he began his retreat and the time factor could have been decisive. In any event the choice was fortuitous and the Greens had peace on that day and again on the 31st as they rode northeastward from Perevesenka toward the border between Saratov and Penza provinces. It may be conjectured that the Reds followed a different course because of a deflection imposed by the river.

Antonov's career had long tried the patience of his good fortune, and now it would desert him. On 1 June, as he and his men were resting in Elan at a considerable distance from the crossing of the Khoper, the "column of fire" burst upon them; part of it knifed into the center of the village while the rest with Kotovski's cavalry closed in from the east and north and opened up with a withering fire. The Greens, taken unawares, fled in panic into a forest losing their entire supply train, three hundred horses, one hundred fifty rifles, two machine guns, and one hundred fifty men killed and wounded.[66] The effort to block movement further to the north ended in failure, for they came to rest in the vicinity of Serdobsk, twenty-five to thirty kilometers north of Elan.

While the rout at Elan may have been less shattering than Red authors like to make it—a loss of one hundred fifty men was not in itself a disaster—worse was to follow. The armored detachment again cut in ahead from the north and Kotovski's brigade came in from the west and the south so that the sorely-pressed Second Army was again threatened with encirclement. In the ensuing cavalry engagement on the Serdoba river, brigade commissar Borisov says that several hundred rebels were thrown into the river. Then he admits that in the fierce fighting the Greens gained the upper hand over one of the two regiments until Kotovski arrived on the scene with the other and a battery of artillery; the cannon fire struck terror into Antonov's men and they fled in ragged order from the river across the prairie, pursued by the Red cavalrymen as long as their steeds could bear them. Once more it seems that disparity of arms decided the issue.

Antonov fell back quickly toward the east—the only line of retreat still open to him—destroying bridges as he crossed them. He was now a hundred miles or so as the crow flies from the Vorona, halfway to the Volga (in a southeasterly direction toward Saratov) with no prospect of more favorable terrain ahead. He reached the village of Bakury where the small stream of that name enters the only slightly larger Serdoba, and there fate overtook him.

Repeating its standard maneuver, the armored detachment got athwart the line of retreat while the cavalry brigades of Kotovski and Kovalev came up from behind, taking the Greens between two fires or even encircling them. The experienced machine gunners took up positions next to one another and poured long bursts of fire into the village; the Greens sought protection in or behind houses and began shooting. One of their number, operating a machine gun from the belfry tower, dosed the detachment with its own medicine until cut down by Fedko in person—according to rehabilitation literature— but not before he had badly wounded the commissar whose name is not given. "In stubborn, cruel fighting the composite insurgent force of 3,000 men was routed."[67]

But a large portion of the entrapped three thousand, if that be their figure, succeeded in breaking out of the encirclement and escaping into Penza province. They lost nearly all their machine guns, many rifles and rounds of ammunition, some eight hundred horses, and nine hundred men killed and wounded, according to the most reliable source;[68] according to another, ten machine guns were lost and only three hundred horses, but nine hundred men were killed.[69] It is obvious that the figure of nine hundred should refer to casualties rather than to dead alone. As usual nothing is said about losses sustained by the Reds.[70]

There is no reason to dissent from the Soviet view that the fighting at Elan, on the Serdoba, and at Bakury marked the ruin of the Tambov uprising in the military sense even as the introduction of the New Economic Policy drained away much of its support. Hitherto Antonov had stood at the head of a well-organized if ill-equipped military force which could be dignified by the term army within its modest frame of reference. Henceforth he would have under him only bands, as the enemy had been describing his forces all along.

The measure of the reverses in Saratov province is very hard to determine, however, even if their cumulative effect is clear. The best surmise is that the action at Elan occurred on 1 June, that on the Serboda the next day, and that at Bakury on 3 June, but the possibility cannot altogether be excluded that the second and third actions were parts of a single engagement occurring on 2 June. Elan has been represented as the undoing of Antonov; thus the assertion that on that day the pursuers had broken up the Special or Guard Regiment, the 3rd Nizovski, the 4th Parevka, the 7th Verkhotsene, the 9th Semenovka, and the 14th Naru–Tambov regiments.[71] But the Special and the 4th had already been annihilated in March [72] and the 14th would cause trouble in the future;[73] besides, the losses at Elan were too light to justify such claims.

The main damage was done at Bakury, it seems reasonably clear, and yet the uncertainty that dogs every step of our way cannot be dispelled even in relation to the most decisive engagement of all. The account we have followed[74] has the Second Army of three thousand men at or in the village of Bakury—an entirely credible figure; if anything it is too low. But a citation for I. K. Danilov, political commissar of the 1st cavalry regiment of Kotovski's brigade, extols his bravery in leading an attack upon a band some four hundred strong in the village of Bakury on 3 July 1921 (*sic*—June is meant).[75]

Where lies the truth: in the version that affirms the presence of a composite force of three thousand or in the version that speaks of a band of four hundred? For Antonov under these circumstances to have distributed his men so as to convert the whole *volost'* of Bakury into the battleground instead of the village would have been foolhardy—an open invitation to destruction in detail. To add to the confusion, another source has Boguslavski slain at Bakury.[76] For once it is possible to take a firm position: this source is wrong.

Finally, it is curious to note that the chairman of the Plenipotentiary Commission in his contemporary report ascribes the main credit for destruction of the Second Army to Konopko and his auto detachment without even mentioning the name of Fedko.[77] Political commissar Borisov, writing forty years later and leaving open the question of whose was the major credit, commends Konopko for his relentless pursuit of the Greens and likewise is silent as to Fedko's role.[78] The divergence in Soviet accounts is rendered less significant when it is borne in mind that the main work was done by I. P. Uborevich, who directed all sections of the striking force and displayed in his swift and resolute action the ability that would lead to high rank in the Soviet military hierarchy and to death at the hands of Stalin.[79]

Mauled in the fighting in Saratov province and stripped of most if not all of the accoutrements that rendered a military force effective, Antonov sought refuge in Penza province, his plans hidden from history as on other occasions by the veil of obliteration that has descended on him and on the movement he headed. If he had any hope of finding a new base of operations nothing betrays it to the investigator, and very soon—if not from the outset—instinct set him on the homeward trail despite the shattering object lesson he had received over the past eight days.

From the little information available,[80] he seems to have ridden an arc from the village of Kliuchi (the name means "springs") to the town of Chembar (now called Belinski) to the village of Chernyshevo and back through Kirsanov *uezd* to his old haunts in the Vorona valley. But which Kliuchi did he go through? The miserable Soviet sources would not think of locating a village and there are as many Kliuchis in Russia as there are Springfields in the United States. Two such villages have been found in Penza province: one to the northeast of Bakury and some distance southeast of Penza city, the other further to the north and west near the town of Chembar and much closer to the Tambov line. If Antonov passed by the first Kliuchi he was swinging on a much wider arc than if he made for the second village of that name, since he would have begun by putting still more distance between himself and Kirsanov *uezd*, as though he had abandoned all thought of returning to the hearth of the insurrection and was making for the

Mordvin forests between the Oka and Volga or else for the steppe.

A not too reliable source[81] has him moving with astonishing rapidity, up to one hundred fifty kilometers (ninety-three miles) in a twenty-four hour period—quite a distance to traverse on horseback and with no respite on succeeding days. If the information is correct it would strengthen the assumption that he moved over the wider arc, as would also the statement by Zhukov that the Greens scattered in the general direction of Penza,[82] by which he presumably means the city rather than the province.

Either because of the swiftness of their retreat or because of uncertainty as to the direction it was taking the Greens managed to elude the armored column, except at Chernyshevo village on 6 June where the main group was overtaken just before entering Kirsanov *uezd* and is said to have sustained a loss of one-fifth of its number.[83] By the next night the survivors of the wreck of the Second Army were back in the Vorona valley hiding in the Shibriaev forest[84] or perhaps in the Sukhotin forest,[85] or else in the Chernavka and Pushchino forests,[86] or maybe in all of these forests and in others besides.

So perished the Second Insurrectionary Army of A. S. Antonov. Fragments were left, in some cases portions of regiments, but no army. How Antonov came through the wreckage and to what extent he directed movements after Bakury are questions that cannot be answered. Those accounts may well be true that have him wounded or struck on the head at Bakury so that he had to be borne off the field,[87] but how seriously he was injured and when he resumed command are points about which there is no information whatever. However that may be, the decision to return to the Vorona valley would seem to have been peculiarly Antonov's, characteristic of his leadership throughout the insurrection.

Meanwhile, Boguslavski at the head of the First Army was reaching precisely the opposite conclusion. We know not whence he came but if he were a native of Tambov, as his standing with Antonov indicates, he was not chained to his habitat and could contemplate operations elsewhere if the prospects at home were so bleak. Unable with a couple of thousand men and in the face of overwhelming odds to take any action that would have helped to avert the fate of the Second Army, Boguslavski now decided not to await a similar blow but to move rapidly southeastward through Voronezh province to the territory of the Don Cossacks in the hope of finding support among chronically disaffected Cossack elements. Hostile sources claim that earlier contact had been made and that White Cossacks had assured him of all possible assistance. How White these Cossacks were and whether contacts had progressed beyond the stage of loose talk are matters that cannot be clarified, but they may be viewed with skepticism.

Nevertheless the First Army entered on its line of march only to be set upon by Kotovski's brigade and a Che-ka armored detachment, the latter presumably taken out of Uborevich's striking force like the cavalry brigade itself. The name of the Red commander is not given but the pursuit was pressed energetically, and on the night of 14 June the Che-ka's armor overtook the First Army at Pospelovka village and inflicted a loss of some one hundred fifty men and four machine guns.[88]

A. A. Vaskin, commander of the Che-ka force—apparently the 1st armored car detachment—received the Order of the Red Banner for bravery and skill displayed in action at the village of Pospelovo.[89] A different version has Boguslavski sustaining the reverse as a result of being surrounded in a forest near a place called Batraki.[90] No Pospelovka or Pospelovo has been located, and no Batraki. But there is a Bratki in Borisoglebsk *uezd* on the Savala river, a tributary of the Khoper, and further up the Savala are the villages of Tugolukovo and Kamenka, respectively one of the strongholds and the capital of the Tambov insurrection. A short distance northwest of Kamenka are the headwaters of the Tsna with the villages of Verkhotsene and Bakharevo—the original position of the First Army at the start of the campaign.

The author believes, therefore, that the route taken by the First Army may be reconstructed: from his original position Boguslavski moved through solidly Green territory over the Oka–Don watershed and down the Savala toward its confluence with the Khoper in Novokhopersk *uezd* of Voronezh province, taking advantage of wooded areas along the Savala. Just beyond lay the Don Cossack region.

By the 17th or 18th of June Boguslavski had reached the lower Khoper somewhere between Novokhopersk and Uriupinskaia; he tried to cross but was taken under fire or pinned to the river and his

First Army virtually annihilated. He himself was either killed in the fighting or taken and shot.[91]

And here we would have to leave the matter in the limbo of uncertainty, as in the case of his predecessor Tokmakov, were it not that the Soviet press contained a passing reference to Boguslavski's fate. Press coverage of the Green phenomenon leaves a vast deal to be desired; in general it offers only scraps of information, but at times these scraps have value.

In the present instance it has a nugget of news that is specific. Boguslavski was taken prisoner in the smash-up of his army. Evidently he successfully concealed his identity, for only after being exhibited with six other captives to peasants in the village of Tugolukovo did the Communists learn whom they had taken. "Justice" followed hard thereafter. "At the peasants' demand he has been shot." Boguslavski, like Tokmakov, was Left Socialist Revolutionary. Yet somehow the "revolution" could no longer tolerate his presence. Only "there, where the Red broom has swept, is established the full revolutionary order."[92]

A paper found on the person of G. N. Pluzhnikov, chairman of the provincial committee of the STK, at the time of his arrest or death on 12 July and purporting to be a secret report to the representative of the SR Central Committee, describes the state of affairs after the loss of Boguslavski's First Army: "our units operating on the 21st and 22nd [of June] in the Don–Khoper region returned in sad condition, dispersed by the armored car detachments, without horses or arms." Lamenting the lack of success at the present time, Pluzhnikov found the root of the evil to lie in the naming of one Mashkov to the Supreme Operational Staff. Whether Pluzhnikov explained his accusation is not known, for the disclosure ends here in tantalizing fashion. The Soviet commentator surmises that either the representative of the Central Committee or that body itself had made the appointment, but the coincidence of his despatch with the SR trial of 1922 suggests a further attempt to blame the Tambov uprising on the jaded SR Central Committee.[93]

The author of this study has conjectured that Mashkov may have been the code name for P. T. (or P. M.) Ektov, until recently staff assistant to Antonov and now agent of the Che-ka. He had been arrested in Moscow and had offered his services to his captors; by this time—12 July—he was back on the local scene in his new capacity. But would Pluzhnikov have learned of the defection already and, if so, why had he not alerted Green units who would soon fall victim to Ektov's betrayal?[94] With only one fixed date the chronology is too vague for a worthwhile judgment and the conjecture must remain a conjecture. Here is a key, however, that might unlock the door behind which are guarded the secrets of the Green command in the most decisive stage of its existence. Unfortunately, absolutely nothing is known about Mashkov beyond this one reference in Pluzhnikov's "report."

With the destruction of the Second and First armies, the campaign against the insurrection changed from open warfare to dispersed action against small guerrilla bands in six different *uezds*. Soviet authorities concerned themselves primarily with the remnants of the Second Army hiding with their leader in the forests and swamps of the Vorona valley, since here the fire might be rekindled most easily. The first major operation was launched with shell fire and chains of infantry against the force of around fifteen hundred which Antonov is said to have gathered already by the second half of June; numbers of rebels were slain or taken captive, including leaders like the brothers Santalov—or at least one of them, Fedor. Successive combings of places of refuge led to successive reductions in the number of rebels still holding out. Operations continued through all of July and into August, culminating in the effort to run Antonov down in his ultimate hideout—the Golden Cage at Snake Lake—not far from Ramza and from Parevka, the latter considered by the Communists as perhaps the village most fanatically devoted to the Green cause.[95]

The campaign of extermination continued to yield results but never the supreme reward: Antonov succeeded in eluding both the Red Army and the Extraordinary Commission. He is supposed to have escaped either by standing up to his neck in water in the shallower reed-infested portion of the lake or else by burrowing into mounds of earth rising here and there in the swamp. Neither method of salvation is very convincing to a person steeped in nature; if standing in water up to his neck, he could have no weapons and would have to make some slight motion among the reeds if only to wave the mosquitoes away from his head. In a deep burrow the water would soon seep in, and in a shallow one the turf above—said to have been removed and then replaced—would have caved in under the weight of a Red Army man. Is all this legend, and was Antonov already there where his life would end: in the Shibriaev forest in Borisoglebsk *uezd*, just beyond his Kirsanov homeland?

But one legend at least seemed valid still when operations trailed off into frustration at the end of the summer:

> Antonov v vode ne tonet, v ogne—ne gorit,
> ego shtyk ne tronet, pulya ne srazit.

> [Antonov does not burn in fire nor in water does he drown,
> the bayonet cannot pierce him, no bullet cuts him down.]

Our Communist commentator observes that the legend had a certain basis in fact, since SR leaders customarily took to their heels at the first sign of danger leaving their followers to face the consequences; no one better exemplified this custom, according to him, or practised it with greater success than Antonov. By fall of 1921 all trace of him had been lost. "It was even assumed that he had left the confines of the province he had plundered and stained with blood."[96]

There are other reasons than concern for his skin to explain Antonov's disappearance. In revolution or in war preservation of the core of leadership is a prime consideration. After all, who among the Communist leaders had a record of incurred risk to compare with Antonov's? There is also reason to think that in this instance Antonov may have had no choice. Apparently he was wounded again in August 1921[97] and could not think of continuing desultory guerrilla action, even if the means had been at hand. One source assigns a specific date for his being wounded—9 August 1921—it is not known on what authority.[98] If the bloodhounds on his trail had wind of his condition they would have been more confused than ever, since even a less serious wound might well have been fatal under the circumstances: Antonov had lost the services of his army physician, Shalaev, who is said to have been taken alive in the same operation that destroyed one or both of the Santalov brothers.[99] Unconfirmed rumors circulated that the leader had perished along with many of his followers in the broken fighting where the dead might not be reclaimed from the depths of the forest or from the waters of the lakes and the marshes.[100] Evidently some of the Soviet huntsmen were inclined to write him off, but others were not.

No sooner are developments painfully reconstructed in this study than it is necessary to back away from them. Not only the terrain, but the whole story of the end of Antonov's fighting career is swampy and affords no certain footing. From the outset the author suspected that Antonov may have been wounded only once, and that the June incident at Bakury was transferred to August or vice versa. And the hypothesis gains support, though not confirmation, from the only section of the primary source that is available—the recollections of the Chekist, S. Polin. No mention of injury at Bakury but only of breaking through the cordon and fleeing into the Saratov steppe—incidentally, an erroneous statement since Serdobsk *uezd* is not steppe country, nor is Petrovsk *uezd* to the east. But in August Polin has Antonov pinned to a village by armored cars and cavalry and sustaining a wound in the head, after which he decamps and abandons his followers to their fate[101]—no mean feat for a man hit in the head.

Armored cars do not operate in marshes, the village must have been Bakury, and Antonov is not likely to have been wounded twice in the head within an interval of two months. It is likely that he was wounded in 1921, but whether in June at the climax of the fighting or in August at its end there is no telling. But the Green leader may be absolved of pusillanimity, for the very same Chekist who brings the charge of abandonment of his followers says on the next page that "Antonov was a man, it is necessary to say, of great bandit effrontery and daring."[102]

The attempt to rally the remnants of the Second Army under Antonov's personal direction had foundered toward the end of June as a result of the blows rained upon him—perhaps also because of his physical condition. His strength splintered into small groups, one of which coalesced under the leadership of I. Kuznetsov. It was considered major by the Soviet authorities, more because of the rank and experience of its leader, it would seem, than because of its size—regarding which there is no estimate whatever.

Kuznetsov, described in the novel as a stout, aging man, had been lieutenant colonel in the Imperial army and had at the outset commanded the Second Army just as Tokmakov commanded the First.[103] Kuznetsov's role in the ill-fated campaign of late May–early June 1921 is a perfect blank; did he remain nominally at the head of the Second Army after Antonov had assumed direction, and to what extent—as an experienced officer—did he advise Antonov regarding the conduct of operations? There is even an intimation that Kuznetsov's band may not have come out of the wreckage of the Second Army but may have resulted from his succeeding the slain Boguslavski in command of whatever was left of the First Army after the debacle on the lower Khoper. The terminology is not clear enough for a definite conclusion, and in any event the matter is not of importance for, as the informant says, nothing was left to command.[104]

Whatever its provenance, Kuznetsov found himself at the head of a band of undetermined strength whose main preoccupation must have been survival, since nothing indicates that it did anything. Indeed, the leader's thoughts had turned to other matters. As a professional soldier, not sprung from the Tambov peasantry, Kuznetsov could see no reason further to serve a hopeless cause. We know from the highest authority that already by 20 July he had opened negotiations for the surrender of himself and his men.[105] Not long thereafter the act was consummated although nothing is known concerning the terms, the number of men involved, the quantity of arms turned in, or the leader's fate.

Probably the commissar of Kotovski's brigade is justified in asserting that the renunciation of further struggle by a leader described by Antonov-Ovseenko as the "right arm" of Antonov and by Ektov as highly respected among the Greens[106] strongly influenced those remaining under arms to discontinue their resistance.[107] It is to be assumed that neither Kuznetsov nor the men under him incurred the death penalty, though to escape under Dzerzhinski in 1921 was no guarantee of escaping under Ezhov in 1936–1938. The silence in the Soviet sources as to this affair, apart from the bare fact of surrender, indicates that Kuznetsov did not turn informer as did others who are praised in these sources.

The second of the two main splinters of Antonov's army still in the field by mid-July 1921[108] is a very different story. All aspects of the

Tambov insurrection suffer from a dearth of information save only the Matiukhin affair. Glorification of Kotovski and the romantic features of this episode explain the blossoming of Soviet accounts in at least this one respect. If the flame had died down in the hearts of Kuznetsov and his men, it burned brightly in the camp of Matiukhin, lighting up its animal vigor and its will to fight to the end.

Ivan S. Matiukhin was an authentic product of the churned-up depths of the Tambov countryside. The defector Ektov—perhaps to ingratiate himself with his captors—characterized him as a man of no ideas and of criminal proclivities, a horsethief before the revolution and a fugitive from Siberian exile or imprisonment. After the revolution he abused peasants as a member of Soviet food detachments; lacking Communist immunity, we may suppose, he was arrested for his wrongdoing but was released by Antonov as head of the Kirsanov *uezd* militia.

It seems that Antonov, like Stalin on a broader scale, was engaged in building up a following of men indebted to him. If so, Matiukhin was too headstrong to be a mere follower and gave Antonov trouble. A *Wachtmeister* (sergeant major) in the old army[109]—something that is not too easily squared with his horsestealing and fugitive status—Matiukhin disposed of qualities that made him commander of the 14th or Naru–Tambov Regiment,[110] one of the elite units of the army of insurrection. He took trophies in battle and refused to share them with other regiments—let them get their own, was his attitude—causing a row with Antonov, whose position Matiukhin is said to have coveted.[111]

This peasant commander is depicted as a man–beast, using his physical strength to twist the heads of Red Army captives.[112] Brigade commissar Borisov warned two emissaries about to be sent to him as bait for a trap to steel themselves and to avoid all drinking, for Matiukhin was "cruel and cunning and not at all stupid."[113] Physically he was a large and powerful man with dark hair and pronounced facial features that were animated by a fierce yet furtive gaze.[114] As already stated, it is a matter of some satisfaction to know how at least one of the Green leaders looked.

In the first part of July and probably since soon after the action at Bakury on the 2nd or 3rd of June, Matiukhin was lurking in the big forest across the Tsna to the east of the city of Tambov with a force of "arch-desperados" variously estimated at from three hundred to four hundred fifty in number.[115] He had been at Bakury and, according to an officer with Kotovski, had extricated his "brigade" without loss from the disaster.[116] A brigade would comprise two regiments, and sure enough Matiukhin had with him in the Tambov forest two regiments: his own—the 14th Naru–Tambov—and another, the 16th of unknown name, commanded by one Nazarov. Only they were sadly decimated regiments as indicated by the above figures, since a full complement for two regiments would have been in the neighborhood of a thousand men. A related source is obviously right in stating that Matiukhin's force consisted of the remnants of these two regiments.[117] There may even have been the remnants of a third, [118] its number and name unknown. Shredded terribly or only badly, these units nevertheless had life simply because they were willing to die.

Matiukhin avoided, it is true, any venture into the open field but—if the novel is to be believed—he sallied forth under cover of darkness with breathtaking daring and "gave heat" to this or that part of Kotovski's brigade,[119] most active of all the Red forces engaged in the work of extirpation. And what the novelist says is confirmed by an early and reliable Soviet source, laudatory of Kotovski yet free of the adulation that later developed: "The liquidation of Matiukhin's band was succeeding not at all. Then Kotovski had recourse to cunning."[120]

Even if it had done nothing but lurk in the forest, the Matiukhin band would have been viewed as a menace because it was only some thirty kilometers—less than twenty miles—from the city and two vital rail lines. The leader himself and at least the men of his own regiment were on home territory; they dominated the terrain absolutely and had solid support in every village out on the plain even though it was occupied by Soviet troops. In the forest recesses they had food, fodder, and arms. In other words, here was a large ember glowing brightly from which the fire at any moment might be rekindled. It was intolerable to leave it there.[121]

But how to extinguish it? Whether because of dread inspired by Matiukhin's savage spirit or because of an unwillingness to incur heavy losses or because of the dimensions of the forest in question, neither Kotovski's brigade nor any other evinced a desire to go into the wilderness after the bear—wounded, but still highly dangerous.

Yet the Red forces had cordoned off areas in the Vorona valley and plunged into the woods after Antonov.

But those were woods in the strict sense of the term, narrow if dense vegetation zones along the streams with open country beyond, whereas east and northeast of Tambov began the real forest, protected from human destruction by the poverty of the soil on which it stood and merging on the north with the Mordvin forests, the mixed forests of the middle Volga, and ultimately with the zone of the northern conifers. The tongue of *podzol* jutting deeply into the fertile black earth as far as Tambov had inhibited the peasants' forebears but would help their present defenders. As one officer under Kotovski says, there was no surrounding the Tambov forest.[122] And another says it was no place for a cavalry brigade to go into action.[123]

And so the decision was taken not to tackle Matiukhin in his lair but to entice him out through a ruse and fall upon him when his guard was down. The conception of the plan is not clear. It is attributed to the Che-ka[124] on the authority of a source[125] later revised to give the main credit to Kotovski.[126] Other accounts do likewise.[127] The Che-ka itself in its published materials confuses the issue, either purposefully or through poor editing: the key document[128] assigns a major role to N. A. Gazhalov, head of the special section of Kotovski's brigade (i.e., the espionage section which had been brought under the Che-ka, not only in this instance but generally), and the commentary makes him the central figure.[129]

It is important to note that the supreme objective was not so much to destroy the band, though that outcome would be sought if feasible, as it was to destroy the core of the leadership.[130] Both the brigade commissar and Tukhachevski himself affirm as the main purpose of the enterprise the extermination of the leaders.[131] To behead the opposition has always been the cardinal aim of Soviet policy, whatever fate is reserved for the rank and file. This feature of the plan and the treachery involved smack of Che-ka inspiration. That the plan went through military channels, from Kotovski in the field to Pavlov in Inzhavino to Tukhachevski in Tambov, [132] may have been for the sake of appearances.

Whether or not Kotovski conceived the notion of disguising himself and his command from something Ektov had said (the Garri version), the scheme called for his brigade[133] to masquerade as a

Cossack force from the Don–Kuban region which somehow had won its way through to Tambov province and wished to concert action against the Communist tyranny with other like-minded elements. He himself would figure as Ataman Frolov—a flesh and blood personage, we are told, not an invention—against whom somewhere in the south Kotovski had fought.[134] Rumors had floated about that such help was on the way, perhaps planted by the Green leaders to sustain morale. Now the Reds would fan such rumors.

As a means of establishing contact with the insurgents and of allaying their suspicions, Kotovski would avail himself of the services of the turncoat Ektov, still under Che-ka guard. Soviet intelligence believed that the news of his arrest and defection had not yet reached the Green leaders, Matiukhin in particular[135] to whom he was well known as a member of Antonov's staff and whose confidence he enjoyed. In this manner, and sparing the details which, moreover, do not agree, it proved feasible to arrange a rendezvous with Matiukhin on the night of 19–20 July at Dmitrovskoe or Kobylinka (Dmitrievka–Kobylenskaia or Kobylenka or Kobylianka—the spelling is free), a village on the edge of the Tambov forest.

Matiukhin has been likened in savagery and cunning to a wolf, a derogation more fitting than most Soviet stereotypes for the opposition. This wolf was powerfully attracted by the bait of reinforcement but extremely wary of the trap that might go with it. Coming out of the forest with some two hundred of his men, his staff, and his colleague Nazarov—commander of whatever was left of the 16th insurrectionary regiment—he insisted on separate quarters for his troops on the ground that friction could be avoided through segregation, since "your men are Ukrainian[136] and ours are Russians." And he gave the order: "Konei ne rassedlyvat' i v koniushni ne stavit'!" [The horses are not to be unsaddled and are not to be put in the stables!] At first his men followed orders and resisted Red solicitude for their horses; eventually, however, the Reds got them into stables or barns on the pretense of feeding them oats and then locked them up, unnoticed by the Greens—or so the commissar says.[137]

Meanwhile the leaders' conference had gotten under way in a kulak's dwelling. There are four basic accounts of what happened:

that of the political commissar of the brigade, Borisov, in an earlier short version and a later expanded one, both written many years later; that of the officer in charge of the field staff, Garri, also written many years later; that of Tukhachevski, undated but written at the time; and that of Kotovski himself, from an interview he gave a correspondent only two years after the Matiukhin episode and two years before his own death.[138]

The accounts have a good deal in common, yet diverge in respect to certain significant matters such as the content of Borisov's report presented at the conference. One of the Green leaders—an SR commissar from Tambov—should have heeded his intuition, for he was the most suspicious of all and flatly refused to occupy a place at the conference table; instead he sat on the floor alongside, facing Kotovski, with his rifle at the ready. Borisov—as representative of the SR Central Committee according to his own account and also to Garri's, but as a member of the Left SR party according to Kotovski's—reported in an optimistic vein about the fortunes of the opposition on the national scene and sounded a call to arms. Garri recounted the heroic exploits of Makhno and his men as the Greens listened with bated breath, the speaker's appearance lending substance to his claim to represent that movement.

In mentioning Garri's oration and even praising it, Kotovski tends to confirm the version that the Reds were deliberately egging the enemy on; yet he asserts that on the basis of his commissar's report he himself urged the Greens to discontinue the armed struggle and to go underground, only to meet with the stern refusal of Matiukhin whom no amount of adversity could deter from his resolution to bring down the "bloodthirsty commune."

After argument over the details of collaboration—the very principle of which was rejected by the SR commissar on the floor—or else after more of the palaver Russians like to engage in animated by libations of moonshine, Kotovski arose to pronounce the end of the "comedy," to disclose his identity, and to dispose of Matiukhin. The flush on his face and the sweat pouring from it should have announced his intention. He whipped out his pistol and aimed at the drunken (?) Green leader. But the problems of Soviet industrialization began early and the new weapon from the Tambov arsenal refused service. Twice it hung fire or maybe three times, enough for the SR commissar on the floor to aim his rifle and smash Kotovski's right arm at the shoulder. Wild shooting ensued, the lamp was extinguished and the room plunged into darkness. Outside the Reds fell upon Matiukhin's band, aided by their knowledge of what was to happen and by the enemy's unreadiness. Apparently the whole brigade was brought into play, although few things are certain about this affray. When it was all over less than a score of the Greens are said to have escaped, for a toll of 90 percent or even more.[139]

There are various reasons why the accounts of the Matiukhin affair, all of them from the Soviet side, leave something to be desired. For one thing, there is the question of transforming an entire brigade into a force so un-Soviet in appearance that it would have been fired upon—as Borisov observes[140]—if it had encountered another part of the Red Army; and this within the space of some three days[141] and without leakage or detection in a countryside swarming with Green sympathizers, where the Reds themselves expected a simulated skirmish to be reported immediately to Matiukhin.[142]

Disregarding the most credible testimony, if only a portion of the brigade had been so disguised, then how could the rest of it have escaped detection as it moved up to the village of Kobylinka? How could Matiukhin have seriously entertained the hope that a friendly force from afar could have penetrated to the heart of Tambov province through a whole army of Red troops blanketing the area of the uprising? After all, what had happened to his movement and why was he holed up in the forest with about 2 percent of its strength?

It is true that he was desperate, eager to clutch at any straw, and that Ektov was a fine decoy; yet desperation sharpens suspicion, and Matiukhin as regimental commander should have known of the mission Antonov had sent to Moscow—if not of its arrest in June [143] or at the end of that month[144]—and should have been prepared for the worst. Ektov must have gone along with this mission and Fedorov-Gorski certainly did. Or if in the turmoil of the time Matiukhin had somehow not been informed, he surely must have known of the assignment and arrest in May of another Antonovist—most likely Ishin—whose disclosures had resulted in the arrest (baseless, as it turned out) of the prominent Moscow Constitutional Democrat, N. M. Kishkin.[145] Matiukhin had been with Antonov at least through the engagement at Bakury in early June. He was not stupid, even the Communists admit, and he had every reason to exercise the utmost caution.

That he would forego posting his own guard around the village upon reassurance from underlings that the "Cossacks" had taken care of the matter seems improbable, as does the eventual disregard by his men of his strict injunctions against stabling the horses, for everything about Matiukhin suggests that he was a man whose orders would be obeyed. Still harder to accept is the Kotovski version which has Matiukhin accepting the quarters placed at his disposal without insisting on keeping his men apart and without thought of keeping their mounts in readiness upon assurance by one of his go-betweens of adequate security arrangements;[146] Kotovski in effect has the Green leader wholly reassured, Borisov only half-reassured.[147]

Borisov's point about the segregation of the two commands along national lines at the demand of the "old tsarist wolf" also offers difficulty; Matiukhin may not have trusted Ukrainians, but as *Wachtmeister* in the old army and as a native of Tambov province, separated by only one thin *uezd* of Voronezh province from the Don Cossack territory, he would have known that these Cossacks were Great Russian, not Ukrainian, even if those from the Kuban might be either.

Another detail that arouses doubt is the closed and bolted state of the windows in the conference room.[148] If Matiukhin were reassured as to security measures why would he have sat for several hours on a July night in a closed room with twenty-six other persons,[149] especially when the commissar who reports these details specifies that it was a warm night[150] and when Matiukhin was imbibing freely and so getting hotter all the time? Doubtless he liked the white mule that had duly made its appearance,[151] if the Kotovski version is to be credited; but if he drank on this occasion he was stupid, and he must have been uncomfortable besides. The conclusion is inescapable that much embroidery adorns these accounts; the question is where does the embroidery end and the substance begin?

By far the main reason for dissatisfaction with accounts of the destruction of Matiukhin's band, however, is the fate of Matiukhin himself, regarding which there are almost as many versions as there are sources. It is generally agreed that most leaders perished on the scene, among them Nazarov, commander of the 16th insurrectionary regiment. But a veil of mystery shrouds the end of the central figure. Some have Matiukhin killed on the spot.[152] Others have him somehow getting away only to perish later, though not in the same way. Thus he is said to have lost his life in a granary that had been set on fire.[153] The value of Kotovski's testimony is lessened by his having ceased to be a primary source when he got it in the shoulder from the SR commissar sitting on the floor. But after being taken to one of the best clinics in Moscow and eventually recovering, he should have learned what happened. Apparently he did not.

There is left to consider the testimony of Kotovski's own commissar, P. A. Borisov, one of the primary actors in this drama. In recollections published long afterward in 1961, the commissar writes that the wounded Matiukhin crawled away from the scene of death only to be taken and shot "after some time."[154] But in the small book published in 1965 Borisov becomes much more definite. Observing that only the escape of the chief figure had dimmed the victory over his band, Borisov says that he later learned that Matiukhin had taken several bullets in the house but had somehow managed to get out the door into the yard and to crawl or creep away. He succeeded in staying alive for two more months before he was killed in a shooting scrape with the Che-ka in the Naru–Tambov forest.[155] Nearly all the other leaders of his band had been slain in the conference room or under the windows out of which they had thrown themselves.

We conclude that official circles, opening up the subject to some extent after nearly half a century yet determined to have no independent investigation, have come to the aid of Borisov's memory. And it has been effective aid, for this 1965 version either establishes what happened or comes very close to the truth. A despatch of long ago lends it support. Noting that most of the "bandit" leaders had either been killed or had surrendered, the Soviet press reported late in September 1921—a little more than two months after the trap had been sprung in Kobylianka village—that

Matiukhin along with Antonov himself and several others had survived. The same despatch announced the killing in the Tambov forest of Boltnev, political commissar of the Tambov "bandit" regiment.[156] A week later the news was repeated.[157] Doubtless the Naru–Tambov Regiment is meant, since we know of no unit with the ambiguous name of Tambov.

Did Boltnev perish in the large Tambov forest as announced, where the band had found refuge, or were the small woods along the Naru–Tambov river—a headwater of the Tsna—the scene of his death? And could Matiukhin have died with his commissar and the news have been withheld by the Che-ka, or the fact not established at the time? These are questions that cannot be answered; no later reference to his fate has been found. As commander of the Naru–Tambov Regiment Matiukhin probably came from one of the villages in the area such as Khitrovo or Koptevo, both strongholds of his movement, and he may have returned there to die.

The Che-ka records as published are no help and only muddy the waters. Obviously in error is the attempt to credit V. G. Belugin with the slaying of Matiukhin, since the time is given as the beginning of 1921 and the citation by Tukhachevski is dated 10 April 1921,[158] whereas Tukhachevski was not appointed until 27 April and did not arrive on the Tambov scene until 6 May. A later document has the right time and setting but deletes the names of the "very eminent leaders" who were marked for destruction and so must be pronounced worthless.[159] Successful operations of the Che-ka do not extend into the field of history.

With the decimation if not destruction of the Matiukhin band, the "largest and most formidable" fragment of Antonov's army had been struck from the list.[160] Most formidable it certainly was, but whether the largest may be doubted; statistics on the Green movement are as wretched in this instance as in any other. The shadowy figure of Averianov again made its appearance, allegedly at the head of six hundred sabers, again to be destroyed by the ever-victorious Kotovski.[161] After this action on 8 July Averianov vanishes into the mist out of which he had never really emerged.

The Burmin band with a reported strength of five hundred early in July would also have been somewhat larger than Matiukhin's if these figures are to be taken seriously. It escaped annihilation, yet had undergone a sad shrinkage by the time of its voluntary surrender when one hundred sixty-one men with the "well-known bandit leaders" Barmin (*sic*), Vorotishchev, Kuldiashev, and Venediktov at their head paraded down the main street in Tambov to the reception awaiting them by the Plenipotentiary Commission, the Red Army, and the Che-ka. Vasiliev—doubtless B. Vasiliev, the provincial party secretary—addressed them in the name of the commission, promising that the lives of all would be spared but warning that they must stand trial for their "grievous crimes."[162] Nothing more is known of the Burmin—or Barmin—band.

Everything has been said that can be said about four of the largest splinters of the Green movement, those headed respectively by Kuznetsov, Matiukhin, Averianov, and Burmin or Barmin. Two of these had given up after an undetermined degree of resistance, a third had either been knocked to pieces or had faded away; only one represented a real fighting force and it had fallen victim to a ruse. Soviet Army archives yield an estimate as of 1 July of twelve groups or bands with a total strength of thirty-eight hundred,[163] of which these four splinters would account for perhaps a half.

The only other sizable band of record is that of Vaska Karas, stated by one source to have consisted of five hundred men.[164] Its line of movement is uncertain, but it was an active force and it held the field to the bitter end. The commissar of repression drew Lenin's attention to its "convulsive activity" at the end of June, resulting in damage to the Tambov–Kirsanov roadbed, the burning of certain stations and bridges, and the plundering of two trains.[165] On 30 June Karas is said to have been routed by the Che-ka's 1st armored detachment at the village of Lavrovka. Taking up the pursuit of his band—now down to one hundred fifty sabres from whatever figure it started with—a Red cavalry force routed him again on 7 July in the Vorontsov forest and drove the remnants into Kozlov *uezd* where they were "completely annihilated" at the village of Malaia Lavrovka, a short distance from the *uezd* center.[166]

There is record of another force, however, not identified as Karas's but rather as Antonov's, which moved out of the rallying point of whatever was left of his Second Army in the Sukhotin forest and proceeded to Zagriazhki in Tambov *uezd*. On 6 July, in a frenzy of activity, it dismantled twenty-six *versts* of the Tambov–Balashov railroad,[167] burned the station of Korpan–Stroganovo, and wrecked a locomotive.[168] But on the next day it was caught and mauled in the woods near the village of Vorontsovka.[169]

All of these place names defy location except Zagriazhki—or better, Zagriazhkoe[170]—a village on the upper Tsna due south of Tambov town and very near the Tambov–Balashov line. From the location of this village where it could readily be on a line of movement out of Kirsanov and Tambov *uezds* into Kozlov, and from the common action on the same day at Vorontsovka or in the Vorontsov forest, we conclude that the two forces are the same. The sources do not necessarily contradict one another because Karas and his command could easily have separated out from Antonov's Second Army in its death throes. The band was destroyed on 15 July 1921 near the town of Kozlov, it is generally agreed, and Karas himself fell in the action.[171]

The seven smaller bands or groups—if that were their number on 1 July[172]—remaining to be run down will not be a subject of investigation if only because next to nothing is available concerning them; it is not possible even to list them. The example of the Zverev band will suffice. It had only some one hundred fifty men when the cavalry squadron of the future marshal Zhukov set upon it and ended its existence except for the leader and four of his men who escaped into a forest under cover of darkness. During the pursuit that preceded the final engagement, several armored cars rushed out of a village to cut in front of what was assumed to be the band but was actually Zhukov's squadron. Knowing that "bandits" had no such equipment Zhukov did not open fire, but reciprocity was not forthcoming from the other side as the commander of the armored cars had no such ready means of distinguishing friend from foe, and only at the last moment did liaison succeed in averting an incident that "could have ended badly." In the front car was none other than I. P. Uborevich, the first occasion on which Zhukov met the man who, but for Stalin, might have played in the second world war the role that devolved upon Zhukov.[173]

As for the rest, it is a story of running to earth individuals or little knots of men holding desperately to some degree of comradeship in the face of disaster, of surrender—voluntary or otherwise—and of suicide. Among cases of collective surrender may be mentioned one of special significance—the remnant of the 4th or Parevka Regiment which counted only a hundred men when it turned itself in sometime in August, still fully armed and with its commander still at its head. Most regrettably he is not named in the despatch.[174] Nor does it explain the surrender of whatever was left of a regiment recruited from the locality more committed to the Green movement and more stubborn in its adherence than perhaps any other. The men of Parevka would seemingly have followed Matiukhin's example and fought it through to the end. Yet a special circumstance accounts for their action, a circumstance that will be noted in due course.[175]

In the same district—unnamed, but presumably in the heart of the Green territory like Parevka itself—eighty or more "prominent bandits" had downed their arms, either individually or in groups (the despatch does not say). Among them were two important leaders: Petrov, commander of the 3rd or Nizovski Regiment, and Frantsuzov, head of the machine gun command of Antonov's army.[176] Nothing more is known about these men.

A sterner figure in the Matiukhin mould was "Grach"—A. Simakov or Finakov, initials unknown—a personal friend of Antonov and leader of a large band. Since for Communists "bandits" can be only in bands, we may assume that "Grach" had been a regimental commander in the heyday of the Green movement and had come to head a band only after the breakup of the First and Second armies, but what regiment and what band is all a perfect blank. In any event, when fate overtook him "Grach" headed nothing; he was a lonely fugitive, fending for himself. The Che-ka caught him in the hayloft or wherever it was he was hiding and he is said to have betrayed fear, but he regained his composure and fortitude, became as hard and stern as before, and did not flinch at the end. Ordinary followers of Antonov might be spared or they might not, but for "Grach" was reserved the "highest form of social retribution." He remained faithful to his comrades in arms; the Che-ka learned nothing from him.[177]

The recitation of woes that beset the Greens in the course of cleanup operations after the shredding of the Second and First armies must not obscure the fact that the picture was not quite so one-sided. Even in their death throes the Greens could hit back hard on occasion. In the language of the commissar of repression, they might score "incidental successes" in their "convulsive movements" to restore the situation.

He tells of the rout of a Red cavalry unit—identified only as Z. V. O., whatever that means—with the loss of two machine guns and forty-five dead. He speaks of a severe setback for cavalry trainees, who lost four machine guns and as many as forty dead. Apparently he refers to the Borisoglebsk cavalry cadets in the action at Fedorovka–Mordovo where apparently—though not certainly—Matiukhin, in breaking out of Kotovski's encirclement with parts of the Zolotoe and his own Naru–Tambov regiments, found the cadets in his path and fell upon them with fury, inflicting—in the words of the sycophant historian—"considerable losses"[178] or—in those of the novelist—"beating them into the dust."[179] In answer to this stinging defeat and the hopes it revived, according to the novelist, Kotovski decided to destroy the band of the "desperately bold" Green commander[180]—but by the ruse related above, we may note, not by going into the Tambov forest after this bear. One may doubt that Matiukhin was a horsethief under the Tsar but one will not question his elevation to warrior status under the Soviet.

In addition to these two setbacks for the Reds, the commissar of repression in his secret memorandum informed Lenin of a third reverse that is the most surprising of all, one about which the published Soviet sources preserve a gravelike silence. On a date not given, in an unnamed place, the Greens mauled a mobile detachment. The human toll is not mentioned but the mechanical loss indicates a severe defeat: five machine guns and three machines, though whether trucks or armored cars is not stated. From another source containing the report of a political commissar in the army it becomes apparent that the action occurred in the Vorona valley between Uvarovo and Borisoglebsk, probably at the end of June, and that the objective of the ill-fated expedition had been the staff of Antonov's Second Army which had been reported hiding in this area very close to the place, it is interesting to note, where Antonov would be killed a year later.[181]

How the Greens managed to triumph over one of the three armored units which had made the struggle so unequal, under whose command they operated, and what units were involved would make an interesting story. But Soviet history is depersonalized before the Stalin era and there is nothing else. Our candidate for the Green commander is either Antonov himself or Matiukhin, and for the worsted mobile detachment one of the two Che-ka units, either the 1st—named for the Petrograd soviet—or the 52nd of unknown name. Together they had six trucks and one armored car[182] so that, assuming a more or less even division, the loss of three machines would have been a wipeout. Perhaps this matter contributed to the singular respect shown Matiukhin in his forest lair.

It may be noted how little precise information is conveyed even in a secret memorandum. Habits of secretiveness and of plain imprecision are not sloughed off even in communicating with the highest source of authority.[183]

But, as the commissar says, occasional successes could not save the Green cause. The struggle proved too unequal in respect to numbers, to military talent, and to equipment, while the New Economic Policy drained the social reservoir from which support had been drawn. Any sort of serious fighting ended with the summer; precisely one month after springing the trap on Matiukhin the Kotovski brigade was withdrawn (19 August) and sent to the western Ukraine where bands loyal to Simon Petliura still troubled Communist rule.[184] The outflow of the formidable strength concentrated against Antonov had begun.

By official estimate, of the twenty-one thousand Greens under arms at the beginning of May, Red intelligence established that only a few hundred remained by mid-July.[185] The figure seems too low for that date, though not for the end of the summer. A more realistic estimate is furnished by Tukhachevski who informed Lenin that by 11 July out of twenty-one thousand "bandits" only twelve hundred sabers were left in the field.[186]

In the fall the Plenipotentiary Commission issued one of its recurrent calls for surrender, setting 5 October as the deadline for "bandits" to turn themselves in for trial on the understanding that their lives would be spared; failing this they would be put outside the law (where had they been before?) and shot out of hand.[187] Over two hundred men—including officers—belonging to the Korobov–Matiunin group responded with voluntary surrender and confession of guilt (the latter always exacted in such cases) during the week 7–15 October.[188] These names mean nothing, and the thought arises from the ease with which Matiunin could be a misprint for Matiukhin whether this occasion might have marked the end of the road for that part of Matiukhin's force which had stayed in the forest and not come out on the fateful night of 19–20 July. It is idle to pose such questions since they cannot be answered.

Nevertheless, the fall and winter of 1921 witnessed activity on the part of holdouts, coalescing here and there to engage in what a Che-ka source calls purely criminal activity. To end their existence became the task of the Che-ka alone; the services of the Red Army were no longer required.[189] Where the work of the Che-ka weakened there trouble appeared, as in Borisoglebsk *uezd* which in December became of concern to the Communist party's provincial committee when it took note of the survival of "small but well-knit" groups, more virulent than elsewhere, and called upon the All-Russian Che-ka not to withdraw personnel from the provincial branch before the spring of 1922.[190] Earlier the southeastern part of Usman *uezd*, an area that had not figured prominently in the insurrection, sheltered some remnants of the uprising whose behavior, according to the Soviet press, was not to be distinguished from that of real bandits.[191]

By December in the province as a whole a few packs still existed totalling some one hundred fifty members, half of them in the more wooded *uezd* of Borisoglebsk.[192] "Banditry" had been ended "almost definitively," Tambov delegate Tretiakov told the 9th All-Russian Congress of Soviets, and in reelections to the local soviets only Communists were chosen.[193] Yet in January 1922 the Communist party committee discerned in spots a certain revival, and in February it passed from imploring Moscow not to weaken the provincial Che-ka to beseeching it to strengthen that organ.[194] It was a very nervous committee. Only later in 1922, at a time that cannot be fixed, did the Green movement draw its last breath.

The ruin of Antonov's armed forces entailed the ruin of the civilian organization behind them. The Union of Toiling Peasantry with its network of committees on three or even four levels and their procurement, recruitment, communication, and security branches had done much to make this probably the best organized peasant uprising in history; Antonov's military talent in the organizational sense had done the rest. Now, in the summer of 1921, the Soviet government—more particularly, the Che-ka—would succeed in dismantling the whole network with the aid of the disclosures of Ishin, Fedorov-Gorski, Ektov, and other captives of lesser rank who thought to mitigate their own punishment by the value of the information furnished the winning side. The occupying forces hunted down organizers, officials, and simply members of the STK with scarcely less zeal than they sought soldiers of Antonov's regiments. Even less is known of this process than of the "taking out" of the military element.

The hardest single blow struck the STK toward the end of June when the village of Kamenka was occupied with the loss of its headquarters, though not of the whole staff of the provincial and district committees as one Soviet source asserts[195] and another intimates.[196] Certainly no total elimination of the STK leadership had occurred when the two main figures escaped: chairman Pluzhnikov into a forest and vice-chairman Shamov, second in command after Ishin's downfall, to Voronezh province. Some *volost'* committees still functioned here and there, according to Tukhachevski in the memorandum he prepared for Lenin on 16 July, though the STK as an effective organization had ceased to exist.[197]

But these local sparks were sooner or later extinguished or fell apart, and the two escaped leaders did not long survive their organization. The contemporary press reported Shamov as still at large in the early fall while mistakenly identifying him as the brother of Antonov.[198] At an unspecified date, however, he was arrested in Voronezh[199] and presumably executed.

Uncertainty also beclouds the way G. N.— or N. G.—Pluzhnikov met his fate, although the fate itself is clear enough. The novel has the head of the Union of Toiling Peasantry taking his own life in his hideaway in the Volkhonshchinski forest where the corpse is found soon after the act by the head of the Green security force, the kulak villain, P. I. Storozhev.[200] But since this villainous kulak did not remove from the body the paper that might unlock the mystery of the last and decisive campaign from the Green side[201] and since a novelist is not an historian, we would under normal circumstances have accepted the press report which—in addition to mentioning the paper found on Pluzhnikov with enough of the contents to whet the appetite—goes on to say quite specifically that he was caught in his forest lair on 12 July 1921 as a result of betrayal by the peasants of Zhuravelka.[202]

Still another version intrudes on the scene, however, to cast a shadow over this rather convincing report, a version that cannot lightly be dismissed since it emanates from the Che-ka. Agents of that institution learn to speak with a forked tongue, and notably on this occasion: Pluzhnikov "fell under a bullet" in a shack in the Kamenka forests.[203] Whose bullet—his own, or the Che-ka's? So perished in one way or another—by suicide, by killing, or by formal execution—the man who had given the Green army a firm social base and whose contribution to the Tambov insurrection had been outweighed only by Antonov's, possibly also by Tokmakov's.

Sequestration of the material resources of the STK accompanied decimation of its personnel. The recent official Soviet study states that along with the action against Kamenka at the end of June Soviet troops seized a large quantity of SR literature and a banner of the Left SR Central Committee.[204] In the light of information from that time this statement is neither complete nor strictly accurate. The victors came on the find—or rather, windfall—not in Kamenka on the Savala but in the village of Khitrovo on the Naru–Tambov river, somewhat to the northwest and closer to Tambov.

Here in the local church they uncovered a stack of SR brochures, manifestos, resolutions of the Kronstadt uprising, and proceedings of the *uezd* congress of the STK, together with the Left SR banner. On red velvet in golden braid were inscribed the slogan common to the SRs and to the Left SRs, "In struggle thou shalt win thy right," and the dedication from the Central Committee of the Left SR Party of Internationalists to the Union of Toiling Peasantry. Not often has a church been the repository of so unusual a relic. The victors also came into possession of something else—the treasury of the insurrection, consisting of five trunks filled with gold and other valuables. The take was complete.[205]

In tracing the lengthening shadow of doom that settled over the Tambov insurrection, we may say that it was at its strongest in the first two months of 1921, that March and April were marked by bloody but indecisive fighting, that the back of the insurrection was broken between the latter part of May and the latter part of June, and that all the larger embers were crushed out by the end of the summer. "In general, August of 1921 may be considered as the month of the definitive rout of the Tambov rebellion led by Antonov."[206] Small-scale activity continued into the fall and winter of 1921 without in any way unsettling the victorious Soviet order. Splinters of bands were confined to out-of-the-way places, to forests and marshlands. Sometime in the first half of 1922 the last flicker of life went out of what had been a well-organized, hard-fought, and withal formidable challenge to that order. At the end of the year *Pravda* could say that for the entire summer of 1922 not a single band had reappeared on the scene.[207]

Only one thing was not to the victor's liking. The leader of the insurrection had not been accounted for. Virtually the entire core of leadership had been eliminated, only not the main figure. The Soviet regime could never reconcile itself to the presence of so dangerous an enemy as A. S. Antonov in the Russian countryside, the combustibility of which, in the last analysis, was due to the regime's own basic attitude toward the peasantry. Despite everything, its victory was not yet complete.

Notes

1. See chapter nine.

2. Typed copy of handwritten note of Sklianski to Lenin and of Lenin's handwritten reply; T–678 of Trotsky Archive. Neither is dated. The notation states that the material is from the archives of Sklianski and that it dates probably from the beginning of June 1921. This attempt to supply a date is clearly a failure. Since Lenin wanted the action taken "tomorrow" and the appointment was made on 27 April, it is reasonable to assume that the exchange of notes took place on or about 26 April. It may be remarked that Lenin's reply to Sklianski has not found a place in any edition of his collected works. What he meant by no publicity "in the center" is not clear, since it is sure there was none in the provinces. The Soviet regime emits words without number, yet without infringing the secretiveness of its most significant actions.

3. Lenin, *Polnoe sobranie sochinenii,* 5th ed., vol. 52, p. 420, n. 352.

4. Donkov, "Organizatsiia razgroma antonovshchiny," *Voprosy Istorii KPSS,* no. 6 (June 1966), p. 70.

5. Tukhachevski, "Zapiska," p. 1.

6. Ibid., p. 2.

7. Virta, *Odinochestvo,* p. 261.

8. Ia. Gorelov, "Zolotoe oruzhie" [Golden arms], *Izvestiia sovetov deputatov trudiashchikhsia SSSR,* no. 307 (13853), 29 December 1961, p. 6. A rehabilitation article, a little more informative than most.

9. G. K. Zhukov, *The Memoirs of Marshal Zhukov,* 1st American ed. (New York, n.d.), pp. 66–70. His account, though a welcome minor oasis in a desert of information, is not free of error.

10. Zhukov does not mention the names of either his regimental or brigade commanders. The latter would have to be either Kovalev or Dmitrienko and certain indirect evidence points to the latter.

11. A. I. Cherepanov, "Nezabyvaemye vstrechi" [Contacts that are not to be forgotten] in *Komandarm Uborevich: vospominaniia druzei i soratnikov* [Army Commander Uborevich: reminiscences of friends and comrades in arms] (Moscow, 1964), p. 105.

12. Information about assignments in Donkov, "Organizatsiia razgroma antonovshchiny," *Voprosy Istorii KPSS,* no. 6 (June 1966), p. 70; see also Trifonov, *Klassy i klassovaia bor'ba,* part 1, pp. 249–50.

13. "Krest'ianskoe dvizhenie," *Volia Rossii,* no. 172, 8 April 1921; anonymous (Podbelski), *Kak tambovskie krest'iane boriatsia za svobodu,* p. 9; Fomichev (Lidin), "Antonovshchina: Iz vospominanii antonovtsa" (Philippines, 1950–1951), p. 33.

14. Zhukov, *Memoirs*, p. 67. To the number of troops as of 1 March 1921 (see above) have been added the seven thousand military trainees brought in in April; see Trifonov, *Klassy i klassovaia bor'ba*, part 1, pp. 248–50.

15. From the article by Tukhachevski in *Voina i revoliutsiia*, no. 8 (1926), p. 6, as cited in Trifonov, *Klassy i klassovaia bor'ba*, part 1, p. 250. Tukhachevski does not mention the size of the force under his command in the memorandum written at the conclusion of the campaign on 16 July 1921 and preserved in the Trotsky Archive.

16. The figure of one hundred thousand relates to Soviet troops in February and so represents more than a twofold inflation; for the Greens the ratio of exaggeration is fifty thousand to twenty-one thousand.

17. Cherepanov, "Nezabyvaemye vstrechi," in *Komandarm Uborevich*, p. 104, reporting a lecture attended by the author which Uborevich gave at the general staff academy in Moscow immediately after the suppression of the uprising. Lieutenant General Cherepanov errs, however, in fixing the date as the spring of 1921, for Uborevich was in the thick of the fighting in June of that year.

18. I. Trutko, "Takticheskie primery iz opyta bor'by s banditizmom: Unichtozhenie bandy Boguslavskogo" [Tactical examples from experience in the struggle with banditry: destruction of the Boguslavski band], *Krasnaia Armiia*, no. 3–4 (1921), pp. 35, 36, as cited in Trifonov, *Klassy i klassovaia bor'ba*, part 1, p. 254.

19. Ibid., p. 253, where the brigades are given as those of Kotovski, Dmitrienko, and M. P. Kovalev.

20. Tukhachevski, "Zapiska," p. 2.

21. N. Kondrat'ev, *Na linii ognia (epizody iz zhizni komandarma Ivana Fed'ko)* [On the firing line (episodes from the life of Army Commander Ivan Fedko)] (Moscow, 1964), pp. 79–80; A. Vladimirov, "Ivan Fed'ko," in *Zhizn' zamechatel' nykh liudei: Geroi grazhdanskoi voiny* [Lives of remarkable people: heroes of the civil war] (Moscow, 1963), pp. 336–37.

22. Kondrat'ev, *Na linii ognia*, p. 80; Vladimirov, "Ivan Fed'ko," in *Geroi grazhdanskoi voiny*, p. 337.

23. Virta, *Odinochestvo*, pp. 264–65.

24. See above.

25. Antonov-Ovseenko, "O banditskom dvizhenii v Tambovskoi gubernii," p. 14. It is clear from the context of this secret memorandum to Lenin that the figure refers to those who were actually in the guerrilla bands. Presumably the names of the members of their families were not included in this total, so that the Soviet authorities had succeeded in registering individually half the soldiers in Antonov's army.

26. Ibid., p. 12.

27. Though the term "right SR" is abused through being applied to what was really the centrist majority of that badly fractured party, it may be used advisedly in respect to the cooperatives staffed by people who were for the most part old-line Populists, relatively conservative, and highly nationalistic.

28. See discussion on the work of the Plenipotentiary Commission above.

29. There was no hope of such action at first; witness the temper of the peasantry at the provincial congress noted above.

30. Donkov, "Organizatsiia razgroma antonovshchiny," *Voprosy Istorii KPSS,* no. 6 (June 1966), p. 69. See above.

31. Antonov-Ovseenko, "O banditskom dvizhenii v Tambovskoi gubernii," p. 18. Information on preparations from the civilian side has been drawn from ibid., pp. 11, 12–13, 14, 15, 18, 21; also from Trifonov, *Klassy i klassovaia bor'ba,* part 1, p. 239.

32. Trifonov, *Klassy i klassovaia bor'ba,* part 1, p. 238.

33. See above. As stated there, five of the military districts corresponded to *uezds,* and the sixth with headquarters at Inzhavino had been carved out especially to include the heart of the "bandit" territory. It was the chief area of concentration for military trainees and had been placed under P. A. Pavlov after Tukhachevski had superseded him in command of the entire province. I. F. Fedko headed the first military district comprising the bulk of Kirsanov *uezd.*

34. It is not clear what was meant here, whether such families were to be protected against reprisals or whether the reference is to households of divided allegiance with one or more members in the Red forces and one or more serving with the Greens—a situation not infrequently encountered in civil wars.

35. See below.

36. See Trifonov, *Klassy i klassovaia bor'ba,* part 1, pp. 219–20, and Donkov, "Organizatsiia razgroma antonovshchiny," *Voprosy Istorii KPSS,* no. 6 (June 1966), p. 70, for language veiling the true import of these decrees.

37. Antonov-Ovseenko, "O banditskom dvizhenii v Tambovskoi gubernii," p. 23. Information on Order No. 130 will be found in ibid., pp. 23–24.

38. Tukhachevski, "Zapiska," p. 2.

39. Antonov-Ovseenko, "O banditskom dvizhenii v Tambovskoi gubernii," pp. 23, 24; Donkov, "Organizatsiia razgroma antonovshchiny," *Voprosy Istorii KPSS,* no. 6 (June 1966), pp. 69, 70.

40. From the Central Party Archives as cited in Trifonov, *Klassy i klassovaia bor'ba,* part 1, p. 219.

41. Antonov-Ovseenko, "O banditskom dvizhenii v Tambovskoi gubernii," p. 27.

42. Ibid., p. 21.

43. Trifonov, *Klassy i klassovaia bor'ba,* part 1, p. 239.

44. Kotovets [A Kotovski man], "Kotovskii vperedi" [Kotovski up in front], *Krasnoarmeets,* no. 109 (no. 16, 20 August 1927), p. 8.

45. Whether Selianski was Averianov, or Averianov Selianski—whether one or both of them bore an assumed name—it is impossible to say. The author has seen no evidence to support the conclusion that either of them was a real person; he leans strongly to the view that Selianski was a fake name for one of Antonov's established lieutenants (see above, chapter eight, text and n. 33), and knows of nothing to make Averianov less ethereal than the mention of his name in the primary local source.

46. Borisov, *Chernym letom,* pp. 3–4, 7, 9, 20–22; Esaulenko, *Revoliutsionnyi put' G. I. Kotovskogo,* pp. 130, 138; Trifonov, *Klassy i klassovaia bor'ba,* part 1, p.

253. The confusion in the Soviet accounts is very great, and yet Borisov and Esaulenko are primary sources (though written long afterwards) and Trifonov had access to all pertinent materials, archival and otherwise.

47. Garri, "Grigorii Kotovskii," in *Polkovodtsy grazhdanskoi voiny,* p. 193. The author mistakenly refers to it as the First Army.

48. Trifonov, *Klassy i klassovaia bor'ba,* part 1, p. 255.

49. Accessible Soviet maps use green to denote low altitude and so do not help.

50. Information on the position of the Green armies without analytical comment from Trifonov, *Klassy i klassovaia bor'ba,* part 1, pp. 253–54.

51. Ibid., p. 255.

52. See above.

53. Virta, *Odinochestvo,* pp. 261–62. Jacob V. Sanfirov, commander of the Guard or Special Regiment, is also opposed to Antonov in this and in other matters, but as the novelist is patently building him up in view of his final betrayal the Sanfirov angle may be dismissed as embellishment, whereas there is some reason to think that friction may well have existed between Antonov and Pluzhnikov, the military and civilian heads of the uprising.

54. Borisov, *Chernym letom,* p. 32.

55. As cited in Trifonov, *Klassy i klassovaia bor'ba,* part 1, p. 248 and n. 27.

56. Ibid., p. 249 and n. 30.

57. Ibid. and n. 34.

58. *Put' Bor'by,* vols. 1, 2 *(Antonovshchina);* Virta, *Odinochestvo.* The Soviet novelist is surprisingly indulgent to Boguslavski.

59. References to Konopko as being in command of the "automobile detachment" in Antonov-Ovseenko, "O banditskom dvizhenii v Tambovskoi gubernii," p. 25; as being in command of the "armored cars" in Borisov, *Chernym letom,* p. 23, and idem, "Konets antonovshchiny," in *Nezabyvaemoe,* p. 289. It is fairly clear that Fedko commanded the vehicular force in general—automobiles, trucks, and armored cars—from which I have concluded that Borisov may be correct in attributing only the armored car leadership to Konopko, thus inferentially subordinating him to Fedko. In general, the account of Antonov-Ovseenko is given preference because it was written at the time and was secret; yet Borisov, who wrote (or was helped to write) many years later, was in the thick of military action as commissar of Kotovski's brigade and his testimony on strictly military matters cannot be waved aside. Whatever Konopko's immediate command, the fact that these disparate sources attest the significance of his role raises the question of whether the rehabilitation of Fedko, who fell victim to Stalin, may have proceeded at Konopko's expense. The failure of other Soviet sources even to mention Konopko's name is one of the many mysteries still shrouding this subject.

60. Virta, *Odinochestvo,* pp. 295–96; Trifonov, *Klassy i klassovaia bor'ba,* part 1, pp. 249–50.

61. Antonov-Ovseenko, "O banditskom dvizhenii v Tambovskoi gubernii," p. 27.

62. Kondrat'ev, *Na linii ognia,* p. 80.

63. Vladimirov, "Ivan Fed'ko," in *Geroi grazhdanskoi voiny,* p. 336.

64. Information on the river from the article in the *Entsiklopedicheskii slovar'* (Brockhaus-Efron), vol. 37, p. 551.

65. Esaulenko, *Revoliutsionnyi put' G. I. Kotovskogo*, p. 130. Esaulenko's account is based in turn on "Voennyi obzor s 28 maia" [A survey of military events since 28 May], *Izvestiia Tambovskogo gubispolkoma*, 22 June 1921, doubtless the best source of all. Unfortunately the author reproduces only a little from this original article in the chief provincial newspaper. But that little is not caked in mud and one can only say that this military man has done better than Soviet historians who have at their command this source and all the others.

66. Esaulenko, *Revoliutsionnyi put' G. I. Kotovskogo*, p. 131. The historian Trifonov, inflating less than customarily, gives a figure of two hundred for killed and wounded, citing a local secondary source; see *Klassy i klassovaia bor'ba*, part 1, p. 254 and n. 66.

67. Kondrat'ev, *Na linii ognia*, p. 80.

68. Esaulenko, *Revoliutsionnyi put' G. I. Kotovskogo*, p. 131.

69. Trifonov, *Klassy i klassovaia bor'ba*, part 1, p. 254.

70. Information about the campaign from the Vorona to Bakury comes from ibid.; Esaulenko, *Revoliutsionnyi put' G. I. Kotovskogo*, pp. 130–31; Borisov, *Chernym letom*, pp. 22–23; idem, "Konets antonovshchiny," in *Nezabyvaemoe*, pp. 288–89; Garri, "Grigorii Kotovskii," in *Polkovodtsy grazhdanskoi voiny*, p. 193; Kondrat'ev, *Na linii ognia*, p. 80; Virta, *Odinochestvo*, p. 296; Zhukov, *Vospominaniia i razmyshleniia* [Reminiscences and reflections] (Moscow, 1969), p. 69. All of these sources can be pooled, and the result is very little. That little, moreover, is not at all free of contradictions.

71. Trifonov, *Klassy i klassovaia bor'ba*, part 1, p. 254.

72. Ibid., p. 249.

73. See below, in relation to the Matiukhin episode.

74. Kondrat'ev, *Na linii ognia*.

75. Esaulenko, *Revoliutsionnyi put' G. I. Kotovskogo*, p. 138. Yet Esaulenko himself places the casualties in the battle at nine hundred (see above, n. 68).

76. Garri, "Grigorii Kotovskii," in *Polkovodtsy grazhdanskoi voiny*, p. 193. Michael Shatov follows Garri's account in his article, "Tambovskie vosstaniia," *Novoe Russkoe Slovo*, 15 February 1966.

77. Antonov-Ovseenko, "O banditskom dvizhenii v Tambovskoi gubernii," p. 25.

78. Borisov, *Chernym letom*, p. 23.

79. Uborevich took part in the fighting and is said to have shown great personal courage; see interesting comment by Zhukov, *Vospominaniia i razmyshleniia*, pp. 69, 71–72.

80. See Trifonov, *Klassy i klassovaia bor'ba*, part 1, p. 254, which draws upon the article by G. Mikhalev in the *Uchenye zapiski* [Scholarly studies] of the Tambov Pedagogical Institute.

81. Ibid.

82. Zhukov, *Vospominaniia i razmyshleniia*, p. 69.

83. Trifonov, *Klassy i klassovaia bor'ba*, part 1, p. 255.

84. Ibid. This surmise has in its favor the fact that here would be Antonov's last place of refuge in 1922; he may have repaired to it on earlier occasions when in dire extremity.

85. Esaulenko, *Revoliutsionnyi put' G. I. Kotovskogo*, p. 132.

86. Virta, *Odinochestvo*, p. 296; likewise Trifonov, *Klassy i klassovaia bor'ba*, part 1, p. 255, who is not at all embarrassed that he has just placed them in the Shibriaev forest.

87. Kondrat'ev, *Na linii ognia*, p. 80; Borisov, *Chernym letom*, p. 23; Garri, "Grigorii Kotovskii," in *Polkovodtsy grazhdanskoi voiny*, p. 193. Kotovski must have been convinced of Antonov's injury "in one of the engagements" (i.e., not necessarily Bakury), for he sought to establish his condition and whereabouts at the time of the confrontation with Antonov's lieutenant Matiukhin. See Esaulenko, *Revoliutsionnyi put' G. I. Kotovskogo*, p. 135.

88. Trifonov, *Klassy i klassovaia bor'ba*, part 1, p. 255.

89. Sofinov, *Ocherki istorii Vserossiiskoi Chrezvychainoi Komissii*, pp. 225–26.

90. See account of the captured captain Ektov in Borisov, *Chernym letom*, p. 32.

91. Ibid.; Esaulenko, *Revoliutsionnyi put' G. I. Kotovskogo*, p. 132; Trifonov, *Klassy i klassovaia bor'ba*, part 1, p. 255.

92. "Na mestakh: bor'ba s banditizmom," *Izvestiia*, no. 167 (1310), 31 July 1921, p. 2. The name of the village appears in the despatch as Tugolugovka.

93. S. E., "Antonovshchina," *Izvestiia*, no. 122 (1561), 3 June 1922, p. 3.

94. See below, the Matiukhin affair.

95. See below.

96. S. E., "Na mestakh: Konets esero-bandita Antonova," *Izvestiia*, no. 145 (1584), 2 July 1922, p. 4.

97. Trifonov, *Klassy i klassovaia bor'ba*, part 1, p. 239, where the information seems to be based on the primary source, *Put' Bor'by*, vols. 1, 2. If so, it may be true.

98. Srechinski, "Zapechatannaia stranitsa," *Novoe Russkoe Slovo*, 28 February 1969.

99. Virta, *Odinochestvo*, p. 325, and see above.

100. Borisov, "Konets antonovshchiny," in *Nezabyvaemoe*, p. 302.

101. Polin, "Poslednie dni esero-bandita Antonova (Iz zapisnoi knizhki chekista)" [The last days of the SR-bandit Antonov (from a Chekist's notebook)], *Put' Bor'by*, vol. 1, p. 48.

102. Ibid., p. 49.

103. Virta, *Odinochestvo*, pp. 89, 100.

104. Testimony of Ektov about certain Green leaders as recalled by commissar Borisov in his *Chernym letom*, p. 32.

105. Antonov-Ovseenko, "O banditskom dvizhenii v Tambovskoi gubernii," p. 25.

106. Borisov, *Chernym letom*, p. 32.

107. Ibid., pp. 74–75.

108. Trifonov, *Klassy i klassovaia bor'ba*, part 1, p. 256.

109. Borisov, *Chernym letom*, p. 28.

110. Polin, "Poslednie dni Antonova," in *Put' Bor'by*, vol. 1, p. 49. To

establish even this simple fact was a task of the utmost difficulty. Borisov has Matiukhin commanding a regiment but fails to specify which one; *Chernym letom*, p. 41.

111. Ektov's observations as given in Borisov, *Chernym letom*, p. 33.

112. Trifonov, *Klassy i klassovaia bor'ba*, part 1, p. 123.

113. Borisov, *Chernym letom*, pp. 46–47.

114. Ibid., pp. 50–51. Here the commissar records a direct impression and is not relaying information received from Ektov.

115. The lower estimate is from ibid., p. 40, and the higher from Trifonov, *Klassy i-klassovaia bor'ba*, part 1, p. 256. The account of Borisov is to be preferred despite the lapse in time.

116. Garri, "Grigorii Kotovskii," in *Polkovodtsy grazhdanskoi voiny*, p. 193.

117. Esaulenko, *Revoliutsionnyi put' G. I. Kotovskogo*, p. 133.

118. Borisov, *Chernym letom*, p. 28.

119. Virta, *Odinochestvo*, p. 326.

120. M. Barsukov, "Kommunist-buntar' (Grigorii Ivanovich Kotovskii)" [A Communist insurrectionist], *Krasnaia Nov'*, book 8 (October 1925), p. 214.

121. Esaulenko, *Revoliutsionnyi put' G. I. Kotovskogo*, p. 133; Borisov, *Chernym letom*, pp. 27–28.

122. Esaulenko, *Revoliutsionnyi put' G. I. Kotovskogo*, p. 133.

123. Garri, "Grigorii Kotovskii," in *Polkovodtsy grazhdanskoi voiny*, p. 193.

124. Trifonov, *Klassy i klassovaia bor'ba*, part 1, p. 239.

125. Borisov, "Konets antonovshchiny," in *Nezabyaemoe*, p. 291. Actually, it is not stated here that the Che-ka thought up the plan; on the contrary, aside from the general charge to get rid of Matiukhin and to use the Che-ka's captive, Ektov, Borisov states here as in the later version (see below, note 126) that the matter was left to Kotovski's initiative; ibid., pp. 291–92.

126. Idem, *Chernym letom*, pp. 28–29.

127. Esaulenko, *Revoliutsionnyi put' G. I. Kotovskogo*, p. 133; Garri, "Grigorii Kotovskii," in *Polkovodtsy grazhdanskoi voiny*, p. 193.

128. No. 343 in *Iz istorii Vserossiiskoi Chrezvychainoi Komissii*, pp. 467–68.

129. Sofinov, *Ocherki istorii VChK*, p. 226.

130. Borisov, *Chernym letom*, p. 28.

131. Tukhachevski, "Opisanie operatsii . . . po likvidatsii bandy Matiukhina" [Description of the operation . . . to liquidate the Matiukhin band], in *G. I. Kotovskii*, document no. 283, appendix 2, p. 363.

132. Borisov, *Chernym letom*, pp. 27–28, 34.

133. In contrast to accounts that make it appear as though only a limited number of picked men were used, commissar Borisov is specific on this point and also speaks of regiments in the plural (there were two in the brigade); "Konets antonovshchiny," in *Nezabyaemoe*, p. 293. The character of the mission leaves little doubt that a full complement was used. And any doubt is removed by Tukhachevski, who says both regiments were involved in the deception; see his report cited above, "Opisanie operatsii," in *G. I. Kotovski*, no. 283, appendix 2, p. 363.

134. Borisov, *Chernym letom*, p. 33. But see Garri, "Grigorii Kotovskii," in *Polkovodtsy grazhdanskoi voiny*, p. 193, for assertion of Frolov's fictitious character.

135. Borisov, "Konets antonovshchiny," in *Nezabyvaemoe*, p. 293.

136. Actually, many of Kotovski's men were Moldavians—that is, Roumanians. See Borisov, *Chernym letom*, p. 62; Esaulenko, *Revoliutsionnyi put' G. I. Kotovskogo*, pp. 137, 138. This national complexion of the brigade had led to the inevitable charge that an essentially alien force was being used to overrun a Russian population, since it would be impervious to their sufferings. See Shatov, "Tambovskie vosstaniia," *Novoe Russkoe Slovo*, 15 February 1966. There may be something in this contention, though there is no indication that the other two cavalry brigades (Dmitrienko's and Kovalev's) associated with Kotovski's in the striking force of Uborevich were other than Russian in composition. Certainly the Kotovski brigade figures more prominently, whether because it was employed more or because it has been given play in order to build up its leader.

137. Borisov, *Chernym letom*, pp. 50–52, 54, 56; idem, "Konets antonovshchiny," in *Nezabyvaemoe*, pp. 297–98. Both versions contain Matiukhin's comment on national segregation and his order; but the second, earlier, and shorter version says nothing about eventual success in stabling the horses.

138. The correspondent's account of the conversation was published under the title of "Tambovskaia operatsiia," in the *Krasnaia Rota*, no. 16 (1923), pp. 26–29. It is used by Esaulenko in his *Revoliutsionnyi put' G. I. Kotovskogo*, pp. 134–36, and is reproduced as document no. 290 in the collection entitled *G. I. Kotovskii*.

139. Tukhachevski, "Opisanie operatsii," in *G. I. Kotovskii*, no. 283, appendix 2, pp. 363–65; Kotovski, "Tambovskaia operatsiia," in ibid., no. 290, pp. 394–401; Barsukov, "Kommunist-buntar'," [A Communist-insurgent (Gregory Ivanovich Kotovski)], *Krasnaia nov'* [Red virgin land], book 8 (October 1925), pp. 214–16; Esaulenko, *Revoliutsionnyi put' G. I. Kotovskogo*, pp. 134–36; Borisov, *Chernym letom*, pp. 53–58, 62; idem, "Konets antonovshchiny," in *Nezabyvaemoe*, pp. 298–301; Garri, "Grigorii Kotovskii," in *Polkovodtsy grazhdanskoi voiny*, pp. 193–94; and the secondary account in Trifonov, *Klassy i klassovaia bor'ba*, part 1, pp. 256–57, based on the Kotovski collection.

140. Borisov, *Chernym letom*, p. 43.

141. Esaulenko gives 16 July 1921 as the date when Kotovski received the order to destroy Matiukhin's band; see *Revoliutsionnyi put' G. I. Kotovskogo*, p. 133. Nothing contradictory is found in Borisov, who is stingy with dates. Tukhachevski dates the first action from 15–16 July.

142. Borisov, *Chernym letom*, p. 44.

143. Polin, "Poslednie dni Antonova," in *Put' Bor'by*, vol. 1, p. 47.

144. "Fabrikatsiia zagovorov: Chrezvychaika o Vserossiiskom Komitete," *Volia Rossii*, no. 307, 16 September 1921, p. 3, on basis of report of the presidium of the Che-ka published in *Izvestiia*, no. 199 (1342), 8 September 1921, p. 3.

145. "Zagovoro-boiazn'," *Volia Rossii*, no. 305, 14 September 1921, p. 1.

146. Kotovski, "Tambovskaia operatsiia," in *G. I. Kotovskii*, no. 290, p. 399; Esaulenko, *Revoliutsionnyi put' G. I. Kotovskogo*, p. 134.

147. Tukhachevski's version agrees with Borisov's—in fact, it goes even further in asserting that Kotovski was secretly advised that the "bandits" were not

going to their quarters and some were not even dismounting. Tukhachevski describes their condition as a "nervous one" as though they had an inkling of the true state of affairs. See "Opisanie operatsii," in *G. I. Kotovskii*, no. 283, appendix 2, p. 365. Tukhachevski was not on the scene, it is true, but as Kotovski's superior he bore the ultimate responsibility and his summary doubtless rested upon solid information which had then been sifted by a far keener mind than Kotovski's.

148. Borisov, *Chernym letom,* p. 53.

149. By rare coincidence, the two sources mentioning the number of those present give precisely the same figure, twenty-seven, though apportioning them differently; Borisov gives twelve Reds and fifteen Greens while Garri divides them eight and nineteen. See ibid., p. 54; Garri, "Grigorii Kotovskii," in *Polkovodtsy grazhdanskoi voiny,* p. 194. Tukhachevski says eight Reds were in the room; the number of Greens he does not specify; "Opisanie operatsii," in *G. I. Kotovskii,* no. 283, appendix 2, p. 364.

150. Borisov, *Chernym letom,* p. 49.

151. Kotovski, "Tambovskaia operatsiia," in *G. I. Kotovskii,* no. 290, pp. 397, 399; Esaulenko, *Revoliutsionnyi put' G. I. Kotovskogo,* p. 134. Here nothing is said about Matiukhin's drunkenness. That charge is found in the least credible source, though also based—as best can be determined—upon materials relating to Kotovski; see Trifonov, *Klassy i klassovaia bor'ba,* part 1, p. 256. Garri says nothing about liquor, much less the drunken state of this hunted man. Borisov has denied in this particular the account of the correspondent to whom Kotovski granted the interview. Borisov says the eating (and drinking?) had been deferred to the end, in a shift from the original plan. But since he seems to take the line that Communists would not sanction drinking we shall disallow his contention. He has a point, however, in protesting the notion that all the Reds had to do was fall upon drunken "bandits" and dispatch them. See *G. I. Kotovskii,* no. 290, p. 399, n. 1.

152. So Kotovski himself in the interview granted in 1923 and reprinted as "Tambovskaia operatsiia," in *G. I. Kotovskii,* no. 290, p. 401; see also Esaulenko, *Revoliutsionnyi put' G. I. Kotovskogo,* p. 136; Garri, "Grigorii Kotovskii," in *Polkovodtsy grazhdanskoi voiny,* p. 194. Likewise the novel (here highly fictionalized) by Virta, *Odinochestvo,* p. 326. Kotovski and Garri were certainly present at the shooting; probably Esaulenko also.

153. Tukhachevski, "Opisanie operatsii," in *G. I. Kotovskii,* no. 283, appendix 2, p. 365. The supreme commander of the troops in Tambov province has Matiukhin and several others jumping through the windows and shutting themselves up in a wooden barn or granary whence they opened a hot rifle fire. Refusal to surrender led to igniting the structure and to their burning up. See also Trifonov, *Klassy i klassovaia bor'ba,* part 1, p. 257. Trifonov may have gotten his information from Tukhachevski (his citation is inaccurate) or possibly from the basic compilation, *Put' Bor'by.* My recollection is that the latter contained something to this effect, but I cannot be certain.

154. Borisov, "Konets antonovshchiny," in *Nezabyvaemoe,* p. 301.

155. Idem, *Chernym letom,* pp. 58–59.

156. "Na mestakh: bor'ba s banditizmom," *Izvestiia,* no. 217 (1360), 29 September 1921, p. 1.

157. Ibid., no. 224 (1367), 7 October 1921, p. 3. Doubtless the same Boltnev had been the emissary of the peasants' congress to the revolting village of Kamenka in August 1920.

158. *Iz istorii Vserossiiskoi Chrezvychainoi Komissii*, document no. 324, p. 438; Sofinov, *Ocherki istorii VChK*, p. 226.

159. *Iz istorii Vserossiiskoi Chrezvychainoi Komissii*, document no. 343, pp. 467–68; Sofinov, *Ocherki istorii VChK*, p. 226. The contradictions in these sources also elicit comment from Shatov, "Tambovskie vosstaniia," *Novoe Russkoe Slovo*, 16 February 1966.

160. Esaulenko, *Revoliutsionnyi put' G. I. Kotovskogo*, p. 136.

161. Trifonov, *Klassy i klassovaia bor'ba*, part 1, pp. 255, 256. For previous action in May ending in "complete rout" of the Averianov band by Kotovski's brigade, see Borisov, *Chernym letom*, pp. 20–22. Now it was "annihilation." It may seriously be doubted that Kotovski fought two engagements against Averianov. Borisov deals with the May engagement, Trifonov with the one in July. The band of five hundred "completely routed" in May had grown to six hundred in July on the eve of its "annihilation." Or it is not to be excluded that the action against the Selianski band on 22 May mentioned by Trifonov (p. 253) and by Esaulenko (*Revoliutsionnyi put' G. I. Kotovskogo*, p. 130) may actually be the same as the one against Averianov referred to by Borisov, who gives no precise date. I rather suspect that Selianski and Averianov are names for the same man, who is enigmatical enough under any name, but there is no firm basis for this identification. It is all too nebulous. The Kotovski collection contains definite information about the actions against Selianski on 22 May and against Averianov on 8 July; see *G. I. Kotovskii*, no. 271, pp. 348–49, and ibid., no. 277, p. 353 (report of commissar Smirnov of 9 July where the strength of Averianov's command is given as four to five hundred sabers instead of six hundred.) Other engagements in May are mentioned but without indication as to whether Averianov was involved; in fact, no Green commanders are named (see nos. 266–69, pp. 345–47). And so the matter trails off into uncertainty.

162. "Na mestakh: Bor'ba s banditizmom," *Izvestiia*, no. 217 (1360), 29 September 1921, p. 1. The date is not given; merely the statement that this novel event occurred "recently." It was all staged, of course.

163. As cited in Trifonov, *Klassy i klassovaia bor'ba*, part 1, p. 255.

164. Esaulenko, *Revoliutsionnyi put' G. I. Kotovskogo*, p. 133.

165. Antonov-Ovseenko, "O banditskom dvizhenii v Tambovskoi gubernii," p. 25.

166. Trifonov, *Klassy i klassovaia bor'ba*, part 1, p. 256, quoting sources that are not available; see also Sofinov, *Ocherki istorii VChK*, p. 225.

167. The author knows nothing of this line, but if it were like the railway he saw between Tsaritsyn or Stalingrad and Rostov in the summer of 1935 it is easy to understand how the band could do so much damage. That line consisted of light rails laid on the bed—or practically on the ground—without ballast or ties; the train had to proceed so cautiously that the traveller felt he could get out and walk with it as it moved along. Maybe the Tambov–Balashov line was a more substantial installation, in which case either the enterprise of the band or the exaggeration of the source is correspondingly magnified.

168. Esaulenko, *Revoliutsionnyi put' G. I. Kotovskogo*, p. 132; the same with minor variations in Trifonov, *Klassy i klassovaia bor'ba*, part 1, p. 116, where the destruction is likewise attributed to "Antonov's band." Could these sources have transferred to the Tambov–Balashov line the damage Antonov-Ovseenko assigns a

week or two earlier to the Tambov–Kirsanov line, or could the commissar himself have reported erroneously to Lenin? Two separate raids, of course, are entirely possible.

169. Esaulenko, *Revoliutsionnyi put' G. I. Kotovskogo,* p. 132.

170. The way it appears on the map of Tambov province in the old encyclopedia. Esaulenko himself has Zagrazhki.

171. Esaulenko, *Revoliutsionnyi put' G. I. Kotovskogo,* p. 133; Trifonov, *Klassy i klassovaia bor'ba,* part 1, p. 256; Antonov-Ovseenko, "O banditskom dvizhenii v Tambovskoi gubernii," p. 25. The leader's name comes from a common noun: *karas'* is a carp with red fins.

172. See above for estimate in the Soviet Army archives.

173. Zhukov, *Vospominaniia i razmyshleniia,* pp. 71–72. The last statement is this author's, not Zhukov's.

174. "Na mestakh: V provintsii: konets banditizma v Tamb. gub." [On the local scene: in the provinces: the end of banditry in Tambov province], *Izvestiia,* no. 189 (1332), 27 August 1921, p. 2.

175. See chapter eleven.

176. "Na mestakh: konets banditizma v Tamb. gub.," *Izvestiia,* no. 189 (1332), 27 August 1921, p. 2.

177. *Put' Bor'by* (volume and page references cannot be recalled); possibly from M. Pokholiukhin, "Po sledam Antonova" [On the trail of Antonov], vol. 2, *Antonovshchina,* pp. 65–91. The Soviet source is not devoid of a certain undertone of respect—still possible in the early 1920s though unthinkable thereafter. "Grach" was seized in the Inusalin district, the location of which is not known. For news of arrest see "Na mestakh: bor'ba s banditizmom," *Izvestiia,* no. 217 (1360), 29 September 1921, p. 1; ibid., no. 224 (1367), 7 October 1921, p. 3. Brief reference to the identity of "Grach" in Trifonov, *Klassy i klassovaia bor'ba,* part 1, p. 79, based on *Put' Bor'by,* vol. 2, *Antonovshchina.*

178. Trifonov, *Klassy i klassovaia bor'ba,* part 1, p. 256. This man takes out insurance by prefacing the words with the information that the cadets "annihilated more than 200 bandits." Neither the commissar nor the novelist mention the two hundred annihilated "bandits."

179. Virta, *Odinochestvo,* p. 325.

180. Ibid., p. 326. If the novelist is correct in naming the other regiment with Matiukhin and giving the locale of Kotovski's attack as the villages of Zolotoe and Khitrovo, then we may identify the 16th regiment under Nazarov, which was soon to be holed up with Matiukhin's in the Tambov forest (see above), as the Zolotoe regiment. The village or *volost* from which it takes its name has not been located but it was near Khitrovo and Khitrovo is on the Naru–Tambov river. Thus Matiukhin had under him a thoroughly homogeneous force from one of the primary hotbeds of the insurrection. No wonder he was formidable. Of equal rank with Matiukhin, Nazarov appears to have been overshadowed by his colleague's dominant personality. If the proper link-up has been made and the 16th and Zolotoe regiments are one and the same, as they probably are, the reader will have gained insight into the tortuous method by which so much of this subject must be reconstructed.

181. From the report of Smirnov, 30 June 1921, in *G. I. Kotovskii,* no. 275, p. 351. The commissar names several villages that could be located. He lists the same

losses as Antonov-Ovseenko, but in addition states that the Reds lost thirty thousand cartridges, two killed, and four wounded. The human loss on the Red side, as usual, seems abnormally low. The Green band that overpowered the machines he estimates at no more than one hundred fifty sabers.

182. From the article of I. Trutko, "Takticheskie primery iz opyta bor'by s banditizmom: Unichtozhenie bandy Bogusłavskogo," *Krasnaia Armiia*, no. 3–4 (1921), pp. 35, 36, as cited in Trifonov, *Klassy i klassovaia bor'ba*, part 1, p. 254.

183. Antonov-Ovseenko, "O banditskom dvizhenii v Tambovskoi gubernii," p. 25. The death toll is given for two of the three reverses, with what accuracy it is impossible to judge, but no information at all is presented regarding the number of wounded and missing.

184. Borisov, *Chernym letom*, p. 75.

185. Antonov-Ovseenko, "O banditskom dvizhenii v Tambovskoi gubernii," p. 25.

186. Tukhachevski, "Zapiska," p. 2.

187. "Na mestakh: bor'ba s banditizmom," *Izvestiia*, no. 224 (1367), 7 October 1921, p. 3.

188. Ibid., no. 249 (1392), 5 November 1921, p. 2.

189. Polin, "Poslednie dni Antonova," in *Put' Bor'by*, vol. 1, p. 49.

190. From the Central Party Archives as rendered by Trifonov, *Klassy i klassovaia bor'ba*, part 1, p. 192.

191. "Na mestakh: bor'ba s banditizmom," *Izvestiia*, no. 217 (1360), 29 September 1921, p. 1.

192. From the Soviet Army Archives as given in Trifonov, *Klassy i klassovaia bor'ba*, part 1, p. 258.

193. "K 9-mu s'ezdu Sovetov: Golos s mest" [At the 9th Congress of Soviets: local opinion], *Izvestiia*, no. 289 (1432), 23 December 1921, p. 1.

194. From the Central Party Archives as reproduced in Trifonov, *Klassy i klassovaia bor'ba*, part 1, pp. 192, 258–59.

195. Trifonov, *Klassy i klassovaia bor'ba*, part 1, p. 255, based on the *Put' Bor'by*, vol. 2, *Antonovshchina*. Despite the paramount importance of the latter source, it is not free of error.

196. Donkov, "Organizatsiia razgroma antonovshchiny," *Voprosy Istorii KPSS*, no. 6 (June 1966), p. 70.

197. Tukhachevski, "Zapiska," pp. 2, 3. On the end of the STK see also Polin, "Poslednie dni Antonova," in *Put' Bor'by*, vol. 1, p. 48; Antonov-Ovseenko, "O banditskom dvizhenii v Tambovskoi gubernii," pp. 28, 29 (this is the second page marked 29 in the manuscript). The commissar says that, together with the STK committees, the "bandits' " lines of supply had been unearthed and blocked.

198. "Na mestakh: bor'ba s banditizmom," *Izvestiia*, no. 217 (1360), 29 September 1921, p. 1.

199. Polin, "Poslednie dni Antonova," in *Put' Bor'by*, vol. 1, p. 49; Virta, *Odinochestvo*, p. 333.

200. Virta, *Odinochestvo*, pp. 318, 333.

201. See above.

202. S. E., "Antonovshchina," *Izvestiia*, no. 122 (1561), 3 June 1922, p. 3. Presumably Zhuravelka was a village near Kamenka; it does not appear on any map I have seen. As the despatch was written nearly a year after Pluzhnikov's arrest or death, enough time had elapsed to clear up any uncertainty.

203. Polin, "Poslednie dni Antonova," in *Put' Bor'by*, vol. 1, p. 48. Commissar Borisov speaks of a campaign launched after Matiukhin's disaster at Kobylinka (19–20 July) to ferret out "bandit" groups elsewhere and more particularly to run down the "old man," as the head of the provincial SR organization was called. Very likely the phrase applies to Pluzhnikov, though actually he headed the STK, whatever his position in the PSR may have been. Borisov says the undertaking was successful but his remarks are so vague as to be of no help; *Chernym letom*, p. 78. Moreover, if the press despatch of 1922 is correct in its date the taking—or killing—of Pluzhnikov antedated Kobylinka by precisely one week.

204. Donkov, "Organizatsiia razgroma antonovshchiny," *Voprosy Istorii KPSS*, no. 6 (June 1966), p. 70.

205. "Na mestakh: bor'ba s banditizmom," *Izvestiia*, no. 177 (1320), 12 August 1921, p. 3. Information taken over and repeated with only two small errors in "Soobshchenie 'Izvestii' o zagovorakh," *Volia Rossii,* no. 290, 27 August 1921, p. 4.

206. Polin, "Poslednie dni Antonova," in *Put' Bor'by*, vol. 1, p. 48. It was at this time that the Plenipotentiary Commission issued its Order No. 284 proclaiming the extinction of "bandit" power. See "Na mestakh: bor'ba s banditizmom," *Izvestiia*, no. 177 (1320), 12 August 1921. p. 3.

207. Iu. A. Poliakov, *Perekhod k nepu i sovetskoe krest'ianstvo* [The transition to the NEP and the Soviet peasantry] (Moscow, 1967), p. 457. The statement in *Pravda* is contained in the issue of 2 December.

— 11 —

Character and Cost of the Insurrection

No study of the Tambov insurrection would be complete without treatment of the mercilessness with which the struggle was conducted on both sides. Civil war usually evokes more savagery than international war—at any rate, prior to the second world war of the twentieth century. And since revolution releases its adherents from traditional inhibitions at the same time that it implants in them a notion of superior virtue, a civil war among revolutionaries may be the worst of all.

The Soviet stereotype, adopted by too many Western intellectuals, denies recognition to SRs and Left SRs alike as revolutionaries, while ordinary Greens are consistently slandered as "bandits." The Communists are probably right in their claim that SRs of all stripes were not really socialists, and certainly right in the case of the Greens. But the question of socialism is not at stake here, only that of revolutionism, and there is no law identifying revolution with socialism. Most revolutions in history have not been socialistic.

The Left SRs, who had more than a little to do with the Tambov insurrection, were highly revolutionary, and the fact that their message has been muted because they did not win should not conceal from the scholar or from any honest-minded person their view on Communists as murderers of the revolution who were erecting a tyranny all the more intolerable because it was masked in revolutionary trappings. As for ordinary Greens, who were untroubled by theory, they were children of the revolution and, like children, could be cruel. The concentrated oppression of the period of militant communism and the revolutionary cast of the Tambov insurrection foreordained it to be bad.

To begin with the Greens, there is no need to idealize peasants. They were cruel. They were capable of actions that explored the ultimate recesses of all that is fiendish in human nature. It was not simply that they engaged in the mass killing[1] of Communists or soviet members or members of Soviet institutions, as in the case of the commune Pchelka (Little Bee) near Rasskazovo, where they are said to have killed everyone, even the young and the aged.[2] It was rather that an assortment of tortures, crude and refined, accompanied these killings.[3] Gorki, who detested peasants—with some reason but no charity—says that in Tambov province they nailed Communists to trees with railroad spikes driven through the left arm and the left leg at a meter's height from the ground and then watched as these purposefully half-crucified people flopped about and dangled in agony.[4]

But one need not turn to an ill-wisher to find a description of such rustic practices. Our only Green source does well enough. Conceding that no mercy was shown participants in punitive expeditions, this witness of barbarities from the Green side describes how captured workers were buried alive up to their necks. Peasants reproached them for religious apostasy as well as for plundering the rural population: "Dig the holes, boys, let them remember God in their suffering." The holes were filled in and the earth packed down; after some minutes faces swelled and eyes became bloodshot. Women came from the village, stood over the victims, raised their skirts and relieved themselves. When the adults had left the children took over and sicked the dogs on those who were slow in dying. The scene closes with the dogs gnawing furiously on the heads sticking out of the ground.[5]

Apparently in Tambov the favored method was to bury straight up or in a sitting position with only the head above ground, whereas Siberian peasants preferred to bury "captive Red Army men head downward, leaving their legs as far as the knees above ground; then gradually filling the hole with earth, they observed from the convulsive movement of the legs who of those undergoing treatment could stand more, who would prove more tenacious of life, who would suffocate more slowly than others."[6]

But burial alive by no means exhausted the resourcefulness of the Tambov peasantry in devising means of retribution on the Reds.

The heading of maiming and mutilation comprised a whole set of practices directed against eyes, ears, noses, limbs, bones, and intestines. Lopping off whatever could be more readily detached from the body seems to have been a basic rule. Flaying made its appearance, though the peasants lacked the thoroughness of the ancient Assyrians in this respect. Disembowelling may be accepted as occurring now and then, though hardly subsequent hanging by the guts[7]—a gut is not that strong, and simple strangulation may have been all that was involved. The peasant P. E. Samorodov underwent quartering in the village of Ponzari in November 1920,[8] thus reviving a well-known form of punishment by no means indigenous to Eastern Europe. The enemy accused Matiukhin of twisting prisoners' heads,[9] a specialty that found few emulators because of the physical strength required. Naturally, Soviet observers laid on the dark colors, but no doubt exists that in more than a few instances peasants did enough to turn Green into black.[10]

The most publicized example of barbarity visited upon a prisoner of war concerns a member of the Red Army's General Staff, Tishchenko, who was chief of the operational division of the troop command in Tambov province. While reconnoitering from the air he had the misfortune to be in a plane that developed motor trouble and had to land in the vicinity of an unnamed village. Instantly he and the aviator were seized by the Greens. They proceeded to carve a red star on Tishchenko's back (he wore the Order of the Red Banner), then to hack off first his right and then his left arm, and—after further torture—finally to behead him. The aviator managed to break loose and flee the scene of horror, only to be overtaken and have the tendons in his feet severed, after which he was taunted and then despatched. The General Staff member relating the incident says that the details of his colleague's fate were confirmed to him at interrogation by a squadron commander of Antonov's Special Regiment.[11]

More damaging to the Green cause must have been the cruelties perpetrated on ordinary Red Army men. Knowledge of the condition of a student from an infantry school lying in bed with a bandage over the empty sockets of his eyes and with only stumps where limbs had been[12] could not fail to strengthen the resolution of his comrades and leave them at best indifferent to the barbarities their own side was committing. Persecution of the families of men serving in the Red Army would have the same effect, not only because of the plundering of their homes but because of that inevitable concommitant of warfare everwhere—rape of the women and girls.[13]

The Greens appealed to soldiers of the Red Army to come over to their side, mixing in even socialist propaganda to the effect that a standing army went against the principle of a people's militia.[14] Much more dangerous to the regime, of course, than an appeal to a socialist consciousness was the appeal to the peasant consciousness of soldiers serving the Communist regime, as is attested by a whole series of revolts of Red Army units in the early 1920s. But the excesses so stupidly committed by the Greens blunted the impact of a bid for class solidarity which, in the last analysis, represented their best chance of success.

Not only prisoners of war or members of families of those serving on the other side fell victim to excesses. The story is told of a group of Komsomol (Communist Youth League) members, fifteen in number and between seventeen and eighteen years of age, who set out from the town of Kozlov to work in a village. Nothing more was heard of them and the rumor circulated that "bandits" had made away with them. Commander Shneerson came to Volchkovo *volost'* to conduct an investigation. He found that a war council of peasants in the village of Matsnevo had taken the Komsomols into custody and had devised for them the worst of fates: it turned them over to the children of the district who proceeded—with the encouragement of their elders—to tie them up and subject them to slow but terrible torture. We are not told what these children did to their peers except that they stuck and cut and did other things. "In the whole history of humanity, more finely spun-out bestialities have not been thought of by any man." The commander takes in too much territory, nor does he say what kind of work in the village the Communist youth undertook—they may have done something to incense the peasants. But it was all bad enough.[15]

The Greens sought to answer the official campaign of terrorism with their own brand. The most drastic means were used to put across mobilization for Antonov's regiments. Already in the fall of 1920, when the spirit of rebellion burned brightly, two villages had been sacked and the population flogged for refusing to volunteer.[16] When the spirit began to droop in the following year after the government put the screws on the peasantry, the Greens resorted to even greater violence; according to the Communist Party Archives,[17] Antonov put through forced mobilization of the inhabitants of Kirsanov *uezd* (May 1921, on the eve of the decisive campaign), accompanied by shooting of those who resisted together with the members of their families.

No statistics are given and one must allow for an element of exaggeration—probably a very large element—yet undoubtedly incidents of this sort did occur. Two demobilized Red Army soldiers in the village of Olshanka paid with their lives for refusing to join up; the Greens killed them in the presence of their mother and then cut her throat.[18] One cannot but feel sympathy for the two ex-soldiers who resisted polarization; having been through the portals of hell they were not minded to reenter through a side gate.

Violence was also employed when things began to go badly in order to hold the mobilized in line in the face of the Soviet summons to surrender and escape the death penalty. Antonov answered the proclamation of the Plenipotentiary Commission with a counter-order, the substance of which is known only as filtered through enemy sources. The Green leader called for a cruel struggle against the Communists "who do not represent the toilers," and concluded by threatening with death all those who were minded to give up, together with the members of their families; their possessions would be confiscated.[19] The order was meant to be lethal yet is somehow pathetic, for the counterterror of the Greens availed little against the full-blown terror of the Reds.

The mercilessness on the Soviet side has already been exemplified in Order No. 130 of the Plenipotentiary Commission.[20] In brief, it provided for a system of reprisals against the families of Green holdouts, consisting of their incarceration in concentration camps as hostages, followed after a short period by exile and confiscation of property; it also authorized the infliction of the death penalty for concealment of arms in the case of the population in general, since every household in "bandit-infested" areas was to be searched. Only the restriction of the death penalty to the senior breadwinner of the household in which a weapon was found mitigated the fury of the phobia of the "workers' and peasants' Red government" against the possession of arms by the workers and peasants.

The whole system of "mass terrorism" (*sic*) established by Order No. 130 went into operation on 1 June 1921. Yet hardly had it been instituted than, according to the commissar of repression, its "inadequacy" became apparent. In a meeting on 9 June representatives of the *uezd* political commissions charged with its execution found that certain developments had vitiated its impact on the rebellious population.

What were these developments? For one thing, the families of Antonov's warriors fled their homes and scattered for protection like so many quail. They prevailed upon relatives to take them in or found other concealment. Captured "bandits" refused to give their names out of fear of what would happen to their families. Very few arms were turned in.

Then there was the counterterror of the STK, which sought to offset Order No. 130 by ordering that hostages be taken from the families of Red Army men and soviet employees in general. Here and there the Greens executed the decree with "maximum cruelty," cutting down soldiers' families by the score; here and there citizens and even units of the Red Army implored the authorities not to touch "bandit" households because of fear inspired by the "white terror."[21]

The outcome of this situation was Order No. 171. If Order No. 130 provided for "mass terrorism," according to its author, what is one to say about Order No. 171? Soviet sources say as little as possible. The sycophant historian permits himself—or is permitted—to speak of "severe measures."[22] The primary source lumps the two decrees together as authorizing the dismantling or burning down of the houses of "malevolent bandits" and as erasing the distinction between sheltering families of "bandits" and sheltering "bandits" themselves.[23] Even the commissar of repression, writing in secret to Lenin, is notably more reticent than with reference to the preceding order and merely summarizes the sequel as stepping up the "Red terror" against "bandits," their families, and those who provided them with means of concealment. However, he does make two highly interesting observations about the execution of the decree.[24]

Locally, at least, the provisions of Order No. 171 had to be publicized and we were indebted to the *Tambovskie Izvestiia* for the text of the decree, which was reproduced as printed in an émigré newspaper. The seven articles of this "truly memorable" decree of 11 June 1921, subsequently identified as Order No. 171, follow herewith:

1. "Bandits" refusing to give their names were to be shot on the spot without trial.

2. Hostages were to be taken from settlements where arms were hidden and were to be shot unless the weapons were given up.

3. From a household where a concealed weapon was found, the oldest worker would be taken and shot out of hand without trial.[25]

4. A family giving shelter to a "bandit" was to be arrested and exiled from the province, its property confiscated, and its eldest breadwinner shot on the spot without trial.

5. A family giving shelter to members of a "bandit's" family or hiding the property of a "bandit" was to be considered itself as "bandit" and would have its eldest breadwinner shot forthwith without trial.

6. In case of the flight of a "bandit's" family, its possessions were to be distributed among peasants loyal to Soviet authority and the dwelling was to be burned.

7. The decree was to be read before village assemblies and was "mercilessly to be carried out."[26]

Order No. 171 is permeated with the principle of collective guilt, the curse of the twentieth century as much as of Tatar times. It followed by a few years the proscription of the Russian nobility and middle class, was contemporaneous with the expulsion of Greek and Turkish populations, and antedated the National Socialist persecution of Jews and the Teheran–Yalta–Potsdam attainder of the German nation. It was a link in a chain of barbarism. It was signed by Antonov-Ovseenko for the Plenipotentiary Commission, by Tukhachevski for the Red Army, and by Lavrov for the Extraordinary Commission, but it could just as well have been signed by Batu or his grandfather for the Mongol hordes of the thirteenth century.

The head of a peasant household taking in a "bandit" waif could incur the death penalty under Order No. 171. As stated above, the commissar of repression glides over its provisions but he reveals plenty concerning the spirit and technique of their application. He instructed the *uezd* political commissions, the key agencies of

Communist vengeance, to avoid spreading their efforts too thinly in order that they might concentrate on localities where a maximum effect could be achieved because of the intimate association of these areas with the "bandit" cause. Here the commissions were to bear down and carry through the provisions of Order No. 171 with "implacable hardness."

As an example to the commissions of how to proceed and to the peasantry of what to expect if the resistance continued, Parevka *volost'* was chosen. This canton of Kirsanov *uezd* in the Vorona valley centering around the village of Parevka had distinguished itself by the strength of its commitment to the Green cause; in the language of the commissar, it was a "stubbornly bandit" *volost'* whose will to fight on must now be broken by "hardline execution" of hostages. And so he caused the victims—many of whom were certainly guilty of hating a regime synonymous in their eyes with extortion and violence and others who were guilty merely of going along, like people everywhere, with whatever pressure was exerted upon them—to be led out and shot in batches as an object lesson to be continued until either all arms had been given up and all "active participants" in the Green bands had surrendered or until the supply of hostages had been exhausted. The commissar adds that military successes and the operations of the Che-ka helped in the execution of the plan.[27] They had not only helped, they made it possible. Such bloodbaths were not feasible as long as the peasants had defenders.

Here, then, is the explanation of the surrender of the men of Parevka, of the remnant of Antonov's 4th or Parevka Regiment referred to above.[28] As the surrender was delayed, however, for over two months, a high toll of hostages must have been exacted or else the shooting in batches had tapered off before final success was achieved. No figure is mentioned for the death toll at Parevka. The commissar in another place in his badly-composed memorandum tones down his disclosure by observing that in this hard-core "bandit" area the peasants began to yield arms and "bandits" only after the shooting of "some kulak hostages."[29]

But Parevka was by no means the only *volost'* to experience this savagery. In Belomestnaia Dvoinia, Tambov *uezd*, where the peasants had persisted in secreting arms and in sheltering "bandits," the shooting of "two groups of kulak hostages" brought an end to their defiance. And now his commissar gives Lenin some figures and we have them from Trotski. "Here in general,"[30] reports the commissar, 154 "bandit hostages" (i.e., not exclusively kulak?) were shot, 227 "bandit families" were seized, 17 dwellings were burned, 24 torn down, and 22 given over to pauper peasants.[31] No date is given for this tragedy, perpetrated in cold blood in a locality some twenty miles due west of Tambov city near the line with Kozlov *uezd* and hence well removed from the main arena of conflict in the southeastern part of the province.

Only once before had Belomestnaia Dvoinia figured in the news: on 21 May 1921 when the band of Vaska Karas had burned the quarters of the soviet and killed up to fifty people, including members of the local soviets.[32] There may have been a connection, not mentioned by the commissar, in which case the ratio of vengeance was better than three to one and had been inflicted vicariously, on the sedentary population instead of on the mobile force that had made the May raid. To convey some idea of what was involved, the nearby village of Soldatskaia Dvoinia or Neznanovka had 291 households at the turn of the century and 2,485 inhabitants;[33] as it was the only village in the vicinity to get into the encyclopedia it was most likely the largest, and certainly was far above the average of over 100 households per settlement in Tambov *uezd*.[34] Hence the "taking" of 227 "bandit families"—that is, throwing them into concentration camps—was equivalent to "taking out" two villages from the *volost'*.[35]

If Belomestnaia Dvoinia witnessed the most drastic action undertaken in Tambov *uezd* against refractory peasant communities—and the commissar assured Lenin this was the case[36]—one is not to think that lightning did not strike elsewhere. Estalskaia *volost'*[37] saw 76 persons executed, 12 houses burned, and 21 houses torn down. But the 76 who lost their lives included captive Green fighters as well as hostages, for whom no separate figure is given. As a result of these exertions in both Belomestnaia Dvoinia and Estalskaia *volosts* 230 Greens were executed and 118 rifles, 25 sawed-off guns, and 10 pistols were removed from the hands of the people.[38]

In Kamenka *volost'* in the southeast, resistance cracked when all males were rounded up. Apparently the females were left desolate by this harsh measure and either they or the hostages revealed the location of stores and hideouts, with the result that many STK committeemen at all four levels could be apprehended in what had been the capital of the Union of Toiling Peasantry. We may be pardoned the suspicion that the shooting of hostages helped to loosen tongues, but the commissar keeps his silence and there is nothing else to go on. In Krivopoliane village, however, he reports 13 hostages slain before the inhabitants would disclose a repository for spare parts of machine guns, hand over some "bandits," and betray the refuge of remnants of Selianski's band.[39]

And that is all we have on the killing of hostages except for a ridiculous figure of 70 for all of Tambov *uezd* during the period 1 June–10 July 1921. Since the commissar on the foregoing page had set the toll at 154 for Belomestnaia Dvoinia *volost'* alone, one might think that the slaughter there occurred later, after 10 July, if he had not noted on the very same page the formation there under Soviet auspices of a peasant defense group before 27 June. Thus a serious possibility exists that this crude half-intellectual, wielding plenipotentiary power over 3.5 million people, had not bothered to harmonize his own statistics, not even on successive pages, in a report to the highest instance of Soviet authority.

After such an exhibition, how much are his figures worth? We give the rest of them without recommendation, since there are no others. He says 549 families were taken as hostages in Tambov *uezd* between 1 June and 10 July, in 296 instances property was definitively confiscated, 80 houses were torn down, 60 houses burned, and 591 "bandits" executed. His complaint about the reluctance of the population to yield arms seems well-grounded, for of 965 "bandits" who voluntarily gave themselves up, 59 appeared with arms and 906 without.[40]

It is not necessary to suppose that the commissar of repression meant purposefully to mislead the head of his party. Lenin would have no squeamishness about shooting hostages. But was the commissar fully reporting such cases or was he merely providing a sampling? And did everything that happened in the field reach his desk? There were 58 *volosts* in this war-wracked *uezd*,[41] and from other terrible things that happened elsewhere it may be concluded that the toll in the four that are mentioned represented only a small part of the whole, even if that particular toll were complete. Kirsanov *uezd* had 37 *volosts*[42] about none of which information is available save Parevka, and about it nothing definite. Treskino, for example, had not yielded to Parevka in degree of support for the Greens and must have suffered comparably. Borisoglebsk *uezd* had been caught up in the insurrection, Morshansk and Kozlov to a lesser extent, while the other seven would not have been unscarred.

Moreover, hostage-taking had not been limited to families directly linked to the Green forces. April had seen the introduction of the system, not in the case of families with members in Antonov's armies but of those who happened to live in villages along a railroad. In June people living beside telegraph lines and near bridges on military highways found themselves drawn into the hostage system. In July the less bothersome technique was employed of not removing hostages from their villages but of designating certain families to suffer first in case of damage to communications.[43]

The order of selecting victims is not stated; presumably kulak families would be first in line of fire, answering for actions that might be totally unrelated to their own. As the Greens sought repeatedly to knock out communications in standard guerrilla fashion this Soviet technique alone may have accounted for a substantial toll among hostages, with no reference to the still greater number of victims chosen because of possession of weapons or refusal of relatives to desert the Green cause.

There is no way of estimating the dimensions of the hostage system as applied in Tambov province, nor the number of deaths it entailed. But it was quite enough to stain the record of a regime that gave itself out to the world as leading the procession on the road to social progress. The only procession it led was that back to barbarism. We have very little official information on four of the fifty-eight *volosts* in Tambov *uezd*, and are told officially that hostages were shot—most likely a sizable number of them—in one of the thirty-seven *volosts* of Kirsanov *uezd*; if we have only an indication of the true state of affairs even in these five cantons, we have no information about the other 376 in Tambov province and are convinced that we have barely raised the hem of the curtain on the scene of horror that ensued there in the wake of the Soviet triumph. Not for nothing does Tukhachevski in his secret memorandum enumerate among the means of sovietization of this conquered

Russian province the use of "terroristic measures" against "bandit" sympathizers.[44]

The application of terrorism through hostage-taking—and slaying—was general, but the intensity of application varied according to the degree of fidelity to the Green cause. The commissar in his secret memorandum at first gives no cumulative total for the province, contenting himself with setting the number of families taken hostage in Tambov *uezd* from 1 June to 10 July at 549 (see above). His commission, however, published the figure of 1,643 for the number of persons (not families) taken hostage from 1 June to 1 July, presumably for the whole province; it asserted that many of these were released to the villages upon the voluntary appearance at army stations of their "bandit" relations.[45]

The figures cannot be matched. And of what use are they anyway—this published deception—when the commissar in his report to Lenin adds as an afterthought, and not in the proper place, the truly valuable information that at the time—20 July 1921—five thousand hostages had been accumulated in the concentration camps awaiting exile, the authorization for which, he complained, had not come through.[46] It would come in due course. And so five thousand victims had been consigned to the camps by the second half of July, not because they were "bandits" themselves but because they were related to "bandits."

These five thousand by no means closed the lists, as can be conclusively demonstrated from at least one official disclosure: in Borisoglebsk *uezd* after its "liberation" by the Red Army, the Central Party Archives reveal the arrest by the very active *uezd* political commission of 3,157 "bandits," 3,024 deserters, and 1,326 hostages during the two-month period from 15 August to 15 October. The commission sentenced a part of those arrested to death by shooting.[47] How many hostages were executed, how many released, and how many exiled there is no telling, but doubtless most of them fell into the third category. There were eleven other *uezds* in the province and what the hostage intake was for them after the middle of July, or for Borisoglebsk *uezd* between mid-July and mid-August, is all a blank.

The doctrine of collective guilt underlying the merciless repression of the Tambov uprising manifested itself in the transplantation of people as well as in the taking of hostages. Here the precedent came down from Ivan III (reigned 1462–1505) in his treatment of the once-free citizenry of Novgorod and from his son, Vasili III (reigned 1505–1533) in the similar case of the republic of Pskov. Some years after the Tambov tragedy and on the eve of a far greater one, the nominal head of the Soviet state, M. I. Kalinin, would say in a public address: "Or take such a matter as the bandit movement of Antonov in Tambov and Voronezh provinces. In the course of that struggle it became necessary to exile to the north the villages most infected with the bandit contagion. Many peasants of Tambov and Voronezh provinces took part in the war between the Soviet order and the old world."[48] The third sentence in the quotation is ambiguous. But the second is definite enough.

The sentence of exile fell upon villages rather than households, not to speak of individuals. As the percentage of voluntary enlistment in the Green force exceeds eighty percent of the male population only in the case of some villages in Kirsanov *uezd*—and fifty percent is high in most instances even according to Soviet estimate[49]—we have here a crystal-clear case of the application of collective guilt, not illogically by a collectivist regime. Likewise in the case of eight *volosts* upon which sentence was pronounced and publicized in 2,300 copies;[50] the commissar does not specify the punishment imposed by the sentence but in all probability it involved exiling all or a part of the population and destroying all or a portion of their domiciles, unless we are to imagine that the population was simply massacred—something that is unlikely but that cannot be entirely excluded.

Neither for the villages mentioned by Kalinin nor for the *volosts* smitten by the Plenipotentiary Commission are any details provided, not even their names—a reticence that is readily understandable. But the two categories doubtless overlap and the number of cantons upon which collective punishment was visited undoubtedly exceed the eight mentioned incidentally under publicational activities. How many suffered without being publicized?

In non-Soviet sources are to be found the names of various villages listed as having been burned to the ground or at least extensively damaged. Three were consigned to the flames: Khitrovo, Koptevo, and Verkhne–Spasskoe.[51] The village of Verkhotsene fell under the ban of Order No. 171, extended in this instance to a community of households rather than to single households or families, to say nothing of individuals. Details are lacking; whatever the punitive expedition did, it left in its wake a devastated locality.[52] A number of villages were shelled and badly damaged, either directly from the cannon or from the ensuing fires. Especially hard hit were Pakhotnyi Ugol and Bondari to the northeast of Tambov city, Znamenka, Karian, and Prokovskoe–Marfino to the south, and the unlocated village of Lavrovo.[53] All ten of the villages named so far were in Tambov *uezd* and eight of them also gave their names to *volosts* or cantons (all except Koptevo and Verkhne-Spasskoe).[54]

Could these have been the eight *volosts* so nonchalantly mentioned by the commissar of repression as having undergone the unstated form of punishment decreed by eight collective sentences? Not necessarily, for he applied the fire and sword technique at will over all of Tambov province and at least one village in Morshansk *uezd*, Raksha—also the core of a *volost'*[55]—had been virtually obliterated by cannon fire.[56] Another village and *volost'* singled out for exceptional treatment was Parevka in Kirsanov *uezd* where more must have happened than the shooting of hostages in batches. Once more Kirsanov *uezd* does not emerge from the void of uncertainty, despite an insurrectionary record that should have caused it—and very likely did cause it—to suffer on the scale of retribution no less than its sister *uezd* to the west.[57]

There is an organic connection between transplantation, the burning or razing of villages, and the sentences passed upon entire cantons in accordance with the Soviet doctrine of collective responsibility. Kalinin—had he been more communicative (or had Stalin permitted it)—could have named all the villages mentioned above and an unknown number of others besides, and Antonov-Ovseenko could have named those *volosts* and added as many more from Kirsanov *uezd*, after which he could have included some from Borisoglebsk and scattered ones from other districts.

In all probability the process consisted of the passing of community sentences, the physical destruction of offending villages, and the "taking out" and transplantation northward of the population or, in simple words, tearing it up and dumping it in some remote and inhospitable region where its fate may be conjectured. The process has to be pieced together as far as the historical record is concerned, since it was carried out and not publicized save—to some extent—on the local scene; but underlying it is a definite pattern of terrorism or planning. Almost none of the particulars have surfaced on the All-Russian scene or that of the world, but there is no doubting the process. We shall return later in this chapter to the topics of transplantation and decimation in weighing the human toll of the repression.

Before continuing with the subject of mercilessness, a word about the credibility of the anti-Soviet sources drawn upon above. Iuri Podbelski was a Populist intellectual, friendly to peasants in a patronizing way but not at all pleased with the escape from Populist tutelage implicit in the Green movement. He addressed his appeal to the chairman of the Moscow soviet, citing three burned villages as evidence of the brutality he was protesting. He would not lie to L. D. Kamenev, a man whose career was based on being a moderate in an extremist party, who knew—or could find out—what was going on in Tambov province, and may well not have liked the measures there employed. Podbelski errs, it is true, in one respect. He asserts that whole villages answered for chance association with Antonov's forces, leaving the implication that the three smitten villages belonged in that category.[58]

They were not that innocent, of course. All three had strongly backed Antonov and had sent many sons into his ranks. According to a Soviet estimate, forty percent of the entire population of Khitrovo had joined the "bands."[59] This figure seems impossibly high; it may actually refer to the percentage of the male population who volunteered, and in any event the author had the impression—when in Moscow with access to the original—that the calculation rested on a fragile foundation. Whatever the degree of participation and despite Podbelski's misstatement of his case, the blunderbuss vengeance exacted by the Soviet fell upon the children and the aged, the women and the crippled, as well as upon the males of military age impressed into service and upon those who had volunteered. If forty percent complicity, it was one hundred percent retribution.

As for the anonymous article on peasant pacification in an émigré journal, it was obviously well-informed from sources on the scene and the degree of exaggeration can be directly checked in one important particular. The author estimated that thousands of arrests had been made in Tambov province;[60] the commissar told Lenin, of course in secret, that five thousand hostages crowded the concentration camps awaiting exile.[61] The article did not exaggerate.

And finally for the SR organ in Prague, the *Volia Rossii* edited by V. I. Lebedev: however one may view his stance in 1917—and he had been one of the tub-thumping, prowar zealots—Lebedev belonged to that small group of people who learn something from history. By 1920 he had sobered up from his war inebriation, his Populist phobias had fallen away, he had come to see the Allies as they were, he could write objectively even about Turkish nationalism, and he flailed the Communists and the reactionaries with admirable impartiality. The author has gone through the *Volia Rossii* with great care hoping to find glimpses of the Tambov scene but reading the commentary on many other subjects; he can say that the *Volia Rossii* during its all too brief span of life was a newspaper conducted with meager resources on a high plane, scrupulously honest, hard-hitting at what needed to be hit hard—an organ of opinion conforming to the best traditions of European (not American) journalism. Its defect lay not in misrepresenting the tragedy in Tambov province but in being able, despite its best efforts, to find out so little about it.

The Soviet predilection for collectivizing guilt as well as agriculture found broader application than that connected with geographical units. It might also be directed against social categories. Anyone could have foretold drastic measures against former members of anti-Communist political parties, all those SRs, Left SRs, Constitutional Democrats, SD Mensheviks, and representatives of lesser parties who once had dominated—or at least shared—the political stage before the October Revolution; but the blackout of information concerning the ill-fated province might have prevented confirmation of their fate had it not been for Stalin's failure to sew things up so tightly by 1929 as to prevent Trotski from taking his papers out of the country. Thus we learn from the commissar himself of the "mass exile" of "suspect philistines," a term he reserves for former members of anti-Soviet parties.[62] Since this element would overlap only slightly with hostages extracted from the peasantry, here is a factor swelling the lists of the arrested and of those condemned to exile beyond the total of five thousand specified in the commissar's memorandum.

Another social category likely to incur punishment consisted of that segment of the working class which had shown sympathy for the uprising, particularly the railroad workers. The Central Inter-departmental Commission for War on Banditry had decided in June to remove from Tambov province *all* persons who were involved in "banditry," including "some railwaymen."[63] Yet either it had moved too slowly or had cast its net too short, for on 20 July the commissar was still complaining that "up to the present" the practical question of transferring these workers to other lines had not been solved[64] (apparently their technical skill afforded them a certain protection against the peasants' fate).

Anyone who persists in regarding Communism as the workers' party should come to grips with such phenomena as the attitude of its plenipotentiary in Tambov province. Only kulaks and presumably capitalists came before the railroad workers on the scale of his disfavor. Previously he had planned purging the means of communication and preparing lists of untrustworthy railwaymen for exchange with other provinces if Moscow would approve.[65] Now in his report to Lenin he termed them flatly the backbone of the counterrevolutionary organization.[66] Inveterate suspicion of the railroad workers haunted the commissar. Unfortunately, no figures whatever have been found as to the number of railroad workers and of oppositional party members who were "taken out" of Tambov society.

Little exists on the use of torture by the Reds, perhaps because most of the sources are Soviet or perhaps because the Reds simply killed without torturing. But on occasion they did quite well also in this field. After wounding eight peasants, soldiers buried them half-alive in the Morshansk cemetery. Four of the peasants are named: Markov, Suchkov, Kostiaev, Kuzmin. "Pacifiers" of the peasantry mutilated fifteen peasants in Ostrov *volost'*, Morshansk *uezd*. A woman had her hair pulled out in the Morshansk prison, and punitive detachments in Spassk *uezd*—a part of Tambov province about which almost nothing is known—flogged villagers in the accepted East European manner.

Unquestionably the high point of ingenuity was attained, however, in Kirsanov *uezd* where a scene was enacted that required more knowledge of bucolic matters than one ordinarily associates with Communists. In an unnamed locality, arrested Greens or

Green sympathizers were locked up for several days in a sty with a breeding boar. A pig is a voracious animal and eats all the time, even when it ought not to be hungry. But this boar had not eaten for some time and availed itself with vigor of the opportunity that came its way. Those incarcerated with it emerged torn and insane.[67]

The merciless character of the struggle having been adequately demonstrated, we may briefly consider two further questions: what element or elements excelled in brutality and in favor of which side does the balance of horror incline?

The Fomichev (Lidin) manuscript leaves the impression that on the Green side the peasants themselves were the main culprits, inflicting primitive tortures upon captives after the Greens had ridden away. The Soviet novelist and Soviet accounts in general, on the other hand, do their best to depict the "bandits" as beasts from hell. Antonov himself, Tokmakov, and I. S. Matiukhin appear as monsters. Neither the Green partisan nor the Soviet writers prove their case. For our part, we are inclined to agree with Fomichev, but we cannot prove anything either. An interesting point is made by an observer from the vantage-ground of commanding Red Army trainees in the theater of operations. He singles out for particular opprobrium the special sections of Antonov's army—the counter-espionage, internal security people. Recruited, as he says, from the most desperate characters, they engaged not only in killing but often left on their victims signs of incredible cruelty.[68]

The Red commander may have a point. The stealthiness, underhandedness, duplicity, falseness, and treachery of such work place a premium upon moral callousness; and the deeper the practitioner is involved, the duller his moral sensibilities become. It either attracts warped individuals or acts as a breeding ground for them. Not only dictatorships face the problem; the proliferation of such activities in "free" societies renders those societies steadily less free. We reject the depiction of Antonov and of Tokmakov as torturers simply because they were fighters. Their work was done in the open field or at least in the forest, not in some cellar chamber. Cruel they may have been, but brave men are less likely to be bestial than are cowards.

The Red commander should have considered also the Che-ka. That institution and its successors may well be the world's chief repository of unusual information. Its very types are unusual. There is, for example, the spectacle of Dzerzhinski becoming exercised over the encroachment of his institution upon a Soviet children's home[69] in the same province where his field workers were seizing "bandit" children, thrusting them into concentration camps, burning their homes, killing their fathers, and sending them and their mothers into distant exile.

Or the spectacle of a man like A. S. Klinkov presiding over a district division of the Che-ka in Tambov *uezd*. Once a big merchant of Tokarevka village, he had been noted for speculative activities before the October Revolution. Other attributes of his were illiteracy, the taking of bribes, and drunkenness. Some Populist moral indignation is mixed in here, in keeping with the source;[70] it is laid on a little thick. His world had gone to pot but he had found another and now, as a Soviet official, there were many arrests in his district and many executions. A business man under the Tsar, a butcher under the Soviet, and a scoundrel under both—such was the record of A. S. Klinkov. Everything is relative, and being in his domain was somewhat better than being in the sty of the breeding boar of Kirsanov *uezd*. The hierarchy and ranks of the Tambov Che-ka would assuredly yield other interesting types if we could pierce the shroud that shielded its operations, those of its sister offices in other provinces, and those of its successors everywhere.

Who were more cruel, the Greens or the Reds? Our impression is that there was an excess of torture on the side of the Greens, an excess of killing on the side of the Reds—battle deaths excluded. But it is only an impression with nothing more in its favor than the general rule that a party weaker in numbers or in weapons resorts to more extreme measures.

Gorki has dealt with the question in words no mere scholar can hope to emulate. His conclusion will come as a surprise to those who think of him as a peasant-hater, as a sympathizer with the Soviet order. He hated the peasants, it is true. In an interview with the London *Daily News* he let himself loose, flaying the Russian peasant as savage and uncouth, as a lowbrow brute—as the enemy of the city and of civilization, of the state and of progress. He agreed with Lenin that the peasant was anarchistic, antistate by nature. "Our peasants are cruel and slothful. Hardly can they be called human. I hate them." The cruelty of the regime, he told the British public, could not be compared to that of the peasantry. The SR paper identifies this attitude with the outlook of the Bolshevik bosses who merely refrained from voicing it publicly. Yet once Gorki had not been so taken with Lenin and had said of him that he held even the workers in contempt, viewing them as "meat for his social experiment."[71]

In a pamphlet published the following year (in Berlin, it should be noted) Gorki had recovered his balance. He still condemned one-sidedly the cruelty of the peasants in Tambov[72] and western Siberia, he still persisted in his color blindness—refusing to distinguish Green: everything that was not Red had to be White. He deepened his observations by linking the recent excesses to age-old sayings among the peasantry exemplifying its heartlessness:

Chem bol'she babu b'esh', tem shchi vkusnee.
[The more the woman is beaten, the tastier is the soup.]

Zhena dvazhdy mila byvaet: kogda v dom vedut, da kogda v mogilu nesut.
[A wife is dear on two occasions: when she is brought into the home, and when she is borne out to the grave.][73]

Commissar of Education A. V. Lunacharski condemned Gorki for his wholesale defamation of the Russian peasantry,[74] just as we condemn the collective Lunacharskis in Moscow for their wholesale decimation of that peasantry. But the independent streak in Gorki which makes him bearable even in the political sense then asserted itself; and when he asks the question, "Who are more cruel—the Reds or the Whites?" he answers, "Most likely it is all the same—both, you see, are Russian."[75] From these words of the great writer that scathe his own people we have no reason to dissent except to observe that insensate cruelty is not a Russian but a human trait.

From the merciless we go to the subject of damage, to the condition of the Tambov countryside after the fighting had ceased and vengeance had been exacted. Both the Soviet and the anti-Soviet sides depict the province as a wasteland; only the responsibility for the catastrophe is disputed, not the prevailing conditions. Tambov in the wake of the insurrection looked as though Mamai's army had gone that way, so great had been the destruction wrought by Antonov and his bands.[76] In reality, Soviet repression had contributed to the appearance of the province, and Batu's army would have made a better figure of speech.

Statements about the enormous damage to the economy[77] contain an element of exaggeration, since half the *uezds* had seen little action; moreover, contemporary accounts tone down the claims of destruction when they proceed to particulars. The same observer who wrote about the "nightmare" of "nearly an entire province" being devastated[78] limits the ruin of the peasant economy to five *uezds*[79] (there were twelve in the province). Still more accurate is the summation of results in the *Tambovskaia Pravda*, where the zone of outright devastation is confined to the three richest *uezds*.[80] There is no reason to question that Tambov, Kirsanov, and Borisoglebsk had been torn up in the course of the swaying warfare over a period of ten and one-half months, interspersed with savage fighting, with destructive raids by the one side and village burning by the other. Probably a Red Army man did not exaggerate when he said it would take years to heal the wounds. And most accurate of all was his admission that at the time no estimate was feasible of the great losses sustained by the economy.[81]

Some information is available regarding damage to industry and to installations. Industrial production in Tambov province for 1921 is placed at only 19.5 percent of the prewar figure,[82] but it should be noted that it was down to 31 percent for the entire country.[83] Cloth-making, the chief branch of industry, amounted to barely one-fourth of normal production, and twelve of the sixteen metal-working plants stood idle.[84] Two distilleries, three beet sugar refineries, one large textile mill, and other unidentified enterprises figured as direct casualties of the insurrection. The indications are that they had been plundered and burned out.[85] Severe damage had been inflicted on the communications network: the Greens had repeatedly destroyed telegraph and telephone installations, they had repeatedly dismantled roadbeds and caused rolling stock to plunge down embankments, they had not only removed rails from miles of trackage but had hauled them away or bent them in order to render them worthless, they had ravaged railroad stations and demolished bridges to the best of their ability, although thoroughness in the last respect may be doubted because of the shortage of explosives.[86]

As Tambov was not an industrially-developed province, the damage to that sector of the economy could not compare to losses in the agrarian sector. How bad things must have been cannot be better illustrated than by the attitude of Antonov-Ovseenko—a typical Communist intellectual with as little interest in agriculture as he had consideration for those engaged in it—who nevertheless felt obliged to urge strongly upon Lenin the need of changing the mind-set of the Food Commissariat. This body viewed Tambov province, despite everything, as a surplus food-producing area from which the entire seed loan of the past year was now to be extracted for the benefit of Samara province. In making it clear that famine existed also in Tambov, the commissar declared that once and for all it must be established that agriculture was in a miserable condition, necessitating not only forbearance in respect to export of grain and fodder but also further alleviation of the tax burden and the transference to Moscow of responsibility for provisioning the forces of repression. Among the measures prescribed by him was permission for the peasants to go to the Ukraine in search of seed, certainly a modest concession to the principle of self-help and one reflecting the grievously fettered condition of Soviet citizens even at that early date.[87]

Some particulars may be offered regarding the state of agriculture in the wake of the insurrection. First in line of fire had been Soviet intrusions into that sector of the economy. "Everything created with such hardship since the founding of the Soviet regime had been plundered, destroyed or dragged away by the SR bandits"[88]—a statement intended to apply to party and soviet organs and to cultural institutions in the rural areas as well as to collective farming enterprises. A thin veneer of regard for popular sovereignty, expressed in adulation of the Constituent Assembly, had overlaid the work of despoliation.[89]

Some sixty state farms succumbed to the onslaught of the Greens, and fifty-eight of the seventy-nine collective farms in the single *uezd* of Borisoglebsk.[90] The thousands of *puds* of grain products and fodder taken from the state farms would not have benefitted the local population in any event, while the low productivity of such enterprises—fourteen of the nineteen state farms in Kozlov *uezd* were rented out to laborers and to cooperatives,[91] a common phenomenon of the time—insured that the loss would be felt more by the Soviet experiment than by the economy. Of much greater consequence had been the pillaging and sometimes burning of repositories for the produce collected under the food levy or the tax in kind, where millions of *puds* of grain intended for hungry workers are said to have been lost.[92] Curiously enough, no specific figures on the destruction of granaries or their contents have been found.

A drastic reduction in the area sown to crops had accompanied the fighting; generally it is ascribed to the terrorism of the Greens in seeking to disrupt all forms of economic activity,[93] even to the extent of flogging plowmen on their bellies.[94] An efficacious method, no doubt, but hardly a farsighted one, for would it not have deprived the Greens as well as others of the means of subsistence? The hopelessness of working under such conditions and in the face of the confiscatory practices of the pre-NEP regime would better explain the unsown fields and the apathy of the peasant population toward farming and toward its own future, viewed by one soviet observer as the worst effect of Antonov's movement.[95] Whoever the responsibility, the sown area is said to have fallen by 44 percent below the pre-war level for the province as a whole,[96] and in Kirsanov *uezd* the fall sowing in 1920 had covered only one-quarter of the area that would be sown in 1921.[97]

The black earth had ceased for the time being to benefit the population, and weeds were growing where crops once had been. In the year of partial recovery, 1922, the center of gravity in respect to farming shifted to the poorer northern *uezds* where Morshansk— black-earth only in its southern reaches—fulfilled the planting quota to the last hectare, in contrast to the fertile but "bandit-ravaged" *uezds* further south which had experienced a severe shortage of seeds.[98]

Losses in livestock weighed upon the sorely-tried rural population no less—perhaps even more—than damage to farming. The draft on horses had been particularly heavy since the Greens needed the best mounts and frequent replacements in order to make up in swiftness of movement what they lacked in weaponry and firepower. The commissar of repression told Lenin that the supply of horses had been sadly depleted in four of the most important districts which he does not name, but it may be conjectured that—in addition to Tambov, Kirsanov, and Borisoglebsk—he meant either Kozlov or Morshansk *uezd*.[99]

For the first three more specific information is available. Although Borisoglebsk had seen less fighting than either Tambov or Kirsanov, for some reason it had sustained the heaviest loss in horses, either because it had more of them or because they were of better breed; the respective diminution in working stock was 50 percent, 38 percent, and 34 percent—a serious handicap to farming operations in all three instances. Over half the peasant households are said to have been without horses, though what proportion had been that way previously and what proportion had been rendered horseless by the upheaval cannot be determined. Often peasants were obliged to hitch up cows and to attempt to get plowing done through the combined efforts of these unwilling animals and themselves; yet even this expedient was hampered by the diminution in the number of cows, estimated to be from 10 to 15 percent of the total stock in the three most affected *uezds*—less severe than in the case of horses but still severe enough.

Losses in other livestock categories cannot be given, but some idea of what was involved can be derived from figures for only four *volosts* in the Sampur area of Tambov *uezd* where the "bandits" are charged with having taken 1,383 horses, 450 cows, 225 pigs, and over 5,500 sheep.[100] The livestock that survived the drought, famine, depredations, and destruction came through in dire condition, little more than skin and bones, until the rains of 1922 restored the meadowlands and the NEP stimulated the incentive of the peasants to care for their cattle. No sector of the economy sustained greater damage than animal husbandry.[101]

If one is to credit Soviet accounts, arson took up where insurrection ended, prolonging the damage done the economy into the period of recovery. In a number of provinces—and not least in Tambov—fires were set with the incidence falling on flour mills, grain collection depots and such; in other words, upon one of the nerve centers of the Soviet system.[102] No doubt sympathizers with the Green movement, in helpless fury over the oppressor's victory, engaged in such actions—the weaker or the vanquished side habitually resorts to measures of desperation—but the presumption remains that in view of the powder-dry conditions prevailing in 1921 some of these fires were of spontaneous origin or resulted from simple carelessness. And the presumption is strengthened by the fact that Lipetsk and Spassk *uezds* are singled out for special mention in this connection, since neither of them ·had been in the forefront of the Green movement and had, in fact, been rather inert throughout the troubled period.

From material damage we proceed to human losses, to a consideration of the death toll of the Tambov insurrection. Here the problem is less the dearth of information—though there are blacked-out areas—than the lack of any system in reporting, the intrusion of an element of gross exaggeration, and the need for bringing some kind of order into a welter of scattered information.

The claim that forty thousand "party men" perished in the Antonov uprising[103] may be dismissed out of hand; on the eve of the uprising in August 1920 the membership of the Communist party in Tambov province, including candidates, stood at 13,490.[104] The conventional estimate in Soviet quarters until recently has been that a thousand or even more than a thousand party members and Soviet employees perished at the hands of the "bandits."[105] This figure seems to have been taken from an estimate made at the time by the provincial committee (of the party?) and the executive committee (of the soviet?) which included, along with Communists and Soviet personnel, nonsympathizers with the Green cause in the village who had been killed by Antonov's men. [106] Recently the figure has been raised to two thousand or more Communists and Soviet workers[107] on the basis of a local and not too reliable study of the 1940's.[108] The original and lower estimate must be preferred. The number of slain in neighboring Voronezh is placed at 691, a suspiciously precise figure, of whom 242 were Communists.[109]

Civilian casualties on the other side cannot even be estimated but doubtless attained a respectable figure. When the local official gazette, the *Tambovskaia Pravda*, speaks of thousands of killed and wounded and tens of thousands of sufferers[110] it did not allude only to battle deaths or even solely to Soviet losses; but for it to have spoken precisely of the toll of the insurrection and of its repression would have imposed too great a strain upon the efficiency of the Soviet administration at that time or upon its honesty at any time.

The record of casualties compiled at Antonov's staff headquarters most likely related only to military engagements and in any event was lost, having been thrown into the Vorona (?) river[111] or otherwise disposed of. Talk of villages in Tambov province that were peopled solely by women and adolescents in 1922 does not ring true, if only because the worst-stricken villages like Verkhotsene in Tambov *uezd* or Parevka in the Vorona valley would have been bereft of the original female population as well, owing to the transplantation attendant upon their destruction. But that the repression had taken a heavy toll of the provincial intelligentsia and that Tambov experienced a dearth of teachers, physicians, medical assistants and such seems entirely plausible, as the intellectuals had for the most part sympathized with the uprising when they had not actually participated in it.[112]

Battle casualties are not a blank but information pertaining to them presents the same broken picture one has come to associate with this entire investigation. Soviet accounts of recent years, now that the taboo has to a limited degree been removed from the subject, give a grossly misleading impression of the fighting as a series of wild routs with heavy losses for the Greens while the Soviet forces emerge only slightly nicked or entirely unscathed.[113] It is not the impression one gets from a sober account written only a few years after the insurrection, in which the campaign of repression is characterized as a hard and stubborn struggle involving more than one hundred fifty clashes over a period of three and one-half months (April/mid-July 1921).[114]

Nor is it the impression conveyed in the memoirs of Marshal Zhukov, who understands that honor is not reflected on one's own arms when the enemy is represented as a pushover. He speaks of especially hard fighting in the Vorona and Khoper valleys at the end of May without giving details, and in general of a number of difficult engagements one of which, near Zherdevka in the spring of 1921, is graven on his memory. On that day he had two horses killed under him and would have lost his life but for the intervention of the commissar; his squadron had ten men killed and fifteen wounded, three of whom died the following day.

Although Zhukov does not give the number of men under him, the casualties would indicate a loss of some fifteen to twenty percent in this unit of a regular army. Antonov's men suffered more acutely because, though numerically superior, they had little to oppose to the four heavy machine guns with unlimited ammunition and the single field piece (76 mm.) of Zhukov's command, the fire from which wrought dreadful execution in their ranks and caused the field to be littered with their dead. Even so, both regiments of the Red cavalry brigade that had undertaken the action found it necessary to fall back on the village that served as their base and had to forego the counterattack they had hoped to deliver.[115]

If this action is indicative of other engagements—and the cumulative if admittedly fragmentary knowledge derived from this study suggests that it is typical of the lengthy period of swaying warfare preceding the knockout blows of early June—the losses in battle are quite enough in themselves to establish the sanguinary character of the Tambov insurrection. Even today, however, after the passage of so much time and with the taboo on discussion partially lifted, there is still no real information as to how costly the repression was to the Red Army. This reticence on the part of the Communist party, while thoroughly in keeping with its secretiveness and its fetish of infallibility, is one good reason for thinking that the losses reflect little credit on its direction of affairs and a good deal of credit on the side that was outnumbered, outgunned, and in every respect outclassed save only in the skill of its leader and the bravery of his followers. Not even in his secret report to the head of the party and of the state did the commissar of repression mention the losses on his side except for a couple of incidents; was he shielding himself or was he simply not minded to dwell on unpleasant facts?

The death toll for the Greens is also unknown and most likely will always remain so, but here there is something more to go on. An émigré source[116] sets at seventeen thousand the number of insurgents killed in "major engagements alone" from the end of December 1920 to the 20th of July 1921. The data is said to be incomplete, though it is not clear whether this is because not all engagements were included or because of the exclusion of the indirect toll in deaths from wounds, from shootings of prisoners and of hostages, and so on. Nor is the basis of computation known. In any event, the figure is defective since it does not cover the first four and one-half months of the insurrection (mid-August to the end of December 1920) and it is unsatisfactory, in the opinion of this author, because it is much too high. The primary local source from the Soviet side contains the report on "bandit" losses presented by the military command to the provincial party conference for the period 28 May to 26 July 1921—that is, for the period of liquidation, when the Greens would have bled most badly. Listed as killed in action are 4,515, 985 as captured on the battlefield, and 5,285 in the manhunts that ensued with the combing of forests and swamps. Virtually eleven thousand Green activists would thus have been accounted for.[117]

There are several reasons for questioning these figures. First, the disproportion between the slain and those taken on the field: unwittingly the Red command paid a high tribute to the "bandits" if such bloodletting resulted in so few prisoners. Our view has been that only desperation and hatred born of altogether exceptional oppression could have raised morale to the level exemplified in the Green movement, but to have the view confirmed from a hostile and on-the-scene source is an unexpected development. Second, there are no figures for wounded. If the Greens were so utterly routed, how could they have borne off and concealed their wounded? Third, 4,515 dead out of a total force of twenty-one thousand (the real strength of the Greens as revealed by Tukhachevski, not the fantastic figure of fifty thousand given in the local source) would have meant a mortality rate of upwards of twenty percent and would have exceeded even on the absolute scale the loss to either side in the sanguinary three-day battle of Gettysburg. For these reasons, and also because of the habitually exaggerated claims from the Soviet side which have already been noted, the statistics of the Red command disclosed at the time to the party conference must be rejected.[118]

The latest word on the subject from the Soviet side represents an attempt to correct the flaw in respect to omission of wounded with the assertion that for the same time period and obviously on the basis of the same figures—without changing the announced totals—the number of killed and wounded came to eleven thousand.[119] Even though such casualties would have amounted to one-half of

Antonov's strength, they would be barely possible under the given circumstances; yet one must wonder how they can be reconciled with the original announcement. Does the total of eleven thousand apply to the killed and wounded or to the killed and captured? Obviously something has slipped, but whether in the original version or in this new effort is not for the exasperated investigator to say.[120]

From this morass of uncertainty we are rescued by Antonov-Ovseenko. The commissar of repression told Lenin that in June and July 1921 as many as two thousand "bandits" had been killed.[121] If his statement is taken literally it would exclude the last four days of May, marked by severe fighting at the beginning of the Tukha-chevski-Uborevich offensive; but in all likelihood Antonov-Ovseenko is referring to the whole offensive, comprising the same time period as the report of the Soviet command to the local party conference.

And so instead of a death toll for the Greens of forty-five hundred fifteen we have one of two thousand. Here at last is a figure both reasonable and authoritative. Here at last is a figure one can accept, even if it is rounded off. The exact number of slain could never be known in any event since not all the corpses would have been noted in the forest nor reclaimed from the river or swamps. The loss of those fighting for freedom is still crushing; in the annals of warfare two thousand dead on the field of battle would constitute a major bloodletting for an army two or even three times the size of Antonov's.[122]

Armed with a firm figure for the decisive campaign, we may now try to reach an estimate for the entire insurrection. At one time the author had thought to add up the losses assigned the enemy in official reports but was forced to abandon the plan, initially because of the unevenness of the reporting (at times casualties would be broken down, at other times given as a lump sum; at times one category would be included, at other times omitted);[123] secondly, because of the incompleteness of the reporting; and thirdly, because the Soviet authorities were trying to create through exaggeration a semblance of success where only stalemate or worse prevailed.

Yet there is nothing else to go on for the five-month period of indecisive fighting between the beginning of 1921 and the end of

May. During this period the Reds would have lost proportionally more and the Greens proportionally less than during the death throes of the insurrection from 28 May to the end of July. On the other hand, the indecisive stage lasted more than twice as long and was marked by a whole series of hard-fought engagements—in this instance indecisiveness must not be confused with lethargy. Just because the sides were more or less at even balance, the superior leadership of the Greens and their familiarity with the terrain offsetting the Red advantage in armaments, the clashes could be as costly in life as when one side was hopelessly overborne. It seems reasonable to conclude, therefore, that as many of Antonov's soldiers died in the first five months of 1921 as in the final campaign.

The period most shrouded in uncertainty is the first stage of the insurrection, from its initial outbreak in August 1920 to the end of that year when the Greens generally held the upper hand outside the towns. Here an estimate involves sheer guesswork. Though the Green army in the strict sense attained its maximum strength only at the end of the year or the beginning of 1921, it can be that these earlier hostilities claimed as many as a thousand lives. If the figure is too high, then the estimate of two thousand dead for the first five months of 1921 may well be too low. We will not be too far wrong, therefore, if we place the killed-in-action total for the Greens at around five thousand.

Battle deaths, of course, were only the most obvious and spectacular component of the blood sacrifice exacted of the Tambov peasantry. Another and quite important component would consist of executions of captured "bandits" and the shooting of hostages. Here so little is known as to require the opening of the secret police archives before any viable estimate can be made. The only thing to go on is Antonov-Ovseenko's report to Lenin that between 1 June and 10 July 1921 in Tambov *uezd* 663 "bandits" and hostages had been shot (divided as 591 "bandits," 70 hostages, and 2 persons who had sheltered bandits).[124] Only with the utmost indulgence can these figures be even partially reconciled with what the commissar has said elsewhere in his report;[125] they apply to only one *uezd* and comprise only a forty-day period, albeit the period of maximum repression. The bloodletting in Kirsanov *uezd* would not have lagged behind; in Borisoglebsk it might have been less though still substantial, while the other *uezds* undoubtedly witnessed some executions.

To this total, whatever it might be, must be added the shootings everywhere before 1 June and after 10 July. They did not await the issuance of Orders No. 130 and 171 as we very definitely know from an incident involving Kotovski's brigade: his men had caught some Green footsoldiers on 22 May at the village of Pokrovskoe, had extracted information from them (one would like to know how), and had then moved on "after shooting the captured bandits."[126] It would be naive to think that this was the first such occasion; it is merely the first occasion of which we have proof.

Similarly at the other end: the Central Party Archives provide the information that after the liberation of Borisoglebsk *uezd* (note the phraseology) a big roundup of "bandits," deserters, and hostages took place between 15 August and 15 October which yielded 7,507 victims, of whom "a part" were then sentenced to death by shooting.[127] We would like to know what part; the silence of the sycophant source that transmits the information, though presumably not of the party archives whence it is derived, only fans the suspicion that it was no insignificant part. There is some basis for thinking that not less than two thousand prisoners and hostages were executed, but the basis is too restricted for even an approximate estimate and the author feels that two thousand does not do justice to the Red terror in Tambov.

The wounded who crawled off to die or who lingered a while before succumbing to their wounds for want of medical attention were another factor swelling the lists of the dead. The hospital with one hundred fifty beds unearthed by Antonov-Ovseenko[128] no doubt was as overtaxed as were the country doctors—nearly all of whom would be either Populist or Constitutional Democrat in sympathy—to look after the stream of victims. If the supply of medicaments for a regiment of Kotovski's elite brigade is described as "bad,"[129] it can be imagined what things were like in the Tambov countryside. The danger of a wound was magnified under the circumstances, and many who in normal times could have been healed without great difficulty no doubt went to the grave.

An undetermined number of participants in the uprising, failing to secure redress of their grievances through a resort to arms, hounded from pillar to post, and expecting no mercy if apprehended, found release from despair and physical hardship in suicide. This phenomenon was distinctly a factor in the loss of life, but how significant a factor one cannot say. Followers of Antonov who chose this way out might escape detection in out-of-the-way places or by employing methods that defied classification such as drowning, but the Soviet press noted instances among roving bandits of suicide by hanging. Ten such cases were established in Morshansk *uezd*.[130]

Transplantation of the disaffected population not only constituted a grievous form of punishment but contributed indirectly to the death toll. Recourse on the part of the Soviet regime to this expedient of Muscovite despotism has already been pointed out;[131] here we must consider its scope and the sacrifice it entailed. As usual in this study, neither can be determined with any degree of accuracy. From the anti-Soviet side we have an estimate of the numbers involved from an informant in the Russian capital who advised the SR newspaper in exile that no less than eighty to one hundred thousand families from Tambov and neighboring provinces and from the Ukraine faced deportation to "far-away places" where they would be subjected to forced labor of an "especially onerous" kind. At the time he wrote—8 July 1921—the first party from Tambov province, consisting of thirty thousand men who were ostensibly deserters and fifty thousand women and children who belonged to "bandit" families and so were hostages, were being sent to the Murman and Ural regions and to the vicinity of the Aral Sea.[132] The first impulse of the author was to reject these figures as grossly exaggerated—but let us see what we have from the Soviet side.

The commissar of repression informed Lenin that from 1 June to 2 July 1,748 "bandits" and 2,452 deserters had been caught while 1,449 "bandits" and 6,672 deserters had voluntarily surrendered, for a total of 12,301 (his addition) in both categories who had been removed from circulation. Adding the haul for the week following—evidently 3–10 July—he raised the total to 16,000 "bandits" and deserters who had been "taken out."[133] The records of the army command cover a more extended period, from 28 May to 26 July. They list 985 "bandits" taken in battle and 5,285 in the ensuing manhunts; they add 7,646 deserters as further yield of the manhunt for a total of 13,916 prisoners.[134] Furthermore, 5,585 "bandits" and about 13,000 deserters voluntarily turned themselves in,[135] for a grand total of 32,501 of these nefarious people who had been apprehended by the "workers' and peasants' " regime. The anti-Soviet source has 30,000 men, "ostensibly deserters," as the victims of transplantation. It is readily apparent that the source strove to be truthful and that it came close to the mark.

The respective figures can be brought even more closely together. Not all of the 32,501 captives in Soviet hands would be transplanted. Of those who had not voluntarily surrendered a goodly number would have been shot. Perhaps a clue as to how many is furnished by the difference between the army command's total of 4,515 "bandits" killed in action, which we have rejected as excessive, and Antonov-Ovseenko's figure of 2,000, which we have accepted as realistic. This difference would be 2,515 which, deducted from 32,501, would leave almost exactly 30,000.

This result is altogether too good, for the anti-Soviet estimate is for early July and the army report extends to nearly the end of a month marked by maximum activity in the rounding up of dissident elements. Yet the suspicion is not dispelled that the figure 4,515 may mask the inclusion of those who were shot after capture with those who were killed in action; the main reason for thinking otherwise would be not the variation of the time period between the two estimates, but the further and stronger suspicion that the number of executions exceeded 2,500.

A wide discrepancy exists, however, in respect to the number of ancillary victims awaiting deportation. The anti-Soviet source speaks of more than fifty thousand women and children, members of "bandit families," as being held in the camps, whereas Antonov-Ovseenko informed Lenin of an accumulation there of five thousand hostages when he complained of the delay in authorization to ship them off.[136] Here we must accept the commissar's word for he would not purposefully have misled the party leader on this matter—five or fifty thousand, it would have been all the same to Lenin; in fact, the higher the number of these accursed peasants who had been corralled the more he would have been pleased, for did he not tell his followers "to rule more harshly than the capitalist had ruled before," in a spirit totally devoid of sentimentality and with no compunction about resorting to means which "even the previous regime" had not employed?[137] Seemingly what happened here is that the anti-Soviet informant of the *Volia Rossii*, who had come so close to the truth in respect to prisoners other than hostages, had in the latter instance again gotten wind of the correct figure distorted by an extra zero—hence the tenfold exaggeration.

In accepting the commissar's estimate, however, we must remember that it reflects the situation in mid-July and that many other hostages from families implicated in the Green movement or simply having a member in its ranks were subsequently added to the lists. In Borisoglebsk *uezd* alone 1,326 hostages had been seized between 15 August and 15 October,[138] and of what happened elsewhere and in the same *uezd* between mid-July and mid-August and after 15 October we are not told.

As for the estimate of eighty to one hundred thousand families awaiting deportation from Tambov and adjacent provinces and from the Ukraine, no way of checking it against other information has been discovered. It may be taken, if not as accurate, at least as indicative of the scope of punitive transplantation. The inclusion of the Ukraine warrants the assumption that large numbers were involved, for the rigor of repression there would not have lagged behind Tambov and would have been applied over a much larger area to a population even more disaffected.

How many of these miserable people—Great Russian and Little Russian—perished in the process may well not be determinable even from the records of the secret police; but the conditions of transportation, the dearth of reception facilities, the callousness at best of the authorities, and the vengefulness that may have dictated what in effect was a veiled sentence of death, provide the framework for a major tragedy. Even without vengeance, the desperate food situation in Russia would have guaranteed a substantial mortality rate. The transplanted families were for the most part used to farming on good land; now they would farm, if at all, under the most adverse circumstances, natural and man-made. We do not know what happened; a veil of silence overhangs the fate of the transplanted. Only one bit of information has come through but it is characteristic: victims of the uprooting process in Tambov province who had been dumped in the Moscow and Vologda areas brought with them the cholera.[139]

Famine and disease complete the list of woes besetting the ravaged province. In both respects Tambov was hard hit, although it did not rank among the areas most tragically afflicted. The cholera began in Usman *uezd*; from 800-odd cases at the outset the number in the province as a whole rose to 1,396 and then to 2,757 as of 20 July 1921. It was a dread disease; of 237 who contracted it in twenty localities, 150 lost their lives.[140] The uprising had been not so much indigenous to Usman *uezd* as it had simply spilled over from neighboring *uezds* further east (Tambov, Borisoglebsk, Kirsanov); nevertheless, the fighting undoubtedly contributed to the spread of the disease if not to its inception by disorganizing the means of containment.

As for famine, the commissar of repression in his report to Lenin had duly noted its onset by midsummer. He admitted serious provisioning difficulties in May and June and conceded that in a number of *volosts* of Usman, Borisoglebsk, Lipetsk, and Kozlov *uezds* people were getting by till the new harvest by eating chaff and bitter weed. And that harvest was not too promising, for the area sown to spring grains had contracted by twelve percent and famine again stalked the countryside.[141]

No better evidence can be cited of how tight things were than that hunger had come even to Kotovski's cavalry brigade: in early August the food supply failed for the 1st cavalry regiment, and while the 2nd for some reason was better off in this respect, 135 of its 537 men were ill, most of them with loose gums (only 12 with venereal disease), and neither regiment had any fodder.[142] Reports in the émigré press of a march of the starving upon Tambov[143] may have been true in the light of Antonov-Ovseenko's report of turbulence among workers in Tambov and elsewhere because of a breakdown in rationing; the authorities dealt with the situation by arrests and dismissals of refractory workers.[144]

If things were bad, worse was to come in the winter of 1921–1922. First on the scale of misfortune came Kirsanov *uezd* and within it the *volosts* of Balyklei, Kalugino, and Ramza—core areas of the insurrection. Here undoubtedly was a direct connection between ravaging, repression, and vengeance on the one hand and the wrecking of agriculture and famine on the other. One hundred fifty thousand people—half the population of the *uezd*—were starving as the first snow fell on the acorns in the forest and made everything worse.[145] Borisoglebsk *uezd* in the southeastern corner of Tambov province and Usman in the southwestern each numbered over one hundred thousand victims of the famine, whereas the northern *uezd* of Spassk, in the smokestack of the province, had only ten thousand. By May 1922 the Communist party archives reveal that in the province as a whole there were two hundred sixteen deaths for every hundred births. From eating chaff, bitter weed, and wild garlic the population had progressed to grass, dogs, and carrion—even infected carrion in the case of horses felled by disease. The situation told on the nerves of the Communist provincial committee which feared that starvation might become the seedbed of revived political opposition.[146]

From the much greater incidence of the famine in the rich but war-ravaged districts of Kirsanov and Borisoglebsk in contrast to the infertile but little damaged *uezd* of Spassk, one is tempted to say that the insurrection and its repression were the primary factors in producing the famine; but before drawing such a conclusion it would be necessary to know the respective atmospheric conditions, to consider the factor of moisture retention in an extensively forested area such as Spassk, and other such aspects. Furthermore, one would have to explain why Usman *uezd*, black-earth like Borisoglebsk but much less torn up by the fighting, would be equally as badly off in respect to the famine.

It is not possible to disentangle the factors and make them stand in isolation; all one can say is that Tambov would have experienced hunger in any event, that it was made worse by the insurrection—but how much worse is a matter of conjecture, all the more so since the number of victims either is not known or has been buried by a regime which can claim with a straight face that "owing to the effective measures of the Soviet state the catastrophic drought of 1921 did not entail the usual grievous consequences."[147] It was rather different in the early years of the Soviet regime when a despatch in the official organ could state that the situation in Tambov province in respect to children was everywhere bad.[148]

No more than the material damage can the toll of life be ascertained or even estimated. But enough is known of the fighting, of the repression, and of the spirit in which both were conducted to

make the Tambov insurrection a memorable chapter in Russian
provincial history. Not that the national history during these years
was less tragic or that other provinces had it much better. Tambov
had been spared the ravages of the Great War and, for the most part,
of the first civil war; moreover, a double tier of provinces separated
it from the outer fringe of the desert of Turkestan and mitigated the
impact of the drought, so that in these respects its interior position
proved to be a blessing.

But woe came to it in full measure with the peasant uprising that
constituted the backbone of the second civil war; and its interior
position, which might conceivably have favored the Green
movement, actually facilitated its repression and doomed absolutely
the leadership of the peasants' cause. But before such doom settled
over it the uprising had forced the Soviet government to change for a
time its agrarian policy, had wrought widespread havoc, and had
cost many thousands of lives.

Notes

1. Anonymous (Podbelski), *Kak tambovskie krest'iane boriatsia za svobodu*, p. 8 (a source sympathetic to peasants); Zybko, *Tambovskaia partiinaia organizatsiia*, p. 38.

2. Trifonov, *Klassy i klassovaia bor'ba*, part 1, p. 123, on the basis of G. Mikhalev's article. A case of one unreliable source citing another.

3. "Banditskie prestupleniia partii eserov: Antonovshchina: Iz besedy s genshtabistom t. Davydovym," *Pravda*, no. 116, 27 May 1922, p. 3; Petrovskii, "Bor'ba s banditizmom i krasnye kursanty," *Izvestiia*, no. 133 (1276), 23 June 1921, p. 1; Hirschfeld, "Tambovskii krovopodtek," ibid., no. 247 (1390), 3 November 1921, p. 1; from a report of the Che-ka, "Partiia s.-r. i banditizm," in *Iz istorii Vserossiiskoi Chrezvychainoi Komissii*, no. 333, p. 457.

4. Maksim Gor'kii, *O russkom krest'ianstve* [Concerning the Russian peasantry] (Berlin, 1922), p. 18; Ekaterina Kuskova, "Maksim Gor'kii o krest'ianstve" [Maxim Gorki on the peasantry], in *Krest'ianskaia Rossiia*, no. 2–3 (Prague, 1923), p. 212.

5. Fomichev (Lidin), "Antonovshchina: Iz vospominanii antonovtsa" (Philippines, 1950-1951), p. 13; see also ibid. (Santiago de Chile, 1955), pp. 18, 21. It is not altogether clear whether the author himself was a witness or learned of what happened from others. The place is not given, the chronology probably faulty. But he personally observed cases of people being buried alive while on the way to Sampur from one of the villages called Nikolskoe (he says Nikolsk); see the ms. written in the Philippines, p. 23. He may refer to this occasion or to some other. In the later ms. the point about the women is not repeated but the dogs figure as before; ibid. (Santiago de Chile, 1955), p. 21.

6. Gor'kii, *O russkom krest'ianstve*, p. 18.

7. S. E., "Antonovshchina," *Izvestiia*, no. 122 (1561), 3 June 1922, p. 3. That SR leaders engaged in such actions as this article charges—it was published at the time of the SR trial—is most unlikely. They were much too fastidious for that sort of thing. Here was something authentically Green, coming from the depths of the people.

8. Ibid., p. 2. For somewhat different version of his fate see Trifonov, *Klassy i klassovaia bor'ba*, part 1, p. 122. Samorodov was a peasant who did not go along.

9. Kotovski, "Tambovskaia operatsiia," in *G. I. Kotovskii*, no. 290, pp. 397, 400; Esaulenko, *Revoliutsionnyi put' G. I. Kotovskogo*, p. 135; Trifonov, *Klassy i klassovaia bor'ba*, part 1, p. 123.

10. On maiming and mutilation see also Fomichev (Lidin), "Antonovshchina: Iz vospominanii antonovtsa" (Philippines, 1950–1951), p. 13; Hirschfeld, "Tambovskii krovopodtek," *Izvestiia*, no. 247 (1390), 3 November 1921, p. 1; Trifonov,

Klassy i klassovaia bor'ba, part 1, p. 122, drawing upon *Put' Bor'by*, vol. 2, *Antonovshchina*, for an episode in the village of Inzhavino in Kirsanov *uezd*.

11. "Banditskie prestupleniia partii eserov: Iz besedy s t. Davydovym," *Pravda*, no. 116, 27 May 1922, p. 3. See also Trifonov, *Klassy i klassovaia bor'ba*, part 1, pp. 122–23 (with inaccuracies as usual); *Iz istorii Vserossiiskoi Chrez- vychainoi Komissii*, no. 333, p. 457 (with the variant that the design of a banner was carved on the breast).

12. Hirschfeld, "Tambovskii krovopodtek," *Izvestiia*, no. 247 (1390), 3 November 1921, p. 1.

13. Esaulenko, *Revoliutsionnyi put' G. I. Kotovskogo*, p. 129, based on the local *Izvestiia* of the Tambov executive committee of soviets.

14. S. E., "Antonovshchina," *Izvestiia*, no. 122 (1561), 3 June 1922, pp. 2–3. The best example of an appeal to Red Army soldiers to come over is in the manifesto of the "Young Lion" (Dmitri S. Antonov) reproduced in the *Put' Bor'by*, vol. 2, *Antonovshchina*, page unknown. See above, chapter four.

15. Shneerson, "Neskol'ko slov o tambovskom esero-banditizme," *Izvestiia*, no. 118 (1557), 30 May 1922, p. 2.

16. S. E., "Antonovshchina," ibid., no. 122 (1561), 3 June 1922, pp. 2–3.

17. Cited in Trifonov, *Klassy i klassovaia bor'ba*, part 1, p. 123.

18. *Put' Bor'by*, vol. 2, *Antonovshchina*, p. 108, as cited in ibid.

19. Shneerson, "Neskol'ko slov o tambovskom esero-banditizme," *Izvestiia*, no. 118 (1557), 30 May 1922, p. 2.

20. See chapter ten.

21. Antonov-Ovseenko, "O banditskom dvizhenii v Tambovskoi gubernii," p. 24. The phrases placed in quotation marks are the commissar's. His phrase describing the system as "mass terrorism" will be found in ibid., p. 23.

22. Trifonov, *Klassy i klassovaia bor'ba*, part 1, pp. 219, 220.

23. *Put'Bor'by*, vol. 2, *Antonovshchina*, pp. 45, 46, as cited in ibid., p. 219.

24. Antonov-Ovseenko, "O banditskom dvizhenii v Tambovskoi gubernii," p. 24. The commissar is at pains to show that it was worked out on the basis of reports of the ebbing tide of banditry within the economic strata of the village (whatever that means).

25. Presumably an extension of Order No. 130, which had made the senior breadwinner subject to execution. But because of the possibility of paraphrasing in either the émigré or the Tambov newspaper, one would have to see the original text of the decree to be sure.

26. Moskvich, "Povstancheskoe dvizhenie (Pis'mo iz Moskvy)" [The insur- rectionary movement (a letter from Moscow)], *Volia Rossii*, no. 264, 27 July 1921, p. 2. The letter is dated 8 July. The decree of 11 June, now identified as Order No. 171, is printed again in all seven articles in "V Tambovskoi gubernii" [In Tambov province], ibid., no. 304, 13 September 1921, p. 4.

27. Antonov-Ovseenko, "O banditskom dvizhenii v Tambovskoi gubernii," p. 24.

28. See chapter ten.

29. Antonov-Ovseenko, "O banditskom dvizhenii v Tambovskoi gubernii," p. 28.

30. The phrase "in general" raised the question whether the statistics might really apply to Tambov *uezd* instead of this one *volost'*. So poorly organized is Antonov-Ovseenko's report and so muddy in expression that the context may not be a sufficient basis for judgment. But in this instance the subsequent figures for the *uezd* (see below) leave no doubt that those given here refer to the single *volost'* (the commissar first makes two *volosts* out of the name [ibid., p. 28] and then reduces it to one [ibid., p. 29]—an example of the sloppiness that pervades his work). The phrase "in general" may indicate shootings of other hostages besides the two "kulak" groups.

31. Ibid., p. 28.

32. Trifonov, *Klassy i klassovaia bor'ba,* part 1, p. 123.

33. *Entsiklopedicheskii slovar'* (Brockhaus-Efron), vol. 20, p. 838.

34. Article on Tambov *uezd* in ibid., vol. 32, p. 568.

35. It may be argued, of course, that a Russian household often included several families in the strict Western sense. But the revolution had reduced the number of multiple family households by allowing younger families to establish households of their own on property seized from the upper classes, and the Red punitive squads would not balk at taking a father, mother, brother, sister, as well as wife and child of the "bandit." The use of the term "senior breadwinner" points clearly to the family in the extended sense, and the provisions of Orders No. 130 and 171 are clearly directed at households where arms, "bandits" or "bandit" families or property were concealed.

36. Antonov-Ovseenko, "O banditskom dvizhenii v Tambovskoi gubernii," p. 28.

37. It has not been possible to locate this *volost'* except that it was in Tambov *uezd*. Apparently it adjoined Belomestnaia Dvoinia.

38. Antonov-Ovseenko, "O banditskom dvizhenii v Tambovskoi gubernii," p. 28.

39. Ibid., p. 29.

40. Ibid.

41. See publication by the People's Commissariat of Internal Affairs of *Sbornik gubernii, uezdov i volostei RSFSR, USSR i SSR Belorussii* [Compilation of the provinces, *uezds* and *volosts* of the RSFSR and of the Ukrainian and Belorussian SSRs] (Moscow, 1921), p. 60.

42. Ibid., p. 59. Borisoglebsk had 33; ibid., p. 58. In all there were 381 *volosts* in Tambov province; ibid., p. 61.

43. Antonov-Ovseenko, "O banditskom dvizhenii v Tambovskoi gubernii," p. 27.

44. Tukhachevski, "Zapiska," p. 2.

45. "Na mestakh: bor'ba s banditizmom," *Izvestiia,* no. 167 (1310), 31 July 1921, p. 2.

46. Antonov-Ovseenko, "O banditskom dvizhenii v Tambovskoi gubernii," p. 30.

47. Cited in Trifonov, *Klassy i klassovaia bor'ba,* part 1, p. 220.

48. From the Central Party Archives as quoted in ibid., p. 94. The year is 1929, other circumstances not known. With reference to Voronezh, Kolesnikov headed the movement, not Antonov.

49. From the Central Party Archives and from *Put' Bor'by*, vol. 2, *Antonovshchina*, p. 24, both as cited in ibid., pp. 93–94.

50. Antonov-Ovseenko, "O banditskom dvizhenii v Tambovskoi gubernii," p. 25.

51. Podbelski, "Predsedateliu moskovskogo soveta r.i k. deputatov," pp. 2–3.

52. "V tambovskoi gubernii," *Volia Rossii*, no. 304, 13 September 1921, p. 4.

53. "Usmirenie krest'ian v Tambovskoi gubernii," *Na chuzhoi storone*, no. 3, p. 130. The author has found a Lavrovo or Lavrovka to the southwest of Prokovskoe-Marfino. Though not bearing an uncommon name for a village, this settlement is probably the one in question.

54. See the list of *volosts* in *Sbornik gubernii*, p. 60 (for Tambov *uezd*).

55. Ibid. (for Morshansk *uezd*).

56. "Usmirenie krest'ian v Tambovskoi gubernii," *Na chuzhoi storone*, no. 3, p. 129.

57. The greater amount of information in the relative sense about Tambov *uezd*, in my opinion, is to be explained by the fact that Tambov town was much less isolated from the Russian intellectual world than the all but exclusively rural *uezd* of Kirsanov. With the exceptions of Raksha and Parevka, all of the villages noted were not far from Tambov, and what little we know about Parevka comes from a secret Soviet memorandum, not from the Populist intellectuals.

58. Podbelski, "Predsedateliu moskovskogo soveta," pp. 2–3.

59. *Put' Bor'by*, vol. 2, *Antonovshchina*, p. 24, as rendered in Trifonov, *Klassy i klassovaia bor'ba*, part 1, 'p. 93.

60. "Usmirenie krest'ian v Tambovskoi gubernii," *Na chuzhoi storone*, no. 3, p. 130.

61. Antonov-Ovseenko, "O banditskom dvizhenii v Tambovskoi gubernii," p. 30, and see above.

62. Ibid., p. 25.

63. Trifonov, *Klassy i klassovaia bor'ba*, part 1, p. 213, apparently drawing on the army archives.

64. Antonov-Ovseenko, "O banditskom dvizhenii v Tambovskoi gubernii," p. 30.

65. Ibid., p. 12.

66. Ibid., p. 30.

67. "Usmirenie krest'ian v Tambovskoi gubernii," *Na chuzhoi storone*, no. 3, pp. 129–30. One or more incidents above might relate to depredations of the committees of the poor or of food detachments before the insurrection proper. But on the whole the indicated chronology is faulty, for the events are supposed to relate to the end of 1919 or to 1920 whereas the chronicle of ruined villages discussed further back undoubtedly belongs to the period of the main insurrection, August 1920 to the fall of 1921. Things often slip a notch in approaching this subject; every source has mistakes.

68. Petrovski, "Bor'ba s banditizmom i krasnye kursanty," *Izvestiia*, no. 133 (1276), 23 June 1921, p. 1. His work in bringing the strength of his charges effectively to bear upon the Greens in the special 6th (Inzhavino–Vorona valley) military district is commended by Antonov-Ovseenko; see "O banditskom dvizhenii v Tambovskoi gubernii," p. 27.

69. See above, chapter nine, text and n. 42.

70. "Usmirenie krest'ian v Tambovskoi gubernii," *Na chuzhoi storone*, no.3, p. 130.

71. "Kleveta na krest'ianstvo" [Defamation of the peasantry], editorial, *Volia Rossii*, no. 324, 6 October 1921, p. 1.

72. See above, this chapter.

73. Gor'kii, *O russkom krest'ianstve*, p. 20.

74. Lunacharskii, *Byvshie liudi: Ocherk istorii partii es-erov* [The have-beens: historical sketch of the party of the SRs] (Moscow, 1922), p. 73.

75. Gor'kii, *O russkom krest'ianstve*, p. 19.

76. "Posle Antonova" [After Antonov], *Izvestiia*, no. 130 (1273), 16 June 1921, p. 2.

77. Most recently by Trifonov in "Antonovshchina," *Bol'shaia sovetskaia entsiklopediia*, 3rd ed., vol. 2, p. 96, col. 276.

78. Dokunin, "Tambovskii schet sotsial-banditam," *Pravda*, no. 123, 4 June 1922, p. 3.

79. V. D. (Vladimir Dokunin), "Pis'ma iz Tambova: 'Budem s khlebom' " [Letters from Tambov: "We shall somehow have bread"], *Pravda*, no. 141, 28 June 1922, p. 6.

80. Quoted by S. Ch. in "Tambovskaia pamiatka ob eserakh," *Izvestiia*, no. 121 (1560), 2 June 1922, p. 1.

81. Interview with General Staff Officer Kazakov, "Banditskie prestupleniia partii eserov: Antonovshchina: Banditskie itogi" [Crimes of banditry of the SR party: the Antonov affair: the toll of banditry], *Pravda*, no. 116, 27 May 1922, p. 3.

82. *Ocherki istorii tambovskoi organizatsii KPSS* [Outline history of the Tambov organization of the Communist party of the Soviet Union] (Voronezh, 1970), p. 128.

83. *Narodnoe khoziaistvo SSSR v 1959 godu: statisticheskii ezhegodnik* [National economy of the USSR for 1959: statistical yearbook] (Moscow, 1960), p. 141.

84. *Ocherki istorii tambovskoi organizatsii KPSS*, pp. 128, 129.

85. Interview with Kazakov, "Banditskie prestupleniia partii eserov: Banditskie itogi," *Pravda*, no. 116, 27 May 1922, p. 3; Borisov, *Chernym letom*, p. 39; Trifonov, *Klassy i klassovaia bor'ba*, part 1, p. 117. It is clear that the other sources had their information from Kazakov.

86. Recitation of damages from Kazakov who, however, does not qualify the harm done to bridges.

87. Antonov-Ovseenko, "O banditskom dvizhenii v Tambovskoi gubernii," pp. 30–31. The passage about the transcendent importance of the food situation has been underlined, most likely by Lenin, since marginal comments are unmistakably in his handwriting.

88. Dokunin, "Tambovskii schet sotsial-banditam," *Pravda*, no. 123, 4 June 1922, p. 3. Despatch from Tambov dated 25 May.

89. Ibid.

90. Interview with Kazakov, "Banditskie prestupleniia: Banditskie itogi," *Pravda*, no. 116, 27 May 1922, p. 3. It is evident that other accounts draw primarily upon this article; see Trifonov, *Klassy i klassovaia bor'ba*, part 1, p. 117; idem, "Antonovshchina," in *Bol'shaia sovetskaia entsiklopediia*, 3rd ed., vol. 2, p. 96, col. 276; "Antonovshchina," *Sovetskaia istoricheskaia entsiklopediia*, vol. 1, p. 636; Borisov, *Chernym letom*, p. 39.

91. Kostinskii, "Tiaga k zemle" [The pull toward land], under the heading "Po sovetskoi federatsii" [About the Soviet federation], *Pravda*, no. 111, 20 May 1922, p. 4.

92. "Posle Antonova," *Izvestiia*, no. 130 (1273), 16 June 1921, p. 2.

93. Ibid.

94. S. E., "Antonovshchina," *Izvestiia*, no. 122 (1561), 3 June 1922, pp. 2–3.

95. Kostinskii, "Tiaga k zemle," *Pravda*, no. 111, 20 May 1922, p. 4.

96. *Ocherki istorii tambovskoi organizatsii KPSS*, p. 129.

97. Interview with Kazakov, "Banditskie prestupleniia: Banditskie itogi," *Pravda*, no. 116, 27 May 1922, p. 3. Trifonov relates the 75 percent drop in Kirsanov *uezd* and, in general, the maximum deficiency period to 1921; *Klassy i klassovaia bor'ba*, part 1, p. 119. Seemingly Kotovski's commissar does likewise, though he is vague as to dates; Borisov, *Chernym letom*, p. 39. But the Kazakov article is primary, both as to author and time, and is accorded the preference. During the fall of 1920 the insurrection had been in full swing, whereas by the fall of 1921 it had been crushed though the damage remained.

98. S. E., "Na mestakh: Tambovskie vesti" [In the localities: news from Tambov], *Izvestiia*, no. 112 (1551), 21 May 1922, p. 4; S. Ch., "Tambovskaia pamiatka ob eserakh," ibid., no. 121 (1560), 2 June 1922, p. 1.

99. Antonov-Ovseenko, "O banditskom dvizhenii v Tambovskoi gubernii," p. 31.

100. Trifonov, *Klassy i klassovaia bor'ba*, part 1, p. 119.

101. See especially the Kazakov interview, "Banditskie prestupleniia: Banditskie itogi," *Pravda*, no. 116, 27 May 1922, p. 3; V. D., "Pis'ma iz Tambova: 'Budem s khlebom,' " ibid., no. 141, 28 June 1922, p. 6; Kostinskii, "Tiaga k zemle," ibid., no. 111, 20 May 1922, p. 4; *Ocherki istorii tambovskoi organizatsii KPSS*, p. 129; Borisov, *Chernym letom*, p. 39.

102. "Podzhigateli ne unimaiutsia!" [Arsonists are not subsiding!], *Izvestiia*, no. 216 (1359), 28 September 1921, p. 2. The article is signed Ilia Lin.

103. Fomichev (Lidin), "Antonovshchina: Iz vospominanii antonovtsa" (Santiago de Chile, 1955), p. 3.

104. Donkov, "Organizatsiia razgroma antonovshchiny," *Voprosy Istorii KPSS*, no. 6 (June 1966), p. 61, n. 12.

105. "Antonovshchina," *Sovetskaia istoricheskaia entsiklopediia*, vol. 1, p. 636; Borisov, *Chernym letom*, p. 38; *Ocherki istorii tambovskoi organizatsii KPSS*, p. 129.

106. "Banditskie prestupleniia partii eserov: Antonovshchina: Iz besedy s genshtabistom t. Davydovym," *Pravda*, no. 116, 27 May 1922, p. 3.

107. Trifonov, "Antonovshchina," in *Bol'shaia sovetskaia entsiklopediia,* 3rd ed., vol. 2, p. 96, col. 276.

108. The source of the estimate appears in idem, *Klassy i klassovaia bor'ba,* part 1, p. 122, n. 328.

109. Information on Voronezh is from the Central Party Archives; see ibid., text and n. 329.

110. Quoted by S. Ch., "Tambovskaia pamiatka ob eserakh," *Izvestiia,* no. 121 (1560), 2 June 1922, p. 1.

111. "Na mestakh: Razgrom antonovskikh band" [The local scene: rout of Antonov's bands], *Izvestiia,* no. 94 (1237), 4 May 1921, p. 2. The despatch relates to the hard but indecisive fighting at the end of April and beginning of May; it grossly exaggerates the Red success. Thus it claims the destruction of the entire main operational staff of the insurrection, only to be refuted by the subsequent course of events. It asserts that the hard-pressed "bandits" threw into the river the records of the staff—without naming the river—an assertion that may or may not reflect the fate of the most important sources from the Green side.

112. Some vague references to these matters in Fomichev (Lidin), "Antonovshchina: Iz vospominanii antonovtsa" (Santiago de Chile, 1955), p. 3.

113. See especially Trifonov, *Klassy i klassovaia bor'ba,* part 1, chapter 5, section 1. Not even Virta's novel is as bad as this hurrah history.

114. Barsukov, "Kommunist-buntar' (Kotovskii)," *Krasnaia Nov',* book 8 (October 1925), p. 214.

115. Zhukov, *Vospominaniia i razmyshleniia,* pp. 64, 66, 67–68.

116. Srechinski, "Zapechatannaia stranitsa," *Novoe Russkoe Slovo,* 28 February 1969.

117. *Put' Bor'by,* vol. 2, *Antonovshchina,* p. 55, as rendered in Trifonov, *Klassy i klassovaia bor'ba,* part 1, p. 257.

118. It is apparent that the novelist has based his account on these figures. See Virta, *Odinochestvo,* p. 298.

119. Trifonov, "Antonovshchina," *Bol'shaia sovetskaia entsiklopediia,* 3rd ed., vol 2, p. 96, col. 276.

120. Still another source of recent date refers to the report of the Soviet command with no mention of wounded nor even of the number of dead and prisoners as given above; it adds the information, however, that about 13,000 deserters and 5,585 "bandits" surrendered voluntarily. See Poliakov, *Perekhod k nepu i sovetskoe krest'ianstvo,* p. 455 and n. 252.

121. Antonov-Ovseenko, "O banditskom dvizhenii v Tambovskoi gubernii," p. 25.

122. For example, in two battles noted for their sanguinary character, 2,614 Russians fell at Kunersdorf (12 August 1759) from an army of 41,000, and 1,734 Unionists at Shiloh (6 April 1862) out of 44,895 who were engaged.

123. See especially Trifonov, *Klassy i klassovaia bor'ba,* part 1, pp. 246–53, where the information is extracted mainly from the Soviet Army Archives. Either the reports from the field, the state of the archives, or the extraction leave a great deal to be desired.

124. Antonov-Ovseenko, "O banditskom dvizhenii v Tambovskoi gubernii," p. 29.

125. See above.

126. G. I. Kotovskii: Dokumenty i materialy, no. 271, p. 348.

127. See Trifonov, Klassy i klassovaia bor'ba, part 1, p. 220; see also above.

128. Antonov-Ovseenko, "O banditskom dvizhenii v Tambovskoi gubernii," p. 28.

129. G. I. Kotovskii: Dokumenty i materialy, no. 284, p. 367. The document is from the army archives and contains the report of Smirnov, chief of the political section, for the period 1–5 August 1921.

130. "Na mestakh: bor'ba s banditizmom," Izvestiia, no. 224 (1367), 7 October 1921, p. 3.

131. See above.

132. Moskvich, "Povstancheskoe dvizhenie (Pis'mo iz Moskvy)," Volia Rossii, no. 264, 27 July 1921, p. 2. The communication is dated Moscow, 8 July. "Moskvich," of course, is an assumed name meaning simply "Muscovite." Could the informant have been Iuri Podbelski?

133. Antonov-Ovseenko, "O banditskom dvizhenii v Tambovskoi gubernii," pp. 27–28.

134. Put' Bor'by, vol. 2, Antonovshchina, p. 55, as reproduced in Trifonov, Klassy i klassovaia bor'ba, part 1, p. 257.

135. Put' Bor'by, vol. 2, Antonovshchina, pp. 17, 36, 55, 105, 114 and passim, as cited in Poliakov, Perekhod k nepu i sovetskoe krest'ianstvo, p. 455. See also Trifonov, Klassy i klassovaia bor'ba, part 1, p. 154.

136. See above.

137. Lenin, "Novaia ekonomicheskaia politika i zadachi politprosvetov," in Polnoe sobranie sochinenii, 5th ed., vol. 44, pp. 166–67. The context of his remarks suggests that Lenin had in mind the Tsarist regime, although technically the previous regime was the short-lived Provisional Government.

138. See above.

139. "Bor'ba s epidemiei" [Efforts to counter the epidemic], Izvestiia, no. 173 (1316), 7 August 1921, p. 2.

140. "Na mestakh," ibid., no. 153 (1296), 15 July 1921, p. 1; "Dvizhenie kholery" [How it goes with cholera], ibid., p. 2; ibid., no. 163 (1306), 27 July 1921, p. 2.

141. Antonov-Ovseenko, "O banditskom dvizhenii v Tambovskoi gubernii," pp. 29, 30.

142. From the report of Smirnov, chief of the political section of the brigade, taken from the Red Army Archives and printed as document no. 284 in G. I. Kotovskii, pp. 366, 367.

143. "Razgrom Tambova" [Destruction of Tambov], Volia Rossii, no. 267, 30 July 1921, p. 1. Red Army men are stated to have refused to fire on the crowd.

144. Antonov-Ovseenko, "O banditskom dvizhenii v Tambovskoi gubernii," p. 29.

145. "V golodnykh mestakh: golod v kirsanovskom uezde" [In the famine-stricken areas: the famine in Kirsanov uezd], Izvestiia, no. 256 (1399), 15 November 1921, p. 1. The despatch refers to "Kaluzino" volost' and Balyklei is likewise

garbled. The number of *volosts* comprised in the estimate of 150,000 victims is given but the figure is blurred beyond recognition.

146. Trifonov, *Klassy i klassovaia bor'ba,* part 1, pp. 120, 192, drawing in part on *Put' Bor'by,* vol. 2, *Antonovshchina,* p. 85, and in part on the party archives; S. E., "Na mestakh: Tambovskie vesti," *Izvestiia,* no. 97 (1536), 4 May 1922, p. 3, where the eating of horses killed by the mange is ascribed to starving peasants in the Stepanov *volost'* of Tambov *uezd*; V. D., "Pis'ma iz Tambova: 'Budem s khlebom,' " *Pravda,* no. 141, 28 June 1922, p. 6.

147. From the article on famine by P. S. Mstislavski in the *Bol'shaia sovetskaia entsiklopediia,* 3rd ed., vol. 7, p. 32, col. 84. This volume of the *Grand Soviet Encyclopedia* was published in 1972.

148. S. E., "Na mestakh: Tambovskie vesti," *Izvestiia,* no. 97 (1536), 4 May 1922, p. 3.

— 12 —

Aftermath of Repression:
Exploitation of the Soviet Victory

The Soviet regime owed its victory only in part to military strength; the New Economic Policy (NEP) had ended whatever chance there may have been for unifying the Green movement and fusing the regional fires into one All-Russian conflagration, while both the NEP and the reappearance of rain in 1922 enabled the long-suffering peasantry to overcome the famine. Lenin's government had maneuvered with skill in extricating itself from a well-nigh impossible situation after having committed the manifold follies that had done so much to create that situation, and good fortune had attended its efforts.

What, then, would the Soviet regime do with its victory? It would abuse it as much as it dared. Hardly had the NEP been inaugurated and the fire of the Tambov, Ukrainian, western Siberian, Kronstadt, and many lesser uprisings been beaten out than its faith-breaking proclivities and the hollowness of its promises became evident.

The new tax in kind under the NEP had been fixed at 5.3 million *puds* of grain in the spring of 1921, when Antonov was still in the field, as against the 11.5 million *puds* supposed to be exacted from the province under the previous food levy for 1920–1921.[1] The alleviation conformed to the generally accepted idea that the food tax was about half the food levy. But already in July 1921 the Food Commissariat, in blind disregard of reality, had classified Tambov once more as a "food-exporting" province[2] and over fifty thousand *puds* of grain were sent by largess of the Soviet government to the starving population of the Volga and Bashkir regions from the starving population of Tambov province.[3] And then in October 1921 a more "precise" determination of what the grain tax should yield caused the figure to be raised from 5.3 million *puds* to 8.5 million, or twenty-nine percent of the gross harvest of grain.[4] Even the original figure was about equal to the amount actually collected under the levy of the previous year, or nearly fifty percent of the assigned quota of 11 million *puds*.[5]

The suspicion may be pardoned that what was involved in hiking the grain tax between spring and fall was not so much precision as calculation that with the insurrection out of the way the Soviet government could do with the peasantry what it willed. It is interesting to note that even in the exceptional year of 1921–1922 the proportion of the crop claimed by the tax in kind—twenty-nine percent—approximated the amount taken by the state under collectivization, which usually is in the range from thirty to forty percent. The replacement of the food levy by the tax in kind in March 1921 represented an alleviation of the burden imposed on the peasantry only in a very relative sense.

The bad faith of the Soviet government in raising the tax in kind after the Greens had been disposed of, and the invincible determination of the Food Commissariat to see in Tambov a food-surplus area, had violated the injunctions of the commissar of repression—the official best able to judge the local situation, whom this study will have revealed as anything but an angel of mercy. Despite an exhibition of ruthlessness that left Lenin no room for complaint, Antonov-Ovseenko had warned the Soviet leader of the ruined state of agriculture in the wake of the insurrection and had pressed upon him the need of a more realistic attitude which would not allow any removal of grain, fodder, or horses from the province and would shift to the center the burden of provisioning the army[6] quartered upon it; the burden of the state tax (presumably the tax in kind is meant) should also be lifted, to be replaced with a local tax of lighter incidence.[7]

Not one of these recommendations was heeded by the Soviet government. As the decision to declare the province food-exporting had been taken—or at least approved—by the Central Committee and by the Council of Labor and Defense,[8] responsibility for disregarding the admonitions of the regime's own representative in the field rests directly upon Lenin who had studied the report and generously underlined many of the points made therein.

The record is not clear as to the reception of the tax in kind in the conquered province. We are told that in Tambov *uezd* the peasants willingly paid the tax[9]—a statement that almost certainly does not accord with reality. One and the same despatch could assert in the first paragraph that all was going well, that everyone agreed the tax would be met on time, in full, and without complications despite the economic disruption stemming from "banditry," while in the next paragraph it conceded a meager intake as yet for the province as a whole and none at all in the northern *uezds* of Spassk, Elatma, and Shatsk—more remiss in this respect than portions of the bandit-ridden *uezd* of Kirsanov.[10] The next day, however, the same newspaper under the same heading announced that more was coming in, with Tambov *uezd* second only to Lipetsk, despite the scars of "banditry."[11] One is tempted to conclude that more came in where maximum coercion could be applied: in the areas blanketed with troops and with Che-ka agents.

On the whole, however, the results must have been discouraging for the authorities, at least for a time. A table ranking the provinces according to the degree of fulfillment of the tax on all produce (standing as of 20 November for grain and of 10 November for other products) reveals Tambov well down in the list with only twenty-five to fifty percent of the tax collected as against docile provinces like Tula, Moscow, Ivanovo-Voznesensk, and Briansk in the category exceeding seventy-five percent.[12] Yet a spokesman for Tambov at the 9th Congress of Soviets would declare only a month later that seventy-five to eighty percent of the food tax had been paid in.[13] Either there had been swift improvement or delegate Tretiakov was lying. So much for contemporary scraps of information.

A source published many years later discloses a surprising degree of resistance to collection of the new tax despite suppression of the uprising. Although eight out of twelve food commissars in the *uezds* had been replaced by men capable of carrying out the official line "by more flexible means," more than a little of former abuses remained and the provincial party committee found it necessary to admonish comrades against approaching peasants with the former attitude of "taking all that was possible"—not, indeed, because of any objection in principle but because such an approach was particularly dangerous in view of the recent past.

On the other hand, the committee sanctioned the formation of shock units consisting of Soviet or party personnel and the village pauperdom in a throwback to the era of committees of the poor. Army units came to the aid of tax collectors when resistance ascribed to kulaks proved especially troublesome or when remnants of the Green bands struck at procurement centers and killed government agents—evidence that sparks from the fire still were glowing. Not for nothing had the Tambov party conference of August 1921 resolved that the campaign to insure collection of the tax must "proceed as in war, in the full sense of the word." Eventually, however, the deed was done, the population tied down hand and foot, the apparatus of tyranny reinstated, and by March 1922 nearly all of the tax is said to have been collected.[14]

The reconstitution of the network of soviets also bears traces of a considerable degree of resistance on the part of the conquered population, although only a blurred picture emerges from the distortion of Soviet sources. Under the Communist system not only was it necessary to uproot the committees of toiling peasants and to replant the soviets, but it was also necessary to insure that the soviets themselves were one-party affairs. Hence the obsequious telegram of greeting sent to Lenin by the 7th soviet congress of Borisoglebsk *uezd*: "We, citizens of Tambov province, having freed ourselves of the Antonov nightmare, pledge ourselves henceforth and forever to stand up firmly for Communist soviets."[15] Not only would they back the soviets, they would back Communist-dominated ones—these people were saying what they had to say. Apparently delegate Tretiakov from Tambov was justified in boasting before the 9th All-Russian Congress of Soviets that in his province "banditry" had virtually been extirpated and only Communists were chosen in reelections to the soviets.[16]

On closer inspection, however, the situation appears in a somewhat different light. Behind the servile Borisoglebsk congress lay a series of local elections that reveal only a very tenuous hold of communism upon an electorate that had experienced no real conversion. Only 50,000 votes were cast in these elections—equivalent at best to about a sixth of the population of the *uezd*. The *volost'* or cantonal soviet executive committees were composed of 44 Communists, 3 candidates (presumably for membership in the

Communist party), and 125 nonpartisans. In the village soviets were 46 Communists and 1,915 nonpartisans. The town soviet, on the other hand, had 50 Communists and 22 nonpartisans.[17]

The claim that only Communists were returned to the soviets is correct only in the sense that no other party secured representation. And for a very definite reason—intimidation—which is also the reason for the tone of the message sent by the *uezd* congress to Lenin. The peasants had been sparing in choosing Communists as members of village soviets. Since they could do nothing else they returned nonpartisans, quite in keeping with the essence of the Green movement. What had happened was that a small, mail-fisted minority had reasserted its sway over the mass by extinguishing any competing minority through the use of superior means of coercion. The sway was already firm in the town, not yet in the villages.

Gradually it became so, however. Already in September 1921 the Council of People's Commissars had removed military units guarding the railroads[18]—firm evidence of pacification—and by spring of 1922 the provincial soviet executive committee decided to disband "as no longer needed at all" the bloody-handed commission to liquidate banditry in Borisoglebsk *uezd*.[19] The regime sought to make the reimposition of its yoke more palatable to the population by affording graphic evidence of its determination to root out abuses in the administration which did not stem from Marxist dogma but merely from human failings.

One example may be cited: a session on circuit of the revolutionary tribunal in Borisoglebsk sentenced nine employees of state mill no. 13 to death by shooting for bribery, theft of flour, and mixing sand with flour.[20] Whether these sentences, if they were carried out, made the population feel any better is not known. By the summer of 1922 all signs of "bandit" activity had disappeared and nothing further ensued to trouble the surface calm in Tambov province.

But until that summer something had remained to trouble the equanimity of the conqueror: A. S. Antonov had not been accounted for. To leave the leader of the Green movement on the loose—or merely to leave a flicker of hope in the heart of his following by failing to establish the fact of his death—accorded ill with the lesson of the past or with Communist designs for the future. So from liquidation of his forces in the field and of the major fragments of those forces, the Soviet authorities turned to tracking down the leader. Without exception Soviet versions of the manhunt accent the enterprise of local Che-ka agents, but in our opinion the implacable pursuit reflects the will of the highest quarters in Moscow, bent on the elimination of peasant leadership with an eye to the time when NEP tactics would have served their purpose and the strategy of collectivization could be resumed.

No firm information is available regarding the movements of Antonov after the debacle in Saratov province in early June 1921 and the return of remnants of his Second Army to the Vorona valley. We have accepted as plausible, though not proven, the version that he had taken refuge in his Golden Cage at Snake Lake and had somehow eluded capture in the combing of this watery fastness.[21] At the latest this operation would carry us into August when he may or may not have sustained a serious injury; but in any event, either at this time or earlier—in July or even in June—he had disappeared from sight like a stone dropped into water.

Among the people and in official quarters speculation was rife as to what had happened: some believed that he had perished by drowning or gunfire in the marshlands bordering the Vorona, while others held that he was still alive but no longer in Tambov province, having fled to some other part of the country or even made his way abroad. After all, as supreme commander he had ready access to gold and documents at staff headquarters and he was supposed to have many connections (in the opinion of this author, he had very few). Nevertheless, the Che-ka did not desist from its search, and success first crowned its efforts in the fall of 1921 when Antonov and his brother returned for rest to his native haunts in Kirsanov *uezd*. But a clumsy approach and failure to reconnoiter adequately spoiled the attempt to trap them, and Antonov vanished as though swallowed up by the earth.

Times had changed since 1919 when he first had taken the field, encountered a reverse, and then holed up for half a year and more to gather strength for a comeback. The Soviet regime no longer was tied down by the first civil war, the NEP had delivered it from the second, the Che-ka had emerged from its fledgling stage and had become a full-blown instrument of tyranny. Antonov faced desperate odds, yet he would be no easy prey; much of his life had been spent in the underground or at penal servitude, and his enemies would never prevail by "approaching him on a she-goat"—such was the tribute the Che-ka paid him. The game was resumed.

Analyzing once more Antonov's past and weighing his actions and habits, particularly his quite extraordinary attachment to his native heath, the men on his trail came to the conclusion that he was still in the province and no further away than the vicinity of the villages of Perevoz and Chernavka in the southern part of Kirsanov *uezd* and Uvarovo at the northern tip of Borisoglebsk *uezd*—all inevitably in the Vorona valley and hardly more than a hundred kilometers east-southeast of Tambov town.

Whether the local Chekists did all this analyzing may be doubted; more likely it was done in Moscow in consultation with local agents, for the presence in Tambov by May 1922—if not before—of Comrade Mosolov as chief of the Political Section[22] argues that a major enterprise was on foot in which the center was directly involved. As an official who had dealt with the Union of Toiling Peasantry (STK) and its uprising in western Siberia, Mosolov was qualified to dig out by the roots the STK in Tambov province and so help in the task of securing the Soviet regime against any recrudescence of the movements in Siberia, Tambov, and Kronstadt that had brought it to its knees in February and March 1921 and forced Lenin for once in his life to defer to the peasant interest.

Nothing is divulged as to how the Che-ka settled on this restricted area in the southeastern part of the province. It lay down the river to the south, at no great distance from the Snake Lake district in Kirsanov *uezd*. Nevertheless, even a modest displacement in habitat was an event in the life of A. S. Antonov. Whatever the reasons for the sleuths' decision, it must have inspired confidence, for the Che-ka–GPU spent the entire winter probing the area.

Then in March–April 1922[23] came the reward for all this effort in the form of quite definite information: Antonov indeed was sitting it out in the vicinity of Uvarovo; he had no intention of going elsewhere but was, in his own words, waiting for a favorable wind to "waft him a match so that everything would go up in flames again."

Adversity had not dampened his spirit. Our Chekist source claims that he and his associates had to arm themselves with "enormous patience" in spreading their net. Knowledge that Antonov had no plans to leave presumably relieved his trackers of any sense of urgency. Moreover, their wish to take him alive must have gravely complicated matters.[24]

Two months or more passed in preparations before finally, on 15 June, the plan was ready. By then all the main facts about Antonov's mode of existence were known and only details remained to be filled in. He had chosen this, his last place of refuge, with accustomed skill. Villages on the black earth tend to be large but the "village" of Uvarovo was enormous, strung out over four or five miles with a population exceeding ten thousand.[25] Around it were forests, hollows, and thickets; to the east the Vorona with its dark, swift-flowing water, on the other side more forest and the modest village of Nizhni or Nizhne (lower) Shibriai (both elements of this place name are spelled freely). It was country where a "whole regiment could be hidden and not soon found."[26]

Antonov and his younger brother secluded themselves during the daytime in the woods along the Vorona and at night came into the village of Nizhni Shibriai to the abode of one or another of his partisans.[27] That he retained a will to fight shows his mettle, for not only was he bereft of a following and reduced to extremity but he was ill—ill with malaria, the attacks of which laid him low and could be surmounted only with Dmitri's assistance.[28] Quinine, of course, was out of the question. Yet he remained as he had been, indomitable in spirit and implacable in his hatred of tyranny.

The hunting party consisted of three GPU men in command and a following of former partisans of Antonov who had surrendered voluntarily or been taken prisoner, had then turned on their movement, and were now displaying their zeal in "atoning" for their "guilt." Several had demonstrated quite exceptional zeal: "Show him to us," they declaimed, "and we will kill him with our bare hands."

For the most part they represented the peasant youth who had been drawn into the insurrection "by deception." Less youthful but much more of a show piece in the hands of his captors was Jacob V. Sanfirov (or Safirov), formerly commander of Antonov's Special

Regiment and now basking in the favor of the GPU as a result of his exploits against one of the last splinters of the Green army, the Utkin band in Lebedian *uezd*. He personally had trailed Utkin with nothing more than an Austrian rifle and three cartridges for a Russian rifle and had brought him down with a shot through the forehead. Now he aspired to be the executor of Soviet vengeance against his comrade-in-arms who had favored him with command of an elite regiment. Only one other of these defectors is known, a man named Yartsevo, who came out of Matiukhin's band.[29] Two more are said to have served under "Grach"[30] but they are not identified.

These Greens-turned-Red were called up by telegram or courier and sent on horseback under a GPU agent named M. Pokaliukhin (or Pokoliukhin) to reconnoiter the village of Nizhni Shibriai and gather down-to-the-minute details on the quarry.[31]

When Sergius Polin of the Tambov GPU and Comrade Benkovski, the commissar in charge of operations and a member of the Tambov political bureau of the Communist party since 1918, drove out from Tambov to Uvarovo on 22 June they found things generally in satisfactory condition. There was, however, one spot of tar in the barrel of honey: Polin was put out to learn that Pokaliukhin had not succeeded in concealing his identity—in Uvarovo it was already known that he was from the GPU.[32] Soon it must also be known in Nizhni Shibriai.

The discovery quickened the pace of events and led to a change of plans. Hitherto Antonov was to have been taken alive, probably for the purpose of a show trial and execution that would have depressed still further the spirit of resistance in the countryside; now the trap had to be sprung quickly—without time for maneuvering to capture him—for in a day or two he would learn what was up and would decamp, shooting agents within reach like chickens as he went.[33] Defamed as he was in Communist circles, deserted and wracked with disease, this man still inspired respect.

On Friday, 23 June 1922, A. S. Antonov had come out of the forest with his brother Dmitri to spend the night at the home of Natalia Katasanova,[34] a peasant woman who lived alone on the edge of the village of Nizhni Shibriai. As best we can tell, her place was once removed from the forest owing to the intrusion of a miller's dwelling with surrounding yard, garden, or potato patch which was separated from her property by a lattice fence. Antonov was not feeling well, the fever gripped him, and he decided not only to pass the night in Katasanova's cottage but to stay there through the next day, taking advantage of the better care a woman can provide and postponing his return to the forest until nightfall. He and his brother were well-armed with two automatic Mausers, two pouches full of shells for each, two Brownings, and one revolver.

Already on 24 June all this had become known to the trappers—it would be interesting to learn how—and the decision was taken to go into action without further delay. The afternoon passed in assembling the hunting party and disguising it in the shabbiest of clothing—presumably not a hard task at the time—to simulate workmen and more particularly carpenters: three carbines were concealed in sacks under the guise of saws, pistols were hidden under blouses, and roles and positions were assigned. The GPU men and their collaborators would not enter Katasanova's cottage; they would surround it, take the Antonovs by surprise and shoot them down, minimizing the danger to themselves.

Toward evening the band of eight or nine men moved through the village, five or so former partisans of Antonov under the leadership of Pokaliukhin, Benkovski, and—less certainly—Polin.[35] Nothing impeded their progress, and toward eight o'clock they had reached their destination and taken up operational positions.

The house was surrounded and all exits covered before the Antonovs grew aware of the danger; even then they did not open fire, thinking perhaps that somehow it was not for them since the encirclement came like thunder from a clear sky. Only when Antonov tried to go out the door and was driven back by bullets did shooting begin that would last for more than an hour according to one account, and for two hours according to another. As a two-hour fusillade would bring us to ten o'clock in the evening there would be no light to fire by, even on one of the longest days of the year; better it is to hold with *Pravda* and say the shooting was "prolonged."

The brothers resisted desperately, maintaining a heavy fire. A stalemate developed with the besiegers unable to close in and the Antonovs unable to get away. The wonder is that in all this shooting no one was hit. Benkovski had it worst, lying behind a pile of manure which was a repeated target with consequent spattering of his eyes and face. As the only hope for the brothers lay in holding out till darkness would let them make a break for the forest, and as the besiegers had no large supply of ammunition—having leaned over backwards to avoid suspicion as they marched or rather ambled through the village—a critical impasse arose which they solved by igniting the thatched roof of Katasanova's cottage. It was soon enveloped in flame and smoke; Antonov and his brother were choking when finally they sprang out of a window straight onto the street, forcing Pokaliukhin to take to his heels.

When others came to his aid, the two men ran back into the yard and mounted the lattice fence. Katasanova saw Antonov's head suddenly droop to one side as a bullet smashed his chin and covered his cheek with blood. Already doomed, he nevertheless made it over the fence with his brother's aid and down into the miller's potato patch. Beyond lay the forest but in between stood Yartsevo, turncoat survivor of Matiukhin's band, who fired at point-blank range, killing first Antonov and then his brother.[36]

From the dead leader the slayers took a map of Tambov province, drenched with his blood, a silver watch, a notebook, some pages from an old Populist journal—something like the *Russkoe Bogatstvo*—and a page from the cover of Mordovtsev's[37] works with the "Young Lion's" rhythmic dedication to his brother of a story of the Tambov insurrection that would never be written. No mention of money or of gold that Antonov might have taken from the treasure hidden in the church at Khitrovo. We have here no conclusive evidence, to be sure, but a rather clear indication of Antonov's probity and of the help he must have been getting in the way of food and lodging from sympathizers in foul weather as in fair, despite the attendant danger and despite the all-pervading misery.

The bodies of Antonov and his brother were taken by car to Tambov where an autopsy was performed. In a final effort to besmirch his name it was disclosed that his hands resembled those of a gentleman, not a toiler, and that he had evidently stored things up for a rainy day and had been living well in the midst of privation—as attested by a substantial layer of fat on his body. The authorities carefully established the identity of the corpse by photographs and descriptions in their possession and by witnesses who had known

Antonov, including his former paramour, Maria Driga.[38] The Soviet regime wanted to be very sure than Antonov was dead.

The peasant reaction to Antonov's death merits comment. All accounts agree that the news brought relief and even joy to members of the class whose standard-bearer he had been. Many were so pleased that they crossed themselves. The GPU agent describes the scene on the way to Tambov:

> For the last time the evil genius of the Tambov peasantry was borne across his domain and curses accompanied his corpse from village to village. Happy and satisfied, they smiled and waved after us—these people who had produced and then destroyed him, his former comrades in arms, the toiling peasantry of Tambov province.[39]

They "warmly greeted" the slayers—fawned upon them, in fact, tailing along behind them and "endlessly thanking" them for the deliverance they had wrought. One remembered that the Greens had taken his mare; another, that they had butchered his cow. During the fight the peasants had sounded the tocsin and, though unarmed (the Soviet had seen to that), had cordoned off the area to form a reserve for the execution party.[40]

These attestations of peasant subservience, it is true, are all from the Soviet side. But they accord all too well with human nature to be rejected in this instance. A thousand years of history had taught the peasants to cringe before the Altaian nomads, the Tsars of Muscovy, and now the Communists. Like the flower whose seeds they were wont to chew, they turned their faces to the conqueror's sun—and their backs to the man who had fought and died for them.

But these were not all of the peasants. It simply is not true to say that Antonov no longer had followers in Nizhni Shibriai or in other villages.[41] The precipitous abandonment of the plan to take him alive in favor of striking at once to gun him down in itself proves the presence of sympathizers; in any event the GPU man states explicitly that "his people" (i.e., Antonov's) would soon have ruined the operation as originally conceived, once the identity of Pokaliukhin became known.[42] No doubt there were many peasants who in their hearts still favored the Green cause but who were not minded to sacrifice themselves to no purpose. They remained on the sidelines and certainly did not cheer the slayers. Heroes they were not, but neither were they swine.

With the death of the brothers Antonov the Communists had achieved their purpose of leaving the peasantry a headless mass in the event of future complications, foreordained by the nature of their regime. We cannot name a single leader who got away—not a surprising result in view of the mercilessness of the struggle and of the interior position of Tambov province. Kuznetsov was the most eminent representative of the minority who had voluntarily surrendered—after all, as a colonel in the Imperial army he would have less dedication to the peasant cause. It is one of the many deficiencies of this study that nothing can be said about what happened later to these men who had thrown themselves upon the mercy of a regime that had no mercy; whether the regime honored its promise not to inflict capital punishment upon them, whether—if it did—suspicion fell upon them later at the time of Stalin's assault on the countryside as may easily have been the case, or whether they perished in the *Ezhovshchina*[43] as is even more likely. Certainly they remained marked men to the end of their days, whenever that end may have come.

As for the hard core of leadership—the desperadoes or "head-cutters" in Soviet parlance and the dyed-in-the-wool partisans in ours—it was not a question of elimination but of extermination. Pluzhnikov, chairman of the Union of Toiling Peasantry and civilian head of the insurrection, had been killed or had committed suicide in his forest hideout in July 1921. Tokmakov, Left SR and second only to Antonov in military matters, had in essence been killed in action, though technically he may have died of wounds. Nazarov, Karas, Utkin, Boltnev, and the brothers Santalov had died in battle. Boguslavski and Simakov ("Grach") had survived the destruction of their units only subsequently to be captured and shot.

There is no reason to doubt that the same fate attended Shamov after being arrested in Voronezh and Maria Kosova after being seized in a village,[44] or that the Che-ka executed Ishin and Fedorov-Gorski after ensnaring them and pumping them dry. Matiukhin had been killed in one way or another. And Antonov had survived his movement for a year and then gone down in blazing battle. Of the regimental commanders[45] only Sanfirov flourished— he had betrayed his cause and his comrades.

It is reasonable to conclude that it was the studied though unannounced purpose of the Communist party to get the leaders on the principle that an organism can be compressed into a different mold if it be deprived of a central nervous system. One of the agents summed up the idea quite well when he observed that for the simple followers of "Grach" there was clemency, but for the "Grach" himself only the "highest form of retribution."[46] The director of military operations in the province had every reason to speak with satisfaction in his report to Lenin of the large number of "bandit" leaders who had been destroyed.[47] And two authoritative sources give as the real reason for devising the strategem to which Matiukhin fell victim the elimination, not so much of the band itself, as of its core of leadership.[48]

A technique was being worked out that would later find broad application beyond the nominal borders of the Soviet Union as well as within them; it consisted of drawing the backbone of an organism to reduce it to a jellylike mass or—changing the figure of speech and with reference to the societies of satellite nations—it consisted of removing the hard shell of the nobility (where existent), of the middle class, and of the German settlers (the best farmers and the models of individual enterprise) in order to get to the soft flesh of the native peasantry beneath.

Notes

1. The levy for 1919–1920 had been set at the "inordinately heavy" figure of 27 million *puds* (the words in quotation marks are Antonov-Ovseenko's).

2. Donkov, "Organizatsiia razgroma antonovshchiny," *Voprosy Istorii KPSS*, no. 6 (June 1966), p. 70.

3. *Ocherki istorii tambovskoi organizatsii KPSS*, p. 135. This source, of course, does not make the juxtaposition of starving populations; it merely says that the grain was sent "in spite of the grievous harvest" in Tambov. It is the contemporary Soviet sources that attest starvation there.

4. Donkov, "Organizatsiia razgroma antonovshchiny," *Voprosy Istorii KPSS*, no. 6 (June 1966), pp. 61 n. 15, 69 n. 60. For Soviet duplicity see Virta, *Odinochestvo*, p. 327. A recent Soviet source, much less authoritative than Donkov, starts with 8.5 million *puds* as the original figure and says that it was lowered as a result of local Communist representations, but without saying to what it was lowered; *Ocherki istorii tambovskoi organizatsii KPSS*, p. 135. Preference is accorded to Donkov.

5. Antonov-Ovseenko, "O banditskom dvizhenii v Tambovskoi gubernii," p. 4. The commissar told Lenin that a grain levy of 11 million *puds* for 1920–1921 had been "entirely beyond the ability" of the province to fulfill. His figure is half a million less than Donkov's; the commissar relates the figure of 11,500,000 *puds* to the levy on potatoes.

6. The commissar called it just that—an army.

7. Antonov-Ovseenko, "O banditskom dvizhenii v Tambovskoi gubernii," pp. 30—31.

8. Donkov, "Organizatsiia razgroma antonovshchiny," *Voprosy Istorii KPSS*, no. 6 (June 1966), p. 70.

9. "Bor'ba s golodom: Pomoshch' golodaiushchim: Semena Povolzh'iu" [Fighting the famine: help to the hungry: seeds to the Volga valley], *Izvestiia*, no. 179 (1322), 14 August 1921, p. 1. The purpose may have been propagandistic—to justify sending seed from where things were very bad to where they were even worse.

10. "Bor'ba s golodom: Sbor prodnaloga" [Fighting the famine: collection of the food tax], ibid., no. 186 (1329), 24 August 1921, p. 2.

11. Ibid., no. 187 (1330), 25 August 1921, p. 1.

12. "Bor'ba s golodom," ibid., no. 275 (1418), 7 December 1921, p. 2.

13. "K 9-mu s'ezdu Sovetov: Golos s mest," ibid., no. 289 (1432), 23 December 1921, p. 1.

14. *Ocherki istorii tambovskoi organizatsii KPSS*, pp. 133–35.

15. "Na mestakh," *Izvestiia*, no. 277 (1420), 9 December 1921, p. 2.

16. "K 9-mu s'ezdu Sovetov: Golos s mest," ibid., no. 289 (1432), 23 December 1921, p. 1.

17. "Na mestakh," ibid., no. 279 (1422), 11 December 1921, p. 2.

18. *Volia Rossii*, no. 308, 17 September 1921, p. 2.

19. Zaezzhii, "Tambovskie vesti," under the column "Na mestakh," *Izvestiia*, no. 75 (1514), 2 April 1922, p. 3.

20. "Bor'ba s golodom: Pomoshch' golodaiushchim: za khishcheniia" [The fight against famine: help for the hungry: on account of thievery], ibid., no. 233 (1376), 18 October 1921, p. 1.

21. See above, chapter ten.

22. In February 1922 the Che-ka was changed—without altering its essence—into the State Political Administration or GPU, after the initial letters in Russian. Subsidiary branches were referred to as political sections or departments. We shall call it the GPU or simply the political or secret police.

23. A journalistic source gives the time of the disclosure as the middle of May; see S. E., "Na mestakh: Konets esero-bandita Antonova," *Izvestiia*, no. 145 (1584), 2 July 1922, p. 4. *Pravda* and the sycophant source simply relate it to the spring of 1922.

24. The above information has been drawn from the account of the Chekist or GPU man, Sergius Polin, "Poslednie dni esero-bandita Antonova" [Last days of the SR bandit Antonov], in *Put' Bor'by*, vol. 1, pp. 49–50. The novelist closely follows Polin save for some embroidery of his own; see Virta, *Odinochestvo*, pp. 353 ff.

25. *Rossiia: Polnoe geograficheskoe opisanie* [Russia: a full geographical description] (St. Petersburg, 1899–1914), vol. 2, *Srednerusskaia chernozemnaia oblast'* [The Central Russian black earth region], p. 422.

26. Polin, "Poslednie dni Antonova," in *Put' Bor'by*, vol. 1, p. 51.

27. K. Pavlov, "Poslednii den' Antonova" [Antonov's last day], *Pravda*, no. 148, 6 July 1922, p. 4. This source mentions only a single abode but the GPU man refers twice to houses in the plural.

28. Polin, "Poslednie dni Antonova," in *Put' Bor'by*, vol. 1, p. 52. It is to the credit of the novelist that he also mentions the illness; Virta, *Odinochestvo*, p. 358. Other Soviet sources do not. Long before coming on this information, the author of this study was on the outlook for evidence confirming his surmise that hiding out in a Russian forest, especially in the vicinity of swamps, would inevitably result in contracting malaria. Never in his experience—not even on the Gulf of Mexico—has the author encountered such swarms of large and warlike mosquitoes as in the forests of Russia near Borisov in White Russia, but also on less swampy terrain between Tver and Petersburg. These mosquitoes make up in concentrated vigor and viciousness for the short growing season allotted them by nature.

29. Trifonov, *Klassy i klassovaia bor'ba*, part 1, p. 239, evidently on the authority of M. Pokaliukhin.

30. According to the novelist; see Virta, *Odinochestvo*, p. 357.

31. Polin, "Poslednie dni Antonova," in *Put' Bor'by*, vol. 1, pp. 50–51; S. E., "Konets esero-bandita Antonova," *Izvestiia*, no. 145 (1584), 2 July 1922, p. 4. The

newspaper source is significant in shedding some further light on the motivation of
those who had turned on their leader: their hatred for him as the one "who had
gotten them into it" is attributed to their having felt the effects of "SR treachery on
their hides"—actually there was no betrayal but only the *force majeure* of the victor
which caused them to cast around for a scapegoat. An example of the customary
decomposition of a losing side.

32. The two operatives appear not to have been fond of one another.

33. Polin, "Poslednie dni Antonova," in *Put' Bor'by*, vol. 1, pp. 51–52.

34. First name also given as Maria; last name also given as Katansonova.

35. The chain of command is not at all clear. Several of the sources assert that
Pokaliukhin was in charge, but he was outranked in title and—more important—in
party standing by Benkovski, the commissar of operations and member of the
party's political bureau.

36. The clearest and best-written account is that of the correspondent K.
Pavlov, "Poslednii den' Antonova" under the general heading "Po Sovetskoi
federatsii" [From the Soviet federation], *Pravda*, no. 148, 6 July 1922, p. 4. The
fullest available account is by another correspondent, S. E., "Konets esero-bandita
Antonova" under the general heading "Na mestakh," *Izvestiia*, no. 145 (1584), 2
July 1922, p. 4. The most authoritative accounts are those of the two GPU agents:
Polin, "Poslednie dni esero-bandita Antonova," in *Put' Bor'by*, vol. 1, pp. 52–53
(for the passage immediately referred to), and M. Pokaliukhin, "Po sledam
Antonova," in ibid., vol. 2, *Antonovshchina*, pp. 90–91—an article read in its
entirety by the author but the notes on which were taken from him. Trifonov,
Klassy i klassovaia bor'ba, part 1, p. 239, incorporates something from
Pokaliukhin, including the information that Yartsevo was the actual slayer;
elsewhere the slayer's name is suppressed, presumably to protect him from
vengeance. The novelist in general stays close to the facts but in striving for
dramatic effect he creates the impression that his hero, Sanfirov, finished off the
"bandit" without actually saying so ("shoots" is the verb used, not "kills," and
there is reference to another who also shot); see Virta, *Odinochestvo*, pp. 361–62.

On the end of Antonov, see also shorter press despatches: "Ubiistvo
Antonova" [Murder of Antonov], *Izvestiia*, no. 142 (1581), 29 June 1922, p. 2;
"Ubiistvo izvestnogo bandita Antonova" [Murder of the well-known bandit
Antonov], *Pravda*, no. 142, 29 June 1922, p. 5; "Podrobnosti ubiistva Antonova"
[Details of the murder of Antonov], ibid. Brief mention of the event also in Borisov,
Chernym letom, p. 72; Zybko, *Tambovskaia partiinaia organizatsiia*, p. 38. From
the Green side there is, as usual, nothing—only the comment of a peasant follower
who was not on the scene yet knew that Antonov had shot it out with his pursuers,
but who erred in saying that he committed suicide. This peasant had been
imprisoned with Fomichev (Lidin) at Nikolsk-Ussuriisk in the Far East; see
Fomichev (Lidin), "Antonovshchina: Iz vospominanii antonovtsa" (Santiago de
Chile, 1955), p. 47.

37. D. L. Mordovtsev (1830–1905).

38. S. E., "Konets esero-bandita Antonova," *Izvestiia*, no. 145 (1584), 2 July
1922, p. 4. See also Virta, *Odinochestvo,* p. 362.

39. Polin, "Poslednie dni Antonova," in *Put' Bor'by*, vol. 1, p. 53.

40. S. E., "Konets esero-bandita Antonova," *Izvestiia*, no. 145 (1584), 2 July
1922, p. 4; "Ubiistvo Antonova," ibid., no. 142 (1581), 29 June 1922, p. 2; Pavlov,

"Poslednii den' Antonova," *Pravda*, no. 148, 6 July 1922, p. 4; and the short despatches in ibid., no. 142, 29 June 1922, p. 5. But see also Virta, *Odinochestvo*, p. 361, for peasant apathy—perhaps a novelist's notion but one not devoid of verisimilitude.

41. "Ubiistvo Antonova," *Izvestiia*, no. 142 (1581), 29 June 1922, p. 2; S. E., "Konets esero-bandita Antonova," ibid., no. 145 (1584), 2 July 1922, p. 4.

42. Polin, "Poslednie dni Antonova," *Put' Bor'by*, vol. 1, p. 52. Green survivors had been active in propagating the legend of the leader's invulnerability; see Pavlov, "Poslednii den' Antonova," *Pravda*, no. 148, 6 July 1922, p. 4.

43. The paroxysm of terror under N. I. Ezhov, blood-beast and scapegoat for Joseph Stalin as head of the NKVD (formerly the GPU) September 1936 to December 1938.

44. According to the novel; see Virta, *Odinochestvo*, p. 333.

45. As stated earlier, it has not been possible to reconstruct the layout of regiments and their commanders. Matiukhin and Nazarov commanded regiments 14 (Naru-Tambov) and 16, respectively. Some of the others mentioned here were in all probability also regimental commanders. Boltnev was political commissar of Matiukhin's Naru-Tambov regiment. Virtually no information exists in respect to Popov, Makarov, Mitin, Sidiaikin, not to mention that will-of-the-wisp Averianov. We know these men had importance—they may have led regiments—but we know nothing else. Even in the absence of information, however, there will be contradictions; thus Popov is reported as having been captured and as having perished in operations in the Vorona valley (assuming that it is the same Popov). See "Na mestakh: Bor'ba s banditizmom," *Izvestiia*, no. 177 (1320), 12 August 1921, p. 3, and Trifonov, *Klassy i klassovaia bor'ba*, part 1, p. 255.

46. Somewhere in *Put' Bor'by*, vol. 1 or 2, *Antonovshchina*, name of author and title of article not remembered.

47. Tukhachevski, "Zapiska," p. 2.

48 Document from the Red Army Archive (TsGAKA), reproduced in *Iz istorii Vserossiiskoi Chrezvychainoi Komissii*, no. 343, pp. 467–68; Borisov, *Chernym letom*, p. 28.

— 13 —

Conclusion

It remains to consider the reasons for the failure of the Tambov insurrection and the question whether there had been any possibility of averting its fate.

Opinion is unanimous that recourse to the New Economic Policy dissolved the foundation upon which Antonov, Tokmakov, and Pluzhnikov had reared the structure of insurrection. Speaking for the country as a whole, A. I. Mikoian told the Nizhni Novgorod provincial conference of his party that the shift to the new policy had swiftly justified itself politically by calming the raging peasant sea.[1] And speaking for Tambov in particular, the provincial party secretary, B. Vasiliev, extolled the new policy as having exerted a powerful disintegrating effect upon the Green army from top to bottom, upon the command as well as the rank and file.[2] Likewise in neighboring Voronezh province, the only one from which Antonov derived any significant outside aid, an observer credits the changeover to the NEP with having put the quietus on "banditry."[3]

Moving from the provincial to the subprovincial level, we learn both from the Tambov Communist committee in September 1921 and from the Borisoglebsk committee in October of the powerful influence of the NEP in dissolving peasant support of the Greens.[4] Quite interesting is the testimony of the commissar of repression, who acknowledges the effect of the "change of state policy" but buries it among a number of other factors accounting for the subsidence of the "bandit" threat as though he found it difficult to give it its full due.[5] Possibly he had been one of those Lenin had in mind when he announced that the 10th Party Conference had been called out of turn to convince the comrades that the New Economic Policy must be followed earnestly over a lengthy period of time without further backing and filling.[6] Or Antonov-Ovseenko may simply have found it more congenial to play up measures taken on the local scene rather than handed down from above, since he did urge adherence to the commitments implicit in the new policy, whatever his original stand may have been.[7] The new line toward the peasantry secured recognition in all quarters as the decisive factor undercutting resistance to the regime.

Before accepting the general verdict an historian must take note of two apparently countervailing considerations. One is Tukhachevski's warning of an undercurrent of peasant distrust: "the peasants definitely do not believe in the sincerity of the decree [instituting] the tax in kind." Hence he recommended among other precautionary measures the maintenance of the army of occupation for a full year beyond suppression of the uprising.[8]

The commanding general's opinion weighs at least as heavily as that of the party functionaries mentioned above. It weighs all the more heavily because it is in keeping with what the population had learned about the nature and promises of the Communist regime after three successive food collection campaigns under the old system. The faith-breaking proclivities inherent in this regime would soon manifest themselves, as we have seen,[9] in a steep increase of the new tax, against which both the general and the commissar—both Tukhachevski and Antonov-Ovseenko—had firmly advised.

The second consideration is the overwhelming force arrayed against Antonov by the end of May 1921, precluding any successful resistance on his part whether or not the food levy had been rescinded in favor of the tax in kind. The force was real, and resistance hopeless. A peasant army in parts of one province had no prospects against the concentrated instruments of coercion at the disposal of a Eurasian state.

Actually, however, in a deeper sense, neither consideration contradicts the thesis that the New Economic Policy proved to be the decisive factor in killing the Green movement. Tukhachevski no doubt correctly appraised the peasant mood as one of distrust, but distrust admits of a ray of hope and does not imply total rejection. The ray of hope allayed the feeling of desperation which alone could have sustained the immeasurable suffering entailed by further resistance. The suffering had for some time been unbearable; only now was it consciously so. Thus the New Economic Policy both weakened the spirit of resistance within the existing movement and blocked its extension to other areas.

As for the military consideration, the disparity of strength rested on the assumption that there would be no defections from the Soviet side. The Kronstadt uprising had rudely shaken this assumption. It was the New Economic Policy that restored its viability. In this deeper and broader sense, therefore, the NEP did in truth ruin the Green movement and save the Soviet regime, even as a badly-scared Lenin had thought it would.

The effects of the famine upon the fortunes of the insurrection defy assessment. It has been contended that the famine more than anything else undermined the spirit of resistance and that the influence of the NEP has been exaggerated by viewing it, in effect, as a bribe whereby the government induced the peasantry to discontinue active resistance.[10] This contention rests upon the enervating influence of famine. It has something to be said for it.

But one may argue just the other way, that famine induces desperation and a *va banque* attitude, that a person facing starvation may very well pose the question: why not take a commissar along, since nothing is lost and a certain satisfaction gained? Bad as conditions were, Tambov did not experience the scenes of horror that came to provinces on the Volga such as Samara and Saratov, where the effect could not fail to deaden any spirit of resistance. In Tambov the lesser horror of the famine might conceivably have quickened that spirit but for the offsetting influence of the concessions embodied in the NEP, which assuredly were not accepted at face value but nevertheless left the rural population with a glimmer of hope.

Probably more than the famine though less than the NEP, the pronounced localism of the insurrection contributed to its failure. Specific manifestations of this localism with reference to coordination with Green movements elsewhere will be considered below, in connection with the possibility of a different outcome. Here the phenomenon will merely be noted under the causes of failure.

Already in this study it has been intimated that more than a little truth resided in the question posed by a local Communist as to whether Antonov had ever thought that there might be people beyond Kirsanov *uezd*. For not only had the insurrection been confined to a single province with some spill-over into Voronezh, but it had been localized in respect to Tambov itself. While the sources list five *uezds* as the locale of the insurrection and record—most unsatisfactorily—desultory action elsewhere, as a matter of fact the Green movement engulfed only the three southeastern *uezds* of Kirsanov, Tambov, and Borisoglebsk, with operations extending into Morshansk and Kozlov and some slight action elsewhere. There were twelve *uezds* in the province. The solid base of the insurrection was confined to three of them, two others witnessed a fair amount of activity, another two an occasional flurry, and the remaining five very little or nothing at all (depending on how one evaluates the silence of the sources). Obviously an element of weakness for the uprising on its own home ground. SRs were everywhere, in varying degrees of fortitude and frustration, yet somehow were able to mount a formidable effort in three districts but not in the other nine of what had been regarded as their patrimony without reference to specific districts.

It is a baffling problem the solution to which lies, in our opinion, in the circumstance that while there were SRs everywhere there was only one Antonov and that it was his insurrection and not theirs. It may well be that Antonov was less limited in outlook than his enemies suggest—he had been separated from Kirsanov *uezd* by Siberian exile and his enemies recognize that he was anything but illiterate—yet his organization and his mind-set as to the conduct of operations limited his effort to the three southeastern *uezds*. He was able to impart depth to the movement he headed but no breadth—unfortunately the one is as important as the other to the success of a movement against an established state.

A fourth and final cause for failure of the Green movement in Tambov province, and one for which Antonov cannot be fairly blamed, inhered in the locale of the insurrection rather than in its localism. In the last analysis local enterprise could give birth only to a guerrilla movement, and guerrilla warfare—to have any prospect of success—must have cover. The early part of this study has set forth how little cover the three southeastern *uezds* afforded such a movement. In the total absence of mountains—a conventional recourse of freedom-seeking individuals against an oppressive

state—forests and swamps would have to compensate for inferiority
of armaments. The stand of forest occupied a little over 10.5 percent
of the area of Tambov *uezd*, 7 percent of Kirsanov *uezd*, and 6.5
percent of Borisoglebsk *uezd*.[11] In Morshansk *uezd*, only to some
extent involved in the uprising, 24.5 percent of the area consisted of
woodlands and in Temnikov *uezd*—not at all involved—no less than
49 percent.[12]

What perversity of fate ordained that the greater the degree of
adherence to the Green standard, the smaller the degree of
protection afforded by nature? Was it the concentration of kulaks
out on the cleared-off fields of black earth? Or the absence there of
Finnish aborigines and Tatars nursing grievances from the past that
predisposed them to favor the Soviet in the forested districts of the
north? Or the presence of Antonov himself as the factor governing
popular acceptance of his movement? Nature had blessed the effort
centering in the *Vendée* to overthrow the first French republic;
nature cursed what the Communists, with customary disregard for
historical accuracy, are pleased to call the Tambov *Vendée*, as it
cursed also the related upheavals in the eastern Ukraine and in
western Siberia.

The operations against Antonov himself and his lieutenant,
Matiukhin, graphically illustrate the importance of adequate cover.
Antonov's elaborate and withal ingenuous hideaway known as the
Golden Cage in the Snake Lake district of the Vorona valley availed
little against his pursuers because the forest belt—though dense and
studded with lovely hardwood, broad-leaved trees—was after all
only a few miles in width, whereas Matiukhin, entrenched in the
great forest on the tongue of *podzol* extending down to the vicinity of
Tambov, could bid defiance to his pursuers. Kotovski's brigade
sealed off the exits from the refuge in the Vorona valley, while the
brunt of combing the woods and swamps fell on the luckless trainees
from various military districts; but the task of going after Matiukhin
beckoned to no one, not even to Kotovski's celebrated and
ever-victorious brigade which had to resort to a dirty Soviet
stratagem to eliminate the threat of Matiukhin's presence so near the
provincial capital. As a Communist source observed, there was no
surrounding the Tambov forest, not only because of its much greater
width, we may add, but because it had no end on the northern side.

In our view, the handicap imposed by nature on the Tambov insurrection doomed it more than any other factor excepting only the change of course on the part of the Soviet government embodied in its New Economic Policy, wrested in no good faith from the hands of the cynical and exceedingly frightened man so widely regarded as the repository of all virtue and wisdom of the party he headed. The handicap of nature combined with the localism inherent in Antonov's conduct of the insurrection to deal it a fateful blow; Antonov had to lead the insurrection wherever it could be fomented, but he chose the wrong place from which never to be separated. This localism conferred substantial advantages in respect to organization and knowledge of the terrain of operations; it also converted that terrain into the graveyard of both the leader and the movement.

A final matter for consideration is whether the Tambov uprising could have had a different outcome. Certainly the best—and very possibly the only chance of success would have come with Communist refusal to change course and to discontinue persecution, if not exploitation, of the rural population. The dogmatic rigidity of Communism was very great and only the severest of crises in February and March 1921 could overcome it. A recent commentator has conceded that it required some time for renunciation of the principle of the food levy to gain ground among party leaders, to say nothing of rank-and-file Communists.[13] And Joseph Stalin with full reason would reproach the comrades—and inferentially the departed Lenin as well—at the 13th Party Conference in 1924 for having been dragged at the tail of events with respect to abolition of the food levy: "Were not developments such as Kronstadt and Tambov needed to make us realize the impossibility of going on living under conditions of war communism?"[14] To which the answer can only be yes indeed, and western Siberia, Makhno, and other developments as well.

Had the Communists not bent before the storm they might have broken—first, because the Green movement would probably have spread to areas as yet untouched or only lightly touched by its example, and second, because there might well have occurred further breaks in the armed forces in addition to the spectacular one in the fleet and the lesser but still serious defections in the Red Army such as Sapozhkov's on the Volga in 1920. But the Communists did bend—even if from the long-range point of view it was a case of *reculer pour mieux sauter*[15]—the desperation of the rural population was allayed, and the whip of war communism that had been driving it into the Green ranks no longer swished so viciously, depriving the insurgents of their best means of recruitment. The peasants might think better days were ahead, and they were—for seven or eight years. Had they been better advised or less earthbound, they would have listened to men in the know like Bukharin when he advised the party membership that the seriousness with which the NEP had been undertaken and the length of time it would be in effect did not mean that it would last forever.[16]

In the course of the insurrection there were two occasions when more capable direction might conceivably have produced a less tragic outcome. The first came at the time of the initial outbreak and lasted for about two months—from mid-August to mid-October 1920—long before the concessions under the NEP had matured, with the members of the Communist party still set like stone against rewarding individual effort in agriculture and with the leader himself still in a quandary as to how to reward better agricultural performance without rewarding the kulak—by his own admission the best performer.[17] No danger of an insurrection being undercut at that time from mitigation of food levy extortions. Moreover it was a time of external crisis, with Soviet Russia at war with Pilsudski's Poland and with the Black Baron breaking out of the Crimea onto the mainland of the Black Sea region. Why did not Antonov strike while the iron was hot and, in the first flush of the insurrection, overrun at least the rest of the province and take possession of Tambov and other towns?

There are three reasons for his failure to do so. In the first place, the spontaneous nature of the insurrection—which we have upheld against the Soviet version of a devilish plot—meant that only the core of Antonov's clandestine force was ready for action and even it had no cannon of serious quality. In accordance with Bonaparte's dictum that God is on the side of the heaviest artillery, the Soviet garrison in Tambov had a distinct advantage: it might have little, but Antonov had none.

In the second place, the element of spontaneity admitted of preparations on Antonov's part to take advantage—in the narrow, tactical sense—of trouble when it came; but not in the broad, strategic sense of coordination with other anti-Soviet movements for which a broader base must be conquered and communications developed. Circumstances of seclusion in his hideaway and lack of external contacts enjoined a defensive strategy upon the Green leader until the insurrection, once it broke out, could be organized and brought to bear upon specific objectives; thereafter it might be possible to go over to the offensive unless the enemy had in the meantime substantially added to his strength.

The third reason for the failure is the most important of all: the insurrection did not engulf the province as a whole. By and large it was confined to five of the twelve *uezds* and achieved formidable strength in only three.

Why the deficiency in this respect; why this fateful handicap, imposed from the start and never overcome? In the case of the northern *uezds* untouched or only slightly affected by the anti-Soviet convulsion it may be argued that the poorer soil and ethnic diversity reduced the incidence of Russian kulaks. We have rejected in this study the contention favored by Communists, yet not strictly adhered to even by them, that it was a kulak insurrection. But the presence of all types of peasants in the Green ranks does not preclude the possibility that kulaks may have constituted the backbone of the movement.

They may have sustained it through thick and thin; they may have created its organizational framework. But they did not direct it. Antonov was not a kulak nor even a peasant, and Tokmakov, Boguslavski, Matiukhin, and Pluzhnikov himself—head of the STK—were not kulaks. At most, kulaks formed the predominant element below the command level, though there is no way of proving that they did. It is a tenable assumption that the three southeastern *uezds* in the vanguard of the insurrection—Tambov, Kirsanov, and Borisoglebsk—had many more kulaks on their rich black earth than would be found on the *podzol* of the northern *uezds* where the Green movement was negligible or nonexistent. The connecting *uezd* of Morshansk, partly *podzol* and partly *chernozem*, partly in the insurrection and partly not, would fit perfectly into such a correlation.

No sooner is the correlation born in the mind of the investigator, however, than further research—and reflection—knock it out. What does one do with Kozlov *uezd*, second only to Tambov in population, contiguous to it on the west, equally endowed with black earth, yet much less involved in the insurrection? What does one do with Usman *uezd*, also black earth and even less involved? And above all, what does one do with Lipetsk and Lebedian *uezds*, westernmost of the provincial subdivisions, black earth except for sand or loam in the Voronezh valley, and scarcely mentioned in the literature of this troubled period?

In all four of these districts there is no reason to assume that the number of kulaks, however defined, would have deviated substantially from the number found in Antonov's southeastern stronghold, yet they were engulfed only imperfectly or not at all in this second civil war. It seems surprising that this paradox should have been ignored in the literature of the insurrection until one remembers Communist dogma with its focus on kulak evil.

On one occasion, however, a Communist official came to grips with the problem. Referring to materials from the economic census of 1917 and from a sampling of individuals which he found adequate but we do not, A. G. Schlichter concluded that 21 percent of the Tambov peasantry could be classified as "more or less" kulak on the basis of household possession of six *desiatinas* or more of sown land. It is true that Kirsanov *uezd* with 25 percent and Borisoglebsk with 28 percent exceeded the average. But what does one do with Lipetsk *uezd*, also 28 percent kulak, and with Lebedian's 29 percent, the highest proportion of such peasants in the province? Schlichter himself singled out for contrast the neighboring *uezds* of Kozlov and Tambov, the one the most pliant in respect to the food levy and hitherto the most peaceful, the other the most turbulent—in fact, the hearth of the "bandit" uprising. Yet Kozlov had 23 percent kulaks and Tambov only 18 percent. The chairman of the provincial soviet committee conceded that the cause of the uprising was complex and that other factors besides the kulak component in the population must be studied.[18] But no amount of study would have induced the Communists to recognize as the primary factor the organizing ability of A. S. Antonov and the moral authority he had acquired over the peasantry in the three southeastern *uezds*.

The default in the western districts prevented the encirclement and reduction of the provincial center; the Communists lost everything in the southeast except a few garrisoned points but they held on to the town of Tambov and remained generally in control of the west and north, blunting the initial onset of the uprising and depriving Antonov of a base of operations sufficiently broad to admit of a link-up with Sapozhkov on the Volga and with Makhno in the Ukraine. The fire had been contained and a deadlock created that was not broken until the late spring and early summer of 1921. Imperfect peasant response to the raising of the Green standard thus accounts in large measure for this initial setback that never could be overcome.

Assuming a response that would have blanketed the entire province instead of only the southeastern section, what could Antonov have accomplished on the All-Russian scene? Hostilities between Greens and Reds were in abeyance in the Ukraine as long as Wrangel posed a threat to both; only with his elimination did serious fighting break out when the Red Army encircled Makhno's headquarters at Guliai Pole on 26 November 1920. Thereafter the left-bank Ukraine burned brightly but before then only indirect support would have been feasible.

By all odds the chief diversion of Soviet forces from peasant repression came on 25 April 1920 with the outbreak of war with Poland. Joseph Pilsudski, of course, had not entered the lists to help Russian peasants or any other Russians, but until the suspension of hostilities on 18 October 1920 Antonov had two months of grace before the reservoir of Soviet strength would begin to be replenished against the large withdrawals that had been made for the western front. The Soviet did not regain a free hand in that sector, in fact, until the signing of the Treaty of Riga, 18 March 1921, an event that duly produced a sharp deterioration of Green fortunes in Tambov and everywhere else.

As for the small but strongly-knit White army of Wrangel, there was never any question of cooperation with it but only of parallel action, encumbered by the knowledge that success would entail a change of front and another civil war the outcome of which would depend on who could engage maximum support from a disintegrating Red Army. This difficult and dangerous maneuver would not have come off in any event because the Greens would never have mustered their full strength even for a parallel action with Wrangel, as the above-cited reluctance of Makhno to make front against Moscow while the White army remained in the field and as his unheard-of cruelty toward officers of Denikin's army[19] conclusively demonstrate.

There was one quarter, however, to which Antonov in the early stage of his insurrection might have—and should have—turned for support. Only a month before the spontaneous upsurge in Tambov province a like event had occurred in Buzuluk *uezd* of Samara province. There a Left SR officer in the service of the Soviet, an ex-lieutenant in the Tsar's army by the name of Sapozhkov— himself the son of a better-to-do peasant in this province of many such peasants—had raised the standard of revolt while engaged in recruiting the 2nd Turkestan cavalry division from deserters who evidently were less repentant than they seemed. He had exercised his own judgment more particularly in picking officers from "anarchistic and SR elements," two of whom—Serov and Usov—would carry on after his death. Sapozhkov began the revolt on 14 or 15 July 1920 with a rather well-armed force of twenty-seven hundred soldiers which he proceeded to arm further at the expense of Red Army stores.[20]

The threat to Samara, Saratov, and Ural provinces, once a major granary of the Russian Empire, evoked a vigorous response from the Communists of the Transvolga region and a violent reaction from their leader in Moscow who cast off restraint in "wielding the plenitude of revolutionary power," decreed the taking of hostages from villages along Sapozhkov's line of march, and ordered Soviet authorities to "cut down at the root" not merely any attempt at cooperation but every manifestation of sympathy with the rebels on the part of the local population.[21]

Sapozhkov himself fell in action on 6 September at Lake Bak–Baul after less than two months of severe fighting, but his successor Serov kept life in his movement and continued the struggle despite crushing blows rained on his head by Communist forces. Although the blows may well have been less crushing than the enemy claims, the remarkable powers of recuperation exhibited by this phase of the Green movement enabled Serov as late as January 1922 to stand at the head of three thousand men,[22] more than Sapozhkov had commanded at the outset. Only late in the summer of that year did Serov finally give up, having held the field for more than two years—longer than any other Green leader excepting only Makhno.[23]

There is no reason to assume any connection between the outbreak of Sapozhkov's uprising in mid-July 1920 and Antonov's on 12 August 1920, aside from peasant exasperation and the presence in both cases of brave and determined Left SR leaders. It may be doubted that Antonov even heard of Sapozhkov's action, much less conceived of any plan of collaboration. A simultaneous blow with the Polish–Soviet war going on and Wrangel back on the mainland, even if that meant no help from Makhno, would have created a very serious situation for the rulers in Moscow, but the idea of coordination from abroad by the White Guard and the capitalist international belongs to the tissue of lies which the Communists have woven about the Green movement.

The spacing of the two insurrections and the failure to develop any kind of mutual assistance—not only during the few weeks between the unfurling of Antonov's banner and Sapozhkov's death in battle but also during the lengthy period of Serov's activity—are further evidence of the spontaneity of the uprisings, while the lack of liaison with Serov is a reflection upon Antonov's leadership. For ties with Sapozhkov and Serov were worth cultivating. The movement they headed lasted twice as long as Antonov's, the resilience it displayed was remarkable, betokening genuine popular support; while it never attained the organization or numerical strength of Antonov's effort, it had the loose support of other bands in the Volga region that in the aggregate approached the size of Antonov's army if they did not equal it.

Two features of the Green movement east of the Volga deserve note by way of contrast with its fortunes in Tambov province. Lack of adequate cover in the areas of maximum strength had hurt the Tambov insurrection, particularly in the later stages when the avalanche descended, whereas the Greens beyond the Volga held out much longer without any cover at all. Is there a contradiction here, or only a paradox that needs to be explained? For one thing, the Transvolga region was not destitute of cover, only it was cover of a different sort. Reeds had grown up around and in the infrequent lakes and especially along the course of the Ural river, affording shelter for hard-pressed "bandits" to the chagrin of their Communist pursuers. Even more important, the vast, arid steppes provided space—if not cover—for guerrillas to disperse and recombine almost at will since bases for pursuit were few and far between, railway lines nothing to compare with Tambov, and Soviet reconnaissance flights still in their infancy.

The second feature concerns the ethnic make-up of the Green bands, in Tambov all but exclusively drawn from the descendants of Great Russian settlers with no appeal to Mordvins and Tatars in the northern *uezds*, yet consisting in part of Altaian elements east of the Volga. At least Serov's band is said to have been composed almost wholly of Tatars and Kirghiz, true hawks of the steppe, with whom he ranged from the Volga to the Sea of Aral and from the shores of the Caspian to the Irgiz river in northwestern Turkestan.[24] The point in Serov's fortunes to which the assertion refers is not clear, whether it is a case of the band at its height or of the hard core at the end. On the other hand, two Tatar regiments of the Red Army—the 202nd and 204th—distinguished themselves in decimating the original force under Sapozhkov.[25] All sides may make too much of ethnic differences, for the most plausible conclusion is that the native peoples, like the Russians themselves, were divided in this second civil war.

Fault must be found with Antonov, if not for failing to link up with Sapozhkov—for which there was hardly enough time—then certainly for making no effort in the succeeding months to conduct joint operations with Serov and other Green leaders of the Volga region. They could have taught him something—for example, how to take a town. Never once did Antonov seize a town in his native province whereas the Volga bands occupied a number of them, at least for a short time: Kamyshin and Khvalynsk on the Volga, the former an important railhead; Novouzensk in southern Samara province, and Gurev at the mouth of the Ural river. Was it a question of exaggerated localism, of a preoccupation with immediate problems to the exclusion of broader objectives? Or was it the shortfall of the insurrection; its inability to encompass more territory, including the whole western and northern parts of its home province, the important towns of Kirsanov and Borisoglebsk in its own southeastern bastion, and above all the nerve-center of the province, the town of Tambov?

Was it, in other words, primarily the fault of the leader or of the class he sought to lead? More probably the latter. Unable to possess himself of such immediate objectives as these three towns, Antonov seems never to have raised his sights in order to develop a broader strategy. And so the opportunity to overrun the Soviet vantage points in the first flush of the uprising while the powerful diversionary influence of the Polish war was being felt came and went unutilized, primarily as a result of peasant apathy in half the province. For success in the southeast must never blind us to the failure of the uprising elsewhere in the province.

The other occasion on which the Green cause might have prevailed, at least regionally, came with the crisis of February–March 1921, a crisis so severe as to force the Soviet government into partial capitulation. The main elements of the crisis have been related; they will bear repetition.

In late January–early February western Siberia went up in flames. On 13 February the Armenian nationalists rose in fury and within five days had seized the capital city of Erevan. On 28 February sailors of the Baltic Fleet at Kronstadt threw off the Communist yoke. All three of these revolts assumed from the outset a formidable character. The one in western Siberia interrupted for three weeks rail communications between the centers of Soviet power and what had now become the chief granary of the country, throwing the regime into dependence on the North Caucasus, itself the scene of vigorous Green action with lines of communication running through Tambov and so making Antonov's movement all the more intolerable. The enterprise of the Armenian nationalists might unhinge the whole situation in the Transcaucasus. The adherence of the Baltic Fleet to the Green movement shook the citadel of tyranny.

And all this against a background of major operations on the left-bank Ukraine and elsewhere against Makhno, on the right bank against Petliura, in the Great Russian heartland against Antonov, on the Volga against a dozen bands, with disturbed conditions everywhere and the armistice with Poland not yet definitively converted into a treaty of peace. No wonder it would be the one occasion in history when the Communists would abate their fanaticism for industrialization and bridle their hatred of an independent peasantry.

For Antonov it was the opportunity to break out of the bloody stalemate that had developed in Tambov by linking up with an outside force, since apparently the limit of expansion had been reached in his home province. His best chance lay to the east, in the direction of the Volga. There the spring of 1921 witnessed the climax of "bandit" activity. A Red Army estimate for April places the Green strength at eleven thousand bayonets and sabers distributed among a dozen bands.[26]

It may have been even more in March. On the 19th of that month the authorities in Saratov province—Martynov as commander of the armed forces, Fedor Ivanov as head of the soviet executive committee, and Smidovich as chairman of the secret police—sent a telegram of desperation to Lenin as head of the government, to Trotski as head of the war department, and to the Central Committee of the Communist party, warning them that "banditry" had gotten out of hand in the province after two and one-half months of futile effort against it and that, in the absence of peremptory and decisive measures from the center, all of Saratov province was going to be lost.[27] All Communist party members and most of the Komsomol (Communist Youth) had been mobilized into the ChON (Units of Special Assignment). It was a crisis of the first magnitude.

The band that gave the most concern was not Serov's, Sapozhkov's successor in the region beyond the Volga, but one that had been formed in December 1920 when a battalion commander of the Red Army by the name of Vakulin had revolted at Mikhailovka in the extreme northern portion of the Don Cossack territory. Though only some hundred miles from Tambov province, this potential accretion of strength was denied to Antonov, for Vakulin had gravitated eastward toward the Volga instead of northward toward the Vorona and had seized Kamyshin between Saratov and Tsaritsyn (Stalingrad, Volgograd) on 5 February 1921. It would be interesting to know why he chose the one line of march and not the other.

Forced out of Kamyshin, Vakulin crossed the Volga and continued eastward into the Ural region. He was now credited by the enemy with having thirty-two hundred men under his command, more than six times as many as in the beginning, so that he had hit pay dirt. He succeeded in taking prisoner a composite Red Army force of eight hundred men. But on 17 February he lost a battle and his life, his command devolving on a Don Cossack, F. Popov, who is also stated to have been an SR (revolutionary Cossacks were by no means rare).

The Popov band moved back into Samara and then into Saratov provinces, bearing to the north and picking up strength as it went until on 17 March 1921 it scored a signal success by capturing Khvalynsk on the Volga, about halfway between the cities of Saratov and Samara. After taking Khvalynsk Popov stood at the head of quite a respectable force, estimated by the Red Army to number six thousand men. It was not enough to hold the outpost on the Volga but sufficed to force its way westward into Petrovsk and Serdobsk *uezds* and to capture an entire battalion of Red Army men. The band had marched up and down and across and back over Saratov and had terrorized nearly all sections of the province. Its feat of 17 March may well have prompted the above-mentioned telegram of desperation two days later. At the end of March the Popov band in conjunction with Serov and another Green leader is said to have contemplated an attack on the city of Saratov.[28]

It might better have been contemplating a march into Tambov and a pooling of resources with Antonov. The exact location of Popov's command in the Petrovsk–Serdobsk area at that time is not known but it was probably somewhere between fifty and a hundred miles of Kirsanov *uezd*. A determined attempt to effect a junction, particularly a combined effort, might well have overwhelmed or squeezed out any Soviet force in between and have ended in success. Antonov would be driven into this same area at the beginning of June, there to meet disaster since no force was awaiting him and Uborevich's armored command was hot on his heels. Quite different had been the situation in March when Antonov without reinforcements enjoyed a standoff, and with reinforcements of six thousand men might have been able to break the deadlock and to gain a decisive advantage in his home province, although too late to bring about a diversion from Kronstadt and with bleak prospect of achieving a victory of broader scope. Nevertheless the effort should have been made—and sooner—to help the Baltic sailors, no matter what the odds may have been and they seem to have been less than insuperable.

Fear existed in Saratov province precisely in regard to a union between Antonov and Popov or other Green leaders, although the Red Army command does not seem to have taken the danger seriously.[29] Since by its own admission, however, the Saratov soviet had succumbed to panic and starvation reigned in the villages, the ability of the authorities to cope with a still graver crisis may be doubted. The moral effect of a union of Green forces accompanied by a serious military reverse for the Reds could conceivably have shaken down the regime in both provinces.

Who bears the responsibility for losing the opportunity we do not know, whether Antonov or the Green leaders further east or all of them together. So favorable a conjuncture would not recur. The Popov band, if we are to believe the Soviet claim, soon was crushed out of existence, but such tub-thumping hurrah history should most likely be set aside in favor of an assumption that it merely ceased to pose a serious menace. Substantial or even heavy reinforcements were sent to Red troops on the Volga including the 27th Omsk rifle division from before Kronstadt, so that the defeat there contributed to Green reverses elsewhere. From all accounts "banditry" in the region waned after the spring of 1921, yet it revived early in 1922 under Serov as the main leader and was not finally extinguished until the end of the summer, having survived the Tambov insurrection by one full year.[30] There had been plenty of activity to the east of Tambov—in the very next province as well as beyond—with which Antonov ought to have been able to forge a link. That he did not remains one of the mysteries of the movement he headed.

Another possible move on Antonov's part to take advantage of the February–March crisis by developing mutual assistance with Green bands elsewhere, and especially by devising a broader strategy, would have been to turn to the south or the southwest. The Vakulin revolt in December 1920 revealed the residue of hostility to the new order that made the Don Cossack region a permanent recruiting ground for anti-Soviet activity. Yet the services of Cossacks to reaction in the past by no means implied their willingness to adhere in large numbers to an offshoot of the revolution employing guerrilla tactics. The Cossacks with landhold-ings that set them apart from ordinary peasants—or with the memory of these privileges—were as little likely to throw in with a peasant movement as they were to adopt tactics so much at variance with their own orthodox military training which would have rendered them easy victims of the powerful conventional forces left over from the first civil war and the Polish war under the command of M. V. Frunze in the southern military district. In general Cossackdom had spent itself in the first civil war and was not minded to become a primary factor in the second.

Quite different was the spirit of the Ukrainian peasantry, unbroken by the repeated ravaging of the first civil war and committed surreptitiously if not openly to the support of the class and national hero, Nestor Makhno. Not the best organizer yet the most resourceful of all the Green leaders, Makhno's strength cannot be gauged from the numbers under his command at any given time since they swelled and contracted like a sponge according to circumstances. Frunze is said to have estimated his total strength at from ten to fifteen thousand in December of 1920[31] after the resumption of hostilities, and certainly credited him with some seven thousand men and eight cannon in mid-December after Makhno had broken through three lines of encirclement in one of his customary feats of self-deliverance. Frunze then has this modest force "destroyed" in a fierce battle with the fourth cordon fencing it in,[32] but the "destroyed" band was presently as destructive as ever, deranging the entire machinery of the food levy program in three *uezds* of Ekaterinoslav and Kherson provinces and engaging in mass slaughter of its personnel.

In one single district Makhno massacred the food commissar, the members of the food committee, and forty-two of the field workers. Under such conditions, said M. Vladimirov, commissar of provisioning, the Red Army and the Donets Basin would have little to eat.[33] It was so bad that, in an action that must have been unique in Communist annals, the central committee of the Ukrainian Communist party, far from regretting the abandonment of the food levy, opposed even the institution of the food tax within its jurisdiction.[34]

Lenin passed Vladimirov's message to Trotski with the observation that interesting things were happening. His own reaction is of interest. He felt the Ukrainian Communists to be wrong, of course.

"The conclusion to be drawn from the facts is not against the tax but in favor of intensification of military measures for the complete annihilation [*sic*] of Makhno and others like him."[35] A standard reaction on his part to a peasant problem.

But Makhno's annihilation, complete or otherwise, was no simple matter. For nine consecutive months the brave and nimble leader, worthy successor to a long line of freedom fighters on behalf of Europe's most luckless population, kept off balance the whole vast, lumbering machinery of repression in an epic of unequal struggle. He fairly ran circles around Frunze and tied the Red Army in knots.

Lenin expressed his disgust to Sklianski, saying that the military command had fallen down shamefully in the performance of duty by letting Makhno escape despite the "enormous superiority" of the forces arrayed against him. What about all the cavalry, the armored trains and cars, the airplanes—how were they being used? Were the armored trains being handled right or were they aimlessly coursing up and down, consuming grain? Broadening his indictment to include other bands he complained that grain, fuel, everything was being wasted because of their depredations while "we have an army of one million men."[36]

Makhno was unbelievably mobile. In a few weeks he ranged through five provinces, whereas Antonov operated for a whole year in a third of one province except for infrequent forays just across the border into two others. Makhno and his men had in truth become nomads,[37] yet nomads of a special kind, for they had only to pass through an area to attract new strength—so strong was the sympathy for them in the matrix from which they came and so dispirited the pursuit of the foe.[38] The five provinces through which he passed in so short a time early in 1921 were Kiev, Poltava, Kharkov, Kursk, and Voronezh. The last two are the most interesting because they were predominantly Great Russian and lay close to Tambov. We know from the Soviet Army Archives that Makhno moved through the Belgorod district,[39] but we know from a foreign source that he penetrated much further into Kursk province than this south-ernmost *uezd*.

In February 1921 the Grand Embassy of the Grand National Assembly of the Turkish liberation movement headed by Mustapha Kemal Pasha proceeded to Moscow by rail from Baku through

Rostov-on-Don, Kharkov, Kursk, Orel, and Tula. Because of special conditions the journey required eleven days, and one of these special conditions was Nestor Makhno. At Rostov the Soviet government put on a machine gun crew in view of the inadequacy of the small Turkish guard of eight men; in addition, from the North Caucasus onward an armored train preceded the passenger train bearing the embassy. It will be noted that both measures were taken on entering Makhno territory. The need for them soon became apparent.

At a station north of Kursk, the name of which the Turkish general could not remember, the armored train went on ahead by itself to the next station; when the passenger train sought to follow, it suddenly came to a stop and the Turkish dignitaries were informed that the track on beyond might have been torn up by a strong Green band. The locomotive was uncoupled to feel out the way, the members of the embassy put their baggage up against the windows to act as a shield, and the Russian machine gun crew with the small Turkish guard took up battle stations. After a while the locomotive came back, having found things in order, and the journey was resumed. The Turks later learned that it was Makhno's band which had placed them in jeopardy. The proximity of the armored train had probably deterred it from raiding the mission and its escort.[40]

For the members of the Grand Embassy it must have been an exciting experience—and for the Soviet government a humiliating one to have foreign guests considered to be quite important endangered by a "bandit" on one of the main railroad lines of the country. The incident took place *Kursk'dan sonra* (beyond Kursk),[41] so that Makhno was in the northern part of the province, off of Ukrainian soil and onto Great Russian some one hundred fifty miles due west of Usman *uezd* in Tambov province. Makhno could just as well have been there had there been any reason to be. For if Antonov would not come to Makhno, Makhno could have come to Antonov. If he could operate so boldly along the trunk line Kharkov–Kursk–Orel–Tula–Moscow there is little doubt he could have made it into Tambov, all the more so since he would in any event soon be in at least the Valuiki *uezd* of Voronezh province.

That there was no junction of the two forces—nor even, so far as we can tell, any attempted junction—must be set down to Antonov's conspicuous failure to coordinate with other Green units. Seemingly he sat there in his bailiwick waiting for the Soviet anaconda to envelop him and crush him to death. His default in this respect is all the more remarkable in that Makhno appears to have made an effort to link up with Green bands in Voronezh, the only outside area with which Antonov maintained ties of any consequence. Moving back into the eastern Ukraine, in early March 1921 Makhno detached from his reinforced "army" Parkhomenko's command and sent it off to the Voronezh area. To our misfortune he does not say for what purpose, but it must have been to establish contact with the Green bands in that province—with Kolesnikov's and the others.

But Makhno did even more. He formed at the same time an independent band under Brova and Maslak for operations in the Don and Kuban regions.[42] And Makhno relates how he himself, when the famine compelled dispersal of his own command, campaigned as far as the Volga and made the rounds of the Don meeting everywhere with like-minded bands and linking them with one another.[43] In short, he was doing precisely what Antonov ought to have been doing.

It seems strange that the Ukrainian leader should not have turned to the best organized peasant uprising in the European part of Great Russia. Did the ethnic difference act as a barrier to collaboration? Or did Makhno make the effort and meet with no success? There is virtually nothing to go on.

Trotski had in his possession a document from the bureau of foreign relations of the Ukrainian nationalist movement headed by Simon Petliura which asserted that Makhno, in his search for allies, had applied to the Don but had found no anti-Bolshevik strength of consequence, had moved into Kursk without evoking sympathy from the population, and had besought support from the east—from Antonov—also without success.[44] And that is all. There is not even that much from the other side. One of the most reliable Soviet sources relates that at the meeting in the peasant's house preceding the destruction of his band Matiukhin had regretted the absence of a representative of Makhno, whereupon the obliging Kotovski had provided him with one in the person of Kotovski's own subordinate, Garri.[45] But by then it was too late—the Tambov uprising lay in shambles.

Antonov and Makhno would have had to concert action in February or at the beginning of March to take advantage of and—even more imperative—to save the western Siberian and Kronstadt insurrections. It was their second and better and last opportunity to avert destruction, perhaps even to gain victory. And it passed unutilized. The opening to the east, linking up with Popov and other bands in Saratov province, appears to have been more problematical; but there was more than a possibility, there was a probability that Makhno and Antonov could have come together.

Leaving aside for a moment the question of what they could have accomplished had they joined forces, it is necessary to say that the fault lay with the sedentary Green leader in Tambov instead of with the free-ranging Green leader from the Ukraine. We have pointed out, to be sure, the extreme mobility of the Tambov Greens within the narrow confines of their stronghold; outside that stronghold, however, they rarely ventured and then only to return as soon as possible. Makhno, on the other hand, possessed a remarkable and even a phenomenal ability to cut loose from his moorings and to campaign over broad distances without any marked diminution of effectiveness on his part or of discomfort for his foe. The explanation of the difference between the two Green movements in this respect will be disclosed below.

In extenuation of this worst mistake of his career, it can only be said that Antonov could not have seen things as clearly as we do now. Locked into his corner of Tambov province by Soviet power as well as by his own inclination, with all means of communication in any broader sense controlled by the enemy, he may well not have realized the uniqueness of his opportunity nor the gravity of the situation confronting the Soviet government. Very likely only an imperfect reflection of events at Kronstadt or in western Siberia got through to him. After all, Petersburg is only a few miles from Kronstadt and the Soviet government, already furiously cultivating the art of withholding the truth from its subjects, so stifled the flow of information even there that the void was filled with monstrous rumors which Trotski thought to dispel by applying to Lenin for permission to say to the Soviet public what he had said two days before—in an interview with foreign press representatives—to the American and British publics.[46]

It is true, on the other hand, that ties existed between Tambov and the fleet. Peasant youths drafted into the fleet from many provinces, including Tambov, had brought peasant discontent to Kronstadt.[47] Sooner or later Antonov would know the truth but the inevitable time lag must not be left out of consideration. Some of the Kronstadt sailors must have gotten through to him, for months later there is record of an engagement on 1 July between Kotovski's cavalry and a small but elite band of Green commanders, SR political workers, and sailors who fought with "striking steadfastness"—the Chekist's tribute to them—until the bitter end, when the few survivors shot their horses and committed suicide.[48] But how, and especially when the news of Kronstadt reached Antonov is not known. The most concrete evidence of a connection between Tambov and Kronstadt was the presence in the village church at Khitrovo, along with the Left SR banner and treasure, of the Kronstadt resolutions.[49] It would be interesting to learn when and by what means they reached Antonov.[50]

If, as may be conjectured, knowledge of Kronstadt came late to Tambov's insurrectionary army, information about western Siberia must have filtered through in still more imperfect and opaque form. It was the penalty peasant fighters have always had to pay because of their restricted vision, geographical dispersion, and relative isolation. But when every allowance has been made for these extenuating circumstances, Antonov cannot be absolved of blame for failure to coordinate the Tambov and Ukrainian Green movements after three full months of fierce and simultaneous hostilities against the Soviet order, to say nothing of previous clandestine possibilities. Even had he been unable—or, more aptly, unwilling—to undertake one campaign away from his anchored position, his prospective confederate Makhno—who had conducted operations from Galicia on the west to the Volga on the east and from the Black Sea coast to Kursk and Chernigov in the north—could have burst into Tambov province had there been any magnet pulling him there. The question then arises, what could the two Green leaders—having effected a junction—have been expected to accomplish?

On the one hand, the lightness of their armaments must be considered; on the other hand, the ability to strike hard and fast—which no one would deny them. They could have altered the balance of forces, broken the deadlock, and taken possession of all or most of Tambov province; thereafter they conceivably could have reclaimed Voronezh province and so thrown a bridge to the Ukraine. Above all, they could without doubt have cut the three southeastern rail lines running through Tambov and linking Saratov, Kamyshin, and Tsaritsyn on the Volga with the wheatfields of the north Caucasus, now the chief granary of Russia since western Siberia had gone up in flames. Nothing could have been better calculated to produce pain in Moscow and a violent reaction from Lenin, with the consequence that had the action come during the three-week interruption of rail communications with Siberia it might even have lifted pressure from Kronstadt and enabled the sailors to hold out longer.

It seems unlikely that Antonov and Makhno could have accomplished anything more unless further defections had occurred in the Soviet armed forces. For them to take place the Communists would have had to persevere in the fanaticism of the food levy program, alleviating in no manner the condition of the peasantry. Approached from this angle as from any other, an appraisal of the situation can lead only to the conclusion that the New Economic Policy saved the Soviet regime.

It had barely escaped with its life as it was. The armed forces had been badly shaken: Sapozhkov had risen on the Volga (July 1920), Vakulin on the Don (December 1920), and Maslak or Maslakov on the left-bank Ukraine (February 1921). The first officer commanded a division, the second a battalion, and the third a brigade. Maslak's revolt and successful junction with Makhno's lieutenant, Brova, meant that the Green movement had reached into the celebrated 1st cavalry army led by Simon Budenny which had been brought into Ekaterinoslav province early in 1921 to run Makhno's bands to earth.[51] The Red Cossack commander with the handlebar moustache, destined to become thrice a hero of the Soviet Union, did not fare so well in this campaign; Makhno loathed him as a "base coward" and made him turn tail on one occasion,[52] while Voroshilov found that continuous pursuit of the light-footed Ukrainian leader (it was not exactly continuous) disorganized and demoralized the 1st cavalry army.[53] Budenny or his commissars, however, managed to prevent any further defections. The main break in the armed forces came, of course, at the end of February with the blow-up in the Baltic fleet.

Since the working class was not insulated from the mood of the sailors and peasants, it is not surprising that Lenin should have confessed (of course, in the bosom of the party), "We are barely holding on."[54] He also acknowledged that the defeat sustained in the spring of 1921, necessitating a "retreat in disorder" from the direct Communist approach to industrialization embodied in the food levy, had been far more serious and dangerous than any sustained in the first civil war.[55]

One concrete and graphic example can be given of how tight things were in Moscow in mid-February 1921, in the midst of the crisis that produced the NEP. Although Lenin, of course, favored subversion of Georgian independence, he resolved that the Central Committee would not allot a single train or even a single car to the 11th Soviet army in the Transcaucasus for support of the Communist take-over in that country, so bad was the food pinch during the period of severance of communications with Siberia.[56] Even after the acute crisis had been allayed, Lenin in his inimitable language, mixing Greek with German while writing in Russian, would describe the position of the Soviet government as *archischwach* (extremely weak).[57]

In the mythology of Communism the Green movement appears only as a further stage in the continuing civil war between Reds and Whites, as a kind of tail that continued to thrash after the back of the counterrevolutionary dragon had been broken. When the White Guard departed the scene, the kulak came on and conducted essentially the same struggle in different guise. But the kulak was not a free agent, only a cat's-paw of the SRs, even as the SRs themselves responded to the will of world-wide capitalist imperialism. All originality and independence of action are denied the Green movement by integrating it into the civil war between Communism and the White Guard as a kind of subhead to the latter.

Iuri Steklov helped evolve this mythology[58] and it received authoritative expression when A. I. Mikoyan, secretary of the southeastern bureau of the Central Committee of the Russian

Communist party, claimed that the latter part of 1922 had witnessed the pacification of the country as a result of the extinction of "political banditry—that appendage and continuation of the civil war against counterrevolution."[59] Of course, all of this is an elaboration of the Marxist–Leninist principle that there is no third force, that the peasantry can never lead itself but is fated to be dominated either by capitalists or by the proletariat.[60] Soviet historians still write in this vein.[61]

The underlying principle has only too much truth in it if it is stripped of its hypocrisy and if "vanguard of the proletariat" is substituted for "proletariat." But the superstructure of mythology should be swept away, for the Green movement was a genuine third force, only not a successful one. Lack of success does not invalidate its essence. It was ever so much closer to the heartbeat of the Russian nation than were either the Communists or the adherents of the old order. Its outbreak marked the advent of a second civil war, not a continuation of the first in different form. In fact, continuation of the first acted as a block to the advent of the second, for it was not until the White Guard had been crushed in the case of Makhno, or virtually crushed in the case of Antonov, that the peasant uprising could gather headway. If the Greens were an appendage of the Whites, why did they wait until the body to which they were attached had had the life beaten out of it before resorting to arms? Why had they not struck in April 1919 when Kolchak had almost reached the Volga, or in October of that year when Denikin had passed Orel in his drive on Moscow?

The answer is clear to anyone but a blind dogmatist or a liar of the stripe of Mikoyan: as long as the Whites had a serious chance of victory the Greens would not lift a finger to help them. They preferred waging a desperate and lonely struggle on their own to helping the oppressors of the past achieve victory over the oppressors of the present. A reactionary gazette published abroad had complained of how Petersburg had been quiet while the civil war raged, only to come to life and start causing trouble when it was over. Just so, observed the SR organ in exile, only when the reaction had been smashed beyond redemption were the people free to rise.[62]

Freed of the nightmare of restoration, the sailors could turn their arms against those who had perverted the revolution and, if they had

had any arms, the workers might have joined them in this second and distinctly people's civil war. The same sentiment gripped the peasantry. In his obsession for dualism where he could not have monism, Lenin insisted it was either-or—either his party's rule or the Tsar's—yet he had to fight two civil wars, not one, because he had two enemies, not one; it was for him good fortune far beyond what he deserved that his two enemies were also enemies of one another and could never go together in a single civil war that would assuredly have brought his regime crashing down in ruin.

The independence of the Green movement in shunning the first civil war and in then staging its own is seen also in the spontaneity of its origin and in the lack of central direction. While it is true that the outbreaks were bunched together on two occasions, the summer of 1920 and February of 1921, suggesting some degree of collusion or of backstage direction, Sapozhkov's revolt in July 1920 and Antonov's in August are quite simply and adequately explained by the onset of the third campaign of peasant despoliation inherent in the food levy program. Antonov had formed the nucleus of a fighting force and was biding his time, to be sure, but the prospect of a third round of confiscation of "surplus" produce applied the torch to the powderhouse of peasant exasperation.

As for the heavy detonations of February 1921, they resulted from the whole hopelessness of the situation created by years of devastation and of puerile Communist experimentation. The failure of the Green movement to achieve any degree of coordination is adequate proof that there was nothing behind it except elemental discontent of the populace and whatever its individual leaders could add on their own. The thorough-going independence of the movement was its undoing; not only was it independent of any extraneous influence, its parts were independent of one another.

Although the free mind can easily distinguish the second from the first civil war, whatever the Communists—abetted by state-worshippers in other lands—may say, it cannot disentangle the fate of the second from the nefarious influence of the first. In their duel with the Whites the Reds succeeded in suborning a key element in the peasantry—the younger men who were brought into the armed forces—and in retaining the allegiance of a sufficient number of them despite mass desertions to have the edge in the second civil war as well as in the first. The peasants in the army, in fact, fell into two categories: those who deserted and ended up—in many instances—in the Green bands, and those who continued to serve the Soviet regime and suppressed those bands.

This split in the peasantry came about as a result not only of Communist organization and discipline but also—and even more—as a result of purposeful creation of a privileged soldierly caste exempt from the sufferings imposed on the bulk of the peasantry. Better food and better living served as the wedge to split off the class from its sons in the army—a class, it must be said, that had never distinguished itself by developing a corporate consciousness.

Lenin's sure instinct for retention of power constituted his immeasurable advantage over the pacifist, rose-water socialists of the West as did also his callousness in respect to the well-being of the civilian population. While the food situation deteriorated to the extent that even the army was affected,[63] Lenin did all in his power to minimize its privations, granting its needs priority over those of industry[64]—for him a tremendous concession—and over those of the centers of power.[65] He had defined the basic purpose of the food levy as supplying the army along with preserving some shreds of industry and so of a working class.[66] The new food tax under the NEP would serve the same basic purpose by covering at least the minimum needs of the army and the proletariat.[67] In the Ukraine Lenin proposed extra rations for soldiers at the expense of the local peasantry as long as the food tax had not been paid.[68] Here was an exceptionally clear case of setting the military over the populace in respect both to function—he would employ soldiers as tax collectors—and to material well-being.[69] Without this nursing of the soldiers more defections would have taken place.

In this second civil war the Tambov uprising occupies a conspicuous position. It was not so spectacular as Kronstadt nor so important as Siberia, and it never attained the amplitude of Ukrainian insurgency; but it stands out from the others because of its solid, organized character and because its suppression necessitated the employment of the ablest military talent at the disposal of the Soviet. One of the less eminent commanders involved in its repression observed that disturbed conditions in the Ukraine, the ebb and flow of political tides, and the endless succession of overturns had created a favorable soil for guerrilla actions but not for a solid, tenacious movement like Antonov's, a leader who had patiently recruited his "army" over a considerable stretch of time and had succeeded in putting down "rather deep roots."[70] There is a measure of truth in this contention, though its worth is lessened by the charge that kulaks and criminals formed the backbone of his army and deserters the reservoir from which the ranks were filled.

Appraising the relative strength of Antonov and Makhno, however, can be done another way. Antonov was so rooted in his environment, his operations were so well organized, that he would not think of going elsewhere except for an occasional thrust across the border into Voronezh or Saratov provinces followed by a swift return to the Vorona valley or an adjacent area. The admirable mobility he displayed did not extend beyond a quite narrow radius of action. For a guerrilla leader, in other words, he carried a heavy cannon of very limited range.

Makhno, on the other hand, did not depend at all on Guliai Pole; he could cut loose and operate with seemingly equal effectiveness in Poltava, Kharkov, or Chernigov as in Ekaterinoslav or Kherson provinces. Both the Green leaders could deliver blows of a severity disproportionate to their numbers and armaments. If Antonov were better organized—and this is an impression rather than a certainty—Makhno had a far wider range of activity; certainly he posed tactically, and perhaps also strategically, the greater danger to the Communists.

In the opinion of the author, the difference is to be accounted for by the greater measure of support the Ukrainian peasantry accorded to Makhno. No matter where he was in the broad stretches of the left-bank Ukraine, Makhno could count on supplies and recruits; in the event of being mauled by Frunze's immensely superior forces he could stamp on the ground and new strength would enable him to resume the struggle. Antonov, as we have seen, never could extend his domain to the rest of his home province. In his infrequent probes of adjoining provinces he does not appear to have received any accretions of strength. The results of his incursions into Voronezh are a matter of conjecture. Once he attempted to recruit strength in Saratov; the effort is known to this author but the information was taken from him—in any event, nothing of consequence. Antonov's venture into Penza (June 1921) was noted only for the speed with which he left it.

Yet the provincial party secretary, Krainov, informed the Central Committee in Moscow that in the summer of 1921 the peasants were still helping the "bandits." Not until autumn of the following year had their mood shifted to one of hostility against continued "bandit" activity—presumably after an intervening period of apathy.

Thus in Penza the key Communist official attests peasant sympathy for the Greens[71] at a time when Antonov went through with bridle down, seeking no contact with the local populace either here or in Saratov out of which he had just come and over which Green bands were swarming. It is true an armored force pursued him, but since he faced certain ruin by returning to his established haunts little would have been lost by a fresh departure in search of additional support. Had he generally been remiss in recruiting strength outside his bailiwick or had the response been too discouraging? The truth would seem to lie in between; Antonov could have done more to rally support but it would not have been comparable to the backing Makhno enjoyed among the Ukrainian peasants.

On the basis of inadequate knowledge, the Tambov phase of the Green movement would appear to have more in common with the western Siberian than with either the Ukrainian or the Transvolga. In both Tambov and western Siberia the STK mobilized the civilian population behind the armed bands in respect to personnel and supply, and in both SRs occupied prominent positions. But there the parallel ends, for the Siberian insurrection spread over a much wider area while being—perhaps for that reason—more loosely organized; Tambov had the superior leadership, much of the initiative and direction coming from the Left SRs who do not appear to have been so much in the foreground in Siberia, perhaps because in general there were fewer of them there than in European Russia.

It is not possible to compare the strain each imposed on the Communist order or the size of the forces each mobilized against it except to say that most energetic countermeasures were evoked in both instances, Lenin's reaction being more immediate and desperate in the case of western Siberia. The Green bands in the

Volga region never coalesced into one force with the potency of
Antonov's; they never overcame their chronic dispersion but they
ranged over a far wider territory and held the field for twice as long.
Other aspects of the Green movement, for example in the north
Caucasus, await further study before meaningful observations can
be made about conformity or nonconformity with those already
mentioned.

An attempt should also be made to place the Tambov experience
in the general setting of peasant upheavals in a country that has
never been without an agrarian problem and has never known a
satisfactory agrarian order, where the rule has been that no matter
what happens the rural population will continue to be oppressed.
Communist rule with its collectivization and second social war in the
village has proved to be a worthy successor of the accursed societies
of Muscovy and Poland–Lithuania, wracked as they were at
periodic intervals by the wild thrashings of the huge but headless
victim class: Bolotnikov's uprising at the beginning of the 1600s,
Razin's in the 1670s, Bulavin's early in the 1700s, Pugachev's under
the Enlightened Empress, its counterpart in the western Ukraine—
the Affair of the Stakes—under the same lady, and—dwarfing all
other peasant rebellions in European history—the Deluge or Slaves'
Fury in the Ukraine, 1648–1654.

All of these social convulsions suffered from certain inherent
weaknesses; they all burdened themselves with a faulty ideology,
they were all badly organized even at the local or unit level, they
were all cursed with poor or miserable if not traitorous leadership,
and they all succumbed in the end to a small but strategically placed,
articulate, and cohesive minority.

An eminent authority in the field of peasant oppression has
commented on the faulty ideology common to all: "In addition,
when speaking of Razin and Pugachev, it must never be forgotten
that they were monarchists; they came out against the landowners
but for a 'good tsar.' "[72] Unable to formulate beliefs for themselves,
the miserable peasants marched under slogans invented by
charlatans and pledging allegiance to some dead or dull-witted
member of the dynasty. The insurrections were directed against the
person of the reigning monarch but not against the monarchy itself,

the institution that served as the main agency of repression. The bad organization could be observed at all levels, not simply at the national or All-Russian, and the force placed in the field at a given moment resembled a mob more than an army. The mob, moreover, was a partial one, for dispersion of effort over a broad area—in part inherent in a peasant movement—resulted not only in failure to gather strength at one point but in failure to bring the diverse and inevitably dispersed elements into flood stage at the same time.

The weaknesses so far cited derived in part from natural conditions and in part from inferior leadership. The insurrections were headed either by men of nonpeasant origin or by former peasants who had become something else—Bolotnikov, Zhelezniak or Zalizniak, Gonta—and whose commitment to the cause of peasant liberation was at best modified by other considerations or at worst was subject to betrayal (Khmelnitski). Not a single skillful leader can be singled out from among these men. The cumulative effect of these weaknesses delivered the peasants into the hands of their natural enemies—in every case but one—by defeat on the battlefield, and in the case of the Slaves' Fury, which had been too big to be crushed in action, by a sell-out on the part of its leadership, the Cossack plutocracy.[73]

Now to see how the insurrection of 1920–1921 headed by A. S. Antonov conforms to this historical pattern. It conforms not at all except in respect to its fate. Not only in this instance but in the other manifestations of the Green movement, not a shred of monarchist ideology remained. Too much water had flowed under the bridge since Pugachev had been vanquished and the Empress had fastened things down good and tight for there to be any trouble on that score.

In fact, the enemies of the Greens taxed them with having no ideology at all,[74] touching unity being achieved in this respect by the Communists[75] and by the right-wing Populist intellectuals.[76] Even centrist Populist intellectuals of the Chernov stripe regretted the "purely negative" aims of the Greens.[77] Positive aims which these people hoped to graft onto the movement involved recognition of the need for representative institutions, especially rededication to the hoary shibboleth of the Constituent Assembly—that is, re-creation of the state which not only Makhno and the Ukrainian anarchists but Left SRs everywhere viewed with well-founded aversion.

If the Greens were in a sense vague as to what they wanted, they were very clear as to what they did not want. If they seemed to waver, at least in Tambov and western Siberia, between soviets and STKs—in the rural areas there would be virtually no difference—they were very clear in their minds that they did not want the soviets as constituted since the middle of 1918, in which the tyranny of the Communist party excluded every other point of view, revolutionary or otherwise.

They were equally determined to have their own peasant army to secure the people's interest, not only against the Communists but against whatever danger materialized thereafter, in sharpest distinction from the right-wing Populist intellectuals whose record between the February revolution and the collapse of their regimes in 1918 and 1919 conclusively demonstrates their intent to have a conventional army, in line with their anti-Japanese, anti-Turk and Tatar, anti-Finn and Magyar, anti-German phobia. Here is the true watershed between Populism and the Green movement. In this respect the political instinct of the Greens was as sure and their will as clear as Lenin's in his policy of putting the army first. With only a rudimentary yet practical ideology, the Greens were healthier and stronger than the Populists.

In addition to emancipation from the self-destructive monarchist ideology of old-line peasant movements, the Greens had made progress in the field of organization. Their forces contrast favorably with the insurrectionary rabble of yore; they offered stern resistance to the levies of the centralized Communist state despite their lighter weaponry. Especially in Tambov and western Siberia but also in the Ukraine a remarkably effective system of supply and replenishment backed up the forces in the field. With regard to dispersion of effort, the Greens effected at least a partial improvement. Coordination of operations never came to pass, yet the various revolts against Communist exploitation did crest at the same time with flood stage being registered in February and March 1921, when the outbreaks in western Siberia and Kronstadt and the Armenian national uprising coincided with the unabated vigor of hostilities in the Ukraine, in Tambov, and on the Volga, and with fitful operations elsewhere.

The conspicuous failure to link up with one another may be cited against the claims of the Green leaders to belong in a different category from the Razins and Pugachevs of the past. And yet the conclusion must be that they differ from their lineal predecessors, and not only in point of dedication but also because of organizational and operational skill. The lumbering apparatus of Alexei Mikhailovich compares very poorly with the Soviet administration, even in 1921; and while Catherine was better served, having in S. I. Sheshkovski a worthy predecessor of the Che-ka, the Pugachev affair caught her desperately short of troops in a war at long-range with Turkey, so that Michelson was greatly outnumbered even in the hour of victory.

In the twentieth century the government always had the advantage of numbers, and nearly always a very great advantage. Its superiority was most pronounced, however, in technical means of warfare. The Communist state disposed of artillery in abundance, of railroads, telegraph, telephone, armored trains, armored cars, and of airplanes, whereas Antonov and Makhno operated on a horse-and-wagon level not too different from the eighteenth century. The ability to maintain the unequal struggle at such a pitch and over a prolonged period of time in the face of odds of this kind bears witness to the skill of the Green commanders.

Antonov and Makhno probably should be awarded first position in respect to talent. The Ukrainian leader excelled as tactician, Antonov as an organizer, though both displayed marked ability in the other's specialty. During five months of bloody deadlock, January to June 1921, Antonov held his own despite a numerical inferiority of one to two during most of the time; Makhno faced even greater odds. As to Antonov's resourcefulness, his daring and personal courage, there can be no question; these qualities are confirmed by the enemy—not the Soviet hacks of later years, writing by prescription, but the enemies who confronted him from the other side of the battle-lines, Communists for whom lying had not become second nature.[78]

On the other side, his cruelty cannot be denied; he committed—or allowed to be committed—barbarities that besmirch his record. The main negative judgment, however, concerns his failure as a strategist. He had no working agreement with Green leaders elsewhere so far as can be discovered, and he evolved no overall plan of strategy raising his sights above the immediate problem in

Tambov province. How then, it may be asked, would he have exploited victory if it had been achieved?

The Green movement in general has been consigned to oblivion since Russians cannot approach its study in any serious manner and Western intellectuals have little interest in peasant affairs. The scant attention it has received has not done it justice for three basic reasons. Those who deal with such matters are in greater or lesser degree worshippers of the state; they revere Revolution with a capital R, usually in a Marxist sense, and—above all—they worship success. They have instinctively disliked the Green movement because it threatened to induce chaos in the Russian state, because it was anti-Marxist to the marrow of its bones, and because it failed.

Let us open a window and air out these biases. Alone of the plunder-empires of history, the Russian still exists. All the others have passed away; why should it be preserved? The subjugation of non-Russian peoples has done violence to their rights, has threatened other European lands or actually arrested their historical development (Poland and Hungary, 1830–1849 and thereafter), and has been of very questionable benefit to the Russian people themselves. The Russian state in the true sense would still be a large entity, inevitably enclosing certain nationalities such as the Mordvins and Kazan Tatars within the zone of Russian settlement. It is not necessary to assume that the Russian people would have lost their unity and independence if power had passed from fanatics of industrialization to leaders of the peasant cause.

All accounts agree that Antonov was running on a small scale a pretty solid system with the embryo even of a secret police. Above all, he had assembled the core of an army that would have put backbone into the people's cause. Success would have brought accretion of strength, but he and the other Green commanders would still have needed to win over large segments of the Red Army from a foundering Communist regime. They might have done so despite the presence in that army of professional elements that could conceivably have aspired to the mantle of General Monk, for the Red Army also contained genuine revolutionary elements uncommitted to Communism *per se* which would have gravitated to the peasant side, aided or propelled by the basic peasant cast of the army itself. There was no parallel with 1659–1660, all the more so since what member of the defunct dynasty remotely approached Charles II in respect to ability? Nor is it necessary to conjecture the return from abroad of the Black Baron on a white horse.

If the defunct Constituent Assembly elected in November 1917 had somehow been resurrected there would assuredly have been a confrontation between the right-wing Populist intellectuals so grossly overrepresented in that body[79] and the Green commanders, whom the intellectuals would have wished to divest of their functions in addition to dissolving their bands preparatory to creating a conventional army. Right-wing Populism was nothing if not sublimated chauvinism compounded with a snobbery which caused its adherents to view with aversion armed forces sprung from the depths of society, like Antonov's, and with horror those both plebeian and antistate—like Makhno's—since they were Ukrainian and anarchistic besides. Considering the temper both of the Green leaders and of their peasant following, the outcome of such a confrontation would have been not a new conventional army but a new constituent assembly or none at all.

Communists have assiduously propagated the calumny that the peasant bands were counterrevolutionary, meaning that they sought to overturn Communist rule, and many besides the Turkish general who ought to know better have tacitly or openly accepted this view. There is no law saying revolutions must be Marxist. History has known many revolutions, only a few of them Marxist. Yet intellectuals in the West, enchanted by the Soviet experiment, have come close to putting across this dogma. Either they have ignored the Greens as standard-bearers of a class that stirs no interest or they have not so much charged as insinuated that the Greens were wholly irresponsible or blindly reactionary with leaders who were to be thought of as Fascists in the making.

As a matter of fact, the Greens represented a simon-pure revolutionary force, elemental and plebeian, unbossed by Marxist, Populist, or conventional intellectuals. They reflected the people as they were, in their crudeness, their cruelty, even in their anti-Semitism. They were revolutionary in their origin, their dress, their organization, and their leadership. Too much has been made of the kulaks among them. Even Lenin conceded in a candid moment that the kulaks themselves had been revolutionary in relation to landowners,[80] and very many Greens were not to be found anywhere within the range of elasticity of that much-abused term. As for the leaders, it is ridiculous to think of them in terms of a Benito Mussolini. Whatever else they may have been they were not buffoons, they did not play at revolution, and they knew how to die bravely. Not one of them betrayed their cause. Indeed, it was not the leaders who failed the peasants but the peasants who failed the leaders by succumbing to the siren promise of the NEP—"seriously and for an extended period, though not forever."[81]

The ultimate indictment of the Greens has been their lack of success. They will never rate with those who see historical validity in terms of being on the winning side. It may be remembered, however, that they did achieve a modest measure of success. In what must be the most violent wrench ever given the Communist conscience, they forced upon that party of devotees of heavy industry the compromise of the New Economic Policy in recognition of the necessity of adjusting to the triumph of the middle peasantry as the unwelcome outcome of the revolution.[82]

Some eight years later Joseph V. Stalin rescinded this concession which was more a landmark of the Green movement than of the economic conditions of the time, and more a result of the western Siberian insurrection than of Tambov or Kronstadt though both, of course, contributed to the result. During this eight-year period of closed season on peasant hunting agriculture recovered from all the ravages of preceding years, and the cow population rose to a level not again attained until 1959 when there would be some 35 million more mouths to feed.

But what are eight good years in the life of a peasantry, it may be asked? And the answer is that in the life of the East European peasantry they are something of import. But that is not all in assessing the significance of the Green movement. The spirit that produced it would burn low in succeeding years, yet never has it been extinguished. The long and valiant stand of the Russian and associated peasantries against reduction from independent tillers of the soil to workers in the field is a powerful factor influencing the history of our times, weakening the Soviet system, necessitating the "theory" of coexistence, safeguarding the independence of what is left of Europe, performing the same function for lands like Turkey and Persia, allowing Red China to seek equality in armaments without being struck in the process, and permitting political mountebanks in America to boast of the détente they have produced.

> The steppe grass grows over the graves of the monsters and base backsliders who did not wish to submit to the will of the toiling people. The grievous sacrifices and righteous blood of champions of the Soviet order, spilled on the fields of battle with the enemies of civilization and progress, have not been in vain. Sacred to succeeding generations is the memory of the heroes who crushed the armed[83] kulak counter-revolution.[84]

In these words the Soviet historian characterizes the fate of the Green warriors—and of history in Soviet Russia. Antonov and his younger brother, Tokmakov, Boguslavski, Matiukhin, Pluzhnikov and others perished with the movement they headed. Not one of the leaders survived the Tambov insurrection. They lie in bloody graves and whether the steppe grass or the forest grows above them, they trouble the regime no longer.

But dead also, it may be remembered, and resting likewise in bloody graves are Antonov-Ovseenko, Tukhachevski, Uborevich, I. F. Fedko, N. N. Krivoruchko, and Trotski himself, the civilian and military heads of the repression in Tambov province, victims of a system they helped to secure—in part on the ruins of the peasant freedom movement of the early 1920s.

Notes

1. Trifonov, *Klassy i klassovaia bor'ba*, part 1, p. 139.

2. *Put' Bor'by*, vol. 2, *Antonovshchina*, p. 16, as cited in Trifonov, *Klassy i klassovaia bor'ba*, part 1, p. 139.

3. Nik. Olegov, "Pis'ma iz Voronezha" [Letters from Voronezh], under the column "Na mestakh," *Izvestiia*, no. 77 (1516), 5 April 1922, p. 3.

4. From the Central Party Archives as cited in Trifonov, *Klassy i klassovaia bor'ba*, part 1, pp. 139–40.

5. Antonov-Ovseenko, "O banditskom dvizhenii v Tambovskoi gubernii," pp. 19–20.

6. Lenin, *Polnoe sobranie sochinenii*, 5th ed., vol. 43, p. 354; from his speech at the 3rd All-Russian food conference, 16 June 1921.

7. Antonov-Ovseenko, "O banditskom dvizhenii v Tambovskoi gubernii," pp. 35, 36.

8. Tukhachevski, "Zapiska," p. 3.

9. See chapter twelve.

10. Shatov, "Tambovskie vosstaniia," *Novoe Russkoe Slovo*, 16 February 1966.

11. *Rossiia: polnoe geograficheskoe opisanie*, vol. 2, *Srednerusskaia chernozemnaia oblast'*, pp. 424–25, 428, 598.

12. Ibid., pp. 494, 340 for the two *uezds* in the order they are given. The figures here presented relate to the end of the nineteenth century; by 1920–1921 the forested zone would have undergone some further encroachment.

13. Poliakov, *Perekhod k nepu i sovetskoe krest'ianstvo*, pp. 201–2.

14. Ibid., p. 233. Later Stalin would recreate such conditions, but his negative approach on this occasion is contrasted unfavorably to Lenin's positive "dialectical" approach which stressed the usefulness of this first assault on capitalism even though it failed; ibid., pp. 233–34. Of what the usefulness consisted we are not told.

15. This consideration is clearly set forth in Lenin's report on the NEP to the 7th Moscow provincial party conference, 29 October 1921, in *Polnoe sobranie sochinenii*, 5th ed., vol. 44, p. 208.

16. "XI Vserossiiskaia konferentsiia R. K. P." [The 11th All-Russian Conference of the Communist Party], *Izvestiia*, no. 287 (1430), 21 December 1921, p. 1.

17. See the very revealing passages connected with the 8th All-Russian Soviet Congress, December 1920, in Lenin, *Polnoe sobranie sochinenii*, 5th ed., vol. 42,

pp. 181, 186–87, 199, and notes 87 and 93 on pp. 474, 475. The Communist delegation had voted down the principle of reward to individuals but backed down under pressure from Lenin, whose own proposal was sufficiently dogma-ridden to avoid giving umbrage to any but the most wild-eyed collectivist. Let anyone who doubts that the NEP was motivated by fear induced by external circumstances read these passages from late December 1920—not even a month and a half before the western Siberian insurrection and not two months before Kronstadt.

18. *Tret'e Gubernskoe Soveshchanie predsedatelei uispolkomov Tambovskoi gubernii: stenograficheskii otchet* [Third Provincial Conference of chairmen of the *uezd* executive committees of Tambov province: stenographic report] (Tambov, 1920), pp. 61–62. For this valuable reference confirming the author's deduction, he is indebted to Professor Peter Scheibert of the University of Marburg.

19. "Makhnovshchina," *Volia Rossii*, no. 24, 9 October 1920, p. 1. The unsigned article is typically that of a right SR intellectual in its studied hostility to the Green movement. Makhno is characterized as an "anarchist of the bandit type"—a statement to which Communists could subscribe with both hands. Here the state-minded Populist intellectuals and the state-minded followers of Lenin are as one.

20. Trifonov, *Klassy i klassovaia bor'ba*, part 1, pp. 163, 259.

21. Lenin, *Polnoe sobranie sochinenii*, 5th ed., vol. 51, pp. 347–48, no. 23 of appendices, with text of telegram to the revolutionary committee of the Ural region and the soviet executive committee of Saratov province. Compare Trifonov, *Klassy i klassovaia bor'ba*, part 1, pp. 162–63, to see how either the sycophant historian or the editors of earlier publications of Lenin's papers have softened his language.

22. Figure taken apparently from Red Army Archives and printed in Trifonov, *Klassy i klassovaia bor'ba*, part 1, p. 262.

23. A. Nevedomski, "V te dni" [In those days], *Izvestiia*, no. 120 (1559), 1 June 1922, p. 2; Iv. Fertov, "Banditizm v Povolzh'e" [Banditry along the Volga], *Pravda*, no. 161, 21 July 1922, p. 4; Trifonov, *Klassy i klassovaia bor'ba*, part 1, pp. 57, 79–80, 90, 105–6, 110, 124, 162–63, 232, 259 ff.; Lenin, *Polnoe sobranie sochinenii*, 5th ed., vol. 51, p. 519 (bare reference to Sapozhkov in name list).

24. Fertov, "Banditizm v Povolzh'e," *Pravda*, no. 161, 21 July 1922, p. 4, under general heading of "Po Sovetskoi federatsii" [Around the Soviet federation].

25. Trifonov, *Klassy i klassovaia bor'ba*, part 1, pp. 259, 260.

26. From the Central State Archives of the Soviet Army, as cited in ibid., p. 261.

27. Copy of telegram in code, ms. of two typed pages, T–650 of the Trotsky Archive.

28. "Po Povolzh'iu: Umen'shenie banditizma" [In the Volga region: a lessening of banditry], *Izvestiia*, no. 160 (1303), 23 July 1921, p. 1; Fertov, "Banditizm v Povolzh'e" *Pravda*, no. 161, 21 July 1922, p. 4; "Polozhenie v Povolzh'i po sovetskim dannym" [The situation on the Volga according to Soviet information], *Volia Rossii*, no. 272, 5 August 1921, p. 1; Trifonov, *Klassy i klassovaia bor'ba*, part 1, pp. 260–61.

29. Conversation of assistant chief of staff Shaposhnikov and chief of staff Kamenev with Kraevski, commander of the Transvolga district, on 23 March 1921, ms. of six typed pages, T–655 of Trotsky Archive.

30. "Po Povolzh'iu: Umen'shenie banditizma," *Izvestiia*, no. 160 (1303), 23 July 1921, p. 1; "Polozhenie v Povolzh'i po sovetskim dannym," *Volia Rossii*, no. 272, 5 August 1921, p. 1. Later the émigré newspaper carried a report from Moscow about a flare-up late in August 1921 in the Krasnyi Kut district east of Saratov in Samara province which had necessitated the despatch of five armored trains; see "Posledniia vesti iz Rossii" [Latest news from Russia], ibid., no. 306, 15 September 1921, p. 3. See also Trifonov, *Klassy i klassovaia bor'ba*, part 1, pp. 261–63.

31. Trifonov, *Klassy i klassovaia bor'ba*, part 1, p. 272.

32. Copy of telegram from Frunze and S. Gusev to the Central Committee, Lenin, and Trotski, dated 17 December 1920 in Kharkov; ms. of a single typed page, T–627 of Trotsky Archive.

33. Copy of coded telegram to A. D. Tsiurupa with copy to Lenin, 2 March 1921; ms. of single typed page, T–640 of Trotsky Archive.

34. Copy of coded telegram, Vladimirov to Tsiurupa with copy to Lenin, 2 March 1921; ms. of a single typed page, T–641 of the Trotsky Archive. This telegram and the one preceding were, or course, secret.

35. Copy of handwritten note dated 3 March 1921; ms. of one typed page, T–644 of Trotsky Archive.

36. Lenin, *Polnoe sobranie sochinenii*, 5th ed., vol. 52, p. 67, no. 117.

37. Trifonov, *Klassy i klassovaia bor'ba*, part 1, p. 272.

38. The sycophant historian concedes as much, referring to a statement by Frunze; ibid., pp. 278–79.

39. Ibid., p. 272.

40. Ali Fuat Cebesoy, *Moskova hatıraları (21/11/1920–2/6/1922)* [Memories of Moscow, 21 November 1920–2 June 1922] (Istanbul, 1955); sections entitled "Moskova yolunda" [On the way to Moscow], "Ihtiyat tedbirleri" [Security measures], and "Bir tehlike" [Danger ahead], pp. 126–27. The Turkish general is a credible source, stiff and honest as he is. He gives the bands their correct name—*zeloni* (green)—but does not avoid confusion in dealing with the Green movement, a failing he shares with nearly everyone else. Thus he refers to the bands as "*mukabil ihtilâl çeteleri*" (counterrevolutionary). They were so in the sense of being against the cast imparted to the revolution by the Communists, but not otherwise. The band active in the Voronezh area under the leadership of a schoolteacher must refer to Makhno himself, but Makhno's band was not based on Voronezh province and Kolesnikov, who was at home there, was not a schoolteacher so far as we know. The band in the "*Rezan*" (Riazan) region formed by a woman named *Marusia* obviously is confused with the band formed in Tambov province by Maria (Marusia) Kosova, whom our novelist makes into Antonov's undesired girl friend; Virta, *Odinochestvo*, passim. Yet for a military man from far away who was being initiated into the affairs of a complex Russian phenomenon the Turkish general does quite well.

41. The historian of the movement states that Makhno crossed the railroad between Kursk and Belgorod—that is, south of the provincial capital. No details are given. See P. Arshinov, *Istoriia makhnovskogo dvizheniia (1918–1921 gg.)* [A history of Makhno's movement, 1918–1921] (Berlin, 1923), p. 193. Makhno himself does not say where he crossed the railroad, only that he occupied the town of Korocha southeast of Kursk. What else he may have occupied is left unsaid. See

lengthy quotation from letter Makhno wrote in exile in ibid. Both Arshinov and Cebesoy are primary sources, but as the Turkish general is much more specific his version is followed.

42. From Makhno's letter to a friend written in exile and printed in ibid., p. 194. The letter was to Arshinov himself we learn from V. M. Eichenbaum (Voline), *La Révolution inconnue* (1917–1921) (Paris, n.d.), p. 654. Here the text of the letter is reproduced in French; ibid., pp. 655–60.

43. Arshinov, *Istoriia makhnovskogo dvizheniia*, p. 199.

44. From Trotski's speech of 27 December 1921 to the 9th All-Russian Congress of Soviets as recorded in the *Izvestiia*, no. 293 (1436), 28 December 1921, p. 1.

45. Barsukov, "Kommunist-buntar' (Grigorii Ivanovich Kotovskii)," *Krasnaia Nov'*, book 8 (October 1925), p. 215.

46. Copy of postal telegram, 15 March 1921; ms. of one typed page, T–647 of Trotsky Archive. To a foreign audience Lenin disparaged Kronstadt as a trifling incident, less dangerous to his regime than Irish guerrillas to the British Empire. See "O kronshtadtskom vosstanii" [As to the Kronstadt uprising], in Lenin, *Polnoe sobranie sochinenii*, 5th ed., vol. 43, p. 129. But privately he was so stung by what had happened that he proposed to Trotski to close down the fleet. Reference is to his remarkable memorandum of 21 March 1921; ms. copy of handwritten original, T–654 of Trotsky Archive.

47. Borisov, *Chernym letom*, pp. 5–6; see also under "Notes," in Lenin, *Polnoe sobranie sochinenii*, 5th ed., vol. 43, pp. 432–33, n. 12.

48. From the report of chief of army political section Smirnov, 5 July 1921, in *G. I. Kotovskii*, p. 352, no. 276. The document is from the Red Army Archives.

49. See above. Report of the discovery in "Na mestakh: Bor'ba s banditizmom," *Izvestiia*, no. 177 (1320), 12 August 1921, p. 3.

50. A Soviet writer claims that Antonov concealed from his followers the news that Kronstadt had fallen; no proof is adduced, so that the assertion may or may not be true. Nor is it disclosed when the news reached Antonov himself. See S. E., "Antonovshchina," *Izvestiia*, no. 122 (1561), 3 June 1922, pp. 2–3. The novelist says merely that Antonov took to heavy drinking at receipt of the news—an eminently safe statement for a novelist concerned with the truth to make; Virta, *Odinochestvo*, p. 261. But it is of no help in respect to the time element.

51. Arshinov, *Istoriia makhnovskogo dvizheniia*, p. 194; Trifonov, *Klassy i klassovaia bor'ba*, part 1, pp. 225, 273.

52. Arshinov, *Istoriia makhnovskogo dvizheniia*, pp. 198–99 (from Makhno's letter to the author).

53. From the Archives of the Soviet Army as rendered in Trifonov, *Klassy i klassovaia bor'ba*, part 1, p. 274.

54. Lenin, "Zakliuchitel'noe slovo . . . 15 marta," in *Polnoe sobranie sochinenii*, 5th ed., vol. 43, p. 82.

55. Idem, "Novaia ekonomicheskaia politika i zadachi politprosvetov," in ibid., vol. 44, pp. 158–59. The date was 17 October 1921.

56. Idem, message of "complete secrecy" to the RVS (Revolutionary War Council) of the 11th army; ms. of one typed page, T–632 of Trotsky Archive. Below is a notation in Lenin's handwriting containing a concession to the army:

"Stalin will send Ordzhonikidze himself." How much consolation that was we cannot say. Someone underlined the notation in red and put a plus sign in the margin: probably Trotski, perturbed over his enemy's forwardness in this affair.

57. Idem, note to L. B. Krasin of 10 May 1921 censuring him for delay in having his department order grain; in *Polnoe sobranie sochinenii*, 5th ed., vol. 52, p. 184, no. 349.

58. See, for example, Steklov's leading editorial, "Derevnia i novaia ekonomicheskaia politika" [The village and the NEP], *Izvestiia*, no. 203 (1346), 18 September 1921, p. 1.

59. Cited by Poliakov, *Perekhod k nepu i sovetskoe krest'ianstvo*, p. 458.

60. For exposition of this principle at some length, see Lenin's speech to the convention of transport workers, 27 March 1921, in *Polnoe sobranie sochinenii*, 5th ed., vol. 43, pp. 136–41. See also ibid., pp. 72, 129, 237–40, and vol. 44, pp. 6, 42–43, 54.

61. Trifonov, *Klassy i klassovaia bor'ba*, part 1, pp. 298–303.

62. "Pomoshchniki bol'shevizma" [Helpers of Bolshevism], *Volia Rossii*, no. 147, 8 March 1921, p. 2.

63. As in the case of one regiment of Kotovski's brigade; see above, chapter eleven. See also chapter nine.

64. Lenin, *Polnoe sobranie sochinenii*, 5th ed., vol. 43, p. 149.

65. Ibid., vol. 52, appendices, no. 34, p. 325.

66. Ibid., vol. 43, pp. 150–51.

67. "O prodovol'stvennom naloge" [About the food tax], ibid., p. 220.

68. Ibid., vol. 53, pp. 101–2, no. 169. Similarly with respect to the Moscow region; ibid., pp. 92–93, no. 154. If anyone doubt that the peasant was to serve as an object of exploitation, let him read these pages. The sale of salt was to be used to extract the tax, thus creating a common bond between Lenin's regime and that of Louis XIV.

69. Other variations on the theme of army priority will be found in Lenin's telegram of 28 May 1921 to the provincial authorities ("grievous food situation least of all to affect feeding of the army . . . army must not experience hunger . . . authorities must attend to provisioning of army by all means at their disposal. . . . bad situation must not affect army . . ., etc.); ibid., vol. 52, appendices, no. 37, p. 327. See also his instructions on matters of economic activity ("not the least let-up in work of meeting one hundred percent the needs of the Red Army, which come first"); ibid., vol. 44, p. 335. The occasion was the 9th All-Russian Congress of Soviets, and the date 28 December 1921.

70. Petrovski, "Bor'ba s banditizmom i krasnye kursanty," *Izvestiia*, no. 133 (1276), 23 June 1921, p. 1. Petrovski commanded these military trainees.

71. From the Central Party Archives as presented in Poliakov, *Perekhod k nepu i sovetskoe krest'ianstvo*, p. 459, n. 270.

72. Joseph V. Stalin, as quoted from Lenin and Stalin, *Sbornik proizvedenii k izucheniiu istorii VKP(b)* [Works collected for a study of the history of the All-Union Communist party (Bolsheviks)], vol. 3, p. 527, in *Istoriia SSSR, I, S drevneishikh vremen do kontsa XVIII veka* [History of the USSR, I, from earliest times to the end of the 18th century], ed. by B. D. Grekov, S. V. Bakhrushin, and V. I. Lebedev, 2nd ed. (n.p., 1948), p. 632.

73. Ukrainian nationalism is badly served when Bogdan Khmelnitski is played up as a national hero. A true national hero, and one thoroughly representative of his people, is Nestor Makhno.

74. See discussion in chapter four.

75. Antonov-Ovseenko, "O banditskom dvizhenii v Tambovskoi gubernii," pp. 31–32. The commissar asserts that without guidance from the parties that spoke for the "industrial bourgeoisie" the Green movement degenerated into anarchistic thrashings and banditlike actions; the narrow, bucolic horizon could not give rise to a clearly-formulated program for the establishment of a bourgeois-democratic state. Naturally not, since the Greens did not intend to erect such a state. Here this crude half-intellectual, having just subordinated the Tambov uprising to the machinations of a counterrevolutionary, White Guard conspiracy, turns around and contradicts himself by recognizing its independent character. One may wonder what clearly-formulated program for the dictatorship of the proletariat he had arrived at when he was led out to execution in 1939 by Stalin's henchmen.

76. Anonymous (Podbelski), *Kak tambovskie krest'iane boriatsia za svobodu*, pp. 11–13, 15–16.

77. "Zadachi i metody Partii Sotsialistov-Revoliutsionerov v derevne" [Tasks and methods of the PSR in the village], *Volia Rossii*, no. 327, 9 October 1921, p. 3.

78. *Put' Bor'by*, vols. 1 and 2, *Antonovshchina*, passim. Both Chekists, Pokaliukhin and Polin, recognize Antonov's qualities.

79. See the analysis of the assembly's membership in Radkey, *The Sickle under the Hammer*.

80. Report on the tax in kind to Moscow party workers in Lenin, *Polnoe sobranie sochinenii*, 5th ed., vol. 43, pp. 156–57.

81. "O vnutrennei i vneshnei politike respubliki: otchet VTsIK i SNK 23 dekabria" [On internal and external policy of the republic: report of the All-Russian Central Executive Committee and the Council of People's Commissars of 23 December]; ibid., vol. 44, p. 311; speech of Bukharin, "XI Vserossiiskaia konferentsiia R. K. P.," *Izvestiia*, no. 287 (1430), 21 December 1921, p. 1.

82. Lenin, *Polnoe sobranie sochinenii*, 5th ed., vol. 43, pp. 156–57; compare also Stanislav V. Kosior's statement in 1930 to the effect that the NEP had been introduced in the interest of the mass of the middle peasantry; Trifonov, *Klassy i klassovaia bor'ba*, part 1, p. 133. Probably an echo of the campaign of rehabilitation of Kosior, who was liquidated on 26 February 1939. A. F. Kerenski told me that a concentration camp victim had told him that Stalin had come personally to interrogate Kosior and that Kosior had spat full in his face.

83. The adverb "lightly" should be placed before "armed."

84. Trifonov, *Klassy i klassovaia bor'ba*, part 1, p. 307.

Glossary

Che-ka: Extraordinary Commission. The secret or political police of the Soviet state. Later GPU, OGPU, NKVD, MVD, and now KGB

chernozem: black earth

chouan: French counterrevolutionary in the Vendée region, 1793–1795

desiatina: 2.7 acres or 1.0925 hectares

dvorovye: menials, courtyard servants before Emancipation

iz'iatie: taking-out, elimination, or sometimes extermination

khitryi: tricky

Komsomol: Communist Youth League

khutor/khutorianin/khutoriane (pl.): farmstead detached from village/ farmer

kolkhoz: Soviet collective farm

kulak: rich peasant (so-called)

mir: village community

muzhik: peasant

NEP: New Economic Policy

okhlos: populace, mob

orman/urman/urema (Turkish): forest

ovragi: hollows or large gullies

podzol: infertile soil in much of Russia, composed mainly of fine grains of quartz

pood/pud: 40 Russian pounds or 36.11 avoirdupois pounds

raion: administrative division of a region in the Soviet Union

sovkhoz: Soviet state farm

uezd: administrative-territorial division of a province in the Russian Empire and earlier Soviet period; district

ukaz: edict

uprava: provincial board

vendéen: French counterrevolutionary of the 1790s in the west

verst: 0.66 miles or 1.0668 kilometers

volost': administrative-territorial division of an *uezd;* canton

yarlyk: label, sanction or letter patent

zemstvo: organ of self-government in Russian Empire after 1864; democratized in 1917; replaced by soviets thereafter

Bibliography

Not everything that has been consulted in this study will be listed below. In a few instances something may be included to which there is no citation in the text. But nothing will be included that has not been read.

Unpublished or Archival Sources

Trotsky Archive, Houghton Library, Harvard University

Trotsky was not directly concerned with the Tambov uprising, but as head of the military establishment he inevitably came into possession of material bearing on its containment and repression. These materials are of transcendent importance though limited in number. As he was able to take his papers with him into exile, this early episode in Soviet history can be approached from the vantage-ground of certainty in respect to the attitudes, decisions, and actions of a regime that locks up the truth and feeds out a general line. Some of the documents contained in the archive are the originals; others are copies. The most valuable are:

Antonov-Ovseenko, V. A. "O banditskom dvizhenii v Tambovskoi gubernii" [About the bandit movement in Tambov province]. T–686 of the archive. Typed manuscript of thirty-six large-sized sheets (really thirty-seven, since two pages are numbered "29"). Original. Dated 20 July 1921 and signed by the author as Chairman of the Plenipotentiary Commission of the All-Russian Soviet Central Executive Committee for War on Banditry in Tambov province. The author, accordingly, may be termed the commissar of repression. Written as a report to Lenin, who marked freely in the margins before sending it on to Trotsky, this account of the chief civilian official charged with ending the insurrection is of inestimable value because of disclosures that would never be publicized. It is poorly organized, however, and suffers from ambiguities and errors that are by no means exclusively typographical. One would expect a report to the head of party and state to have been more carefully prepared.

Sklianski, E. M. Manuscript of one typed page without title or date. T–678 of the archive. Copy of Sklianski's handwritten note to Lenin proposing that Tukhachevski be placed in charge of operations in Tambov despite the sensation that would be caused, and of Lenin's handwritten reply agreeing to the appointment but enjoining secrecy. A notation that the exchange must have taken place at the beginning of June 1921 is wrong; the proposal was certainly made toward the end of April.

Tukhachevski, M. N. "Zapiska" [Memorandum]. Manuscript of three pages typed with blue ribbon; in very good condition. T–685 of the archive. Copy. Dated 16 July 1921. According to a notation, the memorandum is an excerpt from a report on "banditry" in Tambov prepared in compliance with directions from Lenin. It would be more accurate to call it a résumé. A model of succinctness and clarity, the general's memorandum offers a startling contrast to the commissar's.

Russian Archive, Columbia University

Repository of about the only source that can be called Green in the strictest sense.

Fomichev, M. (Michael Lidin). "Antonovshchina: Iz vospominanii antonovtsa" [The Antonov affair: recollections of a follower of Antonov]. Two typed manuscripts, highly interesting but very difficult to evaluate. To begin with, there is supposed to be only one, but I have seen and used two different manuscripts. The first is dated 1950–1951 and the place is given as Tubabao in the Philippines. It consists of thirty-four pages of ordinary size, pp. 1–3 and 16–34 typed with black ribbon and pp. 4–15 with blue ribbon. It was used at Columbia University in 1967. The second manuscript is dated 1955 at Santiago de Chile and was on loan to the Hoover Library, Stanford University, in the summer of 1966. It is typed on longer sheets and appeared to be better organized. The two manuscripts tell basically the same story with certain variations.

The author was an ex-officer who took up with Antonov and served with him till the end of 1920. His knowledge is limited, therefore, to the earlier stage of the insurrection. In not a single instance except for Antonov himself does he refer either to Green or Soviet leaders on the scene by their real names, a circumstance that calls into question the worth of his observations and suggests that many of them rest upon hearsay rather than upon direct experience. His chronology likewise is faulty. A source to be used only by one immersed in the subject, and then with caution.

Nicolaevsky Collection, Hoover Institution

Here there are several documents of unusual interest:

Podbelski, Iuri. "Predsedateliu moskovskogo soveta r. i k. deputatov" [To the chairman of the Moscow Soviet of Workers' and Peasants' Deputies]. Typed manuscript of three single-spaced, legal-size sheets. The appeal of an embattled SR intellectual with roots in Tambov province to L. D. Kamenev, protesting efforts of the Che-ka to link him to Antonov. Date of composition probably late July 1921 since the communication seeks to refute charges made public on 24 July. The notation in the upper left corner of the first page, "15/IX Prague," presumably refers to the date of reception abroad. Valuable information, though Podbelski is capable of twisting the truth.

Proclamation or manifesto purporting to be Antonov's and printed over his name and those of four of his lieutenants in an appeal to Red Army men to desert the Red banner. No date; place and point of assembly given as Tambov, a town strongly garrisoned by the Soviet and swarming with Che-ka agents. The names of the four lieutenants are neither authentic nor assumed; they are fraudulent, in the opinion of this author, and the organizations for which they speak, nonexistent. The pompous, high-flown language about desecrated shrines and relics and the invocation of monarchist heroes of the past betray the real authors. See further in text. Though a forgery, the manifesto is of historic interest as an attempt on the part of reactionaries to make capital out of Antonov's movement.

Published Sources

Newspapers

Izvestiia. Moscow, 1921, 1922 (until fall). Edited by Iuri Steklov.

Pravda. Moscow, 1921, 1922 (until fall). Edited by Nicholas Bukharin. Despite the ideological straitjacket, the distortion and withholding of information, the poor grade of paper and the abominable print, the two main Soviet newspapers have been indispensable to this study. They were then on a higher cultural plane, preserved at least some regard for the truth, and printed reports that were factual as well as propagandistic. The most valuable material comes from the despatches or articles of opinion about the "liquidation" of the uprising in 1921, the proceedings of the SR trial in 1922, the flagellation of the SRs before the trial, and the death of Antonov.

Volia Rossii [Russian freedom]. Prague, 12 September 1920–9 October 1921. Edited by V. I. Lebedev. Organ of the SRs in exile. 327 issues; all examined save the missing no. 259. Despite its best efforts this newspaper assembled only a very limited amount of information on the Green movement, but what it contains is of prime importance. The lifetime of the newspaper coincides closely with the lifetime of the insurrection.

Poslednie Novosti [Latest news]. Paris, 1920–1940. Edited P. N. Miliukov. 6,923 issues. Not searched by the author himself, but pertinent references furnished by his friend, Thomas Riha, who was running the files in connection with his biography of Miliukov. The Constitutional Democratic organ has even less on the Green movement than that of the Socialist Revolutionaries.

Encyclopedias

Bol'shaia sovetskaia entsiklopediia. Moscow. 1st ed., 1926–1947; 65 vols. 2nd ed., 1950–1958; 50 + 1 vols. 3rd ed., 1970–.

Entsiklopedicheskii slovar'. Brockhaus-Efron. St. Petersburg, 1890–1904.
   41 vols. The old encyclopedia offers much on the locale of the uprising,
   though only some of the villages have entries of their own.
Sovetskaia istoricheskaia entsiklopediia. Moscow, 1961–.

Books, Articles, Journals

   Note: Society publications appear under titles, not societies. If there are
only one or two significant articles from a journal the entries will be by
article rather than by journal. If a journal is listed, it means either that more
than two articles from it have been used and are not listed severally, or that
the journal has been inspected and found wanting in material on the subject,
with minor exceptions.
Alekseev, V. *Oktiabr' i grazhdanskaia voina v TsChO* [October and the
   civil war in the Central Black Earth Region]. Voronezh, 1932.
Anonymous (Iuri Podbelski). *Kak tambovskie krest'iane boriatsia za
   svobodu* [How Tambov peasants fight for freedom]. N.p., 1921.
   Published as anonymous pamphlet, but written by Iuri Podbelski. One
   of the basic sources, though only sixteen pages in length and not going
   beyond February 1921. The author combines sympathy for the peasant
   cause with an intellectual's aversion to the Green movement. The same
   account is printed under the title, "Po Rossii: Vozstanie Tambovskikh
   krest'ian (Korrespondentsiia iz Rossii)" [Around Russia: uprising of the
   Tambov peasants (correspondence from Russia)], *Revoliutsionnaia
   Rossiia* (new series), no. 6 (April 1921), pp. 23–28. Here the date is given
   as 10 March 1921 and the author's initials as Iu. P.
Arshinov, P. *Istoriia makhnovskogo dvizheniia (1918–1921 gg.)* [A history
   of Makhno's movement, 1918–1921]. Berlin, 1923.
Barsukov, M. "Kommunist-buntar' (Grigorii Ivanovich Kotovskii)" [A
   Communist-insurgent (Gregory Ivanovich Kotovski)], *Krasnaia Nov'*
   [Red virgin land], book 8 (October 1925), pp. 199–223. Only a few pages
   about the campaign against Antonov, yet one of the best sources. While
   laudatory of Kotovski, Barsukov's account is free of the nauseous
   adulation that developed later.
*Bor'ba rabochikh i krest'ian pod rukovodstvom bol'shevistskoi partii za
   ustanovlenie i uprochenie sovetskoi vlasti v Tambovskoi gubernii
   (1917–1918 gody): Sbornik dokumentov* [The workers' and peasants'
   struggle under the guidance of the Bolshevik party to establish and
   consolidate the Soviet regime in Tambov province (1917–1918): a
   documentary collection]. Tambov, 1957. A disappointing source.
Borisov, P. A. *Chernym letom* [A black summer]. Moscow, 1965. This
   brochure of eighty pages is one of the basic primary sources. Borisov
   was commissar in Kotovski's brigade. Although writing many years
   later, he was provided with competent assistance.
————. "Konets antonovshchiny" [The end of the Antonov affair]. In
   *Nezabyvaemoe: vospominaniia uchastnikov grazhdanskoi voiny v
   SSSR* [What is not being forgotten: recollections of civil war participants

in the Soviet Union]. Moscow, 1961. For this earlier version of his memoirs, the ex-commissar had less competent assistance.

Bykov, D. *Komkor Pavlov* [Corps Commander Pavlov]. Moscow, 1965. Sketch of P. A. Pavlov's career.

Cebesoy, Ali Fuat. *Moskova hatıraları (21/11/1920–2/6/1922)* [Memories of Moscow, 21 November 1920–2 June 1922]. Istanbul, 1955. The Green movement registered on the consciousness even of the Turkish general who headed the Grand Embassy of the Grand National Assembly to the Moscow government.

Chernov, V. M. *Zapiski sotsialista revoliutsionera* [Memories of a Socialist Revolutionary]. Vol. 1. Berlin, St. Petersburg, and Moscow, 1922. On the background of the peasant movement in Tambov province: pp. 249–335.

Donkov, I. P. "Organizatsiia razgroma antonovshchiny" [Organizing to crush the Antonov movement], *Voprosy Istorii KPSS* [Matters concerning the history of the Communist party of the Soviet Union], no. 6 (June 1966), pp. 59–71. Sober and well-informed account from the official point of view, drawing on all those sources closed to the independent investigator, who would have used them differently.

Eichenbaum, V. M. (Voline). *La Révolution inconnue (1917–1921)* [The unknown revolution (1917–1921)]. Paris, n.d.

Eiduck, A. V. *Die russische Hungersnot 1921–1922 und ihre Bekämpfung im Lichte der Tatsachen* [The Russian famine 1921–1922 and its control according to the facts]. Berlin, 1922.

Esaulenko, A. S. *Revoliutsionnyi put' G. I. Kotovskogo* [The revolutionary road of G. I. Kotovski]. Kishinev, 1956. One chapter is devoted to Tambov. The only clear and connected account of military events, but one that is far too brief.

Geroi grazhdanskoi voiny: Sbornik [Heroes of the civil war: a collection]. Moscow, 1963. Issue no. 15 of the series, *Zhizn' zamechatel'nykh liudei* [Lives of noteworthy people].

G. I. Kotovskii: dokumenty i materialy k istorii grazhdanskoi voiny v SSSR [G. I. Kotovski: documents and materials on the history of the civil war in the Soviet Union]. Compiled by M. Chizhova et al. Kishinev, 1956. This collection contains a good deal of valuable but dispersed information on the Tambov uprising (period May–August 1921), drawn from the army archives. There are deficiencies; for example, battle reports for June 1921, the decisive month, are missing (have they been purposefully withheld?).

Gor'kii, Maksim. *O russkom krest'ianstve* [Concerning the Russian peasantry]. Berlin, 1922. Gorki expresses freely his views on the peasantry in Tambov and everywhere else—so freely, in fact, that this pamphlet apparently could not be printed even in Soviet Russia.

Gurevich, M. B. *Golod i sel'skoe khoziaistvo Ukrainy: Ocherk* [Essay on the famine and rural economy of the Ukraine]. Kharkov, 1923.

Istoriia SSSR, I, S drevneishikh vremen do kontsa XVIII veka [History of the USSR, I, from earliest times to the end of the 18th century], ed. by B. D. Grekov, S. V. Bakhrushin, and V. I. Lebedev. 2nd ed. N.p., 1948.

Iz istorii grazhdanskoi voiny v SSSR: Sbornik dokumentov i materialov v trekh tomakh 1918–1922 [From the history of the civil war in the USSR: a collection of documents and materials in three volumes, 1918–1922]. Moscow, 1960–1961. This compilation should have yielded more.

Iz istorii Vserossiiskoi Chrezvychainoi Komissii, 1917–1921 gg: sbornik dokumentov [From the history of the All-Russian Extraordinary Commission, 1917–1921: a collection of documents]. Compiled by A. K. Goncharov et al. Moscow 1958–. Che-ka habits spill over into literary endeavors. Documents that could have been of much significance have been disfigured, either by poor editing or with malice aforethought. Names and dates do not match with known persons and events. Could false names have been inserted for key operatives?

Kak tambovskie krest'iane boriatsia za svobodu. See Anonymous.

Kalinin, M. I. *Izbrannye proizvedeniia* [Selected works]. Moscow, 1960. 3 vols.

———. *Za eti gody: stat'i, besedy, rechi* [During these years: articles conversations, speeches]. Leningrad, 1926–1929. 3 vols. Kalinin's passing references to Tambov can be revealing.

Kazakov, A. *Partiia s.-r. v Tambovskom vosstanii 1920–1921 gg.* [The SR party in the Tambov insurrection of 1920–1921]. Moscow, 1922. While not free of stereotyped denunciation, Kazakov's brochure reveals a deeper understanding of SR affairs than can be found in other Soviet accounts. Important for other aspects of the uprising besides the SR angle. The brochure is seldom cited in this study because the notes on it were taken from the author, but it has added substantially to his knowledge.

Komandarm Uborevich: Vospominaniia druzei i soratnikov [Army Commander Uborevich: reminiscences of friends and comrades in arms]. Moscow, 1964. Rehabilitation of one of Stalin's most talented victims, the man who commanded the armored force against Antonov.

Kondrat'ev, Nikolai. *Na linii ognia (Epizody iz zhizni komandarma Ivana Fed'ko)* [On the firing line (episodes from the life of Army Commander Ivan Fedko)]. Moscow, 1964. More postmortem rehabilitation literature, this time of the man who commanded the armored vehicles against Antonov.

Kotovets. "Kotovskii vperedi (K dvukhletnei godovshchine so dnia smerti)" [Kotovski up in front (on the second anniversary of his death)], *Krasnoarmeets* [The Red Army man], no. 109 (no. 16, 20 August 1927), p. 8. Interesting report by one of Kotovski's men on a fragment of the campaign from which every indication of time and place has been deleted in keeping with the obsession for military secrecy a full five years after the insurrection had drawn its last breath. Recaptures as nothing else the grime and heartbreak of the campaign.

Krest'ianskaia Rossiia [Peasant Russia]. Prague, 1922–1924. Nine issues. Useful for leads more than for information.

Lenin, V. I. *Polnoe sobranie sochinenii* [Full collection of his works]. 5th ed. Moscow, 1958–1965. 55 vols. Especially vols. 42, 43, 44, 51, 52, 53.

The 5th edition is not yet full. Not everything that would tend to show Lenin in a less favorable light has been included, yet the collected works unlock the character and attitudes of the founder of Soviet Russia as no other source can do. They have been extensively used and are indispensable to this study.

Lunacharski, A. V. *Byvshie liudi: ocherk istorii partii es-erov* [The have-beens: historical sketch of the party of the SRs]. Moscow, 1922.

Na Chuzhoi Storone [In foreign parts]. Berlin and Prague, 1923–1925. 13 issues. Contains one important communication from the scene of action (see under "Usmirenie") and some incidental information.

Nezabyvaemoe. See Borisov, P. A. "Konets antonovshchiny."

Obvinitel'noe zakliuchenie po delu tsentral'nogo komiteta i otdel'nykh chlenov inykh organizatsii partii sotsialistov-revoliutsionerov po obvineniiu ikh v vooruzhennoi bor'be protiv Sovetskoi vlasti, organizatsii ubiistv, vooruzhennykh ograblenii i v izmennicheskikh snosheniiakh s inostrannymi gosudarstvami [Summation of the prosecution in the trial of the central committee and individual members of other organizations of the SR Party on charges of engaging in armed struggle against the Soviet regime, assassinations, armed robberies and traitorous relations with foreign states]. Moscow, 1922. Quite limited but significant disclosures concerning Tambov.

Ocherki istorii tambovskoi organizatsii KPSS [Outline history of the Tambov organization of the Communist party of the Soviet Union]. Voronezh, 1970.

Okatov, N. A. *Tambovskaia partiinaia organizatsiia v period vosstanovleniia narodnogo khoziaistva (1921–1925 gg.)* [The Tambov party organization during the period of the restoration of the national economy (1921–1925)]. Tambov, 1961.

Okninski, A. L. *Dva goda sredi krest'ian: vidennoe, slyshannoe, perezhitoe v Tambovskoi gubernii s noiabria 1918 goda do noiabria 1920 goda* [Two years among the peasants: what has been seen, heard, and experienced in Tambov province from November 1918 to November 1920]. Riga, n.d. Preface, 1936. The author records interesting observations that relate more to the background of events than to the events themselves, since his stay in Tambov ended some two months after the insurrection began.

Poliakov, Iu. A. *Perekhod k nepu i sovetskoe krest'ianstvo* [The transition to the NEP and the Soviet peasantry]. Moscow, 1967. Not a great deal on Tambov, but in general one of the better Soviet treatises.

Polkovodtsy grazhdanskoi voiny: sbornik [Military leaders of the civil war: a collection]. Moscow, 1960. Issue no. 11 of the series, *Zhizn' zamechatel' nykh liudei* [Lives of remarkable people].

Put' Bor'by [The path of struggle]. Tambov, 1922–1923. 2 vols. Published under the auspices of the Tambov Provincial Commission for the History of the Communist Party. The second volume appears in Soviet publications under the special title: *Antonovshchina: Stat'i, vospominaniia i drugie materialy k istorii esero-banditizma v Tambovskoi gubernii* [The Antonov affair: articles, reminiscences and other materials on the history of SR banditry in Tambov province]. It was edited by S. Evgenev and O. Minovski, or by O. S. Litovski.

The titling is not only clumsy but inaccurate, because the first volume also contains important material on the uprising. The two volumes together are the point of departure for any study of the subject. The compilers modestly state that the contents are not a history of the insurrection but only the "raw material" for a history. And so they remain to this day—the partial foundation for a history that has never been written. The contents are not free of error and are of uneven value. Besides the reproduction of an authentic Green manifesto—the only one known to this author—the accounts of the two Che-ka or GPU men are of the greatest value: S. Polin, "Poslednie dni esero-bandita Antonova" [The last days of the SR bandit Antonov], vol. 1, pp. 46–53, and M. Pokoliukhin (or Pokaliukhin), "Po sledam Antonova" [On the trail of Antonov], vol. 2, pp. 65–91. These early writings of Soviet participants are decidedly to be preferred to later sources, not only because they are primary and closer to the subject but because they are more truthful.

Radkey, Oliver H. *The Agrarian Foes of Bolshevism: Promise and Default of the Russian Socialist Revolutionaries, February to October, 1917.* New York and London, 1958.

———. *The Election to the Russian Constituent Assembly of 1917.* Cambridge, Mass., 1950.

———. *The Sickle under the Hammer: the Russian Socialist Revolutionaries in the Early Months of Soviet Rule.* New York and London, 1963.

Rakitin, Anton. *Imenem revoliutsii . . . (Ocherki o V. A. Antonove-Ovseenko)* [In the name of the revolution . . . (sketches of V. A. Antonov-Ovseenko)]. Moscow, 1965.

Revoliutsionnaia Rossiia [Revolutionary Russia]. Dorpat, Berlin and Prague, 1920–1931. New series; 78 numbers in all. Only the early issues of this organ of the Socialist Revolutionaries in exile (for the second time) contain materials on the Tambov uprising, mainly in the form of clandestine communications from the scene of action—one is from a peasant and therefore highly to be prized. There is enough to make this source one of the most important, yet only in the relative sense for here, too, as everywhere else, there is no great amount of information.

Rossiia: polnoe geograficheskoe opisanie nashego otechestva [Russia: a full geographical description of our fatherland]. Ed. by V. P. Semenov-Tian-Shanskii. St. Petersburg, 1899–1914. 19 vols., but not all were published. Especially vol. 2, *Srednerusskaia chernozemnaia oblast'* [The Central Russian black earth region], published in 1902. Here will be found a great deal of information about the Tambov countryside, including individual villages that figure in our story and that may or may not appear in the encyclopedias.

Savost'ianov, V., and Egorov, P. *Komandarm pervogo ranga (I. P. Uborevich)* [An army commander of the first rank (I. P. Uborevich)]. Moscow, 1966.

Sbornik gubernii, uezdov i volostei RSFSR, USSR i SSR Belorussii [Compilation of the provinces, *uezds* and *volosts* of the RSFSR and of the Ukrainian and Belorussian SSRs]. Moscow, 1921. Published by the People's Commissariat of Internal Affairs. Very useful reference manual for the administrative subdivisions of the Imperial and earlier Soviet periods.

Shatov, Mikhail. "Tambovskie vosstaniia" [The Tambov Insurrections], *Novoe Russkoe Slovo* [The new Russian word], 15, 16 February 1966.

Singleton, Seth. "The Tambov Revolt (1920–1921)," *Slavic Review*, vol. 25, no. 3 (September 1966), pp. 497–512. Significant as the first published attempt by a Western scholar to penetrate the shroud of the Tambov peasant liberation movement. On the basis of quite limited research and with little detailed knowledge of events (not to imply that anyone, including Russian investigators, has an adequate command of detail), the author nevertheless came out with generally valid conclusions.

Sofinov, P. G. *Ocherki istorii Vserossiiskoi Chrezvychainoi Komissii (1917–1922 gg.)* [Outline history of the All-Russian Extraordinary Commission, 1917–1922]. Moscow, 1960. This commentary on the records of the secret police is of limited use, yet could easily have been of much greater value without damage to the interests of this department of state. The curse of clandestine machinations, of employing any means to an end, extends into every field of endeavor—even into those where different standards would better serve the purpose in mind.

Sovety v epokhu voennogo kommunizma (1918–1921): sbornik dokumentov [Soviets during the period of war communism (1918–1921): a documentary collection]. Ed. by V. P. Antonov-Saratovski. Moscow, 1929. 2 parts. A couple of important statements by Soviet officials in Tambov may be found here, but only for the early stage of the insurrection; nothing is included after the fall of 1920 although the period covered extends into 1921.

Srechinski, Iuri S. "Zapechatannaia stranitsa" [The sealed page], *Novoe Russkoe Slovo*, 25–28 February 1969. Welcome as at least one account sympathetic to the vanquished. The émigré author, however, needs to handle more critically the Soviet sources on which he is forced to rely.

Strygin, A. *Rasplata: Roman* [The reckoning: a novel]. Voronezh, 1965. A down-the-line tub-thumping rendition of the Communist point of view with none of the redeeming features—particularly the intimate knowledge—of the novel by Virta.

Tret'e Gubernskoe Soveshchanie predsedatelei uispolkomov Tambovskoi gubernii: stenograficheskii otchet [Third Provincial Conference of chairmen of the *uezd* executive committees of Tambov province: stenographic report]. Tambov, 1920.

Trifonov, Ivan Ia. *Klassy i klassovaia bor'ba v nachale nepa (1921–1923 gg.). Chast' I. Bor'ba s vooruzhennoi kulatskoi kontr-revoliutsiei* [Classes and the class struggle at the beginning of the NEP (1921–1923). Part 1. The struggle with the armed kulak counterrevolution]. Leningrad, 1964. This book is a reproach to the institution under whose auspices it appeared—the University of Leningrad. With every advantage at his command, with access to the official records denied to others, this author has produced a jumbled study marred with inconsistencies and inaccuracies and impregnated with nauseous servility to the prescription of Communist authorities. He censures other Russian investigators—they are very few—for having given a blurred account of the battle record and then proceeds to do the same. He includes a bibliographical essay of some value.

His study affords a view into archival material closed to foreign scholars and, very likely, to most Russian ones as well. The view is flattering neither to author nor to archives. Non-Soviet sources on the Green movement—none exist for interior regions like Tambov but it is otherwise with respect to the Ukraine and the Caucasus—are almost wholly ignored, and Trotski absolutely ignored. Under the circumstances one must use Trifonov's book, grinding one's teeth every page of the way, but at least no one can deny that here is an outstanding example of how history should not be written.

Tukhachevski, M. N. "Bor'ba s kontrrevoliutsionnymi vosstaniiami: Iskorenenie tipichnogo banditizma (Tambovskoe vosstanie)" [The war on counterrevolutionary uprisings: a case of rooting out banditry of the typical sort (the Tambov rebellion)], *Voina i Revoliutsiia* [War and revolution], no. 8, 1926. This article was read in Moscow but the notes were stolen. It is somewhat disappointing because the general strives to ascend to the plane of military theory instead of presenting a straightforward, down-to-earth account of the repression. The memorandum of only three pages in the Trotsky Archive is a better piece of work (see above).

"Usmirenie krest'ian v Tambovskoi gubernii" [Peasant pacification in Tambov province], *Na chuzhoi storone* [In foreign parts], vol. 3 (1923), pp. 127–30. Information of extreme rarity about the situation in Tambov. The editors of the journal are obviously at sea as to the date of the communication that came into their hands; they relate it to late 1919 or 1920, to the period before the Antonov uprising. Anything from August 1920 would be during the uprising, of course, and at least a part of the information certainly relates by content to the period of combat.

Virta, Nikolai E. *Odinochestvo: Roman* [Loneliness, or the lone wolf: a novel]. Later issue, Moscow, 1962. The Stalin Prize-winning novel about the Antonov insurrection, focusing upon the kulak villain who resisted submergence in the tide of collectivism. The novelist is not lacking in literary talent; he is well-informed, as becomes one who is rooted in the setting and who has witnessed as a boy some of the events he describes. As for the rest, he has studied assiduously the sources—at times it is possible to detect from his diction upon which particular source he is drawing, as, for example, Barsukov's article. The novel can be ignored only with loss to treatment of the subject; the problem is to distinguish fact from fiction. Stalin's judgment, in this case as in some others, was not so bad.

Vospominaniia o Vladimire Il'iche Lenine [Reminiscences about Vladimir Ilich Lenin]. Moscow, 1956–1957. 2 vols.

Zhizn' zamechatel'nykh liudei [Lives of remarkable people]. For entries from this series, see *Geroi grazhdanskoi voiny* and *Polkovodtsy grazhdanskoi voiny*.

Zhukov, G. K. *The Memoirs of Marshal Zhukov*. 1st American ed. New York, n.d.

————. *Vospominaniia i razmyshleniia* [Reminiscences and reflections]. Moscow, 1969. Although Zhukov devotes only a few pages to Tambov, which came at the outset of his military career, his observations are sober and realistic in contrast to the customary Soviet approach. If the same truthfulness holds for the later and major portions of his memoirs, he has made a contribution to historical literature.

Zybko, Nadezhda P. *Tambovskaia partiinaia organizatsiia v gody grazhdanskoi voiny i inostrannoi interventsii (1918–1920 gg.)* [The Tambov party organization in the years of the civil war and foreign intervention (1918–1920)]. Tambov, 1961.

Index

DATE DUE

1-7-77			
JA 27 '77			
GAYLORD			PRINTED IN U.S.A.